ALSO BY JOE JACKSON

BLACK ELK

BLACK ELK

THE LIFE OF
AN AMERICAN VISIONARY

JOE JACKSON

FARRAR, STRAUS AND GIROUX   NEW YORK

Farrar, Straus and Giroux
18 West 18th Street, New York 10011

Grateful acknowledgement is made for permission to reprint material
from the following:
Reprinted from *Black Elk Speaks: The Complete Edition* by John G. Neihardt
by permission of the University of Nebraska Press. Copyright 2014 by the
Board of Regents of the University of Nebraska. Original printings copyright
1932, 1959, 1972 by John G. Neihardt. Copyright 1961 by the John G. Neihardt
Trust. Reprinted from *The Sixth Grandfather: Black Elk's Teachings Given to
John G. Neihardt*, edited and with an introduction by Raymond J. DeMallie,
by permission of the University of Nebraska Press. Copyright 1984 by
the University of Nebraska Press. Reproduced from *Black Elk & Flaming
Rainbow: Personal Memories of the Lakota Holy Man and John Neihardt* by
Hilda Neihardt by permission of the University of Nebraska Press. Copyright
1995 by the University of Nebraska Press.

Library of Congress Cataloging-in-Publication Data
Names: Jackson, Joe, 1955– author.
Title: Black Elk : the life of an American visionary / Joe Jackson.
Description: First edition. | New York : Farrar, Straus and Giroux, [2016] |
    Includes bibliographical references and index.
Identifiers: LCCN 2016016695 | 9780374253301 (hardback) |
    ISBN 9780374709617 (ebook)
Subjects: LCSH: Black Elk, 1863–1950. | Oglala Indians—Biography. | Oglala
    Indians—Religion. | Lakota Indians.
Classification: LCC E99.O3 J33 2016 | DDC 978.004/9752440092—dc23
LC record available at https://lccn.loc.gov/2016016695

Designed by Jonathan D. Lippincott

Our books may be purchased in bulk for promotional, educational, or business use.
Please contact your local bookseller or the Macmillan Corporate and Premium
Sales Department at 1-800-221-7945, extension 5442, or by e-mail
at MacmillanSpecialMarkets@macmillan.com.

www.fsgbooks.com
www.twitter.com/fsgbooks • www.facebook.com/fsgbooks

1   3   5   7   9   10   8   6   4   2

Frontispiece: Black Elk standing at the edge of the Badlands as he addresses the
Grandfathers. Photograph taken by John Neihardt in 1931. (With permission of the
John G. Neihardt Trust)

As always, to Kathy and Nick

But if the vision was true and mighty, as I know, it is true and mighty yet; for such things are of the spirit, and it is in the darkness of their eyes that men get lost.

—Black Elk, *Black Elk Speaks*

I have heard what the prophets said, that prophecy lies in my name, saying, I have dreamed, I have dreamed.

—Jeremiah 23:25

CONTENTS

DRAMATIS PERSONAE

THE LAKOTA AND THEIR ALLIES

Big Foot: Leader of the Minneconjou band massacred at Wounded Knee on December 29, 1890.

Big Road: Leader of the Northern Oglala *tiyospaye*, or large family band, that included the Black Elks. He was named one of the Oglalas' four Deciders prior to the Great Sioux War.

Black Elk (later Nicholas Black Elk, after his Catholic conversion): Oglala holy man, healer, *yuwipi*, and *heyoka*, who fought at the battles of the Little Bighorn and Wounded Knee and performed with Buffalo Bill's Wild West. His collaboration with the Nebraska poet John Neihardt resulted in the 1932 *Black Elk Speaks*, a classic of American literature that scholars have called "an American Indian Rosetta stone."

Black Elk's father (Black Elk Sr. in the text): The third "Black Elk" in the Black Elk clan of bear healers. His famous son would be the fourth Black Elk.

Benjamin Black Elk: Black Elk's only surviving son with his first wife, Katie War Bonnet. Ben Black Elk would serve as the Lakota-English translator during the interviews that produced *Black Elk Speaks*; he would in time become the keeper of his father's legacy and a famous presence in his own right at Mount Rushmore.

Lucy Black Elk: Black Elk's daughter by his second wife, Anna Brings White. Her conversations with the Pine Ridge educator (and later

Jesuit father) Michael Steltenkamp would reveal Black Elk's career during the early 1900s as a Catholic missionary to other tribes and as a lay preacher, or "catechist," well-known in Pine Ridge.

Black Road: The veteran Oglala medicine man to whom Black Elk first revealed his Great Vision and who prescribed as a cure the staging of the Horse Dance from that vision. By doing so, he set Black Elk on course to become one of the most important Oglala holy men during the late nineteenth and twentieth centuries.

Black Shawl: The first wife of Crazy Horse, mother of the doomed Kokipapi.

Anna Brings White: Black Elk's second wife, and mother of Lucy Black Elk.

Chips: One of the most powerful and famous Oglala holy men of the period encompassing the Great Sioux War. The childhood friend of Crazy Horse and four years his elder, Chips would be Crazy Horse's mentor during his spiritual quests and help interpret his famous dreams.

Crazy Horse: The famous Oglala war chief during the Battle of the Little Bighorn and the Great Sioux War; equal in influence to Sitting Bull. Known to the Oglala as Tasunke Witko, he was Black Elk's second cousin and a role model for him as a boy and young man.

Drinks Water: Apocalyptic Lakota prophet, also called Wooden Cup, who died about twenty years before the birth of Black Elk. His most famous prophecy foretold the arrival and dominion of a white nation from the east, whom he called Iktomi men.

Charles Alexander Eastman: Santee Dakota physician educated at Boston University, who served as the Pine Ridge Agency's main doctor during the Massacre at Wounded Knee.

Moses Flying Hawk: A veteran of the Great Sioux War. Flying Hawk served as John Neihardt's interpreter when he first met Black Elk in August 1930.

Gall: Hunkpapa war chief during the Battle of the Little Bighorn. Gall's two wives and several children were killed during Major Marcus Reno's initial attack on the southeast end of the Great Camp.

Good Thunder: One of three Lakota "delegates" sent to meet Wovoka, the Ghost Dance "Messiah," in 1890. Good Thunder was Black Elk's uncle and would marry Black Elk's mother after his father's death. Good Thunder was one of the three main Ghost Dance priests at Pine Ridge, and Black Elk would become his chief lieutenant.

Keeps His Tipi: Black Elk's maternal grandfather; possibly the closest to Black Elk of all his extended family. He helped the nine-year-old Black Elk navigate his resurrection from the eleven-day coma that resulted in his Great Vision and explained to his grandson the meaning of *wasichu*.

Kicking Bear: Crazy Horse's lieutenant at the Little Bighorn and suspected killer of Agency clerk Frank Appleton. Kicking Bear was leader of the three main Ghost Dance priests, and his arrival at Standing Rock Agency precipitated the arrest and death of Sitting Bull.

Leggings Down (later Mary Leggings Down, after her conversion): Black Elk's mother.

Little Big Man: Crazy Horse's lieutenant, who turned against him at Camp Robinson.

One Side: Black Elk's friend, fellow *heyoka*, and informal partner in his healing practice at Pine Ridge.

Charles Picket Pin: Also known as Red Cow. Became lost in Manchester with Black Elk and another Oglala performer from Buffalo Bill's Wild West; all three missed the steamship taking the troupe back to New York. They went to London, were interrogated by police in probable connection with the Whitechapel Murders, and joined Mexican Joe's Western Wilds of America.

Red Cloud: Oglala leader who led his people to victory against the U.S. Army in Red Cloud's War, then led them through the transition into reservation life.

Runs in the Center: Black Elk's half brother. At the beginning of the Reno Valley Fight, Black Elk chased after him with his forgotten gun, and instead found himself drawn into the battle.

Short Bull: One of the three principal Ghost Dance priests during the Sioux "Messiah craze."

Sitting Bull: Hunkpapa leader and holy man whose vision of a U.S. Army defeat inspired his people to victory during the Battle of the Little Bighorn.

Spotted Tail: Brulé chief who became convinced of the futility of fighting the U.S. Army after a year's internment at Fort Leavenworth, so instead devoted himself to peace and fighting for the rights of his tribe. The uncle of Crazy Horse.

Standing Bear (later Stephen Standing Bear, after his conversion):

Black Elk's Minneconjou cousin, who would be his "verifier" as he told John Neihardt of his life and Great Vision, and who would paint the original artwork for *Black Elk Speaks*.

Luther Standing Bear: Oglala author, actor, and chief, educated in the Carlisle Indian Industrial School, remembered today for his many books on Sioux life. One of the first Lakota to act in Hollywood.

Sweet Medicine: Cheyenne apocalyptic prophet who foresaw the conquest of his people by a "good-looking people, with light hair and white skin."

They Are Afraid of Her (Kokipapi): Crazy Horse's only child.

Katie War Bonnet: Black Elk's first wife; mother of Ben Black Elk.

Worm: Crazy Horse's father, related to the Black Elks. Like the senior Black Elk, he, too, was a medicine man, and he, too, passed his original family name—Crazy Horse—down to his more famous son before adopting the Lakota name Wagula, or Worm.

Wovoka (also known as Jack Wilson): The prophet behind the 1890 Ghost Dance, who promised that faithful adherence to the dance would restore the earth to a Golden Age before the arrival of the white nation. Though he never named himself so, his followers called him the "Messiah" and thought of him as a kind of "Red Christ."

THE BLACK ROBES

Father Aloysius Bosch: A Holy Rosary Jesuit priest who was thrown from his horse in 1902 and died five months later, probably of internal injuries, in 1903. Black Elk seemed to indicate that Bosch was one of two Black Robes who interrupted his deathbed ceremonies over a child.

Father Eugene Buechel: The Pine Ridge and Rosebud missionary, linguist, and anthropologist whose main work was the 1939 *A Grammar of Lakota*. After Father Henry Westropp, Black Elk probably worked more closely with Buechel than any other Jesuit missionary.

Father Francis M. Craft: The Jesuit priest, of Mohawk descent, who was wounded by one of Big Foot's warriors during the Wounded Knee Massacre.

Father Florentine Digmann: One of the original Jesuit priests to open missions in the Rosebud and Pine Ridge Agencies. Remembered today as the founder of the St. Francis Mission at Rosebud.

Father Louis Gall: One of the original Jesuit priests at Holy Rosary.

He spoke Lakota and is often considered the historian of the early mission period at Pine Ridge.

Father John B. Jutz: One of the original founders, in 1887, of Holy Rosary Mission; Father Superior in 1890, during the Ghost Dance and Wounded Knee.

Father Joseph Lindebner: A founding priest at Holy Rosary, known as "Little Father" to the Oglala for his short stature. Apparently the Jesuit who converted Black Elk to Catholicism.

Father Aemilius Perrig: Early Holy Rosary missionary whose detailed diary chronicled the Ghost Dance and the Wounded Knee Massacre.

Father Placidus Sialm: Swiss-born Jesuit who served in 1901 as headmaster of the Holy Rosary School and then returned in 1914, after ordination, to take charge of Indian camps and outlying mission stations. Of all the Jesuits, Sialm would be the most vehement critic of *Black Elk Speaks* and its authors for espousing "pagan" ideals.

Father Henry I. Westropp: The young American priest who sponsored Black Elk's work as a catechist and his missionary trips across the nation. Westropp was apparently the first Pine Ridge Jesuit to refer to Black Elk as an "Indian St. Paul."

Father Joseph A. Zimmerman: A younger priest at Holy Rosary who proved to be a close ally of Father Placidus Sialm in his struggle against native religions.

OTHER *WASICHUS* (FRIEND AND FOE)

Captain Frederick Benteen: Commander of D, H, and K Companies of the Seventh U.S. Cavalry during the Battle of the Little Bighorn. His arrival at Reno's Hill is credited with saving the survivors of the Valley Fight; his decision to stay with Reno rather than continue on to Custer was later questioned by critics. Nevertheless, current evidence suggests that Custer was beyond hope by the time Benteen arrived.

Joseph Epes Brown: American scholar whose dedication to Native American religions helped elevate their study into a separate discipline in many colleges and universities. *The Sacred Pipe*, coauthored with Black Elk, would be considered his most important work.

Colonel Henry B. Carrington: Lawyer, professor, author, and commander of the Eighteenth U.S. Infantry during Red Cloud's War. Known also as an engineer, he built a string of forts to protect soldiers and travelers on the Bozeman Trail, but suffered a major defeat at Fort Phil Kearny during the 1886 Fetterman Massacre.

Charlotte, the girlfriend: Black Elk's Parisian girlfriend, whom he first met in the summer of 1888 while performing in Paris with Mexican Joe Shelley's Western Wilds of America. Their relationship is described in *Black Elk Speaks* and John Neihardt's 1951 novel *When the Tree Flowered*, later reissued as *Eagle Voice Remembers*.

William F. "Buffalo Bill" Cody: Scout, Pony Express rider, and showman, whose Buffalo Bill's Wild West traveled to cities throughout the United States and Europe from the 1880s to the early 1900s. The popular image of the Wild West has as much to do with Cody's representation as with any movies, TV shows, or novels that followed. Black Elk performed with the show during its run in New York in 1886–87, then continued to England for the 1887–88 season.

John Collier: American social reformer who served as Commissioner of Indian Affairs in the administration of President Franklin D. Roosevelt from 1933 to 1945. He was chiefly responsible for the Indian Reorganization Act of 1934, in which he tried to end the nation's long-standing policy of cultural assimilation of Indian tribes.

Brigadier General George Crook: The career army soldier, known as "Three Stars" to the Sioux, who fought against the Snake, Apache, and Sioux Indians throughout the Indian wars. In the last years of his life, while serving as commander of the Division of the Missouri, he spoke out regularly against the unjust treatment of his former Indian adversaries. He died suddenly in 1890, and was replaced by his old rival General Nelson A. Miles.

Lieutenant Colonel George Armstrong Custer: Complex and controversial commander of the Seventh U.S. Cavalry, who led his troops into almost total annihilation on June 25, 1876, by attacking a huge Indian camp in the valley of the Little Bighorn River.

Alex Duhamel: Rapid City, South Dakota, businessman who created with Black Elk the Sioux Indian Pageant at his family's recently acquired Sitting Bull Crystal Caverns between Rapid City and Mount Rushmore.

Francis "Bud" Duhamel: Alex Duhamel's nephew, who would become Black Elk's chief chronicler during the years of the Sioux Indian Pageant.

Captain William Judd Fetterman: Civil War veteran and cavalry captain at Fort Phil Kearny, who on December 21, 1866, led his command into a trap on the Bozeman Trail. The entire command of eighty men was wiped out by a huge force of Sioux and Cheyennes under the command of Red Cloud. Black Elk's father was permanently crippled in what the Sioux called the Battle of the Hundred Slain.

Colonel James W. Forsyth: Commander of the Seventh U.S. Cavalry during the December 29, 1890, massacre of Big Foot's followers at Wounded Knee Creek in Pine Ridge.

Frank Grouard: Scout and interpreter for General George Crook, whose misinterpretation of the words of Crazy Horse contributed to the war chief's attempted incarceration at Camp Robinson and subsequent killing.

Eleanor Hinman: The Lincoln, Nebraska, teacher, editor, and journalist who tried to interview Black Elk for a proposed project on the life of Crazy Horse. Black Elk turned her down, but other contemporaries of the war chief did talk to her. Hinman eventually turned over her notes to her friend Mari Sandoz; these would serve as the basis for Sandoz's 1942 *Crazy Horse: The Strange Man of the Oglalas*.

Carl Jung: Famous Swiss psychiatrist and founder of analytical psychology who compared Black Elk's Great Vision to that of some Old Testament prophets. He sought to have *Black Elk Speaks* published in Europe; in 1953, the book was released in German as *Ich rufe mein Volk* (I Call My People).

Helen "Nellie" Larrabee: Crazy Horse's second wife, who advised the war chief that if he left the reservation to visit the U.S. president, he would never be allowed to return.

Dr. Valentine McGillycuddy: Surgeon and controversial Pine Ridge agent who was an early proponent of the assimilation of the Oglala. Though a friend of Crazy Horse, McGillycuddy was despised by Red Cloud.

Major General Nelson A. Miles: Veteran of the Indian wars and commander of the Military Division of the Missouri during the December 29, 1890, Wounded Knee Massacre.

Enid Neihardt: John Neihardt's oldest daughter, who served as stenographer during the May 1931 interviews that resulted in *Black Elk Speaks*.

Hilda Neihardt: John Neihardt's middle daughter, present at the May 1931 interviews of Black Elk, who would eventually write *Black Elk* *and Flaming Rainbow*, a chronicle of the production of *Black Elk Speaks* and of the continuing relationship between her family and the Black Elks.

John Gneisenau Neihardt: Nebraska poet laureate, known during the 1920s and '30s as the "Shakespeare of the Plains," who co-authored *Black Elk Speaks* with the Oglala holy man.

Mona Martinsen Neihardt: John Neihardt's wife, a sculptress, who suggested the title *Black Elk Speaks*.

Sigurd Neihardt: John Neihardt's son, who accompanied him in August 1930 when he first met Black Elk.

Major Marcus Reno: Second-in-command of the Seventh U.S. Cavalry, under Lieutenant Colonel George Armstrong Custer, whose troops were almost overwhelmed by the forces of Crazy Horse during the initial stages of the Battle of the Little Bighorn. Accused of cowardice and drunkenness after the debacle, he demanded a Court of Inquiry and was exonerated; nevertheless, Custer's widow, Elizabeth, blamed Reno for her husband's defeat, and Reno's life and career after the Little Bighorn were ruined.

Dr. Daniel F. Royer: Pine Ridge agent-in-charge whose fear of Indians and bad judgment had disastrous consequences in the weeks leading up to the Wounded Knee Massacre.

Nate Salsbury: Former actor and comedian who became the business force behind William Cody's Buffalo Bill's Wild West.

Colonel Joseph "Mexican Joe" Shelley: Rival and contemporary of Buffalo Bill who sought to create the impression that his "Western Wilds of America" was superior to Cody's show. In fact, Shelley's shows were rougher, more chaotic, and at times dangerous for spectators. Black Elk traveled with Shelley through England, France, Belgium, and Italy during 1888–89.

Lieutenant General Philip Henry Sheridan: Union general during the Civil War and commander of the Military Division of the Missouri during the Great Sioux War. In both the conflicts, he was an advocate of total war.

General William Tecumseh Sherman: Union general during the Civil War and commanding general of the U. S. Army during the Great Sioux War.

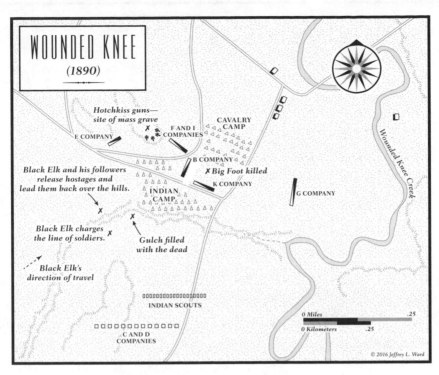

WOUNDED KNEE
(1890)

Hotchkiss guns—
site of mass grave

CAVALRY CAMP

F AND I COMPANIES

E COMPANY

Black Elk and his followers
release hostages and
lead them back over the hills.

B COMPANY

✗ Big Foot killed

INDIAN CAMP

K COMPANY

G COMPANY

Black Elk charges
the line of soldiers.

Gulch filled
with the dead

Black Elk's
direction of travel

Wounded Knee Creek

INDIAN SCOUTS

0 Miles   .25

0 Kilometers   .25

C AND D
COMPANIES

© 2016 Jeffrey L. Ward

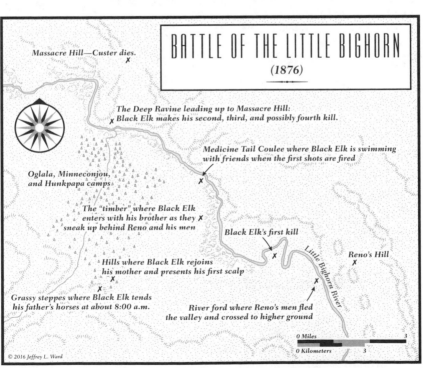

Massacre Hill—Custer dies.
✗

BATTLE OF THE LITTLE BIGHORN
(1876)

The Deep Ravine leading up to Massacre Hill:
✗ Black Elk makes his second, third, and possibly fourth kill.

Medicine Tail Coulee where Black Elk is swimming
with friends when the first shots are fired

Oglala, Minneconjou,
and Hunkpapa camps

The "timber" where Black Elk
enters with his brother as they ✗
sneak up behind Reno and his men

Black Elk's first kill

Reno's Hill
✗

Hills where Black Elk rejoins
his mother and presents his first scalp

Little Bighorn River

Grassy steppes where Black Elk tends
his father's horses at about 8:00 a.m.

River ford where Reno's men fled
the valley and crossed to higher ground

0 Miles   3

0 Kilometers   3

© 2016 Jeffrey L. Ward

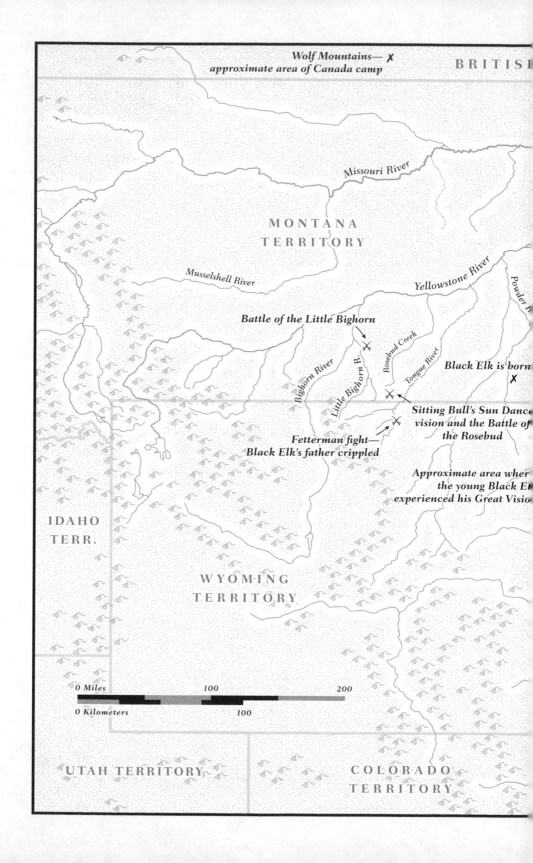

Wolf Mountains— **✗**
approximate area of Canada camp

B R I T I S H

Missouri River

M O N T A N A
T E R R I T O R Y

Musselshell River

Yellowstone River

Powder R.

Battle of the Little Bighorn

Bighorn River

Little Bighorn R.

Rosebud Creek

Tongue River

Black Elk is born
✗

**Sitting Bull's Sun Dance
vision and the Battle of
the Rosebud**

**Fetterman fight—
Black Elk's father crippled**

**Approximate area where
the young Black Elk
experienced his Great Vision**

IDAHO
TERR.

W Y O M I N G
T E R R I T O R Y

0 Miles   100   200

0 Kilometers   100

UTAH TERRITORY

C O L O R A D O
T E R R I T O R Y

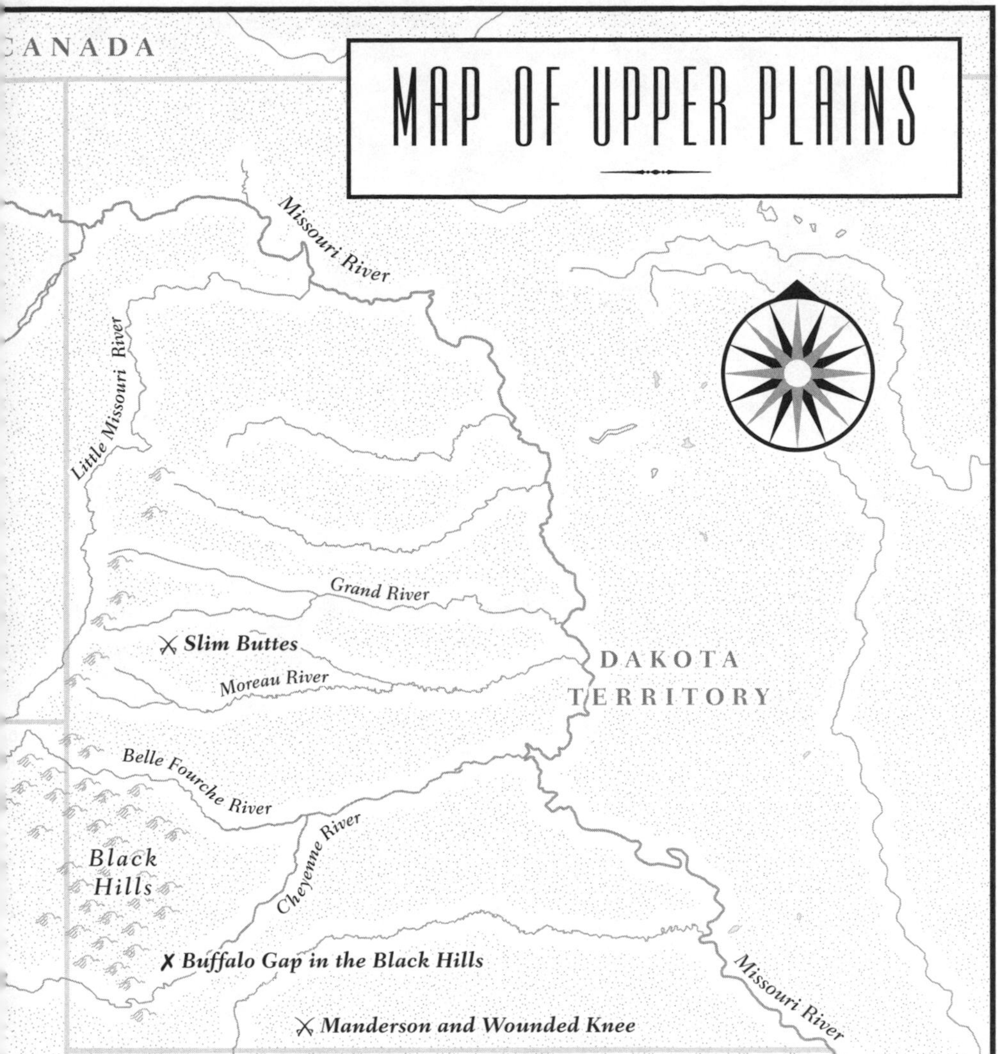

MAP OF UPPER PLAINS
CANADA
Missouri River
Little Missouri River
Grand River
Slim Buttes
Moreau River
DAKOTA TERRITORY
Belle Fourche River
Cheyenne River
Black Hills
Buffalo Gap in the Black Hills
Manderson and Wounded Knee
Missouri River
Niobrara River
Camp Robinson and Red Cloud Agency No. 2—Crazy Horse killed
N. Platte River
NEBRASKA
Platte River
Republican River
© 2016 Jeffrey L. Ward

BLACK ELK

PROLOGUE: "A SORT OF A PREACHER"

In the summer of 1930, the Nebraska poet laureate, John Gneisenau Neihardt, detoured from his intended route to find a holy man. He was headed home after a long and tiring lecture tour, but instead of driving east across the state, he veered north on a whim into Indian Country. Be prepared to cross into another world, he told his son, Sigurd. The Pine Ridge Indian Reservation sprawled for 3,469 square miles across the southwestern corner of South Dakota; split down the middle by the White River, it encompassed more ground than Rhode Island and Delaware combined. But this was harsh country—arid, dry, and poor. The three counties set in its borders consistently appeared in the U.S. Census's annual list of the most impoverished spots in the nation.

Pine Ridge was home to the Oglala Lakota, one of the seven clans of the Teton Sioux. This was the tribe of Crazy Horse, Red Cloud, and American Horse, cousins of Sitting Bull. The Lakota called themselves the People, the true offspring of the Great Mystery. Like wandering Israelites in what was called "the Great American Desert," they'd believed all others—Indian or white—to be their moral and spiritual inferiors. At the same time that American colonists split from Great Britain and began to spread west, the Lakota discovered the horse, turned themselves into consummate riders, and built their own empire.

These were *the* "wild Indians" of popular imagination, the war-bonneted warriors sitting astride painted ponies, watching atop a bluff as a lone stagecoach passed below. At this point in the movie, a chief raised his rifle and with a whoop the horsemen descended upon Claire Trevor, Andy Devine, and John Wayne. It was a stereotype built upon decades of dime novels, Wild West circuses, cliff-hanger movies, and "brewery-distributed cromolithographic fantasies" of Indian fights hanging in saloons across America. At times it seemed that the Sioux were the *only* Indians opposing the white advance, a perception patently untrue. In 1680, the once-peaceful Pueblo rebelled against the Spanish and drove them from New Mexico. The Cheyenne, Kiowa, Blackfeet, Crow, and Arapaho all became formidable horsemen; mounted Apaches terrorized the Southwest for two hundred years. For over a century, the Comanche carved out a 240,000-square-mile empire in the Southern Plains and Southwest, a place where whites survived only in large groups and even then in fear.

Yet no other tribe would be so associated with armed resistance to Manifest Destiny because no other tribe would be so wholly linked to the annihilation of Lieutenant Colonel George Armstrong Custer and his Seventh U.S. Cavalry during the summer of the nation's centennial. Fatal consequences came with that victory. Though the Arapaho and Northern Cheyenne rode with the Sioux on that day, no other tribe would be so blamed for wiping out the 268 officers, enlisted men, and scouts along a line of hills overlooking the Little Bighorn Valley. In death, Custer transcended Custer. He became Saul on Mount Gilboa and King Leonidas at Thermopylae, defending civilization against the savage hordes. The Custer Massacre made the Sioux famous even as it produced a vengeance whose results are still felt today.

Pine Ridge was also home to Wounded Knee Creek, where on December 29, 1890, the last large engagement between U.S. forces and Native Americans ran its sudden and bloody course, marking the end of the western frontier. What happened at Wounded Knee has been called both a battle and a massacre, depending upon one's point of view. According to the historian Rex Alan Smith, "It was mostly a battle, partly a massacre, and entirely a tragic blunder." When the smoke lifted, at least eighty-four Lakota men and sixty-two women and children lay dead, their bodies strewn across miles of frozen prairie, many ridden down by Custer's old regiment. Twenty-five soldiers also lay dying, many from their own crossfire.

Neihardt arrived on a hot August day during the Great Depression:

a two-year drought had wiped out the reservation's small farms, and the first mountain-high cloud of dust rolling across the Plains was barely a month away. He rattled up unannounced to the Pine Ridge Agency's redbrick headquarters and banged through the screen door. Some old Lakota men passing time inside grew quiet as he introduced himself to Field Agent-in-Charge B. G. Courtright and asked a favor. He'd been named poet laureate on the strength of his ongoing narrative cycle: five epic poems covering the western conquest, from the days of the fur traders to the Ghost Dance, the Indian millennial movement that spread like wildfire in 1890 across the West and sought to return the tribes to their former freedom and glory. Neihardt was famous at the time; Courtright pumped his hand and proclaimed himself a fan. The third book—the 1925 *Song of the Indian Wars*—had ended with the death of Crazy Horse at nearby Fort Robinson. Crazy Horse was buried in these hills: many came looking for his grave, but left empty-handed.

Now the poet was five hundred lines into what would become *The Song of the Messiah*, a tale of the "Messiah craze," another term for the Ghost Dance movement. What he wanted, he told Courtright, was to interview an old medicine man who'd been a Ghost Dancer and "who might somehow be induced to talk to me about the deeper spiritual significance of the matter." This was easier said than done: most Indians on the reservation had converted long ago to some form of Christianity, and it was hard to find people still fluent in the old ways. Courtright couldn't think of anyone and turned to the old men. They whispered among themselves in Lakota, then one translated into English. There *was* such a man: Black Elk, or Hehaka Sapa. He was "a sort of a preacher"—a *wicasa wakan*—but he might not be willing to talk. He was a little peculiar.

Neihardt grinned. His face was long and wolfish, his smile slightly unsettling. This was the ritual first step in the West's conversational dance—the test of one's resolve. He'd come this far already, he said. He'd still like to try. Courtright arranged for him to take along seventy-six-year-old Moses Flying Hawk, an old Lakota chief who spoke English. Neihardt would later admit he was not fond of Flying Hawk: the man was too cynical, too "modern," he said. Whether he knew it or not, Flying Hawk was famous in his own right: a first cousin of Crazy Horse and brother of the Ghost Dance leader Kicking Bear, he'd fought in Red Cloud's War, at the Little Bighorn, and at Wounded Knee. From

1898 to 1929, he'd gone "Wild Westing" with Buffalo Bill's Wild West, the Sells Floto Circus, and the Miller Brothers 101 Ranch show. Now old age and bad health had caught up to him.

Neihardt, his son, and Flying Hawk drove sixteen miles northeast from Agency headquarters to the site of the Wounded Knee Massacre, then turned north to the village of Manderson. Though the poet never said whether he stopped this day at the battle site, he would have pointed out the landmarks to Sigurd: the prominent knob where the Hotchkiss guns unlimbered; the small clearing below, where Big Foot's band met the soldiers; the dry gulch where women and children were cut down. A weathered nine-foot obelisk rose from the knob, marking the mass grave of the Indian dead.

A little south of Manderson, Neihardt turned west toward the preacher's one-room cabin. By now the road was barely a wagon track, and his 1929 Gardner kicked up a white cloud of volcanic dust visible for miles. Flying Hawk warned Neihardt not to get his hopes up—the previous week, a "boisterous" lady journalist from Lincoln, Nebraska, had heard that Black Elk was related to Crazy Horse and come to speak to him.

The woman was thirty-year-old Eleanor Hinman, journalist, University of Nebraska stenographer, and daughter of a philosophy professor. That summer, she and her fellow literary club member Mari Sandoz jumped in their Model T coupe and drove the 430 miles from Lincoln to Pine Ridge. Hinman planned to write a biography of Crazy Horse, and during two weeks in July she interviewed several of the war chief's surviving relatives and friends. Though old warriors such as He Dog and Little Killer talked to her through interpreters, others were not as forthcoming. One interpreter, Emil Afraid of Hawk, explained that Crazy Horse's relatives "had repeatedly refused to make any statement about him to white people or indeed to Indians of the opposite faction."

Though Black Elk had been polite, he too was adamant in his refusal. "I took her over, but the old man wouldn't talk," Flying Hawk warned the poet. "He is almost blind, and, after he had squinted at her awhile, he said, 'I can see that you are a nice-looking woman, and I can feel that you are good; but I do not care to talk to you about these things.' Maybe he will talk to you, but I doubt it."

Hinman told the story differently, in two versions. In one, Black Elk demanded two hundred dollars "cash in advance" before he would talk. In another, he suggested she pay two cents a word for an interview that would last two weeks. Either way, she said, "this was taken to be another form of refusal." She later wrote: "At that it was a modest price for what he had to tell. But I would have had to pay the same to everyone else and I did not have it. So that was that."

Now it was Neihardt's turn. The poet had known Indians for about thirty years: he recognized the rhythms of their speech, their long pauses for thought, and seemed to agree with the anthropologist Claude Lévi-Strauss that cultures were like books, each a valuable and unique volume in mankind's great library. Such acceptance was unusual at a time when Native Americans in the West experienced the same kind of intolerance as blacks in the Jim Crow South. Thus, Neihardt often found that he was trusted by Indians.

But this time, he wasn't so sure. Where warriors liked to retell their deeds in all their glory, holy men considered their knowledge sacrosanct. There had been two wars for them: the military campaigns emblazoned in the history books, and a lesser-known but more far-reaching crusade waged by the government and church to eradicate the medicine man and all traces of traditional religion. This war on identity would be the most protracted experiment in social engineering ever conducted in American history, a multigenerational attempt to "kill the Indian in the Indian" for his own good—a failed endeavor to replace the soul of one people with that of another, the ramifications of which still resonate today.

Neihardt's actions that day set into motion events that placed Black Elk in the heart of this conflict, turning him into a symbol of all that was lost and might be regained. Yet at the time, Neihardt was only doing what writers do: following his instincts. He hoped to find and interview an old "long-hair," a member of a dying breed. Though the "Vanishing American" was yet another Indian stereotype, it was also part of the nation's late-blooming realization about the costs of westward expansion. The near-extinction of the buffalo was legendary: recent estimates place 28 to 30 million bison roaming North America before 1800. By 1930, only a few hundred remained in Yellowstone and on private preserves.

The slaughter of the Indian fit the same mold. It is difficult to determine exactly how many Native Americans lived in North America before 1492: modern estimates range from 1.8 to 18 million. Whatever the number, archaeologists do believe that two-thirds of that population was wiped out within 150 years of Columbus's landfall. The numbers continued to fall. By 1800, the population had dropped from millions to 600,000; by 1930, to 332,397. Of all the four horsemen, disease took the greatest toll. When the Puritans landed at Plymouth, they discovered in the surrounding forest scores of deserted Indian villages, a golgotha of corpses where the inhabitants "died on heapes, as they lay in their houses"—victims of what now is believed to be viral hepatitis carried by a shipwrecked French prisoner. The epidemic may have killed 90 percent of the Indians in coastal New England.

Other epidemics would follow, sweeping west across the New World: smallpox, measles, scarlet fever, typhus, typhoid, influenza, cholera, whooping cough, diphtheria, chicken pox, and sexually transmitted diseases. In many tribes, 25 to 50 percent of the population died. It could be worse: from 1780 to 1877, some Plains tribes lost 79 percent of their population through epidemic; in the Upper Plains, tribes such as the Mandan and Arikara saw declines as high as 93 percent. Tuberculosis decimated the twentieth-century reservations, and Neihardt would learn that the old holy man he sought out suffered from the wasting disease.

The three drove up a rutted road through yellow, treeless hills. Flying Hawk indicated an old log cabin at the end; weeds grew from its dirt roof. Two long-hairs who lived in similar cabins watched them pass, then mounted their ponies and followed. A weird feeling overtook Neihardt. This was a country "where little else but weather ever happened," he later wrote: little more "than the sun and moon and stars going over—and there was little for the old men to do but wait for yesterday."

An old, thin Indian stood alone by the cabin, watching the Gardner as it bounced toward him. He was tall, slender, and lithe, with a dark complexion and mobile features. Despite his near-blindness he had "fine eyes," Eleanor Hinman would write: "long, liquid, straight, set to far distances, and deeply crows' footed at the corners." But it was what Black Elk was *not* that struck Neihardt as they drove near. He was not the stereotypical long-hair he'd expected. Instead, Black Elk's graying hair was cut short, and his wrinkled "ready-made" suit had seen years of wear. When the old men at Agency headquarters had said he was "a sort of a preacher," they'd meant that, yes, he had been a *wicasa wakan* during the Ghost Dance, but he'd since become Catholic and was now one of the best-known lay preachers, or catechists, on the reservation.

"*Hau, kola,*" Flying Hawk said as they stepped from the car. The old man replied in Lakota. He went by the baptismal name of Nicholas Black Elk, just as Flying Hawk went by Moses. Though Flying Hawk also addressed him in Lakota, there was always a question about how much English the old man actually understood. Although later letters show he did know some, he was always more comfortable speaking and writing in his native tongue. Some elders also believed it diluted one's power to speak anything but one's own language. It certainly controlled the conversation, especially with those whites one did not trust or know.

Flying Hawk introduced the poet and his son. Neihardt shook the preacher's hand, then gave him cigarettes and other small gifts, making sure to include the old long-hairs squatting by their ponies. He'd come to talk about the old times, he said.

"Ah-h-h!" Black Elk replied.

Experience told Neihardt to move slowly. Impatience was a trait Indians disliked in whites, and considered disrespectful. Around the same period, the renowned Swiss psychologist Carl Jung was talking to an Indian friend in the Southwest who served as governor of a pueblo. "We don't understand the whites," he said, "they are always wanting something—always restless—always looking for something. What is it? We don't know. We can't understand them. They have such sharp noses, such thin, cruel lips, such lines in their faces. We think they are all crazy."

So Neihardt took his time and did not rush his questions. He said he'd heard that Black Elk was a holy man during the Ghost Dance. *He* was a poet, and had just finished a book that ended with the killing of Crazy Horse at nearby Fort Robinson.

The old man had listened politely as Flying Hawk translated, but suddenly interrupted: Tasunke Witko had been his second cousin, he said. Crazy Horse was a great man. Neihardt agreed, adding that he'd once talked with Major Henry Lemley, officer of the guard on the day Crazy Horse was killed. Lemley was so enraged by what he witnessed that he asked to leave the Indian Service. Neihardt paused: good men fought on both sides of that war, he said.

"Hmmm," Black Elk replied. They sat and smoked, and after a while Neihardt asked again about the Ghost Dancers. But Black Elk did not seem interested. His answers were polite but brief; his mind, elsewhere. A couple of times he mentioned a vision he'd had as a youngster, but each time he halted mid-sentence. Something held him back. Locusts whirred in the dry grass around them.

Finally, Black Elk turned to Flying Hawk as if he'd made a decision. "As I sit here, I can feel in this man beside me a strong desire to know the things of the Other World. He has been sent to learn what I know, and I will teach him." The comment came out of nowhere. As he spoke, family members trickled from the house; according to the Pine Ridge census of April 11, 1930, nine people lived in the one-room cabin. Now he waved his hand at a grandson and the boy ducked through the doorway. He returned with a necklace: a leather star tinged with blue, from its center dangling a strip of buffalo hide and an eagle feather. "Here you see the Morning Star," Black Elk explained. "Who sees the Morning Star shall see more, for he shall be wise." The eagle feather stood for *Wakan Tanka*, the Great Mystery, while the hide strip stood for all things given by the earth—food and shelter. This had been his father's. Now he was giving it to the poet, and told him to hang it from his neck. Black Elk smoked his cigarette to the nub, lost in thought again.

When he finally broke the silence, he spoke of the vision that had haunted him all afternoon. The sun was close to setting; it had taken five hours to get this far. He wanted to tell the poet about his Great Vision, which was supposed to save his people. The Vision was central to his identity and long life, a mission given to him by the Grandfathers fifty-eight years earlier, when he was nine. It had guided his choices and actions ever since. Such sacred matters were inviolable, and he'd never revealed the Vision to anyone except during those times when he'd been initiated into sacred mysteries by spiritual mentors. They had been amazed. Revealing it to outsiders would diminish its power, but he was growing old; if he did not pass it on, it would die with him.

But now was not the time—not without preparation, not with all these people around. "There is so much to tell you," he said. "What I know was given to me and it is true and it is beautiful. Soon I shall be under the grass and it will be lost. You were sent to save it." He told the poet to come back in the spring, when the grass was as high as the width of his hand. All would be ready then.

Neihardt felt moved in a way he could not explain. He promised to come back as the old man asked. Black Elk simply nodded.

As they drove off, Flying Hawk shook his head. "That was kind of funny, the way the old man seemed to know you were coming." There were few phones and autos in Pine Ridge; it would have been impossible for someone to phone or ride ahead from Agency headquarters and beat the Gardner. Sigurd agreed—the old man had been looking down the road as they approached. He almost seemed to expect them.

"He's a funny old man," Flying Hawk murmured.

Neihardt returned nine months later, in May 1931. The intervening seasons had devastated Pine Ridge: dust storms, blizzards, droughts, and locusts struck the reservation in nearly uninterrupted succession. Cattle and horses died en masse; according to Black Elk's nephew Frank Fools Crow, "The poultry and the pigs shriveled up and died too." In a land where the average annual family income was $152.80— supplemented by horse meat, wild foods, and meager federal rations— many Lakota barely escaped starvation through contributions from the Red Cross and Mount Rushmore's sculptor, Gutzon Borglum. For the very old and young, this was not enough: sickness set in. Flying Hawk was sick when Neihardt returned, and the poet would never again see his interpreter. The old chief died on Christmas Eve of 1931—the rumored cause, starvation.

Amid such hardship, Black Elk grew convinced that his days on earth were numbered. He was nearing his seventh decade; he'd outlived too many friends and family; he suffered from tuberculosis and a near-blindness brought on by glaucoma and corneal burns. He grew desperate to leave something of value behind for his people. When Neihardt came back with a book contract from New York, the two commenced a project that started as a personal testament of Plains Indian life from the 1860s to 1890 but ended as one of the twentieth century's most important documents on Native American culture and as a classic of world literature. In more than three weeks of interviews that May, Black Elk chronicled a life that spanned a remarkable era of change not only for the Sioux but for all Plains Indians. Born even as the Oglala enjoyed their last days of freedom, he would be witness to the disappearance of the buffalo; the Battle of the Little Bighorn; the death of his second cousin Crazy Horse; travels to the eastern United States and to Europe with Buffalo Bill's Wild West show; the hope and tragedy of the Ghost Dance religion and the Massacre at Wounded Knee; and the ultimate banishment of the Sioux to the reservations.

Throughout, his religious roles were manifold: to the Sioux, he would serve as healer, seer, *yuwipi*, or a kind of medium, and *heyoka*, or a sacred clown; to the Ghost Dancers, as mentor, interpreter of visions, and creator of the "bulletproof" shirts some later blamed for the tragedy; to the Catholic Church, as lay preacher and fervent proselytizer who modeled himself after St. Paul. He passed through each phase and preserved from each what he felt held lasting meaning for his people. As Black Elk told his story, his eldest son translated into English; Neihardt asked questions, and after a round of clarification, the poet's eldest daughter transcribed the old man's words into shorthand. Neihardt was astounded by the unfolding tale, and shaped it into tragic literature.

More than anything else, Black Elk spoke of his Great Vision. He'd received it while still young, as he lingered in a coma near death for eleven days. During that time, he watched himself taken to the spirit world and brought before the Six Grandfathers, the multipartite embodiment of *Wakan Tanka* and the fundamental powers of the universe. Even as he watched, he transformed; he became the Sixth Grandfather, the spirit of the earth and defender of his threatened people. He began an epic quest to save the Sioux, who, like the buffalo, faced extinction. It seemed an impossible task, yet the Grandfathers assured him that buried in the Vision lay the key to salvation. With the powers given by the gods, he would renew the dying Tree of Life and restore the Oglala to their former strength and glory.

The Great Vision shaped Black Elk's life, thoughts, and words. It foreshadowed the choices he would make as a healer, teacher, and thinker. Yet as he grew older, something went wrong: the Vision did not save the Lakota, who, with their defeat by the U.S. government, slipped into decline. Though he never doubted the Vision, he always doubted himself. He feared he was neither prescient nor pure enough to find the Truth hidden in the puzzle-box, and his guilt mounted with the decades. With Neihardt he sensed one last chance: if the poet could understand his teachings, he would pass the Great Vision to the world.

Black Elk Speaks: Being the Life Story of a Holy Man of the Oglala Sioux as told to John G. Neihardt was released by William Morrow and Company in 1932. It was hailed by critics at the time as a "strangely beautiful" book—too strange for public tastes, perhaps, since it did not sell well. Morrow "remaindered" it at forty-five cents a copy, after which it took on an international life of its own. The psychologist Carl Jung compared Black Elk's "remarkable parallel vision" to the Old Testament prophets Ezekiel and Zechariah, and urged its translation into German, a nation strangely addicted to American Indians. In 1953, it was translated as *Ich rufe mein Volk* (I Call My People), and the European cult of Black Elk began. In 1961, the book was finally reprinted in the United States, a rerelease that coincided with the beginning of the counterculture. Yet it wasn't until the April 27, 1971, interview of Neihardt by the TV host Dick Cavett that the nation recognized what it had ignored. Cavett called *Black Elk Speaks* "the greatest book in the history of the American Indian," and Neihardt, who was older now than the old holy man when he'd met him forty years earlier, said he felt himself becoming more Indian as mortality loomed. Like the Lakota, he did not think of death as the end.

Sales of the book spiked after that—it hasn't been out of print since, and has been translated into at least a dozen languages. Today, *Black Elk Speaks* has inspired countless references and articles in literature, popular culture, and the scholarly press. It has been taught in thousands of high school and college classrooms, and has inspired the creation of at least two European institutes devoted to the study of Native American religions. The Sioux social critic Vine Deloria, Jr., claimed that *Black Elk Speaks* struck a chord elevating it to a "Native American bible of all tribes"; the Kiowa author N. Scott Momaday called the book "an extraordinary human document about history and destiny." The anthropologist Raymond J. DeMallie, who transcribed and published the shorthand notes of the 1931 interviews, said that by preserving traditional rites and beliefs, the book served as "an American Indian Rosetta stone." In 1988, the mythologist Joseph Campbell called *Black Elk Speaks* "a key statement in the understanding of myth and symbols"; Philip Zaleski, editor of the *Best Spiritual Writing* series, said that a 1999 poll of experts listed it as one of the top ten spiritual books of the twentieth century.

The most poignant memorial is an unembellished set of words hanging outside the visitors' center at the Little Bighorn National Monument. To the south rises another hilltop obelisk, remarkably similar to the one at Wounded Knee. In its shadow sprout the white grave markers of Custer and the cavalrymen who died around him; farther down Massacre Hill, to the west, more markers cluster in a ravine. It was here that a twelve-year-old Black Elk killed the second of three or four soldiers that chaotic afternoon in 1876, finishing what older warriors had started. Little did he dream that his words would be cast in stainless steel.

They are written in the language of the combatants. In Lakota:

Wowasake kin Slolyapo
Wowahwala he e.
                    —*Hehaka Sapa*

Then, in English:

Know the Power
That is Peace.
                    —Black Elk

———————

What are we to make of all this? How can one understand the flesh-and-blood *wicasa wakan*—with all his triumphs, defeats, loves, and detours—when many consider him the only true American holy man to come out of the twentieth century? The transformation was so swift that one already encounters references to the "historical Black Elk," just as one finds tomes devoted to the "historical Jesus." Though rare, such elevation to cultural sainthood *does* happen—one thinks of Charles Lindbergh and John F. Kennedy. But the debunking began within a decade of their beatification, while Black Elk's star continues to rise.

What does it mean to be "holy"? The concept is nearly impossible to pin down. In the 1917 *The Idea of the Holy*, the German theologian Rudolf Otto saw holiness as a complex of emotions too powerful for words—the chill of the uncanny, the despair of one's insignificance in the presence of God. The stricken grapple with what Otto called the "numinous," a mental state that can "burst from the depths of the soul with spasms or convulsions," or, as mysteriously, "come sweeping like a gentle tide."

Maybe it is easier to be in touch with the holy on the Great Plains. During the day, the light from above is brutal and harsh, but at dusk a "numinous" beauty takes hold. The prairie transforms from a flat whiteness leached of all life to moving shadows of indigo and gold. The land rolls away like waves. One stands atop a hill and understands why Black Elk thought his people lived in a sacred hoop: as the land spreads out in a circle, one encounters peace and sadness, knowing one is part of it, but very small. A longing floods in for something beyond expression, but that is hard to find.

Ironically, the church that once tried to suppress Black Elk's beliefs has now embraced him. The former medicine man's quarter century as a Catholic catechist would lead him to reservations throughout the West and result in hundreds of Native American conversions. Yet, when Neihardt asked the old man why he turned Catholic little more than a decade after Wounded Knee, Black Elk said he did so "because my children have to live in this world." The enigmatic comment suggests an uneasy union.

Neihardt's failure to mention Black Elk's adopted faith in his work created a vacuum that Church commentators have since tried to fill. Today, Catholic writers paint the old man as a bridge between the beliefs of the Old World and the New. On October 21, 2012, the Church named its first North American Indian saint—Kateri Tekakwitha, a Mohican woman converted in the late 1600s whose canonization began in 1884. "With Indian America now having a woman saint, a male counterpart ought to be close behind her," wrote the Jesuit father and author Michael Steltenkamp in 2013. "Nicholas Black Elk is the pre-eminent candidate for that honor."

Not everyone is thrilled by the idea of sainthood. In July 2012, a Lakota woman working in the Catholic mission at the nearby Rosebud reservation flinched at the news. "They [the Catholics] would like that, wouldn't they?" She shook her head in disgust, but refused to say more. Black Elk's great-granddaughter Betty Black Elk O'Rourke stared at me in shock as we dodged ruts in her battered pickup and nearly ran off the road. "Where did that come from?" she shrieked, clearly surprised, barely gaining control of the vehicle. Yet the process has already begun. Two documented "miracles" are required by the Catholic Church to make someone a saint, and the search is under way.

Complicating this all is the fact that concepts of holiness and reality were radically different for Plains Indians and Euro-Americans. People who would be called mentally ill in Western society were readily accepted in tribal cultures as religious healers and shamans. They heard voices, talked to spirits, and visited worlds parallel to our own. This is the kind of behavior diagnosed today by psychiatrists as some form of schizophrenia. In contrast, Lakota society encouraged young men to seek out mystical experiences as a way to aid their people and define their own lives. The boundary between the real and the visionary is fluid for both shamans and schizophrenics; anthropologists have even called schizophrenia the "shaman sickness," since part of the holy man's journey involves entering this alternate reality to seek out medical cures and divine protections for the tribe.

To Black Elk and other *wicasa wakan* of his generation, such talk was academic. The outer world and the inner—the physical world we think we know and the "numinous" mystery beyond—are one. If any characteristic links the holy men and mystics of every age and culture, from today's Amazonian shamans to the vanished, white-clad Essenes of the Dead Sea, it's the conviction that no division exists. The seen and unseen are one.

Black Elk was a haunted man. In the end, that drew me to his story—to the places where he fought and killed to save his people, to the landscape where he watched them die. To the scattered archives and libraries holding tidbits of his life, the mountaintop where he lamented his failure, the little cabin now surrounded by cottonwoods where he died. If there was one overriding pattern to his life, it was the detours he took to reverse destiny. The gods had given him a gift, but one he never fully understood. His search for an answer always seemed in vain. First the Sioux wars, then life on the reservation; "Wild Westing" with Bill Cody, the hope of the Messiah, cattle ranching, Catholicism—each new road was entered with the hope of salvation, but at the end it seemed to fail.

If anything, Black Elk would be what today is called a spiritual seeker—but one with a goal. In the Sioux world, religion was as much a tool as a creed; it conveyed power to the individual and the tribe. In a world laden with mystery and threat, it only made sense to find and employ the right tool. Much has been made of his 1904 conversion to Catholicism and transformation into one of the most effective Indian catechists the Church had ever seen. Yet Catholicism was only one more road. Was he still Catholic when Neihardt drove up, or using the Church as a blind to return to the old and outlawed ways? To say he was wholly one or the other discounts the longer view. Although almost every decade after adulthood encompassed for him a different journey, each was an attempt to unlock his Vision and save his people—the one path he never abandoned.

With Neihardt, Black Elk sensed a final chance. At the end of the interviews, he climbed atop Harney Peak, the highest point in Paha Sapa, and cried out to *Wakan Tanka* like a biblical prophet lamenting the lost glory of his people and their banishment to exile. Neihardt shaped that lament into one of the most famous passages of defeat in American letters: "When I look back now out from this high hill of my old age, I can still see the butchered women and children lying around and scattered all along the crooked gulch as plain as when I saw them with eyes still young. And I can see something else died there in the bloody mud, and was buried in the blizzard. A people's dream died there. It was a beautiful dream."

With that, a light rain began to fall. He was convinced that his days would soon end, but he did not mind. He was tired. He'd fought two wars, feared he'd been defeated in both, and believed such failure would be his legacy. He was a "pitiful old man" wracked with guilt, for he had done nothing with an extraordinary gift and now the moment was past. The "nation's hoop is broken and scattered," he mourned. "There is no center any longer, and the sacred tree is dead."

But Black Elk was wrong. The roots ran deep. Some struggles never end.

PART I

IF YOU'RE NOT GOOD, THE *WASICHUS* WILL GET YOU

If I were an Indian, I often think I would greatly prefer to cast my lot among those of my people [who] adhered to the free open plains, rather than submit to the confined limits of a reservation, there to be the recipient of the blessed benefits of civilization, with its vices thrown in without stint or reserve.

—George Armstrong Custer, *My Life on the Plains* (1874)

CHOSEN

Extinction loomed in his life from the day he was born. It waited over the horizon like the thunderclouds rolling across the Plains. He feared those storms and the gods perched in their black folds. His second cousin Tasunke Witko, whom whites called Crazy Horse, advised him to submit to Their will. He'd been given a gift, a Great Vision to save his people. If he acted on it, all would be well.

He was not alone in such fear. His people, the Oglala Lakota—called the Sioux by their enemies—felt the apocalypse first and foremost with the disappearance of the buffalo. The vast herds remembered fondly by grandparents were doomed by the mid-nineteenth century. By 1842, the annual kill of *Pte* by civilian hunters exceeded 2.5 million; between 1850 and 1885, the railroads transported more than 75 million hides to eastern factories, where they were turned into gun belts and upholstery for high-end furniture. "Kill every buffalo you can," Colonel Richard Irving Dodge told an English sportsman. "Every buffalo dead is an Indian gone."

Perhaps, like a river, *Pte* had drained underground. The Lakota believed that the bison came from the womb of the earth, and in evil times returned. Wind Cave in the Black Hills was that route to the underworld; at least, so said the medicine men, and Black Elk did not question them. His was a family of medicine men, stretching back for generations. Before he was Black Elk, still known by the childhood name Kahnigapi, or

"Chosen," he knew that only the foolish discounted the warnings of seers and holy men. They spoke of a new people who could not be stopped, no matter how many were killed. "They will be a powerful people, strong, tough," the holy men admonished. "They are coming closer all the time."

The most famous prophecy was that of Sweet Medicine, the powerful seer of their friends the Shahila, or Cheyenne. He warned of a "good-looking people, with light hair and white skin" who would come from the east in search of a "certain stone." At first there would be just a few, but more would come, killing off the animals of the earth with an instrument that "makes a noise, and sends a little round stone to kill." They'd replace the old four-leggeds with a new one with white horns and a long tail. They'd bring a drink that drove men crazy, and take the tribe's children to teach them their ways. But these children would learn nothing. They would be shadows, lost between worlds.

Neither resistance nor reason could stop them, Sweet Medicine warned. "What they are going to do they will do." Instead, the People would change: "In the end of your life in those days you will not get up early in the morning; you will never know when day comes; you will lie in bed; you will have disease, and will die suddenly; you will all die off."

The Lakota prophet was no more comforting. Drinks Water—sometimes called Wooden Cup—died about twenty years before Black Elk was born. Black Elk's father told him of the vision, as had *his* father before him. And *he*, the grandfather, had been told by Tries to Be Chief, the old bachelor who served as Drinks Water's helper. Thus, the story had to be true. In this vision, a strange race would weave a spider's web all around the Sioux. In some versions, the web was made of iron. As Black Elk grew older, he recognized this as a variation of the Iktomi, or spider, story, and Drinks Water's dream seems the first reference comparing whites to the Iktomi. At some subconscious level, the image was chilling. Myths are strange and powerful narratives with the ability to "shape and direct [life], for good or ill," wrote Richard Slotkin in an early version of his cultural history *Regeneration Through Violence*. "They are made of words, concepts, images, and they can kill," and Drinks Water's words would be fatal in every way. When the new people finished their web, he said, Oglalas' lives would forever change. They would no longer live in their tipis: a tipi was warm in the winter, cool in the summer, and could be disassembled and moved in a pony drag to follow the herds. If the Grandfathers had meant for man to stay in one place, they would have made the earth stand still. But in the dominion of the Iktomi, the People would live in square gray houses rooted to the earth in a barren land. "When this happens," said Drinks Water, "alongside of those gray houses you shall starve."

The old man lay down after finishing his account and refused to rise. He would die soon, he told his family, and he wished to be cremated so thoroughly that nothing remained. His clan built his bonfire on the prairie west of Paha Sapa, and it burned four days. Its light could be seen from every direction, a grim beacon for a New World his people hoped they would never find.

The child who would become Black Elk was born on a riverbank in the Powder River Country, a fertile rectangle loosely defined as the Powder River Basin of southeastern Montana and northeastern Wyoming. Nestled between the Bighorn Mountains to the west and the Black Hills to the east, it stretches approximately 120 miles east to west and 200 miles north to south; several rivers flow through it to join the Yellowstone, including the Powder, Tongue, Little Bighorn, Little Missouri, Belle Fourche, and Cheyenne. Since the Powder is the longest, it gives the region its name.

Water means life in the West, and the Powder River Country was a game preserve. Migrating herds of buffalo, elk, and antelope passed through. Flocks of waterfowl darkened the sky. Bear, deer, and rabbits lived in the breaks, while trout filled the streams. The valleys were thick with aspen, cottonwood, and willow; the meadows, bursting with cherries, wild strawberries, and plums. The land rose west from the Black Hills in broken steppes, buttoned with strange stone formations like the Missouri Buttes and Devils Tower. Indian trails followed a course northwest from the North Platte River to the Bighorn and Yellowstone Country, where the great herds wintered.

People had lived there thousands of years: each new group called it their own, usually at the expense of the ones already there. In the 1700s, the Powder River Country belonged to the Crow, who soon became the Sioux's favorite enemy. For the next century, bands of Oglala and Brulé spread west, followed quickly by their kinsmen—the Minneconjou, Sans Arc, and Hunkpapa. By the early 1800s, the Crow and Lakota skirmished over hunting rights, and every spring and summer renewed the seasonal cycle of raids and revenge. While the Lakota were excellent horsemen, the Crow were brilliant horse thieves. By the 1850s, a rough balance had been reached: the Crow lived in the mountains; the Lakota, on the Plains.

Most sources place the year of Black Elk's birth as 1863. When Black Elk told Neihardt that he was born when "Four Crows Were Killed on the Tongue," this was the name given to the year in his band's "winter count," the tribal calendar painted on a spiraling pictograph made of hide. Each year was designated by its most significant event, and though winter counts sometimes recorded events of known historical importance, like a comet or battle, more often they reflected the unique experiences of each family band. Thus, to American Horse, 1863 was the year when "Crows Scalped an Oglala Boy Alive." The Minneconjous called it the year when "Eight [Crows] Were Killed"; the Hunkpapa, the "Year of the [Whooping] Cough"; the Yanktonai, the year of "Plenty of Buffalo," an increasing rarity.

The month and day of Black Elk's birth are less certain. This was not unusual: Indians measured time in moons and seasons, and many could make only a rough guess of their age. His mother did say, however, that she gave birth in the month when "the chokecherries were ripe"—late June or July—and one would think that she, if anyone, would remember. Yet Black Elk also told Neihardt he was born on December 6, thus contradicting his mother, and most commentators have accepted that date. He failed to explain that this was the day of his Catholic baptism, when he took the new name Nicholas William Black Elk. At the time, Native American converts literally took the day of their baptism as the day they were "reborn."

Black Elk was apparently the seventh of nine children: five sisters, one older half brother, and two younger brothers are mentioned in the interviews. His half brother, Runs in the Center, or Wicegna Inyanka, was named for his actions in battle. Only two sisters are recorded—Jenny Shot Close and Grace Pretty Bird—and both remained close to Black Elk throughout their lives.

He was heir to a family of medicine men, the fourth Black Elk, though the name did not pass to him until sometime after the onset of his visions. His father was the third Black Elk, a medicine man and warrior hailing from a line of healers. They belonged to the kinship band of Big Road, a Decider, or wise and respected chief, who would be involved in almost every major Oglala decision regarding war and peace in the 1860s and '70s. Black Elk's father shared a grandfather with the father of Crazy Horse, making them first cousins. Finally, the boy's grandfather and great-grandfather were also Black Elks. His grandfather was killed by Pawnees when he was still an infant; of his great-grandfather, no tales remain.

Thus, while stability and a sense of identity reigned in Black Elk's family, so did certain expectations. A medicine man's life was not his own. One was always "on call": to perform tasks demanded by the spirits; to guide young men through their vision quests, interpret dreams, heal wounds and sickness, or provide advice for the tribe. "Specialties" varied, based upon powers granted in a vision or dream.

Black Elk came from a family of bear healers, among the most powerful, and theatrical, of Lakota medicine men. The bear appears in almost every tribal culture as a conduit for medical cures. It came to one in a dream, imparting cures and herbal secrets, passing on its strength to braves headed for war. During rituals, the dreamer was possessed by the spirit of the bear: red clay blew from his mouth with each breath; canines protruded from his lips; he chased people like an angry bear. In the hands of an artist, the performance could be both comic and frightening. Helpers would fill the dreamer's pipe to soothe him, a kindness they hoped the bear spirit would repay in times of war; tribesmen could also purchase cures and protective *wotawe*. He served as a battlefield medic, making him especially important for a martial people like the Sioux: he'd clean out a wound with a sharpened bear claw, apply medicine, and dress the wound. He would stay with his patient through death or recovery.

Generally, medicine men were divided into two classes: the *Zuya-Wakan*, or war prophets, and the *Wapiya* (or *Wapiyapi*), healers of the body and mind. The healers were further subdivided: the *wicasa wakan*, as Black Elk would be called—a holy man whose powers derived from mystical experience; and the *pejuta wicasa*, who healed with plants and other curatives—a term eventually used for white doctors. For all, the goal was similar: interpreting and putting to use that which was *wakan*— that which was supernatural, holy, or beyond comprehension. The medicine man served his Lakota kinsmen like Moses did the Israelites: in direct contact with God, he introduced new rites and declared old ones outdated. He guided them down a perilous path in which the Great Mystery made dangerous and inexplicable demands.

Officially, one could not choose to be a medicine man. One was *chosen*, providing insight into Black Elk's childhood name. One was predestined for the role. Sudden voices or a visit by a spirit tended to reveal the rough outline of one's future. The gods worked through the medicine man, making him their tool.

Unofficially, however, one could start down the medicine path at an early age, often at a parent's urging. Francis La Flesche, an Omaha who would be the first Native American ethnologist, wrote in 1905 that the medicine track "often passed down through the family." Even women could receive the call, though rarely. Catherine Wabose, an Ojibwa who converted to Christianity in the 1840s, described a kind of parental preconditioning: "When I was a girl of about twelve or thirteen years of age, my mother told me to look out for something that would happen to me."

No matter the path, the chosen was trained in the rites, ceremonies, and history of the tribe. In an oral culture, this meant long sessions of repetition and memorization at the feet of respected medicine men. Such professors looked for qualities found more in the scholar than the soldier—an attraction to abstraction and attention to detail; an introversion that transforms into the life of the mind. Where the warrior was tasked with a tribe's day-to-day survival, the tribe's future existence depended upon the accurate performance of those rites and ceremonies necessary for continued favor in the eyes of God.

Thus, tribal elders would be looking, at an early age, for the odd child. The child who heard voices, who saw things at the edge of vision that others could not see. And who was better placed to see this than the mother, especially in a long-standing family of medicine men?

Little is known about Black Elk's mother other than what appears in Neihardt's notes and through family tradition. Her childhood name was White Cow Sees; her adult name, Leggings Down (and after Catholic conversion, Mary Leggings Down). Holy Rosary Mission archives listed her birth as 1844, which made her nineteen when Black Elk was born. Her mother was Plenty Eagle Feathers; her father, Keeps His Tipi, also translated as Refuse to Go. She'd been married earlier to the deceased brother of Black Elk's father; in Sioux society, men were obliged upon a brother's death to support and even marry their former sister-in-law. Thus, Black Elk's older half brother, Runs in the Center, was also his first cousin. Leggings Down was apparently the elder Black Elk's first and only wife; he passed the family name and hereditary calling down to his first natural son. Black Elk records no filial jealousy: it was simply the way things were done.

If Black Elk's father was the mediator between God and the tribe, Black Elk's mother was the mediator between her husband and individual Oglalas. Her marriage to the elder Black Elk made her his assistant: in addition to running a nomadic household, she became chief nurse, office manager, and social secretary. She was tasked with finding many of the secret ingredients used in her husband's cures. The stability of both the business and the household sat squarely on her shoulders: she seems to have handled the responsibility well.

Black Elk's life of ritual began with his mother's labor pains. His father left the lodge to a team of kinswomen, one or several of whom served as midwives. A stake festooned with eagle-down feathers was pounded into the earth; a clean deerskin was spread beside it for Leggings Down to kneel upon. She pressed her hands and knees against the stake. The midwife called for water, grease, and swabs of sweetgrass as the contractions increased in force and duration.

No birth is easy, but no complications were recorded, and so the fourth Black Elk was born. He was washed by an old woman, after which a respected male relative entered the tipi and breathed into his mouth, an act believed to form his character. He would not be named for eight days, and only then given his childhood name, Kahnigapi, or "Chosen."

———•———

Memory is history, but whose memory prevails? We have a tendency to look around at the world as it was when we were children and assume this is the way it has always been. In all the other Sioux autobiographies of the early twentieth century—whether written in collaboration with a white, or by a white-educated Indian—childhood was a happy idyll in an unspoiled but vanished Eden. Charles Alexander Eastman, a Santee Sioux who studied medicine at Boston University and tended casualties at Wounded Knee, called his people "the children of the forest" in his 1902 *Indian Boyhood*. Joseph White Bull, described as "the man who killed Custer," remembered a childhood of buffalo hunts and free-spirited training for war. Luther Standing Bear, one of the first Lakota to act in Hollywood Westerns, remembered his Plains as "a beautiful country" covered with "velvety green grass," where buffalo roamed at will. "Life was full of happiness and contentment for my people," he wrote in his 1931 *My Indian Boyhood*.

Only the Great Plains of Black Elk are governed by fear. His life story begins with the death of his grandfather, the second Black Elk, at the hands of a Pawnee. Then the grandmother dies. *Black Elk Speaks* begins with war and the rumor of war: it was a vague period he remembered "as a man might remember some bad dream," a time of his childhood "when everything seemed troubled and afraid."

More than anything else, he feared the white nation to the east, the one foretold by Sweet Medicine and Drinks Water. His people called them *wasichus*, and since he had never laid eyes on one, he imagined them as bogeymen. Grown-ups called them merciless—an unstoppable force that would "take our country and rub us all out and we should all have to die fighting," he said. In the year of Black Elk's birth, the *wasichus* fought among themselves in a great war to the east: many hoped they would rub one another out and thus spare the Lakota. But that happy chance had not occurred and now they came closer. His mother and others like her wielded this bogeyman like a stick on a disobedient child. "If you are not good, the *wasichus* will get you," they warned.

Only later did he realize that the year of his birth was the cusp when everything changed. In 1862, whites discovered in Montana the yellow metal *mázaska zi* that drove them mad. In June 1863, the failed Colorado gold miner John M. Bozeman probed north through the Powder River Country to blaze a wagon road to reach that gold. The road would not take much space, the miners promised: the width between two wagon wheels and nothing more. But the Lakota had heard similar promises in the Southern and Central Plains. The road itself might not be wide, but the *wasichus* who used it would come in multitudes.

Geographically, the Bozeman Trail was a spur of the better-known Oregon Trail, veering off northwest in Wyoming to the gold in Bannack, Montana. It was an old, well-watered buffalo trail used by Indians to pass north and south since prehistory. Though solitary whites had sometimes traveled its length, the Lakota and Cheyenne believed them harmless wanderers and gave them food. The trail's first recorded mention came in 1804, with Lewis and Clark's Corps of Discovery. On the return trip, Sacagawea guided Clark and a small band over "an old buffalow road" to what is called the Bozeman Pass today.

Until 1863, the old life of following the herds and raiding rival tribes had passed unabated, like the seasons. In Siouan eyes, this was the good life, and they saw no reason to change. The Powder River Country provided everything the tribe could want. Why should they ever leave?

Yet, like the *wasichu*, they were relative newcomers, fellow invaders who'd migrated west in search of a better life, pushing weaker groups aside. The Lakota pushed aside the Mandan and Arikara at the Missouri River, the Cheyenne in the plains to the west, the Kiowa in the Black Hills, the Crow on the Powder River. By the year of Black Elk's birth, their conquered lands stretched from the Missouri River of Dakota to the Bighorn Mountains in Wyoming, from the North Platte River in Nebraska to the Cannonball River of North Dakota. The territory surpassed in square miles that of Pennsylvania and New York combined. Now history seemed ready to repeat itself as the *wasichu* threatened to push *them* aside.

The Sioux first appeared in records in the 1600s, encountered by French explorers and missionaries in the western Great Lakes and upper Mississippi River. The Ottawa called them the "Nátawèsiwok," which the French turned into "Nadouessioux" and shortened to "Sioux." The tribe preferred "Dakota," or "many in one." Some sources called them the "Seven Council Fires": the westernmost of these were the Teton, or "Dwellers on the Plains," also called "Lakota" for their dialect. In time, they divided into seven tribes, or *ospaye*: the Oglala, Brulé, Minneconjou, Hunkpapa, Sans Arc, Blackfoot, and Two Kettles. Their friendship was called *ólakotá*; all others were *tóka*, or "enemies."

The Oglala were the westernmost of the seven, and by the 1850s they'd separated into smaller family bands. These *tiyospaye* averaged about ten to twenty families of fifty to one hundred people each. These split into the Southern Oglala, who ranged as far south as the Republican River, and the Northern Oglala, who made the Black Hills, Powder River Country, and Northern Plains their home. By 1863, the latter numbered about three hundred lodges: their strongest band was the "Bad Faces," that of Red Cloud, Crazy Horse, Big Road, and Black Elk.

To the Lakota, their true origin lay with the Sacred Pipe, the foundation of all society. During a great famine, a beautiful young woman wearing white doeskin appeared to two hunters. When one made a sexual advance, a poisonous cloud reduced him to bones. This was no ordinary woman, the survivor realized, and the woman said, "I am a spirit come to help your people," as if reading his mind. The next morning, White Buffalo Calf Woman arrived at his camp with a bundle containing the first Sacred Pipe, sent by the Grandfathers as a means of prayer and a sign of kinship between Sioux and buffalo. When the People smoked the pipe, the Grandfathers sent bison to them. In their eyes, the Buffalo Calf Pipe signified their covenant with God. Before its bestowal,

it was said, the tribe "ran around the prairies like so many wild animals." Afterward, they were God's Chosen People and all others were
"common men."

A second gift brought power. In the first half of the 1700s, the Lakota
were still a nomadic Stone Age tribe. They traveled on foot in search of
buffalo, transporting possessions by small travois hitched to dogs. That
changed between 1750 and 1820, when they discovered the horse and
transformed into equestrians par excellence with lightning speed.

The mount ridden by the Sioux was nothing like its ancestor *Eohippus*,
a three-toed, dog-sized creature that roamed North America from Florida
to Canada fifty million years ago. It died out, but not before migrating
to central Asia, where evolution and selective breeding turned it into
the horse we know today. In 1493, it reappeared in the land of its origin
when Columbus brought a herd of twenty-five now very different horses
on his second voyage to the New World. As the Spanish spread through
the Americas, so did their steeds. The 1598 expedition of Don Juan de
Oñate to New Mexico introduced the first substantial herd to North
America, and by the 1600s their descendants numbered in the thousands. The Great Pueblo Revolt of 1680 released nearly 1,500 of these
mustangs into the wild and into the hands of the southwestern tribes.

It is not known when the Lakota became a horse nation. In 1630, no
tribes anywhere were mounted; by 1750, most Plains tribes were. Yet
evidence suggests the Lakota were among the last to ride. A 1798–1902
winter count by the Hunkpapa historian Long Soldier named 1801 as
the first year the People bought or stole a horse. They did not *catch* one
until 1809.

Whatever the truth, the horse revolutionized Sioux life. All of a
sudden, they could keep up with buffalo herds. A well-mounted hunter
could ride faster than a bull charging at full tilt, and kill four or five
bison in a single charge. Within a generation, the horse created for the
Sioux a surplus economy: they acquired large stores of food, piles of
buffalo hides, and other valuable goods for transport and trade. A swift
pony became the object of adoration. At early 1800s trading posts, one
could trade a fine racing horse for ten guns; for one fine hunting horse,
several pack animals. A horse conferred status and respect: for the first
time, class divisions appeared, based upon the number of horses owned.
A name that included "horse"—Crazy Horse, American Horse, Man
Afraid of His Horses—signified strength of character. The horse sym-

bolized a fundamental spiritual force that these former foot soldiers found hypnotic: charging horses sounded like thunder, and many Lakota visions included the experience of riding with supernatural warriors in the clouds.

Along the way, hunting skills turned into military prowess, and tribes that dominated the horse dominated unmounted tribes. The Sioux transformed into dazzling cavalrymen. Lakota winter counts from 1810 to 1830 depict battles with the Arikara, Mandan, Pawnee, Crow, Shoshone, and Gros Ventre, as well as occasional sorties with their allies the Cheyenne and Arapaho. Powerful Oglala war chiefs such as Bull Bear drove the Crow from the Black Hills, where they had lived for a century. By 1839, the Oglala and Brulé had pushed south from the Black Hills into the Platte River Valley, driving the Skiri Pawnee from the rolling buffalo lands.

And there these Southern Oglala encountered *wasichu* pilgrims on the Overland Trail. They watched with increasing resentment as the Union Pacific Railroad frightened away the buffalo. In 1849–50, cholera struck the Trail, dealing the Lakota a lethal blow. In 1851, the Americans tried to limit the Sioux to land north of the Platte, but their spokesman Black Hawk protested. The Sioux had the same right to this land as that taken by the United States from Mexico, he said. They owned it by right of conquest. The Americans backed off, at least temporarily, a move that confirmed to the Sioux their right to the land.

Meanwhile, the Northern Oglala spread west, and from 1855 to 1860 pushed the Crow from the Powder River Country and past the Bighorn River. By the time of Black Elk's birth, the Lakota nation numbered eleven thousand people and controlled an area encompassing the present-day states of North and South Dakota west of the Missouri, a good chunk of western Nebraska, northeastern Wyoming, and a large segment of southeastern Montana.

Of all the Sioux, the Oglala were the richest. They lived the farthest west, out on Plains still rumbling with buffalo herds. They were the farthest-removed from white pressure, closest to the horse supplies traveling north along ancient Indian trading routes, closest to wild horse herds still running across the Plains. Their location allowed them to respond quickly to calls by fur companies for buffalo hides. Like another culture that had considered themselves God's Chosen People, they'd reached their Promised Land.

———•◦•———

But great wealth can turn one's head.

By 1863, the Oglala had a reputation for flaunting their power and pride. Their eastern cousins considered them dandies, and their elaborate bead- and quill-work was some of the most sought-after by High Plains traders. The Oglala scorned their poorer cousins, showing contempt by bestowing gifts they knew could never be reciprocated. In battle, they had tremendous esprit de corps. Anything worth doing was done in grand style.

Yet prosperity did not bring peace to the Teton Sioux. There had always been tribal warfare, but by 1832, Prince Alexander Philipp Maximillian of Wied noted during his travels that capturing a horse was more important than conquering the enemy. Wealth was not equally distributed: where some Teton "frequently possess from thirty to forty horses and then are reckoned to be rich," others might not have any. Such disparity brought violence and social disruption.

Winter counts and the journals of visitors such as George Catlin and Francis Parkman, Jr., paint a society in which violence among peers was common. The Oglala winter counts of Ben Kindle, American Horse, and Cloud Shield were especially lurid, recording violence that easily hails from modern newspapers. This included the murder of an unfaithful woman, a killing in a family quarrel, three different deaths by sorcery, the murder of a son-in-law, the dual murder of a husband and wife, a drunken brawl with several killings, and several unspecified killings, woundings, and incidents of the destruction of horses.

By 1850, however, it had become apparent that the fat days of abundance might soon end. Before this date, few *wasichus* coveted their country—it was part of what the whites called the Great American Desert, a land believed so desolate that, according to popular wisdom, even "a buzzard couldn't cross it alive unless he carried provisions." But now the *wasichu* had turned their faces to the west: they, too, believed they were Chosen and had been granted a Promised Land. In 1846, Oregon became part of the United States; the next year, Mormons traveled west to Utah; in 1848, gold was discovered in California. In the summer of 1850, one out of every four hundred Americans— fifty-five thousand people—joined the westbound wagons as they cut a two-thousand-mile set of wheel ruts called the Overland Trail. Sixty-five thousand cattle accompanied them, eating their way through the

Platte Valley and creating a "great dusty ditch" that in places was fifty miles wide.

On August 31, 1851, a council held at Horse Creek near Fort Laramie, Wyoming, officially acknowledged the fact that pressure had built to the point where war between the Sioux and *wasichu* seemed inevitable. But the White Father in Washington wanted peace. The Teton Sioux, Assiniboine, Arikara, Gros Ventre, Cheyenne, Crow, and Arapaho granted the government the right to build roads and military posts through their country in return for fifty thousand dollars in trade goods annually for the next ten years. Soldiers would protect Indians from whites, and whites from Indians. War among ancient enemies must stop; attacks on whites must stop; disputes over grasslands, woodlands, or buffalo would be settled in court. The White Father wanted the tribes to stay within certain boundaries called "reservations," but neither could whites enter without permission. Above all else, Indians must promise not to attack migrants on the Overland Trail.

On September 17, 1851, the first Treaty of Fort Laramie was signed. It would set the mold for all future treaties, though not always as intended. Whites remembered the parts they held important and forgot the rest, as did Indians. The most ridiculous demand to the Lakota was the end of all fighting among tribes. War was the heart of their culture. It was how an older man gained honor and riches; how a younger man earned a name and the attentions of women. This was an impossible thing to ask. As the whites rushed through their lands, the tribes fought as always. Nothing really changed.

———•◦•———

Nevertheless, the decade following the Fort Laramie Treaty would be better for the Northern Lakota than they would ever know again. In general, the *wasichu* did not seriously invade the Powder River Country or the land around the Black Hills. Instead, they passed south, hewing to the Oregon Trail. At the new "Agencies," tribes collected their promised goods. The buffalo still rolled across the hills like a brown, shaggy sea. The Sioux had the things they loved, plus the trade goods given by the White Father. It was the best of two worlds.

But there were portents of trouble. In August 1854, a Mormon migrant allowed an ox to stray into a Sioux camp near Fort Laramie, where it was shot by a brave. When the owner complained at the fort, the commanding officer dispatched Second Lieutenant John L. Grattan, a newcomer who'd boasted he could "whip the combined force of all the Indians on the prairie" with just a few trained men. He rode with twenty-nine soldiers to the Indian camp, ten miles away. By the end of the night, Grattan, his men, and Chief Conquering Bear, who'd tried to keep the peace, lay dead. The next day, the Indians attacked Fort Laramie but were driven away.

The "Grattan Massacre" would be avenged. In late summer of 1855, Agency messengers came to the Sioux camps: all "friendly" Indians must move south of the Platte and report to Fort Laramie. Any band found north of the river would be deemed "hostile." That August, Brigadier General William S. Harney led 600 troops from the fort in search of hostiles. On September 2, 1855, he found them—a band of about 250 Brulés under Chief Little Thunder, camped on the Platte in present-day Garden County, Nebraska. The soldiers killed 86 men, women, and children, and took 70 prisoners. Twenty-seven soldiers died.

Never before in their memory had so many Sioux died in a single fight; never before had an entire camp been destroyed by soldiers. The massacre seemed harsh, but the Sioux understood revenge. It had motivated countless raids on the Crow and Pawnee. The next few years were quiet, and despite an occasional skirmish, the Sioux and *wasichu* left each other alone.

Yet what was called the Battle of Blue Water Creek served as a wake-up call. Before Harney's attack, the Sioux scorned suggestions of organizing against the *wasichu*. War was an individual game of daring and bravery, not a science of tactics and strategy. The Great Sioux Nation feared by the whites was largely a fiction. The Sioux were a collection of interrelated bands that came and went as they pleased; there were no chains of command, no generals. No single chief could order another to fight; a chief could barely order his *own* men into battle. One led by example, and the best one could hope for was to invite or persuade others to join. The only way the Sioux might mount a large force was if a threat touched everyone, not just the unfortunate Brulé.

Yet after Harney's attack, the Lakota began to change. During the 1850s and '60s, observers noticed a new social structure taking shape among the Lakota. The intergroup violence so prevalent in the winter counts began to disappear. No single instance of such violence was recorded from 1855 to 1877, the very years the U.S. government considered the Sioux the greatest threat in the American West. Instead, tribes began to work together in ways contrary to their immediate gain.

The Indian Agents noticed first. In 1862, an agent at Fort Laramie mentioned in his annual report that the "Sioux of the Dakota" had for the first time turned a solid face against the Treaty of 1851. With the exception of a headman named Bear's Rib, chiefs and their bands "actually refused to receive" annual gifts from the agent. And Bear's Rib was worried: by accepting annuities, he told the agent, he put himself and his kinsmen in danger. He was right: days later, a party of Sioux swept from the prairie and slew Bear's Rib and several of his people.

In 1866, a long report submitted by four agents noted a worrisome trend. Though some jealousy still remained among the bands, "they neither fight or quarrel in their families and or villages," they said. "We never see a quarrel or blow among the children or adults."

As the Teton finally recognized the menace massing against them, cooperative values began to replace more contentious ones. Old competitive rituals such as the anointment of a "favorite child" were muted; where revenge killings had been common, now councils of chiefs instituted property settlements between the family of an offender and that of his victim. Before 1850, confederation among bands was little more than a name. Now, it received serious attention. In 1854, an agent observed that chiefs actually commanded little power: "Head chiefs are generally opposed to the young men going to war, but cannot control soldiers," he wrote. "They will put a chief's life in danger if he interpose against their will and design." But starting in the 1860s, leaders such as Red Cloud, Crazy Horse, and Sitting Bull learned to marshal thousands of troops against the U.S. Army—and win.

During this period, the Teton elevated bravery and generosity as their society's two most-vaunted values. On the former rested their best hope of survival against endless waves of *wasichus*; on the latter, the glue that held the People together. During fat times, a warrior's main goal in life seemed a frontier version of conspicuous consumption. Now a man gained more honor by giving than by getting. A chief must be willing to give away everything he owned. Long sermons given at adoption ceremonies and inductions into men's societies emphasized duty to the poor, the weak, and the lame.

Hard times were coming. The Sioux could no longer exist happily as individual atoms blown across the Plains. The famous Sioux Nation must *act* like a nation if it hoped to survive.

2

A CASUALTY OF THE HUNDRED SLAIN

A few months after Black Elk's birth, the Teton Sioux began a debate that would decide the fate of the tribe. That it occurred at all was remarkable: that winter of 1864 was hard, with drifts forty feet deep and bands scattered across thousands of miles. The question began in the north among the Hunkpapa, then traveled south and west via messenger. A man named Red Dog visited the Bad Faces in their winter camp on the Yellowstone. He asked them to consider the problem of white people:

Could they be considered human?

More precisely, was it an honor to kill them in war? For one thing, the Sioux did not quite understand how white men *made* war. Except for the rare individual, the *wasichu* derived no pleasure from it; he fought only to get his way. He sought the spirit of his enemy, not the body: war was an imposition of will, not a stage for testing one's bravery.

Red Dog was arguing for the kind of 180-degree psychological lurch theorists call a "paradigm shift," as a group's world vision heads in a new direction. The work of men in Lakota society was to fight the enemy: to do so was an honor, the highest in life, to which all else was secondary. But if warfare against enemy tribes was a natural state, what about fighting whites? In Teton cosmology there was Lakota and *tóka*—the Sioux and the enemy—but the white man was neither. He was a force: some thought him a kind of pale, vengeful spirit made flesh. But that meant the *wasichus* were not equals—because they were not men. True, the Sioux had killed *wasichus* before, but such acts brought no honor. Their scalps were not valued as trophies.

In essence, Red Dog and the other messengers were asking the People to reconstruct the *wasichu* in order to resist him. They must turn him into an equal whose cause was unjust and whose leaders were criminals, who'd violated the natural order of all that was good and holy. Doing this established his guilt; killing him, in great numbers if necessary, would be a moral act that would restore balance and set the world aright. Doing this legitimized holy war.

Sometimes it is easier to kill a foe seen as a beast or bloodthirsty devil. In the past, the Sioux had built an image of the *wasichu* similar to the one Americans had built of the Indian. Now, they were asked to recognize in whites the fundamental assumptions about the virtues of might and victory that they held about themselves. The people of the United States had relied extensively upon military success for the confirmation of their beliefs, as had the Sioux. They expected victory to be the natural result of their virtues—as did the Sioux. Manifest Destiny was simply the fulfillment of a divine plan: "Away, away, with all these cobweb tissues of rights of discovery, exploration, settlement, contiguity, etc.," wrote the New York newspaperman John O'Sullivan, referring in large part to the rights of Native Americans. "The American claim is by the right of our manifest destiny to overspread and to possess the whole of the continent which Providence has given us." Providence had given the United States the right to occupy the continent, even if that meant pushing old occupants aside. Victory meant expanding to new lands—as it had for the Sioux.

Some opposed the idea of treating the *wasichus* as equals, but recent events lent urgency to such counsel. After a decade of relative quiet, the white world again pressed in. Two years earlier, in 1862, their eastern cousins the Santee Sioux had risen against Minnesotans after decades of hardship; when the "Minnesota Massacre" ended, five hundred settlers, one hundred soldiers, and an unknown number of Indians lay dead. Three hundred three Santee men were arrested and condemned to death; most were released after President Abraham Lincoln intervened, but thirty-eight were still executed. Many Santee fled west; others were shipped to a narrow reservation on the Missouri River where game was scarce and the water unpotable. Of the 1,300 Santees relocated there, fewer than 1,000 survived. The reservation sat immediately east of Hunkpapa territory, and in 1863 several warriors visited their cousins.

One young visitor named Tatanka Yotanka, or Sitting Bull, walked away convinced that the *wasichu* would destroy everything.

The Minnesota Massacre created in the minds of whites an image of the Sioux that drove events for decades. It did not matter that the Santee and Teton were different tribes—to whites, they were both "Sioux." No matter how many treaties were signed, they could never be trusted.

Sitting Bull's fears seemed justified. In the summer of 1863, wagon trains of miners began streaming from the east to reach the recently discovered Montana gold. Hunkpapa war parties attacked, and in 1864 the army responded. Sioux in the west and south felt the noose tighten, too. In Colorado Territory, the Cheyenne and Southern Lakota waged war with the Colorado militia. At daybreak on November 29, 1864, U.S. Army colonel John Milton Chivington and 750 men of the Colorado militia swept upon the sleeping band of the Cheyenne peace chief Black Kettle, camped in a horseshoe bend of Sand Creek near Denver's Fort Logan. As the militia gazed upon the camp, a white flag and Old Glory flew atop Black Kettle's tipi. "Kill and scalp all," Chivington famously told his men as he ordered the charge. "Nits make lice."

Scholars today call the Sand Creek Massacre the turning point in Sioux-white relations. When it was over, 28 Cheyenne men and 105 women and children lay dead. Chivington's men gathered scalps and grisly trophies for the eight-mile ride back to Denver; some stretched the genitals of slain women over their saddle horns or wore them as hat decorations. Even others among Chivington's men were sickened and wrote to Washington, disgracing their leader. But it was too late. By December, Cheyenne runners carried war pipes north to the Lakota. In early 1865, the Cheyenne, Arapaho, and Southern Lakota burned virtually every ranch and stage station along the South Platte River, trading atrocity for atrocity, murdering men, women, and children. The army built more forts and pursued bands of ghosts across the Plains. Troops grew sullen and mutinous, and whole units deserted. By the summer of 1865, the raids moved north and closed the Overland Trail.

So far, the Northern Oglala had not been touched. But they knew such luck would not last long. As Red Dog had argued, they must prepare themselves for a new kind of war: one without mercy, and perhaps without end.

———•◦•———

Thus began the rise of the two principal Oglala militants, both from Black Elk's band. In addition to Sitting Bull of the Hunkpapa, they would be two of the most famous Indians in American history. One would have a war named after him; the other would become a symbol of everything the Oglala held dear. Both would shape Black Elk's destiny.

Of the two, Red Cloud was the most driven by a will to power and prestige. He was in his forties in 1864, a *blota hunka*, or war leader, among the Bad Faces. In his autobiography, he claimed to have fought in some eighty engagements, and "counted many coup," the practice in battle of striking an enemy with the hand, bow, or specially designed "coup stick," then escaping unharmed. There were variations: touching a foe after his death or striking his defensive works also counted as "coup," but far less prestigiously. Though the act ostensibly demonstrated bravery, it also marked one as a little crazy, or at least reckless: it turned warfare into a performance, and the warrior into an actor. Perhaps more prosaically, Red Cloud bragged in his autobiography of slaughtering enemies "without mercy," and a friend of his later years, Captain James H. Cook, confirmed that Red Cloud could indeed be a "terror" in battle.

From 1865 until his death in 1909, Red Cloud would dominate Oglala politics in peace and in war. His most famous photo was taken in his later years. A tall man with a long face and aquiline nose, he sits clad in buckskins and a porcupine-quill breastplate, a cane across his knees. Although by then a chief, he wears in his hair the single feather of a warrior. His calm was formidable: with whites and Indians alike, he could be Machiavellian, always steps ahead.

Red Cloud's origins were shrouded in mystery. Early biographers set his birthday at September 22, 1822, the day a fiery meteor streaked across the northern sky, turning the heavens red. Red Cloud himself said that he was born in May 1821 on Blue Water Creek, site of Harney's revenge. He rose in prominence during the Crow and Pawnee conflicts of the 1840s and '50s, in one case returning from a raid with nearly fifty horses. In 1864, as Red Dog and other messengers descended from the north and Colonel Chivington massacred Cheyennes in the south, Red Cloud's star ascended. Old Man Afraid of His Horses, the titular head of the Northern Oglala, spoke for peace, but younger warriors wanted war and turned to Red Cloud.

He was well placed for leadership. No stranger to whites, he'd been present at the Fort Laramie Treaty and the Grattan Massacre. He could be bold and clever in a pinch: once, during an 1857 raid, he found himself alone in an enemy village. Fighting his way out would have been suicide, so he covered his head and face with a blanket and walked from the village as if he belonged there.

Just as important was his talent for a dramatic and instant eloquence that put words to his people's thoughts while exciting their imaginations. In one famous instance, he rebuked officials at a peace commission for "treating the assembled chiefs as children . . . [and] pretending to negotiate for a country which they had already taken by conquest." The entire year of 1865 was spent attacking soldiers on the Platte, and many of these sorties were led by Red Cloud. He became so well-known in this campaign that when the United States tried to make peace, they singled out the Brulé chief Spotted Tail and Red Cloud, who "ruled the nation."

The fluid nature of Lakota society dictated otherwise. Though he might be powerful, Red Cloud was never king. But Washington always adhered to its concept of "ruling chiefs," and in June 1866 a peace commission met at Fort Laramie with Spotted Tail, Old Man Afraid of His Horses, and Red Cloud. The chiefs did not understand at first that the United States wanted to fortify the Bozeman Trail. Then, in a masterpiece of bad timing, Colonel Henry B. Carrington marched into the fort at the head of the Eighteenth U.S. Infantry.

"Why are these soldiers come?" Red Cloud demanded.

"To open the Montana Trail," replied E. B. Taylor, commissioner of Indian affairs.

Different versions exist of Red Cloud's response, but all summarized a central truth: the Lakota were certain they'd almost been betrayed. According to the most famous, if apocryphal, story, Red Cloud grabbed his rifle and cried, "In this and the Great Spirit I trust for the right." He turned to his tribesmen, boomed that the whites planned to take the last of their land, and declared that rather than capitulate, they should drive out the *wasichu*.

The camp that for days had filled the prairie around the fort dissolved in a twinkling. In that moment, the lead warrior of the Bad Faces was transformed into the general of a mighty Lakota army. For the next two years, Red Cloud led his people on guerilla raids against wagon trains coming up the Bozeman Trail and against soldiers who ventured outside their forts. No white was safe. Red Cloud's War had begun.

———•◦•———

That summer of 1866, as the United States built three new forts in Lakota country, Red Cloud's forces harassed the soldiers inside them and the passing wagons bound for Montana. The southernmost post was the existing Fort Reno in present-day Johnson County, Wyoming; Carrington made improvements, then marched north. He built Fort Phil Kearny near the headwaters of the Powder River. Fort C. F. Smith lay north on the Bighorn River.

Indians made life miserable for soldiers on the Bozeman Trail. They attacked them as they built stockades, harried their work parties, and ambushed the troops sent to relieve them. From July 1 to December 21, 1866, they killed four officers, ninety-one enlisted men, and fifty-eight civilians, and captured huge numbers of horses and mules.

Despite such setbacks, the army believed its superior training and technology would prevail. Generals saw Indians as prehistoric holdouts doomed to extinction: they quoted Charles Darwin to prove that history itself was weighted against the tribes. In the same year that the Bozeman soldiers hid behind their walls, General James H. Carleton, commander of the Department of New Mexico, attributed the decline of Indians in his district to natural selection: "The races of mammoths and mastodons, and the great sloths, came and passed away; the red man of America is Passing away!"

Though the Sioux themselves also had such worries, they did not plan to lie down and die. One sees a phenomenon take shape that has occurred throughout history. In the days leading up to war, people cease to be themselves and become part of something larger and more powerful. This sense of higher purpose brings with it an emotion described as almost holy—a sense of joy. During such periods, leaders rise up in whom their followers invest everything. Their charisma is so great that they are invariably painted in mystic hues. In the fall of 1866, Red Cloud seemed one such individual. But a second and greater one also began to step forward during this period—Black Elk's second cousin Tasunke Witko.

How can one unravel Crazy Horse the legend from Crazy Horse the man? Today, it is nearly impossible. As the historian George S. Hyde wrote in 1961, "One is inclined to ask, what is it all about?" Hyde considered Crazy Horse "morose and savage" even as he was depicted "as the kind of being never seen on earth: a genius at war, yet a lover of peace; a statesman, who apparently never thought of the interests of any human being outside his own camp; a dreamer, a mystic, and a kind of Sioux Christ, who was betrayed in the end by his own disciples." More than fifty years later, little has changed. Each generation produces a new interpretation of the "Sioux Christ." His likeness is chiseled and blasted out of a mountainside in the Black Hills. No one understands him any better as his beatification intensifies.

Everything about him is a mystery, even his name. Given to him in a dream, it was later mistranslated: the Lakota literally means "His horse is crazy," or perhaps "foolish." Then there is the enigma of his birth. Though sources differ on the year, it seems to have occurred between 1840 and 1845 at the foot of Bear Butte, immediately north of present-day Sturgis, South Dakota. His father said he was born in the fall of 1840; Chips, his spiritual mentor, in 1840–41; Black Elk, in 1847. All that can be said with certainty is that Crazy Horse was somewhere between twenty-one and twenty-six during the early days of Red Cloud's War.

Finally, there's the question of his image. At a time when photographs of famous fighting Indians abounded, not a single corroborated portrait exists of the man. Purported photos have popped up, but they are roundly discounted. Most sources question whether he ever posed for a camera. D. F. Barry, a prominent Indian photographer, said he tried to bribe Crazy Horse several times to sit for a photograph, but always without success. Near the end of Tasunke Witko's life, an army surgeon who knew him better than any *wasichu* asked to take his photo. "My friend," said Crazy Horse, "why should you wish to shorten my life by taking from me my shadow?"

Yet plenty of descriptions remain. He was a slender man, anywhere from five feet eight to five feet ten, and 140 pounds; his skin was lighter than most Lakotas', and according to his friend Eagle Elk, "He was a very good looking man—his face was fine." His hair, like his complexion, was light, described as light brown: it was long, down to his hips, and he wore it in braids. In a tribe of dandies he always dressed simply— plain shirt, leggings, and blanket; an eagle-bone whistle; an Iroquois shell necklace around his neck. He was quiet to the point of introversion, and had the habit of looking askance at a person as he talked. Still, as his friend Short Bull added, "he didn't miss much that was going on all the same."

If anything, Crazy Horse was born for war. He rose above himself in battle and was transformed. Like Red Cloud, he was said to have witnessed the Grattan Massacre, and like Red Cloud, he was not directly involved. He was still too young, still going by the nickname "Curly" or "Curly Hair." It was only during the Crow Wars of the 1860s that he gained a reputation for recklessness in battle. By 1865, he rode in war parties up and down the Platte, killing whites, stealing horses, attacking a fort and wiping out an army wagon train; his first documented sighting by Americans was near Fort Laramie that year. By then, he "considered himself cut out for warfare," said the army interpreter Billy Garnett. Chips put it simply: "Crazy Horse was not accounted good for anything among the Indians but to make war; he was expected to do that; he was set apart in their minds to make war, and that was his business."

His coolness under fire made him lethal. His friend He Dog remarked that he was the only Indian he ever saw who would get off his pony in battle, take deliberate aim with his Winchester, and fire. Making the kill was more important than the pleasures of war. Those who rode with him belonged to an organization called *Hoksi hakakta*, or the "Last Child." He'd pick the last son in a family, knowing the boy would be considered the lowliest among male siblings. Suddenly, those who'd been last were now first, and every Last Child was willing to die for his savior.

War can be a spiritual thing. It called to Crazy Horse in visions. The first came when he was fifteen or sixteen, soon after Harney's victory over the Sioux. He feared for his people but was too young to lead, so he requested a vision quest, unusual for one so young. He needed to do this, he told his father: in a dream, the *wakiyan*, or Thunder-beings, promised their blessings if he sought their power.

As with Black Elk, one sees the strong influence of family. Like "Black Elk," "Crazy Horse" was a family name. His father was the second Crazy Horse until giving the name to his son and assuming the new name of Wagula, or Worm. "There were no chiefs in our family before Crazy Horse," Black Elk later said, "but there were holy men," which suggests that Crazy Horse also came from a lineage of bear healers and thunder dreamers. Worm enlisted Chips as his son's mentor for the vision quest; Crazy Horse and the powerful medicine man had grown up together, and Chips was his elder by only four years. In fact, the relationship of Crazy Horse and Chips may well have been similar to that of Black Elk and his cousin Standing Bear, four years his senior: in both cases, the slightly older friend assumed the role of the protective older brother. Chips was well aware of his friend's ambition: "When we were young, all we thought about was going to war with some other nation," he said. "All tried to get their names up the highest . . . and Crazy Horse wanted to get to the highest station."

After a sweat bath, Crazy Horse spent four days fasting at what today is Sylvan Lake at the base of Harney Peak in the Black Hills. On the fourth day, he saw a flash of lightning and heard a peal of thunder, followed by a red-tailed hawk, a messenger from the *wakiyan*. In his vision, Crazy Horse flew to the south, the land of death, then continued west to where the *wakiyan* lived. He received a medicine bundle that would protect him in battle and was told that his guardian spirit was the white owl, the bestower of long life. Before a fight, he must trace a yellow lightning bolt down the left side of his face, then paint his body and face with small white dots resembling hailstones. When he shared his vision with Chips and a council of holy men, they realized the boy had been chosen as a protector of his people.

Black Elk would not get to know Crazy Horse on a daily basis until he was eight and the war chief joined his family band. But who had not heard of Tasunke Witko? Black Elk took great pride that he was a close relative. Given the elder Black Elk's position in the band and the importance Crazy Horse would later place on his council, Black Elk's father was probably part of the group that interpreted Crazy Horse's vision. When Black Elk was older, his father told him the details. When Tasunke Witko dreamed, he entered a world that sounds like Plato's cave, "the real world that is behind this one," Black Elk explained, where "everything we see here is something like a shadow from that world." Crazy Horse rode on his horse in that world: "His horse was standing still there, and yet it danced around like a horse made only of shadow." Everything was light as air. All seemed to float past him.

It was this dream that gave his cousin power, Black Elk later realized. "When he went into a fight, he had only to think of that world to be in it again, so that he could go through anything and not be hurt." Sometime in 1860–61, Crazy Horse experienced a second vision that elaborated upon the original. This was his most famous vision, occurring on the banks of Rosebud Creek: in it, a water spirit rose on horseback from a lake and told him never to wear a war bonnet or tie up his horse's tail before battle, as did other warriors. Instead, he must wear strands of water grass in his hair, then sprinkle himself and his horse with the dust from a gopher's mound. If he followed these strictures, no bullet could kill him. And yet, he must never be captured. If so, he would die of a stab wound, a prospect that haunted him.

By 1866, Crazy Horse's vision had served him well. He'd participated in fights along the Platte, and now like Red Cloud shifted his focus to the forts along the Bozeman Trail. On July 23, a band under Crazy Horse swept down upon an army wagon train approaching Crazy Woman Creek and killed a lieutenant. The following month, Red Cloud tried to entice their old enemy the Crow into putting aside hostilities to join in common cause against the *wasichu*. Though the Crow were hesitant, they called Crazy Horse the bravest Lakota they knew. By October 1866, it seemed generally accepted that Crazy Horse was Red Cloud's principal lieutenant among the Oglala.

All that autumn, Red Cloud kept his eyes peeled for any means of striking a blow against the *wasichu*, something so terrible that they would leave the Powder River Country forever. By October, he had a target in mind.

While not the most isolated fort on the "Montana Road," Fort Phil Kearny, near present-day Sheridan, Wyoming, was the most tempting. It was the largest of the Bozeman forts, and to the Sioux must have looked impregnable. A wooden palisade surrounded the post, a six-hundred-by-eight-hundred-foot rectangle of heavy pine logs standing eight feet tall and tamped three feet deep into a bed of gravel. A banquette, or walkway, encircled the rampart; at every fourth log, a loophole was cut out for rifle fire. Mountain howitzers commanded the surrounding plains from blockhouses in the northeast and southwest corners. Little Piney Creek flowed outside the southern gate; the main gate opened north, commanding a view of the Bozeman Trail.

Red Cloud's warriors surrounded them. Carrington's three hundred soldiers were safe inside the fort, but to survive the Wyoming winter they had to stay warm. Every morning, woodcutting teams headed south to pineries in the hills or west to the largest timber stand at Pine Island. This need to feed the stoves was the fort's Achilles' heel: when the Indians attacked the teams, cavalry predictably charged from the fort to rescue them.

No record remains of how many raids Black Elk's father accompanied, but as the modern-day equivalent of a battlefield medic, he rode in his share. Black Elk's first memories hail from this time. In October, Red Cloud sent word to all bands to collect on the Powder River. By December, about five hundred Sioux lodges had arrived, as well as some Cheyenne and Arapaho. "A horseback could ride through our villages from sunrise until the day was above his head, so far did our camp stretch along the valley of the river," Black Elk recalled.

The strategy was as old as the Punic Wars. A seemingly weak party of Indians would lure the soldiers farther from the fort until reinforcements were too distant and the trap sprung. The plan sounded good in theory, but rarely worked in the field. Ambushes were usually spoiled by overeager young warriors who charged too early and destroyed the element of surprise.

The best place for an ambush was on the Bozeman Trail as it tracked north and west from the fort over rocky Lodge Trail Ridge. The trail dipped to Peno Creek, then rose again to a narrow prominence called Peno Head. The Sioux tried twice to lure the soldiers into this trap. The first attempt occurred on December 6, 1866, as Red Cloud directed his men with signals from a hill. Though a force led by Captain William Judd Fetterman charged the decoys, the trap was sprung too early, resulting in the death of two troopers but the escape of all others. It would seem the young captain learned caution, but not for long. Fetterman had joined the regiment the previous month and, like the young warriors testing their older chiefs, would be a thorn in Carrington's side. He was a handsome man, with dark eyes and carefully clipped muttonchops and mustachio. He'd won numerous combat accolades during the Civil War and, like Lieutenant Grattan a dozen years earlier, was contemptuous of the Indians' fighting ability. With "eighty good men," he said, he could "slice through the whole Sioux nation."

It was a pattern that would repeat itself—Grattan; now Fetterman; Custer in another ten years. It took a decade for soldiers to forget that arrogance meant death on the Plains. On December 21, Red Cloud tried again. A force of 1,500 to 2,000 Oglalas, Minneconjous, and Cheyennes rode up Peno Creek and hid in the deep gullies surrounding the Bozeman Trail. Black Elk's father took position with the Oglalas, Cheyennes, and Arapahos to the southwest, while the Minneconjous hid on the opposite side. When the woodcutting train left the fort around 11:00 a.m., a small group of Indians attacked. Like clockwork, a force of cavalry and infantry numbering eighty to eighty-four men under Fetterman rushed from the gate to relieve them. As Fetterman left, Carrington told him to escort the wood train back to the fort, and nothing more. "Under no circumstances must you cross Lodge Trail Ridge," he commanded.

Ten decoys rode out to meet Fetterman: two Cheyennes, two Arapahos, and six Lakotas. Though Crazy Horse was said to play a major role in the ruse, this was uncorroborated. The small party crested the hills north of the woodcutters' path and taunted the relief force; at least one brave shouted in English, "You sons of bitches!" Fetterman took the bait and charged. The decoys ran, but not very far, always stopping, making obscene gestures, falling back. Fetterman and his men galloped in full pursuit out of sight of Fort Kearny over the forbidden ridge.

And the trap closed. Chiefs hidden in the bushes cried *"Hopo! Hopo!"* Their warriors answered *"Hi-yi-yi!"* and surged upon the soldiers.

One of the men in a gully was Fire Thunder, a "long-hair" present at the Neihardt interviews. He was sixteen at the time. He hid in the bushes with the Oglalas, holding the nose of his pony so it would not whinny as the soldiers charged past. His tribesmen rose as one. The soldiers halted in shock, then fell back up the road. The infantrymen flung themselves behind some large glacial boulders and started firing; the cavalry moved another one hundred yards up the hill. The first wave of Indians rolled over the foot soldiers and surged toward the cavalry.

"I was one of the first to get in among the soldiers," Fire Thunder said. The battle was essentially a series of hand-to-hand scuffles, the kind of mix-up Indians called "stirring gravy." Almost immediately Indians on both sides of the ridge fired up and across with their bows and the air was black with arrows—so many, in fact, that it reminded Fire Thunder of a "cloud of grasshoppers all above and around." It was probably during this chaos that Black Elk's father was wounded. Several Indians were killed that way. Few details remain: the elder Black Elk's right leg was so badly broken that it apparently never set correctly. Black Elk probably would have said if his father had been shot by a soldier. There was no honor in wounds caused by "friendly fire," and an arrowhead lodged in the bone could be one of the most permanent and life-threatening injuries of the Indian wars.

Carrington later told Congress that the firing lasted twenty-one minutes. Then there was silence. He sent up seventy-six men: when they reached the heights, the trail below was filled with Indians gathering their dead and wounded. They pulled out and the relief force found Fetterman and sixty-five others strewn across a space barely forty feet square. Others lay in a line along the Bozeman Trail. Nothing survived but a horse, this so badly wounded that it was put out of its misery. The mutilation of the dead horrified the troops more than the slaughter itself, and Carrington listed the details in his official report: "eyes torn out and laid on rocks; nose cut off; ears cut off . . . ; brains taken out and placed on rocks . . . ; private parts severed." Though his troops had never encountered this kind of butchery, it was very similar to that enacted by Colonel Chivington.

As so often happened, Indian casualties were unknown. Some sources placed the dead at thirteen or fourteen, while the historian Dee Brown estimated sixty Indians killed and up to three hundred wounded. As they left, the storm that had threatened for the last two days finally broke, the temperature plunging to −20 degrees Fahrenheit, killing many more. The ground was too frozen to bury the dead, so the Indians left their corpses on the Tongue, food for coyotes and wolves. Fire Thunder said most of the wounded died while going home. Others were maimed for life, like Black Elk's father.

What was called the Fetterman Massacre by whites would be Wasican Opawinge Wicaktepi, or "A Hundred Whites Were Slain," to the Sioux. It was the largest slaughter of soldiers in the Indian wars since the Grattan Massacre, and would remain the benchmark until Custer rode into the Little Bighorn. News of the tragedy met "with universal horror," Custer wrote in *My Life on the Plains*, "and awakened a bitter feeling toward the savage perpetrators." General William Tecumseh Sherman, commander of the Division of the Missouri, was more blunt: "We must act with vindictive earnestness against the Sioux, even to extermination, men, women, and children. Nothing less will reach the root of the case."

The young Black Elk had more immediate worries. His father barely survived the battle, and the family was forced to break camp before he properly healed. "I can remember my father lying on a pony drag with buffalo robes all around him, like a baby, and my mother riding the pony," Black Elk recalled. The snow was deep; the air, bitter cold. At some point his mother huddled in the robes between Black Elk and his father as the pony trod on.

"I don't know where we went," he said, "but it was west"—as far as they could get from the soldiers' revenge.

3

THE GREAT VISION

They went hungry that winter. The cold months were usually spent in a sheltered hollow close to water and firewood: men made bows and arrows; women tanned hides; medicine men passed down secrets to their successors. Hunters usually entered the forest after elk or buffalo. But this winter the snow was too deep, and the hunters could not find game. The Bad Faces ate acorns, hide scrapings, and their horses, yet were still forced to break camp several times in search of food. Many became snow-blind, and a medicine man named Creeping crept from camp to camp, curing the afflicted. Because of his father's injury, Black Elk's family lagged behind the others in the frequent moves. When they got lost, Black Elk sat straight in the travois, peering to all sides for any glimpse of their people as his mother guided the pony forward. He called out, but his voice was swallowed by the snow.

The Oglala rose slowly from winter like sleepwalkers. With spring, the pasqueflower bloomed in the snowmelt; women gathered beans from the dens of field mice; children and old men tapped rising sap from box elders. Neither the People nor the *wasichu* rushed back to war. Although the Sioux had been victorious, their losses cut too deep, while the American public entered a rare period of soul-searching rather than flock immediately to Sherman's call for extermination. People had grown tired of war. In March 1867, as both sides licked their wounds, Congress

passed a bill calling for a final settlement of the "Indian Problem."
Peace must be made with the tribes and the War Department must not
interfere.

Yet three of the seven appointed as peace commissioners were
generals, and the highest-ranking among them was Sherman, who'd
advocated genocide.

————•◦•————

The wary peace lasted into summer. Though Black Elk's father survived his wound, a bitterness festered inside. The Bad Faces returned
to the Rosebud, a green and winding valley that would become famous
in nine years. "I did not feel so much afraid," said Black Elk, "because
the Wasichus seemed farther away and there was peace in the valley
and there was plenty of meat."

That summer of 1867, Black Elk turned four. With the passage of
the hard winter, life seemed like a lazy camp, where ponies nibbled at
cottonwood bark and one smelled woodsmoke on the breeze. A cozy
place in the lodge was assigned to him: *his* place, with his own bed and
a spot for his belongings. His parents taught him of the family's tradition as healers and holy men; he learned the geography of the country,
the history of his people, the names for plants and animals, a proper
respect for age. He proved trustworthy, eager to please, and so was allowed occasionally to stray away from the tipi and play alone. The un-
hurried sun warmed the earth, and all living things took their time. It
was easy to daydream at such moments, to imagine the day he would
grow up to drive away the *wasichus* or to kill them all. Yet the elders
warned young children that such daydreams were dangerous: one could
fall prey to mischievous spirits at such times. On such a day he played
away from the village; no one was in sight and his mind drifted in the
languid air. He heard voices, as if people called from afar. The sound
was high and sweet, and at first he thought his mother was singing. He
looked around, but no one was near.

The voices spoke to him several times that summer, and when he
heard them, he ran. What did they want? Why didn't they show themselves? He never said whether they spoke to him in Lakota or in *handloglaka,* the language of the spirits, and perhaps over time he forgot. He
always remembered, though, this first time, when he was terrified. His
mother saw his look of fright and asked what scared him. But he would
not say.

Thus began a period in which, as he described it, the spirits either toyed with or tested him. If nothing else, he felt as if he were being observed. The scrutiny stretched five years, culminating finally with the Great Vision when he was nine. But after that first summer, he seemed to lose his fear. He accepted the test, but told no one. Adults would only mock him, say he vied for attention. That was not his purpose. He knew something big was coming, but the time was not yet right. Like everything else on the prairie, it would take its own time.

How much of this was shaped by the forces sculpting his tribe's destiny? It is hard to say—he was, after all, just a small boy. But there were few secrets in a camp, and if he could not understand the details of the events discussed by the adults, he could absorb their emotional effect upon them. A terrible urgency suffused his memories of this period, as if the fate of the Oglala, which once proceeded at its own natural pace, now threatened to career out of control.

That summer of 1867 would be frustrating for both sides in Red Cloud's War. While the Lakota could not oust the soldiers from their forts, they *could* keep them boxed inside. Since the soldiers could not come out, the Bozeman Trail was closed. That July, at the annual Sun Dance, the Sioux and Cheyenne decided to wipe out the soldiers and burn the forts to the ground. On August 1, 500 to 600 Cheyennes under Two Moon and Dull Knife attacked 30 *wasichus* in a long corral in a hayfield two miles from Fort C. F. Smith. The next day, 1,500 Oglalas under Red Cloud and Crazy Horse descended upon 32 men at a woodcutters' camp outside Fort Kearny. Both skirmishes— respectively called the Hayfield and Wagon Box Fights—were defeats for the tribes.

Yet the reasons for defeat would be lessons to the Sioux. A week before the attacks, the soldiers had been armed with new Springfield rifles modified into breechloaders. Where old muzzle-loading rifles fired at a rate of three times a minute, these Springfields could fire ten times during the same period. A soldier only had to eject an empty cartridge and slap a new one in the breech, the work of a moment and previously impossible. No longer could mounted warriors roll over the troops as they paused to reload. Instead, the fire was continuous, and dead braves and horses surrounded the enclosures.

Unlike in the Fetterman fight, the soldiers fought behind shelter

rather than out in the open. Crazy Horse especially absorbed this lesson: the Indian style of fighting was best suited to open spaces, where
wild charges on horseback kept the *wasichus* off-balance and fearful. It
was *not* suited to attacks on fixed positions, where soldiers showed
more discipline and their superior firepower took a greater toll.

By the fall of 1867, a stalemate existed on the Northern Plains. Not so
in Nebraska, where war parties harassed track gangs to the point that
they halted the steady western progress of the Union Pacific Railroad.
President Andrew Johnson faced a dilemma. The United States could
wage all-out war against the Indians, yet after five years of bloody civil
war few Americans favored such an option. Or Washington could create a peace treaty so practical and fair that all problems with the Plains
Indians should end.

In the spring of 1868, Sherman and the commissioners sued for
peace with Red Cloud on his own terms. On July 29, 1868, the troops
at Fort C. F. Smith marched out; the next morning, Red Cloud and his
warriors burned the fort to the ground. One month later, Fort Phil
Kearny was abandoned, and the Cheyenne did the honors.

After two long years, Red Cloud had won his war, the only Indian
chief on record ever to do so against the U.S. Army. On November 4,
1868, Red Cloud rode into Fort Laramie surrounded by his warriors.
Two days later, he strode into the council tent, wiped his hands with
dust from the floor, and grabbed the pen.

The sixteen articles of what was called the Treaty of 1868 would be
the most important and contentious peace treaty ever signed between
the U.S. government and the tribes of the Northern Plains. The government's offer attempted to address the "historic inevitability" of diminishing game—in particular, the buffalo. The old life of wandering was
coming to an end, the government stressed. New sources of food were
required, new ways of living adopted, if the tribes hoped to survive.

Today, when historians and Native Americans say that each new
peace treaty was just another attempt by Washington to rob the Indian
of his land, they are usually correct. Yet the Treaty of 1868 seems an
honest attempt, under hard circumstances, to preserve a separate place
on the Plains for the Lakota at the same time that it hopefully eased
them into modern times. The terms can be divided into three broad
categories:

Land: The present-day state of South Dakota west of the Missouri
River would belong to the Lakota. No white could settle in what was

called the Great Sioux Reserve, and only government emissaries could enter. This important point was repeatedly violated, though in 1868 Washington apparently felt it could control incursions. The Sioux's hunting ground, called the "unceded territory," consisted of all land east of the Bighorn Mountains and above the North Platte. The two together comprised some ninety thousand square miles and would be home to about twenty-five thousand Indians. This was actually land they already occupied: if anything, it seemed to protect the Powder River Country and the Black Hills, the twin poles of their world. All they gave up was the "right" to conquer more land.

Rations and Annuities: For the next thirty years, until 1898, every Indian would receive an annual issue of clothing. Those Indians who continued to "roam and hunt" would receive an annual payment of ten dollars, while those who tried to farm would receive an extra twenty dollars. If an Indian settled permanently and became a farmer, he would receive one pound of meat and one pound of flour per day for four years; he would also receive tools, seed, "one good, well-broken pair of American oxen," and "one good American cow."

"Civilizing" Factors: Above all else, Washington wanted to "civilize" the Sioux. To do so, schoolhouses would be built and teachers provided for every thirty children. In time, it was hoped, all Sioux children would attend reservation schools. Each Indian head-of-household had a right to claim 160 acres; if he farmed it, that amount could double. To aid him, the government would build and operate various mills, and provide doctors, engineers, carpenters, and a "district farmer" to advise the Lakota on planting.

In exchange for these concessions, the White Father asked three things. First, the Sioux would stay within their boundaries. Second, they would no longer attack whites or those tribes friendly to whites. Finally, they would compel their children between ages six and sixteen to attend the white man's schools.

With the Treaty of 1868, Washington hoped that the "Sioux Problem" was finally solved, while in the tribes the adults debated its wisdom among themselves. That spring and summer, as final details were hammered out, the voices called to Black Elk again.

Now he was five. His father had made him a bow and arrow, and he could ride bareback on his pony. One day he was out hunting when a thunderstorm growled near. He ducked into the woods and saw a kingbird perched on a limb. The little birds were hard to miss, blue and white blurs that launched themselves at hawks in defense of their homes. He took aim with his bow and envisioned returning with the feathers to his father when suddenly the bird stared at him, he later said. "Look, the clouds all over are one-sided," it announced, and Black Elk took that to mean that success was heading his way. "Listen," it continued, "a voice is calling you." He glanced toward the north and two men flew toward him from the clouds. They sang as they drew close, while in the west thunder began to drum. They, too, announced that a sacred voice was calling. They were almost upon him when, at the last moment, they wheeled to the west, turned into geese, and entered the storm. The rain fell upon him; the wind roared through the trees.

———•◦•———

"What happened after that until the summer I was nine years old is not a story," Black Elk would say. The seasons passed and the ancient nomadism continued; he grew in height, a thin gangly boy with a ready smile and quiet ways. People liked and seemed drawn to him. He rode horses with the other boys and gained enough skill with a bow that he could shoot rabbits and prairie chickens to add to the family larder. He participated in the rough-and-tumble game of Throw Them Off Their Horses, in which two facing lines of riders tried to unhorse one another; during one such charge, he spilled from his pony and landed in a field of prickly pears. "It took my mother a long while to pick all the stickers out of me," he said.

During those years, the new administration of President Ulysses S. Grant seemed committed to fair dealings with the Sioux. Grant reorganized the Indian Office and instituted a new system of appointing agents based on recommendations from the nation's leading religious bodies, who were thought to be more humanely inclined toward the tribes. Grant's "Peace Policy" was soon called the "Quaker Policy," since so many Friends applied.

Yet even as he promoted peace, Grant appointed to lieutenant general one of America's chief architects of total war. In March 1869, two months after taking office, he gave command of the Division of the Missouri to thirty-eight-year-old Philip Henry Sheridan, the Union general responsible for the U.S. victories at the Shenandoah Valley and the seemingly impregnable Missionary Ridge. Grant made his old friend second-in-command to Sherman, responsible for the vast Indian territory stretching from his headquarters in Chicago to the western borders of Montana, Wyoming, Utah, and New Mexico; from Canada to the Rio Grande. Most of America's unconquered Indians lived within this territory: the Comanche, Arapaho, Ute, Kickapoo, Apache, Kiowa, Northern and Southern Cheyenne, and Sioux.

Sheridan's preferred strategy was always the use of overwhelming force, a requirement he considered necessary for victory and any hope of peace afterward. Although he denied saying it, the infamous quote "The only good Indian is a dead Indian" became synonymous with his Indian policy. What he actually said was more blunt: when the Comanche chief Tosani surrendered in the winter of 1868–69 and said, "Tosani, good Indian," Sheridan replied, "The only good Indians I ever saw were dead."

Just as Sheridan laid waste to the Shenandoah Valley to starve the Confederates, he now determined to destroy the great buffalo herds. Those five years that Black Elk called unimportant instead formed the spine of the Plains Indians' demise. It was the period that saw completion of the Union Pacific Railroad, the years when the great herds dissolved. By November 1867, the *máza chakú*, or "iron road," had reached Cheyenne; in May 1869, it connected with the Central Pacific Railroad at Promontory Point, Utah, thus completing the transcontinental road. Spurs branched from this like the Iktomi webs prophesied by Drinks Water. The bison would not cross the coast-to-coast track, thus dividing the herd. At first, to the Oglala, this did not seem to matter. The buffalo "that stayed in our country with us were more than could be counted," Black Elk said, "and one wandered without trouble in the land."

It was far worse than he knew. The fate of the Northern Lakota could be read in the remains of the southern buffalo herd. Westerners called it the "Buffalo Bone Days": as railroads expanded, they brought in the buffalo hunters who mowed through the herds. In the 1870s, a lone still-hunter would commonly shoot 150 to 200 buffalo without moving from his blind. One man claimed to kill 1,500 in seven days; another claimed to shoot 120 bison in forty minutes. They shipped the hides and tongues back east and left the carcasses for buzzards and wolves. On the Santa Fe Railroad alone, a million animals were left to rot. The Central and Southern Plains became a sepulchre of bones.

During this fragile peace, Washington argued an increased need of distribution points for treaty goods and established three new Agencies along the eastern edge of the Sioux Reserve. It located a new Agency for the Oglala and Brulé thirty-two miles east of Fort Laramie at the present-day town of Henry, Nebraska, in the Platte Valley. In honor of the Oglala chief, it was called the Red Cloud Agency.

But the honor was a hollow one. As the *wasichu* had done with other powerful chiefs, they brought Red Cloud and Spotted Tail to Washington to meet the president. They exposed Red Cloud to the awesome medicine of their military technology, escorting him to the Washington Navy Yard to observe a test firing of one of their big guns. The shell skipped across the Potomac River; Red Cloud measured the gun's muzzle diameter with his fan, then turned away without a word. The man who'd led the Sioux to victory on the Bozeman Trail would never unite them in war again.

By 1872, the Oglala were a shadow of their former fearsome selves. Grown increasingly dependent upon federal handouts, thousands followed Red Cloud to his new Agency on the Platte to be closer to the distribution of gifts and rations. The move split the tribe. Those Bad Faces who stayed behind on the Powder River, like the Black Elks, no longer called Red Cloud their leader; their loyalties shifted to Big Road and Crazy Horse, both of whom refused to move. Seen as stubborn holdouts for a vanishing way of life, they were increasingly referred to in the Indian Office and the press as "non-treaty Indians."

———— ·•· ————

In the midsummer of 1872, at the height of this split, Black Elk turned nine. As his clan moved slowly toward the Rockies for the annual Sun Dance, they camped by a little creek that flowed into the Phežíla Wakpa, or Greasy Grass, known today as the Little Bighorn. A warrior named Man Hip found Black Elk amusing and invited him to share the evening meal in his tipi, a common occurrence in the tribe's communal approach to child rearing. Older men often passed down tribal histories to those they considered promising. As they ate, Black Elk heard a voice. "It's time; now they are calling you," it said. The voice was so loud and clear that the speaker must have been outside. He rose and went out, but no one was there.

As he stood at the entrance, something strange occurred. His thighs began to ache; he snapped alert, as if waking from a dream. The voice vanished, and in its stead he heard a camp's normal summer sounds. He reentered the tipi, but his appetite had vanished. "What is wrong?" Man Hip asked.

"My legs are hurting me."

The next morning, as the Bad Faces broke camp and continued west, Black Elk rode with the other boys. They stopped at a creek: Black Elk dismounted for a drink and his legs crumpled beneath him. He could not rise. His friends helped him onto his horse and stayed with him until that evening. They took him to his parents' tipi. His legs, arms, and face were swollen, and he probably had a high fever.

His parents called Whirlwind Chaser, a medicine man and the uncle of his cousin Standing Bear. Yet this sickness had come on so quickly that even the healer was mystified. Maybe someone at the Sun Dance would have experience in this sort of thing. Whirlwind Chaser did what he could to make Black Elk comfortable; the next morning, his parents padded him with blankets and placed him in a pony drag.

The day passed in a haze. All he could recall years later, when relating it to Neihardt, was that he was very sick, but being dragged across the prairie must have been excruciating. They made camp and his parents settled him in their tipi. His head pounded; he felt as if he were burning alive. His mother mopped his forehead with something cool. Then time stood still.

He entered what is now called a "minimally conscious state," a condition as close to death as one can get yet still survive. What was killing him? It is nearly impossible to diagnose an illness from the historic record. Symptoms alter over time, especially when a "host population" grows resistant over years of exposure. Nevertheless, the swelling and especially the pain in Black Elk's legs are clues. A classic symptom of childhood meningitis—the sudden viral or bacterial inflammation of the lining, or "meninges," of the brain and spinal cord—is pain in the legs. Not *any* pain, but one so intense the child can neither walk nor stand. It hits without warning. Other classic symptoms include cold hands and feet, even during high fever, and a pale, dusky, or blue coloring around the lips—neither of which he reported. But his entire body hurt, especially his pounding head and throbbing legs. He passed in and out of consciousness, his symptoms so advanced only a miracle could save him.

As Black Elk would later relate, he lay staring through the tipi flap when he saw the two warriors approach again from the clouds. They flew headfirst, each with a spear thrust before him, and from each tip flowed lightning. They landed and said the Grandfathers were waiting, then rose back up with Black Elk behind them. His legs no longer hurt, and he seemed light as air. As he left the tipi, a small cloud approached;

he stepped upon it and the cloud raced after the warriors. He remembered glancing back at his mother and father. "I felt sorry to be leaving them," he later said.

Thus began the Great Vision that would dominate Black Elk's life and thought for the next seventy-one years. In some ways, it followed a cultural pattern: a young Lakota man "crying for a vision" was often visited by celestial messengers who took him to a high place where he met a spirit guide. The spirit bestowed a gift, which must be used in prescribed conditions, often lethal or dire. If adhered to strictly, the power of the gift stayed with him forever.

Crazy Horse's vision was one such example: he was given a sacred gift, and shown how to prepare for battle. If he kept the vision close, he would become a great warrior and lead his people to great victories. Black Elk's vision was similar: it, too, was a dream of thunder, and thunder dreaming in Lakota theology was considered the most potent, reckless, and destructive of the gifts from the gods. Like his cousin's, Black Elk's vision was also a dream of horses, the apotheosis and signifier of the Oglala self-image. The horse was swift, proud, powerful, terrible, and mysterious; its sudden appearance in their history had turned them from the last among Plains tribes into the first. It was the living symbol of freedom and war.

But there the similarities ended. Black Elk did not *seek* his vision, as did Crazy Horse. It had shadowed him for years, and it now seemed to pounce on him as if he were its prey. Neither did he torture himself to receive it: the Lakota were famous for the extent to which they endured pain, through fasting, exposure, self-mutilation, or staring at the sun. Instead, the torture fell upon him.

Like many such visions associated with near-death experiences, Black Elk's begins with a flight through the sky. This seems a common denominator in all cultures, the speed and height both glorious and frightening. John Neihardt would experience such a flight during a childhood coma: he flew through space, hands thrust before him as he moved at immeasurable speed. Carl Jung experienced a similar vision in 1944, when a broken bone led to a heart attack and his doctors barely held back death with oxygen and injections of camphor. "I was high up in space," Jung wrote. "Far below I saw the globe of the earth, bathed in a gloriously blue light."

As Black Elk traveled in his cloud, it seemed that nothing existed but the rushing air, the soft cloud that bore him, and the two messengers streaking ahead. They took him to "a great white plain" of clouds surrounded by snowy hills and looming cloud mountains. All seemed very quiet, but if he listened closely, he could hear whispers. In this pause, the messengers pointed to a magnificent bay horse standing in the clouds. "Behold him," they cried, "the horse who has four legs, you shall see."

Suddenly, the bay horse spoke. "Behold me!" it commanded, then pointed to forty-eight glorious horses standing at each of the cardinal directions—black horses to the west, land of the Thunder-beings, with lightning in their manes and thunder in their nostrils; white horses to the north, manes flying in the wind like blizzards; red sorrel horses to the east, with eyes like the morning star; and ocher buckskins to the south, with horns on their heads. He saw before him the entire spectrum of Sioux cosmology. The black horses of the west represented difficulty, evil, and the destructive powers of the storm, but they also stood for the kind of physical and spiritual torment that toughened one. The white horses of the north stood for endurance, physical health, and wisdom; the red horses of the east, the pure light of the dawn, as well as the understanding and peace that came with it. The yellow horses of the south represented growth, innocence, and the promise of renewed life. All were blessed by the sky above them and the earth below.

What Black Elk witnessed was an incarnation of the Sioux medicine wheel, the philosophical framework through which the Sioux understood their world. The son of a medicine man such as Black Elk would have recognized the wheel immediately; it was ingrained. The horses before him stood twelve abreast, dancing in place as had Crazy Horse's mount. As he watched, "great clouds of horses, in all color" seemed to appear behind them—horses without number, stretching as far as he could see. The bay horse neighed and the millions answered back; it neighed again and the millions wheeled around him. Since the horse symbolized to the Sioux strength and hope, Black Elk was witnessing a vision of power and prosperity far beyond imagining.

But if this was the promise, he had to see how it would unfold. "Make haste," said the bay, and the millions led him to a cloud tipi pitched beneath a rainbow gate. It was the home of the Six Grandfathers who directed all things: the spirits of the west, north, east, south, earth, and heaven—the six directions of Sioux belief. The Grandfathers waited in the door. This, too, was a common image, echoing the Cheyenne Camp of the Dead, where the ancestors met in the afterlife, sought out the company of the living, and bestowed to such visitors items that would be sacred in the physical world. Now, as he watched, each Grandfather handed over a gift or prophecy: a cup of water; bow and arrow; Sacred Pipe; holy herb; flaming tree; and powers of the Thunder-beings, which could be used for good or evil. The first five Grandfathers explained their gifts; in addition, the Grandfather of the West, accompanied by four virgins representing the four cardinal directions, explained the meaning of the dancing horses, while the Grandfather of the South showed Black Elk two roads—the good red road of life coursing north and south, and the black road, running east and west, of ruin and fear. Black Elk must lead his people through four "ascents," or generations, this Grandfather told him, traveling both the black and red roads.

To this point, Black Elk described his Vision almost as a breathtaking Technicolor spectacle, but as he approached the Sixth Grandfather, it took on the aspects of nightmare. As he stared in this Grandfather's face, he seemed to recognize him. This old man with white hair looked familiar, and as he watched, the years and wrinkles slipped away. "I stood there for awhile very scared," Black Elk later told Neihardt. As the sixth Grandfather grew younger, "I knew it was myself as a young man."

Black Elk stood rooted in place with fear. When the Sixth Grandfather spoke, his voice was sad. "My boy, have courage," he warned, "for my power shall be yours, and you shall need it, for your nation on earth will have great troubles. Come."

Until now, Black Elk had been the passive recipient of gifts—the powers of life, death, birth, curing, peace, and renewal. Yet henceforth, as he would tell Neihardt, he took an active part in the vision. The Sixth Grandfather and he embarked upon an epic quest to save his world. The horses followed, and at some point turned into the Sioux. They flew on storm clouds to Pikes Peak, "the highest peak in the west," then retraced their route back east to the Black Hills. As he flew, he used the newfound powers of his gifts to save the Lakota. He conquered drought with his bow and arrow in one hand and the cup of water in the other. He saw a famine-stricken village of the future where "all the horses were hide and bone and there you could hear the wail of women and also men." He walked the black road of suffering from the west to the east: the earth radiated silence in "a sick green light" and the hills looked up afraid. "Everywhere about me were the cries of frightened birds and the sounds of fleeing wings." He carried a spear that spit lightning from its tip and with it battled the Spirit of the Water, the creator of chaos everywhere. Though he emerged victorious, he could never quite kill the beast, for it turned into a turtle and hid within its shell, someday to reemerge. Black Elk must be prepared.

At last he arrived at Harney Peak, the highest place in the center of the world. He climbed the mountain and at each ascent received another gift and endured another trial. His tribe and he climbed the mountain together—the four ascents foretold earlier. The first ascent was easy and green, and everyone was happy, but the second was steeper and his people changed into all the animals of the world, which filled everyone with fear. The third ascent was excruciating: each creature went off alone, in a different direction, each following his own, small, incomplete vision. The sacred hoop—the unity that glued the Lakota together as a nation—was broken.

The fourth ascent was by far the hardest. He saw that his people's lifeblood, the buffalo, would disappear, yet as he watched, "another strength" appeared. A man painted red and holding a lance walked to the center of his dying nation. He rolled on the ground and turned into a buffalo. He rolled again and turned into an herb that bloomed in four colors. Black Elk must take this herb and drop it to the earth; where it landed, it would take root, blossom, and turn into the Tree of Life that embodied the heart and health of his tribe. As he watched, this sacred tree sent aloft a ray of light that could be seen from everywhere. With this four-color herb, Black Elk would rejuvenate the dying earth and save his people. As long as the sacred tree lived, even if it was merely the roots, there was still hope, no matter how terrible things might become.

On Harney Peak, Black Elk gained a larger view of life encompassing the entire world. He saw that all creatures must coexist, a hard position to accept for a nine-year-old boy whose people felt threatened with extinction. But that was his command. "I saw that the sacred hoop of my people was one of many hoops that made one circle," he later told Neihardt. In time, this would become the cornerstone of his philosophy: for the Sioux to survive, *all* must survive, even the hated *wasichu*. All must take their appointed place in the Great Medicine Wheel.

Yet contradictions existed in the Great Vision, things he would struggle to understand. At one point in the dream, he received from the Spirit of War an herb that grew only in the Black Hills. He called it the "soldier weed," a plant so terrible that everything near it fell dead. Skeletons surrounded the weed, and no one but Black Elk could touch it, much less recognize it in the wild. The Spirit described it exactly—"a little tree of crinkly leaves, reddish in color." He must pluck it when he turned thirty-seven, when his power would be manifest: the world would tremble at his approach as, with the weed, he destroyed all humans but the Sioux, even down to the women and children. But how did such an apocalypse mesh with the vision of separate but equal hoops all merging into one? He did not understand, and the Spirits did not explain.

In time, the Grandfathers brought him back to the cloud tipi, then down into the stony center of the earth, where they revealed what might be. This was the future, but there were many futures and the choice was his. Once again they bestowed gifts, but two, perhaps, were more important than the others. They gave him a cup of water within which floated a Little Blue Man, or healing spirit; he must drink it down quickly, for this would be his familiar, or *sicun*, to help him with cures when he became a medicine man. Then the messengers again appeared in the east, and between them rose the "daybreak star." They gave him the healing herb he'd seen during the fourth ascent. He called it the "daybreak herb," and with it he knew he could accomplish anything.

Now he understood. This was his mission. This was the reason for his birth and the meaning of his name. The Grandfathers had given him the sacred gifts of life, and with them, "I was going to cure these people." Somehow, in a way he did not yet understand, the sacred tree and the daybreak herb would restore a lost balance. He'd been chosen to save a dying world.

Then the messengers took him home. A spotted eagle led the way. He saw his village in the distance, then his tipi. He felt homesick and started to walk faster. He entered the tipi and "saw a boy lying there dying," then realized he was that boy. The jolt snapped him back to reality. He opened his eyes and his parents bent over him. "The boy is feeling better now," a voice said to the side. As he sat up, his parents hugged him and gave him sips of water. But instead of relief and happiness, he felt sad. He'd been so far away and had seen so much, yet it was something he could not explain. His parents cried and told him he'd hovered at the edge of death for twelve days, and he knew that nothing would ever be the same.

4

RESURRECTION

For the Oglalas in Big Road's band, a miracle had occurred. Not a major miracle—not like the one they would seek two decades hence when in their desperation they turned to the Messiah to rid the world of the *wasichu*. This was more intimate, as the tribe witnessed the resurrection of the lame bear dreamer's son.

Stories collected of near-death experiences such as Black Elk's often follow similar patterns and themes. In 1977, the psychologist Kenneth Ring began interviewing 102 survivors of life-threatening injury or illness: 49 met the criteria for what he called a near-death experience (NDE), and in them he found a basic sequence—a sense of peace; separation from the body; then entering a light. Less universal characteristics included elements from Black Elk's vision—an encounter with a "presence"; making the decision to return. The other commonality Ring noted was an irreversible sense of sadness and change. Many who experienced an NDE did not want to return; they changed their own lives afterward, no longer considering important what they once had. They were no longer the same person. "You can't put that wine back into the bottle," quipped Ring. "It's broken."

Carl Jung felt a similar sense of loss when he returned from his coma. He'd reveled in his free-floating "primal form," but when he came back, "a good three weeks were still to pass before I could truly make up my mind to live again." Food no longer held interest; the beautiful view of the city and mountains from his hospital window now seemed a flat, painted sheet hiding the reality he'd glimpsed from above. The life he'd once enjoyed seemed a prison, a little box hung in space by a thread.

So it was for young Kahnigapi. His face and extremities were still badly swollen, yet the night after waking he felt strangely energized and begged his parents to let him leave his bed. They refused, thus beginning a protectiveness that surfaced repeatedly. Members of the clan filed into the tipi to pay witness to his resurrection, and the attention saddened him. He lay still as they passed and remembered the places he'd visited; he could not shake the Vision from his mind. Everyone should know of it, yet he held back from describing what he'd seen, afraid that people would think he was still sick, or worse, crazy. Even the act of putting his Vision to words made it slip away. "I could see it all again and feel the meaning with a part of me like a strange power glowing in my body," he later told Neihardt, but any attempt to tell others "would be like fog and get away from me."

This and other aspects of his return greatly angered him. People stared at him like a curiosity. He watched his father give Whirlwind Chaser his best horse for curing his son; he wanted to yell that the Grandfathers and the Vision had saved him, not the medicine man. But he held his tongue. Even so, Whirlwind Chaser seemed to realize the credit was not entirely his. Something had occurred outside his understanding. He'd stare hard at his patient, trying to divine the mystery. The boy had been chosen—but for what, he did not know.

The next morning, the clan moved a day's ride west to Willow Creek; they'd missed the Sun Dance during Black Elk's coma, and instead now headed to buffalo country. To Black Elk's surprise, his swelling had vanished and he could ride. Though he felt fine physically, he still felt disjointed and strange—separate, as if he no longer belonged.

At one point during that day, his cousin Standing Bear rode back to visit. As one of the older boys, he rode close to the front, while smaller boys like Black Elk took up the rear. He trotted back and spotted Black Elk astride one of his father's bays. "*Hau*," he said, reining up. Black Elk answered in kind. Standing Bear smiled. "Younger brother, after all, you got well?"

"Yes, I'm not sick at all now," Black Elk replied. But Standing Bear could tell that something had changed. Around them, the other boys played their endless game of Throw Them Off Their Horses, the air filled with raucous cries. But a bubble of silence surrounded his cousin, and it struck Standing Bear that Black Elk seemed more a man than a boy.

For the next twelve days, the clan traveled north in search of buffalo. And during that period, Black Elk's silence and distance grew. He remembered the land of his Vision and the beings who dwelt in the clouds; he gazed at his friends and family as if they were strangers. Each evening as they made camp, or during the day if they stayed in one place, he might come home for meals, but he no longer was hungry. Once he'd loved his mother's cooking; now what he did eat tasted like ashes. Afterward, he rode alone into the prairie. He searched the skies for the winged messengers, but they never came.

His distance worried his parents as much as had his disease. One evening, Black Elk's father came to Standing Bear's lodge. He looked upset and was invited to stay for the meal. As they ate, the elder Black Elk poured out his soul. He'd been prepared to lose his son during his sickness, he said, but when the boy returned their grief should have ended. Instead, it remained. All of his experience as a bear dreamer had not prepared him for Kahnigapi's change. Standing Bear realized that the once-doting father seemed almost afraid of his son. The boy had "queer ways," he whispered. "He is not the boy he used to be."

In fact, Black Elk would tell Neihardt, the *only* person he wanted to be around was his grandfather, Keeps His Tipi. He tried to tell the old man about his Vision, but the words dried up in his throat. He sat in silence, as silent as the dusk, and Keeps His Tipi realized that whatever had visited his grandson had not completely disappeared. The boy had been changed, but to what extent? Keeps His Tipi sat as silent as Black Elk, waiting him out, wondering what would come.

Finally, Black Elk asked about the coming of the *wasichu*, which he'd come to sense was the real subject of his dream. He asked his grandfather why, in the old days, the word didn't refer to the white man at all. "*Wasichu*" referred to the buffalo, but only in great numbers, when the herds were so endless it seemed they would flow on forever. At that time, scouts returned to camp and said the bison were *wasichu*. Now they said the same of the whites, that they would not stop and kept getting closer. "What does it mean?"

"That they are many," his grandfather said. Too many to count, even to comprehend.

During this time, his grandfather made him a bow and arrow, and he often went hunting with it in the woods. He liked this: it gave him an excuse to be alone, almost as if Keeps His Tipi had known. As he stalked, his mind returned to his Vision and the feeling of strangeness crept over him again. It seemed as if the bow and arrow had been given to him by the First Grandfather, yet he felt foolish and tried to convince himself that he'd just experienced a fever dream. He came upon a bush where a wren flitted from branch to branch: he should just kill something, and that would put an end to this confusion. But as he took aim, he remembered how the Grandfathers told him he was related to the birds. He eased up on the bowstring. But this angered him even more. He walked along a creek and spotted a green frog. He shot and killed it, then picked its body up by the legs. It dangled before him. *I have killed him now*, he thought, his first kill with this bow and arrow. But instead of feeling pride, he wanted to cry.

How long such confusion could last was anyone's guess. Yet soon after Standing Bear's visit, the scouts returned from their search. They'd sighted a huge bison herd, the one thing guaranteed to bring any disoriented Plains nomad back to hard reality.

Hunting was not the diversion it is today. A bison hunt was a matter of survival. For most of the year, the bison wandered through the grassland in groups as small as five or as large as a hundred. They traveled in two types of groups: "cow groups," consisting of cows, calves, and a few young bulls, and "bull groups," made up of bulls four years or older. But in the summer, when the shortgrass was thickest and most nutritious, the two groups merged for the rutting season, creating the huge herds.

Even though these summer herds could be gigantic, it was still hard to find them on the undulating prairie. The scouts had hunted twelve days after Black Elk's resurrection, and always without luck. At the end of an unsuccessful day, they would slip back into camp without fanfare. They used any clue, including the black horned ground beetle. The twin horns on its head could move in all directions, but during the summer they pointed toward the closest herd, possibly drawn by the vibrations of hundreds or thousands of hooves too distant for human ears.

On this day, the scouts returned with good news. They rode over a hill and through the crowds to the big tipi in the village center. Everyone ran to hear the news. Black Elk crept close enough to peer between the legs of the man in front of him. The scouts sat before the tipi door and a headman filled a pipe with *kinnikinnick*, the inner bark of the red dogwood tree. He lit it and offered it to the four compass points, passed it to the scouts, and asked what they had seen. "There was nothing but bison all over the country," the lead scout replied.

The sun burned overhead when the band rode out to the herd. Since Black Elk was too young to participate in the hunt, his job was to assist in the butchering and bring up the pack horses. But Standing Bear was thirteen and supposed to be a man. He'd killed a calf in a previous hunt, but this time meant to bag a yearling. The most common plan of attack was a two-group surround. The night before the hunt, his father gave him pointers. The most important thing to remember was to closely watch the buffalo. If the ground was level and *Pte* ran straight, you could ride up close to one and shoot immediately behind his left shoulder, a good way to strike the heart. But you had to watch his eyes. If he watched you from the corners, he might dip his head and hook those horns into your horse. For beginners such as Standing Bear, it was safer to aim behind the short ribs, then shoot again at the joint of the hips so the bison began to tire.

Standing Bear told his father he would remember, but when the leader cried *"Hoka hey!"* it was hard to remember anything. A great shout rose from all throats, and both sides charged. Standing Bear entered a cloud of swirling dust where he could barely see anything. He passed through and found himself surrounded by hundreds of bison. The ground trembled from their hooves. He realized how small he was and felt a moment of fear, but then spotted a yearling pounding down a draw and dug his heels into the sides of his pony. He notched an arrow and loosed; it struck, but the yearling did not seem affected. He notched another and this one penetrated halfway up the shaft. The yearling wobbled; blood ran from its nostrils; he must have hit its heart. Hunters cried *"Yuhoo!"* when they made a kill, but he was so excited he just kept yelling. He realized later his people must have thought he had slaughtered an entire herd.

It was a good hunt, and all were happy. Black Elk and his people feasted that night, danced and sang. They stayed in camp for several days. The women cut the meat into strips, then hung these on wooden racks to dry. Red meat hung everywhere. The boys played war games. In one, they built a grass village outside the adult camp and at night crawled back to steal strips of drying buffalo. If they returned without getting caught, they held a feast and danced, bragging of their deeds just as warriors did after a battle.

In this way, Black Elk finally returned from the other world. As he ranged with his friends away from camp, he took his new bow and arrow. He was turning into a good shot and could easily knock down a bird. For the moment, he forgot his Vision and the disorienting separation and sadness. He came back to his people and was himself again.

But sometimes, when a thunderstorm threatened from the west, he would remember. At those moments he felt happy, but in a different way. As the clouds approached, he watched the skies for messengers. They did not come, but someday, he knew, they would.

———— • • ————

The summers of 1872 and 1873 would be the last time that the High Plains Paradise the Sioux called their birthright would appear uninterrupted in Black Elk's memoirs. Although white pressure continued from the north and south, the greater number of Northern Sioux would still not have felt it, flushed as they were with good buffalo hunts and the sense of invincibility left over from their victory in Red Cloud's War. But in Black Elk's family, one notes a subtle change in 1873 that may have affected many. Instead of heading northwest as in the past in pursuit of the great herds, they turned south at a leisurely pace to the Red Cloud Agency.

At first, the change seems inexplicable. Black Elk's father hates whites, a hatred that only grows. Yet he is lame. The family is always a little slower than the rest, drifting into villages later than the others, breaking camp early so they won't be left behind. It happens enough that it can't be occasional. Black Elk's father is a cripple, and that slows them all.

The fact led to compromises that must have grated on him. Due to his injury he could no longer hunt, yet he still had to provide for his family. If he could not keep up with the tribe, he'd be too late to provide timely service as a bear healer. This means that the only other consistent source of food was the treaty rations, and the elder Black Elk had to feed his children. It was a humiliating turn in his life, and as his dependence on the *wasichu* grew, so did his hatred.

Yet the Black Elks were not alone. These years seem to have been a tipping point—it was no longer easy to find food in the hunting grounds.

Though the young and strong could still fare well enough, they had to range farther in the hunt. But the old, the lame, and the sick who could not maintain the pace turned in their need to the Agencies.

The Black Elks and others like them were the first glimpse of the future. At this point, they were probably in denial. As Black Elk portrayed it, theirs was merely a leisurely detour to "Soldiers' Town" to participate in a family reunion. "Some of our relatives were there and we wanted to see them," he said. A favorite aunt lived on the Agency outskirts, and they all looked forward to a feast. The visitors would bring buffalo meat, but according to Black Elk, "we wanted bread and coffee!"

That summer, as most of Big Road's people headed north to the Yellowstone Country and the Black Elks turned south, the government completed the move of the Red Cloud Agency from its first location on the Platte to the Sand Hills country of northwestern Nebraska. Red Cloud Agency No. 2 was situated in a land of sculpted limestone buttes and stunted trees, near the present-day town of Crawford. Built on a hill overlooking the White River, the Agency included a large warehouse, offices, homes for the agent and his staff, and a blacksmith shop and stables. A log stockade enclosed the Agency, creating a two-hundred-by-four-hundred-foot "safe zone" from the Indians; its walls were ten feet high.

It was the first time Black Elk had seen the *wasichu*, and at first he felt afraid. They seemed to him pale and sick, almost insubstantial. He remembered the old prophecies and feared they might rub him out. But as time passed and nothing happened, he grew used to them.

What he could not know from a child's perspective were the streams of antagonism flowing through the new Agency from both the Lakota and the *wasichu*. Agency politics were complex: there were the Northern Oglala, like the Black Elks; the permanent residents led by Red Cloud, whom the northern visitors called Loafers; and the whites married to Indian women, known as "squawmen." The Northern Oglala thought the Loafers were always drunk; Agency Indians considered the visitors arrogant and liable to make trouble. Both hated the squawmen, who took the best jobs. They traded bad whiskey with Agency Indians for blankets, flour, and bacon, then resold these at higher prices.

These enmities grew obvious on ration days. At the old Agency, Indians flocked to headquarters every fifth day, and while there they told the agent exactly what they thought of him. The aversions only worsened at Agency No. 2. The Episcopal Church selected a new agent, the Denver physician Dr. J. J. Saville, and like most new appointees, he had no idea what he was facing. That fall, an estimated four hundred Oglala and Brulé families left the hunting grounds to spend the cold months receiving rations and gifts. Ration days were always tense: beef cattle were delivered on the hoof and hunted down in a sad imitation of the buffalo hunt; flour and bacon were often spoiled. Beans, coffee, and sugar sometimes fell short, while some Indians exaggerated their family numbers to increase their entitlements. When that October's annuity did not include firearms, the Northern Lakota shot up the Agency. When the Indian Office ordered an accurate census, the visitors told Agent Saville that he would be killed if he tried to count them.

In February 1874, war parties set out for cattle raids to the south. Within ten days, a hunter named King was shot at Laramie Fork, a teamster killed at Running Water, and U.S. Army Lieutenant Levi Robinson and Corporal John Coleman killed near Laramie Peak. At the Agency, Agent Saville received death threats. He asked for troops, but the army refused, believing their presence might incite war.

On February 8, Saville temporarily left the Agency, placing his nephew Frank Appleton in charge. Appleton was already chief clerk; the wild northern visitors fascinated and appalled him. He seemed amazed that he "would be out here among the infernal *Red skins*," he wrote on his birthday, January 7, and described a dance in which a hundred squaws clubbed a dog "till I suppose there was no bone left in him large enough to be broken." Yet he had friends among the Lakota, one of whom warned him never to answer his door after sundown. A white man had killed a Sioux raider during one of the war parties, and it was customary to seek revenge.

But Appleton paid no heed. Around 2:00 a.m. on February 9, he opened his door and a Minneconjou warrior shot him point-blank with a rifle, immediately killing him. Some thought the killer was Black Elk's uncle Kicking Bear, but this was never proven. Nevertheless, Kicking Bear immediately fled north from the Agency, Black Elk said.

On March 8, 1874, the army finally established the cavalry post requested by Saville. Named after the recently slain lieutenant, Camp Robinson would always seem fated for tragedy.

———•◦•———

Those who headed north with Crazy Horse in 1872 and 1873 looked forward to summers filled with buffalo hunts and autumns devoted to winter preparations. They hoped that illusion of the old, free life would sustain them for at least another year.

They underestimated the persistence of the U.S. Army and the Northern Pacific Railroad. On June 20, 1873, a military expedition escorting Northern Pacific surveyors departed from Fort Rice on the Missouri. Though most of the railroad's route would run north of Sioux lands, one segment through Montana crossed the Yellowstone in violation of the 1868 treaty. Nearly two thousand soldiers and civilian contractors were assigned to Colonel D. S. Stanley, wartime cavalry commander of the Army of the Cumberland. Stanley's cavalry unit was the Seventh Regiment; their commander, Lieutenant Colonel George Armstrong Custer, the dashing "boy general" of the late Rebellion.

Custer was thirty-three years old, ten months older than Crazy Horse, and already known as an Indian fighter. As with Crazy Horse, Custer brooked no middle ground. To supporters, he was peerless; to detractors, a braggart squandering soldiers' lives. With his red shirt, gold-braided uniform, and blond hair cascading in shoulder-length ringlets, he was hard to forget. Custer cast himself as a Plains Romantic, a cavalier in buckskin. He sympathized with the Indian even as he subjugated him, and saw the Plains as a huge arena for personal glory. He would have agreed with the old Latin epigram *Audentes fortuna juvat*. Fortune favors the bold.

The Battle of the Washita was as important for establishing Custer's reputation as an Indian fighter as it was for his evolution as a Plains tactician. It determined his fate, and that of his men: the strategy that on November 29, 1868, resulted in the death of 103 Cheyennes and the capture of hundreds of ponies would be repeated seven years and seven months later at the Little Bighorn. Custer swept down from the heights on the forty-seven-lodge village of Black Kettle—the same peace chief of the Sand Creek Massacre. Though he'd survived Chivington, Black Kettle would not survive Custer: he was shot through the stomach and back as he fled with his wife on a pony.

Yet the gunfire brought a swarm of Arapahos from neighboring villages, and their numbers multiplied. Custer fell back without searching for the twenty doomed cavalrymen who'd pursued some fleeing Cheyennes. Though there'd be no official charges of cowardice, their loss tainted his victory and many in the Seventh distrusted their commander to pull them from a jam.

Colonel Stanley also harbored uncertainties about his young

commander. Sherman placed a lot of hope in the Yellowstone Expedition; he fully expected that the Northern Pacific would "bring the Indian problem to a final solution," and Stanley did not want to disappoint him. In a letter to his wife, Stanley worried that "I will try but am not sure I can avoid trouble with [Custer]." Soon he added: "I have seen enough of him to convince me that he is a cold-blooded, untruthful and unprincipled man."

If anything, the Yellowstone Expedition was the first time Custer and Crazy Horse met in the field. On August 4, 1873—around the same time that Black Elk arrived at Red Cloud Agency No. 2—about three hundred Hunkpapas and Oglalas led by Crazy Horse tried to snare Custer with the same ruse that had doomed Fetterman. But Custer did not take the bait. His advance column dug into a line of timber near the Tongue River and, though outnumbered three to one, held off the Sioux for about three hours until the arrival of Stanley's main force.

Nevertheless, Custer and his officers were impressed by their first contact with the Sioux. Custer wrote in his report that the Indians charged "in perfect line, and with as seeming good order and alignment as the best drilled cavalry." One officer admired the way the warriors moved in strict order; their battle lines revealed "a very extraordinary control and discipline," he said.

Within days, Stanley's column veered west, out of Lakota country. Though the Sioux had not turned back the surveyors, they did win a reprieve. That fall, as Black Elk camped at the Agency and Crazy Horse returned to his village, the financial crisis known as the Panic of 1873 sent shock waves through Europe and North America. Banks closed; businesses shuttered. The Northern Pacific's new "end-of-track" was a boomtown called Bismarck; at its outskirts, the army built a new outpost, Fort Abraham Lincoln, where Custer and his Seventh Cavalry were permanently stationed. Thousands of immigrant settlers washed against this eastern edge of the Sioux Reserve and stopped. They gazed west, dreaming of the riches going to waste in the land of the Sioux.

—⋆—

Crazy Horse should have returned from the Yellowstone in triumph. He found heartbreak instead.

What happened now to the war chief echoed his life's course over the previous six years. When honors befell him, tragedy followed, often by his own hand. Such fortune marks a person, and this at the moment he became an important—if everyday—part of Black Elk's life. Kahnigapi's front-row seat to his cousin's fate would shape his entire future: his identity as a Lakota, his growing sense of doom and duty, and his determination to save the Sioux.

Crazy Horse's transformation began in the summer of 1867, after the Battle of the Hundred Slain. His success in that fight and others led his people to name him, with three others, an *Ogle Tanka Un*, or "Shirt Wearer"—a head warrior of his clan. The ceremony took place at the yearly tribal council at Bear Butte, the lonely prominence north of the Black Hills that served as a holy site for both Cheyenne and Sioux. The appointment held meaning: Crazy Horse was no longer Red Cloud's lieutenant but a commander in his own right, his people's defender, as he'd foreseen in his thunder dream.

Although an honor, the appointment held expectations. Shirt Wearers were future chiefs: they must show strength, forbearance, and generosity, especially to widows, orphans, and the poor. Like chiefs, they must work for the tribe's harmony: old rivalries, sexual jealousy—all must be put aside. Even if a rival seduced his wife, the Shirt Wearer must pay no more attention than if a dog urinated against his tipi. One must be "big-hearted": "Do not give way to anger, even if relatives lay in blood around you," admonished the orator. Shirt Wearers were warriors, but also mediators, for the path upon which they led their people was "narrow and full of thorns." Finally, Shirt Wearers must "look after the land." Since the land was the heart of all the Sioux held sacred, they must preserve and protect all sacred ways.

Yet harmony eluded Tasunke Witko: excitement and change were his siren songs. In May 1870, he invited Black Buffalo Woman, wife of Chief No Water, to accompany him on a buffalo hunt to Slim Buttes in present-day northwestern South Dakota. In some versions, she went willingly; in others, she was abducted. No Water was a heavy drinker, said to abuse the beautiful Black Buffalo Woman. Divorces were easy in Lakota society—a woman placed her husband's belongings outside their tipi, then moved in with a relative or another man. If the latter, some compensation was expected.

But Black Buffalo Woman left without preamble, and the *manner* of the split humiliated No Water. So he tracked the couple down. He called from outside the tipi, and when Crazy Horse answered, No Water stepped through the flap and said, "My friend, I have come." Crazy Horse rose, drawing his knife; his friend Little Big Man, seated near the entrance, saw the gun in No Water's hand and grabbed for it, deflecting the jealous husband's aim. Nevertheless, No Water stood a mere three or four feet away when he pulled the trigger, and the bullet struck Crazy Horse below the left nostril, followed the line of his front teeth, and fractured his upper jaw before leaving the back of his skull. Black Buffalo Woman screamed and fled to her relatives. No Water fled to his own village, suddenly realizing the kind of revenge that could follow an attack on such a powerful man.

Crazy Horse barely survived, drifting for months in and out of fever. The wound and the severe powder burns never really healed, leaving a scar that lifted his cheek in a sinister parody of a smile. Several elders stepped forward, demanding that no more blood be shed. In compensation for the shooting, No Water gave Crazy Horse three horses; he left his village and resettled in the new Red Cloud Agency.

But Crazy Horse had stolen another man's wife, putting his own desires before the welfare of the tribe. For this, he was stripped of his status as Shirt Wearer. "I'd rather be a plain warrior," Crazy Horse said. A few months later, after the furor had passed, the Oglalas made him tribal war leader, supplanting Red Cloud after his move to the Agency.

Crazy Horse had gotten what he'd wanted, if not in the way he'd imagined. Still, his father decided he must settle down. Before his son's affair with Black Buffalo Woman, Worm had begun marriage negotiations with Old Red Feather, the father of the attractive Black Shawl. Worm reopened negotiations, and in 1871, Crazy Horse married Black Shawl and went to live with her family in Big Road's band.

The move brought Crazy Horse directly into the life of Black Elk. Before this, Black Elk knew of his second cousin by reputation. Now, he encountered this strange man every day. He saw firsthand what others said: in camp, his cousin rarely seemed excited, and was always measured in his ways.

At first, Black Elk was only one in the loud gaggle of village boys, and Crazy Horse probably paid him little mind. But after Black Elk's resurrection, Crazy Horse became very aware of this strange, silent boy. Before the Great Vision, there is no mention in Black Elk's memoirs of contact with Crazy Horse. After the Vision, the famous cousin becomes part of the village fabric for Kahnigapi. "Now and then he would notice me and speak to me," Black Elk said, "and sometimes he would have the crier call me into his tepee to eat with him. Then he would say things to tease me, but I would not say anything back, because I think I was a little afraid of him." Many seemed intimidated by this quiet, "queer man." He always seemed to be thinking hard about something, as if "he was always part way into the world of his vision."

Soon after Crazy Horse's wedding, bad luck struck again. As the No Water debacle unfolded, Tasunke Witko's younger brother, Little Hawk, was killed on the far side of the Rockies in a foray against the Ute. In Big Road's band, however, most people blamed white settlers. The news reached Crazy Horse just after he wed. Instead of a honeymoon, the couple traveled to Little Hawk's grave. Crazy Horse shot his brother's favorite horse over the bier, collected his bones, and went on a killing spree. He camped in a high place overlooking the settlement and stayed for nine days. He shot anyone he saw below: it is not known how many settlers died. Soldiers rode out and he lay in wait, killing two. On the return trip, he chased down a party and killed two more. Death demanded death, but it took many to satiate Crazy Horse before he decided to come home.

Black Shawl conceived a child during this time of revenge, and later that year bore a daughter. They named her Kokipapi, or They Are Afraid of Her. Crazy Horse was a doting father, and soon the Bad Faces noticed a change. Though Crazy Horse still acted distracted, Black Elk noticed that his cousin had begun to pay special attention to little children. His mood lightened around them, and he began once more to joke with others. On the warpath, he did what he could "to make his warriors feel good."

But if life as a father lightened the war chief, the state would not last long. Within a month of the Yellowstone fight, Crazy Horse led the annual late-season raid against the Crow. He wasn't gone long before They Are Afraid of Her contracted an unidentified illness; Worm and others tried to nurse her back to health, but Kokipapi's condition deteriorated. Within days, Crazy Horse's two-and-a-half-year-old daughter died. Black Shawl was disconsolate: she hacked off her hair, dressed in ragged clothing, slashed her thighs and shins with a butcher knife, and possibly chopped off the first joint of her little finger. The Bad Faces wrapped the toddler in robes and blankets, erected a scaffold, and lashed her to the bier. Black Shawl howled in grief as the tribe headed east. Black Elk heard her howls.

Several days later, Crazy Horse returned. His party had come back with several stolen horses, but nothing mattered when he heard the news. When people told him where they'd left his daughter, he decided to backtrack the seventy miles to Kokipapi's grave.

An account exists of that trip, if it can be believed. Frank Grouard was a teenage mail rider on the Upper Missouri Pony Express route when he'd been captured by the Hunkpapa and become a ward of Sitting Bull. He was one of those strange characters who seemed to populate the Plains: in time he would become an army scout and famous western "personality." Now twenty-two, he'd been accepted by the Oglala and befriended the war chief. Crazy Horse asked Grouard to accompany him to his daughter's grave.

The trip took two days. They rode to the girl's scaffold, erected high in the outcrops overlooking the Little Bighorn River. Crazy Horse asked Grouard to prepare camp. As he left with the ponies, Grouard glanced back and saw the war chief clamber up the scaffold and lie down beside the tiny bundle. For the next three days, as Grouard huddled by the campfire, he could hear the loud keens of Crazy Horse "mourning for the departed one."

At sunrise of the fourth day, Crazy Horse knelt beside the sleeping Grouard. The scout looked up; his friend's face was a spectral mask. He said he was ready to go. As Grouard readied the horses, Crazy Horse broke his three-day fast: he ate sparingly and sipped from a waterskin. They rode in silence back to the Bad Faces, and to the mourning of Black Shawl.

5

THE BLACK HILLS

In March 1874, the soldiers came to the Red Cloud Agency and built Camp Robinson, a mile and a half west of the Agency on the White River. A ridge of limestone buttes separated it from the town of Crawford. The whitewashed headquarters building, stables, and barracks rose from the shortgrass like stumps, open to the plains.

When the troops moved in, the Lakota moved out, though how much was in reaction to the soldiers and how much the annual spring migration to the hunting grounds was hard to say. In early April, Black Elk's family and thirty others trekked sixty miles north to the Black Hills.

The Lakota built their lives around this strange geographical formation: it was the place where young Lakota men "cried for a vision," the center of the earth where Black Elk had come in his coma. Paha Sapa resembles a forested black island rising four thousand feet from a grassy sea; the blackness is caused by its carpet of ponderosa pine. This alien landscape of buttes, hogbacks, granite ridges, and lava columns forms the easternmost extension of the Rocky Mountains, a massive six-thousand-square-mile stone ellipse that extends 120 miles north to south and 40 to 50 miles east to west. It thrust up from the earth 60 to 70 million years ago; the sediments eroded, exposing twisted igneous rock said to be 2.5 billion years old. If true, this makes it the oldest geological formation in North America. Such ancient cores formed what today

are the Black Hills' highest peaks—Mount Rushmore, Custer Peak, and
the granite towers known as the Cathedral Spires. At 7,242 feet, the
highest point is Harney Peak: to stand here on a clear day and see the
Plains spread in all directions is to understand why the Lakota considered the place holy. One becomes an omniscient eye.

Even whites considered the Hills strange. "The Black Hills has been
to the plains traveler the embodiment of the fullest idea of the mysterious and the unknown," Colonel Richard Irving Dodge wrote in 1876.
The weather could change in an instant; black storms appeared out of
nowhere, shot through with lightning; hailstorms could be lethal unless
one sought proper cover. The place was home to noises that seemed to
have no natural origin: their first mention appeared in the journals of
Lewis and Clark. In an entry dated October 1804, the fur trapper Jean
Valle told them that every summer "a great noise is heard frequently."
Other explorers recorded "mysterious boomings and bangings," and
miners conjectured it might be the release of hydrogen from subterra-
nean beds of burning coal. The Sioux claimed they were the groans of
a Great White Giant, condemned to lie forever beneath the mountains
for invading Lakota hunting grounds. The source was never discovered—
after 1833, the rumblings ceased and explorers no longer mentioned
hearing them.

Paha Sapa's first mention in Lakota history occurs in 1775–76: an
Oglala war party under Chief Standing Bull came upon them during
the tribe's slow march from the Missouri country. Within a century, the
Lakotas' spiritual link to the Hills was firmly established. As a boy,
Black Elk heard tales of the half-human, half-celestial hero Falling Star,
who lived in the Hills. In the legends, Falling Star visited seven "Star
Villages" that existed simultaneously in the Hills and the Big Dipper,
straddling both worlds.

The Black Elks traveled three days to Pte Tali Yapa, the Buffalo Gap
or Buffalo Gate at the ellipse's southeast edge, the place where for ages
great herds of buffalo entered the Hills in the fall and departed in the
spring. The People believed the gap was formed as the herds emerged
from their birthplace, Wind Cave. This was a good place to camp: game
was plentiful, and to the south bubbled Mnikahta, the hot springs where
sick and lame people drank the holy water. Maybe it would help Black
Elk's father. People swallowed four mouthfuls and prayed; supposedly,
it tasted different each time.

Soon after they camped, Black Elk and his father went hunting. They climbed up a hill and peered south to the western curve of the Cheyenne River. It was a hard climb for his father: the pain in his right leg was so great that he often had to sit. When they reached the top, his father spotted some deer in the distance. "We'll catch them," he said. "I'll round them up and you wait for me here."

But Black Elk knew his father was in pain. As head of the family, he must provide for all of them, but there were times when he could barely get around. Without thinking, Black Elk answered, "No, Father, you stay here, they are bringing them to us and we'll get them here."

Then they stared at each other, surprised. It was the first time Black Elk revealed his contacts with the spirit world to a family member. Who else could "they" be but spirits? Without meaning to, he'd given his father a glimpse of his inner world, and though his son's words may not have made sense at first, the older man had encountered such subtleties before. As a bear dreamer, he knew the ways in which spirits were revealed. His wife and he had known their boy was "different" ever since his resurrection, but in the months that followed he'd begun to act like his old self again.

If Black Elk's father did not rebuke his son for what could have been seen as disrespect, he also did not rejoice when the boy gave himself away. He knew the costs of possession and quietly studied his son. He "looked at me in a queer manner," Black Elk said, then told his son to secure the horses and come back up to watch the herd. They lay flat in the grass and watched it draw close; they could see now that they were antelope, notoriously skittish, prone to bolt at the least sound. His father's limp made him a clumsy hunter; in all probability, he would have spooked the herd. They separated briefly and, after a moment, Black Elk heard two shots. His father rose from his hiding place and said he'd downed a pair. Black Elk brought up the horses and they rode to the animals. To their surprise, four antelope lay dead. When they returned to camp, everyone cheered.

They spent the first half of that summer in Buffalo Gap, from May until June 1874. The boys hunted and fished: whenever they caught a fish too small to keep, they kissed it and threw it back, hoping it would tell bigger fish to come. Whenever Black Elk brought home game, his mother was proud: "I made up my mind to do this so that everyone would think lots of me," he said. They moved deeper into the hills, looking for the long, slim lodgepole pines that made the best tipi poles. Sometimes the storms emerged from behind the crests and split-tail swallows scattered before the wind. His people seemed content—until the day everything changed.

It happened suddenly, with slight warning. After the men and boys had cut and dressed the lodgepoles, they sat in camp, boiling bear meat and chatting. Some men helped Chips build a sweat lodge. A sense of unease had come upon the medicine man, and he hoped to discover the cause. People listened to Chips: he was probably the band's most powerful thunder dreamer, a mentor of countless young men in their vision quests, and the *wicasa wakan* who'd made the sacred ornament for Crazy Horse that kept him bulletproof in battle. The men bent a dome of limber willow poles, and over that draped buffalo hides. They dug a small pit, or *iniowaspe*, in the center for heating stones; around this they spread a thick blanket of sage. Chips shed his clothing and crawled inside; he took a paunch of water, and with a spoon carved from the horn of a mountain sheep flicked water upon the stones. Clouds of steam rose up; Chips flicked water on the stones four times. He sang verses from his visions, wiped himself with sage leaves as the sweat poured out, and waited for the Thunder-beings to speak to him.

At the other end of camp, Black Elk's friends asked him to go out and shoot squirrels. They were hard to hit, and seemed warier than usual. Suddenly, Black Elk felt nauseous and had to sit. All seemed too quiet, like the silence accompanying snowfall. Then a voice rang from that silence: "Go at once. Go home," it said.

We should leave for camp, he told the other boys. Though the adults might not yet know what to think of Black Elk, his friends knew that when he spoke like this, it was best to listen. But when they returned, all was in chaos. The adults were breaking camp, catching ponies, loading drags. As Chips sat in the sweat lodge, images passed before his eyes. A voice had spoken in his ear, he said. The band must flee at once: if it did not, something terrible would happen. Black Elk felt odd: Was this the same voice that had spoken to him?

They left before sundown and headed south, riding all night until they were out of the Hills. They stopped at Good River long enough to eat, then started again. That evening, they camped at the mouth of Horsehead Creek, the same place they'd camped two or three months earlier on their way to Paha Sapa. It was a good place to stop, but the scouts rode up. *You must leave,* they told them. *You are in danger.* Soldiers had ridden from the north. Despite the treaty, the *wasichu* had come to the Black Hills.

Army Special Orders No. 17 would officially describe the Black Hills Expedition as an exploratory reconnaissance-in-force to determine the best site for a fort to guard the planned Northern Pacific Railroad. Between Fort Abraham Lincoln at Bismarck and Fort Ellis near Bozeman, Montana, nothing existed—a defensive gap of 550 miles. Sheridan had long ago decided that the Black Hills were an ideal spot for a fort: the fact that building one would violate the 1868 treaty did not matter. Sheridan anticipated objections: Article 2 of that treaty allowed an exception to passage by "officers, agents, and employees of the Government . . . in discharge of duties enjoined by law."

Yet the column's sheer massiveness belied this explanation; it would be one of the largest cavalcades ever assembled in the Northern Plains. It numbered 1,200 souls, 900 of them military, the remainder Indian scouts, guides, scientists, engineers, two "practical miners," a photographer, and three reporters from newspapers in Chicago, New York, and Bismarck. One hundred ten wagons hauled equipment; drovers herded three hundred beef cattle. The president's twenty-four-year-old son Colonel Fred Grant rode as "acting aide."

It was all led by Custer, now called Pahuska—or Long Hair—by the Sioux. He'd come far since the Yellowstone survey. There, he was commanded by the "squat, humorless" Stanley. Now, Custer commanded. The press portrayed him as a frontier D'Artagnan, epitomized by his long blond hair "swing[ing] below his shoulders perfumed with cinnamon oil." As he impatiently awaited the end of winter in snowbound Fort Lincoln, he finished up *My Life on the Plains*, his autobiographical account of army life in Kansas and Oklahoma. "I expect to visit a region of country as yet unseen by human eyes," he wrote, "except those of the Indian."

The expedition left Fort Lincoln on July 2, 1874, accompanied by a sixteen-piece brass band riding white horses. They played the regimental theme "Garry Owen," the same played during the attack at the Washita. Every morning, the band serenaded the troops with popular tunes for the first two or three miles. They entered the Hills on the western circumference on July 25, and marched south, encountering few Indians except for twenty-five to thirty Oglalas who'd just killed some deer. Custer gave them flour, coffee, and sugar in exchange for information, but when four tried to slip off, Custer's scouts followed and possibly wounded one of them. They found some abandoned camps and other signs of Indians, but the single band of Oglalas was all the Lakotas they encountered. Later oral evidence suggests the Sioux had either fled or were simply unaware of the column's presence as they went about their daily lives.

On July 31, Custer and his companions climbed Harney Peak. The climb took most of the day: though Custer nearly made the summit, "a mass of granite forty feet in height" blocked the final ascent. Its "perpendicular sides . . . forbade any attempt to scale them without the aid of rope and ladder," wrote Captain William Ludlow, the chief engineer. Just the same, the view was breathtaking: they spotted Bear Butte, forty miles north, and the forks of the Cheyenne. Custer's pulse rose to 112; he drank a toast to General Harney and fired at distant cliffs in celebration.

They descended, elated. Custer led five cavalry troops southwest to the south fork of the Cheyenne, Paha Sapa's southernmost boundary. He sent another two troops southeast from Harney Peak, a course that would take them down Buffalo Gap. These were probably the troops from whom Black Elk's band barely escaped. Chips and Black Elk firmly believed that the spirits had warned them about the soldiers riding from the north, and so they fled.

———————

Meanwhile, Custer's "practical miners" and geologists searched for gold. On August 2, 1874, they found it near present-day Custer, South Dakota. The prospector Horatio N. Ross and the ambulance driver "Antelope" Fred Snow examined a streambed near French Creek; when they spotted a telltale color in the grit, they dug a hole and came up with a fine-grained dust sparkling with occasional nuggets about the size of a pinhead. This was tested in all the accepted ways—washing with acid, mixing with mercury, tasting, cutting, cleaning. They wrapped their find in the torn leaves of a journal and took it to Custer and Major G. A. Forsyth, commander of the Ninth U.S. Cavalry. Ross would later recall that he had never seen two "better pleased" officers in his entire life. When asked the worth of this pinch of dust, he answered, "About ten cents."

A dime's worth of what Black Elk would later call "the yellow metal that makes the Wasichus crazy." Everyone associated with the expedition, from Custer to the lowliest mule skinner, knew what this portended. First would come a stampede of whites through Dakota Territory; next, the Sioux would kill miners and attack wagon trains. The army would retaliate. There would be war.

It did not matter. Not to the hordes of men ruined by the economic depression, nor to the companies organized to outfit them. There had been rumors of gold in the Black Hills for decades. A prospector named Crazy Hank Joplin told of meeting an Indian boy who used gold-tipped arrows. In 1833, four miners from Laramie entered the Hills and disappeared, but afterward a message found scratched on a sandstone slab read, "Killed by Inds beyond the high hills got our gold June 1834." In 1852, thirty prospectors entered the hills and eight came back. They'd seen gold, but also more traces of Indians than seemed healthy. Except for a memorandum book and two skeletons, the rest of the party disappeared.

Black Elk was right—*mázaska zi* made whites crazy. The metaphor of lunacy recurs throughout the mid- to late 1800s' history of gold. Chroniclers compared miners to the sick and insane. During the California gold rush, witnesses said that news of a strike caused temporary derangement. In May 1849, displays of gold in San Francisco reduced the population from one thousand to fewer than one hundred as inhabitants stampeded for placer mines near Sutter's Mill. All of a sudden, the lowliest and poorest could dream of untold riches. In 1849 alone, rumors of gold brought 55,000 to California's goldfields by land and another 25,000 by sea. The state's non-Indian population increased from about 14,000 in 1848 to 223,856 in 1852. The California rush was followed by one to Nevada in 1858; to Colorado in 1859; to Idaho and Montana in the 1860s; and to the Dakota Territory, now. Gold madness girdled the globe: prospectors came from China, Mexico, Peru, and Chile. In the 1880s, men rushed to strikes in Australia and the Transvaal; to Alaska in 1898. Though most went "bust," the tales of huge nuggets were legendary—the "Castle Ravine" nugget found in 1853 near Downieville, California, worth $49,000; the "Ryan & Haultmus" found in New South Wales, Australia, in 1872, worth nearly $149,000.

The simple rumor of gold could change a place forever. On June 17, 1874—two weeks before Custer's march—*The Bismarck Tribune* justified what was to come: "Humanitarians may weep" for the Indian, wrote the editor, "and tell the wrongs he has suffered, but he is passing away":

> The American people need the country the Indians now occupy;
> many of our people are out of employment; the masses need
> some new excitement. The war is over, and the era of railroad
> building has been brought to a termination by the greed of capi-
> talists and the folly of the grangers; and depression prevails on
> every hand. An Indian war would do no harm, for it must come,
> sooner or later.

There would be no closing the floodgates once opened. Custer could
see that in his own men. On August 3, one day after examining the
sample of gold dust, he dispatched scout "Lonesome" Charley Reynolds
to Fort Laramie with the news. "I have upon my table forty or fifty particles of pure gold," Custer wrote, "in size averaging that of a small
pinhead, and most of it obtained today from one panful of earth." He
would not speculate upon its worth, or greater quantity, until a more
detailed analysis was made. That same day, wrote the chief geologist,
Custer's soldiers caught gold fever: "The fact of the existence of gold
caused considerable excitement . . . and quite a number were busily
engaged in prospecting along the creek, sinking holes to the bed-rock
wherever there was the slightest indication of a deposit of gravel." On
the whole, "the results of their labor was so discouraging . . . that after
a few days they abandoned the search." Yet this did not discourage the
three correspondents from sending dispatches to their own newspapers
reporting that "from the grass roots down it was 'pay dirt.'"

On August 7, Custer backtracked north, and seven days later he left
the Black Hills. The column returned to Fort Lincoln on August 30,
having logged 894¾ miles in sixty-one days. The news of the gold strike
preceded them by weeks. "STRUCK IT AT LAST!" blared a Dakota paper.
"A Region of Gold and Silver Mines and Lovely Valleys Discovered,"
announced page 1 of the August 11 New York World.

———•·•———

Almost immediately, prospectors organized to invade Lakota land.
Having opened the door, the army could not close it again. Sherman announced that any whites found on the reservation could be driven out at
gunpoint, but few officers observed such stringent commands. Instead,
they turned them over to the nearest civil authorities. It was nearly impossible to stop a determined miner; he simply turned around and started
back. "I have been captured and sent out from the Hills four times," one

man said. "I give the troops more trouble in catching me each time, and I guess I can stand it as long as they can." By the summer of 1875, hundreds of men were panning for gold in the Black Hills. The Lakota were furious and called Custer "the Chief of all the Thieves." His route into Paha Sapa was dubbed "the Thieves' Trail."

That spring, Sitting Bull addressed his people at the annual council on the Powder River. Along with Crazy Horse, he now led the hostiles: as with Red Cloud in an earlier age, Sitting Bull's oratory and intellect could not be denied. Standing Bear was present: now fifteen, he was old enough to fight, and everyone knew a fight was coming. Sitting Bull addressed the importance of the Black Hills to their survival. Paha Sapa was "just like a food pack, and therefore the Indians should stick to it," he said. As Standing Bear thought about it, he could see that Sitting Bull was right—the Hills were full of "fish, animals, and lots of water." Indians could roam where they wanted, "but when they were in need of something, they could just go in there and get it." It was their fallback; their insurance policy.

Yet that could be ending. The annihilation foretold by the prophets was coming to pass; Sitting Bull updated the threat for any who'd forgotten their words. "Yet hear me, people, we have now to deal with another race," he said. His voice rang out; he walked with a limp from an old bullet wound. He might be stocky and unassuming, but everyone knew him. "The enemy was small and feeble when our fathers first met them, but now great and overbearing." They had a religion "in which the poor weep, but the rich will not." They claimed the earth, but defiled it with buildings and garbage. "That nation is like a spring freshet that overruns its banks and destroys all who are in its path," he said.

The old policy of living side by side with the wasichu had failed. They'd tried that ever since Red Cloud's War, and where had it gotten them? "We cannot dwell side by side," Sitting Bull cried. "Only seven years ago we made a treaty by which we were assured that the buffalo country should be left to us forever. Now they threaten to take that from us. My brothers, shall we submit, or shall we say to them: 'First kill me before you take possession of my fatherland!'"

—•—

Since the government could not keep its citizens out, it turned to the Indian Office to legalize the invasion. In the summer of 1875, as Sitting Bull addressed his people, the secretary of the interior appointed a commission to negotiate a revision of the Fort Laramie treaty. Specifically, they wanted to buy the Black Hills. Senator William Allison of Iowa was chairman; the commissioners included other congressmen and Major General Alfred Terry, commander of the Department of the Dakota. Though they were a distinguished group, the Lakota were not impressed. Later, when the Sioux told of Iktomi men from Washington, this would be their prime example.

Negotiations fell apart from the beginning. When the commissioners arrived at Camp Robinson on September 20, 1875, warriors surrounded them with leveled guns. Little Big Man, the friend of Crazy Horse, echoed the words of both Sitting Bull and *The Bismarck Tribune* when he said this was as good a time as any to start a war. Two lines of cavalry formed with carbines ready—then waited silently for the slightest hostile move. The tension eased when the Brulé peace chief Spotted Tail interceded.

War was averted, but not old antagonisms. From September 20 to 28, the Allison Commission and five thousand Lakotas, Yanktons, Arapahos, Santees, and Cheyennes, met about eight miles east of the Red Cloud Agency. Red Cloud, Spotted Tail, Little Bear, and other chiefs spoke for the tribes; Crazy Horse and Sitting Bull did not attend. The tribes knew they had to parley: by now, only the foolish could pretend that the buffalo was not in decline. That winter of 1874–75, a large hunting party from the Agencies spent several weeks hunting bison along the Republican River. In the recent past, such a party would have killed thousands and come back with a year's supply. This time, they found a hundred. The only thing that stood between the tribes and starvation was Agency rations.

Though Black Elk watched, he did not understand the proceedings. The commissioners sat in a circle under a big shade tree; a crowd milled around them. They wrangled for days, but to Black Elk it seemed "just like wind blowing in the end." He asked his father what they talked about. The Grandfather in Washington wanted to buy or lease the Black Hills so that miners could look for *mázaska zi*, his father replied. The soldier chief, Terry, threatened that if the tribes did not do as asked, the *wasichu* would take the country anyway.

If Terry hoped to intimidate the Sioux with threats, he instead merely angered them. A rumor began that at night soldiers crept between camps, filling the chiefs with whiskey. Drunk, they would be pliable; though never verified, the rumors appeared in several Indian accounts. In response to the threats, the chiefs began making what the commissioners considered outrageous demands. Red Cloud said $600 million seemed a fair price for the Hills. Spotted Bear proposed $70 million: "Our Great Father has a big safe, and so have we," he said. "This hill is our safe."

The commissioners realized early on that the Sioux "would demand an exorbitant sum for the Hills," they later reported. What surprised them, however, was the intransigence and resentment displayed by every chief beneath the shade tree. In the past, commissioners were able to play one chief against another. Not this time. In the end, the Allison Commission offered to buy the Black Hills for $6 million—one one-hundredth of Red Cloud's offer—or purchase mining rights for $400,000 annually. On September 29, the chiefs rejected both offers.

The commissioners returned to Washington, smarting from the experience. Unfortunately for the Lakota, they also wielded considerable influence. The Indians had done "absolutely nothing but eat, drink, smoke, and sleep" for the past six years while living on "appropriations from the national Treasury," the commissioners complained, then recommended that the government name a price for the Hills and hand it to the Indians "as a finality." Rejection would put an end to rations and annuities. Teach the Sioux a lesson—let them sell, or starve.

The Black Hills council ended so acrimoniously that Black Elk's father decided it was safer to leave Soldiers' Town. Trouble was brewing, he said. A few days later, the family broke camp to join Crazy Horse on the Tongue. They headed north to Horsehead Creek, then swung west on a route that put them in sight of the soldiers' road into the Black Hills from Fort Laramie. They paralleled this as it skirted the western edge of the Hills; they then veered west across the Plains. Some Loafers who'd been traveling with them now realized that the Bad Faces meant to winter with Crazy Horse. The war chief would fight if hostilities developed, and the Loafers did not want to be in the midst of such fighting. So they headed back to Soldiers' Town.

One day as the band traveled west, Black Elk and a friend named Steal Horses rode ahead. They came across the moccasin prints of a lone Indian; they followed the trail across Kills Himself Creek and up a rocky knoll. At the top they found an old man named Root of the Tail who'd started a few days ahead of them. He was afoot, and when people asked where he was headed, he said he meant to visit some relatives on the Tongue. Old folks who felt their death approach would sometimes say "I am going away to see my people," as if one could pass through the barrier to the Hereafter and live with the dead. They'd all wondered, but let him go. He'd made it this far but must have felt death closing, so he climbed the knoll and lay down. He looked very peaceful to Black Elk; he must have faded out like this, the sun or the stars on his face, and perhaps his body had felt as light as Black Elk's when he'd gone to see the Grandfathers. As if he rose to the clouds.

The best they could do was cover the old man with rocks and leave him alone on the hill.

The next day, the band continued west toward Powder River. The feeling that trouble followed was never far behind. They were right. The mechanics of war became official.

The decision was reached in early November at a meeting attended by President Grant, the secretary of war, the secretary of the interior, the assistant secretary of the interior, and G. W. Manypenny, the commissioner of Indian affairs. By sending troops against the Sioux in the Powder River Country, Washington hoped to force the tribes to relinquish the Hills. Few if any in the room believed the Indians would put up a serious fight.

All that was needed was an excuse, and that was found in the November 9, 1875, report of Indian Inspector General E. C. Watkins describing Sioux attacks on whites and the Crow. Reports such as this had been made to the Indian Office every year since 1866, but now the timing was right and the Watkins report was just what they needed. The Powder River Country, Watkins wrote, "is probably the best hunting grounds in the United States, a 'Paradise' for Indians, affording game in such variety and abundance that the need of Government Supplies is not felt. Perhaps for this reason they have never accepted aid or been brought under control." The Lakota there openly defied "all law and authority and boast that the United States authorities are not strong enough to conquer them."

But Paradise could be used against them. "In my judgment," Watkins wrote, "one thousand men, under the command of an experienced officer, sent into their country in the winter, when the Indians are nearly always in camp and at which season of the year they are the most helpless, would be amply sufficient for their capture or punishment." Winter hindered the Sioux's mobility, their one great advantage over the army. Winter raids had broken the power of the Southern Cheyenne during attacks at the Washita in November 1868, at Soldier Springs one month later, and at Summit Springs in July 1869. Now the tactic could be used against the Sioux.

A final report by Watkins landed on the desks of Sherman and Sheridan on November 27, 1875. Just before Christmas, an ultimatum reached the Sioux Agencies: the misdeeds of the nontreaty Indians would no longer be tolerated. They had until January 31, 1876, to come to the Agencies. If they did not, they would be deemed "hostile." And that was all the reason the army needed to march into Paradise and cast out the Sioux.

6

"IT IS WAR"

New Year's Day 1876 was a time for taking stock. Editorials posed the questions that would be asked increasingly in the nation's centennial year: Who are we? Where are we going? Where have we been? In one hundred years, the United States had survived four wars, including the recent War of the Rebellion, in which more than half a million combatants died. It had survived a succession of political and economic crises. Its population had increased from 2.5 to 46 million, drawn from every continent on earth; thirty-eight states stretched from ocean to ocean, connected by thirty-five thousand miles of railroad track. It had changed from a simple agrarian society to one that was aggressively industrial, and had done so with such speed that few could grasp its complexity. A decade earlier, Lincoln had warned: "The dogmas of the quiet past are inadequate to the stormy present." Walt Whitman put it differently: "Unwieldy and immense, who shall hold in behemoth? Who bridle leviathan?"

George Custer and his wife, Elizabeth, spent New Year's Day enjoying the civilized delights of New York City. They made a glamorous pair—Custer with his long blond locks and starry blue eyes, Libby with her wit and serene beauty. Long ago, Custer had learned the value of publicity. *My Life on the Plains*, in which he criticized Grant's Indian policy, had come out to glowing reviews; the Redpath Lecturing Agency had offered a contract for a speaking tour that would have made him a wealthy man. But that was curtailed, at least for now. Orders to return to Fort Lincoln for the Indian campaign would arrive soon.

Custer understood the power of the pen. He usually arranged for at least one journalist to ride along on an expedition, and was always open to interviews. On February 13, 1876, reporters quizzed the couple at the Palmer House Hotel in Chicago. How many Indians might the army face? they asked. Probably eight to ten thousand warriors loyal to Sitting Bull, Custer said. They turned to Elizabeth Custer. Was she worried?

"Not in the least," she replied.

On the Sioux Reserve, New Year's dawned white and cold. Messengers from the Agencies struggled across the Plains in the very worst weather, tasked with delivering the army's ultimatum to nontreaty camps before the January 31, 1876, deadline. The wind blew like a scythe; the Indians they hunted were laced up tight in their tipis, their small villages hidden in forested ravines or protected gullies, sheltered from the killing winds.

But the messengers knew their tribes. The runner from Standing Rock Agency found Sitting Bull's people near the mouth of the Powder River; he was well treated, but could not make it back with an answer until February 11, nearly two weeks after the deadline. Agent James S. Hastings at Red Cloud Agency said his runner found Crazy Horse near Bear Butte and told him there would be trouble if his people did not come in. "But it was foolish to say that, because it was very cold and many of our people and ponies would have died in the snow," Black Elk stated, no doubt echoing the adults. Runners who found Cheyenne tribes one hundred miles beyond Bear Butte had not returned. The fact that the messengers themselves could not plow across the Plains and back within the given time revealed Washington's cynicism.

Crazy Horse and his people apparently sensed this, for in late January an early thaw occurred. The Oglala took advantage of the break to leave Bear Butte and head to the hunting grounds. About one hundred lodges camped approximately ten miles north of the Tongue, the Black Elks among them. Within a few days, Big Road's people shifted some miles west, where they felt safer, but here, in this "Paradise of Indians," enemies were everywhere. A day or two earlier, Crows had surrounded and massacred a party of Loafers. Now the Oglala were on guard. A man named Crow Nose pitched his tipi near the entrance of the pony corral; it was night, and Crow Nose heard a noise. He peeked out and saw a man creeping among the horses. When the thief lifted the bar and began to mount, Crow Nose shot him with his rifle and the thief dropped among the herd.

The shot resounded through the camp. Black Elk ran outside. When he reached the fallen Crow, "what I saw was horrible." The Crow's arms and legs had been chopped off and he'd been scalped—in Sioux warfare, the man who killed an enemy must not touch him. Another must count coup while a third did the scalping. As Black Elk ran up, someone told him to strike the dead thief with a coup stick; he did as told, adding his stick to a pile beside the body. But he took no pleasure in the act, which held for him no hint of honor. As he watched, women cut up the body with axes and scattered the pieces. War was not as glorious as he'd heard.

The thaw continued, and in February about thirty-five families, including Black Elk's, turned back to Soldiers' Town. They struck southeast and crossed the knoll where Root of the Tail had died, but once again the cold grew lethal and they hunkered down. This act of survival made them vulnerable to a winter attack. By missing the deadline, they'd become "hostiles." In fact, by January 31, only one small band had managed to come in.

—◦—

If all went as planned, Sheridan hoped to squeeze the Sioux between three converging columns as winter locked them in place in their tipis. Brigadier General George Crook would move from the south at the head of 800 men; Major General Alfred Terry would lead a force of 925 from the east, including Custer's Seventh Cavalry; and from the west, Colonel John Gibbon would lead 450 soldiers from Fort Ellis in Montana Territory. The three prongs totaled slightly more than 2,100 men. They'd meet near the junction of the Bighorn and Yellowstone Rivers, surrounding and compressing the hostiles until they either surrendered or died.

But the weather failed to cooperate with Sheridan's plans. Crook's was the only column to actually leave quarters, marching north on the Powder on days so cold that the mercury froze in his thermometer. The Indians called him "Three Stars"—one star sewn on each shoulder and one on his hat. He was the most unpretentious of the generals, abjuring a uniform in the field, preferring instead a canvas suit and cork helmet. He wove his forked blond beard into braids and tied them behind his neck; when given the choice, he rode a mule. On March 17, 1876, six of his cavalry companies under Colonel Joseph Reynolds swept down upon a Cheyenne village on the Powder, but what at first seemed a victory turned into retreat when nearby Oglalas, reportedly under Crazy Horse, counterattacked. Crook retreated back to his base camp close to the remains of Fort Kearny. Sheridan's master plan to subdue the hostiles would have to wait until summer.

Sometime during this period, the Black Elks crept unnoticed and unpunished into Soldiers' Town. Hobbled by the cold until late February, they most probably arrived in March and did not hear of the events on the Powder until long afterward. Just as in the hunting grounds, the most absorbing topic of debate all that winter was the *wasichus'* illegal seizure of the Hills. That long winter of discontent drove opposing factions together as rarely before. In fact, such obvious cracks were showing in the reservation system that every Indian—"hostile" and "friendly"—might have abandoned the Agencies if not for the necessity of the rations. Disease and famine filled the camps: from September to November 1873, smallpox killed sixty people in the Santee Agency, while in late February 1876 a beef shortage caused near rebellion. Corruption was rampant: there were more than seventy Indian Agents, each making about $1,500 annually. Many added to that by defrauding the Indians; the most common scheme was to shortchange them on treaty goods, then sell the surplus back at higher prices or even off-reservation.

Such treatment stoked the anger of the Sioux. By April 1876, the Northern Lakota began leaving for the Powder River in great numbers. They did so openly, and neither the agent nor the soldiers at Camp Robinson seemed to realize the true scope of the migration. By the 1920s, old long-hairs spoke of a "summons" from Sitting Bull.

In early April, Crazy Horse sent Little Big Man to the Red Cloud Agency on a recruiting mission. Messengers headed to other agencies, inviting all to come to a Sun Dance on the Rosebud in early June. "It is war," they said. In the second week of May, Little Big Man left the Agency with approximately one hundred Oglala families. Soon afterward, another twenty Oglala and fifty Brulé lodges followed, and the Black Elks were among these stragglers. They were going back to Crazy Horse, his father told him. They were going to have to fight, "because there was no other way to keep our country."

The decision to leave may have been the entire family's. Before they left, an aunt (or an older sister) who'd opted to stay with the Loafers gave Black Elk a six-shot revolver like the soldiers carried. He must always keep it close, she said; now he was a man. Weapons conveyed status, but this was indeed an expensive gift. No arms had been sold at the Agency for two years; though an underground trade existed in arms and ammunition, Agency Indians were virtual paupers, and arms smugglers charged exorbitant prices. In all likelihood this revolver was a spoil of war.

A terrible urgency gripped them all. They started in the dark and traveled fast; Red Cloud's young son Jack rode with them, bringing along the Winchester given to his father by the president and engraved with the words "Red Cloud." As they camped at War Bonnet Creek, some Cheyennes joined their band. Their hearts "were bad like ours," Black Elk said. Later he learned that many bands made the same journey.

As they broke camp the next morning, two scouts appeared. They'd ridden ahead and seen a wagon train heading north to Paha Sapa. A miner fired a shot; then the wagons curved into a circle. They resembled a big white bull's-eye from the overlooking hills.

Such a target was hard to resist. Little Big Man was riding back to Powder River with them, still seething over the confrontation with the Black Hills Commission. His feelings about war had not changed, and Little Big Man always liked a brawl. In the spring of 1865, he'd teamed with Crazy Horse for raids along the Platte, killing whites and stealing horses. The two seemed inseparable, and he was known as Crazy Horse's lieutenant during Red Cloud's War. But where Crazy Horse was quiet and introspective, Little Big Man was bombastic and loud. Veneration did not attach to him as easily as to his famous friend. He stood five feet five but had a strong physique; his broad chest was laced with Sun Dance scars where the pinions had torn free of the muscle. He circled the scars in red paint so all would know that he could endure any pain.

The warriors decided to attack the wagon train. Little Big Man stared at Black Elk, his cousin Jumping Horse, and some other boys and said they, too, would ride. That past summer of 1875, Black Elk had turned twelve: in most cases, he would have been beneath the notice of a warrior such as Little Big Man, but these were perilous times. Maybe Little Big Man was aware of Black Elk's new six-shooter; maybe he knew the tales of his strange behavior ever since returning from the dead.

One can feel the hesitation in the gang of boys. They hadn't even killed a buffalo yet; hadn't chosen a mentor for a vision quest; had not participated in the initiations that turned a boy into a man. Now Little Big Man was telling them to ride with him and possibly get killed. Black Elk seemed to step outside himself and realized he was rather small for his age. Yet he and his friends had practiced endurance, they were good riders, and he could shoot straight with both a gun and a bow. Maybe he was small, "but I thought I shall have to be a man anyway." He turned to his friends and told them he was going with the war party. "I made up my mind that, small as I was, I might as well die there, and if I did, maybe I'd be known."

So they went, holding on to their horses for dear life. Black Elk circled the wagons once to see if he would survive. "All I could do was to hang on to my horse barely and the bullets would just whiz over me," he later said. The miners pumped shells at them from the wagons; he peered from beneath his pony's neck as shots cracked close and puffs of dust rose on the ground around him. But no one was hit, not even the horses or the miners' oxen.

As they circled a second time, Black Elk recalled his Vision. He seemed inside it again—the sensations in this fight were somehow like riding on a cloud. The fear left him and he realized it must be his power that kept them from getting hurt. He was bulletproof, like his famous cousin, and the protection spread to those around him.

Two circuits were enough. As they rode off, Black Elk realized that he and Jumping Horse had been the youngest in the attack. A Cheyenne warrior noticed and said they were brave boys. Another proclaimed in sign language that they should fight in all future battles.

He thought often about his first warpath—how he'd been afraid at first but then the fear vanished in the whirlwind of battle; how he'd heard the bullets crack as they passed but no one was hit, and there had to be a greater reason for this than luck alone. He thought about ways of fighting—how the attacking horse soldiers massed together in such a big group that it was easy to hit them as they charged. But the Lakota charged as if they rode on the backs of antelope, weaving across the Plains. It was hard to hang on to the side of your pony and shoot beneath its neck even if your legs were long; his were short, but somehow he'd held on. They'd ridden in two circles around the wagons—one inner, one outside—each going in opposite directions. It seemed a beautiful thing, a dance almost, lifted from a dream.

They traveled fast—north to Bear Butte, west toward Devils Tower, past that to the Rosebud Valley. Riders passed with news that three great columns of soldiers had left their bases. Gibbon departed first on

March 30, followed on May 17 by Terry and Custer, then Crook from the
south on May 29. Each march was long—Crook's would take him 150
miles north, while Gibbon marched 200 miles and Terry, 250. Yet the
area where they planned to meet was only about one hundred miles
square.

As the Black Elks traveled west, they met more bands, all going to the
same place, all driven by anger. Soon the bands mixed together. They
climbed a steep ridge and Black Elk saw below him a valley of tipis.
They stood on the eastern edge of the Rosebud Valley, a narrow corridor stretching north and south through which the slow, shallow Rosebud meandered like a blind lizard. The scouts said that all bands were
there—Oglalas, Minneconjous, Hunkpapas, Blackfeet, Sans Arcs, and
Brulés; even their eastern cousins the Yanktonais and Santees. Bands
of Arapahos and Cheyennes had also come. Somewhere down below
were all the great chiefs of what some were calling the "Northern
Nation"—Crazy Horse and their own Big Road of the Oglalas; Sitting
Bull, Gall, Black Moon, and Crow King of the Hunkpapas; Spotted Eagle of the Sans Arcs; the younger Hump and Fast Bull of the Minneconjous; Dull Knife and Ice Bear of the Cheyennes; Inkpaduta of the
Yanktonais and Santees.

Sometime between May 21 and 24, Sitting Bull received a sign. He
felt drawn to the top of a butte, where he communed with *Wakan Tanka*.
As he sat on a moss-covered rock, he fell asleep and dreamed. He saw a
great dust storm approaching from the east, leading a host of soldiers.
Sailing from the opposite direction he saw a cloud resembling an Indian village. The two collided in a maelstrom that shook the mountains.
Soon the storm died out: the dust disappeared, as did the soldiers. Only
the village-shaped cloud remained.

Sitting Bull returned to the tribes and spoke of his dream. The twin
forces, of course, were the soldiers and the Sioux—the soldiers were
coming to wipe them out, but they would fail. Yet more was needed to
ensure this, to see into the *heart* of his vision, and so he pledged to *Wakan
Tanka* a Sun Dance to propitiate the gods. He vowed to give flesh so that
his people might live.

The dance would be held in June, the Moon of Making Fat, the time
of year when the sun was at its zenith and "the growing power of the
world is strongest," Black Elk was told. By June 4, 1876, the whole village had moved a short distance north to a place where the valley was
wide and flat and lodges could be erected in a great oval with the river

running through the center. It formed a kind of parade ground. In its center the medicine men and their assistants built a circular dance bower of willow branches; its door faced east toward the rising sun. And in the center of the bower—in the very center of the center—they erected the *waga chun*, the holy tree, a soaring cottonwood stripped of all branches and sanctified by a series of rituals.

The dance was called *Wiwanyong Wachipi*, the "dance looking at the sun." It was entirely a Hunkpapa affair held over four days, from June 4 to 8, though people from the other bands gathered to watch. The dance was already infamous throughout the West for the degree of self-torture the participants endured. Every dancer fasted and purified himself in the sweat lodge during the days and nights of the dance, sucking only on moist roots or leaves to slake the nagging thirst. Each day centered about a different "degree" of dance, with escalating stages of pain, yet each degree included some bodily sacrifice and called for the dancer to stare directly into the sun. Actually, the dancer stared right beneath it to save his eyes, but the light was still harsh enough to temporarily blind him.

The dancers sacrificed themselves to enter into a direct relationship with the Great Holy and win the favor of the gods. But it was also a communal event. As spectators gathered to watch, they identified with the dancers, who suffered for the group. The sacrifice was made so that *all* could receive the blessings of the sun.

"Mortification of the flesh" is not unique among the world's religions: such penance or sacrifice has been practiced by Christians, Muslims, Hindus, Buddhists, various indigenous tribes, and even by today's Church of Body Modification. Among Western religions, the faith with the most extreme and dramatic form of mortification was Catholicism, the faith that would go to the greatest lengths to stamp out the Sun Dance and medicine men. Methods used by Catholic and early Christian ascetics included flagellation, donning a "hair shirt," and wearing a cilice—a small metal chain with inward-pointing spikes worn around the upper thigh. Pain, said penitents, strengthened the bond between the body and the spirit, creating an altered state of awareness.

Yet the Lakota form of mortification *was* unique in the way it had evolved from penance or sacrifice into a sheer public spectacle of pain—a dance of punishment in which the Sioux demonstrated to themselves and others that they were the most formidable people on the Plains. One could certainly believe that when considering the most severe form of

Sun Dance torture—the one that had become legendary throughout the West, and that occurred on the fourth and last day. Dancers were suspended from the pole attached to wooden skewers thrust through the muscles of their back and chest. The bravest and most honored were those who tore themselves loose, yet to do so was unbelievably brutal, and those outsiders allowed to witness such a moment often could not believe their eyes. In 1880, the Nebraska rancher Edgar Beecher Bronson witnessed a Sioux Sun Dance, which he described in his 1908 *Reminiscences of a Ranchman*:

> Each candidate in turn was laid at the foot of the Sun Pole. The chief medicine man then drew his narrow-bladed knife, bent over the candidate, and passed the blade beneath and through a narrow strip of flesh on each breast. A hardwood skewer was placed through each of the two openings and looped each of the two ends of one to the hanging ropes over each of the two skewers. This finished, the candidate was helped to his feet and given a long, stout staff—to help him at his terrible task of rending his own flesh till the skewers were torn from their lodgement in his breast! Some pulled slowly but steadily and strongly backward, aided by their staffs, until the flesh of their breasts was drawn out 18 inches, while that of their backs was as tight as a drum head. Others jumped and bucked on their ropes like a bronco suffering the indignity of his first saddle. Yet no cry escaped their lips, no eye showed pain.

Pain focused the mind as it swayed the gods. In the coming fight against the *wasichu*, the Lakota and their allies would need to wield powers far greater than any they'd tapped before. On June 6, the second day of the dance, Sitting Bull entered the circle alone. It had rained that morning, and some dancers preceded him. Naked from his purification in the sweat lodge, he offered the pipe to the powers and tribal leaders and then sat with his back to the dance pole. He extended his legs and let his arms rest on the ground against his thighs. Buffalo robes were piled around him and the pole—another gift to *Wakan Tanka*. His adopted brother Jumping Bull approached with an awl in his hand.

What happened next brought a gasp of disbelief from the spectators. Beginning at the bottom of Sitting Bull's left arm, Jumping Bull inserted the awl under the skin and removed a piece of flesh about the size of a match head. He worked his way up until fifty pieces of flesh had been gouged from Sitting Bull's arm. He began on the right arm, gouging out another fifty pieces. Sitting Bull cried in pain as blood poured from the wounds. The cuts were made together in rows and then rubbed with pine ash to stop the bleeding. The entire process took thirty minutes.

Then Sitting Bull rose and danced around the pole. He danced what was called the "first form," without piercing or suspension, though the scars on his back and chest bore witness to earlier such dances. He gazed at the sun. For hours he danced like this, until finally he stopped in his tracks. Onlookers assumed he had lost consciousness; he began to sway. He looked up at the sun once more, then staggered. Assistants and bystanders rushed forward and eased him to the ground. Someone sprinkled water on his face. Sitting Bull opened his eyes and took a sip, then turned to Black Moon, his cousin and an accomplished Hunkpapa holy man. He told him what he had seen; then his eyes rolled back and he finally passed out.

Black Moon told the assembly what his cousin had seen. After hours of dancing, a voice had told him to stare at an image directly beneath the sun. His eyes hurt, but he focused and saw figures fall from the sky. Some were Indians, but the great majority were soldiers and their horses. They fell toward the village, their heads to the earth and feet in the air. The foreordained battle was coming, and though the Lakota had warned the soldiers they would fight, they never listened. They rode in their great blue columns, sure of their power. A great victory was coming, and Sitting Bull had seen the finale. The *wasichu* in their arrogance would attack and die.

"I give you these," the voice told Sitting Bull, "because they have no ears."

7

WHEN THE *WASICHUS* COME

A gathering as large as the Sun Dance camp ate quickly through grass and game. Every three or four days, it had to pick up and move. On June 8, after the dance, it moved twelve miles up Rosebud Valley to Muddy Creek, where it sat tight through three days of rain. On June 12, it moved another dozen miles to the mouth of a western tributary that rose in a gap in the Wolf Mountains and offered easy access to the Greasy Grass. On June 15, the village left the Rosebud for good and on the night of the 16th they pitched camp twenty-one miles away at what is now called Reno Creek, but was then called the Ash. The Greasy Grass was still six or seven miles off; the valley stretching north and west was prime buffalo country, and the Lakota hoped for good hunting.

In reality, *they* were the hunted. Sheridan's columns drew closer. On May 27, Lieutenant J. H. Bradley, with Gibbon, saw the smoke of the great camp on the Rosebud. On June 7 or 8, Major Marcus A. Reno, second-in-command of the Seventh under Custer, scouted ahead with six companies when he barely missed the Sun Dance camp; soon afterward, he saw its enormous trail branch toward the Little Bighorn. The Sioux were in fact camping past the divide not far to the west; the fact that neither group spotted the other attests to the power of chance in the Plains' folds and ravines. Reno rode north to report his discovery to Terry.

Though the Lakota seemed less aware of the soldiers in the north, they were well aware of those approaching from the opposite direction. As he had in March, Crook moved north, now at the head of nearly 1,300 men. At first, he followed the empty Bozeman Trail past the ruins of the abandoned forts; when scouts reported Sioux on the Rosebud, he angled in that direction. But Crook was being watched, too, and on June 16 some Cheyenne spied his column near the head of the Rosebud. They arrived that night at the camp, which still lay on Reno Creek. Criers announced the sighting, and about a thousand warriors set out toward the Rosebud.

Black Elk prepared as well. Crazy Horse was going and he wished to join him. He'd ridden with Little Big Man in the wagon-train attack and felt he was ready for war. But when he appeared at the war party, an uncle pulled him aside. "Nephew," he said, "you must not go. Stay and look at the helpless; stay here and fight."

So he stayed behind. It was galling. He'd proven himself, but people still treated him as if fragile. "Maybe my uncle thought I was too little to do much," he said, "and might get killed."

The war party traveled all night. A thirty-mile ride separated the two armies, and on the morning of June 17, they came together. Crook's men had started before dawn; at 8:00 a.m., they stopped in a wide grassy spot ten miles upstream to eat breakfast and make coffee. Crook played whist with some of his officers. His Crow and Shoshone scouts, sensing the enemy, ranged north; they topped a hill and nearly collided with some advance Sioux riders. The two sides traded shots: hearing the noise, the main body of Cheyennes and Lakotas rode up and the valley beneath Crook's scouts teemed with the enemy. They wheeled and galloped back to Crook, screaming "Lakota! Lakota!" and "Heap Sioux!" Right on their tails raced a line of painted warriors, riding straight for Crook's left. Officers rallied their men, but they would have been wiped out if the scouts had not turned around and fired point-blank into the charging Sioux. Crook was able to form a skirmish line, but for twenty minutes the battle hung in the balance. And when he finally pushed these Sioux back and seized the surrounding bluffs, another wave poured down the hills to his right, opening a new phase of the battle.

The conflict flared through the morning and into the afternoon, a running, confused melee of charge, retreat, and countercharge. The fight was literally every man for himself. "Our Indians fought and ran away, fought and ran away," recalled the Lakota Wooden Leg. "The soldiers and their scouts did the same. Sometimes we chased them, sometimes they chased us." Yet where in the past warriors would spar with troops and then ride off, now they pressed close with a ferocity that amazed the soldiers. Though Indian accounts suggest that no leadership existed in a military sense, something had so changed that Crook was shaken. Under Crazy Horse, the attackers knew enough to avoid massed infantry and seek weak places in the line. He seemed everywhere—*na hel ake Tasunke Witko lila wohitika*: "And there again Crazy Horse was very brave," said the young Thunder Tail, son of the Oglala warrior Black Twin.

But as the afternoon waned, the attack ran out of steam. The Lakota called off the fight: they'd ridden all night, fought all day, and finally turned home. The correspondent Robert Strahorn wrote that the soldiers had fired "over ten thousand rounds of ammunition"; the Indians, "from a third to a half more." If true, both sides were abysmal shots. The Cheyennes and Lakotas lost thirty to forty warriors; Crazy Horse said thirty-six. Army losses came to nine dead and twenty-three wounded; the scouts suffered one killed, seven wounded. Crook claimed a victory: "The command finally drove the Indians back in great confusion," he wrote in his report, but the fight so unnerved him that he turned back to his supply base at Goose Creek and would not venture out for another six weeks, taking him out of the equation for what would soon follow.

The next day, Standing Bear and twenty friends rode to the Rosebud to view the scene of the battle. Black Elk's cousin had not been in the fight; like Black Elk, he had been told by an older relative to stay behind. They rode the thirty miles and first came upon a dead horse. Then several dead horses. Then a dead soldier beside his horse; then a soldier full of arrows. They came to the hastily dug grave of the army dead and unearthed the mound. The soldiers were laid one atop the other, each wrapped in an army-issue wool blanket. Standing Bear and his friends argued over the spoils. One brave cut the diamond ring from the finger of a slain lieutenant; someone scalped a corpse and took it home.

Standing Bear took a blanket and figured that was enough. In the distance, dust rose from Crook's retreat. A silence pervaded the valley. They were no longer curious and headed home.

———•◦•———

Home had shifted while they were gone. On the morning of June 18, as Standing Bear headed back, the women struck the tipis and loaded them on travois. They left behind a single lodge—the burial site of a Sans Arc warrior killed at the Rosebud—then journeyed down Reno

Creek almost to its mouth. They then angled north-northwest along the valley of the Little Bighorn River, which flowed north to the Bighorn at Hardin, Montana.

The new village was laid out from south to north, from "upper camp" to "lower," in a spot about two miles below the mouth of Reno Creek and eight miles from that morning's starting point. Compared with the narrow Rosebud Valley, this one was wide and grassy, with more than adequate room for the sprawling congeries of tipis. To the west, the grassland rose in low benches where ponies could graze; to the immediate east, the river wound among thick stands of cottonwood. Though the Little Bighorn usually flowed a lazy path, it was now swollen with spring meltwater from the southern mountains, making it deeper and wilder than usual. Across the river, on the east bank, a series of ragged bluffs rose to about three hundred feet. The Indians could see everything coming from the west, south, and northwest, but from the east, they were blind.

How big was this "Great Camp" on the Little Bighorn? Its dimensions and population are debated today. How many Indians streamed into it during the seven days of rest and feasting from June 18 to 25? And how many were warriors? The greater the population, the easier to believe that what befell Custer was the result of being vastly outnumbered. But a smaller population meant that Custer was outgeneraled. And there was a flip side: the greater the population, the more insane it seems to attack such an overwhelming foe.

Indians and whites have both added to the confusion. The Blackfoot chief Kill Eagle said the camp was six miles long by one mile wide; the historian Robert Utley in 1960 estimated the population at fifteen thousand, with more than three thousand of them warriors. Yet currently, estimates have contracted. The historian Gregory Michno has concluded that the village ran a mile and a half along the river and about three hundred yards back, for an area of one-quarter to one-half square mile. He surmised about a thousand lodges, for a population of about five thousand people and fifteen hundred fighting men. The Little Bighorn battlefield historian Michael Donahue concluded from an analysis of Indian and army maps that the camp stretched a mile and a half from the dry cut in the south now known as Shoulder Blade Creek to Medicine Tail Coulee in the north, which opened across the river.

To Black Elk, the village was simply huge. There were so many tipis "we couldn't count them," and "ten thousand ponies" grazed to the west—that is, beyond number. The tipis were arranged in six circles, though "circles" may have been a commonplace for any big group of lodges. The southernmost circle contained the Hunkpapa lodges of Sitting Bull, Rain in the Face, Hump, and Gall. The Minneconjous were to their immediate north, at the ford at Medicine Tail Coulee. The Oglalas pitched their tipis between the Hunkpapas and Minneconjous, giving them the best view of the wide river bottom opening south. To their north camped the Blackfeet, Brulés, and Sans Arcs. Most accounts place the Cheyennes at the far north, though Black Elk placed the Santees and Yanktonais there instead.

For six days, the village celebrated the retreat of Three Stars. They danced, feasted, told of glorious deeds, laughed at near escapes, visited the wounded, and mourned the dead. Hunting parties reported buffalo herds in the south and antelope herds to the northwest. Decisions had to be made that balanced security against the need to feed so many.

On June 24, a bear healer named Hairy Chin needed Black Elk for a ritual. A man named Rattling Hawk had been shot through the hip, and people thought he would die. Black Elk had just greased himself down for a swim when Hairy Chin said he required a sixth boy—dressed as a bear—for a healing ceremony. The other five were his sons, already painted red from head to toe. Hairy Chin was about to do the same to Black Elk, but then stared at him quietly and painted him yellow, with black stripes drawn from his eyes to his nose. Black Elk concluded from this that Hairy Chin sensed his power. He tied up Black Elk's locks to resemble bear ears, then stuck eagle plumes in his hair.

As Hairy Chin began to sing, Black Elk started to feel as if he was floating overhead. This worried him, since the same had occurred right before his Great Vision. All felt disconnected and murky, as if "I knew more things than I could tell." Two women entered the tipi, one holding a cup, the other, an herb. He realized that someday he might perform this ritual himself, and with that last flash of lucidity the ceremony blasted off into strange and hallucinatory realms. The two women gave Rattling Hawk a red stick and led him from the tipi. The five painted boys growled; as they did, Black Elk seemed to see colored feathers flow from their mouths. He barely had time to wonder what was happening when Hairy Chin grabbed his face, blew some kind of chewed herb into his mouth, and threw him to the ground. The wounded man began to walk, and Black Elk bounced up on his haunches like a bear. He certainly felt more bear than human: "I made a cry and it was a genuine bear sound and I felt like a bear and wanted to grab someone." The women passed around raw dog meat, and Black Elk wolfed it down. After a while, the boys walked to the river and washed off, but behind them in the village the party had just begun.

Meanwhile, three exhausted riders approached the village. They'd returned from a wide-ranging scout; two days earlier, on June 22, they'd spotted a troop of cavalry riding south from the Yellowstone—most certainly an advance unit of Custer's men. They'd shadowed these soldiers until 6:30 this morning, when they'd discovered the remains of the Sun Dance camp and galloped back north in alarm. The Sioux scouts were convinced they'd spied the vanguard of soldiers foretold in Sitting Bull's dream. If the main body of soldiers still lay north, as most seemed to think, the scouts predicted they should arrive at the Great Village within two days—by the 26th. But if they rode all night to warn their comrades, the main column could arrive as early as noon on June 25.

According to tradition, the news distressed Crazy Horse. He rode among the camps, urging vigilance, but most chiefs seemed unconcerned. Sitting Bull was troubled, too. No two men were less alike: Crazy Horse was "always taciturn and rarely jokes or smiles," said Crook's aide John Bourke, who knew both, while Sitting Bull was a "great talker and very fond of his joke." But on this night, the prophet and the war chief were equally worried. The old seer painted his face and asked his nephew One Bull to accompany him up a high ridge across the river. The valley swept below him; the river snaked from the south, a carpet of tipis lining its west bank. The two men climbed to the crest where the *wasichus* would later erect a white stone monument. Sitting Bull presented to *Wakan Tanka* his offerings—a buffalo robe, a ceremonial pipe, and bits of tobacco wrapped in buckskin. "Father, save the tribe, I beg you," Sitting Bull prayed. "We want to live."

The sun flowed beneath the horizon. Around the fires, nightlong dances and kill-talks began. Black Elk brought the ponies close to camp, then strolled among the fires, listening to warriors' boasts, watching the young men flirt with girls. The trill of crickets and frogs rose from the river. Night deepened and he grew sleepy. He returned to his tipi and snuggled into bed.

June 25, 1876, dawned calm and clear. On the Gregorian calendar, it
was the 177th day of the year; on the Lakota calendar, it fell near the
end of the month called the Moon of the Blooming Turnip. In nine
days, the nation would celebrate its hundredth birthday. A month and a
half had passed since the May 10 opening of Philadelphia's Centennial
Exhibition, and on most mornings, thousands of people "were packed
like herrings in a box" as they crowded the main gate. They ran in herds
like sheep, said Makoto Fukui, the Japanese commissioner to the Exhibition: They "run here, run there, run everywhere, one man start, one
thousand follow," he said. "All rush, push, tear, shout, make plenty noise,
say 'damn' great many times, get very tired, and go home." Every thirty
seconds, trains rolled from the three platforms of the new Pennsylvania
Railroad depot; thousands, dressed in their best suits and bustles, joined
the waiting throngs to marvel at Alexander Graham Bell's telephone
or the 1,400 horsepower Corliss "Centennial Engine" dominating Ma-
chinery Hall. But this was a Sunday, and the Exhibition was closed: the
streets deserted for the Sabbath; the wooden stalls hawking lemonade,
hot roasted potatoes, and oranges, empty. Visitors from New York,
Baltimore, and points north and south often did not know this. They'd
assumed the gates were always open and were outraged.

On the Little Bighorn, all was quiet and lazy. Slivers of light crept
through the flaps of the east-facing tipis. Ponies grazed to the west,
watched over by a few sleepy boys. Wandering dogs yipped at one another without urgency. Early risers stoked the breakfast fires. The smoke
curled up and was caught by a slight northerly breeze.

Black Elk's father woke the boy at daybreak to take the ponies to
graze. A cousin joined him; before they left, his father took him aside.
Be careful today, he said. Keep a rope on at least one horse so it will
be easy to catch; keep an eye on the camp. Watch for something strange.
"If anything happens bring the horses back to camp right away as soon
as you can," he warned.

That worried him. Black Elk revered his father, but always felt his
sadness running beneath the surface. He wanted to take off some of
that weight, but what could he do? A constellation of factors—his youth
and slight build; his parents' overprotectiveness—always stood in the
way. He never measured up, never did his part in times of danger. He'd
been surprised by his success at the previous day's bear ceremony, since
his usual opinion of himself was that "I was so young yet and I wasn't
very dependable." This was the time of year when his mother said he'd

been born; he was very close to turning thirteen, if he had not done so already. He wanted to make people proud of him, but no one thought him a man.

Where were the soldiers? No one seemed to know. Everyone knew they were out there, hunting for them, but the prairie swallowed them up. Riders pass like ghosts on the Great Plains.

He didn't know it, but they were staring at him. When the Seventh Cavalry left the Yellowstone on June 22, Custer was ordered to ride south to the huge trail discovered by Reno, then continue south to the headwaters of the Rosebud. Once there, he must swing west, then backtrack north along the Little Bighorn. Gibbon would march south along the same stream. Custer's rate of speed was planned to coincide with Gibbon's; they would meet on the 26th, squeezing the Sioux between them. Timing was everything.

Estimates vary on the size of Custer's force, but a common figure among sources lists 31 officers, 586 soldiers, and 35 to 40 Crow and Arikara scouts. Twenty civilians also rode along: guides, interpreters, packers, and the newspaper reporter Mark Kellogg of *The Bismarck Tribune*. Twelve companies comprised the regiment, all under-strength. The column rode hard on June 22 and 23 and by the evening of the 24th hit the wide trail of the Sun Dance camp as it cut west toward the Little Bighorn. Rather than follow orders and continue south, Custer succumbed to temptation. He roused his cursing soldiers at midnight, and at 12:30 a.m. on June 25, 1876, the exhausted Seventh rode west over the Wolf Mountains behind a screen of native scouts.

These Crows and Arikaras were worried. They'd seen sand drawings depicting soldiers falling from the sky. At dawn, they climbed a high point at the divide between the Rosebud and the Little Bighorn; called the Crow's Nest, it overlooked the western valley and was a vantage the Crow often used in raids against the Sioux. Early daylight revealed to them the smoke of many cookfires. The interpreter Mitch Bouyer and guide "Lonesome" Charley Reynolds, who'd carried the news of Custer's Black Hills gold, also saw a dark spot by the river that seemed to move— the immense pony herd where, even then, Black Elk tended his father's horses. They pointed this out to the chief of scouts, Lieutenant Charles A. Varnum, but after seventy hours in the saddle, Varnum could barely make out anything. Reynolds and Bouyer tried again. "Look for worms in the grass," one said.

In the valley, it was 8:00 or 9:00 a.m. It had grown warm among the ponies, and Black Elk watched with envy as women passed west to dig turnips and hunters rode off in search of pronghorn. His stomach growled. He suggested to his cousin that they head for the river to water the horses, and along the way stop for breakfast at their tipis.

By every sign, it was another lazy, windless day. The sun crept up the midmorning sky; more boys abandoned the steppes for the river, and some of Black Elk's friends were already swimming. They called for him to come in. His cousin offered to stay with the horses, so Black Elk greased himself with buffalo fat and jumped in.

In the Minneconjou camp, Standing Bear rose shortly before noon after a long night spent flirting with girls. He was sixteen and life was good. Only an uncle and an old, feeble grandmother remained in the tipi when he woke. He stumbled to the river for his morning ablutions, returned to camp, threw on a shirt, and braided his hair. Grandmother fried some meat in the ashes. "After you are through eating," said his uncle, "you had better go and get the horses, because something might happen all at once, we can never tell." Standing Bear did not appreciate lectures, especially during breakfast. He shrugged and kept eating.

The night had been long for the soldiers crossing the Wolf Mountains. At dawn, when Black Elk rose to tend the horses, Custer learned that some Sioux had discovered a hardtack box fallen from the pack train. Around noon, as Standing Bear braided his hair, the civilian scout Frank Gerard climbed a knoll and in the north spied a cloud of dust. "Here are your Indians, General," he said. "Running like devils." Though Gerard was mistaken, Custer feared the worst—he'd been discovered and the Indians had fled. He'd hoped for a successful "dawn attack" like that on the Washita, but here it was noon already, the Indians were awake, and they were escaping. He'd have to surprise them by some other means.

So Pahuska split his forces into four units: 112 men in A, G, and M Companies, under Reno; 125 men in H, D, and K Companies, under Captain Frederick Benteen; and 225 men in C, E, F, I, and L Companies, under Custer himself. The 130 men in B Company were sent back to guard the pack train. Each cavalryman received one hundred rounds for his carbine—fifty in his belt and fifty in his saddlebags. Each carried twenty-four rounds for his Colt Single Action Army revolver, six in the pistol itself, eighteen in a belt pouch. Benteen was told to veer south to some ridges on the column's far left and "pitch into" any Indians that he might find. Reno would ford the stream they were following to where it met the Little Bighorn; he would cross into the valley and hit the village at its southern end. Custer would swing right, along the high ridges east of the river. His course was most nebulous: he'd either find a way across the river and hit the village on its flank during Reno's attack, or circle to the north and attack the Sioux from behind.

Most scholars think today that the battle started around 3:00 p.m. Custer's men rode past the funeral lodge containing the lone Sans Arc warrior, and onto the ford, where Custer split off from Reno. They were still close enough to maintain communication via mounted messengers. Reno flushed a small party of Sioux; they rode in panic toward the village, still hidden from the soldiers by a high ridge and thick stands of trees. Custer sent his adjutant, First Lieutenant William W. Cooke, with a message that he believed the Indians were running away. The adjutant told Reno "to move forward at as rapid a gait as I thought prudent and to charge afterwards, and that the whole outfit would support me," Reno later testified. He apparently interpreted this as support from the rear rather than Custer's plan of a flank attack, but would quickly learn otherwise.

Reno's force forded the river at what is now called Reno's Crossing. The 112 soldiers were augmented by three civilians—including Charley Reynolds and the black interpreter Isaiah Dorman—and twenty-five Indian scouts, including Custer's favorite, Bloody Knife. The thirsty horses stopped to drink, causing the command to "mushroom," in the words of one soldier. It took about ten minutes for Reno to re-form his lines. He placed Lieutenant Varnum and the Indian scouts up front with A and M Companies, while G Company was held in reserve. They trotted north up the valley, separated from Custer by the river and trees. This line of cottonwoods stretched all along the river: though not wide, it was dense, choked in places with brush and fallen branches.

The Hunkpapa circle lay two miles beyond the ford. Reno saw more Indians as he advanced and sent two messages to Custer that the Indians "were strong." By now, Frank Gerard, the scout who'd erroneously told Custer that the Indians were "running like devils," had revised his opinion: "Custer was under the impression that the Indians were running away," he later said, "and it was important for him to know that the Indians were not running away."

It was shortly after 3:00 p.m. when the south end of the village erupted in shouts of alarm. At the river near the Hunkpapa camp, Black Elk heard criers shout, "They are charging, the chargers are coming!" Soldiers had been seen back at the funeral lodge! Alarms rolled north through the tipis like a receding echo. All around him, boys and warriors splashed through the river to retrieve their horses: Black Elk grabbed his mare and hurried back to his father.

In the Minneconjou camp, Standing Bear heard the same uproar. A crier added that someone had been killed. Soldiers fired upon two boys eating the hardtack they'd dropped: a boy named Deeds was killed, and his friend ran to camp with the news. "I told you this would happen," snapped Standing Bear's uncle. "You'd better go right away and get the horses."

Black Elk's cousin dove barefoot through the tipi flap and ran downstream. His older brother Beard and other warriors were already there, herding horses across the ford at Medicine Tail Coulee. He cut across the river until the water was up to his chest, then emerged on the opposite bank and climbed a steep hill called Black Butte. He gasped for breath and bent forward for relief. In that brief space, he looked around.

The opening stages of the battle unfolded before him. In the camps, women screamed. Babies cried. Men called for their horses, while others sang their death songs. Gunfire in the south sent the noncombatants in the opposite direction—north down the river, toward the Cheyennes. Others streamed across the river at Medicine Tail Coulee, where Standing Bear had just crossed. Within minutes they'd realize their folly and backtrack, screaming louder than ever.

When Standing Bear gazed south, he saw Reno's soldiers. They'd come down the gentle slope toward the village and formed a skirmish line. At this distance it looked like beautiful clockwork, a drill common to cavalry worldwide. Three men dismounted to open fire while a fourth, the "horse-holder," held their mounts in the rear. The left flank of the line stretched toward the steppes where the ponies had grazed; the right flank was anchored in the cottonwoods. The first bullets rattled through Hunkpapa tipi tops; the first warriors galloped through the dust to meet Reno. The dry wash called Shoulder Blade Creek cut across the valley to the south of the Hunkpapa lodges, and there the first warriors collected to make a stand.

By the soldiers' chronometers, the time was 3:18. Standing Bear had to get back, but suddenly realized the folly of diving from his tipi without moccasins. He stood in a patch of cactus, and picked a careful path downhill. As he watched, Reno's line advanced another one hundred yards, stopping near a bend in the river but still short of the dry wash and first tipis. They planted their guidons. He glanced over his shoulder and saw *more* soldiers riding from the south, but this time on his side of the river. A small group studied him from a high hill. He didn't know it yet, but it was Custer, advancing for a flank attack with his 225 men.

Standing Bear forgot caution and ran barefoot through the cacti.

By now, Black Elk had made it back to his father's lodge. People screamed around him; it was hard to keep from panicking, too. A light breeze blew through the tipis, kicking up a dust cloud. His cousin arrived from the river with the horses; his older half brother, Runs in the Center, bridled his sorrel and charged toward the enemy. Just as he vanished, his father ran up holding a revolver. "Your brother has gone to the Hunkpapas without his gun," he cried. "Catch him and give it to him. Then come right back to me!"

With those words, Black Elk remembered his own gun. Sometime during the confusion he'd grabbed his six-shooter; he jumped on his buckskin and turned toward the battle. The dust lifted and he saw rising smoke to the south; it was the soldiers, "big and husky and tall," still three hundred to six hundred yards short of the Hunkpapa camp—the farthest they would advance that afternoon. They stopped and started firing. Before this moment Black Elk had heard solitary *pops*, but now their volley ripped into the southern curve of lodges. Those warriors in the front fell back, while others crouched and ran to the shelter of the dry wash, keeping low. Some of Reno's Arikara scouts had made it through the timber to the wash; there they cut off and killed ten women and children. Two were the wives of the war chief Gall; three, his young children. Black Elk found it hard to think. All he wanted was to find Runs in the Center and give him his gun.

Out of nowhere, his brother found him. He grabbed the revolver and told Black Elk to go home. Black Elk watched as he wheeled his horse and raced to a stand of timber just south of the tipis. Several warriors were gathering and his brother disappeared among them. It dawned on him they were also gathering their courage before charging the soldiers through the trees.

He froze atop his horse, a still target as the world pirouetted around him. His brother and father both had ordered him to return home. They always told him that, always fearful of his safety, always certain something would kill him. He always did as they said: he might not feel proud about it later, but he was an obedient son. Yet they did not understand. They did not know he had been chosen, and he looked down at his six-shooter. He did not know who these soldiers were or who led them, but before him lay that *wasichu* threat that he'd heard about since birth—the extinguishing force foretold by the prophets. He glanced at his parents' lodge, then down at the gun. Then upstream to the timber where his brother had disappeared.

He kicked his pony in the sides and raced toward the sounds of battle.

———•—•———

This period would be a turning point in the fight in the valley. Reno's men had drawn close enough to get within killing range; a normal trooper could fire up to seventeen times a minute, with accuracy up to 250 yards. Bullets rattled among the Hunkpapa and Blackfoot tipis and shattered the lodge poles. The highest concentration of Indian casualties occurred during these first minutes: warriors were shot as they charged toward the skirmish line, noncombatants hit as they fled in panic from the tipis.

If a hundred soldiers fired only half their carbine ammunition during this stage of the fight, more than five thousand rounds would have been expended. Yet the troopers fired high. The tipis lay on a lower elevation than the valley south of the dry wash. The Springfield's relatively slow muzzle velocity of 1,150 feet per second meant it was hard to hit what you aimed for. The soldiers, especially the new recruits, tended to flinch and jerk up when pulling the trigger.

"Fire is everything, the rest is nothing," an old army adage proclaimed. "Fire discipline," stated the drill regulations, was "the unhesitating habit, developed by instruction and training," of directed and regulated fire on command. At the beginning of a firefight, at extreme ranges, volleys were most effective; at closer distances, regulations allowed for rapid fire. Yet multiple sources asserted that the army's green recruits did not receive regular training. Thus, no such thing as "fire discipline" existed. "Our regiments of cavalry are composed of men about three-fourths of whom are recruits, who have never fought with Indians," wrote Lieutenant Edward Maguire, Corps of Engineers, in his July 10, 1876, report to Congress. "They were never drilled at firing on horseback, and the consequence is that the horses are as unused to fighting as the men themselves, and become unruly in action."

Due in part to this lack of training, Reno's men grew terrified. Almost every Indian massing against them was a seasoned warrior who'd gone on the warpath several times since early adolescence, and would continue to do so until he was too old to fight. As a rule, he was cooler under fire than the soldier, and by then the army had grudgingly acknowledged that they were fighting what many called the best light cavalry in the world. As Reno's men spread out in a skirmish line, two of their fellows were carried into the village by their panicking steeds. They died there immediately. Of the remainder, eighty-four to ninety-one men were strung east to west along the valley floor. The warriors trapped in Shoulder Blade Creek turned west and spilled from the depression. They began to ride around Reno's unsecured left, beyond the edge of the firing line. It became obvious they would soon flank the troops and get behind them. Reno's position was untenable. Where was Custer's promised support? It was later estimated that ninety riflemen faced seven hundred Sioux. As Reno would say in his defense, "The very earth seemed to grow Indians."

Despite the odds against them, the soldiers at this point still maintained their positions and fired. Yet by now a few of their number had dropped; by now, more Indians rode around their open flank, kicking up dust and making their position impossible. After about fifteen minutes of fighting, Reno pulled the skirmish line into the trees along the riverbank. The firing line was now at right angles to its original position, with G Company farthest north, closest to the camp, near an old, dry loop in the river. M Company anchored the south, while A Company filled the middle. The new line stretched about one hundred yards through the trees, a crescent-shaped mix of cottonwoods and undergrowth that followed the steep western riverbank, in some places twelve feet high. This "timber" stretched twenty-five feet from river to valley, and in the center lay a small glade where many of the soldiers' horses were held.

Black Elk headed for these woods. A number of warriors had collected there, hoping to attack the soldiers from the rear. This was where he found his brother. Runs in the Center snapped at him again to turn back, but Black Elk crawled into the brush after him. He could not see anything, could only hear shooting, but as they crawled deeper the soldiers sensed their advance and started to fire. The warriors around Black Elk admonished one another to be brave. "Take courage, don't be like a woman," one man cried.

But the soldiers still fired overhead. Bullets clipped the leaves, which floated down upon him. He was mesmerized. Shafts of sunlight pierced the canopy, dappling the forest in yellows and greens. He thought of his Vision, how maybe his people had borrowed his power without his knowledge and had transformed into Thunder-beings. As the leaves floated around him, he wondered why the soldiers had attacked. It made no sense, yet his Vision gave him courage. If he were a conduit and his power somehow radiated out, his people would wipe out the *wasichu*.

Then he heard a cry: "Crazy Horse is coming!" From the west, beyond the trees, he heard the pounding of hooves and the shrill call of the eagle-bone whistle. "*Hoka hey!*" cried the warriors around him, and in the distance he heard the tremolo of advancing riders.

Black Elk was right—it was his cousin. Tasunke Witko had taken his time. As the troops fired into camp, Crazy Horse prepared. Wearing only moccasins and a breechclout, he painted his face and body yellow, then dabbed on his skin white pigment like hail. He tied the stone war charm, or *wotawa*, beneath his left arm, fastened a hawk feather in his loosened hair, grabbed his Winchester and a stone-headed war club, and talked with a holy man. He sprinkled gopher dust on his body and hair. Horses were brought up and he selected a white-faced pinto, streaked its flanks with earth, and traced wavy blue lines down its legs. The preparations had taken more than twenty minutes, but Crazy Horse would not be rushed. He sprang upon his pinto's back and stretched his arms to the sun, asking the help of *Wakan Tanka*. He turned to his loyal but fidgeting men.

He rode along the line of mounted warriors and told them to hold their attack until he gave the word. He wanted Reno's men to fire their Springfields until they started to heat up and the shell ejectors jammed. "Do your best," he cried, "and let us kill them all off today, that they may not trouble us anymore." He turned his pony south and leapt forward.

The time was about 3:45 p.m. Crazy Horse and his men sliced into the timber, across the front of Reno's firing line. The war chief rode first; he would not allow anyone in front of him. Close behind rode Kicking Bear, the alleged killer of the unlucky Frank Appleton. They pumped rapid fire into the startled soldiers; according to one account, Kicking Bear felled Bloody Knife with a single shot, spraying his blood and brains upon Reno beside him. Other accounts said the killing shot came from behind as the Hunkpapas burst through the brush and opened a murderous crossfire. Whichever was true, Reno apparently panicked—he ordered his troops to mount, dismount, mount again, and "charge to the rear." Many in G Company—the company farthest from Reno—did not hear the orders.

Whatever cohesion Reno's battalion had maintained to this point instantly dissolved. The charge to the rear became a rout as soldiers leapt on their horses and galloped south in hopes of fording the river and escaping to the hills. The flight was so sudden that it hit a line of Indians slicing from the south and threw them into confusion. About a dozen men in G Company got left behind in the woods. Isaiah Dorman and Charley Reynolds were thrown or shot from their horses and died at the spot where they fell. Fleeing soldiers were shot between the shoulders, pulled from their saddles, filled with arrows, or brained with war clubs. Warriors wove between them, selecting unhorsed targets and riding them down. Forty of Reno's men were killed in the valley—most during this period. "It was like chasing buffalo," one warrior recalled.

The soldiers charged the tide of Indians four abreast, firing their pistols: the Sioux gave way to let them pass, then closed in. Reno rode back upstream, hoping to reach the original ford, but the weight of Indians upon his right was so great that he swerved left toward the river. To Lieutenant George D. Wallace of G Company, the Sioux seemed "as thick as trees in an apple orchard or thicker." If a man did not use his pistol, a warrior rode in close and fired. Sometimes the warriors hung off about fifty to one hundred yards on the flank, laid their rifles across their saddle pommels, and fired.

Reno's panicking men finally hit a second ford about a mile downstream from the first; on the other side of the river rose a set of steep, commanding hills. Yet surviving a crossing here seemed impossible. A sharply eroded cut-bank bordered the river, followed by a six-foot drop. The first horses balked and refused to jump, and those coming up slammed into them. Men and horses spilled over the side. The river here was four feet deep: the horses floundered across, their riders hanging on as best they could. Indians fired into the mob from all sides. The river ran red.

Black Elk was in the middle of this, amazed that he still lived. He'd burst from the timber, always working to the left, when the cyclone of fleeing men and horses enveloped him. Right ahead, a warrior grabbed a soldier's bridle. The soldier fired point-blank with his revolver and his attacker pitched from his horse; the *wasichu* swiveled and shot two more Lakotas before Black Elk realized he'd be next. He ducked and ran past, joining two boys his age. Incredibly, they still had their ponies, so he mounted one and followed the rout upstream. He noticed something shining in the mud and scooped it up—another soldier's revolver. Now he had two! He held it up and thought he might shoot a passing soldier, but the blur of bodies around him was so thick he could not focus—his pony whirled in the excitement and he'd just as easily shoot a kinsman as a foe. He felt small and vulnerable and charged south along the river until coming to a gravel flat strewn with corpses. A small number of *wasichus* leaving the timber had tried to cross the river north of the main body and had been cut down like dogs. Pistols, rifles, and ammunition littered the flat. Black Elk and the two other boys stared in wonder at this treasure horde.

Then he saw a soldier lying a short distance off at the fringe of timber, twitching from his wounds. All got quiet, and Black Elk stared. He rode close and a shadow reared above him. He looked up; it was a brave he did not know. "Boy," the man snapped, "get off and scalp him!" Black Elk looked down at the soldier, then up at the brave. A lump formed in his throat. He slid off his pony's back and fingered the hilt of his knife.

In the hands of an experienced warrior, taking a scalp was swift and surgical. The scalp itself is about a quarter-inch thick and fits snugly to the skull. The warrior makes a horizontal cut near the forehead and lifts up, ripping free a carpet of hair and scalp about the size of one's palm. A scalp has to include the crown to be acceptable: since the hair radiates from this central point, taking the crown usually meant taking it all.

But Black Elk was no expert at this game. It was his first scalp, and the soldier had short hair. Black Elk made his cut and started to lift, but the knife was not very sharp and the man was still very much alive. He ground his teeth and thrashed as Black Elk sawed back and forth with his dull blade. The river gurgled past; more shots and screams came from upstream. Black Elk felt very sick and knew the man beneath him was in pain. He drew his pistol from his belt and placed it to the soldier's forehead. He pulled the trigger and put him out of his misery.

Who was this unlucky fellow? We can, of course, never know. But some conjectures are possible. Six white enlisted men were known to have fallen in this area, but the most likely candidate is Private William Moodie, a thirty-five-year-old Scotsman born in Edinburgh. He had gray eyes, brown hair, a florid complexion, stood at five feet eight, and listed his occupation as "coachman" when he enlisted in New York City on December 13, 1874. If so, Black Elk killed a Scotsman, a martial race like his. Both came from a nomadic race that responded to unequal force with guerilla tactics—and that paid dearly afterward. Both had more in common than they would ever know.

But Black Elk took little pleasure in his first kill. He was tired and somewhat dispirited. Behind him to the south, Reno's remaining soldiers rushed up the slope to what would become their fragile redoubt; they formed a lopsided circle within a hilltop crease and made a barricade of anything that might stop a bullet or an arrow—breadboxes, saddles, blankets, sacks filled with oats or hay. These were followed by horses and mules, which, within the next two days, were infested with maggots and carrion beetles shining like dark jewels. The soldiers attacked the ground with sticks, jackknives, coffee cups—anything to dig themselves in. Soon Benteen and his troops rode up from their useless reconnaissance to the south, followed by B Company with the pack train. All heard firing from Custer's direction; they wondered what had happened to the larger force, and when it would return to save them.

Three miles to the north, the fate of Custer and his 225 men was nearly sealed. Black Elk could watch their final moments more easily than Reno's men. He backtracked the course of his last few hours: down the river past the timber, past his father's lodge, into the hills where the ponies had grazed. He passed a wounded man sitting in the dust with his gun and lance, singing a tune of regret that he could no longer fight: "Friends, what you are doing, I cannot do." He passed a pretty maiden, singing encouragement to the young men: "Take courage. Would you see me taken captive?" He climbed the grassy steppes and found his mother.

As he approached, he held up the Scotsman's scalp for her to see. She smiled and felt proud for her son. In all this blood and madness, her fragile Chosen had prevailed. It did not matter how. She broke into a shrill tremolo, the ululation of victory that women sang for their warriors to lift their spirits after the excitement passed and horror began to find them. As her voice blended with the voices of other women on the hills, she watched as his step seemed a little lighter. Her eyes teared up. Her poor boy had proven himself a man.

———•·•·•———

By then it was 4:30 p.m. For the next hour and a half, Black Elk and his mother watched as, to the east, far across the river, a small and diminishing clutch of soldiers clung to the top of the prominence where Sitting Bull had prayed. Custer and his remaining few clung like ants to this last holdout, fighting for their lives. At that distance, it was hard to see: the dust rose up like smoke, bullets zipped, shots cracked. The women's voices trembled in the air. He watched his tribesmen swarm around and below the hill like flocks of swallows wheeling with one mind.

Nothing had gone right for Custer since leaving Reno. He'd traveled parallel to the course of the Greasy Grass, but behind bluffs so high he could not see what played out in the valley. Twice he called a halt to climb high overlooks; during one halt, he may have seen a lone brave on his side of the river, standing in a cactus patch. A mile separated the two ridges, and at the second he beheld for the first time the largest encampment of Indians ever recorded in North America. Why he did not turn back at that point to save Reno has been *the* psychological mystery since that day. Maybe he thought he'd caught the Sioux napping, for he sent a note to the rear with the Italian trumpeter Giovanni Martini—"Benteen: Come on. Big village. Be quick. Bring packs"— and ordered a charge down Medicine Tail Coulee, immediately north of the second ridge. They hit the river right across from the Minneconjou camp and were repulsed by hordes of Indians; it was here that the first of his men fell. Another ravine opened at a forty-five-degree angle to the right and they galloped up, charging north along a grassy hogback under heavy fire toward what today is called Massacre Ridge.

These were the soldiers Black Elk watched from the western steppes, but the bodies of others were strung behind these ridges for about three-quarters of a mile. Two crushing waves of warriors—one led by Gall, the other by Crazy Horse and the Cheyenne chief Two Moon— poured from the village and overwhelmed entire companies. By the time Black Elk joined his mother, only a few *wasichus* were left: Custer, three relatives, and forty-seven others, their numbers dwindling in the rain of bullets and arrows.

Black Elk wondered which of his relatives might be in the midst of this fight; even then, Standing Bear wondered if he'd emerge alive. He'd ridden late to the battle: it kept shifting north as he approached, always higher toward the summit; he'd pass a soldier's body, then another, until suddenly he was in the thick of the fight and dust and smoke enveloped him. Warriors flew around him like shadows; the noise of hooves and guns and dying men that had been so loud as he approached was now soaked up by the dust cloud. "The voice seemed to be on top of the cloud," he later remembered. "It was like a bad dream."

Black Elk and his mother watched until nearly sundown. Somewhere in the carnage lay Custer, a bullet in his chest, another in his temple. Either could have killed him. Only small pockets of fighting remained, and as Black Elk watched, women and children began to climb the ridges to strip bodies and collect prizes. He could see wounded Indians being led down. Though he did not know it yet, one was his cousin Black Wasichu; a bullet had plowed through his right shoulder and down and across his body until lodging in his left hip. Black Elk's father was already climbing the ridge; he was with Black Wasichu's father when they heard of the news. The two men seemed to go crazy and butchered a white man lying nearby. They cut him open: the man was fat and the exposed meat glistened like buffalo. Black Elk never heard whether the man was still alive. His father *did* say the meat looked good enough to eat. He hoped they didn't do that—he tried to tell himself they wouldn't—but the madness and hatred made him uncertain and he preferred not to dwell on it too long.

Shortly after 6:00 p.m., six of his friends rode up and asked him to go with them. Black Elk glanced at his mother, who waved him on. He rode across the valley to a northern ford, then started up a gulch later called the Deep Ravine. As the boys rode up, Black Elk heard shots; he kicked his pony in the sides and climbed the embankment just as gray horses with empty saddles stampeded past him toward the water. Each company of the Seventh rode matching mounts for easy identification in battle: E Company rode gray horses. Black Elk assumed their riders were dead, but then the dust parted and near the top of the gulch he could see them. Their eyes were not right; they were so consumed by terror that they'd lost control of their limbs, pumping their arms as if running in a race when in fact their gait was that of sleepwalkers. Indians crowded the sides of the gulch and rained bullets and arrows upon them.

Black Elk picked his way farther up the gulch, followed by the younger boys. By the time they reached the top, most of the gray horse troops were dead. But not all. The boys surrounded those retaining the slightest spark of life, shot them full of arrows, pushed those already in their bodies farther in. Black Elk continued on. He noticed a dying soldier with an engraved gold watch hanging from his belt; he took the watch and shot the dying man. He ascended the hill to where greater numbers of soldiers lay in clumps and guessed this was where the fight had ended. One of the boys ran up and asked him to scalp a soldier; Black Elk handed over the scalp and the boy ran off to show his mother. Another man writhed before him, flapping his arms and groaning in pain. Black Elk shot a blunt arrow into the soldier's forehead and the man toppled backward. His limbs quivered and stopped. Black Elk kept climbing. He'd made three or four kills this day, but now each kill was like the other. He later told John Neihardt that he took no pleasure in them.

He was not the only one to witness the aftermath with such a detached eye. Kate Bighead, a Northern Cheyenne, had fled with the other women when Reno first appeared. But when the battle whirled around Custer, she borrowed her brother's pony and rode close so she could sing strongheart songs for the men. As she crossed the river, thousands of arrows blackened the sky. They stuck into horses and cavalrymen. She hoped they did not drop into braves. She neared the top and noticed the strangest thing: the few remaining soldiers seemed to have gone crazy with fear. She watched as they jumped up in panic and ran down the Deep Ravine to their deaths, no doubt the same men encountered by Black Elk. She watched in amazement as other soldiers shot one another. One *wasichu* sat on the ground, rubbing his head as if he could not understand what unfolded around him. Three Sioux ran up and stretched him flat on his back. Two held his arms while the third drew his sheath knife and sawed off his head.

As Black Elk watched, he knew he should feel happy. His Vision had said this would happen: the *wasichus* had come to kill them and this was what they deserved. But as he walked, he smelled the blood and gunpowder. Smoke and dust nearly blotted out the sun. His stomach clenched and he felt sick.

He turned down the ravine toward the river and camp, and left the dead behind.

PART II

CHILDHOOD'S END

I circle around God, around the primordial tower.
I've been circling for thousands of years.
And still I don't know: am I a falcon,
a storm, or a great song?
—Rainer Maria Rilke, *The Book of Hours*

8

THE BURNING ROAD

The sun went down as a red ball. Reno's troops looked down on the Great Camp from their vantage point above the valley; it sparkled with light from hundreds of campfires. They listened to a camp alive with barking dogs, beating drums, the howls and shouts of what they assumed were celebrating braves. Heat lightning throbbed overhead in the clouds.

It seemed that everyone was up all night, but Black Elk knew the clamor was not all festive. The Lakota lamented their dead: warriors cropped their hair in grief; Cheyenne men untied their braids; women gashed themselves. The bonfires seen on the hill were often the towering flames of burial lodges; the songs, dirges, punctuated by kill-songs.

How many Indians died that day? *The Bismarck Tribune* would write that Custer's men sold their lives dearly: since this was the first paper to run the story and the closest to the massacre site, other papers followed suit. "The Indian dead were great in number," it claimed. Lonesome Charley himself nearly wiped out an entire platoon. It was all wishful thinking; in time, the most liberal accounting put the ratio at one dead Indian for every fifteen whites. The estimates of Indian dead would run from twenty-six to forty-three: David Humphreys Miller, who corralled dozens of old warriors, produced a list of thirty-two casualties. Five were Oglalas, all warriors Black Elk's family would have known. Kate Bighead counted six Cheyennes dead, and twenty-four Sioux. More Indians would have died, she added, if the soldiers had not killed one another.

The shouts nearly unhinged some soldiers on the ridge. One private believed he saw renegade whites circling their flimsy breastworks, daring them to stand and fight. Others saw troop columns approach and heard the bugle of Custer's trumpeter. Despite surrounding snipers, some leapt to their feet and fired into the air to signal their rescuers. One trumpeter blew "Taps" to guide in the phantoms. "Custer was coming at last," one survivor said.

Dawn broke with a light rain. Black Elk and his mother joined a war party to relieve those surrounding Reno; it had the air of a picnic, and his mother "rode a mare with a little colt tied beside her." The colt trotted beside its mother like Black Elk beside his. They could see the ring of dead mules and horses on the hilltop, but the soldiers were too dug in. He noticed down the hill a boy named Round Fool's Impersonation pointing at the bulberries. "There is a white man there in the bush," he cried.

There were actually two soldiers in the berry thicket—Lieutenant Carlo Camilius DeRudio and Private Thomas O'Neal—abandoned with sixteen others when Reno fled the timber. Two were killed immediately, fourteen others made it back to Reno's hilltop, and DeRudio and O'Neal were the last two refugees. Though Black Elk and his friends would spend considerable time trying to flush the two and kill them, they never succeeded. They were too well hidden, and Round Fool's Impersonation grew bored.

So he coaxed the boys over to the other side of Reno's Hill. They crept through the grass toward the breastworks, but did not realize how close they had come. During the two days of siege, ambitious braves would wriggle to within a few yards of the line; some crawled close enough to throw clods of dirt, and a Sans Arc named Long Robe killed a soldier and then counted coup with a stick ten to twelve feet long. For this act of bravado, he was shot by Reno's men. Black Elk suddenly realized they'd crept within three hundred yards of the soldiers; they saw the men's heads just as they began to fire at them. This was too hot for Black Elk, and he ran back down the hill.

By then, his mother had seen mirrors flashing in camp, so they rode down the hill on their ponies. Soldiers began shooting as they crossed the river; bullets pattered around them. They bent close to the necks of their mounts and galloped back as fast as possible.

Soon it was sundown. Scouts returned from the north with news that the forces of Terry and Gibbon had camped nine miles downriver. They must move by nightfall. They fled all night, south along the Greasy

Grass, into the Bighorn Mountains. Black Elk and his two younger brothers rode in a pony drag. His mother put some puppies in with them and all night they tried to escape. He'd grab one every time it crawled out and throw it back in the drag. Then another would attempt a getaway. His brothers slept well that night, but "I didn't sleep much," he said.

———•◦•———

Reno's men saw them go—thousands and thousands, more Indians than seemed humanly possible. The valley was set afire; amid rising smoke, the Great Camp moved. Reno's men watched in awe. This was no rabble, but a military deployment—each band moving as a unit, men, women, and children on horseback, possessions on pony drags. A river of horses moved southwest over the steppes toward the Bighorn Mountains. In time, Reno's men buried their dead, expecting the return of the Sioux. They moved closer to the river for better access to water and to escape the stink of dead horses. DeRudio and O'Neal finally crept back to their friends.

That morning, Terry and Gibbon drew closer. The previous evening, near sunset, Gibbon's scouts spotted "strange-looking objects" like white boulders on a ridge to the east. They argued about their identity, unaware it was the stripped, bloating bodies of Custer's command. During the advance they'd seen hundreds of Indians heading south; warriors would race their ponies past the soldiers, but never fired. When the troops rose on the 27th, "there was not an Indian in view anywhere in that region," one soldier said.

The column quickly covered the last nine miles. The northern limits of the campsite lay abandoned. A few tipis were left, some with dead warriors. In one they found five bodies "laid out carefully with all of their best costumings and favorite face paintings and personal belongings"; in another, they found three bodies. They counted seven burial scaffolds. Cooking implements, moccasins, blankets were scattered around.

But as they continued south through the camp, the remains turned disheartening. First they found clothing—a buckskin jacket; a pair of gloves inscribed with "Yates, 7th Cav."—then dead bodies of soldiers, some filled with arrows. The severed head of Private John Armstrong, whose panicking horse carried him into the village early in the Valley Fight, was impaled on a stake. Another head had been dragged around the camp by leather thongs. Across the river, a lieutenant and ten men were scaling the high ridge when those in the valley saw them dismount, "as for a rest." One of them galloped down the slope, waving his hat, and pounded to a halt before Terry. Custer was wiped out, he told the general. All were dead.

All that morning, the survivors on Reno's Hill watched the approaching dust, but could not tell whether it was from soldiers or returning Indians. As the column neared, they could see Terry's headquarters flag—blue, with a white star in the center. They cheered. Lieutenants Hare and Wallace were sent out; they galloped up, found Terry and Gibbon at the head of the column, and saluted. "Where is Custer?" one cried.

By now that answer had become gruesomely obvious. When Terry and his staff rode to relieve Reno, the survivors gave him three cheers. Terry "cried like a child when he told of Custer's sad fate," said Daniel Kanipe, a sergeant in C Company. The next two days would be spent removing Reno's wounded to the valley, exploring the Indian village, and burying the dead. The carnage was worse than most had ever experienced in war. The dead were stripped and cut up; in some cases, the mutilation went beyond horrifying. Private George Glenn of H Company discovered the body of his former bunkie Tom Tweed split down the middle with an ax, one leg thrown over his shoulder, and shot with arrows in both eyes. Tom Custer's body was treated with extraordinary ferocity—his back spiked with arrows, head bashed in, scalp ripped down to the nape of his neck, entrails emerging. He was unrecognizable, but tattoos on one arm of a flag, the goddess of liberty, and the initials "TWC" identified him.

Though stripped of clothing, Custer's body was undisturbed; he was found sitting up, leaning upon two dead soldiers. Some unpublished letters detailed slit ears and arrows fired into the groin, but these ran counter to the majority of observations and may have been held back to spare Custer's widow. He'd also escaped scalping, and the story would circulate that it was in homage to his courage. Later Indian interviews painted a different picture: his hair was sparse due to premature balding and the fact that he'd cut it short. From a warrior's point of view, Custer's scalp was no prize.

June 28 was spent burying the dead. The setting's weird colors seared into their minds: "the marble white bodies," "somber brown" of slain horses and ponies, reddish-brown tufts of grass on the "ashy-white" soil. "Oh, how white they look! White!" cried Captain Thomas Weir of the corpses. Bodies were so deteriorated that burials were little more than respectful gestures. "In burying the dead, the smell was so bad we had to be relieved every five minutes," recalled Private John Lattman. Few spades were available, so they used knives, bayonets, and cups to scrape shallow depressions for graves. In other cases, bodies were simply straightened out—when possible—then "covered with sagebrush and a little dirt and sand," one trooper said. Officers' remains were marked with tipi poles cut short and then scored with a Roman numeral. Enlisted men remained anonymous. Custer's body was buried beneath a large mound.

They left on the night of the 28th, carrying the wounded in hand-litters, and completed the seventeen-mile trek to the river's mouth by June 30. The wounded were loaded aboard the *Far West* for the seven-hundred-mile journey to the hospital at Fort Abraham Lincoln. By then, Terry had sent his report to Sheridan. "It is my painful duty to report that day before yesterday, the twenty fifth inst., a great disaster overtook Gen. Custer and the troops under his Command," he wrote late on the 27th, when all the horrors of the defeat had been revealed. He read the report by candlelight to his staff, and sent it by the rider "Muggins" Taylor to Fort Ellis, the nearest army post. From there it went to Bozeman, site of the nearest telegraph station. A second report—marked "Confidential" and citing Terry's belief that Custer disobeyed orders—would be sent to Sheridan on July 2 from Bismarck, where the telegraph operator spent hours tapping the news.

Yet word had leaked by then. In Wyoming, ranchers heard tales from friendly Indians that Custer had suffered a great defeat, but few gave credence to the story. Late on July 2, a paper in Helena, Montana, received a brief dispatch from Stillwater County, about fifty miles west of the battlefield, summarizing the dispatch carried by Muggins Taylor. The Helena paper wired the report to Salt Lake City, which transmitted the first bulletin to eastern papers on July 6 at 3:00 a.m. As elsewhere, the first response was one of disbelief, and it was only when a more detailed report appeared later in the day from Bismarck that disbelief turned into national mourning.

The "Custer Massacre" profoundly shocked a nation two days past its centennial. Had he lived, Custer probably would have faced a court-martial for disobeying orders; in defeat, he became—like Hector, Leonidas, and Achilles—a martyr, ushered by death into mythology. The survivors—Reno, Benteen—were branded cowards, despite the petitions of their men and public hearings concluding otherwise. When Fetterman and his men were similarly dispatched, the nation stepped back and reconsidered its course; now, the nation was awash in patriotic paeans to a glorious future. It was unthinkable that God's Chosen People could be so shamed by savages.

Western papers howled for revenge. The *Bismarck Weekly Tribune* called for an end to all treaties, Agencies, and annuities, replaced instead by punitive action. The St. Paul and Minneapolis *Pioneer Press & Tribune* wanted "the Indians exterminated root and branch, old and young, male and female," echoing Sherman's words after the Fetterman Massacre. Any sympathy for the Indian triggered fighting words. When the *Union* of Springfield, Massachusetts, suggested that the Sioux were not the aggressors in this fight, the *Pioneer Press* fired back that the *Union* either was "inexcusably ignorant" or "maliciously misstated the facts."

Regions differed in their responses: in general, those towns closest to Indian Country were least inclined to mercy. Where many western newspapers called for annihilation, eastern papers seemed more measured. A July 12, 1876, editorial in *The New York Times* mourned for the "gallant men" and the "dauntless Custer"; though it called for war waged in a "sharp, vigorous manner," it did not call for genocide. "It is neither just nor decent that a Christian nation should yield itself to homicidal frenzy, and clamor for the instant extermination of the savages by whose unexpected bravery we have been so sadly baffled." To do otherwise, it counseled, would be "more worthy of savages than of civilized men."

But few heeded these words. Custer's defeat "shows that all the old spirit of brutality is still alive in the hearts of the Indians," claimed *Frank Leslie's Illustrated Newspaper*, one of the most widely read weeklies of the day. Put an end to all treaties, it advised. If anyone benefited from such talk, it was Sheridan and his army. Since spring, he had argued that reservation Sioux were giving aid and arms to their hostile relatives in the hunting grounds; he lobbied unsuccessfully to return control of the Agencies to the army. After the Little Bighorn, on July 22, he got his wish. Wires streamed from the Indian Office to the agents: in coming weeks, the army would assume control of the Great Sioux Reserve.

The encomiums to Custer would last days, weeks, months—down through the years. Newspapers published special editions adding more details until, by July 8, most of the story drawn from white survivors and battlefield evidence was as complete as it would be until the late twentieth-century advent of forensic archaeology. The Indian side of the battle would wait decades. By July 10, Walt Whitman had published in the *New-York Tribune* his twenty-six-line "Death Song for Custer": "Thou of the tawny flowing hair . . . bearing a bright sword in thy hand." Three days later, the same paper lamented, "The youngest of our generals, the *beau sabreur* of the Army of the Potomac, the golden-haired chief whom the Sioux had learned to dread, has fought his last fight." Public prayers were held for Custer, funds raised for Custer monuments, bills passed for pensions for Custer's mother and father. *What*, Congress demanded, *would be done to the Sioux?*

The Lakota and Cheyenne could not be forgiven. They'd committed two unpardonable sins that dusty June day. They'd won too overwhelmingly. And they'd done so at the worst possible time. One hundred years after the War of Independence, Americans saw their land as a beacon of opportunity and liberty, an industrial powerhouse soon to take its place on the world stage. The victory over Custer suggested otherwise. Humiliation was worse than defeat, and the hatred burned for decades.

—————•◦•—————

By late July, Black Elk's father had told him a hard truth. The victory at the Greasy Grass meant nothing. More soldiers would come. Their people were trickling back to the Agencies. Some Loafers and their chiefs still planned to sell the Black Hills.

At first it seemed they might be left alone. Terry's demoralized troops remained north on the Yellowstone; Crook stayed in his camp at Goose Creek. For a while, the Powder River Country was soldier-free. By the morning of June 28, the bands had stopped at a dry creek southwest of the Greasy Grass, roasted meat, then moved on. By midafternoon, the Great Camp reached the foot of the Bighorns and halted. They still worried about pursuit, and rose in alarm when someone yelled "The soldiers are coming!" Soldiers indeed were seen, a suicidally small contingent riding from the direction of battle. But then they laughed: it was only pranksters wearing captured uniforms. They brought with them the welcome news that the troops had turned around.

They got down to the serious business of celebrating victory. By now they'd learned that Pahuska had led the fallen troops, and he figured prominently in their songs. Standing Bear's favorite hinted at the fateful ties between too-similar enemies:

A charger, he is coming.
I made him come.
When he came, I wiped him out.
He did not like my ways; that is why.

During this period, the mortally wounded dropped away. Black
Wasichu died in agony, as did a man named Three Bears, whose pain
made him delusional. He screamed "Geneny!" and then went into convulsions and died. No one knew what he meant, and for long afterward
people would refer to the spot as Geneny Creek.

For three days, the Lakota took their ease. Black Elk and his friends
fished and stalked small game. During this time, the scope of the battle
unfolded as participants narrated their experiences. Big Road and Low
Dog, another Decider, had led independent parties of warriors; the
Hunkpapa chief Crow King led eighty men. Yet nearly two hundred
braves had followed Crazy Horse against Reno, and that number grew
when he crossed the river to rub out Pahuska. The Little Bighorn "brought
Crazy Horse more prominently before all the Indians than any one
else," wrote Lieutenant William Philo Clark after debriefing returning
Sioux. "Before then he had a great reputation," but after the victory "he
gained a greater prestige than any other Indian in the camp."

Throughout July, the Great Camp wandered in search of game. It
generally drifted east, always hidden in the slot between Crook and Terry.
In mid-July, they caught up with the bison herd. The hunt was so successful that it seemed it might provide for the winter ahead. Yet even
with this, it had become apparent by August 3 that it would be too daunting to feed such a great mass of people much longer. The Great Camp
finally started to disband. Some Hunkpapas headed north; the Cheyennes turned south toward the Bighorns. Small family bands drifted to
the Agencies. The majority still followed Crazy Horse, heading east
across the Little Missouri in search of deer herds migrating to the
uplands north of the Black Hills.

On August 5, Crook left Goose Creek and headed north for what
would be called the "Bighorn and Yellowstone Expedition." He commanded more than 1,800 troops, as well as 250 Shoshone scouts and
200 packers and guides. With them rode the thirty-year-old William
Frederick Cody—the army scout, buffalo hunter, and showman already
known as "Buffalo Bill."

Black Elk's life would be so tied up with Cody's that he deserves serious examination. With the Bighorn and Yellowstone Expedition, the linkage began. The man whose transatlantic interpretation of America's West would shape Hehaka Sapa's life and thought was now charged with rubbing out his people. Like Black Elk, Cody was an enigma—and like Black Elk, much of that mystery was tied to the *show*.

Even as Crook's scout, Cody was at core a showman. In the April 1971 Dick Cavett interview, John Neihardt was convinced that this was the central truth of the man. "Was he a phony?" Cavett asked, and the poet smiled. In 1908, while working on a series of magazine articles about the Missouri River that would eventually become *The River and I*, Neihardt spent time on the *Far West* and asked Captain Grant T. Marsh the same question. Marsh laughed and recalled an instance, when instead of leading his horse down the gangplank like any sane horseman, Cody straddled its back and waved his hat, and man and mount leapt to shore, a feat that took considerable equestrian skill. This was, of course, the whole point. "Indeed he wasn't" a phony, said Marsh. "He was a show-off, but he wasn't a phony."

Cody was already famous when he and the others trailed Custer's executioners. After the Civil War, he supplied buffalo meat to the workers on the Kansas Pacific Railroad. In one eighteen-month period during 1867–68, he supposedly killed 4,282 bison. He earned the right to use the sobriquet "Buffalo Bill," he claimed, after an eight-hour buffalo shooting match against his fellow hunter William "Medicine Bill" Comstock: Cody killed sixty-eight bison to Comstock's forty-eight. Yet historians doubt that it happened this way. No credible eyewitnesses ever surfaced, but more important, Comstock was wanted for murder and would not have shown himself so publicly.

Yet for all the embellishments, there were reasons for Cody's rising star. From 1868 to 1872, he was employed as an army scout, and in 1872 he was awarded the Medal of Honor for "gallantry in action" with the Third Cavalry in Nebraska. In December 1869, the first of many Buffalo Bill dime novels—*Buffalo Bill: King of the Border Men*—was published in the *New York Weekly*, written by Edward Z. C. Judson, better known as Ned Buntline. In December 1872, Cody appeared with his friend "Texas Jack" Omohundro in the Chicago debut of the Ned Buntline–produced play *The Scouts of the Prairie*. This was followed in 1873–74 by *The Scouts of the Plains*, featuring Cody, Omohundro, and James Butler Hickok, known as "Wild Bill."

By 1876, Cody would scout in the summer and act in the winter.

In early June of that year, he joined the Fifth Cavalry as it tried to keep straggling Lakotas and Cheyennes from joining up with Crazy Horse and Sitting Bull. By early July, the Fifth got word that up to eight hundred Cheyennes had left the Red Cloud Agency and were somewhere west of the Black Hills. The news of Custer's defeat would not reach them until July 7; Cody carried the news.

Two days later, on July 9, Cody famously exacted revenge. That day, the regiment charged a party of Cheyennes at War Bonnet Creek as they tried to ambush two couriers. Dressed in a stage costume of black velvet slashed with scarlet and trimmed with silver buttons, Cody reportedly shot and scalped a young Cheyenne subchief named Yellow Hair, later mistranslated as Yellow Hand. The Fifth Cavalry's adjutant, Lieutenant Charles King, would later describe the scene: "I see Buffalo Bill closing on a superbly accoutered warrior. It is the work of a minute; the Indian has fired and missed. Cody's bullet tears through the rider's leg, into his pony's heart, and they tumble in [a] confused heap on the prairie. The Cheyenne struggles to his feet for another shot, but Cody's second bullet crashes through his brain, and the young chief, Yellow Hand, drops lifeless in his tracks."

That's not how Cody would tell it. Soon after returning to Fort Laramie, Cody coaxed King and a reporter from *The New York Herald* to wire reports to the eastern press in which Cody and the young Cheyenne charged each other like knights between observant ranks of soldiers and Indians. The two fired and both horses fell. They fired again, and "Yellow Hand" died. Cody "scientifically" scalped the Indian as two hundred Cheyennes closed in to kill him, but the soldiers rode to his rescue. "As the soldiers came up I swung the Indian chieftain's top-knot and bonnet in the air, and shouted: 'The first scalp for Custer.'" That fall, he acted out the fatal duel in the premiere of his *The Red Right Hand: Or, Buffalo Bill's First Scalp for Custer*.

Even Cody's friends acknowledged he often played a role. If one story can be believed, the merger of role and reality sometimes bothered Cody. G. W. Beardsley was an old-time bull-whacker who worked the route between Denver and North Platte, Nebraska. Once, as his outfit bedded down for the night, Cody rode up to warn them that they were being watched by Indians. The warriors would attack if the outfit lowered its guard. Cody probably saved their lives, and the two men became close friends.

During a visit years after the Yellow Hand incident, the two talked until 2:00 a.m. Beardsley asked why he allowed "those goddamn stories to be printed when he knew they were lies." Cody smiled and said they were good for his Wild West show. They were mostly the tall tales all old-timers loved to feed to tenderfeet, never thinking they might become historical fact. Beardsley asked about Yellow Hand.

"I never fired a shot in that battle, and I don't know who killed Yellow Hand," Cody said. "I think it was a red-necked Irishman [among the line of soldiers]. I never scalped an Indian in my life and killed dern few, if any. Any Indian killed was in battle." He did have Yellow Hand's war bonnet and what was reportedly his scalp, but he'd gotten them through other means, not as described in the famous tale.

———•◦•———

Cody's duel with Yellow Hair would be one of the few moments of contact for the rest of that summer between the army and its prey. Again, Crook marched north on the Rosebud; three days later, on August 8, Terry marched south with 1,600 men. The strategy was as earlier: two huge forces would box the Indians between them. But the Sioux refused to cooperate. On August 10, the columns came together in a cloud of alkali dust and confusion. "And then it is," wrote King, "that the question is asked, in comical perplexity, 'Why, where on earth are the Indians?'"

They had slipped to the east, to Dakota Territory. The two generals stayed together for a couple of weeks, getting on each other's nerves. Cody was irritated, too, and headed to Chicago for the theater season. Crook was convinced the Oglalas would head into what is now North Dakota, then veer south to the Black Hills, where boomtowns such as Custer City, Deadwood, and Crook City had sprung up like mushrooms. In five short months, Paha Sapa had become one of the most densely populated sections of real estate west of the Mississippi.

On August 26, Crook's column followed the month-old Sioux trail. Knowing he would probably come, the Lakotas set fire to the grass behind them so the soldiers' horses would have nothing to eat. Then rain fell for twenty-six days. History came to know the pursuit as the Horsemeat March for obvious reasons. The starving men were forced to slaughter and eat their starving horses, an expedient that seemed "cannibalistic" to cavalrymen.

Three months after starting out, Three Stars stumbled upon the Sioux. On September 7, Crook sent a contingent of 154 men under Captain

Anson Mills due south from their position in the upper Dakotas to Deadwood for desperately needed supplies. Mills's route took him through a low-lying range of limestone spires called the Slim Buttes that arced through the region. Unknown to the soldiers, this was the Sioux's traditional fall hunting zone. Crazy Horse's followers, including the Black Elks, had pitched two large villages among the chalk-white buttes: one of about four hundred lodges, a second of about three hundred. Ten or more small groups camped at the fringes.

One of these, a small clutch of thirty-seven tipis following the Minneconjou chief Iron Shield, was tucked away in a depression on the eastern edge. The little group was wet, tired, and dispirited: relatives from Sitting Bull's band had just joined them, and they discussed surrender as they sat laced up in their rain-soaked tipis. Mills discovered the soggy camp on the afternoon of September 8 and attacked the next morning. His soldiers killed two men and a woman, captured four hundred ponies, and confiscated three tons of dried meat, dried fruit, and flour, which would be manna for Crook's starving men.

They also found proof that these Indians had been at the Little Bighorn: a locket, a picture of Captain Miles Keogh, a pair of ivory-handled revolvers, and a Spencer hunting rifle. Most of the Indians escaped and took the news to Crazy Horse, camped twenty miles away. But the mortally wounded Iron Shield and twenty-six others hid in a ravine. By midafternoon, Crook arrived and the survivors were persuaded to surrender. At 4:15 p.m., Crazy Horse attacked. But he'd expected Mills's small detachment, and crashed instead against the largest force he'd encountered during the war. For the rest of the day and into the next, his men sniped at the soldiers as they limped south to Deadwood.

The Bighorn and Yellowstone Expedition was over—for both exhausted armies. As the Indians trailed Crook, they confirmed what had only been rumors: Paha Sapa boomed with new settlements, linked by roads, small-gauge railroads, and telegraph lines. The *wasichu* had seized the heart of their world. Though Three Stars had not won this long fight, neither had Crazy Horse. What whites dubbed the Battle of Slim Buttes, the Oglala called "The Fight Where We Lost the Black Hills."

———•◦•———

By the end of September 1876, it was evident to both sides that this conflict would be a war of attrition. There would be no more grand victories like the Greasy Grass, no simple strategy to entrap and destroy the Lakota. "Wherever we went, the soldiers came to kill us, and it was our own country," Black Elk said, in his voice a tired note of despair. It no longer mattered that the land had been ceded to them by treaty. "They were chasing us now because we remembered and they forgot," he said.

Around this time some statistics began to circulate in the eastern newspapers. The Great Sioux War had cost the United States $1 million to kill each Indian and $2 million a year to feed and maintain the soldiers who killed them. Historians find these figures suspect: they seem too nicely rounded. But they were repeated enough at the time to become folk wisdom, and reflected the fact that the conflict had become more expensive in lives and matériel than the army had ever anticipated. Before its end, nearly one-quarter of America's regular army would be sent to the Northern Plains; blood would be shed at twenty-two places in Nebraska, Wyoming, Montana, and both Dakotas. The Bighorn and Yellowstone Expedition proved a perfect example: the government spent several million dollars to kill a few women and warriors and one infant, and burn up some tipis and buffalo robes.

The Great Camp disbanded by September's end, never to form again. The Northern Nation, as Sitting Bull and Crazy Horse had once called it, was dead. The Lakotas' traditional roving lifestyle simply could not provision so many people, and even more horses, at one place for any length of time. As many as 465 lodges followed Sitting Bull on a plodding course northeast, while just as many Cheyennes and Oglalas followed Crazy Horse back to the Powder River Country.

Others gave up and returned to the Agencies. But life was no easier there. At least six native-language newspapers were then being published in the United States: the Sioux newspaper was Iapi Oaye, or The Word Carrier, printed monthly in English and Sioux out of Santee, Nebraska, by the Presbyterian and Congregational churches. Its stories from the far-flung Sioux Agencies were litanies of despair. In April 1873, snows killed one hundred ponies and forty to fifty oxen and cattle; in November 1873, smallpox killed sixty people at the Santee Agency; in July 1876, locusts descended "like a snowstorm," destroying crops, ensuring famine. "These Indians must suffer," a missionary wrote. "They are suffering now. They have had no help from the government since early in the spring; and just when their new corn and potatoes were coming to their relief, the grasshoppers have, in one night, swept away their hopes. May God help them!"

In October 1876, as Black Elk returned to Powder River, Commissioner of Indian Affairs J. Q. Smith saw nothing but doom for the Indians. "No new hunting grounds remain," he wrote in his annual report, "and the civilization or the utter destruction of the Indians is inevitable."

The only lasting salvation, warned Smith, was in the "individual ownership of land," the only recourse by which an Indian could receive "all the guarantees which law can devise." Landownership inspired "men to put forth their best exertions," he said: it was a transformative faith, *the* guiding principle of the frontier. "What then is the American, this new man?" famously asked J. Hector St. John de Crèvecœur in his 1784 *Letters from an American Farmer.* His answer hinged upon the Latin dictum *"Ubi panis ibi patria"*: "Where there is bread, there is my country."

It was happening just as Black Elk's father predicted. The Greasy Grass had not changed anything. In the fall of 1876, a new commission of Iktomi men arrived at the Agencies with the ultimatum that all rations would cease unless the tribes handed over the Black Hills. By the end of October, the commissioners had the marks of 10 percent of all Lakota men living in the Agencies, not the three-quarters required by law. Though U.S. courts would acknowledge the swindle, it would not be for another forty-seven years.

Winter came early that year for the Black Elks. "It snowed much; game was hard to find, and it was a hungry time for us. Ponies died, and we ate them," Black Elk said. On November 25, soldiers under Colonel Ranald S. Mackenzie fell upon the Cheyenne camp of Dull Knife, nestled beneath the Bighorns. The attack killed more than forty people and drove half-clad survivors into the mountains. Fourteen papooses were later found frozen in their mothers' arms. On December 6, the survivors limped into Crazy Horse's camp on Beaver Creek. His people did what they could, but they were nearly paupers themselves. After a while, the Cheyennes had no recourse but to leave for Camp Robinson. Now, said Black Elk, "we were all alone."

9

KILLING CRAZY HORSE

A new general now entered the picture: Nelson Appleton Miles, who would help shape Black Elk's fate for the next two decades. In the fall of 1876, Sherman sent the veteran of the Civil and Red River Wars to repair the shambles of the Custer Massacre. Top army brass saw the death or surrender of Sioux leaders as the best path to victory, and Miles came to the Yellowstone Country to bring in Sitting Bull. In October 1876, the Sioux watched a new fort rise where the Tongue met the Yellowstone: in addition to the Fifth Infantry and Fifth Cavalry, Fort Keogh housed two companies of the Twenty-Second Infantry, some artillery, and a small number of scouts, interpreters, and Crows.

This was not friendly country. The temperature often plunged to −60 degrees Fahrenheit, and Miles measured it once at −66 degrees. The fort and its supply train were harassed by war parties; during one such attack, two bullets pierced Miles's tent just above his bed. In mid-October, Miles received a message. "I want to know what you are doing on this road," it said:

> You scare all of the buffalo away. I want to hunt in this place. I want you to turn back from here. If you don't, I will fight you again. I want you to leave what you have got here, and turn back from here. I am your friend.
>
> —Sitting Bull

On October 21, 1876, the two men met about three days' ride north-east of Fort Keogh. Hunkpapas covered "the hills and adjacent plains to the number of a thousand or more warriors," Miles wrote, and this first sight of the Sioux en masse inspired in him both admiration and alarm. The Indians seemed armed with rifles, "were gorgeously decorated with feathers, beadwork, and war paint, were well supplied with fur robes and splendidly mounted on their fleet, hardy war ponies." These were not a people to be trifled with, Miles realized.

The two came together in a declivity between two hills, each accompanied by six men. Sitting Bull, wrote Miles, "was a man of powerful physique, with a large, broad head, strong features, and few words, which were uttered with great deliberation; a man evidently of decision and positive convictions." Miles sported his waxed mustachio and wore a long coat trimmed with bear fur. From thenceforth, he would be Bear Coat to the Sioux.

Why, Miles asked, was Sitting Bull in the Yellowstone Country?

To hunt buffalo before the winter, the seer replied. The Sioux had done this forever, long before the white man arrived.

Well, said Bear Coat, the white man *had* arrived, and it was useless to fight him. His numbers were great and would never stop; the Sioux's only chance of survival lay on the reservation. But Sitting Bull brushed aside such talk. He'd spend the winter wherever he pleased.

Though nothing was resolved, they agreed to meet the next day. But this time they simply bickered. Sitting Bull said the fighting would not stop until the *wasichu* left the hunting grounds; Miles countered it would end only when the Sioux entered the reservation. Sitting Bull's patience ended with these words. He snapped that "Almighty God had made him an Indian, but not an *Agency* Indian, and he did not intend to be one," Miles later wrote. "He said there never was a white man who did not hate the Indians, and there never was an Indian who did not hate the white man."

So there it was, two hundred years of Indian-white relations distilled into one moment of rage. The next day saw fifteen minutes of gunfire, followed by two days of pursuit until Miles called a halt. To Sitting Bull, the future was clear. He could no longer live in this country. The Hunkpapa drifted north through the winter toward Canada. Though messages passed between Sitting Bull and Crazy Horse, they would not meet again until January 1877. One month later, Sitting Bull and his people crossed the border into Grandmother's Land.

With Sitting Bull out of reach, the hunt focused on Crazy Horse. That winter, the pressure began to kill him by slow degrees. Until that point, Sitting Bull personified for most Americans the face of the hostiles. Though they knew the name "Crazy Horse," he was just another Indian. Yet by 1877, awareness of Tasunke Witko had taken shape, largely because of Crook's mysterious scout Frank Grouard. Crook seemed the first general to grasp the importance of Crazy Horse: "The chief fighting man is Crazy Horse, as a chief; Sitting Bull is looked upon more as a Council Chief," his aide Lieutenant Walter S. Schuyler told the *Chicago Tribune*.

That winter, Black Elk watched his cousin turn strange. His father noticed first, then confided his fears to his son. The man who'd led by example became a tyrant; who'd always been a loner, sank into a hermit's shell.

Crazy Horse was thirty-six and ruled what remained of the Great Village with an iron hand. After the December attack on Dull Knife, his determination hardened against any compromise with Americans. His tribal council prohibited all movement to the Agencies; his *akicitas*, or tribal police, beat those who attempted a break, destroying their property and killing their horses, making survival unlikely if they abandoned the tribe. Yet even Crazy Horse and his enforcers could not restrain the cold and hunger that wore steadily at the old and young.

After the attack on Dull Knife, the Oglala moved north, away from Crook but closer to Miles. As more tribesmen sickened and died, a large group of chiefs announced that it was time to hear Bear Coat's terms. Crazy Horse had little power over so many headmen, and on December 16, 1876, he watched thirty chiefs and warriors ride to a hill overlooking Fort Keogh. Eight rode on, bearing aloft a white cloth tied to a lance. They neared the fort, passing a Crow camp pitched outside the walls.

Now fate played a hand. One delegate—probably the Minneconjou chief Gets Fat with Beef—rode the horse of a woman killed in autumn raids against the Crow. The Crows "approached them in a friendly manner," wrote Miles in his report, "said 'How!', shook hands with them"— then maneuvered them behind a woodpile, where they surrounded the group and fired. Most accounts said that three Sioux escaped while the other five died. Even Miles was shocked; he sent out riders, but the killers fled across the frozen river and into the hills.

The murder solidified Crazy Horse's hold over the approximately eight hundred lodges still with him: only betrayal and death awaited those who trusted the *wasichu*, he said. But the Sioux were not as united as they had been under Red Cloud or Sitting Bull. Crazy Horse's vow "to save the land" flew in the face of reality. No rivers of Lakota flowed to his camp, as they had before the Greasy Grass. Agency Sioux called Crazy Horse "big trouble," a man willing to ignite a holocaust that none could survive. Former allies came to the camp and pleaded with him to surrender. Yet when they tried to lead some weary families back to the Agencies, Crazy Horse appeared with his *akicitas*; they shot the families' horses, took their weapons and possessions, and said that *now*, if they still wanted to go, they were free—an almost certain death sentence in the killing cold.

Perhaps it was still possible that Tasunke Witko would prevail. On the same day that he drove off the peace chiefs, his guerillas drove off 150 cattle. Three days later, on December 29, Bear Coat seemed to take the bait, leaving Fort Keogh with 436 riflemen—and two mountain cannons hidden in his supply wagons. The snow lay a foot deep and the streams were frozen solid; the Indians headed south, and Miles followed.

Bear Coat was three hundred miles from the nearest settlement and four hundred miles from the nearest railroad—more isolated than Custer at the Little Bighorn. But he did not split his forces, and he brought artillery. On January 8, he caught up with Crazy Horse in a narrow valley in the Wolf Mountains. Black Elk's father told his son it was a good day to die because their ammunition was running low. The Indians commanded the heights, but Miles unlimbered his artillery and assaulted a high bluff to his left where Crazy Horse had concentrated his forces. A blizzard quickened above them.

The battle lasted four hours. Though the artillery pounded the heights, the shells often failed to explode. "I stayed with some boys" on the bluffs "and we saw a cannon ball coming and we threw ourselves down," Black Elk said. When a ball passed overhead, one boy "went out and picked it up and brought it home." Black Elk watched as a Cheyenne named Big Crow walked along the ridge, defying the soldiers to kill him. They found his range and obliged. By afternoon, the blizzard finally broke and both sides withdrew. The dying Big Crow asked to be wrapped in his buffalo robe and left behind; his body was found the next spring, still swathed in the robe.

The next day, Bear Coat and his weary troops trudged home to Fort Keogh. Though Miles described in his memoirs the Indians' "panic and rout," the Battle of Wolf Mountain was a stalemate. Two Sioux and the Cheyenne Big Crow were killed; Miles reported one soldier killed and nine wounded. If anything, one trooper wrote, "we wasted an awful lot of ammunition."

———·•·———

After Wolf Mountain, the remnants of the Great Northern Nation parted at the seams. The 800 lodges still with Crazy Horse in December dwindled to 350 by the end of January. Peace delegations siphoned some away; others packed up in the cover of night and departed. On February 3, the Great Village divided one last time. The majority headed west after buffalo, while others turned south, eventually bound for the Red Cloud Agency.

Only two *tiyospaye* stayed with Crazy Horse—some ten families, including the Black Elks. But the changes Black Elk saw in his cousin frightened him. Tasunke Witko was a beaten man. The reserves of willpower that drove him to fight Miles and hold together the tribe finally dissipated. Friends would find him alone in the snow outside the village and beg him to come back. He would not, and issued unheeded dictates and orders. "He was always a queer man," said Black Elk, "but that winter he was queerer than ever. Maybe he had seen that he would soon be dead and was thinking how to help us when he would not be with us any more." He turned to the holy men for help—since so few were left, that would have included Black Elk's father.

A political skirmish ensued between Miles and Crook over who would "bag" Crazy Horse, but Crook had a hole card: Tasunke Witko's uncle Spotted Tail. On February 15, 1877, the peace chief set out with 250 warriors to find his nephew, and by late February or early March he discovered his camp straddling today's border between Montana and Wyoming.

But Crazy Horse had left, telling his father that he would ride alone into the hills with Black Shawl. His wife had the coughing sickness; he would go into the caves to fast and pray, to cry for a vision that might save his wife and people. *Be good to my uncle*, he told Worm. But Crazy Horse would not meet with him.

Black Elk watched as Spotted Tail rode into the village. By then Black Elk was fourteen and reflected much of his father's anger. He immediately disliked the peace chief: "He was fat with Wasichu food and we were lean with famine." Where was the justice in that? How could the Grandfathers reward such betrayal? "How could men get fat by being bad," he wondered, "and starve by being good?"

When Spotted Tail asked Worm about Crazy Horse, the old man replied that his son "was out hunting by himself . . . [but] shakes hands through his father." He gave Spotted Tail a pony as a peace token, adding that Crazy Horse's sole commitment was to his people. Spotted Tail repeated Three Stars' promise that no harm would come to those who surrendered. And, he added, Three Stars promised Crazy Horse a reservation in the Powder River Country if he surrendered to him.

Then Spotted Tail rode around the country, convincing about 160 lodges of various bands to turn themselves in at his or Red Cloud's Agency in the spring. On March 26, his work done, he turned home. He'd accomplished much, but his greatest feat perhaps was to placate Worm: soon after his departure, Worm and his kin departed for the Powder River, followed almost immediately by another four lodges. The Great Village that overwhelmed Custer had dwindled to the two lodges of Crazy Horse, standing alone in the snow drifts of the Little Powder.

Sometime in late March or early April, the Black Elks began a slow journey back to Camp Robinson. During the trek, they found Crazy Horse alone on a creek with Black Shawl. He'd asked the gods for answers, he said, but the gods had yet to reply. Black Elk and his family would be the sole eyewitnesses of Crazy Horse's disintegration during this period. Crazy Horse was gaunt and pale, and Black Shawl seemed to be dying. Black Elk's father begged him to join them, but Crazy Horse refused. "Uncle, you might have noticed me, how I act, but it is for the good of the people," he said. "I don't care where the people go. They can go where they wish. There are lots of caves and this shows that I cannot be found." He still had many things to figure out. When the spirits answered, he would return.

Crazy Horse paused at this point, as if it were imperative to be understood. By his uncle. By the strange little cousin who revered him. "This country is ours, therefore I am doing this," he said. Then, almost to himself, he added, "All is lost anyway."

In the end, the gods did not come. The once-potent medicine had faded. On March 26, 1877—the day of Spotted Tail's return—the headmen of the last hostile bands met at Pumpkin Butte with delegates from the Red Cloud and Cheyenne River Agencies. No one was being punished for his role in the war, the delegates reiterated. Three Stars kept his promises. All eyes turned to Crazy Horse, who'd limped from the wilderness to attend. Perhaps the gods had answered his entreaties. Instead, his reply was short: "This day I have untied my horse's tail and laid my gun aside and I have sat down."

There would be no more war. Tasunke Witko was beaten. As one witness later recalled, "Crazy Horse said whatever all the rest decided to do, he would do."

In mid-April, Crook learned that approximately a thousand Indians had gathered at Devils Tower. Most were Oglalas, interspersed with some Brulés, Minneconjous and Sans Arcs. Their leaders were already picked: Big Road, Little Big Man, Old Heart, and Little Hawk were Deciders; Crazy Horse's friend He Dog led the *akicitas*; Iron Hawk was village herald. But what about Crazy Horse? His status remained ambiguous; his intentions, unclear.

On the night of April 12–13, Crook sent Red Cloud with seventy men to find out once and for all whether this was a war or peace council. He found them within a week, and explained without equivocation Crook's terms. If they surrendered at Red Cloud Agency, their ponies, numbering about 2,300 head, would be handed over to officials and then redistributed equally through the village. No one would be punished for the war—not even for the Little Bighorn. Yet on the question of guns, there would be no compromise. All must be turned over to the soldiers.

The council grew quiet. No war chief had been chosen for this gathering; nevertheless, the final word belonged to Tasunke Witko. All knew what this meant. Without guns, he was vulnerable. Enemies were everywhere. But he'd also vowed to follow his people's wishes. "All right, let them have them," he finally conceded. And then, to himself, as he had to Black Elk, he added, "I am aware that I will not live."

The next day, Crazy Horse rose from his council seat, spread out a buffalo robe for Red Cloud, and draped over his old captain's shoulders his hair-fringed shirt, symbol of his status as war chief. Red Cloud sent back news that Crazy Horse would soon surrender. After some delays, by Saturday, May 5, 1877, Crazy Horse's people had camped in the hills north of the Agency, and at daylight the next morning, the final march began.

Crazy Horse rode upon a white horse at the head of the column. They crossed Soldier Creek, where twenty blue-coated Oglala scouts awaited them. At their head rode Lieutenant William Philo Clark, known to the Sioux as White Hat for the bright white campaign hat he wore. As Crook's head of scouts, Clark often got to know the Indians first and best: he certainly would serve as an important intermediary between Crazy Horse and government officials. At 10:00 a.m., the two groups met in a valley between long, sloping bluffs. "All bad feelings of the past must be buried," Clark said.

At noon, the procession rode the last five miles to the Agency. Clark wore He Dog's headdress, given to him as a gift: the lieutenant "looked so comical" that some warriors could not help but laugh, one Lakota said. Clark and another officer, Lieutenant J. Wesley Rosenquest, rode out front, followed by the army scouts, Red Cloud, and his envoys. There was a quarter-mile gap, then a row of six—Crazy Horse, He Dog, and the Deciders. While the other chiefs wore their war bonnets, Crazy Horse wore the single eagle feather given to him by Chips years earlier. As the valley widened, three hundred warriors formed into the five disciplined ranks of the warrior societies. They sat astride their painted ponies, dressed in their finery: blankets, headdresses, ornaments made of silver, brass, glass, and tin. It was a bright spring day, and the ornaments shone in the sun. After them came a column two miles long. On cue, a man began to sing, and all took up a solemn peace song.

"By God!" exclaimed an officer, watching from a distance through field glasses. "This is a triumphal march, not a surrender!"

————◦◦◦————

They pitched their lodges in a crescent, about three-quarters of a mile from the Agency stockade. Once camp was set, the warriors surrendered their horses and guns. This was followed by the recording of names, as well as the number of wives, children, and other dependents per lodge, all entered in a lined two-hundred-page ledger book bound between marble and maroon covers.

Known today as the *Crazy Horse Surrender Ledger*, the booklet contains the 1877 Indian census of the entire Red Cloud Agency. Approximately 1,500 names are entered: two-thirds Lakota, with 300 Cheyennes and 200 Arapahos. Crazy Horse's band fills up the May 6, 1877, entry on pages 163–70: the acting agent, Lieutenant Charles A. Johnson, recorded a total of 899 Indians: 217 men, 312 women, 186 boys, and 184 girls. It is the most comprehensive listing of the war chief's followers ever found. Crazy Horse appears on page 162; he lodges with the warrior Tall Bull, three unidentified women, and two boys.

The Black Elks also appear, though the listing presents a bit of a mystery. In *Black Elk Speaks* and the transcripts of John Neihardt's interviews, Black Elk said they left ahead of the others for Soldiers' Town in April, then arrived at Camp Robinson around May. They stayed a few days until hearing that Crazy Horse approached, so they must have ridden out and returned with the "triumphal" procession. The soldiers and Lakota police were formed in lines when they rode up; the soldiers and their mounts were well fed, but "our people and the ponies were only skin and bones."

Black Elk's household is registered on page 159. It contains one adult male (Black Elk's father); one adult female (his mother); and three male children (Black Elk and his two younger brothers). The half brother, Runs in the Center, was by now old enough to live apart; the older sisters would have married and been listed with their husbands' lodges.

Sprinkled among the entries are several scatological names: Tanned Nuts, Snatch Stealer, Soft Prick, Shits on His Hand, Pisses in the Horn, and others. Some have suggested this reflects the Sioux habit of enlisting a male cross-dresser, called a *winkte*, to give a child a "joke name" at birth. Yet given the circumstances, a more likely explanation is simply one of disrespect. The Lakota had a lively, if sometimes coarse, sense of humor. To sign one's name as "Singing Prick" during the solemn rite of surrender is a quiet form of protest. The fact that the soldiers took it down for posterity made it all the more absurd.

Then it was over. The dreaded capitulation had come and gone. "We had enough to eat now," said Black Elk, "and we boys could play without being afraid of anything." True, the soldiers were always watching, and the grown-ups could feel their stares. The old life was over; the new one, still unknown. The last battle of the Great Sioux War occurred one day after the surrender. On May 7, 1877, Bear Coat found the camp of the Minneconjou chief Lame Deer, tucked away on Muddy Creek, seventy miles from Fort Keogh. Miles commanded 470 men; Lame Deer, sixty-one lodges, or about 488 people. Miles and Lame Deer rode out to talk, but a tussle ensued and shots were fired. When Lame Deer leveled his Spencer rifle at Miles and pulled the trigger, Miles spurred his horse and the chief was cut down by a fusillade from Miles's guard. By 9:00 a.m., the shooting had ended. Fourteen Indians were killed, and four soldiers. The villagers scattered, and most surrendered at the Agencies later that year.

What unfolded that summer at the Red Cloud Agency did so with an air of tragic inevitability. Crazy Horse and his people—including the Black Elks—camped several miles northeast on Cottonwood Creek, a small White River tributary between the Red Cloud and Spotted Tail Agencies. It was a pleasant spot, cool and breezy, yet even so, Crazy Horse grew disenchanted. This was no life for a warrior. In place of buffalo, the government gave them stringy beef; skin tipis had been replaced by canvas tents; days of industry and excitement were replaced by lingering hunger and quarrels. Crook's promise of a Powder River reservation proved a chimera, its creation blocked by bureaucracy, indifference, and hatred. Aware of Tasunke Witko's restlessness, Crook offered him leave for a fall buffalo hunt, but many advised against it, including Spotted Tail: What prevented his nephew from crossing into Grandmother's Land? Intercepted messages from Sitting Bull urged that very thing.

But Crazy Horse's first concern was the fragile health of Black Shawl. As soon as he made camp, he asked to see the post doctor. Dr. Valentine T. McGillycuddy was no stranger to Indians. He'd served as Crook's physician during the Rosebud fight and the Horsemeat March; now he held the rank of major and served as assistant post surgeon. He was hard to miss—the ends of his waxed mustache drooped like pruned vines two inches below his lower lip, for which the Lakota dubbed him Putin hi Chikala, or "Little Whiskers." McGillycuddy rode regular rounds through the camps, often accompanied by his wife, Fanny; while the doctor saw to Black Shawl, Fanny chatted with the women and children. The visits developed into friendship, but anyone who was the friend of Crazy Horse could not be the friend of Red Cloud.

At least the old religion remained. As all else vanished, the Lakotas' relationship to *Wakan Tanka* could give them courage. In June 1877, they held the largest Sun Dance ever seen to that point on a reservation. It occurred on a small creek midway between the two Agencies: twenty thousand Indians were said to be present, many making the trip for days. It was held in honor of Crazy Horse, one year after his victory on the Greasy Grass, and to offer up prayers for him in the days ahead. Although Tasunke Witko attended, he did not dance; he mingled with his people, some of whom he had not seen for a long time.

A favorite part of the Sun Dance was a sham battle, and what happened now reflected the seismic anger lingering beneath the surface at the Agency. The battle would represent the Custer fight: the Crazy Horse tribesmen who fought at the Greasy Grass squared off against Agency Indians representing Custer. William Garnett—son of an army officer and a Sioux woman and perhaps the best interpreter at the post—lined up with Custer. "When the fight was on," he later said, "instead of striking the Custer party lightly as was usual, some of the [Crazy Horse Indians] struck their opponents with clubs and war clubs hard blows." Garnett and the others drew their pistols and started shooting; William Clark rushed down a hill "and stopped the firing and prevented what might have been a serious affair."

Despite such undertones, evidence suggests that Crazy Horse tried to get along with old foes. He joined the Indian scouts to serve as mediator with those Lakotas still living away from the Agencies. Many saw him as a yet-unsubdued warrior who'd surrendered to bring peace to his people, but at great personal cost. "The expression of his countenance was one of quiet dignity," said Crook's aide John Bourke, now acting agent at Spotted Tail, "but morose, dogged, tenacious, and melancholy."

Yet his old allies would prove his greatest threat. All that summer, civilian and military officials lobbied Crazy Horse to visit the Great Father, but he always demurred. He'd seen how Red Cloud and Spotted Tail changed after their Washington visits, and hoped to preserve a shred of integrity. But the requests increased, and he realized he must comply. An audience with the Great Father seemed inevitable. He questioned Billy Garnett about white etiquette: How did one use a fork? "He said he had got to do it," Garnett said.

This seemingly benign decision turned the Agencies into a swamp of intrigue. A visit to the Great Father was a sign of respect: with this, both Red Cloud and Spotted Tail feared that Crazy Horse's star would rise too high and he might supplant them. Neither man had anticipated the hero worship forming around Tasunke Witko. As he walked alone among the camps, Indian youths stopped their hoop games. They sympathized with him and disparaged their own leaders. Both old chiefs saw Crazy Horse as a danger as long as he lived.

Rumors began to circulate that Washington was a trap: if Crazy

Horse left the reservation, he would never return. He'd end up in Florida in chains. The source of this rumor remains uncertain: though some have blamed Red Cloud, speculation about imprisonment was common. In 1875, seventy-two prisoners of the Red River War had been jailed at Fort Marion in Saint Augustine, Florida: prisoners included chiefs, warriors, and members of their families. In the 1880s, hundreds of Apache prisoners would be sent there.

Friends and family advised against a visit—Black Elk's father, for one. Because of his injury, the elder Black Elk had become "an inveterate hater of the encroaching whites," said Billy Garnett: possessed of "the same type of spirit as Crazy Horse to whom he would most naturally become endeared through association and sympathy, [he] added his own vicious suggestions . . . [and] repeated substantially the same silly falsehoods." John Provost, an Indian scout married to one of Black Elk's sisters, "likewise had the chief's ear into which he, too, poured the same misleading strain." A Minneconjou uncle, Spotted Crow, seconded both men.

But the person whom Crazy Horse heeded most was a young woman. Eighteen-year-old Helen "Nellie" Larrabee (or Laravie) was the daughter of the French tracker "Long Joe" Larrabee and his Cheyenne wife; she was well-known at Red Cloud and called Ištağiwin, or "Brown Eyes Woman." Crazy Horse fell hard. He courted her openly, visited her house, brought ponies to her father. For her part, Larrabee visited Black Shawl in her tipi and asked her consent to be the war chief's second wife. The ailing Black Shawl said that a new wife might "enliven [Crazy Horse's] spirit," and by midsummer Larrabee moved into Tasunke Witko's lodge.

Garnett painted the eighteen-year-old Larrabee as a siren, and blamed her influence for Crazy Horse's paranoia. When she fixed "her captivating gaze" on the war chief, "disaffection began to assert itself over him," Garnett claimed. "She told him the trip to Washington was a trick to get him out of his country and keep him; that if he went away he would not be allowed to return." Garnett said that both John Provost and the elder Black Elk agreed that he might be "placed upon some island in the sea." Doubtless Crazy Horse expected betrayal at the Agency. He'd never trusted whites, and knew well the machinations of jealous chiefs such as Red Cloud. On August 7, 1877, he told White Hat that "there was no Great Father between him and the Great Spirit" and that he had changed his mind. He would not visit Washington after all. Distrust breeds distrust: Clark admired Crazy Horse, but such sudden recalcitrance convinced him that the war chief endangered the peaceful settlement of the Sioux. Still, he tried one last time and sent Frank Grouard and John Bourke to change his mind. It was not the wisest choice: the Indians despised Grouard. Sitting Bull and Crazy Horse had taken him into their tipis; in payment, he'd led soldiers to them during the wars. He tended to panic, or at least get flustered and not think clearly. Yet Grouard had also accompanied the distraught Crazy Horse to the grave of his daughter and had seen him at his most vulnerable. "Frank is the only one whom Crazy Horse seems at all glad to see," wrote Bourke. When they entered the tipi, Crazy Horse grasped their hands and told them that he'd just woken from a troubling dream. Crazy Horse "was looking for death," said Grouard, "and believed it would soon come for him." In the dream, he'd been standing atop a mountain watching as an eagle soared overhead. It floated alone in the sky, then folded its wings. "The eagle's body fell at his feet and when he looked upon it, it was himself," Grouard said. "An arrow had pierced its body, and its life was gone." The war chief recalled the vision in which it was foretold that no bullet would kill him, yet if ever captured, he would be fatally stabbed. This no longer frightened him, as it had when he was younger. Instead, said Grouard, the dream promised "eternal quietude."

The turmoil around Crazy Horse spread to his own band. Black Elk's father was deeply troubled by events. Close allies such as He Dog and Little Big Man moved closer to the Agency. According to Chips, Crazy Horse and Little Big Man "got in a fight over [a woman] and were never friends again." Given the timing, that woman was probably Nellie Larrabee. He Dog moved closer to relatives, but apparently felt guilty and asked his old friend whether this made them enemies. "I am no white man," Crazy Horse said. "They are the only people that make rules for other people." He laughed. "Camp where you please."

If anything, Crazy Horse retreated into silence. After a while, "he did not want to go anywhere or talk to anyone," He Dog observed. He seemed to realize that his mere presence created discord. Even whites sympathized. After a visit, Major George M. Randall felt sorry for the man. People "talked to him too much," he said. If only "they would let him alone and not 'buzz' him so much, he shall come out all right."

But the buzzing never stopped. He was surrounded by people who would not shut up, who easily took offense, who wanted him to do one thing, who wanted him to do another. The camp seemed equally divided between those who feared and those who revered him. All he longed for was surcease; everybody wanted something from him, but what he had to give was not enough. It would never be enough. There had been a time when the gifts he could give his people were as simple as death or victory. But those days were over, and life was more complex. Everyone had an agenda, and to get what they wanted, many were willing to lie.

In late August, the final, most damaging incident occurred after the Nez Perce left their reservation and headed for Canada. Crook wanted to stop them, and White Hat told Crazy Horse and Touch the Clouds, a Minneconjou chief who may have been the war chief's cousin, to get their men ready. Both chiefs were reluctant but during an August 31 meeting in Clark's quarters agreed to go. But Crazy Horse added a codicil: *first* he would take his warriors on that long-promised buffalo hunt. Then he would track the Nez Perce. When Clark insisted otherwise, Crazy Horse taunted him: "If the white man could not conquer his enemies, he [Crazy Horse] would do it for him."

As the exchange grew heated, Frank Grouard made it worse by repeatedly mistranslating Crazy Horse's words. When Crazy Horse told Clark, "We are tired of war; we came in for peace, but now that the Great Father asks for our help, we will go north and fight until there is not a Nez Perce left," the flustered Grouard translated the final clause as "we will go north and fight until not a white man is left." With this mistake, the room erupted. Clark leapt to his feet; Three Bears, one of Clark's most trusted scouts, roared that if Crazy Horse "wanted to kill anybody, to kill him." Crazy Horse froze: he apparently had no idea what had just happened.

Grouard concluded things were "too hot for him" and left the room. He met Billy Garnett and told him to take over. Garnett saw immediately that Crazy Horse was "not right." Though he corrected Grouard's mistake, Crazy Horse's blood was up. He'd been accused unjustly: the *wasichu* and their Loafers thought him capable of *any* perfidy. Why should he risk his life for such men? He'd changed his mind, he told them: he would *not* fight the Nez Perce. "You are too soft," he snarled at Clark. "You can't fight." He rose and left the room.

The incident cemented the long-held opinion that Crazy Horse would go on the warpath at the least provocation. Sheridan ordered Crook to investigate; Crook arrived on September 2, received a briefing, and called a meeting the next day. He sent gifts and two oxen for a feast. Crazy Horse declined, but apologized through He Dog: "Tell my friend that I thank him and am grateful, but some people over there have said too much. I don't want to talk to them anymore, no good would come of it." Yet he did agree to talk with Crook the next day.

Now the last piece fell into place. On the morning of September 3, as Crook prepared for the meeting, Garnett and the scout Baptiste "Big Bat" Pourier waited outside as escorts when a scout named Woman's Dress walked up and "unraveled a tale which brought the most important affair of the day to sudden pause," Garnett said. Crazy Horse planned to arrive at the meeting with sixty men; he would shake Crook's hand, but hold on firm as his men slaughtered Three Stars and everyone with him. Garnett and Pourier took the scout to Crook, and Woman's Dress repeated the story. Clark advised the general to cancel the meeting; Crook had been the target of an earlier ambush, and so he opted for caution. Crook ordered the arrest of Crazy Horse and then departed for Cheyenne.

Before leaving, however, Crook called a meeting of the principal chiefs: Red Cloud, Little Wound, Young Man Afraid of His Horses, and Crazy Horse's old foe No Water. While Red Cloud and No Water hated Crazy Horse, Young Man Afraid captained the Indian police and hoped to avoid bloodshed. Clark repeated the story, and all seemed surprised. Some proposed killing Crazy Horse on the spot, but Crook said "it would be murder." Instead, Crazy Horse must be jailed. The man who subdued him would receive two hundred dollars and a fine racing pony, he said.

Ten years later, Garnett and Pourier discovered that Woman's Dress was a nephew of Red Cloud and that his story of a murder plot was an elaborate lie. Garnett diplomatically said that the motives lay "in the secret corners and crevices of the human mind," but he clearly suspected Red Cloud. If he was right, the plan worked brilliantly. On the morning of September 4, 1877, eight companies of cavalry, four hundred Indians, and one piece of field artillery—nearly a thousand people—rode the six miles to Crazy Horse's village.

But the war chief and his people had disappeared.

Late that night, Black Elk was wakened from his dreams. "We broke camp . . . without making any noise, and started," he recalled. "My father told me we were going to Spotted Tail's camp," about forty miles to the east, "but he did not tell me why until later. We traveled most of the night and then we camped." They rose early the next day and continued.

Several of Red Cloud's scouts had followed them. They caught up and warned "there would be bad trouble if we did not come back right away," but the majority stayed with Crazy Horse on his flight to Spotted Tail. Black Elk understood that his cousin might feel safer with his uncle; family was a shelter, but Crazy Horse was in for a surprise. A group of Brulés and soldiers awaited the refugees outside the Agency outpost, Camp Sheridan. They escorted Crazy Horse through the gates, where Spotted Tail stood ramrod-straight on the parade ground.

If Crazy Horse expected help, his hopes were dashed immediately. Spotted Tail began screaming before his nephew reined his horse. "We never make trouble here!" he cried. "The sky is clear; the air is still and free from dust. You have come here and you must listen to me and my people! *I am chief here!* We keep the peace! We, the Brulés, do this! They obey ME! Every Indian who comes *here*, must obey me! You say you want to come to this Agency to live peaceably. If you stay here, you must listen to me! That is all!"

Without responding, Crazy Horse dismounted and accompanied Spotted Tail, Touch the Clouds, and a group of officers into the adjutant's office. "Crazy Horse seemed to realize his helplessness" after Spotted Tail's tirade, said Lieutenant Jesse M. Lee, the military agent-in-charge. All of the stuffing seemed to have gone out of him; the depth of his betrayal and isolation was now pitifully clear. He'd come to Spotted Tail to protect his sick wife and because he thought his people could live there in peace. His uncle's outburst caught even the officers by surprise. There was something pathetic in how friends and family abandoned Crazy Horse to save their own skins. Lee turned to Spotted Tail and tried to calm him; he talked softly to Crazy Horse, showing him a respect that had grown increasingly rare. He could not just leave Red Cloud Agency unannounced, Lee explained. Those days were over. But if he would return to Camp Robinson to explain his desire to relocate, Lee would ride along and see that he came to no harm.

They left the next morning, September 5, and arrived at Camp Robinson around 6:00 p.m. Crazy Horse had been accompanied all that day by a small group of friends, including He Dog. Black Elk and his father had ridden ahead and camped outside the Agency. Black Elk watched as the party rode past; Crazy Horse "was riding his horse alone a little way ahead." It was a lonely sight: hundreds, if not thousands, of Oglalas were drifting in throughout the Agency, aware that something momentous was about to occur. They watched in silence as the party rode to Soldiers' Town. "My father and I went along with many others to see what they were going to do."

Yet once there, it was nearly impossible to get close enough to see. "When we got over there, we could not see Crazy Horse," he said. "There were soldiers and Lakota policemen all around where he was and people crowding outside." This was an open camp, not a stockade like the Agency, so hordes of Lakotas pressed onto the outer edges of the crowd. McGillycuddy thought that ten thousand had gathered; more conservative estimates ranged from three thousand to six thousand. The crowd was so dense that few actually witnessed the events of the next few minutes in their entirety; those who saw anything mostly remembered strobic flashes. Most were like Black Elk, too far back, small atoms in the growing crowd.

Few of the participants fully understood the circumstances into which the war chief now strode. During that day, Camp Robinson's commander had received a telegram from Crook: Crazy Horse was to be arrested and sent under armed guard to Fort Laramie. From there, he'd speed by train to the railroad nexus at Omaha, then either to Fort Marion in Saint Augustine or, worse, to America's Devil's Island—the Dry Tortugas, a chain of islands sixty-seven miles west of Key West, Florida. The fears of Nellie Larrabee and Black Elk's father were not fantasies, but a cold, ruthless reality.

Crazy Horse reined his pony. Armed Loafers, whom he knew as foes, and his own supporters filled the parade ground. On the northeast edge, the post commander, Luther P. Bradley, paced his whitewashed veranda; to his left, the two-story officers' quarters overlooked the quadrangle. The adjutant's office and guardhouse, both little more than log cabins, were planted before him in the center of the parade ground.

He Dog reined beside Crazy Horse, cradling his shotgun. Crazy Horse wore beaded moccasins, buckskin leggings, and a white cotton shirt. He'd tied a red blanket around his waist, and under that carried a white-handled revolver in a holster. "You should have listened to me and we could have gone to Washington," He Dog chided. "Instead, you listened to your people lie." He studied the churning mob. "Look out," he said, "watch your step. You are going into a dangerous place."

As Crazy Horse dismounted, a short figure in a red shirt pushed through the crowd. It was Little Big Man, his former lieutenant, but alliances shifted quickly in the toxic politics at Red Cloud. He assumed "a rather superior manner, as though he was running the business," observed the interpreter Louis Bordeaux, who'd ridden beside He Dog. Little Big Man plucked at Crazy Horse's sleeve and snapped, "Come on, you coward!" Crazy Horse seemed irritated, but said nothing, and followed Little Big Man into the adjutant's office.

Jesse Lee was already there, talking to the adjutant, Lieutenant Frederick Calhoun, whose brother had been killed at the Little Bighorn. Crazy Horse must be turned over to the officer of the day, Captain James Kennington, Calhoun demanded. Lee countered that he first wanted to speak to the post commander about Crazy Horse's request for a transfer to his Agency, but when he crossed the parade ground, Commander Bradley was adamant—he had his orders from Crook and Sheridan. Crazy Horse must be placed in the guardhouse for transfer to Omaha and prison.

But Lee persisted. Circumstances had changed, he tried to explain. Crazy Horse had not fled the reservation as originally thought; he'd come to the Spotted Tail Agency for protection. You could not blame a man for that. Bradley did not care: his orders permitted no latitude. When Lee begged for clemency, Bradley snapped that the time for talk was past. Lee returned to the adjutant's office, sickened by how the army could so easily wash its hands of an innocent man by hiding behind the command structure. He gazed at the mob, dreading what might come.

At this point, Crazy Horse was still ignorant of his fate, but the chiefs and subchiefs were being told in twos and threes. Captain Kennington grabbed Crazy Horse by the right hand; Little Big Man grabbed his left. They stepped from the adjutant's office onto the parade ground. Indians were everywhere, all mixed up, friend and foe. As the three stepped out, McGillycuddy pushed up and Crazy Horse greeted him with a friendly *"Hau kola!"* It dawned on the doctor that the famous war chief had still not grasped what was about to happen to him.

Two guards on parade snapped to attention, shouldered their rifles, and fell in behind Crazy Horse. As the little group turned left toward the guardhouse, the mob grew restive.

Black Elk worked his way forward through the crowd. He could not see, but knew that something terrible was happening. Word had spread: Tasunke Witko's supporters streamed into camp on foot, on horseback, and in wagons. "Rescue him!" someone shouted. Several braves surged toward the guardhouse and cocked their rifles, but a group of mounted scouts rode up, hands raised for peace, and the men fell back. The guardhouse door opened, and Crazy Horse, Captain Kennington, and Little Big Man pushed their way inside. Some Indian scouts slipped in next, followed by Chips and Turning Bear. The door slammed behind them.

An officer turned to McGillycuddy and said the arrest had gone smoothly after all.

But in the guardhouse, events unfolded precipitously. Only a few witnessed what happened next, and their accounts were at times confused. One was Lieutenant Henry R. Lemley, the officer of the guard who later talked to Neihardt; Chips and Turning Bear would also be important witnesses. They watched as Crazy Horse was pushed forward; his whole demeanor changed as, for the first time, he realized that he was in the front room of a jailhouse, separated from the cell beyond by an iron door. "What kind of place is this?" he demanded. Turning Bear burst through the guardhouse door and screamed to the parade ground, "It's the jail! It's the jail!"

By then, Crazy Horse had begun to struggle. "I won't go in there," he cried. He grabbed one of Little Big Man's braids, braced his arms against the door, and thrust backward. The red blanket at his waist ripped loose; he reached for the revolver at his hip but a scout knocked it away. He drew a butcher knife, snatched loose Little Big Man's scabbard knife, spun, and dove for the outer door. The space was too tight for bayonets; as Captain Kennington drew his sword, Crazy Horse sprang and sliced the air with both knives. Steel clanged on steel. When a tribesman leapt between them, Crazy Horse used the diversion to dive through the door.

Outside, Black Elk had squirmed close to the front, but still could not see. It was the tightest crowd he'd ever experienced; tribesmen towered above him like granite blocks; the human walls pressed together and it was hard to breathe. Suddenly above it all he heard a voice— "Don't touch me! I am Crazy Horse!"—and he pushed back, growing frantic, beating those around him with his fists, screaming that his power could save his cousin, that they must let him through.

And then . . . all stopped. The parade ground grew quiet. Something went through the crowd "like a big wind that strikes all the trees at once," Black Elk said.

For they witnessed the unthinkable. Little Big Man and Crazy Horse crashed through the guardhouse door, fighting like pit dogs in the arena formed by the crowd. Crazy Horse freed his right hand and cut Little Big Man between the thumb and forefinger of his left; he slashed again, opening a gash on Little Big Man's forearm. Kennington emerged behind them and screamed, "Kill the son of a bitch! Kill the son of a bitch!" Crazy Horse broke from his former lieutenant, cried *"H'gun"*—the warrior's cry for courage—and sprinted for the crowd. But enemies grabbed him and shoved him back toward the jail.

Private William Gentles of F Company, Fourteenth Infantry, stood beside the door at Guard Post Number One. A twenty-year veteran, he assumed the "guard" position when Kennington shouted, thrusting his rifle forward so that the butt lodged tightly against his waist. What happened next has been a subject of debate ever since. Some witnesses swore that Gentles thrust out; others, that Crazy Horse's momentum carried him backward into the triangular bayonet, driving the four-foot blade deep between his kidneys and piercing his intestines. Gentles tugged back, but in the tight space the rifle butt banged against the guardhouse wall. Intentionally or by accident, he delivered a second thrust, this one entering the war chief's right lower back, piercing the ribs and the right lung.

He Dog still stood outside the adjutant's office as his old friend burst through the door. He watched Crazy Horse stagger back after the second thrust; watched as Little Big Man still somehow managed to hang on to his arm. An uncle of Crazy Horse knocked Little Big Man to the ground with his rifle and screamed, "You are always in the way!" Crazy Horse wavered for a moment, then sank to the ground.

It happened in seconds, then silence wrapped the crowd. "I stood there, ready to drop," He Dog recalled, then leapt to the side of his friend. "They have stabbed me," gasped Crazy Horse. "See where I am hurt. I can feel the blood flowing."

He Dog lifted his chief's white shirt even as McGillycuddy rushed up and knelt by the wounded man. Blood trickled from the war chief's right hip; froth oozed from his lips; his pulse dropped rapidly. "I am sorry that man got it as bad as he did," Private Gentles stammered behind them. "It was not my intention. I only wanted to stop him, to make him be still."

Confusion took over. Black Elk asked what had happened, but no one knew: "I heard that Crazy Horse was killed, that he was hurt, that he was sick." He felt the crowd's anger rise around him like that of the

Thunder-beings—mindless, destructive, enraged. "It seemed to me we might all begin fighting right away."

McGillycuddy worked his way to the guardhouse door and told Kennington of Crazy Horse's injuries. But the captain did not care. His orders had been to move the war chief into the guardhouse, and that's what he meant to do. They would carry him inside. As Kennington spoke, American Horse rode up and sat mounted above them. An ally of Red Cloud, American Horse was no friend of Crazy Horse. But he stared at Kennington and spoke simply and clearly. A chief did not die in jail, he said.

American Horse dismounted and spread his blanket on the ground beside Tasunke Witko. He motioned his young men forward; they lifted the blanket and carried Crazy Horse inside the adjutant's office.

He lingered several hours, recalling to his friends the old prophecy that he would be killed if ever taken into custody. In time he descended into delusion, and McGillycuddy injected him with morphine to ease the pain. Someone lit a kerosene lamp, and in the night Worm and his wife arrived. "Son, I am here," he said.

"Father," gasped Crazy Horse, "it is no use to depend on me. I am going to die." He sank back to the floor. His stepmother sobbed. Worm and Touch the Clouds began to cry.

Others came and went during those long hours: Agent Jesse Lee, Post Surgeon Charles E. Munn, the interpreters Louis Bordeaux and Big Bat Pourier, the *akicitas* Spider and White Bird. Worm began his eulogy. Outside, a sentry passed: the melancholy call of "Taps" marked the end of day. At one point, Crazy Horse roused slightly and murmured something. McGillycuddy bent close and thought he heard him say "*Sante wasaku*," the call forward to battle.

At 11:40 p.m., McGillycuddy rose from his crouch and crossed the room. He felt for the war chief's pulse. But there was nothing. Crazy Horse had quietly died.

McGillycuddy's body language conveyed the message without words. The little room grew quiet, then Worm said, "My son is dead without revenging himself." Touch the Clouds stooped over his friend's body and drew the blanket over his face. "It is good," he said softly. "He has looked for death, and it has come."

During the long night, the soldiers made Indians holding vigil leave camp and go home. Black Elk and his father returned to their tipi outside the Agency. "That night I heard mourning somewhere, and then there was more and more mourning." Soon it was all over the camp, all over the reservation, wails and cries like the high lonesome howls of wolves that did not seem to end. McGillycuddy heard it, too: "In some mysterious manner, word of the death of the chief spread in an incredibly short time into the surrounding camp of the Indians, and from miles about arose the death wail, hideously gloomy in the darkness."

Black Elk's cousin was dead. "He was brave and good and wise," he would tell Neihardt. "He never wanted anything but to save his people," and in ways more profound than Black Elk then realized, he modeled himself after the man.

But that would be later. Now there was only heartbreak. "I cried all night," Black Elk said, "and so did my father."

10

GRANDMOTHER'S LAND

Crazy Horse's father made his preparations, then returned at dawn to claim his son's body. A mule-driven ambulance moved in a hush from Camp Robinson, past soldiers and their wives. Worm and his first wife led the way to the Oglala village; two scouts drove the ambulance; a detail of scouts took up the rear. The uncle who'd flattened Little Big Man strode up and leveled his rifle at the drivers, but he was talked from such madness and lowered his gun.

Black Elk watched the procession stop before Worm's tipi. The family stripped and cleaned the body. As kinsmen filed in, Worm said he intended to perform what is called the Ghost Owning or Spirit Keeping ceremony, one of the seven sacred ceremonies handed down by White Buffalo Calf Woman. By so doing, he released his son's soul to the place where it was born; it "need not wander all the earth as is the case with the souls of bad people," Black Elk said. Worm also pledged himself to months of self-denial. He could not commit, nor even witness, an act of violence; he must meditate daily, and his household must be generous with everything. He braided a long lock of his son's hair behind the crown, tied it at both ends, and severed it close to the scalp with a knife purified in sweetgrass smoke. The braid now contained his son's spirit. He purified the lock in the smoke and tied it in a buckskin pouch. He must keep this with him at all times, living in a way that made him worthy to be its keeper.

The family dressed Crazy Horse in his best clothes. At noon, Worm threw back the flap and mourners carried the body outside. Worm announced his son's dying request to be buried at Spotted Tail, a slap in the face to the Oglala. "Red Cloud Agency is not on hallowed ground," Worm cried. The body was bundled in a buffalo robe and laid on a pony drag. Worm took the reins and led the pony through the camp as Black Shawl and other mourners followed.

The next morning, they arrived at Camp Sheridan. On a bluff opposite the post, they built a high scaffold; they laid the body on top, swaddled in a vermilion blanket, and mourned for three days. On September 11, Agent Lee's wife took hot food and coffee to the family; Worm said he feared wandering cattle might upset the scaffold, so Lee and the fort carpenter surrounded it with a fence. Camp Sheridan provided "the best coffin the Quartermaster's department could turn out," Lee later wrote, and on September 13, eight days after his death, Crazy Horse was placed inside. A pipe and tobacco, bow and arrows, loaded carbine and pistol, coffee, sugar, and hard bread were placed beside him. Tasunke Witko's favorite pony was led over the coffin and killed.

But Crazy Horse's journey was not over. Even as the mourning continued, the government threatened the Oglala and Brulé with starvation unless they moved to new Agencies along the Missouri. This was unfinished business from the Treaty of 1868 calling for a single Sioux agency in the Dakotas; in what was becoming a ritual, Red Cloud and Spotted Tail left for Washington to meet with President Rutherford B. Hayes. The president compromised: if the Lakota moved just for the winter where rations had already been stockpiled, the chiefs could choose alternate sites come the spring.

In late October 1877, some eight thousand people pulled up stakes. The Oglalas moved first: on October 25, they massed behind two cavalry companies and headed northeast to the mouth of Yellow Medicine Creek, about fifty miles south of Pierre, South Dakota. Four days later, the Brulés headed east for the former Ponca Indian Agency. The two columns were about a day apart, Black Elk said.

The Black Elks and Crazy Horse's family traveled together, first with the Brulés, then shifting over to the Oglalas. Worm tied his son's coffin to a pony drag and trailed the eight-mile column. Most credible sources, including Black Elk, say that Crazy Horse remained in the coffin for the entire journey. On November 7, a beef issue held for both groups near Butte Cache created such confusion that in the darkness, Worm and his people dragged Crazy Horse away.

Black Elk watched them go. "Nobody followed them," he said. "I can see them going yet." A buckskin pulled the pony drag; Worm rode a white-faced bay with white legs; his wife, a brown mare with her bay colt. They angled back south along the White Clay Valley. It was a small group, only ten: Worm, his two wives, and his widowed sister Big Woman; Black Shawl; two warriors, Kills Enemy and Iron Between Horns; two unidentified boys; and Chips. Nellie Larabee apparently stayed with her parents. After a space, another half-dozen familes followed.

Where did they go? The old people never told where they took the body. "Nobody knows today where he lies," Black Elk said. Though many burial locations were rumored, scholars suspect that most were feints to fool fortune hunters. Worm especially feared treachery. Before Crazy Horse's death, when Crook offered the two-hundred-dollar reward for his capture, whites described the bounty as a "price on his head." Worm misunderstood and thought someone actually wanted his son's skull. Not surprisingly, the hidden grave became the stuff of legends.

But Black Elk had his suspicions. In 1907, Chips would tell the Chadron, Nebraska, newspaper editor Eli S. Ricker that Crazy Horse was buried first on White Horse Creek, then moved south to a place near Caŋkpe Opi Wakpala, or Wounded Knee Creek. Chips helped "put the bones in a black blanket and laid them in a little rock cave" in the bluffs by Beaver Creek; the spot was marked by three weathered limestone pinnacles and concealed by pines and cedars. "It does not matter where his body lies, for it is grass," Black Elk later told Neihardt, "but where his spirit is, it will be good to be."

A feeling of lost opportunity and guilt informed such rumors. In a council held before his death, Tasunke Witko described the vision of the falling eagle and said he would die soon. But if his body was painted head-to-toe in red and then plunged in fresh water, he would return. The five warrior cousins who'd sacrificed blood and flesh to Crazy Horse during the 1877 Sun Dance pledged to do this for him. But they forgot in the confusion and heartbreak following his death, and for long afterward struggled with despair. They'd failed their cousin and their tribe, and were certain that if they'd followed Crazy Horse's instructions, he would have returned.

Yet Crazy Horse had also seen their failure in the dream. All was not lost even then, he said. His spirit would still rise to *Wakan Tanka* and he would not be doomed to wander the earth as a lost soul. But his joints would turn to flint, his bones to hard stone. His skeleton would petrify, just like the ancient monsters frequently unearthed in the Badlands.

———•◦•———

Ten days after Worm's departure, the Black Elks left for Grandmother's Land. By then, the column had slowed to a crawl. Rain, sleet, and snow churned the route into a morass; each night, tipis stretched for three miles. By this time, Sitting Bull's messengers had infiltrated their ranks, promising a better life where *Pte* was abundant and they could live as they pleased. Black Elk's father believed them. Canada represented a chance to regain the glory that had destroyed Custer. It was their final opportunity to be free.

On November 17, one hundred lodges, or about six hundred people, left the Red Cloud column. They left openly, relying upon their numbers and the army's disorganization for their getaway. Though a few moderate Indians and some scouts begged them to stop, the tipis were struck and heralds issued commands. They headed for Cedar Pass, a route north of the Badlands, then traveled fast to the northeast past Slim Buttes, over the Little Missouri and Yellowstone Rivers, swinging wide of Fort Keogh. Sherman and Sheridan were furious, and Black Elk later learned that another hundred lodges followed the first group. In January 1878, they reached what his people called the "Medicine Line" separating the United States from its northern neighbor.

In the 1870s, the Medicine Line was both a physical and a psychological reality. The border at the 49th Parallel originated in the era of the Louisiana Purchase and was ratified in the Treaty of 1818, which clarified border issues after the War of 1812. The portion that most affected Plains Indians ran from the Lake of the Woods in Minnesota west to the Rockies. The area north of the line was historically controlled by fur traders with the Hudson's Bay Company; Indians who lived on the border crossed the line easily to trade furs for hardware, blankets, liquor, and guns. The Hunkpapa were among them: it was easy for Sitting Bull to relocate his people to a land they had long known.

The Medicine Line acquired a physical presence when American and Canadian surveyors platted the border. They erected eight-foot iron pylons along the Minnesota-Manitoba border, and five- to eight-foot stone cairns or mounds of earth every three miles on the line separating Dakota and Montana from the Northwest Territories. No fence or checkpoint connected the points, yet the border still possessed strong medicine. It had the power to stop the U.S. Army.

This was a good place to run. These northern prairies were interspersed with unique highlands that still offered excellent hunting. Though the Sweet Grass Hills and Bear's Paw Mountains dotted the American side, the region's dominant features lay north in Canada. Most notable were the Cypress Hills, a broad upland on the western edge of today's Saskatchewan. This rose 1,900 feet above the prairie and was well watered and timbered. The Cypress Hills were very much like the Black Hills, if on a smaller scale. Wood Mountain rose 160 miles to the east, and between the two stretched a vast, nutritious expanse of shortgrass. In 1878, buffalo still drifted here in considerable numbers, but the Canadian tribes and *Pte* existed in a delicate balance. It would not take much to upset the equilibrium.

Canadian authorities—and specifically, the North-West Mounted Police—worked hard to preserve the peace. The Mounties had come to these western territories two years earlier, in 1875, to extend Canadian law to a region long overrun by American whiskey dealers. Liquor had created chaos among Canadian tribes. The Mounties built the palisaded Fort Welsh in the Cypress Hills and the smaller Wood Mountain Post to the west; to them, preserving the peace meant treating the tribes with respect, which meant honoring treaties. A treaty violation like Custer's Black Hills Expedition would not occur under the Mounties.

Nevertheless, Canada feared this influx of American refugees. Damaged relations with its contentious southern neighbor seemed likely: although no bans were issued, the government in Ottawa preferred that the Sioux stay home. But neither did they want to return them to certain subjugation. A balance must be met. As long as the newcomers kept the peace and did not use Canada as a base for raids into the United States, they could stay. If not, they must go.

The responsibility for maintaining this balance fell to Major James M. Walsh, the Mounties' regional commander. Canadian Indians called him "White Forehead," but Sitting Bull called him "Long Lance" after the red-and-white pennants attached to Mounties' lances on parade. Americans called him "almost Custer-like" in appearance, and he certainly did not lack courage. The first time he met Sitting Bull, Walsh's party of seven rode through the Indian pickets, dismounted, and set up their own camp at the edge of the village. White men had never dared approach this close; Sitting Bull held a council that afternoon. The Hunkpapa prophet recited at length the misdeeds inflicted by Americans on his people; Walsh replied that the Sioux were now in the land of the Great White Mother whose laws protected every person, regardless of color, but also punished those who broke them. The Sioux must obey: any brave who crossed the Medicine Line to kill or steal forfeited all rights of asylum.

Walsh kept his word, and time would prove to Sitting Bull that in the Mounties he had discovered trustworthy white officials. Within weeks, the Mounties were able to exert extraordinary influence over the refugees, yet the presence of Sitting Bull unnerved American officials. They feared Canada would turn into a supply base from which a growing body of Lakotas would one day swoop south and wreak revenge. The Canadians should either adopt the Sioux as their own "or force them back to our side of the line before they recuperate their ponies and collect new supplies of ammunition," Sherman wrote in July 1877. "If the Sioux renewed their war from over the border, it would be the same as if Canada herself had started hostilities."

———•◦•———

In December 1877, as Black Elk made his way to sanctuary, the U.S. Senate asked General Sherman to give an accurate tally of the human and financial costs of the Sioux War. The nation had spent $2,312,531, Sherman reported, or about $52.6 million in 2014 dollars. Sixteen officers had been killed and 2 wounded; 265 enlisted men killed and 122 wounded—for a total of 405 casualties. Later scholarship added interpreters, Indian scouts, and civilians, for a total of 431 killed and wounded.

Sherman did not estimate the costs to the Sioux and Northern Cheyenne. The Senate did not ask for such figures, and Indian casualties were difficult to measure. Soldiers and journalists tended to inflate the number of Indian dead, while Indians themselves rarely kept tallies. Yet modern scholarship, aided by later Indian accounts, gave a figure of 162 recorded dead during seventeen of the twenty-eight Sioux War engagements from March 3, 1876, to July 3, 1877. Another 236 were wounded. Large battles accounted for larger numbers: 36 dead and 63 wounded at the Rosebud; 43 dead and 60 wounded at the Little Bighorn; 40 dead and 80 wounded on November 25, 1876, at the Red Fork of the Powder River, a Cheyenne affair.

Such losses were not devastating: the ratio of army to Indian dead was slightly more than three to one. More insidious and long-lasting were cultural losses. In soldier attacks at Slim Buttes, Powder River, Cedar Creek, Red Fork, and Muddy Creek, Indian possessions were completely destroyed, including religious and cultural finery, family belongings, clothing, utensils, tipis, and food. At Slim Buttes, Crook's men confiscated 175 ponies, more than 5,500 pounds of dried meat, and, according to Captain Anson Mills, "large quantities of dried fruit, robes, ammunition, and arms, and clothing." The pony herd at the Greasy Grass was estimated at 20,000 head: such wealth would never be seen again. When Crazy Horse's band of eight hundred surrendered at Camp Robinson, they relinquished 1,200 ponies. A portion was handed back, but when they fled to Canada they lost it all. Before the war, the Oglala were the most prosperous Indians on the Northern Plains. At war's end, they limped into sanctuary as beggars.

At first, Grandmother's Land seemed a place where the Black Elks could happily end their days. Buffalo were plentiful; the hunting was good. They camped at Freedmen's River, close to the villages of Sitting Bull and Gall. U.S. soldiers could not reach them; they no longer feared dawn raids. As long as they adhered to the law of Long Lance Walsh, there was no reason to return south to the Agencies.

Black Elk thought often about his Great Vision during this time. The Grandfathers had shown him how his people would walk the black road of hardship; how the sacred hoop would break and the flaming tree at its center wither. All had happened just as the Grandfathers said. Now he awaited the second half: the growth of his own power, so he could close the hoop again. He watched for a sign, and kept silent. "What can you do if even Sitting Bull can do nothing?" his people would laugh if he revealed anything to them.

By now, a pattern had formed: his concerns for his people were often attended by visions or voices. And trouble was brewing again. In the spring of 1878, more Lakotas crossed the border, peaking the exiles at five hundred lodges, of which forty-five were Nez Perce. This translated into more than three thousand refugees. Beginning with that spring, the hunt for the Canadian bison turned a corner, creating a pressure that led to its virtual extinction a few years before that of its American cousin. As the herds dwindled, Canadian Indians blamed the Sioux.

That spring, Black Elk was big enough to ride with the men. One day he rode alone with his uncle Running Horse in search of *Pte*. The two crossed a creek when suddenly Black Elk felt the strange sensation that often preceded danger. "I have a queer feeling that something is going to happen today," he told his uncle. "It has been told to me that it will happen, so, you shall chase the buffalo alone and I'll not hunt. You just get one." They should make quick work of butchering and then leave.

His uncle gazed at him. It was the first time he'd made such a pronouncement to anyone but his father. Though the Lakota professed belief in the power of visions, their appearance still seemed to take them by surprise. Though few people said it, Black Elk's caution suggests that visions were professed too often and loosely. Their "truth" was scrutinized. In an era of radical change, many hoped to be touched by the gods. One could either buy such pronouncements at face value, or adopt a wait-and-see attitude. Running Horse seemed inclined toward the latter.

They came to a ridge and spotted bison grazing in the valley below. Black Elk held the two pack horses while his uncle charged down the hill and felled a fat cow. Black Elk rode up and helped butcher it, but something made him nervous and he kept the horses close. They were nearly finished when he thought he heard a voice: "Raise your head!"

Running Horse noticed Black Elk's discomfort and suspected that all was not well. "Nephew, get on your horse and get up on that hill and look," he said. "I feel something."

Black Elk rode to the crest and watched as two hunters in the next valley over chased a buffalo herd toward a bluff. Just as they rode out of sight, his horse pricked up its ears and sniffed the air. He heard three shots, then the sound of galloping horses—then even more gunfire. He galloped back to his uncle. They'd loaded some meat when two more shots rang over the hill. They backtracked fast; when they reached the opposite ridge, they saw behind them fifty to sixty members of the Canadian branch of the Crow. "*Unnley!*" one yelled—which meant they'd killed and scalped the two riders. Black Elk and his uncle galloped home, warning other hunters they passed. Running Horse told everyone what had happened. "This showed that my power was growing," said Black Elk, "and I was glad."

The voices found him again in June 1878. Sitting Bull and Gall held a Sun Dance—the second since they'd come to Canada—and afterward the Black Elks went hunting along Freedmen's River. That month, he turned fifteen and increasingly did his part to protect and provide for his family. Running Horse had apparently taken a leading role: he told Black Elk and Iron Tail, the herald's son, to kill a buffalo and return with just the fat while the rest broke camp. The two ran one down and butchered it, but when they turned back thunderclouds swept up and the rain poured. Out of the storm Black Elk seemed to hear a voice: "Make haste! Before the day is out, something will happen."

He told Iron Tail. They did not hesitate, leaving everything behind but the fat and riding hard through the rain. They returned and told everyone to flee. By now, Black Elk's people apparently believed his predictions. They finished breaking camp and forded Freedmen's River, but the rain had swollen the watercourse and the horses mired in the mud. And now the foretold threat materialized—the Crow, in greater numbers than the Black Elks could survive. The Crows shrieked and fired from the far bank as the Oglalas straggled across. Black Elk stayed with the rear guard, firing blindly at the enemy.

Finally all had made it across except for an old couple and their beautiful daughter; their travois had mired mid-river. A warrior named Brave Wolf jumped from his horse, lifted the girl on its back, and told her to ride. The old man dropped in his tracks from a bullet; the current carried him downstream. Brave Wolf told the old woman to stand behind him. He stood his ground in the middle of the river, but the Crows overwhelmed him and both were cut down.

Now Black Elk's cousin Hard to Hit turned back. This was both brave and suicidal; he was selling his life to buy time for the clan. Black Elk called out to stop—too many cousins were dying—but before he could lift a hand Hard to Hit charged at the Crows. One warrior took aim from a nearby bush. Hard to Hit and the Crow fired simultaneously, and both fell dead.

That left Black Elk at the tail end of his band. The rest of his people had made it atop a knoll; it was a great defensive position, but they still needed time to dig in. Only Black Elk stood between his family and the enemy. He jumped off his horse and hid in some brush; he cocked his rifle and peered through the rainfall, ready to sell himself dearly. Someday his people would sing of his bravery. He awaited the onslaught, but where were the Crows? Time dragged on; he tried to stay alert in the cold rain.

And then . . . he woke. What had happened? He jumped up, confused. If the Crows had been around, they would have killed him. But *no one* was around. The Crows had vanished from the river plain; his people were gone from the hill. His little pony hobbled toward him—at least *he* had waited. He must have passed out from adrenaline and exhaustion: both sides decided they'd had enough and melted from the field of battle, leaving him in the rain between them, snoozing peacefully.

At times such as this, Black Elk seemed to realize that if he *were* going to make a mark, it would not be as a great warrior. It wasn't that he lacked courage; rather, he just seemed hapless sometimes. Some men seem destined for greatness; others, for absurdity, at least in their own eyes. It would surprise no one when a few years later he became a *heyoka*, or sacred clown, a divinely chosen court jester who lampooned the pretenses of a rigid society.

But first he must survive this most confusing day. He'd finally gotten his bearings and started to follow his people's tracks when he heard crying. He crept close and peered over the hill. In a bush crouched the wife of his slain cousin Hard to Hit, moaning. Wives often stayed behind to mourn the deaths of their husbands; they would cut themselves like religious penitents, mix their sadness with blood, then reappear in camp without warning. It was her duty to mourn and his duty to protect her, but he feared that the Crows might still be close enough to hear her sobs. He told her to be quiet, but she kept moaning; he helped her on her horse and led her off as quietly as he could. Suddenly her sobs stopped.

"There are some men coming," she said.

How did she know? How could anyone hear or see *anything* in this rain? He jumped off his pony, grabbed both halters, and led them forward, but it was too dark to see. Lightning flashed, revealing what looked like ten men riding toward their hill. If he'd seen them, they'd seen him; they were coming too fast to be outridden. If he hadn't been killed when he'd dropped asleep, he surely would be now. He turned to his cousin's widow and told her to hang on to the side of her horse in case she had to sprint off. He grabbed his six-shooter and rifle. He had one slim advantage, and that was the dark: the approaching riders could not tell how many stood against them. If he started shooting wildly, they might think he was legion and turn away.

So he stood his ground. By now he could hear their horses; their shadows began to take shape. He did not recognize them, so surely they must be enemy. Luckily, they were a little more savvy—and calm— than the frightened fifteen-year-old standing before them. They were friendly Nez Perces, whom the Lakota called Cut-Noses, and they recognized him from camp. They were exiles, too, remnants of Chief Joseph's tribe. They joked with the mud-covered teenager and asked whether he had enough bullets to kill them all. Where were he and the young woman headed? they asked, then graciously escorted them back to their band.

When they returned, everyone wrapped their arms around one another and commenced to mourn. It was custom that Black Elk must mourn for the fallen all day. But he was very tired. It might have been the longest day he ever remembered. *"Howanh, howanh,"* he wailed. "My cousin, he thought lots of me and I thought lots of him." But now he was dead. Crying all day could not bring his cousin back, but it was expected and if he did not do so, he brought shame on his family. "I had to do it," he groused, "all day."

———•◦•———

The attacks by the Crow were just the beginning. By the winter of 1878–79, it was obvious that the exiles and the Canadian Indians would compete for the dwindling supply of food. The Canadian tribes begged the Mounties to send the refugees back over the border—but it was something they would not do. New rivalries sprang up; old ones renewed. On October 10, 1878, a party of Assiniboines surprised some Sioux south of the Cypress Hills, killing eight. In January 1878, a party of Assiniboines or Gros Ventres stole fifty-nine Sioux horses. In February 1879, the Assiniboines attacked six Lakotas on the Milk River, killing all but one. The Sioux struck back, and by mid-May 1879, four Gros Ventres and two Assiniboines were slain.

That summer of 1879, the first Oglala and Brulé exiles began heading back south, barely one year after fleeing to Grandmother's Land. Hunger trumped everything, and the shortage of buffalo had caught up with them. They left alone or in small groups: relatives had sent word that they'd moved to their new Agencies south of the White River. The Red Cloud Agency was renamed Pine Ridge; Spotted Tail was Rosebud. Four smaller Agencies stretched north to south: Standing Rock, Cheyenne River, Lower Brulé, and Crow Creek.

But the Black Elks stayed in Grandmother's Land during the autumn of 1879, into Black Elk's sixteenth year. Fighting between the Crow and Lakota continued; skirmishes spread to the Blackfeet and Piegan. But famine was deadlier than the raids. The blizzards seemed endless; the

dried meat was all eaten up; the game disappeared. Small hunting parties dispersed to all points, and one day Black Elk and his father started
out alone. They made a shelter with their buffalo robes against the bank
of Little River Creek and lit a small fire. Black Elk spotted a rabbit run
into a hollow tree; he trudged over, chopped down the tree, and found
four rabbits huddled inside. The snow was too deep for them to escape;
he felt sorry, but his father and he were starving and he killed all four.
Father and son roasted and ate them before they went to bed.

The wind died that night and Black Elk listened to the still, crisp
world around him. It was easy to imagine they were the last Lakotas. He
listened to the regular breathing of his father as he slept, to the slight
susurration of the trees. Fairly close a coyote howled, as if it talked to
him: "Two-legged one, on the big ridge west of you there are bison." But
before he found them, he was told, he would encounter two people.

He woke his father and repeated what the coyote said. By now, his
father realized that his son had "some kind of queer power." His promised
powers had not yet budded, but *something* was working in him, something his family accepted. He needed to accept it as patiently as they.

At daybreak, the wind rose again. They started west, as the voice
directed, but could see only a few feet ahead. They crested a ridge and
spotted two horses below, their heads hung down, their tails to the wind.
They stood beside some brush, and as Black Elk drew close he could
make out a small shelter of buffalo robes. A boy and his grandfather
huddled inside, Lakotas from another band: they'd come out two days
earlier, but with no luck. Now they were losing strength, and in such
circumstances people died. They coaxed them up the ridge to a deeper
stand of timber that would at least shelter them from the wind: all the
two could talk about was their hunger and their starving kin. Sometimes,
when Black Elk heard the wind abate, he crept to the edge of the timber.
The whiteout conditions would lift in these brief periods and he could
see for miles. But there was still no sign of buffalo. He saw only white,
endless miles of white, stretching into the distance until the white sky
and white hills merged.

How long they stayed in that cold camp was never said. The haze
would lift, then close, again and again. Suddenly it lifted and Black Elk
spotted a dark blot against the white. As he watched, it formed into the
shaggy head of a bull buffalo emerging from the draw they'd struggled
up to reach this stand of timber. Seven more bison trudged slowly behind
the bull. Then the wind picked up and white covered the distance—but

now this could be an advantage. If he could not see the bison, they could not see him. Since they drifted with the wind behind them, there was no danger that they would catch his scent on the breeze.

It was just as the voice seemed to tell him: first they found the tribesmen, then the buffalo. The four gave thanks, then mounted their horses and rode to the mouth of the draw; the bison would have to pass this point if they continued before the wind. The two older men would shoot as they trudged past; then Black Elk and the boy would chase down the wounded. The older men fired, but hit only one. "*Huka!*" they cried, the signal to follow. The boys emerged from hiding just as the herd backtracked, and Black Elk charged after the bellowing herd.

But there was a problem with this plan. The white haze was so thick he could not see in front of him; a dark bulk appeared, then disappeared in an explosion of snow. The entire herd had plunged into a snow-filled gulch, and Black Elk and his pony dropped in right behind them. Luckily, the packed snow cushioned their fall. But that was little comfort when he found himself surrounded by four floundering bison and his pony, all kicking and thrashing wildly. He pulled his carbine from its scabbard and managed to back off a little, firing repeatedly until the four bison were down. But in the excitement, he'd thrown off his mittens; he now discovered that the gun had frozen to his hands. He was forced to rip it free, tearing off the top layer of skin.

He clawed from the gully and found that the other boy had killed the remaining three bison. All lay dead in the snow. His father and the old man butchered the animals; Black Elk could do nothing, since his torn hands were frozen and raw. They had time to butcher only four before the cold became too much: they placed the meat in a cache, built a shelter, and made a big fire. They cooked some of the meat and fed cottonwood bark to the horses. Night fell suddenly, as it does in the north; they fed the fire and their hunger all night long. They expected wolves with so much meat, but their only visitors were a lost mob of porcupines whimpering from the cold. They huddled as close as they dared to the far side of the fire, and the humans left them alone. By morning, the porcupines were gone.

The next day was spent butchering the remaining buffalo. They stayed one more night, divided the meat evenly, and set off for their separate villages. It took two days for Black Elk and his father to return. His people rejoiced when they saw so much meat, and the kill probably saved their small band.

That brutal winter accomplished what the Canadian tribes and the U.S. Army both failed to do. In 1880, the Lakota began to head south for home. By the end of April, more than 1,100 Lakotas had come to Fort Peck and surrendered their horses and guns.

Black Elk's band held on as long as possible, but their numbers had dwindled to the point where it was foolish to go on. Only two families remained in their group, with nine adults between them. Three of these were men—Black Elk, his father, and a medicine man named Chased by Spiders; the six women included Black Elk's mother and probably Hard to Hit's widow. No children were mentioned, so we do not know whether Black Elk's two younger brothers survived the brutal winter. The two lodges counted five horses between them: all others had died in the snow or been eaten. They'd leave Grandmother's Land as paupers, and if they were attacked on the way they'd be easily overrun and killed.

In early May 1880, two years and four months after arrival, Black Elk and his family once again crossed the Medicine Line. They would surrender at a fort, and this time, surrender would be final. They were out of options. There were no other places to run. By turning south, they turned away finally from the last illusion of freedom represented by Grandmother's Land.

11

THE FEAR

In May 1880, as Black Elk's family trudged south from Wood Mountain, the United States was entering the decade when the frontier died. Its official obituary would not be written until a decade later, first by the 1890 census, then more famously by the scholar Frederick Jackson Turner, whose 1893 "The Significance of the Frontier in American History" asserted that the wilderness shaped the nation: one saw in the long march west the evolution of attitudes, practices, and institutions that defined everything American. Yet by the time Turner published his thesis, the frontier had already begun to fade. By 1887, the cattle drive—the soul of the cowboy mystique—had vanished: cattlemen had learned that the tough and hardy longhorn could survive the Northern Plains, obviating the need for long cattle drives. This was the decade of barbed wire: although invented in 1874, it began to be used in the 1880s to enclose huge tracts of land, ending the image of the "open" range. By 1880, almost every single Indian in the United States lived on a reservation; that year, as Black Elk crept home, nearly sixteen thousand Lakotas lived on the remnants of the Great Sioux Reserve.

In 1880, the American activist Helen Hunt Jackson put the finishing touches on *A Century of Dishonor*, her chronicle of the government's legacy of broken treaties with seven Indian tribes. Within a year of its 1881 publication, the book helped create the powerful and often misguided Indian Rights Association; although the term "Vanishing

American" had surfaced previously, Jackson's book gave it wings. "It makes little difference," she wrote, "where one opens the record of the history of the Indians; every page and every year has its dark stain. The story of one tribe is the story of all, varied only by the differences of time and place; but neither time nor place makes any difference in the main facts. Colorado is as greedy and unjust in 1880 as was Georgia in 1830, and Ohio in 1795; and the United States Government breaks promises now as deftly as then, and with an added ingenuity from long practice."

———·•·———

The flight to surrender proved nearly as deadly as the struggle to stay free.

The first worry was the Blackfeet, an ancient enemy. The two families in Black Elk's group moved slowly—easy prey. Fort Peak, the closest Soldiers' Town, lay sixty miles south at present-day Poplar, Montana; they made their first U.S. camp at a place called All Gone Tree Creek, halfway between the fort and the border. There'd once been a stand of timber, but the soldiers cut it down—thus, the name. Black Elk did not like this place: it was too open, too vulnerable. As he grazed their five remaining horses, the voice again came to him. "Be careful and watch. You shall see."

Though he did not understand the warning, the voice had saved them several times already and he knew to take heed. He staked the horses and studied a tall bluff with two high, horn-like points rising a short distance away. He climbed to the highest point, settled among some boulders, and gazed over the grasslands. He saw their tipis; the women lighting cookfires with wet wood. A few cottony clouds scudded across the sky. It worried him when he heard the voice but saw no threat, as if he'd simply made it up. People were known to do that. Sometimes he feared he was crazy; other times, a desperate boy.

Then something moved—just barely, behind the other point, lower down. He froze. In a minute he saw two men crawl forward on their bellies; Blackfeet! he realized. Many Blackfeet in this region were aligned with the powerful chief Crowfoot, with whom Sitting Bull had sued for peace several times. But peace never gelled. The Blackfeet were the most vocal in blaming *Pte*'s disappearance on the newcomers; in 1879, Crowfoot begged the Canadians to "drive away the Sioux, and make a hole so that the Buffalo can come in." This had not happened, and soon both tribes preyed upon each other just as they did upon *Pte*.

Black Elk watched as the two studied his band. One peeped over the rocks and motioned his comrade forward. If he moved an inch, they would see him. If he had his rifle, he could end the threat, but he'd left it in the tipi. They crawled down backward, ran downhill, and disappeared. Their intent was clear. He crawled down the opposite side, sat for a second at the bottom, and prayed for guidance. He ran back to the tipis and reported his sighting.

They all had to flee immediately, he said. They could not take the time to strike the tents: they could only take horses and the bare essentials. They traveled fast until they hit a roaring creek, swollen with the rains. Black Elk and another swam across, hanging fast to rawhide ropes; the old people tied themselves to the other ends and the young men pulled them through the deep water. Others climbed atop horses; the young and healthy swam across on their own.

As they fled, a thundercloud slid up from behind. The sky blackened; lightning flashed inside the cloud. Black Elk heard the cry of thunderbirds. Gunfire erupted from their camp: the Blackfeet had probably surrounded the tipis and started shooting, thinking they were inside. They ran until the cloud moved on; by then, they were far enough away that there was no danger of being seen. He wondered if the thundercloud had come to save his family; if so, it was the first time one of his prayers had been answered. They camped on the prairie that night, but Black Elk was not afraid. The next morning, they continued to Soldiers' Town.

Fort Peak had just that year become an Agency. There was a trading post, which Sitting Bull had visited before crossing into Canada, and two villages—Minneconjou and Assiniboine. They made uneasy neighbors, quick to anger, prone to revenge. In their exhaustion, the Black Elks camped close to the Assiniboines.

Instead of welcoming the newcomers, the tribe surrounded them with drawn guns. The Black Elks had walked into an intertribal rivalry that demanded vengeance. Before they'd arrived, two Lakotas had been killed for unexplained reasons; an Assiniboine of the Brave Hearts, an important warrior society, blackened his face, walked to the Minneconjou camp, and admitted killing the men. So the Minneconjous stabbed him. As he died, he sang his Brave Heart song: "Friends, difficulties I seek. Difficulties I have now." He took one more step and added, "Friends, I was an Indian, too. You should not have done this to me." Then he toppled and died.

Why the Assiniboines thought the Black Elks had anything to do with this fracas is hard to fathom. Most likely, they did not think at all. The Black Elks were newcomers without nearby family; if they happened to die in the blood debt, no one would mourn or demand reprisals. At the last moment, a small Assiniboine man wearing a red blanket said the band was Oglala, not Minneconjou. They had nothing to do with this madness, not even by blood. They should be fed instead. The Black Elks ate and slept as hospitality warranted, but decided it was safer among the Minneconjous.

It was not long before they decided that nowhere was safe in Fort Peak. The next morning, they joined some Minneconjous heading south to Fort Keogh. This journey became for Black Elk a symbolic nightmare. They rode to where the Poplar met the Missouri and crossed over on a paddlewheeler. He joined three others for a hunt; they bagged a buffalo and some deer, and the next morning headed back. On the way they witnessed something that convinced him that more than just the world of man was falling apart. Nature itself was out of joint. Chaos reigned. They'd happened upon three male buffalo challenging an older bull with a cow. One by one, the young males charged their elder and butted heads; one by one, they died. It was as if the challengers willingly threw themselves to their deaths, yet the lengthy battle took its toll. After the last challenger died, the old bull groaned and fell to the dirt, mortally injured.

Black Elk's companions seemed as distressed as he. Like the Lakota, the buffalo belonged to a tribe—the "buffalo nation." But the four had murdered one another. The Lakota term for murder, *ti wicakte*, meant "he kills his home," and the "worst thing to an Indian is murder" within the tribe, Black Elk said. In murder, two deaths occurred: the death of the body and the death of one upon whom others relied. The Brave Heart's last words at Fort Peak—"Friends, I was an Indian, too"— evoked the same relationships. Black Elk remembered the murder of Crazy Horse: though a soldier's bayonet had pierced his cousin, it had been guided by family and friends. It was a betrayal of trust, the glue that had made their nation strong.

But now that trust had failed. His people killed one another in an endless cycle, just like the four buffalo who threw themselves to their deaths. The *wasichu* had truly won.

He rode back to his family, depressed and confused. If others accepted the chaos, must he accept it, too? The Grandfathers had given him a calling—a Vision of how things were *supposed* to be. But how does one reconcile the harsh world of the flesh with that of the spirit? How does one navigate darkness without becoming tainted, too?

He could see now that the days of the warrior were ending, and once he surrendered at Fort Keogh, his chances of ever becoming a warrior would also end. Though he'd been in battle, he'd never authentically counted coup. True, he'd scalped the dying at the Greasy Grass, but there was no honor in that, no chance to show his bravery to his tribe.

Once, on a hunting trip, he spied six unfamiliar warriors through his spyglass and told his friends that he planned to count coup. The older men laughed: he realized that even as he longed for things that he'd never experience, they longed for things they would never experience again. "Take courage," one said, "there are only six and if we try we will probably get all of them."

Then the older men charged. As the youngest and smallest, he was told to stay back and hold the horses, even if it had been his idea. When he heard firing, he no longer cared. He jumped upon his horse and charged. "I made up my mind that I was going to coup the first one [even] if I got killed doing it," he said. "I thought it would be a great honor and I really wanted an honor very much." He charged into the confusion and dust, and had couped two men when he came out the other side.

This was good, he thought. His mother would sing for him, as she had at the Greasy Grass. His father would be proud. His party wheeled for a second pass, but then pulled up. One older man started laughing. The "enemy" had been Lakota. He'd couped two Sioux.

———•———

Although the coup episode was humorous, it reflected the ambiguity of the changing Sioux world. The tribe was the basis of one's identity, but a world in which that identity could be so easily mistaken was one that was disintegrating. The older men treated it as a joke, but Black Elk saw it as an indication of worse things. The only other time this kind of misidentification occurs in *Black Elk Speaks* or the transcripts is Standing Bear's account of mistakenly scalping the body of a fellow Sioux during the chaos of Last Stand Hill. Both of them reacted with shock: such things did not happen in an ordered world. Standing Bear simply left the scene, but Black Elk tended to see meaning where others did not. As he had done in the past, he reacted spiritually. He would say later, "A terrible time began for me then."

In June 1880, the Black Elks finally made it to Fort Keogh, 125 miles south of Fort Peak, where they surrendered to Bear Coat Miles. Soldiers took their guns and horses, then returned two horses per lodge. They moved three miles downriver and camped with some Cheyenne friends. This was a more peaceful place than Fort Peak, and they stayed here nearly a year.

It was wild country still. Small-scale skirmishes between soldiers and renegades were not rare. On March 8, 1880, a battle with the Sioux forty miles west of the fort ended with the capture of the tribe's livestock; on April 1, a battle near O'Fallon's Creek resulted in the surrender of five Lakotas, the capture of forty horses, and the death of a sergeant in the Second Cavalry. On May 27, two men were killed at a stage station on the Bismarck–to–Fort Keogh mail line, both shot through the head. A month after Black Elk surrendered, another stage driver was killed.

Even so, the region had "civilized" since Black Elk roamed here as a child. By 1880, Miles City had grown up outside the fort, and it had everything that made the West notorious: cowboys, liquor, gambling, girls. According to the March 13, 1880, *Yellowstone Journal*, the population was 550, served by one church and twenty-three saloons. The construction of saloons outpaced that of churches: by 1881, there would be forty-three saloons, and they served one thousand bottles of beer a day. The ladies, though accommodating, "were certainly not beautiful." When the soldiers were not fighting Indians, they fought townsmen, one another, and cowboys. "A row in which about 30 men, mostly soldiers, engaged in, occurred in Frank Reese's dance hall on Thursday night," ran a typical news item: "Broken glass, chairs, tables, etc., were strewn promiscuously around, and had it not been for the prompt appearance of the officers, loss of life might have resulted."

Nevertheless, a measure of tribal independence remained outside the fort, at least for those Lakotas who endured and survived. The temperatures fluctuated between −40 degrees Fahrenheit in the winter and 110 degrees Fahrenheit in the summer; the wind could be brutal, transforming into thunderstorms, microbursts, and hail. Such weather killed livestock like an abattoir. Each spring, ranchers found skeletons of cattle lodged in tree branches six feet up, the level of that winter's snowfall. There were creeks where, it was said, one could walk end to end on cattle bones. Yet game was still plentiful, a boon for the Indians: they hunted mule and whitetail deer, elk, antelope, and even a few buffalo. Coyotes prowled the country; mountain lions preyed on the ranches.

That June, Black Elk turned seventeen. He had not yet fulfilled any commands of the Grandfathers, yet he believed that their prophecies were coming true. The voices had not abandoned him; they spoke in times of need. They'd led his father and him to big game twice when his people were hungry. They'd warned him of approaching enemies, allowing his people time to escape slaughter at their hands.

Yet he always felt a sense of failure, of never being good enough. He was too small, too sick, too frail, too young. He had not performed his duty to his people, had not worked the medicine that would turn his Great Vision into flesh. In June, soon after his band's surrender, a Sun Dance was held at the Agency. When it was over, all he could think about was his Great Vision and how he did not know what the Grandfathers expected of him.

Signs of his failure were everywhere. Before daybreak he would leave the tipi, afraid of the stillness when everyone else slept. As the sky lightened, low voices murmured in the east. The daybreak star would sing:

> In this manner you shall walk!
> Your nation shall behold you!

The coyotes and crows called in the day and night: "It is time! It is time!"

But time for what? He did not know. Flocks of birds twittered en masse, "It is time! It is time!" He thought he was going mad. He was assailed by countless voices, but could tell no one, not even his parents; he could not bear to be around anyone who might bear witness to his disintegration. He rode far from camp to compare everything in the earth and sky with the world of his Vision and finally understood why Crazy Horse chose to live by himself in the wilderness. The four-leggeds and the birds would see him riding and shout and warble to one another in mockery. "Behold him! Behold him!" they cried.

Modern psychiatry would call the voices "auditory hallucinations," a common sign of schizophrenia, and even Black Elk would concede he was slipping into a psychic chaos entirely new to him. But in the Lakota world, such voices came from without, not within; they were considered not a sign of advancing insanity, but dire warnings from the spirit world.

Yet the warnings were so loud, so constant, so *insistent* that they filled his mind to the exclusion of all else—and in the process drove him a little mad.

The unease only grew worse whenever he saw a cloud. At such times, Thunder-beings called. Lightning and thunder terrified him. The storms were no longer a haven; now they hunted him. When the Grandfathers found him, he would be destroyed.

He prayed for relief with the first frosts of autumn, a signal that storms would abate until spring. But he was wrong. Sometimes the crying of the coyotes at night terrified him to the point where he ran from one tipi to another until he finally collapsed from exhaustion and into oblivion. Maybe he *was* going crazy, and he would live out his days like the madwoman on Crazy Woman Creek, whom all feared. His parents were distraught: "It is the strange sickness he had the time when we gave the horse to Whirlwind Chaser for curing him," they told others. It had not helped. He had not been permanently cured.

Then came the spring storms. Just as the grass showed its face, a cloud blew up and cried "*Oo! Oohey!*" A pronouncement was being made. "It is time," declared the voices. "It is time!" And he would run all night long from lodge to lodge, screaming for release, for interpretation, for understanding, until finally he passed out from fear and pain.

By then, his mother and father could take no more. They sent for an old medicine man named after the path of suffering—Black Road. They suggested he ask Black Elk if he'd ever had a vision. If he had, perhaps Black Road could deliver him from a life of fear.

So Black Road isolated Black Elk in his tipi and asked what troubled him. In the past, Black Elk would dissemble at this question, fearing people would think he was crazy or sought attention like a child. Now, he no longer cared. He was afraid. Afraid of everything, of being afraid of everything, and he could not go on. He broke down and told Black Road his Great Vision in its entirety—from the moment the cloud messengers appeared to the gifts of the Six Grandfathers; from the vision of the dancing horses to the battle with the water spirit; from the breaking of the sacred hoop to the gift of the deadly and merciless soldier weed. Now his people were dying and the Grandfathers demanded action, yet they never said what or how. Now the Thunder-beings spoke, and if he did not act soon he knew a horrible death awaited.

All this time, Black Road's eyes grew wide. He'd expected a simple malady, not something so . . . profound. "Ahh," he finally sighed. "Nephew,

I know what the trouble is. You must do what the bay horse in your vision wanted you to do." He must perform for his people on earth the Horse Dance, as he had seen it performed in his fever dream. Only by such reenactment could he save himself. "Then the fear will leave you, but if you do not do this, something very bad will happen to you."

By prescribing this, Black Road saddled Black Elk with both a cure and a curse. If the boy replicated the equine spectacle, he might save himself and his people. If not, he would be annihilated by the Thunder-beings. Yet on the surface, Black Elk's visionary dance seemed impossible to stage. Today, a dancer garbed in horsehair mane and tail steps forward and back like a prancing stallion. A 1931 Horse Dance described by Black Elk's nephew Frank Fools Crow involved a charge and dance by four riders on four horses, performed against a backdrop of thunder and lightning. That was impressive enough, but Black Elk's vision of spirit horses was cinematic in scope: forty-eight black, white, sorrel, and buckskin horses, with manes of lightning and thunder, dancing in place and leading "great clouds of horses, of all colors" that stretched as far as the eye could see. How could such a vision be reproduced? It seemed destined to fail.

And even then, Black Road did not tell him the whole truth—a terrifying truth he would have known. When Black Elk spoke of hearing the Thunder-beings, this was *wakan* indeed. To dream of thunder was to be imbued with the highest power, yet it bestowed a responsibility both difficult and frightening. Crazy Horse had been a thunder dreamer, and look what happened to him. He must act "anti-natural"—not unnatural or abnormal so much as consciously *opposed* to Nature, as if mocking the known world. Some thunder dreamers became sacred clowns, but there was nothing funny about it. Many led a lonely existence, avoided and ridiculed. Only the strongest commanded reverence.

And all died alone.

12

DANCES WITH THUNDER

When Black Road gave his troubled patient the seemingly impossible task of re-creating the Horse Dance, he knew that life for the Sioux had irrevocably changed. The return from Canada was the expression of a profound truth: the unconquerable Lakota had been conquered. After decades of treaties, bribes, broken promises, and war, the *wasichu* had finally corralled them on reservations. They must live there or perish. No other choice remained.

With 1880, a new kind of war began—a subtle and insidious war for identity, one still being waged today. The U.S. government would endeavor to obliterate all that made the Indian "Indian"—and religion lay at the heart of that struggle. If the Indian as an entity was dying out, salvation meant replacing his soul with that of his conqueror. Men like Black Elk, Black Road, Frank Fools Crow, and other *wicasa wakan* would be central to the struggle, though at first they only felt it instinctively. As late as 1969, as *Black Elk Speaks* experienced a countercultural rebirth, the Siouan social critic Vine Deloria, Jr., would assert that "Indian religion appears to many of us as the only ultimate salvation for the Indian people." Although the term in greater modern use would be "identity," on the reservation that and religion were often the same.

Despite the victories at the Rosebud and the Greasy Grass, it was now painfully apparent that the Lakota would not be saved by military means. Their most brilliant military strategist had been murdered; too many warriors had been killed or wounded; the nation had been ground down by years of total war. Earthly means of power had failed them. Another source was necessary.

To understand what would take shape in Sioux culture over the next decade—and how Black Elk fit into it—one must grapple with the Lakota concept of power. As Black Elk would one day tell a disciple, one found power in truth, and that truth was "the oneness of all things." To the Lakota, Nature could be neither fully known nor controlled; the best a man could hope was to venerate Nature's power, then use it to the best of his abilities. Man could not stand apart from Nature, for he was part of it; though his role was to understand vast forces, he could never realistically seek to dominate them. One dared not stand above and outside Nature's sacred hoop, for such a stance was the arrogance of fools. Since one could exist only inside the hoop, one must try to direct the flow of power from *within*. If anything, said the modern holy man John Fire Lame Deer, such an approach was "a way of looking at and understanding this earth, a sense of what it is all about." It was, above all else, "a state of mind."

After decades of fighting the army, the Sioux had come to suspect that this was the basic difference between the *wasichu* and them. Time had proved that the *wasichu* were human enough, not the maleficent spirits some feared during the tribewide debates of 1864. They bled like human beings, died like human beings, ran like cowards or fought as bravely as any warrior. Their parts were the same: they even bred and bore children by Lakota squaws.

The difference lay in the way they approached Nature: in essence, how they attained power. They stood *outside* the hoop and sought dominion. Their trains and fire-boats, guns and gunpowder, talking wires strung across the prairie—none were of this world. They might hail from forces teased from Nature, but none existed naturally. The consequences could be devastating: look what they had done to the buffalo. A people that could destroy something as limitless as *Pte* could destroy anything.

The Lakota, on the other hand, tried to work within Nature. To them, *Wakan Tanka*—understood generally as the "power of the universe"— could not be isolated from the natural world. No separation existed between the sacred and the secular. Every object had a spirit, called *tonwan*; thus, every object was holy, or *wakan*. Find a way to use *tonwan* and one found the power to do *wakan* things.

It was the shamans who tapped such power. The Lakota called them *wicasa wakan*; whites, "the *wakan* man." Every Lakota individual sought spiritual power to some extent, usually through vision quests and dreams; such power could lend an advantage in battle, hunting, or healing. The shaman, on the other hand, was distinguished and separated from the rest of society by the intensity of his experiences. There were all kinds of healers; the shaman healed, too, but on a grander scale. He specialized in the trance in which his soul left his body and journeyed across the spirit world. He went to the very source of *Wakan Tanka*. Most cultures had a myth or belief that a time once existed when a bridge spanned the gulf between heaven and earth, and communication was common between men and gods. But something happened and the connection crumbled. The *wicasa wakan* could reestablish connection. He was the bridge.

Throughout Plains tribes—in fact, throughout the world—similarities existed in how shamans were "made." Guides such as Black Road knew what to look for in the young. The first hint of power often came in a dream state that resembled death; after a time, the dreamer was resurrected. In his dream, he encountered divine messengers that escorted him to an animal guide, which in turn took him to the Center of the World. There he found the World Tree, guarded by the Cosmic Lord, who bestowed upon him some kind of innate power or handed him a powerful tool.

All this had been manifested in Black Elk, yet a certain timing was still necessary. The first signs of power often appeared with maturity. Among the Yakut of Siberia, the future shaman grew frenzied, lost consciousness, withdrew to the forest, flung himself into fire or water, slashed himself with knives—just like Black Elk when thunder called. The family appealed to an old shaman, as the Black Elks did to Black Road; the shaman attempted to teach the sufferer that this was merely a stage. Thus began his apprenticeship. Black Elk must learn the names and attributes of the various *tonwan*, how to summon and control them. Though merely a start, such steps brought relief. They showed the initiate that he was going through a process—and not going crazy. Initiation was the cure.

———•·•———

In the spring of 1881, Black Elk was seventeen. The winter had been harsh; many Sioux horses froze to death, and with the first thaws more

Lakotas crossed the Medicine Line. Even Sitting Bull's lieutenants Crow King and Gall came south to surrender. They arrived almost daily—tiny, battered bands. When Black Road ordered the staging of the Horse Dance as a kind of therapy, the cure was not for Black Elk alone. His people needed hope. Black Elk had the same inkling. All that winter, the voices whispered: "It is time."

Black Road made his plans. He asked for help from an ancient medicine man named Bear Sings, who was apparently a kind of holy stage manager of complex religious rituals. Both knew this would be an important affair. In a culture and time devoid of almost every other form of mass communication or entertainment, a ritual dance fulfilled several purposes. At the simplest level it was fun—the drums, the voices, the dancers in their costumes and paint, all added up to a kind of theater that could best be described as spectacle. If done right, it would be exhilarating.

But more than that, it spoke to them. Many scholars believe that dance was humanity's first "high art"; it was narrative, imagistic, musical, emotive, aesthetic, and, if carried to extremes, hypnotic. The dancers wove inner nature and Nature together in an inseparable tapestry; if the dance was the representation of a shaman's Great Vision, the spectators gazed straight through his eyes into the mind of God.

An event such as Black Elk's Horse Dance was part of a social movement that had moved slowly east from the Pacific Northwest since the mid-1870s. "Dream Dances" were first chronicled in Oregon tribes in 1875. If a man experienced a powerful dream, he must sing of it in front of others or he would sicken and possibly die. Simple songs evolved into song-and-dance, changing from narrative to performance. If a dream dance was good, people from other tribes would hear about it and come to watch. There would be food and fun. Chiefs would build dance houses and invite dancers from other tribes. Local amateur dream-dancers would serve as warm-up acts, followed by the featured performer. In at least one case in Oregon in the 1880s, a chief charged admission for imported dancers.

Thus, Black Elk's dance was an anticipated event: the audience would have expectations. If this was indeed a dream of true power, as the medicine men said, then it must meet and exceed cultural standards—just like a blockbuster movie today. For such an event, a special venue was required. Black Road and Bear Sings created a camp circle a little distance from Fort Keogh, and in its center erected a sacred tipi of bison hide. On the hide they painted pictures from the Great Vision—animals representing the four cardinal directions, Black Elk's sacred gifts, a rainbow painted over the door. It took the entire day to do this, during which time Black Elk fasted. That evening, they told him to dress in his regalia and come to the painted tipi. They asked if he'd heard any songs during his Vision; if he had, he must teach them to them. He remembered several songs from his eleven-day coma, so it took all night to teach Black Road and Bear Sings.

Meanwhile, Black Elk's mother and father helped prepare. They rounded up sixteen horses—four black ones to represent the western powers; four white for the north; four sorrels for the east; and four buckskins for the south—each with a young rider. They purchased a bay horse for Black Elk, just as he'd ridden in his Vision. They asked "four of the most beautiful maidens in the village" to take part, and enlisted six very old men to portray the Grandfathers.

On the morning of the dance, the two sponsors sent a crier through Fort Keogh's various campsites, telling the people to camp that day in a large circle around the sacred tipi. From later descriptions it sounds as if several hundred Lakotas arrived. Black Elk spent the day alone in the sweat lodge, then was joined by his mentors. They practiced the songs from Black Elk's Vision.

Now it was time for the dancers to prepare. As Bear Sings and Black Road repeated the songs, Black Elk, the four virgins, the sixteen horses and their sixteen riders faced the sacred tipi. Black Elk was painted entirely in red, with black lightning on his limbs; he wore a black mask, and a single eagle feather lay across his forehead, reminiscent of Tasunke Witko before battle. Black Elk's bay had bright streaks of lightning painted on his legs, and across his back, on the rider's seat, a spotted eagle with outstretched wings. The four virgins braided their hair, wore red dresses, and painted their faces red; each wore a sage wreath pierced with an eagle feather. The black-horse riders were painted black with blue lightning stripes and white hail on their hips; the white-horse riders, white with red streaks and plumes of horse hair; the sorrel riders, red with black streaks; the buckskin riders, yellow streaked with black lightning. Every horse was also streaked with white lightning. Black Elk gazed at the horses and riders when they were painted. They looked beautiful, "but they looked fearful too."

By now it was evening, and tension was building. The horses were the first indication. The riders would sing a vision song as they faced the tipi and were painted; as they sang, the sixteen horses neighed and pawed the earth. Suddenly, horses in the surrounding camp also neighed, as if in reply. The Lakotas had begun to gather in a wide circle. Swift breezes swept through the camp. Black Elk looked to the west and could see thunderclouds.

Black Elk and the maidens entered the tipi to confront the Grandfathers. The old men had been busy. They'd drawn a circle in the dirt, and two roads crossed the circle: a red road of holiness running north and south, while east to west ran the black road of suffering. At each point they'd placed symbols of the Grandfathers' gifts; the four girls took their places and lifted the representations. By doing so, they "held in their hands the life of the nation." Black Elk carried a red-painted stick representing the sacred arrow given to him by the Sixth Grandfather. This held the power of life and death itself, "the power of the thunder beings."

The dance began. All exited the tipi and took their places outside, the riders to their points, the maidens to theirs. The drums began to throb; the Six Grandfathers took their place in the center, by Black Elk's horse, and chanted their sacred songs. As they sang, each troop of horses wheeled in place and came to stand, four abreast, before the Grandfathers. Black Elk mounted his bay. They all faced west, toward the thunder, and pranced in place; the bay reared up and pranced to the sound of the song.

Now strange things occurred. The whole village was on horseback as they watched, and as the inner circle of performers wheeled and sang, so did the outer circle of spectators, wheels within wheels. But when the dancers in the inner circle faced west toward the storm, a silence fell over all. Silence seemed to cover the earth, except for low thunder, and Black Elk improvised. He held out his hand and cried four times, "Hey-a-a-hey!" The Grandfathers pitched in, and suddenly his bay horse pricked up its ears. It raised its tail, pawed the earth, and neighed long and loud to the approaching storm. The other horses in the inner circle answered, then the horses in the outer circle, those in the village still tied up, even those beyond—grazing in the valley and on the surrounding hills. They raised their heads and neighed together, as the millions had done in his Vision. His eyes pierced the clouds and he saw the world of his Vision—the cloud tipi sewn with lightning, the flaming-rainbow door, the one million cloud horses dancing. There he was again, outside the holy lodge, once again astride the thunderous bay.

He gazed about him and it was as Crazy Horse had once said. "What we were then doing," he realized, "was like a shadow cast upon the earth from yonder vision in the heavens, so bright it was and clear." Reality lay in the clouds and the heavens. Darker dreams lay here.

His Vision faded, and in its place the storm rushed upon them with lightning in the forefront and the voices of gods growling inside. Split-tail swallows swooped above the dance circle and past, fleeing the storm. People ran through the village to tie down their tipis. "I, myself, made them fear," sang the black-horse riders, raising their voices above the rolling drums, pitting their voices against the wind:

> Myself I wore an eagle relic.
> I, myself, made them fear.
> I, myself, made them fear.

And the storm appeared to listen. The hail and rain came down in sheets, but the edge of the storm stopped short of the village and instead they received a light sprinkling and cool breeze. The anvil-shaped cloud loomed motionless, roaring internally all the way to the summit but advancing no farther upon the village, as if the Thunder-beings had come to watch and were gladdened by what they saw.

Surely it was a sign! The universe celebrated, and now the people did, too. Four times the riders and their horses wheeled around the circle, crying *"Hey-hey! Hey-hey!"* Four times they visited the sacred points, and more villagers hopped on their horses and spun with the dancers, a great wheel rotating tighter and tighter until finally the entire camp was a wheel of prancing ponies and others dancing afoot, all singing Black Elk's words. In the end, the horses charged the sacred tipi and the riders screamed *"Hoka hey!"* His horse plunged in like the rest, but many were ahead of him, coup sticks *thwap*ing the painted bison skin.

The Horse Dance was over. Black Elk dismounted, but seemed to float above the ground. People crowded about him to tell how before the dance their relatives had felt sick, but had now been mysteriously cured. They pressed on him little gifts, and he felt a power grow inside; his people looked healthier and even the horses seemed happier. His fear of thunder vanished; instead, it seemed like family, and he was glad when storm clouds came. Medicine men from the several camps came to talk, fascinated and amazed by his dreams.

He was at peace, a peace he had not known for a very long time. He would wake before dawn and go out to await the appearance of the daybreak star. Soon others learned what he was doing and rose with him. They'd sit on the prairie and watch the eastern sky turn from black to purple, with thin streaks of turquoise. They watched in silence, as if awaiting a miracle.

Then it rose, as it always would. "Behold the star of wisdom," they said.

PART III

THE MESSIAH
WILL COME AGAIN

My father told me the earth was getting old and worn out, and the people getting bad, and that I was to renew everything as it used to be, and make it better. —Wovoka, "The Messiah"

I am coming! —Placard for the 1889 Paris opening of Buffalo Bill's Wild West

13

THE LAND OF DARKNESS

In late June 1881, after the Horse Dance, the Black Elks and other Lakotas at Fort Keogh—in all, 2,766 Sioux—were sent by steamboat down the Missouri to Fort Yates in the Standing Rock Agency. This was to be the home of the Hunkpapa; those whose tribes had settled at other Agencies were encouraged to return to their people. That summer, Black Elk and three friends talked about returning south to the new Oglala and Brulé Agencies along the White Clay River. He was nearing eighteen, and this would be the first time he'd ever left his family.

As they prepared to depart, they learned that Sitting Bull and 186 followers had left Canada to surrender on July 19 at Fort Buford, the closest American post to the border. They arrived like beggars: Sitting Bull's clothing was ragged, and a calico handkerchief covered an infected eye. "Let it be known that I am the last one of my tribe to surrender my rifle," he said as he handed over his Winchester.

At first it was thought that the great chief would return to Standing Rock with his people; that may have been why Black Elk lingered. He had not seen Sitting Bull since leaving Grandmother's Land. Like many Lakotas, he held the seer in awe. Black Elk's powers were growing, and he probably hoped for a chance to "talk shop" with the famous holy man. But it was not to be. Soon after surrendering, Sitting Bull heard that the promised amnesty would not apply to him. He was sent to Fort

Randall, farther down the Missouri, where he would stay two years as a prisoner of war.

Black Elk and the others left in early September for a 232-mile journey home. They traveled a week, averaging 33 miles a day. They walked, since the soldiers had taken their ponies, and hunted with bows and arrows, since the soldiers had taken their guns.

Much had changed in the four years since Black Elk slipped into Grandmother's Land. The winnowing of the Great Sioux Reserve had begun. When the Teton lost the wars of 1876–77, they'd relinquished the Powder River Country and the Black Hills. During his stay, the United States altered the reservation's western boundary from the 104th to the 103rd meridian. A 50-mile strip of land abutting the Black Hills was sliced off, as well as a lush triangle between the forks of the Cheyenne River. All that remained of Black Elk's childhood paradise was an anvil-shaped block—35,000 square miles between the 103rd meridian and the Missouri River that had been deemed virtually worthless by surveyors.

The "Great Dakota Boom" had started in 1878, the year after Black Elk fled, and would last a decade. The 1877 Black Hills "agreement" carved a wedge out of Paha Sapa that soon filled up with miners and settlers. Deadwood was its economic center, a narrow strip of saloons, brothels, opium dens, and outfitters, named either for the dead trees crowding both sides of the gulch or for the discards in a poker game. Murder was rife; justice, unequal; smallpox and syphilis, widespread. The place that once represented the Lakota Good Life now spelled death for any foolish enough to visit.

To feed the miners, cattlemen moved their herds into the grassy foothills between the Cheyenne and Belle Fourche Rivers; the range filtered north of the Black Hills and west into the Yellowstone Valley. The buffalo were gone; in their place grazed hundreds of thousands of Texas longhorns, a fierce breed adept at goring cowboys with their four-foot horns. They were skinny and dusty, their dun-colored hides splotched or ringed in red, yellow, cream, or mulberry blue. Where *Pte's* meat was streaked with fat, the longhorn's was stringy, but they were the Lakotas' rations when the Agencies held their "beef issue" days.

Cattle ranching had become big business in the Dakotas. As Black Elk walked south, he crossed the ranches of eastern and European investors who'd realized that a Great Plains cleared of buffalo and Indians meant millions of acres of nearly free grassland. A series of wet years east of the Missouri had turned the prairie verdant; what had been tan and sere was now green. The new money included English lords, Scottish linen magnates, Boston bank presidents, and lawyers from Edinburgh. As refrigerated steamships opened Europe to American beef, more investors arrived: a book titled *The Beef Bonanza: Or, How to Get Rich on the Plains* by General James S. Brisbin claimed that an investment in cattle would double in five years and pay an annual dividend of at least 10 percent. By 1884, three years after Black Elk's journey south, foreign investors controlled more than twenty million acres of Plains ranchland.

Open land not claimed by cattlemen was promised to homesteaders. The Homestead Act of 1862 stated that on surveyed but unclaimed public land, a citizen or immigrant intending to become a citizen could claim 160 acres—a "quarter section"—and own it outright after residing and improving upon it for five years. A nation of independent farmers should create a strong republic, an idea as old as the nation and one that became the driving philosophical force behind "Americanizing" the Indian. But the idea would prove disastrous for both whites and Native Americans: the Northern Plains was a region where animals and Indians had traveled hundreds of miles in search of food; where water was precious, and the extremes of climate destroyed crops indiscriminately. Before the decade was over, abandoned farmsteads and sod houses dotted the landscape like lost buttons, mute testament to the homesteaders who went broke, lost their crops to grasshoppers, or watched them wither in the sun. They sold their farms and left, something Indians shackled to reservations could not do.

The new invaders followed the railroad. The Panic of 1873 had finally subsided; railroad promoters looked to develop the Black Hills and the western lands beyond. By 1879, graders for the Northern Pacific pushed west from Bismarck across the Missouri. To the south, the Chicago & Northwestern and Chicago, Milwaukee & St. Paul railroads aimed for Lakota lands. In 1870, all of the Dakota Territory had held fewer than 5,000 *wasichus*. In 1880, 17,000 whites mined gold in the Black Hills while another 117,000 crowded the borders, awaiting the chance to stream in.

Black Elk would have seen much of this as he walked south with his friends—the empty sod houses, dangerous longhorns, strands of barbed wire, abandoned windmills clacking in the breeze. Near the beginning of their trip, the four crossed the Grand River and camped for the night;

they discovered a plum bush heavy with ripe fruit—a lucky find, since this would be their only source of food for the entire journey. A small hill bordered the camp and Black Elk climbed to its crest. He sat and faced west "as though I waited to see somebody."

The evening was warm and still, and it seemed as if the entire world awaited a message. He rose and sang the first song from his Vision, sung by the spirit messengers. As he did so, he seemed to see them again in the west, flying straight toward him. It was as if they'd listened for his call. As before, they pointed their bows and arrows at him, but he was not afraid. They came to a halt and floated upright, bows raised overhead; though they stared in silence, he knew what they wanted. It was time: he must do his duty. Then they turned back, streaking into the sun.

His friends asked what he'd seen. They knew of his power and had heard his song. He answered, "I was only singing to some people I know in the outer world."

They traveled south to the new homes of the Oglala and Brulé. After their 1878 return from the Missouri, the people of Red Cloud and Spotted Tail had settled at the Reserve's southern edge, jammed against the northern border of Nebraska. The Oglala moved to the southwest corner at Wazi Ahanhan, or Pine Ridge. The Brulé settled east along the Little White River and called their Agency the Rosebud.

Black Elk's little band first came to Rosebud. They crossed a plateau that plummeted into a deep valley intersected by a small stream and surrounded by sand hills. The agent's house rose upon one of these hills; tipis and pony herds spread out in every direction. Though a pastoral vision, the Agency was in turmoil. Peace had not come with the move from the Missouri. The Brulé patriarch Spotted Tail had been murdered a month earlier.

There was something Shakespearian in Spotted Tail's fate: he'd grown imperious and greedy, as if the almost absolute power granted by the *wasichu* had corrupted him. His treatment of Crazy Horse was a harbinger. He walked around the Agency with a loaded Winchester to intimidate rivals and "brooked no opposition," the agent noted in his report. He used the Indian police to settle old scores, and was accused, probably falsely, of accepting bribes from the railroads. On August 5, while Black Elk and his friends still lingered at Standing Rock, the captain of the Indian police, Crow Dog, publicly accused Spotted Tail of stealing another man's wife. On a lonely road two miles out of town, the two men pulled their guns. Crow Dog fired first, killing Spotted Tail. Now he lingered in prison at Deadwood, awaiting trial.

Black Elk and his companions arrived at Rosebud during the mourning period. His friends stayed with their kin, but Black Elk moved on. He rode west past Spotted Tail's home, a three-story palace that cost the government five thousand dollars and proved such a source of jealousy that many believed it the real cause of the chief's murder. Now it perched atop a hill overlooking the Agency, stripped of furniture, abandoned. He averted his eyes as he rode past. "I came on alone."

———

He rode at a leisurely pace over the hills separating Rosebud from Pine Ridge. At first, it seemed that he'd gone back in time; that he'd come to a land where his people were nomads again. He saw small clusters of tipis pitched beside the narrow creeks or in the shelter of white limestone buttes; passed small groups of Oglalas on horseback, rifles balanced on their saddle bows. Their bare heads were decorated with feathers or trinkets, their faces striped in white or spotted in vermilion and ocher. But these were not war parties, just scouts looking for stray ponies. He greeted old friends and rode on.

Soon this impression changed. He rode through a plain of gray sand and yellow grass; from its center rose Agency headquarters, also called Pine Ridge Village. Tipis grew thick; children peeped shyly from inside. Traders' stores clustered around the main gate: old men in blankets lounged outside. He entered the stockade enclosing the agent's house, hospital, and ration office. A cross-crowned Episcopal church stood beside them on the dusty street. Mixed-blood residents and whites entered its doors.

From the start, Pine Ridge Agency was a testament to contention. Boundaries were not officially set until 1889, but were generally understood as running from the Rosebud to the east, the foothills of Paha Sapa in the west, the Nebraska line to the south, and to the north, the lunar Badlands. The Agency was named after a great ridge of pines that lay in northern Nebraska; it was *not* named after Red Cloud, since Washington sought to diminish the importance of chiefs, nor after the tribe, since no one could spell "Oglala." Headquarters lay two miles north of the Nebraska line: Red Cloud had already set up camp here when the government got around to choosing an operations center, and he refused to move. The Oglalas called the Agency *owákpamni*, or "Distribution Place," but due to an error in transcription, John Neihardt would call it "the Place Where Everything Is Disputed." The error would prove as true as anything else in the Agency's troubled history.

One thing that Pine Ridge was *not* was farmland, a problem for a philosophical construct determined to turn former warriors into "yeoman farmers." Of Pine Ridge's 2.2 million acres of land, only 84,000 acres, or 3.8 percent, was arable. Like the rest of the Upper Plains, the "normal" climate was one of extremes—hot, cold, dry, or stormy, punctuated by blizzards, floods, droughts, and lightning-sparked fires. The higher elevations in the Agency's northern section were covered with windblown sand and soda ash; the south was prairie grassland, more favorable for grazing than for farming, broken by white-faced buttes, dotted with cedars and yellow pines. Like everything else in reservation life, Pine Ridge was a limbo. Ecologists call it a transitional zone, located between the moist tall-grass prairie of the east and the arid short-grass prairie of the west. One crosses a ridge of ankle-high grass into a valley where it grows to the waist. Then it flattens to a pancake vista where grass crunches under one's heels.

The reservation's most eerie feature lies in the north: Mako Sica— the Badlands. Where one goes *up* into the mountains, one goes *down* into the Badlands, a grand basin of white, soapy sediment twenty-five miles wide by one hundred miles long. The remnant of an ancient sea sixty million years old, it would erode over the millennia into a labyrinth of great perpendicular peaks, mammoth white cones, minarets, and deep ravines. It is a secluded place where silence reigns; a gnarled wall, forty-five to fifty miles long, forms the north border, and few passes allow access between high and low ground. Bear, deer, and mountain sheep inhabit the gorges, but hunting them is nearly impossible. Deer or sheep shot on a narrow peak fall off the opposite side. Bears lurk in the cedar thickets; they spring on the hunter before he knows he is doomed.

The Agency was in flux when Black Elk arrived. In 1881, its Oglala population stood at about 4,800, largely composed of the clans that had returned with Red Cloud from the Missouri. According to the historian George Hyde, the population would swell in a year to 7,202, a 150 percent increase that was either an accounting error or the result of far-flung Oglalas such as Black Elk drifting home. From 1878 to 1880, most Lakotas lived within a short ride of the Agency village, yet as the numbers increased they settled with their *tiyospaye* along the narrow, wooded waterways. The White River flowed from west to east, and several narrow creeks flowed north into the river: Big White Clay Creek, Wounded Knee, Porcupine, Medicine, Pumpkin, Corn, Bear Run, Eagle Nest, and Pass. On a map, these creeks resemble the thin tines of a comb. The tipi clusters perched along them evolved into small communities, then districts, each supervised by a subagent, or "Farmer," the first line in "civilizing" the Indian. He was aided in this grand purpose by an assistant, some Indian police, and any missionaries who settled nearby.

Like everyone else, Black Elk first pitched his lodge in sight of the Agency. The winter of 1881–82 was hard, "just like one long night, with me lying awake, waiting and waiting and waiting for daybreak." But dawn never came. Thunderstorms ended with the frosts, and the Thunder-beings who felt like his "relatives" departed until the spring storms. Without their power, Black Elk felt lost and alone. Few of his people at Pine Ridge had been present for the Fort Keogh Horse Dance, so few knew of his power and Vision. They all seemed "heavy and dark," and moved through their new lives like sleepwalkers.

He discovered quickly that life had no meaning here. Existence boiled down to the bimonthly distribution of rations. Every Indian family received a ration ticket printed on heavy paper: the lower third proclaimed the dates for collecting food and clothing; a number scrawled in an upper corner indicated the number of individuals covered by the card. Once the visit was complete, the date was punched with a cross-shaped hole.

Though some Oglalas tried to imitate whites, the attempt was killing them. A few erected the square houses of which the Cheyenne prophet Sweet Medicine warned; they moved into these first log cabins in hopes that the simple act of doing so would give them more power. Yet the one-room houses were cramped, low, dark, and dank; the air was stuffy compared with that of a tipi, whose wind flaps managed airflow. Germs bred in the dirt floors and closed space, the tuberculosis bacillus especially; soon the coughing sickness swept through every *tiyospaye* and the death rate increased. For many, death seemed more hopeful than life. "Am I to die?" was a common deathbed retort. "Good! So much the sooner I can see my grandmother again!"

The old ways were being discarded even as Black Elk returned. The Sioux had been defeated militarily, and now the government waged economic, social, and political war. The old approach of isolating Native Americans on nearly worthless land had not solved the "Indian problem."

Now the solution was more complex: the government believed that the only way to save the Indian was to turn him into a white man.

Thus, the 1880s would be an era of banned folkways and new rules, an almost titular faith in the power of regulation and law to remake humanity. Government was the sculptor; the Indian, the clay; the School, Church, and Farm, the tools. Life in the modern world would be defined for the Oglala by the death of their ancient identity. By dint of what he practiced—and later sought to preserve—Black Elk would become a criminal.

The process of change started in earnest two years before Black Elk's return, with the advent of the new agent-in-charge. The four-year appointment paid $1,500 annually, and corruption was the norm. Popular wisdom held that new agents arrived at their sinecures men of modest means and, thanks to graft and kickbacks, left wealthy. They brought with them a small army of "whisky-sellers, bar-room loungers, debauchers," all beholden for their positions, lamented Bishop Whipple of Minnesota in a letter to President Lincoln. "It needs more than one honest man to watch one Indian Agent," Lincoln replied.

Valentine Trant McGillycuddy was the opposite—an honest but intractable man. After standing vigil over the dying Crazy Horse in 1877, then in 1878 watching a band of imprisoned Cheyennes under Dull Knife escape Camp Robinson and try to fight their way home to Montana, McGillycuddy complained in Washington about the treatment of the Indians. The new secretary of the interior, Carl Schurz, was so impressed by the post surgeon that to everyone's surprise he appointed him agent-in-charge of Pine Ridge.

McGillycuddy was convinced the Indians were dying out, and their only salvation lay in Washington's plans for assimilation. When he arrived at Pine Ridge on March 10, 1879, his mustache had grown longer and more rigid, the great inverted "V" favored by cavalry officers of the day. It was a badge of status and rank, and the Oglala immediately recalled his nickname "Little Whiskers." They also remembered him as Tasunke Witko Kola, or "Crazy Horse's Friend."

The latter, to Red Cloud, was not endearing, and the two clashed at their very first meeting. Two narratives exist: in the Indian version, Red Cloud told his subchiefs to listen to their new Father, while the agent's account paints Red Cloud as an impediment from the opening line: "I am Red Cloud, the great warrior chief of the Oglalas. When Red Cloud speaks, everybody listens. I have not asked you white men to come here." McGillycuddy describes his own response as more politic: he desired Red Cloud's assistance, but would go to younger chiefs if it was not forthcoming. The days of handouts were over, he said: the future lay in farming the fertile valleys of Pine Ridge.

Not surprisingly, Red Cloud was not happy. It took no great insight to see that this meant an end to the rations and annuities promised in the treaty negotiated at the end of *his* war. He rose from his seat and laid out the gulf between the Lakota and *wasichu* views of the future. "Father," he said, "the Great Spirit did not make us to work. He made us to hunt and fish. He gave us the great prairies and hills and covered them with buffalo, deer, and antelope. He filled the rivers and streams with fish. The white man can work if he wants to, but the Great Spirit did not make us to work. The white man owes us a living for the lands he has taken from us." Tilling the soil was women's work, and besides, the 1868 treaty promised rations without labor for another seventeen or eighteen years.

True, conceded McGillycuddy, but the winds were changing in Washington. For the moment, however, he let Red Cloud's objections stand. He had a bigger purpose—the establishment of a mounted police force composed entirely of Indians. He proposed hiring fifty men and giving them uniforms and guns; they would answer to the agent, and replace the army as the Agency's principal lawmen.

With these words, Red Cloud immediately understood that what had started as a discussion of the future was really a bid for power. In the past, agents were paper tigers, their only power a vague threat of withheld rations. Red Cloud liked the status quo. Pine Ridge had no need of such a force, he countered, since his *akicitas* kept the peace already.

McGillycuddy now showed he could be as strong-willed as Red Cloud. Without a police force, he said, the agent had no way to enforce federal regulations. With one, he could evict liquor peddlers, drive out horse thieves and cattle rustlers, and arrest white fugitives and other lawbreakers. He could bring order where there was chaos, yet failed to mention an equal purpose: social control. A native policeman wore a white man's uniform, lived in a frame house, and earned a monthly salary at a time when his fellows lived off government rations. Such status and income could be a powerful "civilizing" influence, and the officer could be a major force in ending traditional practices such as dancing, polygamy, and the power of the medicine men.

Yet even friendly chiefs resisted the native police, and it seemed at first that Red Cloud had won this initial test of wills. In the face of this impasse, McGillycuddy proposed other expedients he hoped would modernize his Oglala, and in the process sway subchiefs and younger tribesmen to his side. He introduced stock-raising, which showed early promise as an alternative to farming: the Sioux took good care of their cattle, and preferred ranching to plowing and weeding. And he encouraged hauling freight, because Lakota freighters could work for less than the local teamsters.

Yet both expedients hit a snag. Obsessed with the idea of farming, the government never sent enough breeding stock to allow Lakotas to compete with surrounding white ranchers. And politically connected freighters put an end to the idea of Indian competition.

These impediments were not McGillycuddy's fault; in fact, he showed himself more open to new ideas than his superiors in Washington. Given more patience and a little luck, he might have set "his" Oglala on a successful course toward self-sufficiency. Yet sit him opposite Red Cloud and his wants, and this broad-mindedness disappeared. The two brought out the worst in each other: where compromise could have formed a partnership that eased the Oglala into the twentieth century, these two powerful personalities created a legacy of distrust that remains today. Red Cloud would cede no power; in response, an angry McGillycuddy demanded slavish adherence to Washington.

Within a year of McGillycuddy's arrival, the Pine Ridge Lakota were divided into two camps: the "progressives," who believed that salvation lay in cooperation with whites; and the "non-progressives," determined at all costs to hang on to the "old ways." The progressives were led by American Horse and Young Man Afraid of His Horses, both notable warriors during the Indian wars; the non-progressives, by Red Cloud, Little Wound, and Big Road, the leader of Black Elk's band.

If McGillycuddy made one great mistake, it was that he changed too much, too soon. Ever since the eighteenth century, reformers had seen education as the ultimate solution to the "Indian problem," but it was not until 1879 that the federally run Carlisle Indian Industrial School came into being. The nation's first, it would be the model for the Bureau of Indian Affairs' twenty-five boarding schools built across fifteen states and territories by 1902. Carlisle inhabited an abandoned army barracks in the same Pennsylvania town as the U.S. Army War College; the school's founder, the Civil War veteran Captain Richard Henry Pratt, created what he proclaimed to be a social experiment to remove native children from their parents, teach them English, put them in uniform, and force them to live by military protocols. Such "assimilation through total immersion" was the only way to break tribal bonds, he preached, a strategy derived from the belief in the plasticity of all men. Since the Indian was "born a blank like the rest of us," assimilation should be easy, Pratt said. In an 1892 speech he summed up his philosophy in three famous lines: "A great general has said that the only good Indian is a dead one. In a sense, I agree with the sentiment, but only in this: that all the Indian there is in the race should be dead. Kill the Indian in him and save the man."

Thus, Sherman's call to kill the Indian to save the West evolved into Pratt's and the government's dictum to kill the "Indian inside" to save the Indian. It was a faith that would reign in the Indian Office for the next fifty years. About a month after McGillycuddy's first meeting with Red Cloud, Pratt visited the Agencies to recruit children for his new school. He was big-nosed, self-assured, and stern; he visited Rosebud first and persuaded Spotted Tail to enroll four children and two grandchildren. Red Cloud was more stubborn, but did allow Pratt to recruit Oglala children. In the end, Pratt took a total of sixty boys and twenty-four girls from both Agencies, leaving behind anguished parents who feared they would lose their children forever.

The wisest course for McGillycuddy after something so wrenching would have been a compromise, even a slight one. But not so. On April 29, 1879, the Catholic father Meinrad McCarthy arrived with a letter from the "Father Superior of the Benedictine Missions among the Dakotas," asking to build a mission at Pine Ridge. Red Cloud had often asked for Catholic priests: ever since the early work of the Belgian Jesuit Pierre-Jean De Smet, many Oglalas preferred Catholic to Protestant missionaries. They called them *Sina Sapa*, the "Black Robes," after their long black soutanes, and saw them as *wasichu* medicine men.

McGillycuddy sensed that a Catholic mission would be well received. Its appeal "for the red man [was] greater than any other form of worship," he told Father McCarthy. "They liked the chanting, the burning of incense, and the bell-ringing; it was like medicine-making to the Indians." Yet under the terms of Grant's peace plan, Pine Ridge belonged to Episcopal priests—the "White Robes," or *Ska Un*. When McCarthy replied that he'd start a mission anyway, the new agent responded in character: any Catholic found attempting such a thing would be tossed from Pine Ridge. Given Red Cloud's temper, that might lead to violence: "Would you like to read in the press that a priest of the Church had caused an outbreak among the Sioux while opposing the government?" McCarthy backed down, but not before informing Red Cloud of the meeting.

The old chief was enraged. On May 1, he wrote to the president and demanded McGillycuddy's instant removal; the letter was signed by twenty-one chiefs and was followed twenty-five days later by a demand that they be allowed to have Catholic teachers. "The Great Father and also the Commissioner told me that whenever and wherever I selected my place for a home," Red Cloud wrote, "that there I should have school houses and churches with men in them in black gowns." But his pleas fell on deaf ears.

Thus began alternating attempts by Red Cloud and McGillycuddy to "depose" each other for the next seven years. One would conspire unsuccessfully to unseat the other, then the other would try. The battle of wills bewildered the Oglala, but it was one that was carried out on reservations throughout the West. At Standing Rock, Agent James S. McLaughlin waged similar war against Sitting Bull when the seer returned from captivity in 1883. At a time when the Lakotas' future was being set, trust became a casualty, conflict the norm.

With the death of trust came suspicion of all things white, including Indian schools. In June 1880, Red Cloud, Spotted Tail, and other chiefs visited Pratt's school in Carlisle. When Spotted Tail saw that his childrens' long hair had been cut and they'd been forced to wear military uniforms, he remembered Sweet Medicine's prophecy of the shadow children who would fit into neither world. He dragged his children from the school, and other chiefs followed. Hair-cutting became a symbolic flashpoint: when parents entered the first day at the Oglala Boarding School and discovered the principal, Emma Sickles, cutting the boys' hair, every male was withdrawn. The school would not reopen for months, and only after the badly shaken Sickles fled to a safer job in Nebraska.

Only one of McGillycuddy's initiatives met with success—and this for reasons outside his control. From March to July 1879, only one Oglala joined his new police force—and this a member of Red Cloud's band. Then, in August, thirty-two men enlisted at once. One month later, another thirteen signed on.

Why the sudden turn? In some ways, the Oglala had no choice. During that spring and summer, horse and cattle thieves from Nebraska and the Black Hills preyed upon Oglala herds. In May, rustlers hit the camps of American Horse, Young Man Afraid of His Horses, and Little Wound, making off with more than one hundred ponies. Little Wound alone lost more than six hundred horses; losses for all of Pine Ridge in 1879 totaled more than three thousand head. Although Red Cloud's *akicitas* had the power to police their own tribesmen, they lacked the authority to arrest whites, just as McGillycuddy had warned. Neither would the military help, while U.S. marshals were spread too thin. If the Sioux hoped to protect the one reservation industry that showed any early promise of turning a profit, they would have to do it themselves.

Soon afterward, McGillycuddy appointed as chief of police Man Who Carries the Sword—better known today as George Sword. He was one of the younger Oglalas who'd come of age after the *wasichu* prevailed. Yet George Sword was no turncoat: he'd been a *wicasa wakan*, or holy man; a *pejuta wicasa*, or medicine man; a *wakicoze*, or camp administrator; and a *blota hunka*, or war leader. He'd taken part in the Sun Dance; fought the Crow, Pawnee, and Americans; and was wounded four times. Yet sometime in the 1870s he started to assist the *wasichu*, helping to conduct the annual census and serving as an army scout after the Little Bighorn. He'd been one of the emissaries to Crazy Horse during the winter talks, and watched Tasunke Witko surrender.

The appointment of George Sword as police chief made the most intransigent Oglalas examine the direction of their lives. For Sword, accepting the captaincy was a personal choice, a crossroads Black Elk would one day face. Sword cropped his hair, donned white man's clothes, and pinned a silver badge to his chest. His choice boiled down to power: his own personal power, rather than that of his conquerors. When the Great Sioux War brought his people repeated defeats, he questioned his own spiritual power and that of the Lakota. How powerful were the Grandfathers, he wondered, if the *wasichu* always prevailed?

14

THE MAKING OF A MEDICINE MAN

The change by McGillycuddy that most directly affected Black Elk began two months before he walked home. On June 22, 1881, Pine Ridge's "last great Sun Dance" was held at Sun Dance Flats, a level bench of land a mile south of Agency headquarters. The participants did not call it that at the time, and only slowly realized it as, over the next couple of years, momentum built in Washington to end this centerpiece of their religion. Most of Pine Ridge's Oglalas and two thousand Brulés from Rosebud turned out, for an estimated twelve thousand to fifteen thousand Sioux. Only a few whites attended, including McGillycuddy and his wife, all guarded by George Sword's men. McGillycuddy feared the worst; the Sioux always worked themselves into a fever during these dances, he wrote, remembering the near-riot at the dance for Crazy Horse before he died.

But nothing happened. On the third day, nine warriors danced desperately to free themselves from the Sun Dance pole. In the end, eight had weakened to the point that their skewers were cut loose by medicine men. Only one had the strength to keep going. He staggered to the center pole, then ran hard to the end of his tether, hitting it with such force that he was lifted off his feet. The impact tore him free. All grew quiet; then his friends and a medicine man rushed to his side to treat his wounds and revive him.

The dire winter of 1881 convinced Black Elk that his people would die out if he did not resort to drastic means. Starvation rampaged through the western reservations: appropriations geared for simple subsistence plummeted below Interior's requested levels. Cattle issued to the Sioux in February and March were little more than skin and bones. The army and Indian Office both agreed that something must be done to head off famine, yet to the typical late-nineteenth-century congressman, the idea of issuing free rations to grown men and women seemed obscene. As Congress debated, Indians starved.

That spring, when grass began to carpet the prairie, Black Elk once more heard the voices of Thunder-beings and felt the Grandfathers' power coursing through him. "It is time to do the work of your Grandfathers," the Thunder-beings said: time to start the final stage of his transformation. He must seek the guidance of older medicine men and cry for a vision.

He was eighteen, and it was his first formal act of lamentation. All else had been spontaneous; this would be guided and controlled. Black Elk chose a medicine man named Few Tails. He filled his pipe, held its stem before him, entered Few Tails' lodge, and sat before the old man. He placed the pipe on the ground with the stem reversed, indicating he wished to gain knowledge. Few Tails raised his hands to the four directions and asked Black Elk his wishes. "I wish to lament and offer my pipe to *Wakan Tanka*," he said. "I need your help and guidance, and wish you to send a voice for me to the Powers above."

"It is good," the old man said. He told Black Elk that he must fast four days, and could only have water. The first couple of days were not bad: one grew hungry in proportion to the amount eaten beforehand. But by the third day, hunger was inescapable. His metabolism changed when the body no longer receives energy from outside, it robs from that stored in the muscles. By the fourth day he'd passed the worst part, but had begun to grow weak. Heatstroke was a danger: he sat in the tipi's shade and tied up the back for a cool breeze.

The chief advantage of fasting was solitude. Isolation focused the mind on spiritual matters. As his horizons shrank, so did his ego. He saw his smallness in the face of God.

On the fifth day, Few Tails led him to a sweat bath. Black Elk shed his clothes and unbraided his hair, two signs of supplication. The more pitiful he made himself, lower than even the ants, the better his chances

of winning the spirits' sympathy. Few Tails poured water on the hot
rocks and steam rose up; he told Black Elk to inform the spirits what he
wanted from them.

Now he was ready. He took only his pipe and wore only a buffalo
robe. They rode to a high place four or five miles northwest, arriving near
sundown. He held the pipe before him as they climbed to the top; Few
Tails spread sage to make the site holy, thrust a flowering stick in the
center, and at each compass point placed sacred offerings. Black Elk
must stand in the center and pray, said his mentor, then walk slowly to
the west quarter and mourn. He would mourn in each quarter, back up
to the center stick, advance to the next quarter, and so on all night long.

This was considered the most profound ritual in the Lakota canon,
and the vision elicited would shape the young man's future. One of the
best prayers repeated during the night was *Tunkasila onsimala ye*, or
"Grandfather, pity me." It rolled off the tongue like a mantra, and cleared
one's mind. After the prayer, one should grow quiet—wait, watch, and
listen, paying attention to everything. Even the smallest creature could
convey a message, through either its voice, its appearance, or its behavior. From time to time one should return to prayers, asking always that
the People would live.

After a while, Black Elk noticed some changes. Birds began to
gather outside the sacred circle as if watching him. A spotted eagle
perched on a pine branch to his east and made its shrill whistle. A
chicken hawk hovered overhead, then lit on a branch to the south. A black
swallow flitted about until also landing in the east; he enjoyed its continuous trill, yet as he listened, its song called up in him a lingering
sadness about what was and what might be. Until this point, he'd only
been trying to weep, just going through the motions. But now the tears
streamed down his face and he could not stop them. He thought of his
relatives, now dead, and how they must have been when young. He remembered Crazy Horse and missed him desperately. For the longest
time they'd placed their hopes in Tasunke Witko, but he was just a man.
Yet that hope had been their strength, and he was gone. They were all
gone. Now they lived in a place of sorrow and death and the light would
never come. His sobs came from deep within, from so deep they hurt,
and he thought he might very well die from crying.

Then he heard a faint rustling in the south, and as he watched, a
delicate cloud of yellow dust floated toward him. As it drew closer, the

dust separated into butterflies of all size and hue. He walked backward to the flowering stick; the butterflies hovered overhead and then descended, covering him so thick he could not see beyond them. The eagle spoke in its shrill voice: "Behold these!" it said. "They are your people. They are in great difficulty and you shall help them." He heard the whispers of the butterflies. They lifted up and swirled back to the south; as they vanished, the chicken hawk told him to listen for the Grandfathers.

And they were coming, for a storm scudded in the west, its heavy clouds swathing the land. He heard the neighing of horses and saw bolts of fire. The two messengers separated from its roaring blindness and approached, headfirst as always like arrows.

But as they neared the earth, a dust cloud rose up and from it emerged the head of a dog. In camp, dogs were the symbol of sacrifice, since they willingly gave themselves for slaughter. Everyone loved the taste of dog. He watched as one messenger, then the other, plunged his lightning arrow into the dog's head. They rose with it toward the cloud, but as they drew close the head turned into that of a man. The storm blotted out the world and rolled at him spitting lightning and hail. He raised his robe and crouched underneath; there was often a test of courage in the vision quest and he must stay calm. The rain flooded the dry gulches around his hill and the giants cried *"Hey-a-hey!"* Yet the hail and lightning did not penetrate his sacred circle, and as the storm passed east, he dozed and dreamed.

In the dream, he saw his people from above, as he had in the Great Vision. They sat in a huge tipi, weary, sick, and sad. He recognized their despair. As he watched, a light leapt skyward—a strange, sparkling, many-colored light that briefly touched the heavens and then disappeared. In its place he saw an herb. He studied it carefully so not to forget; he saw the morning star rise slowly, glittering in a cloud of faces. He heard the voices of birds, mixed with those of bison and deer. As the cries reached a frightening crescendo, he passed into oblivion.

After an unknown time, a voice again summoned him. "Wake up," it commanded. "I've come after you!" Yet this time, the voice belonged to Few Tails. Black Elk blinked in the morning light, unsure at first whether this was not just another part of the dream. Few Tails led him downhill to their mounts, and they rode back to the sweat lodge. Inside sat several old medicine men. They presented the sacred pipe and then told Black Elk to detail the experiences and dreams of his vision quest, without exaggerations or lies. He told them all he had seen and heard. Then, unbidden, he told them of his Great Vision when he was nine.

When he finished, silence settled over the sweat lodge. They had never heard of such a thing, they said. They discussed among themselves how the Great Vision seemed made of seven parts: the call by the messengers, welcome by the Horse Nation, first gift-giving by the Grandfathers, Black Elk's trial down the black and red roads and then up the four ascents of Harney Peak, the final ascent where all things came together, the return to the Grandfathers, and his resurrection. Many Plains visions contained such elements—power gifts, forecasts of the future, spirit people or animals, predictions of one's own future. But Black Elk's Vision contained them all. And he'd borne it since he was nine. How was it possible that one so young could have a vision imbued with the whole of Sioux cosmology?

"You will be a great man," they finally said. But he must immediately use his gift, for "it was now time to do these things on earth to help mankind." Before this moment, he'd understood his responsibility in a more limited sense—he was meant to save his nation, and that alone. But now the elders gave his Vision a more universal interpretation: his mission was not for the Sioux alone, but all mankind. They added, "Many are called, but few are chosen," echoing the Christian teachings then filtering through Pine Ridge.

Yet no joy resounded in that sweat lodge. Black Elk must enact the dog vision on earth as he had the Horse Dance, but he must do so as a *heyoka*, a sacred fool. The possibility had apparently never occurred to him, and he does not mention in the interviews that any of the other ancestral Black Elks had been *heyokas*. In some way he should have guessed, for only those with the most dangerous visions—those involving thunder or lightning—were chosen. Their obligations were daunting: they were expected to mock normality, and always play the clown. They must live in ragged lodges, sleep without robes in the winter, dress in stifling motley on the hottest days. They must grab meat from boiling water barehanded to show they were not like other men. The thunder blessing of the *heyoka* was the most ambivalent blessing a man could receive from the gods, and it could not be turned down if one hoped to survive. The dreams of buffalo, bear, wolf, elk, or even deer—none conferred the confused mix of power and sadness as that conferred by a *heyoka* dream. Only the most able could live a normal life, yet even they were scarred.

Few Tails regarded his young pupil somberly and told him he had thirty days to prepare.

———•·•———

Black Elk performed the ceremony of the *heyoka*—the "contrary," or Thunder Clown—sometime after mid-May 1882. It was one month after Jesse James was shot from behind in Missouri by his gang member Robert Ford; the year the Indian Office ruled that Agencies no longer "belonged" to any one religious denomination and the Jesuits requested by Red Cloud could finally stream in. The sacred fool had a long history in most religious cultures: though his role was religious and ceremonial, his "purpose" was to dissipate excesses of power by mocking them. By behaving in a contrary or backward manner, it was believed, the fools wove a reverse magic that dissipated malevolent forces and countered the dangers of lightning and storm. Yet such visible threats were but the dim reflection of powers that sometimes peeked from the spirit world. What one could *not* see was worse—the apocalyptic wrath of *wakan sica*, the "evil mystery spirit," that had somehow jumped the divide and now wrapped Pine Ridge in a dark, destructive shroud.

The early *heyoka* of legend were fearsome indeed: warriors with extraordinary powers and no restraint who killed hundreds in the service of the tribe. In that respect, Crazy Horse was the modern equivalent, though Tasunke Witko never deigned to act the clown. At what point in the Sioux's westward trek the *heyoka* evolved from a death-dealing juggernaut to a pain-defying satirist is not certain: where once the power to deal pain was directed *out*, at the enemy, now the direction was reversed, to the individual Oglala.

All Lakota rituals took themselves seriously, unlike others, however, *heyoka* rituals were not staged with anything resembling solemnity. Modern *heyokas* wore round buckskin masks recognizable by a sharp, pointed beak or a ridiculous bulbous nose. The purpose of any mask is to preserve anonymity, but everyone knew the *heyokas*. One could not hide a life modeled on the contrary code. Since a strict adherence to that code would be suicidal, it seems that most were selective in self-torture, adopting the full-blown lifestyle only at certain times. Though Chips was a *heyoka*, accounts of his life rarely mentioned his "contrariness" and he lived to a ripe old age. Many *heyokas* seemed to limit the extremes to the ceremony itself; at the same time, they reserved for themselves the role of social commentator, almost like a stand-up comedian. In Sioux society, social control was maintained by ridicule and shame; the pressure for conformity was great in a close-knit community where a puritanical code prevailed. The *heyoka* acted as a counterbalance; his attacks on pretense were shocking and biting, like the fool in *King Lear*.

It makes sense that Black Elk would become a *heyoka*. He'd always been a bit of a clown. He'd play the games of war and fall into a cactus patch; plunge into a pool so ludicrously while spearfishing that an old man couldn't look at him without laughing; drop out of a tree when a man yelled at thieving dogs. His was always a physical humor, even when unintentional; when not worried about his health, his parents knew that people felt happier near this oddball little comedian. In later years, he became a master of the unexpected, launching into an absurd tale of a young man's near-fatal attempts at courtship, or building a sweat lodge in a dingy hotel out of loose bricks, chairs, and unwashed bedding.

At least Black Elk would not perform this sacred comedy alone. His friend Kills the Enemy had also dreamed of thunder, so they'd perform together. They approached a man named Poor, or Wachpauna, to be intercessor; he was a *heyoka* himself and knew the ritual's intricacies. He told the people to circle up in a field near the Agency; they pitched a sacred tipi in the center and next to that a pot of boiling water. Black Elk and Kills the Enemy painted their bodies red with black streaks; they shaved the right side of their heads, while the hair on the left side hung long. Such nakedness showed humility before the gods. Kills the Enemy liked the look so much that he changed his name to One Side. Black Elk was not as impressed and kept his old name.

As with the Horse Dance, Black Elk had to reenact his dog vision. One Side and he portrayed his vision's messengers: both carried long and crooked bows; the arrows were so bent they were not usable. Their sorrel horses were painted red and black to match their riders. Black Elk knew it all looked "crazy," but then, that was the purpose.

The ceremony began. Wachpauna offered sweetgrass to the west as he sat beside a fire and prayed. As he sprinkled grass on the fire, sweet-smelling smoke rose up. As it burned, he sang.

Offstage, two *heyokas* killed a dog. They slipped a noose around its neck and gently pulled the ends three times. The dog thought it was a game. On the fourth try, they pulled hard enough to break the dog's neck, then Wachpauna washed and singed the body. He cut away everything

but the head, spine, and tail, walked six steps to the pot, offered the sacrifice to the Thunder-beings, and threw everything, including entrails
and meat, into the boiling water.

During the sacrifice, thirty *heyokas* entertained the crowd. Two came
up to a shallow puddle and acted as if it were a wide, deep river. One
plunged in and floundered; his partner tried to save him and was dragged
in, too. Another group nocked a crooked arrow to one of the useless bows
and loosed it at the scattering crowd. The arrow, made of soft rawhide,
flopped at their feet, as useless as the bow.

As these sideshows played out, Black Elk and One Side began the
main ritual. They charged the boiling pot on horseback with their long,
jagged arrows thrust before them. Black Elk impaled the head; One
Side, the heart. They held them aloft, then the other *heyokas* rushed up
and thrust their hands and arms into the boiling water. This was a trick:
they'd rubbed themselves with a chewed paste of red false mallow
root, which briefly protected the skin. Everyone tried to get a piece of
meat, considered sacred medicine; the other *heyokas* chased Black Elk
and One Side for the heart and head. A hailstorm swept from the
east and the ceremony dissolved into a drenched, joyous melee.

Word of Black Elk's power spread. He'd proven himself a visionary. But
to truly help his people, he must become a *pejuta wicasa*, able to heal.

In June 1882, one month after the *heyoka* ceremony, he moved north
to Wounded Knee. Many of Crazy Horse's people had relocated there:
Chips, He Dog, Little Wolf, and Kicking Bear. Several of Big Road's
clan moved there, too, erecting cabins in a narrow valley with high hills
to the west and limestone buttes to the east rising like knobs of vertebrae.
The tallest was Porcupine Butte and from its top one could see the Black
Hills. The little village would eventually be called Manderson, though
at this point it was little more than a store. By the summer of 1882, Black
Elk's parents had come from Standing Rock and moved here among
their kin.

One Side also built a cabin nearby. One day Black Elk invited his
friend to eat and mentioned that in a dream he'd seen a curing herb. He
did not say that this was the daybreak herb of his Vision, but did admit
that he needed a powerful herb if he hoped to become a healer. One
Side was as new to healing and as ambitious for success as Black Elk;
they would help each other so often that in time they formed a kind of

partnership. One Side was more than happy to search the hills and gullies with his friend for a miracle cure.

As the son of a bear healer, Black Elk would have known the importance of medicinal herbs. Lakota healers used the willow leaf and bark for reducing fever; sycamore, as a laxative; and sunflower and skunk cabbage, to fight colds and open air passages. They cured snakebite with a poultice of snakeroot, plantain, purple cornflower, and white ash. Bear healers were a brotherhood and passed on their cures. For each medicine, called *pejuta*, there existed a song. The medicine man sang the words in time to a drum or rattle; the hypnotic chant pleased the *wakan* and calmed the afflicted.

Black Elk and One Side rode eight miles north to Grass Creek until cresting a hill that looked familiar from Black Elk's visions. They sang some *heyoka* tunes, then spotted a number of birds circling to the west. They rode there and found a dry wash where four or five gulches converged like a star; the birds flapped off, and Black Elk saw growing from the bank the daybreak herb.

He'd never seen such a plant. The root was long and deep and, at the top, thicker than his thumb. The plant had two stems, bearing blooms of blue, white, red, and yellow. Black Elk offered a prayer, cut off a foot of taproot, wrapped the herb in sage, and rode home.

No flowering plant found today in Pine Ridge exactly matches Black Elk's daybreak herb. But two come close. Lupine, or *Lupinus sp.*, is a tall wildflower native to the area, with a long root and flowering conical spike, or spadix, which produces blooms of various colors. The flowers near the bottom open first, often in blue or red, but as the cone narrows, the colors change to white tinged with yellow. Most important is the fact that it yields sparteine, an oily alkaloid that is toxic to livestock but in humans acts as a heart stimulant. The second candidate is hound's-tongue, *Cynoglossum officinale L.*, which bloomed throughout the reservation from March to June. It, too, has multicolored flowers— blue, pink, white, and reddish-purple; it, too, has a taproot and yields a powerful medicine. Hound's-tongue could be boiled or powdered to produce an anti-irritant and mild sedative, but was best known for its use against coughs and bronchial problems. Though lupine was more prevalent on Pine Ridge, hound's-tongue is intriguing due to the epidemic of pertussis, or whooping cough, then sweeping through all Plains reservations. Along with measles, pertussis was one of the great killers of Indian children in the 1880s; the violent coughing fits could lead to hemorrhages, rib fractures, fainting, and pneumothorax—a hole blown through the lung. The coughs could last for six weeks, by which time a child was so weak that death was not unlikely.

Black Elk never divulged the preparation of his daybreak herb: according to George Sword, a good prairie doctor guards his secrets well. Most likely, he produced an extract by boiling the flowers or beans, or ground them down. No doubt he experimented. On this night, however, he did not have that luxury. He and One Side returned from their search, and as he ate supper with his parents, his father may have given him some pointers on how to make *pejuta* from his herb. Yet before the meal was finished, a neighbor named Cuts to Pieces appeared: "I have a boy of mine and he is very sick and I don't expect him to live," he said, in real distress. "I thought since you had so much power in the horse dance, *heyoka*, etc., that you might have the power to cure my son."

For Black Elk, time stood still. He told Cuts to Pieces that he must bring back a pipe tied with an eagle feather as a kind of contract; in all likelihood, Black Elk just needed time to gather his wits. What must he do? The thought scared him. Everything—his Great Vision and vision quest, the horse and *heyoka* dances, all of the hopes for himself and his people—depended upon whether he could cure that little boy. He'd known such a moment would come, but not so soon. In the middle of what had seemed an everyday family supper, the world had turned. This was an all-or-nothing moment. Everything would begin—or end—with this child.

Cuts to Pieces returned with the pipe as instructed. Black Elk passed it to the four quarters, then to his parents and a dinner guest. As they smoked, he thought of his Great Vision: the secrets of his healing powers lay in its riddles. He grabbed his drum and beat out a low rhythm like distant thunder that reassured him. He sent for One Side to assist, then walked to Cuts to Pieces' lodge. To his surprise, Standing Bear was already inside, watching with the same intensity as when they were boys and he'd returned from the dead.

Forty-nine years later he told John Neihardt, "That evening was to be my first performance in medicine." It was an interesting choice of words. This was the element dwelt upon by detractors—the performance, the theater, of the "*wakan*-man's" art. "Ignorance is emphatically the mother of credulity," wrote the Presbyterian missionary Gideon Pond, who lived among the Dakota in the 1840s and '50s, "and no absurdity is too great to be heartily received by an ignorant savage, when proposed by one of artful cunning." Yet modern studies have likened such healing "performances" to group therapy; have shown that, in fact, the "therapeutic skills" of Dakota shamans stretched as far back as the Pleistocene era. In tribal life, the afflicted was not alone. He or she was part of the body of the tribe. Treating an individual cell of the body would be ridiculous. Treating the entire body cured both the individual *and* the tribe.

It was a terrifying position for a young man of barely nineteen, made worse by his belief that he'd been chosen to save his people. Black Elk took a deep breath and entered the stage. He ducked through the flap and circled the tipi from left to right, then sat with One Side to the west, place of the Thunder-beings. He studied the patient in his bed. The boy moaned and sweated from fever. Black Elk had brought his pipe, drum, and four-colored herb—all had happened so fast that he'd had no time to assemble a medicine bag. He asked for a cup of water and an eagle whistle, as he'd seen in his Vision. Someone placed a cup before him, and he grew silent. "I had to think awhile, because I had never done this before and I was in doubt," he later said.

He remembered his Vision, then handed the whistle to One Side and told him to play; the sound would help him enter the world of the Grandfathers. He filled his pipe with red willow bark, or *kinnikinnick*, and handed that to Cuts to Pieces' pretty young daughter, who reminded him of his Vision's Virgin of the East. He beat on the drum and four times cried *"Hey-a-a-hey!"* A feeling spread through him from his feet up. He started to sing:

> In a sacred manner I have made them walk.
> A sacred nation lies low.
> In a sacred manner I have made them walk.
> A sacred two-legged, he lies low.
> In a sacred manner I have made him walk.

Now things become hallucinatory, just as during the bear dance the night before Custer attacked. We enter the realm of the unreal. "I could feel something queer in my body and I wanted to cry," he recalled. In his anxiety, he called upon all the powers of the earth, only realizing later that just the thunder power was necessary. It was, he admitted, overkill. He rose and walked to the west, where the cup of water had been set, and as he passed, the boy looked up and smiled. The boy's innocent assurance was electric, and to Black Elk it meant everything. "Then I knew that I had the power and that I would cure him," he said. He made an offering, took a puff on the pipe, drank part of the water, and completed the circle back to the boy. No one else moved. He felt something move in his chest, and he knew it was the Little Blue Man from his Great Vision—his familiar, his *sicun*, come to help him, as promised by the Grandfathers. He stomped on the ground four times, then put his lips to the boy's stomach and "drew the north wind through him." He wiped his mouth with a white cloth and saw blood, which suggested that he'd drawn poison from the boy's body. He washed his mouth with water, then started the medical segment of the cure.

He cut off some of the daybreak herb and ground it into powder, then sprinkled this into a cup of hot water. He mixed it up, took a sip, blew it over the boy in four directions, and had him drink the rest. Cuts to Pieces' daughter helped her brother rise, and they walked slowly from the south and around the cardinal points until returning to his bed. The boy was very tired and weak; they laid him down gently and covered him with robes.

Then Black Elk left. Whether the boy lived or died was up to the Grandfathers.

The next day, Cuts to Pieces came to Black Elk's lodge. His boy was feeling better, he said. He was sitting up and even eating, if only a little, but it was still more than he had done in days. In two more days, he could walk; by the end of the summer, he was well. Just as his own parents had done for Whirlwind Chaser, Cuts to Pieces offered Black Elk a horse in payment. The gift was an honor, but Black Elk would not accept it until four days had passed and he knew for certain that the boy was cured.

Word spread quickly. Soon others came for help. "I was busy most of the time," he said.

As his reputation spread, Black Elk increased his power by adding to his résumé what could be considered "specialties." Later that summer, he performed the buffalo ceremony from his Vision; this represented the getting of wisdom. In the spring of 1884 or 1885, he performed the Elk Dance, which represented the source of all life and the mystery of birth. During this time, he fought tuberculosis and other diseases, often with One Side's help; people brought them their sick children—and there were many. He realized that if he could see the patient smiling in the water cup, there was a good chance of success; if not, the afflicted was too far into sickness to be saved. He no longer doubted his power. For the first time in his life, he felt like a man.

Yet even as his power grew, his people declined. He might battle the symptoms, but he must somehow confront the cause. But what was it? Where did it lie?

In 1883, McGillycuddy bragged in his annual report that life was getting better for the Oglala: they'd spread through the reservation, built 625 homes, used 500 wagons for freighting, laid 135 miles of tele-graph line, and opened 6 day schools. The cattle herd had grown to 1,500 cows and bulls; they put up hay with 40 mowing machines; they'd received a winter beef herd of 6,000 animals, and operated saw-, corn, planing, and shingle mills. In the four years of his tenure, his Lakotas had "advanced in every respect in civilization."

Black Elk saw the truth from the inside. His people weren't thriving, but dying. The number of sick appearing at his tipi flap—especially children—belied the official line. He'd take his sacred dances to places where the greatest number could participate, the flats just outside Agency headquarters. Despite the risk, he felt an obligation. Yet even as they danced, he could read defeat in their faces.

If anything thrived at Pine Ridge, it was dogs. By 1883, McGillycuddy estimated that twenty to thirty thousand ran free. Like the Lakota, they were always hungry. Unlike the Lakota, they preyed on cows and their calves. They ran in packs, encircling cows in labor and dragging them down. When asked by Congress what might be done, McGillycuddy sug-gested that the army "be called in to have a big dog hunt," knowing full well it would never happen.

This was the decade that saw the final winnowing of the Great Sioux Reserve. In 1883, as Black Elk revealed his power, Dakota's con-gressional delegate, Richard F. Pettigrew, slipped a rider into unrelated legislation calling for the Sioux to exchange their one large reservation for six smaller ones, each to be home to a principal *ospaye*. Thus, Stand-ing Rock belonged to the Hunkpapa, Rosebud to the Brulé, and Pine Ridge to the Oglala. The chiefs liked the idea of each major tribe having exclusive control of its own reservation, uncomplicated by the common ownership of all Lakota. But Pettigrew's bill had a catch. All unfarmed "surplus" left from the breakup—nearly twenty-two million acres— would be up for sale. Some was arable, some forested, and nearly all perfect for grazing. The largest strip lay between the Cheyenne River

Agency and the northern borders of Pine Ridge and Rosebud. Land boomers and ranchers coveted this land. Although the rider was detected and the bill killed before it could pass, the controversy marked the area for subsequent attempts and left the Lakota fearful of future "land reform."

More than anything else, this was the period that ushered in a massive psychological assault upon Indian identity—a war waged upon all tribes on all western reservations. Ever since Grant's Peace Policy, reformers and Indian "friends" hoped to prevent extermination by turning the Indians into Christians: "The religion of our blessed Savior is believed to be the most effective tool for the civilization of any people" was a common refrain. Since Christianization called for the extermination of native religions, the easiest and most obvious place to start was through suppression of the large sacred dances.

From 1879 to 1882, agents at all six Sioux reservations called for an end to the Sun Dance, and often used the Indian police to stop residents from attending dances on other reservations. In December 1882, the perennial cry to end the dance was given teeth when the newly appointed secretary of the interior, Henry Moore Teller, asked Hiram Price, commissioner of Indian affairs, to finally outlaw all dances, polygamy, and medicine men. The dances "stimulate the warlike passions," he wrote, and must be banned. He was just as determined to exterminate the medicine man:

> Another great hindrance to the civilization of the Indians is the influence of the medicine men, who are always found with the anti-progressive party. The medicine men resort to various artifices and devices to keep the people under their influence, and are especially active in preventing the attendance of the children at the public schools, using their conjurors' arts to prevent people from abandoning their heathenish rites and customs. While they profess to cure diseases by the administering of a few simple remedies, still they rely mostly on their art of conjuring.

The 1882 Indian Religious Crime Code turned Teller's personal dislikes into reservation law. Tribes were ordered to surrender sacred objects; these then made their way into museums and private collections. On April 10, 1883, the government's "Rules for Indian Courts" was released, which allowed for the establishment of a Court of Indian

Offenses and the codification of penalties. Any Indian found guilty of engaging in "the sun dance, scalp dance, or war dance, or any other similar feast," would be punished for the first offense by the withholding of rations or an imprisonment of ten days. Punishments were harsher for medicine men: first offenses drew ten to thirty days' imprisonment; subsequent offenses, up to six months.

In addition, any white found guilty of supporting the dances would be expelled, a move apparently directed at curious whites willing to pay for staged dances. Yet one of the first to be thrown out was the Jesuit father Francis M. Craft, who'd attended dances at Rosebud. Craft had already incurred the wrath of Agent James G. Wright for telling the Brulé that everything they'd learned under Episcopal missionaries was incorrect, and for urging them to oppose the Indian industrial schools. Craft, said Wright, held himself "above all civil law." In a November 25, 1883, letter to Secretary Teller, Carlisle's Richard Pratt wrote: "I heard it from a halfbreed at Rosebud who claimed to be an eyewitness that Father Craft solicited the privilege from the Indians of opening the ceremonies of the Sun dance last summer with prayer, and from my sources, that he wore eagle feathers in his cap throughout these ceremonies, and entered into them to the full extent allowed by the Indians."

Armed with his Indian police, Indian Court, and new set of regulations, McGillycuddy would withhold rations from any full-blood Indian who danced, imprison any mixed-blood, and expel any white man. Red Cloud and his allies threatened to rebel against the edicts, but McGillycuddy called these threats "but a last bid for authority." After the big 1881 dance, McGillycuddy boasted that the Sun Dance at Pine Ridge was completely obliterated.

This does not seem entirely true. Offhand remarks by agents suggest that it lived on surreptitiously. As late as 1914, Agent Albert H. Kneale indicated that the dance persisted at Standing Rock. When asked how the Hunkpapa "fritter away the summer months," Kneale stated that "July was devoted to the Sun Dance," this some thirty years after McGillycuddy declared it dead. It would be naive to think that the same situation did not apply on other reservations.

Yet, even if the dance persisted, it had changed. What had been the great annual festival that united the Lakota and affirmed their identity was now transformed into a small, underground performance held in outlying areas. For the older *wicasa wakan*, the ban was an economic blow. Dancers hired holy men to act as spiritual guides and intercessors during their trials; at larger dances, like the one in 1881, as many as fifty holy men could be employed. Participation conferred high status, since not all were considered qualified. The ban hit the holy men hard, and if only for that, Teller's edict could be considered successful.

Since Black Elk entered the profession just as the ban took place, these were economic blows he probably never felt. One cannot miss what one has never had. In addition, his participation in the underground Sun Dance seems to have been limited. He certainly understood its rites, but later photos do not show any telltale scars lacing his body. Although the accompanying ban on native medicine sounded dire, the reality was that it was much harder to enforce. For agents and the Indian police, it was easier to look aside.

Still, the ban on the Sun Dance would have created a depth of despair that Black Elk could not ignore. It had been the centerpiece of Sioux social and religious life; now all that was left was a void. Without the Sun Dance, the Sioux lost the powerful connection to *Wakan Tanka* they'd once had. Through the dancers' terrible sacrifice, the tribe would win God's protection for another year. They'd gained the sense of power that made them a force to be feared.

In its place, confusion and resentment ruled. As late as 1946, the suppression of the Sun Dance would be blamed for the disintegration of Dakota society. The central drama of Oglala life had been stripped off, and with it the means of passing values to the next generation. If the elders no longer knew who they were, what hope could be held for their children? Like Sweet Medicine and Drinks Water long before him, the sociologist Gordon Macgregor would lament a land stained by "the crumbling of Dakota culture."

Black Elk's Vision had warned him of this. His duty, as he saw it, was to stop the spread of such poison. But how? He might treat the symptoms, but he must look elsewhere for a cure.

15

THE "SHOW MAN"

From 1883 to 1886, Black Elk doctored Pine Ridge's sick—healed their bodies and their souls. His hands were always full; many who came to him sick left happy and "made over." An Agency doctor practiced in the village, but many did not trust him. Already a suspicion had formed: white men were dangerous and unpredictable. The first thing an Indian said to himself when confronted by a white was "*takto kahta he*": "What's going to happen?" How long before I am betrayed?

They did not trust the white way of medicine because it was hard to understand. In modern terms, Indian medicine was holistic; white medicine, reductive. White medicine did not address the whole person— it treated a heart, or a kidney. A patient was transformed into a "coronary problem" or "renal problem." A Lakota medicine man wouldn't recognize a renal problem if he saw one, but he would know the whole person. At the same time that he attacked the root of the ailment—an upset stomach, or endless cough—he spread out in wider circles to heal the individual, his family, friends, and tribe. Since everyone participated, the patient had a responsibility to get well.

Yet Oglalas did *not* get better, even as more things changed. Agents insisted they live in log houses and abandon their tipis; the Indian Office insisted that children attend the new schools, which increased in number slowly but steadily. By 1885, eight government day schools were built around the reservation: each had one teacher and space for

45 students. At Agency headquarters, a large boarding school boasted a superintendent, 7 teachers, and 225 pupils. Compulsory education was the norm: when a child was absent without good reason, the entire family's rations were cut off until he returned.

But cooperation with the *wasichu* was never enough. They always wanted more. By now, more and more of Black Elk's people lived in the square houses: by 1886, about 1,900 were spread across the Agency, up from 625 in 1883. By 1886, 5,080 full-blooded Oglalas lived at Pine Ridge, down from the probably incorrect earlier estimate of about 7,000. Now was the time to farm, they were told. Rainfall had increased in the early 1880s, and a popular theory held that rainfall increased in an area as more people settled there and farmed, wrote J. D. Harrison, an observer for the Indian Rights Association. Prophets of Indian farming believed this would occur in Pine Ridge, yet this was an empty optimism, since only one-eighth of the Agency's two million acres was arable. Most was "as barren and useless as the central desolation of the Sahara," wrote Harrison. The only land that *could* be cultivated lay in narrow valleys, but during storms, alkali soil—or "gumbo"—washed down from the heights and destroyed the crops entirely. The soil that remained required a special kind of care. When wet, it turned into a paste with the consistency of wax or cement. If the farmer did not "stir" this paste within a few hours of the downpour, it would harden into a surface "as impervious to air as glass or slate, and which would bake as hard as a brick in the sun."

If anything, Black Elk grew weary. When he treated the sick, their despair and illness sprang back up like weeds. His people tried to live the white man's way, and it was killing them. They'd forgotten the ways of their ancestors. "I got so disgusted with the wrong road that my people were along now," he said. "I was trying to get them to go back on the good road," but they would not listen.

Finally, Black Elk could take no more. When a chance to see the world outside Pine Ridge presented itself, "I made up my mind I was going away from them to see the white man's ways." If those ways proved better, perhaps his people should live by them. If he did discover the secret of this power, he would bring it back to close the sacred hoop and renew the holy tree.

And to do this, he must become an *oskata wicasa*—a "show man."

If 1883 was the year U.S. authorities banned all Indian religious traditions, it was also the year that those endangered practices entered a national—and soon international—arena. This year saw the conception of Buffalo Bill's Wild West, and by taking part in it, Black Elk and his fellow Oglala would shape and define the image of the West as it came to be known worldwide.

Its impresario was the former sworn enemy of the Sioux. William F. Cody had not been idle since his days scouting for Three Stars. The dime novels written in his name created such notoriety that in 1872 the Western melodrama *The Scouts of the Prairie* opened in Chicago. He'd earned $150 a month as an army scout, a sporadic $1,000 a month as a hunting guide—and $6,000 in six easy months on the stage. To Cody, the message was clear: 1876 saw the end of his days as a scout and the beginning of his career as a full-time showman.

A major factor in his success—the very feature that drew millions to the Wild West from its inception until its 1913 bankruptcy—was the practice of using "real" Indians as actors. Yet that very formula has done the most to discomfit historians. Were the Indian performers duped, extorted, or abused? Robert Altman's 1976 *Buffalo Bill and the Indians* portrayed Cody as a self-promoting drunk who fooled the Indians into a kind of Native American blackface buffoonery. "Altman, like many others," wrote Louis Warren in his 2005 *Buffalo Bill's America*, "presumes that Indians were simple, naive victims of Cody's chicanery," the same kind of charge leveled at Neihardt after the publication of *Black Elk Speaks*.

Cody *did* drink. Just as for many native performers, alcohol was his Achilles' heel. As early as 1882, his manager and business partner, Nate Salsbury, berated him for a drinking binge. Cody was contrite: "This drinking surely ends today," he wrote, a promise he never kept. Sometime after 1901, Salsbury would write in his unpublished memoir that while "Cody makes a virtue of keeping sober most of the time during the summer season," he would abandon that vow in the off-season and forget "honor, reputation, friends, and obligation, in his mad eagerness to fill his hide with rot gut of any kind."

Concerning his dealings with show Indians, however, Cody would prove a man of his word. Although performers such as Black Elk might dislike their parts in such staged set pieces as "The Attack on the Deadwood Stage" or "Custer's Last Stand," they rarely, if ever, had anything bad to say about the man. Black Elk called him Pahuska, another Long

Hair, but unlike the Pahuska his people rubbed out, Black Elk had only praise for Cody. Over its thirty-three-year run, more than a thousand Indians chose to sign up with the Wild West; Cody's good humor and generosity became legend among the Sioux and Cheyenne. George Dull Knife, a son of the Cheyenne chief allied with Crazy Horse, would ride with the Wild West during most of the 1890s; he told stories of Cody sleeping in Sioux tipis and how Pahuska would entertain Indian children with a trick pony that fell down and played dead.

Cody's change of heart toward his former enemies can be seen as early as October 25, 1879, when in a *Washington Post* interview he said unequivocally, "I think I can sum up my policy in a single sentence. It is this: Never make a single promise to the Indians that is not fulfilled." Cody did not prohibit or constrain traditional religion in camp; except for the Sun Dance, which would have been too blatant, such banned social performances as the Omaha Grass Dance could have faded from memory if not for their preservation in Cody's camps and shows.

There had been Western shows before Cody's. In 1842, P. T. Barnum staged a "Grand Buffalo Hunt" in New Jersey, complete with native dancers. In 1855–56, "Tyler's Indian Exhibition" toured the country with circuses. Displays of cowboy skill were staged as early as 1847 in Santa Fe, and on July 4, 1882, Cody hosted the extravagant "Old Glory Blow Out"—a combination parade, rodeo, and horse race—at his "Scout's Rest Ranch" in North Platte. The next year, he joined with Dr. William Frank Carver—the dentist, marksman, and entertainer who billed himself as the "Champion Shot of the World." That partnership ended badly, and soon afterward Cody partnered with Salsbury to midwife what became the Wild West.

Cody apparently tried to hire a number of Pine Ridge Oglalas for his first show. As early as February 28, 1884, he wrote Acting Agent Charles Penney that he'd received permission from the Interior Department to contract with his Indians. By this point, McGillycuddy was embroiled in the politics that would end in his 1886 ouster. Penney, his stand-in, was more sympathetic to Cody. On March 17, 1884, Cody wrote that he'd printed five hundred contracts in advance and hoped to arrive at Pine Ridge in early April. Yet something held up his visit, and for his show's inaugural season he instead hired Pawnees.

It was just as well for the Oglalas. En route to the first show, Cody's Mississippi steamboat collided with another a few miles above Memphis. The boat sank within an hour, taking with it the Wild West's wagons, camping gear, arms, ammunition, several buffalo and donkeys, and one elk—a total loss of twenty thousand dollars. The troupe limped into New Orleans and days of rain scared away the crowds. An accident killed the scout who'd liaisoned with the Pawnees. "Fate if there is such a thing is against me," Cody wrote to Salsbury. "I am a damn condemned Joner [Jonah] and the sooner you get clear from me the better for you."

Cody calculated his losses at about sixty thousand dollars that first year. Yet even then, the Wild West appealed to a nostalgia that would be felt by audiences around the world. In 1884, a Denver reviewer said that Cody portrayed "incidents that are passing away *never more to return.*" The show's promotional literature called the stagecoach used in the robbery scene a "relic," and dubbed the buffalo the "fast-disappearing monarch of the plains." Cody produced what one historian called "memory showmanship" even as it emerged as something new in world entertainment. As late as 1902, the program declared the days of America's West numbered: "Soon the dark clouds of the future will descend upon the present, and behind them will disappear the Wild West with all its glories, forever made mere memories." From the beginning, Cody styled his show as a *preserver of memories,* the same claim Black Elk would make with the release of his oral memoir.

In 1885, Cody hired Annie Oakley, who became an instant favorite; more important for the Lakotas, she helped recruit Sitting Bull. The Sioux chief had seen her the previous year in a show at St. Paul, then exchanged gifts and gave her the Sioux name Watanya Cecilla, or "Little Sure Shot." Their inclusion gave the Wild West a tremendous promotional boost; to the Lakota, Sitting Bull's participation gave it instant legitimacy.

The tour played in more than a dozen cities, half of these in Canada, and Cody and Sitting Bull became fast friends. A series of photographs taken in Montreal and titled "Foes in '76, Friends in '85" showed the two clasping hands. Rather than parading around as the "Slayer of Custer" or participating in the battle tableaus, Sitting Bull rode in parades, greeted visitors in his lodge, and sat impassively on his horse at the beginning of each performance. Each appearance stole the show. He detested this part of his duties, but loved new experiences such as his discovery of oyster stew. He sent most of his earnings back to his family, and gave the remainder to newsboys and street urchins. He could not understand how a nation of such wealth could let children starve; that whites would let children suffer convinced him that the *wasichu* would do nothing for the Indian but destroy him.

The season ended in St. Louis on October 3, 1885, and Sitting Bull went home. As a parting gift, Cody gave him a light gray trick horse he'd ridden in the parades and a big white sombrero. He kept them the rest of his days. The 1885 tour had been such a success that the Wild West made a profit for the first time. Cody hired a new scriptwriter, dreamed up new acts, and returned to Pine Ridge for performers. He envisioned great things for the 1886 season.

———•◦•———

In the early fall of 1886, Black Elk heard that Cody was hiring again. At first, he was reluctant to go. Many Oglalas still needed healing—the trail of sick to his door never ended. His relatives—and probably his parents—argued against his departure. Whether by choice or necessity, medicine men tended to be homebodies. Duty demanded that they stay with the tribe.

Yet the temptations to go were legion. He was single, healthy, restless, and twenty-three years old; this would be a chance to see the fabled wonders of the *wasichu* world, a chance that might never come again. He was not alone: He Dog would go with Cody that year to "see the lands where the palefaces originally came from." Many discovered they were happier on the road than on the reservation: they were nomads again—honored and useful. Black Elk had even heard rumors that the show "was going across the great water." Cody, for his part, would say that although "the idea of transplanting our exhibition to England had frequently occurred to us," there were no specific plans at the moment for an ocean voyage. Nevertheless, more than ten of Black Elk's close friends had signed up, and one envisions this as the Lakota version of a road trip.

He could also make good money, better than anything else a full-blooded Lakota could make at the Agency. The standard contract for a Native American performer with the Wild West paid $25 a month, or $300 a year; this seems low for an era when the national average for all Americans was $20 a week, or $1,040 annually. But Cody also paid food, travel, clothing, shelter, full medical coverage, and other incidentals, benefits with an estimated worth of $300 annually. Thus, although Cody's Indian performers made two-thirds the income of an average white worker, their benefits surpassed those of many Americans.

They'd certainly earn more with Cody than if they stayed at Pine Ridge. The annual salary of the captain of Indian police was only $144. There were higher salaries: the Agency interpreter made $500 annually; a day-school teacher, $600; the Agency physician, $1,200. But these jobs were filled by mixed-bloods and whites, not full-blooded Oglalas.

Unlike Cody's first attempt to sign the Oglalas, no impediments seemed to exist when Black Elk put his pen to paper. In May 1886, the embittered McGillycuddy retired from Pine Ridge, the victim of rancor, rumor, and the political house-cleaning that occurred whenever a new presidential administration swept out the old. Two agents followed: Acting Agent Captain James M. Bell, from May 1 to September 31, 1886; and the former Union officer Hugh D. Gallagher, who started on October 1. Black Elk signed two contracts that year: one dated January 17, 1886; the other, December 17. The January 17 contract was probably a print run of predated contracts that served as a statement of intent; the second served as the actual contract once the troupe was on the road. Black Elk signed both with his boyhood name, Kahnigapi, the same way he was listed on the census rolls. He signed for two years, and since baptism in the Episcopal Church was required of all Indian performers, he agreed to that, too. The formality meant so little to him that he failed to mention it in the Neihardt interviews.

According to the show's 1887 program and a list of cast members, 119 Pine Ridge Lakotas signed up that season with Buffalo Bill. Men and women both signed: women were paid ten dollars a month. Although they did not ride in the show, they participated in the "authentic" Indian camp visited by ticket holders between performances. Children accompanied their parents, but were neither listed in the records nor paid. Black Elk's friend One Side signed up, as did Eagle Elk, an older friend who would be interviewed in 1944 by Neihardt for what became the semifictional *When the Tree Flowered*. The notorious Little Big Man signed, as did Standing Bear. Black Elk's older cousin was thirty, with a wife and daughter, neither of whom accompanied him. This was not unusual: traveling with the Wild West could be dangerous. Cody was bonded by the Indian Office; the terms included sending the bulk of one's wages back to the family.

Black Elk packed his best outfit—beaded moccasins, buckskin suit, porcupine quill vest, and war bonnet—and in mid-November eight wagons hired by the Wild West arrived at Agency headquarters to take the Indians to the Union Pacific station in Rushville. His family begged him once more to stay. There were whoops of joy as the wagons pulled off, but he focused on the tears of his parents; as their figures dwindled, he wondered if he'd see them again. They reached Rushville by sundown. The train awaited their arrival, engine huffing. He felt like hopping from the wagon and running back to Pine Ridge. The Sioux staged a dance, then he boarded a car with his friends. The locomotive reversed and with a bump coupled with the cars. It lurched forward and they headed east over the iron road.

They ran all night and by morning were in Long Pine, Nebraska; they ran all day and by evening were in Omaha. The miles rolled beneath them, and in a day they were in Chicago. One day of rest, then clattering days without number. As the miles piled up, he became convinced that something terrible would happen to his people while he was gone.

They roared across a landscape in which time itself was divorced from reality. To a child raised on the Plains, time had meaning: it might not be exact, but it progressed with the sun. Not so on the railroad. As the miles of track spread into a national network, trains ran a crazy quilt of schedules based on mean local sun times. If Black Elk had made this journey three years earlier, noon in Chicago would have been 11:27 a.m. in Omaha, 11:50 in St. Louis, 12:17 in Toledo, and 12:31 in Pittsburgh. The Buffalo station had three clocks, each with a different time; there were twenty-seven local times in Illinois and thirty-eight in Wisconsin. As early as 1870, the *Railroad Gazette* urged a single standard time for the entire nation, but this found little support. Finally, on Sunday, November 18, 1883, the railroads chopped the nation into four wide time belts divided at the 75th, 90th, 105th, and 120th meridians. The public adjusted, but the U.S. government would not adopt standard time until 1918.

But this was 1886, a year when anything seemed possible. They devoured the 1,600 miles between Rushville and the eastern edge of the continent in four or five days. Two months earlier, on September 4, Bear Coat Miles had tracked and forced the surrender of the Chiricahua Apache chief Geronimo, an event many hoped would spell the end of the Indian wars. Geronimo had fought for thirty years and was imprisoned in Pensacola, Florida. He would never go home, the same fate that awaited Crazy Horse, if he had lived.

The troupe arrived at Manhattan's Pennsylvania Station, shouldered their gear, and walked the eight or nine blocks southeast along West Thirty-Second and Broadway to what had once been P. T. Barnum's

"Monster Classical & Geological Hippodrome" at East Twenty-Sixth and Madison Avenue. Now it was more modestly called Madison Square Garden. Spectators lined the streets for the impromptu parade. "The long talked of, anxiously looked forward to Wild West show parading the streets," reported the November 25, 1886, *New York Herald*, "was a collection of fiercely painted, gaily gotten up Sioux, Pawnees, cowboys, vaqueros . . . a vision of flowing locks, flowing trousers, flowing hat brims, and, in fact, everything in the flow style." They filed to the Hippodrome and with a whoop Pawnees who'd arrived early descended upon them. "They couped us in a friendly way and we just had to hurry out of there," Black Elk said. Former enemies, now fellow thespians. Perhaps nothing else showed how things had changed.

For the next three months—from November 24, 1886, to February 22, 1887—the huge open-air arena would be their home. The roofless oval was 420 by 200 feet, and hosted boxing matches, an ice carnival, circuses, and the Westminster Kennel Club Dog Show. Unfortunately, it was also hot in the summer and cold in the winter, and *Harper's Weekly* called it a "patched-up, grumy, drafty, combustible old shell." The underground quarters for the animals were bleak and chilly, and the buffalo contracted pneumonia. Sixteen died.

The show opened on November 25 to a packed house—estimates ranged from five to fifteen thousand. Dignitaries in the twelve-dollar box seats included General Sherman; New York's governor, David Hill; and the Reverend Henry Ward Beecher and his wife. Past shows had basically been a collection of scenes from Cody's dime novels—an Indian attack on a settler's hut, a stage robbery, Indian dances, et cetera—but for Madison Square Garden he hired the New York dramatist James Morrison Steele MacKaye to adapt and reshuffle the acts into a spectacle of American expansion called *The Drama of Civilization*, complete with huge scenic backdrops painted by the popular British artist Matthew Somerville Morgan. The show was divided into four acts, or "epochs." The first focused on the "Primeval Forest": Black Elk and the Lakotas danced in the forest when suddenly they were attacked by the Pawnees. Act Two shifted to the "Prairie": a dozen buffalo drank at a watering hole. Buffalo Bill yelped and fired his Winchester; the buffalo ran off, followed by a wagon train; night came, interrupted by a prairie fire and mad stampede of Indians, whites, and animals. Act Three: a cattle ranch; an Indian attack; cowboys ride up "and the noble red men are sent to the happy hunting grounds in a body." Act Four: a mining camp—a stagecoach robbery, a gunfight, and a Pony Express rider, ending finally with a cyclone created by a patented "hurricane raiser" that kicked up a sixty-mile-per-hour gale and whirled "several dummies . . . wildly in midair."

Black Elk enjoyed the Indian segments, "but I did not care much about the white people's parts" in which they rode in and sent the "noble red man" to the "happy hunting grounds." He excelled at dancing: his training of the last few years turned him into one of Cody's best dancers for the 1886–87 season. The audience—especially the women—loved him. "The dancing of the Indians," wrote *The New York Herald*, "aroused particular attention. The frescoed sons of the forest tossed off their blankets and the fair sex did not know whether to look with interest upon the dancers or to glance at the roof. Sixty almost entirely nude braves, with their hides tinted according to the latest thing in war paint, danced to the accompaniment of some very weird music."

Opening night was a hit, though all did not go smoothly. When the curtain rose on a forest scene augmented by a "herd" of elk, one bull forgot his cue. He strolled past the net separating wilderness from audience, sauntered down the stands, and inspected "the pretty girls in the boxes with critical stares." When a warrior tried to herd him back, the elk dipped his antlers and charged. The warrior climbed a rail into the nearest box, frightening a "brown-eyed girl in a white tailor-made jacket." Meanwhile, the elk trotted to another box, where a little girl patted it on the head until a red-shirted cowboy rode out and drove it offstage.

Cody claimed that the show's two daily performances "nearly always played to crowded houses," but this does not seem true. Annie Oakley's husband, Frank Butler, also a marksman, wrote in letters home that although people were turned away at first, by mid-December "the show was not paying well." To drum up interest, Cody added "Custer's Last Rally." On a canvas 440 feet long by 40 feet high, the Montana prairie sweeps to a bend in the Little Bighorn River. Mounted Sioux ride out of the painting toward Cody's cowboys, dressed as Custer's doomed men. There is a fight; smoke rises; the Sioux circle the soldiers until the last one falls. The Sioux disappear into the wings. Cody and others ride up and hang their heads in sorrow. A transparency bearing the words "Too Late" drops from the rafters.

Did Black Elk know what Cody was doing with "Custer's Last Rally"? He never says. But the tableau was so surreal and ironic that he and his friends must have talked among themselves. The suggestion that Cody might have saved Custer inflates and distorts his own place in history. No longer does he take "the first scalp for Custer"; he's evolved to a more mythic role. By this point, he's begun to resemble Custer, donning for shows and photographs the fringed buckskin suit, broad-brimmed hat, and high boots the Boy General always wore in popular depictions of the massacre. He even trimmed his long hair, beard, and mustache to resemble Custer's. Many of the "dead" warriors still on the battlefield when Cody rides up were, like Black Elk, actual participants in the showdown. In one theatrical flourish, Cody transforms himself from Custer's avenger to Custer Reborn.

But why? No one actually believed the historical accuracy of such a portrayal, and Cody never spelled it out explicitly. Yet in rewriting history, he was creating a moral truth of the frontier—and thus, of America itself. He expanded the doctrine of Manifest Destiny to include the claim that total war was necessary to civilize the Plains. The 1887 program states it bluntly, in an essay titled "The Rifle as an Aid to Civilization":

> [While it is] a trite saying that "the pen is mightier than the sword," it is equally true that the bullet is the pioneer of civilization, for it has gone hand in hand with the axe that cleared the forest, and with the family Bible and school book. Deadly as has been its mission in one sense, it has been merciful in another; for without the rifle ball we of America would not be to-day in the possession of a free and united country, and mighty in our strength.

A gloom settled over Black Elk as the show continued. It snowed all winter, but the piles of snow shoveled aside turned gray, not white like the drifts on the Plains. There was nothing here for his people. He would not find the secret to the power of the whites in Manhattan.

Once, before the end of the season, the troupe visited New York's penitentiary and asylum, both housed on Blackwell's Island in the East River. Why they chose such a place for an outing is anyone's guess; perhaps they succumbed to the universal fascination with the macabre. Between 1839 and 1887, thousands of New York's criminals, poor, and mentally ill were confined to the complex on the 120-acre sliver of land. Designed to cure inmates with the latest theories of moral therapy, the island asylum was the city's first publicly funded mental hospital and the first such facility in the nation. Yet by 1887, the good intentions had soured and Blackwell's Island was a brutal place, where convicts from the penitentiary served as attendants, and where torment, beatings, and neglect were the primary methods of treating the insane.

For the Sioux, comparisons to Pine Ridge were hard to ignore. Guards pointed guns at the inmates and herded them around like animals. Soldiers pointed guns at the Lakotas and ordered them to abandon everything they held dear. Just like the prisoners on Blackwell's, Black Elk's people were penned up on islands—islands of grass called reservations. Maybe this was the way the *wasichu* treated all whom they deemed different. They penned them out of sight and threw away the key.

<hr />

The show closed on February 22, 1887, and with its end some Oglalas went home. Some tried convincing Black Elk to go with them, and it was hard to refuse. So far, he'd found nothing that his people could use to rebuild the sacred hoop; neither had he seen anything that convinced him to follow the *wasichu* road. There were marvels, but these seemed dangerous and beyond comprehension. The city lights at night shone so brightly he could never see the stars. He'd heard that they glowed with the power of lightning and thunder created by something called a "dynamo," but losing touch with the stars was just another way to lose touch with *Wakan Tanka*. The sight of the poor begging on the street depressed him. Perhaps his parents had been right when they told him to stay in Pine Ridge.

Yet by March 1887, the rumor that they might cross the Atlantic to meet Grandmother England was confirmed. Two years earlier, the English entrepreneur John R. Whitley imagined a series of grand expositions staged in central London's Earl's Court; each would feature a separate nation's achievements in science, technology, and the arts, and all would be modeled after the World's Fairs that had enjoyed such success after London's 1851 Crystal Palace Exhibition. The first would showcase the United States. Whitley approached Cody and Salsbury: if they invested in this first "American Exhibition of Arts, Inventions, Manufactures, and Resources of the United States," he would guarantee a percentage of gate receipts. The fact that it would coincide with the fiftieth-anniversary celebration of Queen Victoria's ascension to the British throne promised high returns.

Cody had dreamed of such a venture. In *The Wild West in England,* published in 1888, he claimed that he had been urged repeatedly by "prominent persons of America" to take the show abroad. One was Mark Twain. "It is often said on the other side of the water that none of the exhibitions that we send to England are purely and distinctly American," Twain wrote to Cody in 1884. "If you will take the Wild West show over there, you can remove that reproach." Significantly, when the show opened in Manhattan, Cody and Salsbury billed it "America's National Entertainment."

Yet, the show's *Americanness*—its claim to authenticity and hope for financial success—depended upon Indian performers such as Black Elk. To Europeans, the idea of the New World, and the fantasies that went with it, were bound up with Native Americans. They reflected virtues the Europeans ascribed to themselves: Hungarians extolled the Indians' horsemanship; Germans, their military prowess; the French, the beauty of Indian maidens. The British and French courted them as allies during their own colonial wars.

Cody's Lakota and Pawnee performers were not the first Native Americans to visit the Old World. In 1608, the Virginia Algonquin ruler Powhatan sent a subject named Namontack to England to give a first-hand account of the place and its people; eight years later, he sent the temple priest Uttamatomakin to keep count of all the trees and people by making notches on a stick. In the 1720s, two "American princes" bearing the titles of Creek chiefs revealed, for the price of admission, their extensive tattoos.

But never before had so many Indians come to Europe at one time to appear in one venue. Cody may have instinctively understood this, but by 1898 he was well aware of their importance: "My Indians are the principal feature of this show," he said, "and they are the one people I will not allow to be misused or neglected." On March 31, 1887, the 209 members of the Wild West boarded the SS *State of Nebraska* for the voyage to England. Of that complement, 133 men, women, and children—or nearly 64 percent—were Lakota, Cheyenne, Kiowa, Arapaho, or Pawnee. Belowdecks were corralled 180 horses, 18 bison, 10 mules, 10 elk, 5 Texas longhorns, and an unspecified number of donkeys, deer, and bear. The *Nebraska* was a three-masted steamship, 3,986 gross tons, 385 feet long by 43 feet wide; this combination of sail and steam was common up to the end of the century as a kind of insurance should the engines fail. Launched on September 6, 1880, in Glasgow for the State Line, she typically made the voyage from Belfast to New York in seven days, and had done so at least forty-five times.

None of this was particularly comforting to Black Elk as he stood at the foot of the gangway. He and three others—Little Bull, Cut Meat, and Poor Dog—refused to board. They'd been told that crossing the great water would be beneficial to the Lakotas, but Black Elk wasn't so sure. He believed, as did many tribesmen, that any Indian attempting to cross the ocean would die. There was a logic to this, since of the few Native Americans who had crossed in the past, even fewer returned. Most succumbed to disease. Black Elk and his friends did not know this; instead, they reacted to the more common belief that soon after casting off, a man's flesh would wither day by day until dropping from his bones. Only the skeleton would be left, and that would be dumped in the sea; without proper burial, their spirits would wander the earth forever. It didn't help when Captain Braes pulled the steam whistle; Black Elk was already intimidated by the huge "fireboat," and when he heard the "big voice, I got scared." Cody sent down two trusted show members—a cowboy, "Squawman" Johnny Nelson, and the interpreter "Bronco Bill" Irving—and the two persuaded Black Elk and the others to board.

Something else may have added to their uncertainty. A few days earlier, the Indian performers had undergone a major shift in personnel. Throughout the stay at Madison Square Garden, their head chief had been the Oglala Rocky Bear, yet he was replaced soon before sailing by Ógle Lúta, or Red Shirt, a "progressive" aligned with McGillycuddy. Where Rocky Bear was a major Pine Ridge chief, Red Shirt was the leader of a small band of Loafers who lived near Agency headquarters. Enraged and insulted, Rocky Bear went home.

With the help of Cody's promotion and an enchanted European press, Red Shirt would become one of the leading Indians in the European show. He was tall, handsome, and portrayed in news stories as a ladies' man. He was turned by Cody's press corps into a veteran of the Custer fight and a warrior "second only in influence to Sitting Bull himself": a short time before joining the Wild West, he'd supposedly quelled an Oglala uprising by killing a rival for his chieftaincy. None of these claims can be confirmed. What *is* known is that he'd been an Indian scout opposed to Crazy Horse during the Great Sioux War, had enrolled his children in Carlisle's first class, served with the Indian police, and was an 1880 Lakota delegate to Washington. He stood for all the things Black Elk stood against. Though Black Elk never mentions discord, neither is there loyalty.

Their departure had all the hallmarks of forced gaiety. The Indians danced, the cowboys whooped, the show's Cowboy Band played "The Girl I Left Behind Me." The pier crowded with well-wishers. Cody, his daughter Arta, and Salsbury waved their hats "in sad farewell."

For Black Elk, there was nothing but "water, water, water." As they steamed from the harbor he gazed to the east, where the sky met the sea in an impenetrable barrier. Maybe they'd keep going until "we would drop off somewhere." He glanced back over the stern and "there was nothing but mist behind." Even Cody seemed cowed. He realized that "we were out upon the deep, for the first time in my life."

They had good reason for concern. They traveled the same route that would claim the *Titanic* a quarter century later. The North Atlantic was one of Nature's great battlegrounds, where warm air masses heading north crashed into the polar air mass heading south; a realm of bleak winds and monstrous waves. More ships lie at its bottom than at any other place on earth, their hulls split open by mountains of water, or tossed about like toy boats until capsized. The Norsemen, who sailed these waters before anyone else, saw the end of the world in those waves. According to Norse myth, Ragnarok, the apocalypse, would start in this ocean waste where the winds were "so keen and piercing, that there is no joy in the sun."

The winds came for them that evening. At first, only the Indians despaired. Black Elk battled nausea in a steerage compartment with sixteen others; the waves knocked them from side to side and the decks rolled. People around him cried, vomited, or sang their death songs. They'd unhooked their swaying hammocks from the ceiling hooks and tried to lie flat; instead, they rolled from one end of the room to the other as the ship climbed each giant swell and dropped down the other side. The whites laughed. But when the *Nebraska*'s rudder was damaged, the ship lost headway. They were tossed about like sticks, and they, too, grew terrified.

At one point, a crewman shoved life belts at the Lakotas, certain that the ship was about to go down. Black Elk tossed his life belt aside. He did not want to float like a willow branch on the breakers. He donned his best clothing and resolved to face death like a warrior. He and some others began to sing. They'd wanted adventure and that, by God, was what they were getting: "We wanted to know this and now we were learning it," he wryly observed. If he'd regretted coming earlier, he was *really* sorry now. Even Cody felt "sick as a cow," and though he tried to buck up their spirits, it did little good. Though the worst of the storm abated that night, the rolling continued and most of the troupe was seasick for two more days.

The storm passed on the third day of the voyage. Repairs were made to the rudder, and the *Nebraska* regained some stability. Though Black Elk was able to climb on deck and watch the sunrise, nothing he ate would stay down. They steamed slowly through a realm of chimeras and mist, where sailors historically reported phantom islands and wild storms disgorged giant squid. During this period, he spotted a "big black thing . . . his body was in the middle and his tail and head were way on either end of him"—probably a whale. The carcasses of buffalo and elk that had died in the storm were dragged from the holds and shoved overboard. He stood at the rail and watched the buffalo sink out of sight. "It looked as though they were throwing part of the power of the Indian overboard," he mourned.

On Thursday, April 14, the *State of Nebraska* entered the Thames and anchored at Gravesend, customs port for London. It had snowed that morning. The ocean voyage had taken two weeks, one week longer than usual; the storm had blown them off course, and they'd limped in on their damaged rudder. Black Elk and his tribesmen wrapped themselves in their blankets as a tug filled with curious quarantine officials chugged up for inspection. The ship moved slowly upriver to London's Limehouse Basin, where it was pulled through Regent's Canal to the Royal Albert Docks. The livestock would stay aboard for a few more days to guarantee against rinderpest and foot-and-mouth disease, but on April 16, Black Elk and the others disembarked into the heart of London. "They took us," he said, "to a place they called the Show."

———•◦•———

Life moved quickly after two weeks at sea. That Saturday morning, when they finally left the ship, "we still felt dizzy as though we were on water still." The troupe boarded three trains at the docks; they clattered twelve miles to Earl's Court in London's West End. Black Elk watched the city pass: each house seemed stacked one atop the next, and the people who lived in them filled the streets in an endless stream. With 4.25 million inhabitants, London was the most populous city on earth—the world center for finance and transport. Like Rome two hundred centuries earlier, all roads led here. Monuments of limestone and plate glass towered above his coach; electricity had been introduced in 1878, and electric lights glowed everywhere. New avenues such as Charing Cross Road had been opened for the Queen's Jubilee; these were crammed with horse-drawn trolleys, horse-drawn carriages, and horse-drawn omnibuses. There was so much manure that sanitary workers could not keep up; it was pushed to the roadside in mounting piles until shoveled into carts and wheeled away.

The train deposited them at the Midland depot, which abutted the Wild West showground. Americans had invested $165,000 in the entire encampment, with $130,000 of that relegated to the arena, stands, and refreshment area. The arena was still under construction when they arrived: it tracked a third of a mile in circumference; the entire showground, seven acres. The arena boasted twenty thousand seats, with sheltered stands for ten thousand ticket holders and open-air standing room for another ten thousand. Stables for horses and mules had already been built; corrals for the buffalo, elk, and antelope would soon be finished. A causeway led west from Cody's extravaganza to the Main Exhibition Hall, an iron-and-glass edifice measuring 400 yards high by 150 yards wide. There Londoners could ogle a switchback railway, an early form of roller coaster, a New England toboggan slide, and a scale model of New York City and the Statue of Liberty. Although the Wild West would get all the press, the two attractions would complement each other. As the Exhibition approached its closing date in November 1887, *The Times* of London would write: "Those who went to be amused often stayed to be instructed. It must be acknowledged that the Show was the attraction which made the fortune of the Exhibition."

The performers did not rest when they reached the showground. By 4:00 p.m., the horses were all stabled, watered, and fed; by 6:00 p.m., tents and tipis were going up, equipment and bedding distributed, and an American supper of "beef, mutton, corn-bread, ham" laid out in the open air. Thousands of Londoners watched from surrounding rooftops, walls, and streets, and Cody wanted the British to say that "the Yankees mean business." The American flag was hoisted overhead and the Cowboy Band played the national anthem. Then, in a public relations masterstroke, it launched into "God Save the Queen." The crowd roared its approval.

Opening Day was set for May 9. For the next three weeks, they worked feverishly to get everything ready. A spot by the railroad tracks was reserved for the construction of a "wilderness." Seventeen thousand carloads of rock and earth were dumped, and for ten days the show's roustabouts sculpted it into hilly terrain and planted trees. This was the location of the Indian camp, where Black Elk would live in a "state of nature." Nearly three thousand employees and hired laborers worked on the grounds. Black Elk rehearsed frequently, honing his dance steps and memorizing cues for the attacks on the stagecoach and settler's cabin; Cody's press agent in chief, "Major" John M. Burke, and his publicity army plastered the city with posters; the Wild West held "Indian breakfasts" and rib roast dinners for journalists and dignitaries. Whenever there was a break, cowboys and Indians visited theaters, churches, and other public places.

In fact, like tourists everywhere, the Lakotas "did" the sights of London. It turned into free publicity. If the Wild West did not catch fire in London, said *The New York Dramatic Mirror*, "it certainly will not be for want of gilt-edge advertising. Never was a show better boomed. Within the last ten days, the cowboys and Indians have been the round of London theatres, on free seats, which have been placed at their disposal by enterprising managers." The Oglalas visited the Tower of London, sat in box seats at the Lyceum Theatre for Sir Henry Irving's production of Goethe's *Faust,* and attended services at Westminster Abbey, which Red Shirt called the "Great Spirit Lodge." The lofty spires and winged cherubs on the stained-glass windows convinced him that he'd experienced a sacred vision.

A steady procession of distinguished visitors brought even more attention to the show. On April 25, the former prime minister William Gladstone and his wife toured the camp and were treated to a short preview. On May 5, after officially opening the Exhibition, Albert Edward and his wife, Alexandra, the Prince and Princess of Wales, climbed into the grandstand. The forty-five-year-old heir apparent was plainspoken, pleasant, of medium height, and "rather inclined to corpulency," Cody observed; he liked cards, mistresses, fine food, clothes, and horses, and he and Cody hit it off instantly. "Bertie's" popularity waxed and waned as various scandals hit the papers, but his natural affability smoothed all waters and everyone—the British public, politicians, and even his wife—eventually forgave him. All except his mother, the Queen, who blamed her husband's December 1861 death on her son's latest peccadillo. As she told her eldest daughter, "I never can, or shall, look at him without a shudder."

But for all his faults, Bertie was one of the few European sovereigns of the colonial era to even suggest that a man's race did not determine his worth. During an eight-month tour of the Indian subcontinent in 1875–76, his retinue and advisors began to remark upon his unusual habit of treating all people the same, regardless of color or station. In letters home, he complained of the treatment native Indians received at the hands of British officials: "Because a man has a black face and a different religion from our own, there is no reason why he should be treated as a brute," he wrote to Lord Granville, the future secretary of state for foreign affairs.

Now the Prince was about to meet America's Indians. Cody escorted the Prince and his guests to their box and left them in the hands of Major Burke to explain the various acts of the performance. The arena was almost complete. The field sloped up to a painted backdrop of a mountain pass, five hundred feet in length and designed to block out the urban vista of London. The performers burst from a hidden entrance into the arena. The mounted Indians, "yelling like fiends," galloped toward the box and "swept around the enclosure like a whirlwind." The effect was "electric," Cody said, beaming. The Prince leaned over the front rail of the box; the Princess and the rest of the party seemed thrilled. "Cody," he said to himself, "you have fetched 'em!"

He'd fetched 'em all right, or at least the Indians had. When the royal party toured the Indian camp, the Princess of Wales crooned over a newborn papoose. The Prince conversed with Red Shirt, then made him a gift of cigarettes from his cigarette case. He fetched all of London, and newspapers estimated that 28,000 ticket holders streamed through the gates on May 9, Opening Day. They were treated to what one English paper called "a sort of a savage circus, and a rough and ready theatre." They were awed by the opening procession, horse races, "Cowboy Fun," the Pony Express, sharpshooting demonstrations, Indian dances, a buffalo hunt, stunts by Mexican vaqueros, and an Indian attack on a settler's cabin. There were female trick shots and cowgirls, an assault on a wagon train, a demonstration of Indian women setting up tipis, and bronco bustin'. The arena was filled with "shooting, war cries, action, color, the strains of the Cowboy Band, the huge voice of Frank Richmond." According to the *Illustrated Sporting and Dramatic News*, the

English were most fond of the trick shooting and horse racing segments, since they could make "heavy bets" on them.

But more than anything else, Cody knew he'd fetched 'em when, on May 10, he received a request from Buckingham Palace to provide a private performance the next day "by command of Her Majesty, the Queen." Her son had piqued her interest, and for once she planned to break a decades-long seclusion. "One day we were told 'that Majesty is coming,'" Black Elk said. Grandmother England would come to the show.

———•◦•———

By May 11, 1887, Victoria had occupied the British throne for nearly fifty years. Her Jubilee Celebration, planned for June 20–21, would be the triumph of her career. To that point, her reign had been the longest of any British monarch and of any queen regent in world history. She was compared to Elizabeth, but Elizabeth had ruled a little island of five million people while Victoria ruled nearly half the world. When British subjects acted out their separate dramas for empire—when the Light Cavalry Brigade rode to destruction in the Crimea, or General George Gordon died at Khartoum—at some point they thought of Victoria and ransomed their lives to her. This was the "Pax Britannica," Britain's "imperial century," when the British Empire controlled some thirteen million square miles of territory, almost a quarter of the earth's surface, and held sway over roughly four hundred million people, or one-fifth of the world's population. Great Britain's was the largest, most powerful empire in history, dwarfing that of her predecessor Rome.

On May 11, 1887, Victoria was thirteen days shy of her sixty-eighth birthday. She did not wear the years well. The death of her husband, Prince Albert, twenty-six years earlier had been the turning point of her life. She felt that her true self had died with her husband. Contemporaries seemed to agree. Lord Clarendon spoke of Albert's death as "a natural calamity of far greater importance than the public dream of." She'd dressed in mourning since that day. Her short, stout figure, draped in folds of black velvet with muslin streamers; the heavy pearls hanging about the heavy neck: all became a dour symbol of the age. She rarely went out—to Parliament, seldom; to theaters, never. Her knowledge of her kingdom's great actors and actresses was gleaned from private performances at Windsor Castle, where they'd been "commanded" to entertain the Queen.

But the Wild West was too big to fit in Windsor Castle. So, due largely to Bertie's coaxing, she went to them. "Her Majesty will arrive," Cody was told, "at five o'clock," and expected to see the entire show in an hour. A dais was built, draped with crimson velvet and decorated with orchids. For this day alone, the public was banned from the show.

She arrived on the hour, as forewarned. Fifty horse-drawn carriages pulled into the arena, bearing the Queen and "a collection of uniformed celebrities and brilliantly attired fair ladies," Cody said. Soldiers in red tunics surrounded the Queen. Gunfire usually filled the arena during the opening, but no shooting was allowed on this day. Cody would later tell the world that Victoria rose from her seat and bowed to the American flag when it was presented on horseback, and his version passed into legend. Yet the British press told a different story. Protocol dictated that foreign flags should dip before the throne; the monarch then acknowledged this with a nod, and the flag was raised. And that was what happened. According to *The World*: "When, in the course of the performance, Serjeant [sic] Bates brought down the 'star-spangled banner' . . . and lowered it before the Queen, she inclined her head twice in recognition of courtesy."

Such emotion-packed moments fall easy prey to memory. For Black Elk, it all passed in a blur. By now he was one of the Wild West's best dancers, and he'd been chosen as one of five Indians to dance before the Queen. He was tall and limber, an extremely handsome young man with long dark hair and an expression as direct as a child's. He'd crossed the great water to find the source of the *wasichus'* power; he'd been pointed here like a lodestone, coming to the world's largest city in the most powerful nation on earth. Now he was about to dance for the ruler of that nation, arguably the most powerful person in the *wasichu* world.

Dance, in the Lakota world, was a means of communication to and from the gods. The dancer was the conduit: the vision of that truer reality could be transmitted only through the music and motion of the dance. They had chosen to perform the Omaha Grass Dance, one of the oldest dances on the Plains, nearly three hundred years old. According to legend, a lame boy, yearning to dance, was told by his mentor to seek inspiration in nature; he limped into the prairie and saw himself dancing like the grasses that swayed in the constant wind. Movement was life on the prairie, and one only stayed rooted to one spot when one died. He shared the vision with his village, and it touched something in them. Soon, the Grass Dance was common to all tribes.

And so Black Elk danced before Grandmother England. A large

drum was beat slowly, then faster. He stomped the grass to one side, then the other, and turned: three toe taps and then drop the heel, left and right foot alternating. Some said this was the true origin of the dance—that in order to secure a meeting spot, high grasses must be stomped flat, but the steps meant more. Balance and symmetry were essential in life—what the body did on one side it must do on the other. As Black Elk danced, his body swayed. Three toe taps and drop the heel. Every piece of his regalia was adorned with sweeping lengths of yarn, from the fringed cape to the apron and leggings. The yarn swayed like grass blown by the wind. It swung with every step until *he* was the grass, *he* was the world, *he* was the wind. The world's balance had been broken and must be repaired. The Queen would watch other performers during her visit—Pahuska himself, Little Sure Shot, Chief Red Shirt—but right now there were only two people present: Black Elk, the bearer of truth, and Grandmother England.

And then the drumbeat ended. The swaying stopped. The dancers stood still in a row. Victoria came down from her dais and shook hands with each one. In Black Elk's memory she shook hands only with the dancers, though in truth she offered her hand to others. She was little and fat, and her hands were as soft as a baby's; he liked her because she seemed good. "I am sixty-seven years old," she said. "All over the world, I have seen all kinds of people, and I have seen all kinds of countries, too, and I've heard about some people that were in America and I heard they called them American Indians. Now I have seen them today."

She smiled. "I have seen all kinds of people, but today I have seen the best-looking—the Indians." She gazed up into Black Elk's eyes. "If I owned you Indians, you good looking people, I would never take you on a show like this." The Grandfather in Washington should not allow it, a big war was coming soon, and all people needed to be treated decently before it was too late and the war destroyed them all. She grew silent, almost pensive, and pointed at Black Elk. "I wish that I had owned you people, for I would not carry you around as beasts to show to the people." She raised her hand. Her speech was over.

The time was 6:45 p.m. She'd watched the performance and wandered through camp for an hour and forty-five minutes, three-quarters of an hour longer than intended, a rarity for Victoria. An eternity. She added in afterthought, "It's up to you to come and see me now." Then she and her retinue entered the carriages and drove away.

16

THE ENTRANCE TO HELL

Black Elk would think about his dance before the throne of empire for a long time. He'd danced for the salvation of the Oglala, and he believed she'd listened. Victoria had been touched by the beauty of the dance, and for an instant had a glimpse of a place beyond the barrier of language. She came down from her dais, grabbed his hand, and spoke as if he were a cherished son. At 210 words it is the longest speech given by any white in *Black Elk Speaks* or in the oral interviews, yet Black Elk's rendition is too convoluted and Victoria's words cannot be taken verbatim. After fifty years as regent, Victoria was practiced at public speaking. She might burble like a girl in her diaries, but she was commanding in front of crowds. Neither can we trust his memory of her forecast of "the big war in the future." No other account corroborates this vision of a world war still twenty-seven years away. No biographers credit Victoria with the gift of prophecy.

Something else occurred—something Black Elk struggled with for forty-four years. We must break it down to understand. Of all the people she'd encountered in her travels, the American Indians were the best-looking. The Grandfather in Washington should not let them be treated like "beasts to show to the people." *If I owned you, I would have treated you better.*

It was a rebuke, ostensibly of Cody but more accurately of American culture—a remarkable rebuke, considering the British Empire's myriad little wars throughout the world that conquered people like the Sioux. By May 11, 1887, the empire had fought in more than 150 wars, relief expeditions, and police actions that Rudyard Kipling called the "savage wars of peace," and as Black Elk danced, two were under way: the war with Arab slavers in Nyasa, and the Third Burma War. Though somewhat hypocritical, Victoria reacted viscerally, just as Bertie had in India. Neither spoke officially, as Queen or heir apparent. Both spoke from the heart of the treatment of man by man.

Though Black Elk had touched Victoria, her words had no teeth, something she seemed to realize. *If* the United States were still part of the Commonwealth; *if* America treated Indians as fairly as Canada, adhering to treaties, not breaking its word. One hears regret in her statement, which Black Elk echoes: "Maybe if she had been our Grandmother, it would have been better for our people." But in the end, that's all it was—more words.

For now, however, he was swept up in the excitement of the Queen's Jubilee. Victoria marked the fiftieth anniversary of her accession on June 20: she breakfasted under the willows at Frogmore Estate adjoining Windsor Castle, where Albert lay in the Royal Mausoleum. She traveled by train from Windsor to Paddington Station, then on to Buckingham Palace, where she'd host a royal banquet that night attended by fifty kings, queens, princes, princesses, and the governing heads of Britain's overseas dominions.

That morning, as Victoria made her stately way to Buckingham, the Prince of Wales escorted the royal guests to the Wild West's morning show. Since this was Bertie's second visit, Cody determined that something new was in order. He placed the Prince—along with the rulers of Belgium, Denmark, Greece, and Saxony—in the Deadwood Stage, a refurbished derelict coach that had been abandoned after the driver and passengers were massacred. Bertie sat in the driver's box with Cody, who told his Indians to "whoop 'em up" and sweep down upon the stage. According to an oft-told tale, the Prince turned to Cody after the attack and said, "Colonel, did you ever hold four kings like that before?" The most colorful version of Cody's response came from his sister Helen: "I have held four kings more than once, . . . but, your Highness, I never held four kings and the royal joker before."

The next day, it was the Indians' turn to be honored. Victoria made good on her words "It's up to you to come and see me now." The show boss told the Indians to don their finery; chariots transported them to grandstands built at Windsor Castle. Victoria emerged in a procession of open landaus escorted by Bengal cavalry; the parade wound through London's streets to render thanks at Westminster Abbey, then returned to Windsor. The Queen's gold-and-silver coach "looked like fire coming" as it approached the stand of Sioux. All around the Indians, the English stamped their feet and cried "Victoria!" and "Jubilee!"

Then the confirmation occurred. The Queen's carriage passed, then stopped and backed up to that place where the Indians sat in the grandstands. "All her people bowed to her, but she bowed to us Indians," Black Elk recalled. They returned the honor, men and women raising a tremolo until it seemed they might suffocate, then breaking into song. Black Elk would always remember this moment. "This was the most happy time!" he said.

It seemed so, too, for Victoria. She would always miss her Prince, but the long mourning had ended. The English lining the streets and packing the grandstands hailed their Queen "as the mother of her people and as the embodied symbol of their imperial greatness," wrote the Edwardian biographer Lytton Strachey, and she responded in kind: she knew that "England and the people of England . . . were, in some wonderful and yet quite simple manner, *hers*." That night, after the return to Buckingham, after the appearance on the balcony, the fireworks and cheers, she was asked how she held up. "I'm very tired," she said, "but very happy."

The Wild West closed in London on October 31, 1887. For the entirety of its stay, Londoners could not get enough of the Indians. They learned that they liked roast dog and were fattening a white stray for that culinary purpose; worried over false rumors that smallpox and scarlet fever were decimating the native performers; chuckled at the report in *The Evening News* that Indians had purchased opera glasses and were now watching spectators in the stands. When the London run ended, these spectators had bought 2.5 million tickets, for an average daily attendance of 30,000 to 40,000. Cody said they made a "barrel of money."

At first the show was fun. There would be "shouting and war-cries and a great deal of hoofs"; Black Elk and his pals would get killed and fall in the dust; then their friends would ride by, pluck them up, and take them from the arena. They'd laugh about it afterward. The curious would gather as they stood together between shows. "Sometimes we would growl and the people near us would rush back, and we would look angry, but we were laughing inside."

But soon, time dragged. The weather was nothing like that of the Plains: "terrible fogs" descended upon London for three or four days, so thick one could not see across the street; it was hard to breathe, and one coughed up black phlegm. This would be followed by prolonged rain. Fights broke out: in late July, the show member Jack Ross was charged with being drunk in public and breaking a plate-glass window at the Old House Revived public house. A few days later, in early August, the "Giant Cowboy" Dick Johnson got into a fistfight at a London pub. Two constables arrived and one was sent to the hospital. Johnson was convicted of assault and sentenced to six months of hard labor at Pentonville Prison.

On November 5, the Wild West moved to Birmingham, a sooty warren of redbrick workshops, heart of the island's Industrial Revolution. Time took a toll on the Indians. Red Shirt spoke of England's "great villages which have no end, where the pale faces swarm like insects in the summer sun." It might be a big country, said Black Elk, but "it is always full of white men."

Cody seemed aware of his Indians' homesickness and restlessness, and tried to steer clear of acts that might offend them. During this period, he dropped the duel with Yellow Hand, and when a reporter suggested "the introduction of a little scalping," Cody grew irate: if the gentleman had been involved in frontier warfare, "he would not be so zealous for realism. Nothing but a real massacre, with genuine blood flowing and a comfortable array of corpses," would satiate such armchair adventurers.

On the whole, the Indians were given considerable freedom, a situation that occasionally resulted in their getting lost or in trouble. In London, no Indian had been allowed outside the grounds unless accompanied by a white for fear of liquor consumption, but this rule was relaxed in Birmingham. "There is apparently no restraint imposed on the movements of either Indians or cross-breeds," one reporter noted. "The untutored children of the prairie stalk about in their gorgeously colored blankets, and seem quite indifferent to the sensation they are causing."

Sometimes their travels ended in a pub, which brought up the issue of Indians and alcohol. Today, alcohol-related deaths among Native Americans are about four times greater than in the general population, but no one really understands why. History and culture are no doubt contributors, yet decades of research have also focused on the role of alcohol-metabolizing enzymes. When a person drinks, ethanol is turned into water by an enzyme called alcohol dehydrogenase (ADH); the more ADH one produces, the faster alcohol is metabolized, or broken down. Many geneticists suspect that Native Americans do not produce ADH at the same rate as the larger population, a chromosomal deficit that might account for up to 50 or 60 percent of the problem. Yet no specific gene that might be responsible has yet been found.

Cody might not have known the causes, but by 1898 he had enough experience with the problem to appoint a chief over native performers; he kept track of their peregrinations and limited the amount of money available to spend at pubs. But in 1887 the system was not in place. Freedom had its consequences.

On Monday, November 28, Black Elk and a friend identified as Black Bird visited some pubs along the city's Lichfield Road. Neither went by their regular names during the incident: Black Elk went by "Choice," while no Black Bird was listed in the roster, which suggests he, too, went by a childhood name. At some point during the night, they separated and ended up in different pubs. Black Bird went to the Reservoir Tavern, where sometime after 5:00 p.m. constables found him "behaving in an indecent manner, foaming at the mouth, and very drunk," according to *The Birmingham Daily Post.* "He was nearly naked, having divested himself of his blanket and other clothing," and had to be held down by five or six bystanders while officers handcuffed and rolled him to the station in a handcart. Forty-five minutes had passed: when they tried to take him to lockup, Black Bird began fighting again, this time throwing a "Police-sergeant Parker" to the ground, tearing off the sleeve of his coat and ripping the knee of his trousers. The police slammed the cell door behind Black Bird and let him sleep off his bender.

Soon afterward, constables received word of another inebriated Indian, this one in the Crown Inn on Church Lane. Constable Parker was sent out again. He found Black Elk propped on a bench, asleep, far more docile than his friend. Parker "aroused him and found that he was helplessly drunk." He, too, spent the night in a cell.

The next morning—Tuesday, November 29—Black Elk and Black

Bird appeared before a three-judge panel of "Messrs. Hill, Cooper, and Weiss" at Aston Police Court. "Bronco Bill" Irving—the same cowboy who coaxed Black Elk up the *Nebraska*'s gangway—served as interpreter. Both men admitted to drinking too much, but neither could remember what followed. The judges dismissed the charges of public drunkenness, but Black Bird was fined two pounds, five shillings, to mend the sergeant's uniform.

The show next moved to Manchester. Six million miners and mill-hands lived in "Cottonopolis," divided into towns of ten to one hundred thousand and linked to the industrial hub by a spider's web of rails. The performers had no choice but to stay indoors. The English winter—rain, drizzle, fog, frost, snow, and cutting east winds—was hard on the Americans, and could kill the livestock. The Manchester race course—actually located in the neighboring borough of Salford, on the banks of an "inky ditch" called the Irwell—would serve as their winter quarters. A new £15,000 wood-and-brick building was built for the Wild West, huge by the standards of the day—six hundred feet long, two hundred feet wide, and eighty feet high with rafters painted white and red, heated by steam and electrically lit. Its eight thousand seats were arranged around an amphitheater and rose forty feet. The Indians camped inside the building, while livestock was stabled in the rear. The walls were hung with mounted horns and hunting trophies to give the interior a "Western" feel. The show was scheduled to start on December 17, but tragedy struck the week before opening. During rehearsals, twenty-two-year-old Surrounded by the Enemy—a six-foot-seven Oglala who performed "daring gun-slinging and horse-riding stunts"—died of a "lung infection," apparently Cody's first performer to die overseas. No other details were available, and Cody did not mention his death in various accounts of the tour. "Lung infection" often meant pneumonia, a common malady in the English cold. According to Salford lore, a traditional burial was held. Red Shirt and Black Elk officiated, which suggests he still served as the Oglalas' *wicasa wakan*. Surrounded by the Enemy's body was taken to Salford's Hope Hospital and supposedly buried in a pauper's grave on hospital grounds. Yet records discovered years later stated he was buried on December 15, 1887, in Brompton Cemetery near Earl's Court, the site of the London shows. The mystery was never explained.

January 1888 proved harsh, with dense fogs and gales. In February, the
snow was so deep that roads and railroads closed. Black Elk was happy
to hunker down in his steam-heated building and study the white man.
On February 15, 1888, he wrote of his experiences to his people in a
letter printed in *Iapi Oaye*, the Lakota-language newspaper published in
Nebraska's Santee Agency. He no longer feared nor hated the *wasichu*,
he said: "Now I know the white man's customs well. One custom is very
good whoever believes in God will find good ways." England was very
different: "The days are all dark. It is always smoky so we never see the
sun clearly." And he adds: "Whoever has no country will die in the
wilderness. . . . That which makes me happy is always land."

What does he mean? In one way, like Crazy Horse, he expresses a
mystic connection to the land. In England, that connection seems severed; the cities were smoky industrial hubs where the sea of faces went
on forever. Those he observes seem like lost souls. This was not a path
his people should take. Something essential was missing.

If anything, he seems tired. He'd crossed the ocean, danced before
the seat of power, touched Grandmother England herself, and on a daily
basis witnessed thousands rejoice as he performed. But what did it mean?
Where were the secrets he'd come to learn? There were no secrets—
that was the secret—and the people in these gray industrial cities were
no more free than the Oglala at Pine Ridge. The factories were their
reservations—if not the factories, then the cities themselves. They were
beaten down and dirty, a tribe as hungry and sickly as his own.

It was time to go home, time to see his friends and family and tell
them what he had learned. That was all he could think about, but it
was not to be. The Buffalo Bill Wild West gave its closing indoor performance in Manchester on April 30, 1888, and the crowds gave Cody an
extended standing ovation, refusing to let him leave. From May 1 to the
morning of the 4th, the performers were free to do as they pleased.
They had to be back by Friday morning to board a special train to the
port city of Hull on the River Humber, where the SS *Persian Monarch*
waited to take them home.

Cody's first European tour had been a financial and critical success.
The Wild West's 1887 earnings were estimated at more than half a million dollars. Though his total 1888 earnings are unavailable, his gross
receipts upon his return to New York totaled almost $250,000. His daily
expenses, including salaries, came to about $2,000; thus, his 1888 New
York profits have been estimated at $100,000.

But Black Elk and his three companions in Manchester would not be present to enjoy the American accolades. For three days—from the last Manchester show until the morning they were supposed to board the train—they painted the town. While we do not know their itinerary, we do know that Cottonopolis gave the Indians a send-off in grand style. A period photo suggests a Mardi Gras atmosphere. A two-decker Manchester Corporation Tramways car is crammed, top to bottom, with Indians in their war bonnets and eagle feathers. They hang from the windows and wave at the crowd, jingling past power lines and "adverts" for Lipton's Jams & Marmalades and Yorkshire relish. It was a three-day party, and Black Elk and his companions—High Bear, Two Elk, and Charles Picket Pin, also known as Red Cow—got lost in Manchester.

They had no idea where they were, could speak no English beyond a few simple words. Black Elk's earlier drunkenness charge raises the question of whether they partook of John Barleycorn too freely; whatever the case, they apparently panicked when they realized their predicament, knowing the show would leave without them. The British were friendly, but could not speak Lakota. "We roamed around there and we found a resting place and stayed all night in a rooming house." Maybe someone would help them the next morning.

At 10:00 a.m. on May 4, a special train of eighteen wagons filled with livestock pulled from the Windsor Bridge Station of the Lancashire & Yorkshire Railway, bound for Hull. A second train of nine cars pulled up for Cody and his entourage. The crowds sang "Auld Lang Syne" as Cody stepped into the saloon carriage; his daughter Arta was handed several huge bouquets. "The leave-taking was a prolonged one," reported the *Manchester Weekly Times*, "for every member of the troupe, including the Indians, seemed to have numerous friends, from whom they were loth [sic] to part." By 11:00 a.m., this second train moved out, followed by a third carrying baggage and the Deadwood Stage. By 2:20 p.m., the trains had arrived at Hull's Alexandra Dock, where all was loaded onto the waiting steamer. On May 5, the Wild West gave a farewell performance. At 3:15 a.m. on May 6, the *Persian Monarch* left with the tide.

Black Elk was not with them. His little group had missed the boat and was left behind.

—•◦•—

They had one last chance to reunite, and that was to take a train from Manchester to the Portland Breakwater, far south in Dorset, where the *Persian Monarch* would let off journalists, dignitaries, and four young stowaways, and continue west into the North Atlantic. This expedient had been explained to cast members should they, in the confusion, miss the train to Hull. There was plenty of time. The *Persian Monarch* entered the North Sea from the mouth of the Humber, turned south through the Straits of Dover, then sailed along the southern coast of England at a leisurely pace. It dropped anchor off the Breakwater at 11:00 p.m. on Monday, May 7, but no Sioux waited. At daybreak on May 8, the shore boat containing the last guests cast off, and the steamship sailed for New York and home.

Perhaps Black Elk and the others tried to rejoin their friends. "We could not speak English," he reiterated. Two other performers, who have remained unidentified, had also gotten separated and joined the four in the rooming house. Now there were six Buffalo Bill refugees left behind in England; the additional two may have been Indians, since Black Elk described one as an "English speaker" and not a *wasichu*. Luckily, this fellow spoke passable English, and they took a train to London. Yet continuing south through the megalopolis was simply too confusing. The six stayed in London, "where we roamed around for three days," in effect missing their last chance to return to the United States with Buffalo Bill.

By now, they were low on funds and even lower on ideas about getting home. One option, they decided, was "to make some money to go home by giving shows"; in all likelihood, the unidentified "English speaker" had heard of rival Wild West shows drawn to London by Cody's success. In fact, news of a "Red Indian invasion of England" had flooded all points of the Sceptered Isle. "There are rumors that a few more Cowboy Colonels are coming to our Tom Tiddler's Ground now this style of thing has caught on," wrote the *North-Eastern Daily Gazette* on August 16, 1887:

> Texas Jack, Jericho Jim, Timbuctoo Tom, Arizona Alf, Nebraska Ned, Frisco Fred, and Sacramento Sam will all be coming over with wild men of the woods, and will crowd the metropolis. One never knows what great events from little causes spring, and the wholesale introduction of Red Indians into the country may

have a notable effect on our race. . . . The Londoner of the future may be more like a Red Indian than a Cockney.

At the moment, posters and handbills plastered up around town advertised something called "Mexican Joe's Western Wilds of America," scheduled to run May 21 through June 9 at the grand reopening of the Alexandra Palace in North London.

The six found housing in what Black Elk called the "English speaker's place." But since this fellow was also a refugee, it is more likely that they stayed at a lodging house similar to that in Manchester. Black Elk did not know its location, but it's probable that they stayed in the Whitechapel district of London's East End, an area characterized by poverty, poor housing, drunkenness, homelessness, and violent crime. Lodging houses overran Whitechapel, providing cheap common quarters for the destitute and desperate. Constables walked beats down foggy alleys. Prostitutes were everywhere.

On the third day of their stay, during the second week of May, "a policeman came to us and took us to the courthouse and asked us where we were the night before." In a compact district such as Whitechapel, the presence of six lost Lakotas in a lodging house would have been common knowledge. The six were confused: "We did not know but what we were arrested."

Black Elk was certainly frightened. He'd seen the lockups at Blackwell's Island and could imagine that he'd be jailed forever in one of the *wasichus'* metal cages. "They questioned us about everything," he said. The English speaker told the police where they'd been for the last three days and what they were trying to do. Given the confused repetition in Black Elk's account, they were probably questioned for hours and then released without explanation. They never learned details, but the police "probably blamed us with something that had happened."

What could that have been? Because of the approximate time and specific place, most commentators have assumed they were suspects in the horrific slayings by the unidentified serial killer Jack the Ripper. But the chronology for that is wrong; later, all western performers in their troupe *would* be suspects, but not now. The five women universally acknowledged today as Jack's victims—Mary Ann Nichols, Annie Chapman, Elizabeth Stride, Catherine Eddowes, and Mary Jane Kelly—were all murdered in the period from August 31, 1888, when Nichols was found with her throat cut, to November 9, 1888, when Kelly was found butchered in her room. "Jack" did not even identify himself as such until the infamous "Dear Boss" letter dated "25 Sept. 1888" and sent to the offices of the Central News Agency on September 27.

But something else was happening, something authorities only slowly comprehended. Despite Whitechapel's rampant crime, murder itself was rare. The Annual Report of the Sanitary Conditions of White-chapel listed no murders in the district for the two preceding years, 1886 and 1887. The report *did* list seventy-one violent deaths in 1887, but sixty-nine were blamed on accidents, two on suicide. Nineteenth-century London coroners were loath to classify a death as homicide without solid proof, which meant a confession or eyewitness testimony. Yet, be-ginning in 1888, the streets of Whitechapel became deadly for women.

From Tuesday, April 3, 1888, until Friday, February 13, 1891, eleven women were murdered, and it was not known whether the crimes were committed by a single killer. Even today, there is wide doubt concern-ing which were the Ripper's victims, and which belonged to copycats. All eleven deaths were gathered in a single file referred to in the police docket as the "Whitechapel Murders," and despite the best efforts of the Metropolitan Police, City of London Police, private organizations such as the Whitechapel Vigilance Committee, and hundreds of pro-fessional and armchair investigators, not a single one of these eleven has been solved.

The first had already occurred when Black Elk rented lodging. On April 3, 1888, forty-five-year-old Emma Elizabeth Smith was attacked at about 1:30 a.m. by three men near Whitechapel Church. She stumbled the three hundred yards to her lodging house at 18 George Street, and two neighbors helped her to the London Hospital, where she died at 9:00 a.m. The coroner attributed her death to peritonitis: her abdomen was injured and peritoneum ruptured by a blunt instrument thrust up her "woman's passage." Although Detective Constable Walter Dew later thought she was the Ripper's first victim, his colleagues believed she was attacked by a gang of pimps assaulting lone prostitutes who were not part of their "stable."

Smith's murder was probably the reason Black Elk was interrogated. Once the constables accepted that the six were in Manchester on the day of the murder, they were released. Yet the belief in Indian cruelty had been planted by the Wild West: journalists depicted the Oglalas as fierce and dangerous men. As Ripper hysteria heightened, the press echoed imagery from Cody's "Attack on the Settler's Cabin": every shadow held a savage, and women were spared rape and murder only by the presence of armed white protectors.

Black Elk and his original companions joined Mexican Joe soon after their interrogation. Though it was a smaller show, the pay was better: Mexican Joe paid thirty dollars a month, compared with Buffalo Bill's twenty-five dollars. Still, Black Elk seemed to feel it was a step down in status upon discovering that the show's bloodthirsty Apache were "nothing . . . but Omahas." They moved to the Indian Village erected on the Alexandra Park Racecourse and stayed there until June 9; the show then moved to Paris and played there from June 23 to July 20. It was originally slated to return to London, but the Paris run had been so lucrative that it moved instead to the Grand Concours in Brussels, where it opened on Sunday, August 5, as part of the Exposition Universelle. It stayed on the Continent until early October, then returned to England and opened in Birmingham on October 18.

And during this period, the Ripper became a worldwide obsession. On August 7, two days after Black Elk opened in Brussels, thirty-six-year-old Martha Tabram was found faceup in a pool of blood on a first-floor landing in Whitechapel's George Yard, stabbed thirty-nine times. Many today think she was the Ripper's first victim. The "signature" characteristics of Tabram's murder were similar to those of the Ripper's five acknowledged victims: in all six cases, the killer preyed on white female prostitutes in a one-square-mile area of Whitechapel. When the women hiked their skirts up for sex, he grabbed their throats and strangled them; lowered them to the ground with their heads pointing to his left; then cut their throats to the left. This gave way to a frenzy of stabbing and slashing with a sharpened long knife, an act that grew worse with each murder.

About three weeks before Black Elk's troupe opened in Birmingham, the Ripper wrote the "Dear Boss" letter in which he introduced himself to the world:

Dear Boss:
                                                  25 Sept. 1888.
    I keep hearing the police have caught me but they wont fix me just yet. I have laughed when they look so clever and talk about

being on the right track. That joke about Leather Apron gave me real fits. I am down on whores and I shant quit ripping them till I do get buckled. Grand work the last job was. I gave the lady no time to squeal. How can they catch me now. I love my work and want to start again. You will soon hear of me with my funny little games. I saved some of the proper <u>red</u> stuff in a ginger beer bottle over the last job to write with but it went thick like glue and I cant use it. Red ink is fit enough I hope <u>ha ha</u>.

He signed it, "yours truly, Jack the Ripper," and at right angles to the rest added: "wasnt good enough to post this before I got all the red ink off my hands curse it. No luck yet. They say I'm a doctor now <u>ha ha</u>."

Although no murders attributed to Jack occurred in October, it was a busy letter-writing season. "Dear Boss" unleashed a flood. As many as eighty letters purportedly by the Ripper arrived at police and press offices; hundreds more came in from citizens. A three-way conversation ensued among the Ripper, the authorities, and the people of London. As it continued, a new theme arose: the Ripper was American. Not only that, but a westerner.

The first hint of this theme appeared on Wednesday, October 3, fifteen days before Black Elk's opening in Birmingham. A small news story carried in the *Star of the East* compared the Ripper murders to similar ones in Texas. It quoted an undated editorial in *The Atlanta Constitution* noting that, even though the "mysterious crimes in Texas have ceased . . . they have commenced in London: Is the man from Texas at the bottom of them all? If he is a monster or lunatic he may be expected to appear anywhere. The fact that he is no longer at work in Texas argues his presence somewhere else."

Almost instantly, a letter dated October 4 and signed "Spring Heel Jack, The Whitechapel Murderer" appeared: "I am an American I have been in London the last ten months and have Murdered no less than six women I mean to make a dozen of it now."

Experts now believe this a hoax, but it cemented the American connection in everyone's mind. On October 5, a letter signed "Observer" appeared in *The Daily Telegraph*. This almost exclusively analyzed "Dear Boss," focusing on Jack's use of slang: "His letters favour far more of American slang than of home. They are the exact reprint of the Texas Rough's style, and probably the Texas solution of the mystery is the true one."

What exactly was this American slang? Some 250 "Ripper letters" survive at the Public Record Office and the Corporation of London Records Office; most are furious, mocking, and spiteful, and most, police believed, were hoaxes or the products of unbalanced minds. Americanisms abound: "Catch me if you can"; "coppers"; "You donkeys, you double-faced asses"; "You see I am still knocking about. Ha. Ha." The one phrase most repeated was that final *Ha. Ha.* "'Ha ha' was much more American than English," wrote Patricia Cornwell in her analysis of the Ripper letters. It grated on the ears. "One can read hundreds of letters written by Victorians and not see a single 'ha ha,' but the Ripper letters are filled with them."

The police, for one, took the American connection seriously, returning in the autumn of 1888 to the theory that had led them to Black Elk in May: Americans, and especially westerners, were more savage than Englishmen. And where would there be the greatest concentration of westerners but in the Wild West shows? Buffalo Bill was back in the United States, but Mexican Joe's cowboys and Indians had returned to England shortly before the final killing, of Mary Jane Kelly on November 9. According to an October 19 report by Chief Inspector Donald Swanson of the Home Office, police by then had interviewed more than two thousand people in the Ripper case, investigated three hundred, and detained eighty-eight. A widespread belief had taken hold by then that Jack could not be an Englishman. He must be an outsider. Suspicion fell upon the East End's recently settled Jewish community, "Asiatics," "Greek Gipsies," "butchers and slaughterers," and American cowboys and Indians. "Three of the persons calling themselves Cowboys who belonged to the American Exhibition were traced and satisfactorily accounted for themselves," Swanson declared.

There would be more. On October 21, *The Echo* of London reported that "Colorado Charley" of Mexican Joe's Western Wilds of America had been detained by police for questioning. "He was said to have been seen in the Battersea Park Road, and to answer the description of the supposed murderer." Colorado Charley was released, but demanded exoneration. "A smart, well knit fellow, he was very indignant at the idea of any suspicion attending to him. He stated that he had himself called at Scotland Yard, that his explanation had been deemed satisfactory, and that they made no effort to detain him."

By October 1888, Black Elk may have dodged the suspicions cast by the Ripper. But it would be another six or seven months before he escaped the chaos surrounding Mexican Joe.

Little is remembered today of Mexican Joe's Western Wilds of America. John Neihardt devotes four paragraphs to Mexican Joe in *Black Elk Speaks*; Black Elk, one in the 1931 interviews, then one more in a letter printed in the December 1889 issue of *Iapi Oaye*. Despite such scant mention, Black Elk traveled with the show from May 1888 until April or early May 1889—almost a year, nearly the same length of time he spent with Buffalo Bill. The historians Don Russell and Louis Warren call Mexican Joe's show a pale shadow of Cody's, yet the Mexican Joe Western Wilds toured the British Isles almost continuously from its Liverpool arrival in the summer of 1887 until its 1894 collapse. In comparison, the Buffalo Bill Wild West made only three trips to Europe: the 1887–88 tour limited to Great Britain; an 1889–90 tour that opened in Paris and ranged the Continent; and the final tour in 1893. And though historians say that Mexican Joe was ignored in his time, contemporary newspapers prove otherwise. "'Mexican Joe' has arrived in this city with a Wild West show which is to rival Buffalo Bill's," crowed the *North-Eastern Daily Gazette* of August 16, 1887. After four weeks in Edinburgh, reported *The Era* of June 15, 1889, "Colonel Shelley and his frontiersmen and Indians have made themselves immense favorites, and the entertainment has secured a great and well-deserved success."

By his own telling, Colonel Joseph "Mexican Joe" Shelley was "understandably one of the most notorious and remarkable men of the nineteenth century." Born in Georgia in 1845, he called himself a descendant of the Romantic poet Percy Bysshe Shelley and said he'd soldiered under three flags. He claimed to have founded the famous Texas Rangers, and to have killed more Indians than the entire commands of General Ord, Crook, and Miles combined." He took credit for shooting the Union general James B. McPherson through the heart during the 1864 Battle of Atlanta; for killing the outlaw Sam Bass in Texas in 1876; for rescuing fifty-eight women and children from "bloodthirsty Apaches"; and for killing the Apache chief Victorio in single-handed combat that ended with the chief's drop from a 150-foot ledge. As a Texas Ranger, "he decked the woods about San Antonio with horse thieves as one hangs trinkets on a Christmas tree"; in revenge for the death of his wife, three children, and entire herd of cattle, he killed so many Apaches they called him the "Red Eagle of the Sierras." He was the "greatest running shot in the world." His adopted Apache daughter was named "Black Mountain Daisy." And he was "a modest unassuming natural gentleman."

Such a regimen surely tires a man. He said that he'd received so many injuries fighting Apaches that in 1886 he retired to Chicago, where for five hundred dollars a week he exhibited his war trophies in the city's many museums. But when he heard of Cody's plans to tour England, his life changed. "Feeling desirous of visiting the old country, the home of my forefathers, I returned to Texas," he said in an 1894 interview, "and there selected some of my old comrades and brought them over to Liverpool under a special engagement with the Jubilee Exhibition Committee." In July 1887, he sailed from Baltimore aboard the SS *Italy* and opened on August 17, 1887, at the Liverpool Exhibition, playing at the same time that Cody performed in London for the Queen's Jubilee.

Mexican Joe's timing would always be bad. He was short, barely taller than some of the women in his troupe, always depicted wearing a black sombrero with a star in the crown that bore the inscription "Shelley's Texas Rangers Capt. 6th." His thick walrus mustache gave his face a sad, vaguely comic cast, and it was rumored he was bald. It rained on Opening Day, "a dispiriting circumstance to all concerned," yet despite the downpour the *Liverpool Mercury* rated his effort "fairly" successful, even if one segment, dubbed "The Death of the Lone Scout," occurred in a large open space "covered to the depth of three or four inches" with rainwater, which turned the attempted realism into "a realistic absurdity." Because he arrived in England three months after Cody; because his troupe was smaller—an average of thirty to forty performers to Cody's two hundred—he was often compared unfavorably with Buffalo Bill. As one reviewer lamented, Mexican Joe's program "contains many of the features made familiar to our readers by a long course of 'Buffalo Bill.'" Though inevitable, this was slightly unfair. Shelley would break new theatrical trails, reaching Scotland, Paris, and other parts of the Continent years before Cody. His herd of wild mustangs was a genuine crowd-pleaser. A segment featuring the lynching of a horse thief was more graphic than anything found in Cody's West. His whole show, he bragged, "was more gory than" Cody's, and he designed it especially "to suit the English taste!"

None of that mattered. He always existed in Cody's shadow, and it grated on him. By September 1887, he'd written a program book expressing "his unbelief in the genuineness of scouts who are blessed with flowing locks, wear pointed moustachios, and don sombreros." By

December 24, 1887, he claimed on his handbills that his show was "the only genuine one of its kind in the world." Inquired the *Pall Mall Gazette*: "Then what about Buffalo Bill? Were we all wrong?" Years later, in 1894, "the canker-worm, jealousy," still gnawed at him. He abhorred those "swash-bucklers who pass for 'scouts' [and] display themselves in buckskin suits, with long hair and broad sombreros." Though he never named the poseur who'd been "a worthless fellow in the field, and a hero only in dime novels," it was easy to guess his identity.

No records indicate that Cody responded. Though Nate Salsbury probably paid close attention to Shelley's success in Scotland and on the Continent, Cody was not interested in a public squabble. Shelley insisted he was the real thing, and such was the public's enthusiasm for this new kind of circus that they took him at his word. Regarding his claims as an Indian fighter, said the *Liverpool Mercury*, "we have no reason to doubt their accuracy." In truth, his claims would have been hard to verify, given the distance and state of communications.

Yet verification was possible, had the audience cared. There were problems with Joe's claims. The poet Shelley had only one boy survive to adulthood—Percy Florence Shelley, Third Baronet of Castle Goring, Sussex—who died without issue, discrediting Joe's claims of ancestry. Sam Bass was shot on July 20, 1878, by Texas Rangers George Herold and Richard Ware, and died the next day—not in 1876, as Shelley claimed. Victorio was surrounded and killed by Mexican soldiers on October 18, 1880, in Mexico's Tres Castillos Mountains. The only claim impossible to disprove was the death of General McPherson, surprised and killed by Confederate skirmishers during the Atlanta campaign. It was hard to say *who* shot him.

Of course, such claims lay in the realm of western embellishment. The credo was simple: never let facts stand in the way of a good story. But criminal behavior was another matter. On February 18, 1887, five months before the Liverpool opening, Shelley was charged with indecent behavior toward a child. His show was playing in Fort Wayne, Ohio, when, according to the town newspaper, a "Mrs. Kelker of Ewing Street" accused him of taking liberties with "her ten-year-old niece, Blanche Hart." Shelley pled guilty to simple assault, paid a fine, and left town.

Then there was the theft of another man's identity. There was indeed a "Joseph Shelley," a lieutenant and later captain of F Company, First Battalion, of the Texas Rangers. But he was ten years younger than

Mexican Joe; at six feet one, taller; a farmer and native of Bexar County, Texas; and he spelled his last name "Shely." On August 2, 1888—while Mexican Joe toured the Continent—the *San Antonio Daily Light* exposed the imposter:

> A contemporary tells us that "Captain Joe Shely has returned after an absence of some months in the south-west. He says the sensational individual who appropriated his name and took a wild west show to England was prosecuted by Buffalo Bill, and after being robbed of his false plumes dropped into and became a part of Bison William's combination." But the Paris correspondent of the London (Eng.) Weekly Budget, July 27th, says that "Mexican Joe" is in Paris, France, and is doing enormous business there in his wild west show.

The negative coverage turned few spectators away.

By May 1888, when Black Elk signed up, Mexican Joe's Western Wilds of America had cut a swath through southern England like nothing seen in that country before or since. "While Mexican Joe's company was only a tenth the size of Buffalo Bill's," wrote the Scottish Buffalo Bill scholar Tom F. Cunningham, "it generated ten times as much business, both criminal and civil, for the courts of law. A spirit of chaotic malignance was its presiding genius." If the true American West was wild, horrific, lethal, random, absurd, and hilarious, then the mad version of Mexican Joe was closer to reality than the sanitized portrayal by Buffalo Bill.

Disasters dogged Shelley's circus every step of the way. Even before Black Elk signed up, Mexican Joe had cast a toxic fascination over English audiences: one's survival was never certain when Mexican Joe arrived in town. On September 3, 1887, Shelley's cook tried to kill a cowboy in the dining tent during an argument over Joe's adopted daughter, Black Mountain Daisy: "Revolvers and bowie-knives were quickly produced, and it looked as if a general meleé of a sanguinary character was about to take place," wrote the *Hampshire Telegraph & Sussex Chronicle*. On September 30, a publicity stunt went badly wrong: the "Tombstone Coach" was driving full-speed through Liverpool when it overturned, seriously injuring four passengers. On October 4, a bucking bronco threw itself down while being shod and died of its injuries. On October 8, a boy named John Joseph Dinash was killed when another bucking bronco broke loose, dashed among the spectators, and kicked a barricade to splinters, striking Dinash in the head. In late October, the cursed "Tombstone Coach" struck again: one of its spoked wheels fell off during a parade in Wolverhampton, pitching two squaws through the door of a residence, bowling over a young mother with her baby. On November 3, "Lasso Mack" was called before a Wolverhampton judge for making improper advances to girls under sixteen. During a Sheffield performance on November 28, an Indian named Running Wolf shot Shelley during the "Lone Scout" segment: "Instead of using a blank cartridge," reported the *Leeds Mercury*, "the Indian had used a hard substance, which struck Colonel Shelley under the left eye and inflicted a slight wound, from which blood flowed rather freely." It was the third or fourth time that he tried to shoot Shelley, and always under the influence of alcohol. On December 2, a Sheffield man was sent to the hospital with a concussion and broken leg after yet another fight with a cowboy, this time over a horse.

Thus ended 1887, and the New Year promised to be as exciting. On January 11, 1888, a second Indian tried to kill Shelley with a stiletto in Battersea. And so on, throughout the year.

Young men and boys were drawn into Mexican Joe's orbit, "inspiring them to a broad range of delinquent behavior, including horse theft, absconding from home, and even firearm offenses," wrote Cunningham. A London youth somehow procured a dagger, revolver, and bowie knife, and journeyed to Liverpool to join the show. Two teenage boys in Everton secured revolvers; as they imitated Mexican Joe, one shot the other in the hand. A boy stole money from his parents to attend the show. A letter signed by eight boys in Liverpool begged Shelley to take them back to America so they could become cowboys. Two other "young fellows" wrote, "We are fair shots with the rifle, and can ride well."

Girls and young women could not control themselves. There were at least two "cowboy weddings" during the period before Black Elk signed up—"Montana Bill" to Mary Carry and "Yellowstone Vic" to Eva Johnstone, both young Liverpudlians. Girls hung around the gates or wrote letters: the erotic component was barely concealed, though in the early part of the show such lust and love was focused entirely on cowboys and did not yet cross racial lines. "Dear Sir," wrote a seventeen-year-old Liverpool maiden, "As I am in want of a husband, will you mind asking all the cowboys you have at the exhibition, and those you know in America, if they want a wife." When Mexican Joe left Liverpool on

October 16, 1887, the crowd that assembled to see him off numbered two to three hundred, "a considerable portion of which belonged to the tender sex." In mid-November 1887, four "young and respectable look-ing girls" were brought up on charges of loitering about the doors of the show: they'd wandered from Wolverhampton to Sheffield "in search of their sombrero-covered Orlandos."

Mexican Joe's performers were reckless with life and love, and that very recklessness released a longing in the tight-laced Victorian soul. It had not calmed down by the time Black Elk, Two Elk, High Bear, and Charles Picket Pin signed on. If anything, the troupe became more reckless, more libidinous, more strange. The things that happened in Joe Shelley's version of the West did not happen in William Cody's, and if they did, they were kept from public display. Black Elk joined Chief Black Hawk, Running Wolf, Texas Jack, Lasso Mack, Señorita Marvella, Suspender Charlie, Texas Rosy, Black Mountain Daisy, Wild-Horse Harry, and others as they rampaged through Great Britain and the Con-tinent. Nor were the Sioux the only refugees from Cody's entourage: in 1888–90, mention is made in the press of the former Cody cowboys Bronco Charlie Miller, Pedro Esquival, Richard Chester Dere, and John Dunn, some traveling with Colonel Shelley, some seeking adventure on their own.

Mexican Joe opened at Alexandra Palace on May 12, 1888. After seven years of renovation, the "People's Palace" held its grand reopening on the May 21 Whit Monday holiday. Sixty thousand visitors enjoyed the perfect spring weather as Mexican Joe and his troupe gave five performances at two-hour intervals. For the rest of the season, they played two shows daily, in the afternoon and at night. Only one seri-ous incident occurred during this period. a cowboy sustained grave in-juries when a bronco pitched backward on him in the stable. The fate of the man, and the horse, is unknown.

Every Saturday night, a "pyrotechnical representation" of Edward Bulwer-Lytton's hugely popular *The Last Days of Pompeii* would erupt in the park's central lagoon. The "pyrodrama" awed Black Elk and just about everyone else in London: the eruption of Mount Vesuvius, the cataclysmic destruction of Pompeii, unfolded as a sign of God's judg-ment for Rome's decadence and ruthlessness in subjugating the less powerful. Two hundred actors and extras portrayed the doomed resi-dents; as the painted apocalypse scrolled across 180,000 square feet of backlit canvas, it presented a spectacle as outsized and engrossing as any multimillion-dollar movie epic of later years. The ersatz Vesuvius vomited "forth flames and smoke, quickly overwhelming the city, whose people rushed wildly about mad with terror, the whole making a very effective picture, and one well worth seeing," concluded a reviewer for *Fair-Trade*.

Black Elk thought about each Saturday's devastation. He'd come to England to learn the power of the whites; instead, they portrayed a power greater than their own. This was supposed to be a re-creation of a true event when, he said, "some people had disappeared on the earth a long time ago." Were such things possible? Did the *wasichu* God truly rain fire and death upon the unjust? If it happened once, could it do so again?

Shelley's show closed in London on June 9 and opened on June 15 or 16 at the Porte-Maillot arena in Neuilly, on the western outskirts of Paris. By now his complement had grown to fifty performers and just as many horses. He planned to return to Alexandra Palace on July 20, but the Paris reception was so overwhelming that he remained on the Continent until October.

By all indications, his was the first Wild West show to open in the City of Light, and his performers reverted to their old reckless ways. At least one incident made international news. A sixteen-year-old English girl identified as "Jenny F." fell in love with a brave named Eagle Eye, whom she'd seen performing on horseback in Mexican Joe's London show; she followed him to Paris and moved into his tipi, in effect becoming his wife. The family sent a detective to Paris to bring her home: French authorities and Mexican Joe fought Eagle Eye to a standstill as the detective "seized the girl in his arms" and spirited her back to London.

The sexual attraction that young white women were discovering for native performers was both unprecedented and carefully handled by the courts and press corps. During Buffalo Bill's London visit, such attraction was painted as a joke: the women—not the Indians—were portrayed as predators. In France, however, romance was part of the alchemy. The popular stereotype of the Indian as a dying race took on new meaning on the Continent. Nothing could be more poignant than the resignation of a man condemned to die.

In Paris, Black Elk also fell in love. At the same time that Eagle Elk's drama played out so publicly, "there was a Wasichu girl who came to the show very often," he said. "She liked me and took me home to see her mother and father. They liked me, too, and were good to me. I could not talk their language. I made signs, and the girl learned a few Lakota words."

By late July or early August, the show closed in Neuilly. Yet it had done so well that plans were made to include it in next year's Paris Exhibition. Black Elk left his girlfriend behind, but promised to return. He did not know how prophetic that statement would be. He was beginning to hate the constant forward motion: "I did not feel right and I thought the best thing to do was to stick with this show so I could get money to go home with." Yet the longer he stayed, the farther from home he seemed.

Confusion shows in his voice. "From Paris we went to Germany," he said, yet a close study of schedules and newspaper articles shows that Mexican Joe opened next in Brussels, on August 5, 1888. They stayed ten weeks and moved on, but not before Shelley was dragged into court over an alleged nonpayment to a Belgian saddler. They moved on to Naples in Italy: "Then we went to the place where the earth was on fire—there was a big butte here in a cone shape," he said. Black Elk learned that Pompeii's destruction in A.D. 79 and the instant, excruciating death of sixteen thousand people was not just a story. Such things *were* possible.

He approached the edge of the rim as if hypnotized. He felt the heat on his face, the deep rumbles beneath the earth, as if a caged animal fought to break free. The last major eruption had occurred in April 1872, when an immense lava flow destroyed major segments of the villages of Massa di Somme and San Sebastiano, and twenty people died. The beast had lain dormant since then, but this year, throughout 1888, the volcano had become active once more. A new lava cone was building thirty to forty yards to the southwest of the original, and a fissure crept across the mountain's face a little more each day. Volcanologists believed that another eruption was due.

During this period, tourists could take a cable car to within a hundred feet of the crater, then walk around the rim. Black Elk was amazed. This was God's power, and he stood at its edge. Below him lay the power of the earth, greater than the soft hand of Grandmother England, than all the guns of the soldiers—greater even than the destructive forces foretold by Drinks Water and Sweet Medicine. In an instant the earth's center could shoot up and out, covering *wasichu* and Lakota alike in a lake of fire.

The potential for destruction was as absolute as anything he'd seen in his Great Vision. It seems to have frightened him. One can imagine his reaction. Three years later, J. F. Christie, a cowboy returning to America from Cody's 1891 Continental tour, said he'd visited this same spot with Cody's Indians. He had watched as the Indians gathered around the crater and prayed to the Great Spirit.

"They imagined," he said, "the crater was the entrance to hell."

17

LA BELLE ÉPOQUE

The pace was killing him. When the troupe returned to England, they moved to Birmingham in October, to Sheffield in the first week of November, back to Liverpool in mid-December, and on to Manchester in February 1889. Throughout this period, Shelley continued his run-ins with the law. All charges stemmed from nonpayment for services. In Sheffield, he failed to pay £17 owed for posting publicity posters; in Wolverhampton, £110 owed to a carpenter in back wages. With the earlier nonpayment suit in Brussels, one suspects that the Western Wilds teetered near bankruptcy. He shed performers, possibly from nonpayment of wages. The hint comes from a cowboy named Carver, who advertised in the October 13, 1888, *Era* that he would take any position: "CARVER, one of the Best Riders at Mexican Joe's Show, is open for a Situation. Suit a Circus. Address to me."

One of Black Elk's friends also left: Charles Picket Pin, one of the Oglala refugees. He'd traveled with Mexican Joe at least until Paris; after that, his peregrinations are not recorded. But on February 15, 1889, he turned up penniless in London, "almost wholly ignorant of the language," but dressed in the latest Paris fashions. He came to the attention of American expatriates, who collected £10 for steerage passage aboard the New York–bound *Tower Hill*. He was listed on the passenger list as "Mr. Picket Pin," age thirty-two, destination "Pine Ridge Agency,

Dakota." He carried two pieces of luggage and spent the trip in the "Starboard alleyway." His "calling": "Sioux Indian going home."

The *Tower Hill* docked at Columbia Stores, Brooklyn, on Thursday, February 28, 1889. A crowd of journalists pushed aboard and found near the saloon companionway a man "6 feet in height, with broad shoulders, and a muscular form" who could sign his name and say "Buffalo Bill" and "Pine Ridge Agency." The reporter for *The New York Times* was mystified:

> He was dressed in a black Prince Albert coat, black vest and light trousers, and brown derby hat somewhat worn. A large linked gold chain, on which was a heavy seal, presented to him in Paris, adorned the outside of his vest. On his hands he wore a buff-colored pair of white gloves, which he removed while talking to the reporters, disclosing two rings on the little finger of his left hand, in each of which blazed five large Parisian diamonds.

According to the reporter, Picket Pin had returned because he was "disgusted with all things that smelled of Europe" and missed his people. "He will be turned over to the local representative of the Interior Department, who will send him home."

Two days before Picket Pin's landing, tragedy befell his former employer. At about 10:00 p.m. on Tuesday, February 26, a fire started near the entrance of the Royal Circus on Manchester's Chepstow Street, where Shelley's renamed New Wild West Company had played since mid-month. The wooden Circus lay in the heart of the crowded downtown: one side edged against King & Co., a cotton mill; on the other lay the Chepstow Buildings, a large square block of several businesses, separated by a narrow lane. Every Indian and some of the cowboys lived in tents and tipis pitched inside; the show's horses and mules were stabled beneath the gallery, and costumes, guns, sets, and props were stored in the wings.

The last performance had ended and the audience was filing out when someone lit a pipe and dropped the burning match to the floor. A fire ignited near the entrance and had "obtained a good hold before anyone discovered it," reported *The Manchester Weekly Times*. "A smell of burning wood was first experienced, and then smoke gathered rapidly and floated through the passages."

"Fire!" several people screamed. The blaze roared up the walls and grandstands; the arena filled with smoke; a giant pile of straw exploded in flame. Black Elk entered the arena and found his friends Two Elk and High Bear: the roar and crack of the arching furnace, shouts of horrified performers, shrill screams of horses—all filled their ears. According to one account, the Indians tried to save the horses until the cowboys took charge. They freed those they could from their stalls and dragged them to the arena; they herded them down a corridor and then clambered up a staircase to the open air. "The cries of the poor animals whilst they were in danger, and the delight they mutely seemed to express at being rescued from the burning building was exceedingly affecting," the newspaper reported. The hose station was a few hundred yards away and the entire firefighting force had assembled by the time the horses emerged, yet by then the Circus was doomed. Hundreds of spectators gathered; flames shot from the roof; the night glowed red. Firemen pumped water onto adjoining structures "and at the same time poured volumes of water into the centre of the Circus." Although the surrounding structures and town center were saved, within thirty minutes the Circus was "a charred wreck."

Incredibly, no one died or was seriously injured. But there were close calls. A female performer "nearly lost her life in trying to rescue her pony, and acted like a mad woman until the animal was safely led into the street," Shelley told *The Manchester Weekly Times*. Shelley himself was nearly killed fighting with one pony until he finally led it outside.

The fire was a financial disaster for Mexican Joe. Total losses amounted to £2,800. Eleven horses and a donkey burned to death, or nearly a third of the show's livestock; most of the company's guns, several cases of Indian relics, and all the props, saddles, and other gear were consumed. The Indians lost everything, since all was stored in their tipis. Nothing was insured.

The people of Manchester came to their aid, contributing clothes and other relief as Shelley moved to the Grand Circus on Peter Street and announced plans to resume performances. Yet, as always, trouble found him. An eight-year-old boy named John Hancock was charged and convicted of stealing a gold watch and revolver during the fire: Shelley told the court the items had come from the body of Victorio after their merciless fight to the death, and they held great meaning for him. The court was moved and sent John Hancock "to gaol for three months with hard labour."

Disquiet and disorder orbited Mexican Joe. On the night of the fire, a paper manufacturer named John Fletcher was found in a hansom cab abandoned near the conflagration; he had been robbed, and died of unspecified injuries. A few days later, a female performer named "Idareata" left the circus to buy some sweetmeats when a gang of ruffians knocked her insensible. Shelley called the attack "revenge for his resistance" to attempted extortion. No arrests were made in either crime. Meanwhile, Shelley moved on. On March 16, the show opened at Victoria Hall in Nottingham; on April 6, once again in Manchester; on May 20, at Newsome's Circus in Edinburgh, the first time he—or any Wild West show—crossed the border into Scotland.

By now, Black Elk had left the show. Though we do not know exactly when, it was probably sometime in April. The circumstances have confounded scholars since they began studying the holy man. In the 1931 interviews, Black Elk said, "We went back to Paris again and I was very sick and couldn't go on with this show," and John Neihardt concluded that he dropped out during a second visit by Mexican Joe to the City of Light. Yet the detective work by the Scottish scholar Tom Cunningham proves otherwise. Mexican Joe remained in England after he returned from the Continent in October 1888. Black Elk returned to Paris alone.

But why would he backtrack to Paris rather than ship to New York from London or Liverpool? He had money, but he was alone and wanted to be someplace where he was not a stranger. He was far too sick to keep up with Shelley's schedule, and depressed beyond measure. He wanted some semblance of home.

There was also the matter of Buffalo Bill. Though Black Elk does not mention it, there is good reason to suspect he knew his old employer planned to return. In the summer of 1888, Shelley told the press he would come to Paris in May 1889 as part of the Exposition Universelle, a World's Fair commemorating the hundredth anniversary of the storming of the Bastille that featured the official unveiling of Alexandre Gustave Boenickhausen-Eiffel's nearly thousand-foot tower. Yet by April 1889, Mexican Joe had been usurped by Buffalo Bill. Given Shelley's envy of all things Cody, the arrival of the Buffalo Bill Wild West in Paris was probably a frequent topic of conversation in the Mexican Joe revue.

Scholars have always assumed that Black Elk was homesick, but his condition was in fact far worse. Lost in a small *Pittsburg Dispatch* report dated June 18, 1889, and titled "Black Elk's Accident," one finds a telling detail: "Mr. Black Elk, a Dakota Chief who was badly hurt at Buffalo Bill's Wild West Show, in Paris, by being trampled by his mustang."

Given the confusions of transatlantic journalism, it is easy to see what happened. Though Cody *would* eventually save him, Black Elk was not performing with his former employer, but with Mexican Joe that year. Sometime between the Manchester fire of February 16, 1889, and his arrival in Paris in April or May, he'd been trampled by one of Shelley's prized broncos. Was it during the chaos of the fire, or afterward, in Nottingham or during the return date in Manchester? We do not know.

All we know is this: Black Elk was one more victim of Mexican Joe Shelley's Circus of Madness. And when he arrived at his girlfriend's house in Paris, he wavered at death's door.

———•—•———

Her name was Charlotte and when Black Elk fell in love with her she was in her late teens or early twenties. Long after Black Elk's death, his Parisian love resonated as a kind of legend at Pine Ridge. Black Elk would sometimes drift back into the past: he suspected that when he left "Pars," his girlfriend was pregnant with his child. Not much else was known until Black Elk's great-granddaughter, the activist Charlotte Black Elk, played detective. "I'm named after my great grandpa's chick," she told the author Ian Frazier in his 2000 *On the Rez*. Although the Parisian girl's given name was no secret, she'd also heard a surname.

Sometime during the 1980s or '90s, Charlotte Black Elk tracked down the Parisian descendants of her great-grandfather's lost love. "They were very surprised," she said in a phone interview. They showed her their ancestor's photo and revealed intimate details, but only with the promise that she respect their privacy and never reveal the family name.

The original Charlotte was petite, with lustrous black hair. Her family owned a three-story mansion outside the old Paris walls: it was a grand estate, with an attic, servants' quarters, grounds to rival any public park, and towering trees. Her father was, in all probability, a wealthy merchant, and his daughter was well educated in a private school.

Given the garbled nature of Black Elk's account, scholars have been divided about the girlfriend. Was she English, and accompanied him back to Paris to see Cody? Was she French, and Black Elk met her when he performed in Paris with Mexican Joe? Charlotte Black Elk's detective work confirms the latter. And one thing is certain—she was not shy. This was not Victorian England, where women corseted their sexuality; this was Paris on the cusp of what the English called the Gay Nineties and the French, *la belle époque*—the era of the Eiffel Tower, Toulouse-Lautrec, high fashion, and the New Woman, the *nouvelle femme* who was not afraid to show her fascination in a man. It was that period in France when romantic love made a comeback; when Paris seemed determined in an almost tribal sense to prove that it was the universal home of art, fashion, literature, and, above all else, love.

No other place on earth rivaled Paris as the city of love. The Seine coursed through its center like an artery, both sides lined with restaurants, theaters, shops, and parks where men and women of every social class could promenade and fall in love. Popular journals seemed obsessed with the singular topic of who was bedding whom. As Pierre Darblay wrote in his 1889 *Physiologie de l'amour*, "A man gets respect depending upon the mistress he has." The same may have applied for the female of the species.

If English girls could not keep away from Mexican Joe's performers, what, then, was to stop French women? Lakota men were dark, exotic, mysterious, sensual, and, as a race, presumably doomed. When Neihardt visited Black Elk in 1944 for a series of final interviews, the old man's memories of Paris would be used in Neihardt's last book on the Sioux, the 1951 novel *When the Tree Flowered*; in it, the main character, Eagle Voice, was modeled after the old holy man. Black Elk still remembered Charlotte's face and "the way she looked up at me." The Lakota actors would wait outside the tent when they were not performing, and the *wasichu* girls would crowd around. He remembered one who visited— and then returned. "She looked up at me and I saw her face," and something electric passed between them. She returned again and the passage is related so vividly in the novel that there's a very good chance it comes directly from memory. "It was in the night when she came back," he said. "She came out of the shadow. One of her hands was on my naked arm and one upon my breast—thin white hands—and she was looking up at me." It is as if he describes it as it happens, lamenting the passage of time. "Her look was soft and kind. There was a power that went through me from her hands.'"

Did they have a child? Family tales suggest as much, and the rumor took a later comic turn. The Parisian family apparently told Charlotte Black Elk, but also exacted a promise that she never reveal the truth. But Eagle Voice, Black Elk's surrogate in Neihardt's novel, describes what sounds like a lover's tryst: "Her mouth was over my face; her hair was on my eyes; her hands were about my neck. I did not know what she was saying again and again, but it was like singing; and I could smell young grass when rain had fallen and the sun comes out."

We may never know the truth. It is relegated to that intersection of truth and legend, like Crazy Horse's grave. Black Elk returned to "Pars" and Charlotte saw how sick he was. Her family took him in and gave him a room; we have no idea how long he took to recuperate, but it must have been at least a couple of weeks, time enough to get his strength back and feel healed. Charlotte's parents were in the house, as were two sisters: the parents brought in a doctor and then a tailor to measure him for a full set of the latest "white-man's" fashion, like Charles Picket Pin. The three girls must have fluttered around their injured warrior like little birds.

One morning, he donned his Paris suit and shoes, unbraided his hair and combed it back so that it hung down. He sat next to Charlotte at the long table for breakfast; the father sat at the head, the mother and two other girls chattered around him. The servants set his place and he felt happy. He looked overhead and the ceiling seemed to move. As he watched, the house spun like a top from that hub. He stared in fascination as that point rose and receded.

Then he saw the familiar cloud. It filled the space between the breakfast table and the receding ceiling. It lingered a second, then began to descend. It was coming for him, just as it had in his Great Vision, and he did not even have time to glance over at Charlotte before he smiled peacefully, keeled over backward, and his eyes rolled up in his head.

Once again he calmly watched as he left the earth behind. Charlotte tried to catch him, but it happened so fast and the family hopped around his body like startled antelope. The girls screamed. He lay still. Meanwhile, his spirit rose through the mansion roof and over Pars. He saw the spiraling steel structure by the man called Eiffel that was nearly finished; the gray cathedral with monsters and eyeless stone saints perched on its towers, watching the mortals below. He rose higher than these; as the cloud sped west, he climbed to the top and clung hard. Houses, towers, and green fields passed underneath; he flew over the English Channel, over the city where Grandmother England lived. Once again he crossed the endless ocean, but did not get sick this time. He kept speeding west, over New York, over Chicago, over the Mississippi and Missouri, and began to recognize landmarks. This was his country and he felt happy. From the distance he saw the black dome of Paha Sapa. The cloud came to Pine Ridge and descended.

But it did not drop far. He was still high enough that if he jumped he would not survive. He could see for miles. All the various bands had gathered outside Agency headquarters, but this was no celebration. Something was wrong. His people were agitated. He strained to hear but was too high up. He pushed at the cloud but it would not respond.

He searched for the tipi of his parents and finally found it among the crowd. They had a cookfire going and sat cross-legged eating something—maybe stew. He missed them so much and wanted to step off and be with them again. He'd never felt so alone. They'd been right when they begged him not to go with Pahuska; something important was taking place and he should be there. He waved his arms to get his mother's attention; he cried out, and she seemed to look up. He thought she saw him, and he really started to yell.

But then the cloud scooted sideways and up, and took him the way he had come. He zoomed back over America, back over the coast until only water flashed past and the night came without stars. He was alone in a black world. Maybe he would not return this time. Perhaps he'd been given one final glimpse of home because this time he would die. All his hopes of learning the *wasichus'* secrets, of saving his people and understanding the gifts of the Grandfathers—all were in vain. He'd die without fulfilling his purpose. He started to cry.

Then the green fields flashed past, and he knew he'd returned. The cloud came to Pars and there was the house of his girlfriend, rising to meet him like a welcoming friend. The roof spire pierced the cloud and dragged him back inside. All grew quiet. Bells rang in his ears.

"He's alive," someone said.

———————

He lay on his back in bed. A doctor bent over him and took his pulse; his girlfriend and her family watched a few steps away. He'd been unconscious nearly twenty-four hours. They'd run for a doctor after he dropped; he looked dead when the healer came back, but his body was still warm. The doctor put his ear to Black Elk's chest and occasionally "my heart would beat a little beat," as if he were hibernating. Other doctors came to the house and they, too, listened and concluded "that there wasn't enough life in me to bring me to." As the hours passed, his pulse grew more faint; in their opinion, he wouldn't last another day. Charlotte's family bought an expensive casket and placed it in the room beside him, awaiting the inevitable.

Then he rose. This scared Charlotte's sisters almost as much as when he'd dropped over; they screamed and ran into the hall. Charlotte herself turned white; the doctor told him not to get up, he needed rest, he had no idea how close he'd come to dying. He eyed the coffin and saw that it looked pretty nice; maybe he should have taken advantage of their kindness, he joked, and stayed dead. "I wish I'd died then, as I would have had a good coffin," he later told Neihardt, "but as it is, I won't have a good one."

And just as had happened after his Great Vision, he knew no one would believe him and so did not divulge where he had been or what he had seen.

Charlotte's family "took good care of me during this time," he said. Yet life in the mansion must have been strained. Since the doctors had no idea what triggered his seizure, they had no idea whether it could happen again. He'd risen again like Lazarus, but his resurrection this time was not treated as a miracle. It was, in itself, an end. It was obvious he could never fit into European society: he was a curiosity, a beautiful freak, and though loved, what could he do? The only place he fit—would ever fit—was back on the Plains. There he was needed, had power, could do some good. If Black Elk and Charlotte had built a fairy castle about themselves in the spirit of *la belle époque*, if they'd believed their love could conquer all differences, his seizure and near-death knocked out the castle's supports and sent it crashing.

When Charlotte told him that Buffalo Bill had opened on May 17 at the Exposition, she knew what it meant. If her lover reunited with Cody's troupe, he would go home. He'd saved some money from his Mexican Joe wages; he hung on to what he could, never knowing the cost of a sea passage, simply trusting to fate. "I told the folks that I was going over there and I told my girl that I would go first and she could come afterwards." But she knew better. If she took him to Buffalo Bill, she would lose him forever. But he would live.

Perhaps no American's advent in Paris had ever been as greatly anticipated as Buffalo Bill's. Posters plastered the city with images of a charging bison, and in a circle set dead-center in the animal's body, Cody gazed upon this new frontier. Emblazoned across the posters was the simple message "*Je viens*": "I am coming!" Never before had Parisians seen such an advertising blitz, and many found it distasteful. But one thing was certain—the Americans were in town.

They came like famous Americans always seemed to come to Paris—like conquering heroes. They left New York Harbor on April 28 aboard the *Persian Monarch*, the same ship that had taken them home from Hull. The company totaled 218 persons, including "half a dozen pretty women who can ride or shoot"; 48 cowboys, 16 of them musicians; Mexican vaqueros, property men, camp officers, et cetera; and 115 Indians, most from Pine Ridge and Rosebud. They brought nearly 250 animals, including 20 buffalo, 25 mustangs, 186 horses, and 8 "Esquimaux dogs" under the care of 2 Canadian trappers. To handle the language barrier, Cody hired a platoon of French-speaking secretaries, press agents, and interpreters. They marched through the Arc de Triomphe, two by two, Cody at the head. The Lakotas were painted for victory, their ponies, too; next came the cowboys, lariats looped on their saddles. The Parisians lined the streets. From a thousand throats it seemed to the Indians that they cried "Bufflo Beel! Bufflo Beel!"

The Wild West set up in the Parc du Neuilly, the same suburb where Mexican Joe had been located. Two streets were closed; grandstands were built to hold twenty thousand. As in London, visitors could spend one or two hours strolling through the stables and Indian Village before passing into the hippodrome. Opening Day was held on May 17, an invitation-only affair. In the absence of French royalty, it was attended by Marie François Sadi Carnot, the fourth president of the Third Republic, and a retinue of dignitaries estimated at fifteen thousand. The Cowboy Band played "La Marseillaise." The French flag appeared beside the American during the grand entry, and Frank Richmond tried yelling the script in a phonetic approximation of French so garbled that he was finally hooted off the stage.

We do not know when Black Elk and Charlotte attended, but it had to have been in late May or early June 1889. They attended the 11:00 a.m. show and sat up in the stands. Black Elk now saw the production as others had. The crowds increased until the stands were packed; the Cowboy Band played behind the canvas surrounding the arena. A dark red awning stretched overhead to shade them from the midday sun. Flags of all nations popped above the canopy. The long rectangular arena stretched to the left and right, with spectators on three sides.

As punctual as ever, the Cowboy Band launched into "The Star

Spangled Banner" and the backdrop fell away. Screaming and yelling, a clutch of painted Lakotas charged into the arena astride their little ponies, followed by a second group wearing feathered headdresses. Cowboys charged after them . . . Mexican vaqueros . . . more cowboys and Indians . . . until the arena became a seething mass of horsemen. The riders circled the hippodrome three or four times, then slowed their horses and formed into regular lines.

And then a lone figure entered from the back, riding in a lazy canter on a big gray horse. The crowd hushed; their eyes followed the man, so familiar, even to those who'd never seen him before. "Pahuska!" Black Elk whispered, not realizing until that moment how much he'd missed him. He watched as he rode slowly from the back to the front, his hair as long and golden as ever, dressed in the famous light buckskins and wide-brimmed sombrero. He'd put on a few more pounds since Black Elk had last seen him, but that was the only obvious change. A cheer rose from the audience as Cody urged his horse forward and halted before the nearest line of horsemen. He swept off his hat with one hand, saluted the crowd, and cried, "Children, Ladies and Gentlemen, allow me to introduce you to Buffalo Bill's Wild West!"

"Pahuska!" Black Elk might have cried as all others screamed "Buffalo Bill!" A wave of happiness swept over him. He was a child again.

And if there were any lingering doubts for Charlotte, they all disappeared. She watched her young holy man and knew that she'd lost him. Nothing could stop him from going home.

When the show was over, they went down to the camp to see his friends. Standing Bear and One Side, Little Wolf and Red Shirt—they were all there. They gawked at him in his Paris fashions as if they beheld a well-dressed ghost; they started to laugh, remarking that Kahnigapi had once again returned from the dead. He told them all that had passed: how he and the others had missed the fireboat; how the police had questioned them for something awful; how he'd seen the world with Mexican Joe. As they talked, word made it to Cody of the return of this prodigal son. A messenger came back: Cody would like to see him. Black Elk and Charlotte probably went to the dining tent, the largest enclosed space, for when they got there Cody had gathered all his performers and "they gave me four big cheers." The Buffalo Bill Wild West had lost several performers by this point in its history, but by all accounts, Black Elk was the first to return so unexpectedly. Cody studied his talented dancer sagely, and saw that time had been hard on him.

Though he probably already guessed the answer, he asked Black Elk what he wanted to do. Did he want to travel with the show for the rest of the season? Or did he want to go home?

"I told him that I was going home," Black Elk said.

Pahuska held a big dinner for him, and it may well have been at its conclusion that Charlotte and Black Elk parted. He apparently told her again that he would send for her, but she knew better by now. She returned to her world; he, to his. She returned to her mansion, got married, had children, Charlotte Black Elk would one day be told. There are no records of letters sent or received. If, forty-three years later, word drifted back that his memories of Paris had been published in a book, neither she nor her descendants ever commented.

Cody bought a ticket back to America for Black Elk and gave him ninety dollars in traveling money. They sent for his luggage: the quickest means would have been to send Black Elk's lover home in a hansom, then bring his bags on the return. But whether on the Plains or in Paris, the Lakota traveled light and there probably was not much to collect. A gendarme took him to the railroad station and showed him where to buy a ticket to Le Havre. He spent the night in a seaport rooming house, then rose the next morning to board the fireboat and cross the great water.

At about 9:00 a.m. on June 10, 1889, "B. Elk," age twenty-five, sailed from Le Havre aboard the White Star Line's *La Normandie*. His occupation was recorded as "none." The passage was easy: whereas the *State of Nebraska* had hit a huge storm, damaged its rudder, and made the trip in a tortoise-slow two weeks, this passage lasted only eight days. "I was sick part of the way, but I was not sad because I was going home." He arrived in New York on either June 17 or 18. No crowd of reporters awaited him as they had for Charles Picket Pin. One reporter was present, and he muddled the facts: "Mr. Black Elk, a Dakota chief who was badly hurt at Buffalo Bill's Wild West Show, in Paris, by being trampled by his mustang, returned to his native soil to-day on the steamship Normandie. He is going to Pine Ridge. He has a letter from Nate Salisbury to the Baltimore and Ohio railroad Company, requesting them to send him through, but to give him no money."

18

THE MESSIAH WILL COME AGAIN

When Black Elk stepped off *La Normandie* in New York Harbor, he did not waste time. He caught a night train to Chicago, arrived there the next evening, caught a night train to Omaha, and arrived the next morning. He started from Omaha immediately. He arrived in Rushville at 5:00 a.m. on June 21, 1889, nearly three years after leaving there with his friends. No one knew he was coming, so he climbed aboard a regular mule train loaded with rations for the Agency.

Much had changed. Soon after his fall 1886 departure, Agent Hugh D. Gallagher prohibited the funeral "giveaway," the distribution of possessions that ensured that one's soul entered the spirit world with honor when one died. In February 1889, South Dakota, Montana, North Dakota, and Washington were made states: the Upper Plains was becoming civilized. In 1889, Red Shirt's younger sister committed suicide; such an act rarely happened before the People's banishment to reservations.

By now, Black Elk's was the most closely controlled tribe in America. The army administered a vast area once owned by the Sioux. Military forts rose on or near every reservation: Forts Niobrara and Robinson watched over Rosebud and Pine Ridge; Fort Yates guarded Standing Rock; Fort Bennett kept tabs on Cheyenne River. All were connected by telegraph and rail.

When Black Elk returned, the twenty-two-million-acre Great Sioux Reserve was being whittled away. During his absence, Congress passed two acts designed to turn the Sioux into farmers and break up tribal lands. The Dawes Act of 1887 "allotted" 160 acres to every Lakota head-of-household; the Sioux Act of 1889 doubled that to 320. The acts were then merged and rewritten, and now awaited passage by at least three-quarters of all eligible Sioux males. If they signed the treaty, the United States promised to distribute one thousand bulls and twenty-five thousand "good American cows" throughout the reservations, or about five cows per family. Each household would receive a span of mares, enough seed to plant five acres for two years, and fifty dollars to put up "a little house" instead of a tipi. Those who started farming would receive a wagon, tools, and other goods. The rations and annuities promised since 1868 would continue, but for how long frequently seemed to change.

"Allotment" was the brainchild of the humanitarian groups collectively called the "Friends of the Indians." They, like the Indian Office, believed in the agrarian "narrative of progress": a nation of independent "citizen farmers" ensured a strong democracy. Give the Indian land and he would be wedded to that land instead of to his tribe. His assimilation as a citizen would be certain, a philosophy so self-evident as to seem beyond debate.

Yet the mathematics of allotment revealed a calculated greed. Everyone wanted the Indians' land, and here was a way to get it that on the surface seemed fair. After allotments were complete, eleven million acres of the original Great Sioux Reserve would still remain: this "surplus" could be sold to non-Indians at $1.25 per acre. Most would be taken by white cattle ranchers.

In the summer of 1889, the Sioux debated whether to accept the treaty. A land commission headed by Three Stars moved among Agencies, cajoling the Lakota to sign. The Sioux trusted Crook; he was direct and plainspoken. He presented the *wasichus'* lust for their land as an unstoppable force; the treaty was the best deal they would get, an all-or-nothing proposition. But many were not convinced. Red Cloud, for one, recited a string of unfulfilled promises: 882 commandeered ponies never returned; $28,600 in damages never paid. The Oglala understood that land was their last leverage: once the government took that, it could also slash their rations. The commissioners vowed otherwise: rations were fixed by past treaties and had nothing to do with the new land agreement. Rations, they said, would stay the same.

On August 5, 1889, the final vote was taken. Out of 5,678 Sioux males in all six Agencies, 4,463 signed away their land—just slightly more than three-quarters. "The Sioux Nation Consents," *The New York Herald* declared:

> At last the Sioux nation has surrendered, and its autonomy is gone. The vast reservation on the west bank of the Missouri—as large as the State of Indiana—is to be split up. Eleven million acres of soil will be thrown open to white settlers presently.
>
> This consent of the Indians to the sale of their land for four-teen million dollars is one of the most important events in the later history of the Northwest. There is room for perhaps seventy thousand families in the new public domain thus acquired. The earth is fat and prolific. A vast multitude of pioneers is camped about the borders awaiting the official signal that they may enter upon their inheritance.

Two weeks after the vote, Washington reduced the annual beef issue, just as the Sioux had feared. It was cut at Rosebud by two million pounds; at Pine Ridge, by one million; at the four other Agencies, pro-portionately. Congress, searching for ways to slash the budget, ordered a 10 percent reduction in funds for Sioux "subsistence and civilization." For the fiscal year 1890, Congress allocated just $900,000 for the Sioux—$100,000 less than in the previous two years and the smallest appropriation since 1877. The Indian Office slashed rations, recalculat-ing individual beef consumption from 3 pounds daily to 1.9. Crook was mortified: "It will be impossible to convince them that this is not one result of their signing," he warned, but it did little good. "They made us many promises," said one old Lakota, "more than I can remember, but they never kept but one; they promised to take our land and they took it."

Black Elk returned to Pine Ridge in the midst of this debate. His mother's tipi was just as he'd seen it from above. He told his parents all that he'd experienced, and when his mother said that she'd dreamed he'd return on a cloud, "I was supposed to be a man, but my tears came out anyway." If he did arrive home on June 21, the Crook Land Com-mission was still ongoing. He apparently did not vote, and may have been too exhausted after his journey to enter the debates. The proceedings at Pine Ridge were the most contentious of all the Agencies, and when the final vote of more than 1,500 eligible Oglala and Cheyenne males was tallied on June 28, only 614 gave their consent, or less than 50 percent. The Crook Commission moved north to Lower Brulé, where they received a friendlier reception.

The Oglala now found themselves caught in a swift accretion of miseries. This was saying a lot, considering all they'd been through. Before Black Elk's return, they'd suffered crop failures: Pine Ridge's rainfall was historically sparse, "and it seems almost a waste of time and money to try and make" the land productive, conceded Interior's *Indians Taxed and Not Taxed*: "The little land that is arable will not sustain a large population. There is but little water, and the small streams running through the reservation" could not sustain agriculture.

By the time he returned, famine gripped Pine Ridge. "Before I went some of my people were looking well," he said, "but when I got back they all looked pitiful." Though the chiefs complained that their tribesmen were always hungry, "this complaint of an Indian is not always heeded because to be hungry seems to be his normal condition," Interior said.

If one thing had kept the Oglala from starvation, it was their beef ration, but now that was cut to the bone. Following the winters of 1886–88, an outbreak of deadly black-leg raced through the cattle herd. Tribesmen who attended the land debates found upon returning their crops withered and cattle stolen or killed. When the beef ration was cut, they were forced to slaughter more than three times as many of their own young cattle, further depleting the Agency's livestock trade. Soon, they began to kill the range cattle of white ranchers. "Men will take desperate remedies sooner than suffer from hunger," warned Indian Inspector Frank Armstrong.

Weakened by hunger, the People sickened and died. That summer and autumn, measles, influenza, and whooping cough swept through Pine Ridge, especially striking down children. "The people said their children were all dying from the face of the earth, and they might as well be killed at once," one resident told the Smithsonian ethnographer James Mooney. By winter, disease killed as many as forty-five people per month, or nearly 1 percent of the population. While overseas, Black Elk had mourned the loss of his power and felt "like a dead man moving around most of the time." Now, in the face of such crisis, he had no choice but to try healing again. "Just after I came back, some people asked me to cure a sick person, and I was afraid the power would not come back to me, but it did." Yet even the best healer could not revive the People's dying spirit. "Anyone who understands the Indian character needs not the testimony of witnesses to know the mental effect this produced," Mooney said. "Sullenness and gloom, amounting almost to despair, settled down on the Sioux."

Everyone knew someone who died. In addition to those he tried to save but could not, the waves of sickness decimated Black Elk's own family. One brother escaped by signing up with Cody's Wild West, bound again for Europe, but that fall he lost a sister and at least two other brothers to disease. Then came the hardest blow.

In his interviews, Black Elk's greatest personal sorrows were often the least mentioned. One imagines a flatness of affect, as if he could not face the pain. That fall, "I lost my father and I was fatherless on this earth," he said. The elder Black Elk was placed on a scaffold, and his son entered a mourning period that would continue to the spring or summer of the next year. In all likelihood he performed a spirit-keeping ceremony, just as Worm had performed for the slain Tasunke Witko. Black Elk would mourn daily and commit himself to months of self-denial; the spirit bundle containing the soul of his father was always by his side. He would also perform a giveaway, in defiance of the law. By doing this, he guaranteed that his father's spirit need not wander the earth forever, but would return to the sacred place where it was born.

We will never know the influence that Black Elk's father wielded within the tribe. Yet his closeness to Worm and Crazy Horse; the intimate details he knew of the war chief's life and visions; his role as a bear healer in a long line of bear healers; his fateful advice to Crazy Horse shortly before his death—all suggest that his influence was great and that he was a counselor to kings. His influence over his son could not be denied. He was the first to sense his son's strange powers; the one to guide him through preparations for the Horse Dance and beyond. Duty, he preached, was everything.

With his father's death, Black Elk found himself the family's primary provider. The bimonthly rations were listed in his name, as were all future land allotment decisions. Luckily, his income was not the sole resource: the brother who'd joined the Wild West would send some of his pay back home. It was still customary for one of a deceased man's kin to marry his widow, so for the third time Leggings Down would wed a member of the Black Elk clan—this time her husband's second cousin, the medicine man Good Thunder. But even with this help, the main responsibility for Black Elk's mother devolved to him.

To make ends meet, he took a job as clerk at the Manderson store. Such businesses were government concessions that went to whites or squawmen; the owners were not exactly absentee, but they often held several contracts at once and left daily operations to their Indian clerks. The original store owner at Wounded Knee, for example, was George E. Bartlett: at the same time that he owned the concession, he served as deputy U.S. marshal, postmaster, and inspector for the Black Hills Live Stock Association. The Manderson store was probably run the same way.

It was a good position for a young medicine man. As the people of Manderson and Wounded Knee came to the store, they could arrange with Black Elk for his services. He'd hear their stories, gossip, and news. He heard how, on February 10, 1890, President William Henry Harrison opened the Sioux's "surplus" land to settlers ahead of schedule— this, instead of waiting until a proper survey protected those Indians already living there. The Lakota were furious, but what could they do? He heard how people could no longer ride north to visit friends at Cheyenne River, Lower Brulé, or Standing Rock; these were now separate reservations, and one needed a permit to leave Pine Ridge. Black Elk listened as former allies turned against one another: traditionalists like Red Cloud turned upon "progressives," calling them "fools and dupes" for agreeing to the land settlement. Resentment grew.

Black Elk was not the only one aware of such anger. The government's 1890 census takers heard many things. The young men were restless, especially when reciting stories of old heroes. The Sioux were an intelligent people, "and freely discuss all matters relating to the tribe or themselves," they wrote in *Indians Taxed and Not Taxed*. "They know every move made by the government, and watch every change of policy."

The census takers knew that anger simmered just below the surface, and it would not take much for it to catch fire. South Dakota's Sioux, they concluded, "are some of the most dangerous Indians on the American continent."

———•—•———

Most of all, Black Elk came to see that his Oglala were besieged by competing faiths. Of all the reservation's tugs-of-war for men's allegiance, the spiritual engaged him most. After all, he'd concluded since age nine that the only way to save his people was through religion.

At this moment, more religions competed for men's souls in Pine Ridge than ever before. This said a lot for a people as spiritually conscious as the Lakota. There were "quiet" traditionalists—the worshippers of *Wakan Tanka*. There were Episcopals—the reservation's original stewards under Grant's Peace Policy. Vague rumors floated from the west of an Indian Messiah. Strange visitations occurred closer to home. Some Arapahos appeared on the reservation: they'd run out of food and water after a long, unsuccessful hunt and prayed to the Great Spirit for relief. "Jesus is said to have appeared to them with his wounds, the crown of thorns . . . a piece of cloth around the loins and all covered with blood," wrote the Jesuit father Aemilius Perrig in his diary for September 9, 1889. "Where Jesus stood, there the dust flew up and a spray of water sprang up to quench Their Thirst."

And there were the Catholics, to whom Perrig belonged. If the growing sightings of an Indian Messiah would have the most immediate effects, the Catholic Church would have the most long-lasting. Both would have equal weight in Black Elk's life and thought. The failure of one would drive him into the arms of the other.

The Catholics officially arrived in Pine Ridge while Black Elk traveled with Buffalo Bill and Mexican Joe. Perhaps even then they intrigued him. Though to this point he'd never mentioned them in the Neihardt interviews, he had shown an interest in Christianity while overseas: he favorably mentioned Englishmen's faith in the February 1888 letter home from Manchester, and there are hints that he visited Anglican or Catholic cathedrals in England, France, or Italy.

After the lifting of Grant's Peace Policy, the Catholic Church almost immediately moved in. Jesuit priests and brothers and several Franciscan nuns arrived at Rosebud in 1886 to found the St. Francis Mission and Boarding School. One year later, the Philadelphia heiress Katharine Drexel donated sixty thousand dollars for a similar mission in Pine Ridge. The Jesuits built a church and boarding school four miles west of the Agency village in a wooded curve of White Clay Creek, a narrow valley hemmed by high, arid hills. Originally called Drexel Mission, the facility would soon be known as Holy Rosary; Father Perrig was school superintendent, reporting to Father Superior John B. Jutz. When four Sisters of St. Francis of Penance and Christian Charity arrived in 1888, the Lakota thought they were the wives of "Blackrobe" Jutz. The Sisters explained they "came only for the sake of the Indians."

Many Sioux had already converted by the time the Jesuits arrived. Spotted Tail and Red Cloud had both trusted Father De Smet; Sitting Bull, the Benedictine father Martin Marty. Red Cloud's desire for Black Robes was one more flashpoint in his feud with McGillycuddy. He believed that while God had sent His son, Jesus, to the *wasichu*, He'd sent His daughter, Buffalo Calf Woman, to the Lakota. The Indians treated her better. Buffalo Calf Woman had revealed that Indians and whites would one day merge into one race; Red Cloud believed that now was the prophesied time. He wanted the priests to "teach our people how to read and write" in English. Conversion was a way to adapt to the white world.

Thus, the road had already been paved for the holy order nicknamed "God's Marines," after their willingness to go anywhere at the Pope's command. Jesuit explorers had founded the city of São Paulo, charted the Amazon and Mississippi Rivers, located the source of the Blue Nile, and brought vanilla, quinine, ginseng, and rhubarb to the West from Asia and South America. The first Jesuits to Holy Rosary were Germans and Austrians: like Jutz and Perrig, the fathers Eugene Buechel, Louis Gall, and Florentine Digmann all spoke Lakota. Some became so proficient that they preached their sermons in Sioux. The more effective and enlightened, such as Buechel, taught about the Catholic faith as if it were an outgrowth of Lakota tradition. God was *Wakan Tanka*; the Eucharist was the "holy food," or *yatapi wakan*; the church was a "sacred house," or *tipi wakan*. The devil, or "evil mystery spirit," was *wakan sica*.

Each religion proclaimed that it alone possessed the Truth. Each promised Eternal Life as an escape from the current world of death and pain.

————•◦•————

America has always been a millennial land. Gripped by apocalyptic fervor, the Puritans fled the Land of Bondage and crossed a watery waste to the Promised Land. This was the New Jerusalem of Revelations, John Winthrop's "city upon a hill." Since these millennial beginnings, hundreds of revivals, communities, cults, and institutions have sprung up, merging biblical text with ecstatic dreams of the End. Short-lived or long-lasting, violent or peaceful, all have at their root the hope that the Messiah will come soon, and with His arrival begins a Golden Age enjoyed only by the elect and the resurrected dead.

Along with war, revitalization and messianic movements are among the most recurrent features of human history. According to the scholar Frank K. Flinn, the United States has spawned more millennial cults than any other modern nation on earth: they course through our history like rivers, some drying up, others branching off to separate streams— the Shakers, Oneida community, and the Second Great Awakening and Burned-Over District; Millerites, Mormons, and Jehovah's Witnesses. The urge has not faltered in recent times: the Nation of Islam, Jonestown, Branch Davidians, and Heaven's Gate. Most have been peaceful: non-believers might vanish from the earth, but for this to happen believers need only watch and pray.

The *wasichu* God was a god of time: he acted in history and would come to judge the righteous and unrighteous, the quick and the dead. The late 1880s had its share of prophets and saviors. In the summer of 1888, a minister in Soddy, Tennessee, outside Chattanooga, announced that Christ had come again as his assistant, A. J. Brown, who fasted in the mountains for forty days. That same year, the Methodist minister George J. Schweinfurth of Rockford, Illinois, announced that the divine spirit of the Risen Lord Dora Beekman passed into him at the moment that she died. "To-day he is worshiped by hundreds," wrote *The New York Times*, "not merely as the Christ returned to the flesh, but as the maker and ruler of the earth as well."

The Indian God was a god of space, not time. Whereas the white God called people forward to a future kingdom, the Indian God was ever-present, in the plains and lakes, not so much imminent as always there. When present-day commentators call Indian theology environmentalist, this is what they mean: God did not make the forest so much as He *is* the forest, and one did not move in with double-bladed axes to strip the land of God.

There had been Indian Messiahs in the past, but theirs were restorative movements pointing *back* to a hallowed age before the white man appeared. Such Messiahs almost always emerged after several generations of exposure to Europeans, usually after the exploitation accompanying colonialism. In Central and South America and the American Southwest, that was slavery; farther north, disease, severely depleted game, and loss of land. In 1762, a prophet named Neolin appeared among the Delawares preaching a union of all tribes. Return to the old ways, he promised, and the whites would disappear. From 1752 to 1775, a Maumee Indian preached the same message along the Susquehanna and Allegheny Valleys; from 1740 to 1775, eight native prophets—two of them women—carried similar beliefs through the eastern woodlands. A new world was coming, but only for Indians.

In 1869, the year the Iron Road finally stretched from coast to coast, a Paiute, or "Fish-eater," spoke of a vision he'd received as a young man. His name was Wodziwub, and he lived in Mason Valley, Nevada, a mining region sixty miles south of Virginia City near the Walker River Indian Reservation. During a trance, he was addressed by the Great Holy: the spirits of dead Indians would create a paradise without a single white; all would be young again and live forever. But this would not happen unless believers performed the Dance of the Souls Departing, also called the Ghost Dance, a round dance held on moonless nights outside the light of fire. The Ghost Dance of 1870 spread quickly through western Nevada and nearer parts of Oregon and California, largely due to the work of several disciples. One was a Paiute shaman named Tavivo, whose son, born in 1856, was named Wovoka, or "the Cutter."

Wodziwub died three or four years after starting the Ghost Dance, and by 1873, his Golden Age had not appeared. By 1875, interest in his dance had faded. By then, the Cutter was nineteen: he'd been adopted by the farmer David Wilson and was known as Jack Wilson.

In 1889, word spread of a Messiah living among the Fish-eaters. It traveled east, from the Shoshoni to the Crow, then to the Arapaho and Cheyenne. By summer, stories made it to the Sioux. On July 23, 1889, Elaine Goodale, a young white woman just appointed South Dakota's superintendent of Indian education, was camping in the Nebraska sand-hills on an antelope hunt when a Brulé named Chasing Crane visited her camp. Christ had just appeared among the Crow, he said, a story similar to the one Father Perrig would hear in September from the wandering Arapaho. Within a month, more stories spread through the Agency, and they sounded so much like those told from the pulpit by Catholic and Episcopal priests that they could not be ignored. A council headed by Red Cloud, Young Man Afraid of His Horses, Little Wound, and American Horse appointed delegates to investigate. The delegation included Good Thunder and three others from Pine Ridge; Short Bull and another from Rosebud; and Kicking Bear from Cheyenne River.

Black Elk was related directly or by marriage to all three. Kicking Bear was probably best-known. A mystic and medicine man, he'd fought beside Crazy Horse at the Rosebud and the Greasy Grass and was implicated in the 1874 murder of the Red Cloud clerk Frank Appleton. Born an Oglala, he'd become chief of a small northern Minneconjou band after marrying Woodpecker Woman, niece of the headman Big Foot. Now forty-one, Kicking Bear was an angry man. Like Black Elk's father, he hated whites. Though Black Elk called him uncle, the relationship is not clear.

Short Bull was a few years older than his brother-in-law Kicking Bear. Once a notable warrior, he was now a leading medicine man. Dr. James Walker, the Pine Ridge physician, called him "open, generous, and kindhearted," but uncompromising in his defense of the old ways.

Good Thunder was the oldest and the one whom Black Elk knew best. He'd helped Black Elk mourn when his father died; his prestige as a Pine Ridge holy man helped reestablish Black Elk as a healer when he returned from Buffalo Bill. "He was an old man of winning appearance, with hoary locks, that hung nearly to his waist," wrote Elaine Goodale, "and the soft voice and ingratiating manner of many old-time Sioux." He'd been in Grandmother's Land with the Black Elks and had returned to the Agencies to persuade friends to join them. According to an Indian Office letter dated November 8, 1890, Good Thunder assured them that "the Queen told him that the United States was cheating the Indians out of their land and robbing them of their rights, and that if the Indians would come to the English Government that they would be protected."

The delegates started west, by train. They sent back letters at each stop, relating tales of a man living near the base of the Sierras who said he was the son of God and bore on his body the scars of crucifixion. He would wipe all whites from the earth, then bring back the buffalo and the dead. The number of delegates increased with each whistle-stop, all sent by their tribes to investigate the Messiah.

Black Elk would hear the story of the delegates' journey from Good Thunder. They traveled until the railroad stopped, where two Indians greeted them as brothers. They gave them meat and bread, supplied them with horses, and told them to ride four days to Mason Valley then on to Walker Lake if they hoped to see the Messiah. There they found hundreds of Indians in an open field, speaking in dozens of tongues. A disciple came forward and said they must wait two more days; at sundown on the third, the Paiutes built a huge bonfire. Only then, after the long buildup, did the Messiah appear.

It was Wovoka, the Cutter. Now thirty-four, he was nearly six feet tall, with a dark complexion and close-cropped hair. He wore *wasichu* clothes and a wide-brimmed hat; he was known as a hard worker, and the Wilsons treated him like family. Beginning with the Wilsons' daily Bible readings, he'd grown intrigued with different forms of Christianity. He talked to Mormon missionaries, then worked in Northern California's hops fields, where he met the Shakers.

One day in 1886 or 1887, he was cutting wood in the mountains when he heard a great noise overhead. When he went to investigate, he said that he "fell down dead." God took him up to Heaven and before him stretched a vista of Indians and whites, all young. The country was bountiful and green; people danced and played sports; they'd been brought here as a reward for their virtue. God made them young again and promised eternal life. Then Wovoka woke. He returned to camp and crawled fever-stricken into bed.

That night, God came to him again. He commanded Wovoka to tell all people they must not fight; peace must reign in the world. People were all brothers now. When Wovoka had finished spreading this message, God would come again.

The Cutter heard no more from God for three years. During this time, he preached to the Indians. Because no one initially believed his claims, he announced that in July 1888 he would make ice appear on the Walker River. Afraid that Jack would lose face, the two Wilson brothers hauled a wagonload of ice from their father's icehouse and dumped it upstream. When the ice floated past, the Paiutes were convinced—as was Jack Wilson. His reputation spread.

On January 1, 1889, a total solar eclipse darkened the sky. It was *Anpa wi wan te* in Short Man's winter count, or the year "a sun died." Wovoka crawled into his wikiup and lost consciousness, probably from scarlet fever. This time, he climbed a mountain and met a beautiful woman in white who said the Master of Life waited at the summit for him. He stripped off his clothes, plunged into a frigid stream, and appeared thus reborn before God. The Creator's instructions were different and more apocalyptic this time. The old world would be destroyed and replaced by a new one in the spring of 1891; the dead would return, happy and young. God gave Wovoka control of the elements with five songs; he must call together the tribes, admonish them not to fight with whites or one another, and teach them the Ghost Dance, which they must dance for five days every three months. When Wovoka was satisfied that the Indians had followed his teachings, he would begin the new millennium.

This was the first step, the gathering of the tribes as God had commanded. Though he never called himself the Messiah, others did. He'd become what the biblical scholar James Tabor called an "inspired interpreter," the necessary prophet equipped with proper insight to prepare his followers for the Second Coming. By so doing, he joined the ranks of such American prophets as William Miller, Joseph Smith, and Tenskwatawa. As the delegates watched, Wovoka sat by the bonfire for several hours, then rose. For the first time, they could plainly see that he was not white, but Indian. He was going to show them a dance, and he wanted them to learn it with him. They all danced the Dance of the Ghosts until late into the night. They resumed the next morning, and sometimes during the dances he would go into a trance for twelve to fourteen hours. "He wasn't shamming," said E. A. Dyer, a white contemporary. "His body was as rigid as a board . . . and he showed no reaction to pain inducing experiments." When he recovered, he told the assembled that the Messiah was coming to the Indians. One must merely dance, and wait, and it would happen.

During the long trances, delegates would debate the nature of an Indian Christ. Was such a thing possible? When Christ first came to earth, whites had rejected and finally killed Him. Now it made sense that the New Christ returned as an Indian and rejected the *wasichu*. Some delegates were troubled by the fact that although Wovoka bore a scar on his body and another on his face, they were not the same as the stigmata described in the Bible. Others felt it did not matter that the scars were not the same.

What seemed most important was his message. "My father told me the earth was getting old and worn out," Wovoka said after coming from his trance, "and the people getting bad, and that I was to renew everything as it used to be, and make it better." He gave the delegates some sacred red and white paint to be worn while dancing, two holy eagle feathers to help bring back the dead, and a bundle of green grass as a reminder of all he'd preached. He also gave each delegate a letter to read when they returned to their tribes.

After a few more days, Good Thunder and the others started home. They split up during the return. Kicking Bear stopped in Wyoming to learn more from the Arapahos, already dancing hard. Good Thunder took a train to Oregon, where *another* Messiah was said to have surfaced, but he never found him. Short Bull went straight home. By April 1890, all had returned.

Agent Gallagher also heard of the delegation. Though he had few details, he knew the Indians were excited about *something* and ordered his police to bring in the leaders. Good Thunder was questioned for two days, but revealed nothing. Kicking Bear and Short Bull told the Indian police what they had seen and heard. The chiefs called a council to hear their reports, but away from the agent in a little-used bend of White Clay Creek. The delegates spoke of Wovoka's commandments and read his letter to the tribes: "Do not tell the white people about this. Jesus is now upon the earth. He appears like a cloud. The dead are all alive again. I do not know when they will be here; maybe this fall or in the spring. When the time comes there will be no more sickness and everyone will be young again."

All that spring and summer, Wovoka's Ghost Dance spread. The doctrine, basically unchanged from his father's in 1870, was known by different names to different tribes, and that very flexibility allowed his message to succeed where others had failed. By summer, the dance had spread south from the Paiute to the Hualapai, and east to the Bannock, Shoshone, Arapaho, Cheyenne, Caddo, Pawnee, and Sioux. A religion that called for a return to the old way of life could spread so rapidly because of modern innovations. The concentration of tribes at the Agencies allowed adherents to communicate more easily; the railroad, telegraph, and expanding postal service helped spread the word. Young Indians educated by Colonel Pratt could communicate with other tribes in English, the new lingua franca.

How many Native Americans believed? Modern scholars estimate that by the late summer or early fall of 1890, as many as twenty thousand Indians practiced the Ghost Dance religion. But no one really knows. The Smithsonian's James Mooney, upon whose work all later studies depended, believed that the Ghost Dance of 1890 was accepted by only 13.7 percent of the Indians west of the Missouri. But in those tribes that embraced it most enthusiastically—the Pauite, Shoshone, Arapaho, Cheyenne, Caddo, Pawnee—the converts counted for as many as a third.

Then there were the Sioux. Mooney claimed that 50 percent, or 13,000, of the 26,000 Lakotas living in the Agencies took an active part in the Ghost Dance, yet the Interior census of June 1, 1890, counted only 19,068 Lakotas that year. Using Mooney's 50 percent estimate, this placed the number closer to 9,500 dancers, and later studies lower the totals more. Yet firm numbers require strict adherents, and many Lakotas may well have adopted Little Wound's practical advice: "My friends, if this is a good thing, we should have it. If it is not, it will fall to earth itself." It was best to learn the dance, he counseled, "so if the Messiah does come, he will not pass us by." One thing is clear: no other Plains tribe embraced the Ghost Dance as fully as the Lakota, and no other Lakota band converted in such numbers as the Oglala of Pine Ridge.

Why them? This was a mystery even to Mooney, and remains a puzzle today. Still, it makes sense. This was the tribe of Red Cloud and Crazy Horse, who'd fought the combined might of the U.S. Army to a standstill. They'd waged an honorable war and kept the terms of the Great Father's peace; in return they'd been swindled, betrayed, starved, and forced to watch their children die. The Ghost Dance leaders remembered the glory of the Greasy Grass, especially Crazy Horse's former lieutenant Kicking Bear. The insulting land sales and ration cuts had finally been too much. Many felt they had nothing more to lose, and everything to gain.

All that summer, Black Elk heard talk of *Wanagi Wacipi*—the "Ghost Dance"—but he stayed away. People came to the store and talked about the dance and the Messiah. Another world was coming, but only for Indians; by donning the sacred paint and dancing the right steps, one would be saved. The paint and dance would draw believers up like magnets when the new world roared by. It was the "rapture" without using the term. Descriptions of the Promised Land varied: it could be as massive as a planet, or as nebulous as a cloud. Whites would be left behind, or crushed, or buried alive.

One day in June, Good Thunder came to the store. He'd been away a long time and could think of little else but Wovoka, but he was happy to see his nephew. Kicking Bear and he were arranging a Ghost Dance south of Manderson, and they needed tobacco and bits of colored cloth to prepare. He told Black Elk of the miracles he'd witnessed in the land of the Fish-eaters. Once, Wovoka held out his hat: "We saw the whole world and all that is wonderful," Good Thunder claimed. Another time, he led them to the spirit world, where they hunted buffalo with departed loved ones. "The Messiah told them to take everything but the head, tail, and four feet, and then the buffalo would come to life again."

But Black Elk was puzzled. Such tales seemed similar to his own Great Vision, though not in every detail. Something bothered him about it, so he stayed away.

Finally, in August 1890, Kicking Bear held the first local Ghost Dance, north of Pine Ridge at the head of Cheyenne Creek. It was a small affair, not well attended. Soon afterward, Good Thunder staged a larger dance to the south at Wounded Knee Creek, organized specifically to proselytize Big Road's band. When Black Elk heard, he could no longer resist. His curiosity got the best of him. He saddled his horse and rode the ten miles south on the Manderson Road until he came to some high hills. And there he stopped and looked down into the Valley of the Wounded Knee.

19

DANCES WITH GHOSTS

Black Elk gazed south into a large natural amphitheater surrounded by high hills, his vantage point a long eroded butte called Lookout Hill, the last of the White Buttes stretching north from here. The north-south road from Pine Ridge Village cut the basin in half; that road lay to his left, and continued north to Porcupine. Near it squatted Bartlett's Store, now owned by the French and Indian mixed-blood Louis Mousseau. Wounded Knee Creek snaked behind that, gouging a ragged north-south gash in the basin. A dry streambed cut west midway down its course, a deep gully with high crumbling walls. Chokeberry bushes clumped in its curves.

No one knew how the creek got its name. No battles or duels could be recalled. The best guess was that it had been named after George Bartlett, the store's original owner, who'd earned a bad knee riding with the Pony Express. The Oglala called him Huste, or "Wounded Knee." But was he named after the creek, or the creek after him? No one could say.

The camp of the Ghost Dancers nestled in the pocket between this hill and the gully. It was early evening and about 250 men and women swung in a great circle from right to left, hand in hand. Most dressed in white, which glowed weirdly in the twilight blue. According to Good Thunder, the dancers would have fasted and purified themselves in sweat lodges. Their songs were monotonous and simple:

> Here we shall hunt the buffalo—
> So says the Earth!

This was broken occasionally by brief invocations from Good Thunder or the wailing of women. As Black Elk watched, a woman spun from the ring and dropped to the ground. The circle closed up; dancers barely lifted their feet as they stepped over her. Others were also strewn about, all apparently senseless. Some would rise and shout what they had seen: visions of dead family, a prairie black with buffalo. "How can I bear this life?" They were answered by cries and groans.

As Black Elk rode close, he could barely believe his eyes. In the circle's center stood a dead tree, its trunk, branches, and leaves painted brilliant red. It was exactly as he'd seen in his Great Vision: a dying tree around which men and women held hands, hoping to re-form the hoop and make the tree bloom again. Sacred articles tied to its branches were also painted scarlet, as were the dancers' faces. Good Thunder held a pipe and eagle feathers—all as in his Vision.

As he watched, he felt helpless and sad. Everything resembling his Vision reminded him of how much was left undone. "Boy, take courage!" the Grandfathers had said. They'd given him so many gifts and so much power, but what had he done with them? His people were lost and dying. He was as lost as they.

But as he sat there, joy overtook him. He realized that the convergence between his Vision and this dance could not be a coincidence. Perhaps the man called the Messiah was really a messenger from the Grandfathers "to remind me to get to work again to bring my people back into the hoop and the old religion." The Grandfathers had said he would be an intercessor for his people. When God's power flowed through him, the Lakota would once again be whole.

When the dance ended, he asked Good Thunder and Kicking Bear if he could stay the night and join in the next morning. The Ghost Dance had transformed both men, and not always for the better. Now regarded as the leader, Kicking Bear had already initiated the Minneconjou bands of Big Foot, Hump, and Eagle Bear into the Dance; these were all to the north, across the Cheyenne River. He could not rest until the Oglala danced, too. He'd become a fanatic, and it worried his friends. Eagle Elk, who lived near Black Elk in Manderson, found Kicking Bear frightening. He moved among the dancers like a ghost—a gaunt, unfamiliar specter who condemned unbelievers and seemed possessed. The body looked familiar, but the mind was not his own.

But Good Thunder seemed liberated. He moved among the fallen and ministered to their needs. Good Thunder most fully grasped the value of Black Elk's participation. He'd heard hints of Black Elk's coma-vision from his father; the sickly boy had become with manhood one of the Agency's most powerful *wicasa wakan*. If he joined the dance, others would, too.

The next morning, Black Elk dressed in white and Good Thunder led him to the bright vermilion tree. "Father, behold me," he cried, "this by your ways he shall see, and the people shall know him." As Good Thunder began to weep, Black Elk remembered his father. The elder Black Elk had always believed in his son, yet he'd never fulfilled the promise the older man had seen. He, too, began to weep, then knelt beside the withered tree. He lifted up his face to keep the tears from coursing out, but it did little good. He thought of his people—how they'd taken the wrong road, the white man's road, and all they'd found was death and poverty. How long could this continue? Maybe this dance was the answer, after all.

Suddenly, he began to shiver, but not from cold. Good Thunder and Kicking Bear lifted him up, each by an elbow, and they moved into the dance's early phase. They sang together:

> What is it that comes to us now?
> One who seeks his father!

They danced the entire day. In general, dances proceeded similarly. Good Thunder spoke a few words, then the dancers turned their faces south, raised their hands, and sang at the top of their lungs. This lasted for two or three minutes, until they faced the holy tree and joined hands. They moved in a circle, eyes closed or staring hard at the ground. The pace quickened; everyone sang. After about twenty minutes, some dancers began to moan and roll their eyes. They fell in or out of the circle, rolling in the dust until completely exhausted. Next came un-consciousness, which they called "dying." This lasted for about thirty minutes as others fell around them or kept dancing. Holy men moved among the fallen as they came from the depths, asking what they'd seen. This continued for another ninety minutes until they paused to rest and the medicine men related the visions of the fallen. Two hours later, they started again.

Black Elk danced all that day, praying for a revelation. He begged *Wakan Tanka* to let him see his father and to hunt bison with him. Sometimes as Black Elk danced he felt consumed by the old "queer feeling" that often preceeded his visions, but this always passed. He danced until his legs ached and he shivered from exhaustion. But no vision was granted him that day.

The next morning, he tried again. Kicking Bear gave the invocation. "Father, behold me!" he cried. "These people shall go forth today. They shall see the relatives that they may be happy over there day after day and there will be no end to that happiness." As if on cue, dancers surrounding Black Elk began to wail and cry.

All that morning Black Elk danced, but he could not reach the visionary stage. This is an important distinction: Black Elk was not a stereotypical cultist, more than willing to feign religious ecstasy. The Ghost Dance must be *proven* before he called it real. As he danced, more Oglalas fell out of the circle: some laughed, others cried; some lay silent while others staggered about. But Black Elk did not succumb: if he was meant to receive a vision, it must be genuine.

So Black Elk danced into the afternoon, nearing exhaustion, close to what anthropologists call a "possession trance," that long-term physical punishment that begins to change the brain. The fact that Black Elk danced so long and hard shows that he was desperate to believe. He danced and danced, his eyes shut tight, Good Thunder at one elbow, Kicking Bear at the other. They *needed* his conversion: it validated them. The wails of the fallen filled his ears. Another queer feeling tingled through him and he seemed to glide forward and swing back, a human pendulum marking the passage of time. Good Thunder and Kicking Bear no doubt assisted, rocking him as he danced, knowing he was prone to strong visions and hoping to aid the process. He began to pant, and they released him at the end of an arc. He fell forward, as if flying.

And as he fell, he saw again in his mind the sacred eagle feather given to him by the Grandfathers long ago. "I fell as though I had fallen off a swing and gone into the air," he later said. His arms were out straight and he flew over the tipis, over the hills surrounding the valley, over the beautiful land of the dead. He came to a dream camp in which the sacred tree was blooming, and the spirits, dressed in what he would call "ghost shirts," came out to meet him. "It is not yet time to see your father," they said, "but we shall present to you something that you will carry home to your people." He was lifted back into the air and returned to his body at Wounded Knee Creek. He opened his eyes as dancers crowded around him, eager to learn what he'd seen. He told them of his vision and of the holy garments. He thought that, if his people learned something from his vision, perhaps the tree *would* bloom again.

No one was more excited by Black Elk's vision than Kicking Bear. He said he'd had a similar vision; more important, Wovoka had worn a shirt like the one Black Elk described. The Cutter stood upon a blanket while a tribesman fired a double-barrel shotgun from ten paces away. Kicking Bear clapped twice to mimic the discharge. "My relatives, you know me well," he said, the eerie light of belief in his eyes. "My tongue is straight. But I tell you this: *The shirt had not a single hole in it!*" Wovoka stepped away from the blanket unharmed. "All over the blanket upon which he had been standing were the scattered buckshot from the gun." Kicking Bear drew from his tobacco bag several tiny shot that he rolled on his palms. "I tell you, my cousins, that holy shirt has the power to turn away bullets!"

Thus began the belief in the "bulletproof" ghost shirts, at least in Black Elk's version. Faith in their efficacy would have disastrous consequences and play a major role in what was to come. Yet the shirt, as Wovoka would tell Mooney, was not part of the original dance. While many claimed that such "armor" pushed the Lakota past worship into militancy, an analysis by the Finnish historian Rani-Henrik Andersson of recorded Sioux ghost songs detected no such anti-white bias: the bulletproof shirts were purely defensive, like the shields and charms taken into battle. But the fact remains—though other ghost-dancing tribes created similar shirts, only the Lakota endowed them with claims of invulnerability.

Black Elk spent the rest of that day making ghost shirts patterned after those in his vision. Made of unbleached muslin or government-issued canvas, they were cut like old-time ceremonial war shirts, fringed and shaped alike but with distinctive markings. On most, the picture of a young eagle with outstretched wings was painted in blue on the back; beyond that, they varied. Black Elk painted a blue star on the left shoulder; from it, the rainbow of his Great Vision stretched across the chest and down to the right hip. Another rainbow circled the neck like a necklace, and a star dangled like a pendant. He attached eagle feathers to the shoulders, elbows, and wrists, and haphazardly painted red streaks like lightning. He made the first shirt for a dancer named Afraid of Hawk; the second, for the son of Big Road. That evening, he painted a stick bright red and fastened to it an eagle feather. This was for his own use in future ceremonies.

He led the dance on the fourth day. Everyone faced west and the ceremony began with Black Elk's prayer: "Father, Great Spirit, behold me!" he cried. "The nation that I have is in despair. The new earth you promised you have shown me. Let my nation also behold it." They raised their right hands to the west and began to weep; some fainted at once, even before the dance began.

Once again, Kicking Bear and Good Thunder danced beside him, each holding an arm. Once again, he began to fly. Up ahead he saw fire and smoke, and as he flew close recognized the volcano he'd seen with Mexican Joe—Vesuvius, destroyer of empires, exterminating the unjust as the Messiah promised to do again. He glided over six villages, and twelve men emerged. They would take him to their chief, they said. They took him to the village center, where once again he saw the sacred tree in bloom.

Against the tree, he saw a man. His arms were out, palms open. "I looked hard at him," Black Elk said. Though the man might be Indian, he was unsure. His hair was long and loose, and an eagle feather hung from it in the same fashion as with Black Elk and Crazy Horse. The man had painted his body red. Because he was bathed in light, it was hard to see his features. Black Elk knew, however, that he was "a very fine holy man."

The man spoke in a voice that sounded like song. "My life is such that all earthly beings and growing things belong to me," he said. "My Father has said this. You must say this." As he spoke, he transformed. As the light blazed around him, his body glowed with rainbow colors. As the light grew brighter, Black Elk thought he saw wounds form in the man's palms.

"Then he went out, like a light in the wind." The twelve men told Black Elk to "turn around and behold your nation." He turned, and the heavens were yellow; the earth, green; his people, young. In an instant, all had changed.

He would not be the only dancer to report such a vision of the crucified *wanikiye*, the Red Christ, during these summer dances. Kicking Bear claimed to have had a vision in which he, too, saw a man marked by stigmata. Iron Hail, later known as Dewey Beard, would wear his hair in the style of the Red Christ until the day he died. The visions were similar: the Red Christ would come in the spring, when the grass was about two inches high. He would save his Indian children and destroy the *wasichu* and every trace of their civilization.

Black Elk never reported seeing his real father again. He'd apparently replaced him with the Red Christ, a vision potent enough to imbue him with an increased sense of mission. The dance ended on this day, and Kicking Bear moved to Rosebud to instruct the Brulé dancers. Good Thunder and Black Elk were left in charge of the Ghost Dancers at Pine Ridge.

———•◦•———

All that summer, Black Elk and Good Thunder led the dance at Wounded Knee, adding converts to the ranks of believers. His innate spirituality blossomed in this role; he had the power to incite visions in others, and often all he had to do was shake his "red flowering stick" and dancers would collapse into convulsive dreams. As word of his power grew, the Brulés at Rosebud asked him to lead their dances, too.

The Ghost Dance spread to tribes throughout the Plains during that summer. Dancers believed that the end would come by various means: a passing planet, cleansing cloud, sea of mud, or wave of fire unleashed from the moon. But in all versions, the cataclysm would occur if believers danced and prayed faithfully. Sometimes there were competing Messiahs. The first inkling that official Washington knew of the "Messiah Craze" appeared in a June 1890 War Department memo quoting the "Cheyenne medicine man, Porcupine." On August 20, 1890, the agent of Montana's Tongue River Agency reported that Porcupine had declared himself the "new Messiah." He warned doubters that their disbelief would call down "the curse of the 'Mighty Porcupine.'" Yet nowhere were the dances as prevalent as at Pine Ridge and Rosebud. Estimates of their numbers varied between a quarter and a third of the population. Whole families joined. While husbands and wives danced, children played inside the dance circle. At Rosebud, it seemed to Carlisle-educated Luther Standing Bear that the majority of Indians had joined. The dances were held daily on a flat about eight miles west of Agency headquarters. He could hear the drumbeat and "plainly locate the dancers from the dust they raised." Though his father had not yet joined the dancers, two brothers-in-law held high positions among them.

This family split was not uncommon. The Ghost Dance sparked a great internal debate among Lakota throughout the six Agencies. Leaders who cooperated with the government—such as Young Man Afraid of His Horses, Gall, and George Sword—feared the new movement would lead to violence. Others, such as Crow Dog and Sitting Bull, encouraged the dancers. Red Cloud steered a middle course: he did not believe the Ghost Dance would work and feared a crackdown; however, he supported the dancers' right to worship. After all, weren't many of the teachings identical to those of Christianity?

Some of the very first whites to grasp the hold of the Ghost Dance were missionaries. Father Aemilius Perrig noted that throughout the month of August 1890 "that silly talk about the apparitions of Jesus Christ" was common. In the Catholic boarding school, Father Superior John Jutz saw a strange change in the boys and girls. They were "just crazy over the Ghost Dance, and as soon as they thought they were not being observed, they danced it," he wrote.

On most reservations across the West, agents and army officials decided to let the dance play out: when the Messiah did *not* come, belief would dissipate, as it had in 1870. But the Sioux were seen as different. That August, further cuts came to the beef ration: if the Lakotas remained in the dance camps and did not tend their crops and livestock, the usual winter shortages could turn deadly. Sioux agents saw in the dance a mass hysteria that could spawn angry mobs; given a charismatic leader such as Kicking Bear or Sitting Bull, that mob could be organized into an army. The Indian Office still regarded the Sioux as a barely controlled threat, and these new tales of ghost shirts did nothing to dispel that image. Sioux agents worried they could be derelict if they did not stop the "Messiah Craze."

Thus began the steps that pulled both sides toward tragedy. That August, Agent Gallagher heard that more than six hundred Indians danced at No Water's camp, twenty miles northwest of Agency headquarters. He sent a squad of Indian police to break it up, but the dancers refused to budge. Gallagher called all white men at the Agency to an emergency meeting, then, on August 24, 1890, rode with a force of twenty to thirty Indian police to the dance camp in the Badlands.

But lookouts were everywhere, and Gallagher's force was outnumbered and outgunned. Whether through actual addition or due to the kind of inflation often seen in government reports, the number of dancers had jumped from six hundred to two thousand. They arrived at what seemed a deserted camp when armed dancers materialized from behind trees and out of creek beds. Though accounts vary, two constants emerge. The cool heads of the interpreter Philip Wells and the police commander Young Man Afraid of His Horses prevented bloodshed. And dancers refused to disperse, telling Gallagher that they planned to keep dancing.

To his credit, the agent did not demand revenge. Such open defiance was a hard pill to swallow, but he listened to reason. Yes, the dancers were emboldened by the standoff: they were safe in numbers *and* they had their ghost shirts and Winchesters. Yet this had happened only during a direct confrontation. There had been no reports of threats as long as the dancers were left alone. Interior's general policy at this point was "wait-and-see": the coming harsh winter would break up the gatherings, driving the Sioux to their lodges. Time, and the failure of Wovoka's prophecy, would send the Ghost Dance to a peaceful grave.

Late that summer, Black Elk journeyed to a Brulé dance at Cut Meat Creek, twenty five miles northwest of Rosebud headquarters, where Kicking Bear, Short Bull, and a chief named Mash the Kettle led the dancers. He brought with him six ghost shirts he'd made at Wounded Knee. He joined the dance and soon felt unsteady. Though he no longer seemed to pass out, he would grow dizzy and dream. He envisioned a flaming rainbow in the west that pierced a cloud tipi like the one in his Great Vision. A spotted eagle soared above it. "Remember this!" it chided.

He surfaced troubled, but did not know why. He could not divine the meaning of his vision, so mentioned it to Kicking Bear. The head priest was stumped: sometimes, he said, it was best to ignore those things one did not understand. Kicking Bear kept dancing and advised his young protégé to do the same.

But Black Elk recognized such foreboding. He'd felt it many times— before the soldiers arrived in Buffalo Gap; during those months when he'd feared obliteration by the Thunder-beings. He was missing something important, and it troubled him.

Only later did he understand. The dream had been a warning not to abandon his Great Vision for a lesser one. He had not trusted his instincts; he'd depended instead upon the red-painted stick, which he'd misinterpreted as a symbolic substitute for the sacred tree. "It is hard to follow one great vision in this world of darkness and of many changing shadows," he later told Neihardt. "Among these shadows, men get lost."

The September 1890 lull proved deadly. Though the summer's tensions seemed to abate, individual missteps occurred. At Rosebud, dancers killed breeding stock for food and sold their property for guns and ammunition. On September 26, settlers living west of the Cheyenne River Agency petitioned the Indian Office for the "protection of our lives and our children and our homes and our property": the closest Sioux to them was a small band of Minneconjous led by the old peace chief Big Foot. In Standing Rock, Sitting Bull acquiesced to his followers and sent a message to Kicking Bear, asking him to tell the Hunkpapa of the Messiah. Kicking Bear headed north with six followers. Whether Sitting Bull believed in the Messiah is unknown. Some historians claim he was a convert; others, that he tolerated the movement since his people believed. He never danced himself, and never directed the dances. Yet as a *wicasa wakan* who'd devoted his life to his people, he felt obligated to test the new creed.

At Rosebud, Cheyenne River, and Pine Ridge, experienced agents were replaced by neophytes who knew nothing about Indians. The revolving door at Pine Ridge would prove most fateful. Hugh Gallagher may not have been a saint, but he could be unflappable when cool heads were needed. Sadly for the Oglala, he was not a Republican. His replacement, Dr. Daniel F. Royer—a thirty-six-year-old physician-pharmacist from Alpena, South Dakota—would illustrate everything disastrous about the nineteenth-century political spoils system. Though he knew nothing about reservations, he'd helped elect Richard F. Pettigrew as South Dakota's first U.S. senator in 1889. Before Royer's appointment, Pettigrew outlined his plans: "If you secure the appointment I shall want to clean out the whole force of farmers, teachers, and clerks as far as possible and put in Dakota men."

But where other appointees may have known nothing about Indians, Royer feared them. Feared them so much that the Sioux named him Lakota Kopegle Koskala, or "Young Man Afraid of Lakota." Short, pudgy, sporting a walrus mustache, and often wearing a high-crowned Stetson, he came to Pine Ridge expecting a $183-a-month sinecure in which he'd do little more than keep records and hand out rations. Instead, his job entailed keeping order among several thousand angry and hungry Sioux. He was so easily buffaloed that his charges faced him down for the sheer joy of watching him lock himself in his house and refuse to emerge. Soon, Agency whites reported his erratic behavior to Washington. Time would reveal a possible explanation—like many frontier doctors, he abused the very drugs he prescribed, and some years later lost his medical license due to substance abuse.

Though history paints him as a fool, Royer's letters to Washington portray a man dominated by fear. Appointed on October 1, 1890, he received orders two days later to stop the Ghost Dance at Pine Ridge. Pettigrew made clear that Royer had no discretion and must do as told. When Royer arrived with his family on October 9, he found the order impossible; when he told Ghost Dancers to stop, they told him to mind his own business. According to one story, Royer surrounded himself with armed men before confronting dancers. One Indian walked up, unarmed and unafraid. Whites danced when they wanted, he said, and so would the Sioux. What did he intend to do with that pistol? Had he ever killed an Indian? "Here, kill me," he shouted, baring his breast, "for I am going to dance!"

Three days later, on October 12, Royer wrote Commissioner Thomas J. Morgan that "I have been carefully investigating the [Ghost Dance] and I find I have an elephant on my hands." More than half the Indians at Pine Ridge danced, he erroneously reported. The police had lost control and the chiefs were unhelpful; soldiers should be sent to protect him. The Indian Office replied that he should handle matters through tact, but nevertheless sent Major General Nelson Miles to investigate. Newly appointed as commander of the Department of the Missouri after the March 1890 death of George Crook, Miles had reached the pinnacle of his ambitions. He was now in charge.

All that October, Black Elk made more ghost shirts and led the dancers at Wounded Knee. He was so busy that he did not seem cognizant of the growing excitement a mere twenty miles away. The Jesuits at Drexel Mission, on the other hand, were very aware. "Not one Indian attended Mass," wrote Father Perrig in his October 17 diary entry. "They are dancing again." Unlike Royer, however, the Jesuits were not afraid. There had been no physical threats to them or any other white—rather, what seemed to be forming was an internal debate over religious freedom. "Christian Dakota constantly pointed out to their wilder kin," wrote Elaine Goodale, "the unreality and utter impossibility of the Messiah superstition." In response, the dancers essentially answered: *Just let us dance, then we'll see.*

On October 27, Miles arrived at Pine Ridge. The ambition of Fort

Keogh's young commander had been tempered by time. After unsuccessfully chasing Crazy Horse and Sitting Bull, he'd chased and beaten the Nez Perce, Bannock, and Geronimo's Apache. Victory had given him insight into his Indian foes: these days he preferred negotiation to bloodshed. Like other veteran Indian hands, he believed the "craze" largely one of starvation. Feed the Lakota as promised, let winter come, and the Agencies had nothing to fear.

Nevertheless, Miles met with dance leaders when he arrived. End the dance, he advised. So far there'd been no panic among settlers— but what if that changed? They knew how easy it was for any little incident to set off a war. In response, Little Wound—an Oglala chief and converted Episcopal—stood up to him. The Lakota would no longer live like whites; they'd tried, and all they'd gotten were broken promises and suffering. They would live and dance as they pleased. He invited Bear Coat to join him in a feast and dance, then tell the Great Father of his participation.

When Miles left Pine Ridge on the 28th, he tried to assure Royer that the dance would subside. Others who'd lived among the Lakota echoed his words. Valentine McGillycuddy, now a Black Hills banker brought in as peace commissioner, counseled, "As for the ghost dance, too much attention has been paid to it." James McLaughlin, longtime agent at Standing Rock, saw no need to panic: when spring came and the prophecies had not come true, the dance would stop of its own accord. If the Ghost Dance was dangerous, it was only so in terms of the Sioux' progress. "What is God going to bring out of it" when the craze subsides? asked C. G. Sterling, a Presbyterian missionary. "What is to fill that vacuum? The world-spirit of despair?"

Yet the investigation itself disturbed the system observed. Both sides became so instantly intractable that one cannot help but see a link to Miles's brief and rather innocent inquiry. Royer thought Miles had not gone far enough and on October 30 complained to Washington that *two-thirds* of the reservation Indians—not the one-half of earlier— were out of control. He called again for the military. The next day, on October 31, Short Bull told his followers that because the *wasichu* were interfering so much, he would shorten the time for the end of the world. Instead of next spring, everything foretold would happen after one more moon. He took upon himself the role of Messiah. All must dance together for a month at Pass Creek, a place "where the tree is sprouting" between Rosebud and Pine Ridge. If soldiers came, they would die: if the dancers wore their ghost shirts, they would live. In one more month, Indians would inherit the earth. As for whites, "There will be only five thousand of them left living on the earth," he said.

During this period, the Jesuits tried to convince dancers that such a course would be fatal. To them the frenzied singing and dancing was the devil's work, but with the agent's panic, a sense of perilous urgency arose. A major dance camp had set up four miles from the mission; on an unspecified day, Father Jutz entered the whirling circle and tried to reason with the dancers, many of whom were friends. Jutz knelt beside a reviving dancer and asked what he'd seen. "Do you not realize now yourselves how there is absolutely nothing in what you believe," he pleaded, "and that you cannot speak with your dead friends, or see them?" The Oglalas liked the elderly Black Robe, who spoke with an odd accent and whose gray beard sank below his collar, but in the end he was just another *wasichu* who could not understand. Jutz offered five dollars to any who described his vision. No one took his offer.

On November 6, 1890, the first snow of the season fell on Pine Ridge. On November 8, Father Perrig wrote that it was "getting snowy all day," covering the Plains in white icing, muffling the ghost drums. At the Agency, Elaine Goodale enjoyed the attentions of Charles Eastman, a Harvard-educated Santee Sioux who served as Agency physician; he would soon propose. At the mission school, the boys spent most of November 9 sledding down the hills.

The snow did not soften Daniel Royer's fears. On November 8, the day of the snowfall, he wired Washington that four major dance camps existed in Pine Ridge: 600 people danced at nearby White Clay Creek, 300 at Medicine Root Creek, 250 at Wounded Knee Creek, and 130 on the Porcupine. Altogether, nearly 1,300 Lakotas were dancing, and it would just get worse, he said. He begged to come to Washington to describe the situation, but his superiors responded that it was best for an agent to remain at his post if conditions were as bad as he claimed.

Wednesday, November 12, was the beef-issue day, when Oglalas swarmed headquarters. In the building that served as both dispensary and police station, Dr. Eastman saw patients from the outlying districts; as they always did during "Big Issue," the chiefs held a council in the same building. Suddenly, they heard a tumult outside: Indian police had tried to arrest an Oglala named Little wanted for cattle theft. Instead, two hundred Ghost Dancers led by Jack Red Cloud seized the police. They freed Little, who drew a knife on a police lieutenant. The

Ghost Dancers threatened to burn down the Agency and kill every white inside.

"Perhaps I was never in greater danger than at that moment," Elaine Goodale wrote. As she crossed the Agency's wide, muddy plaza, she saw a large crowd and heard cries of "Kill the soldiers! Kill them all!" A tall Indian stood unarmed in the office door. The tall Indian was American Horse, a progressive chief, who'd been in the council. They could kill the policemen, he said, but they and their families would be wiped out in the vengeance that followed. Is that what they wanted? Jack Red Cloud thrust a cocked pistol in the chief's face. "It is you and your kind that have brought us to this condition!" he cried. American Horse's eyes filled with disdain. He glanced at Red Cloud's son, turned his back, and walked inside. The crowd fell silent and dispersed, taking Little with them.

Though American Horse had averted a massacre, he could not avert Royer's panic. The next day, on November 13, Little sent a message to Royer demanding that the policeman who tried to arrest him be fired. If not, Royer wired, "I could expect trouble, and I was given four weeks to do it." Two days after that, on November 15, he sent an urgent telegram to Acting Commissioner of Indian Affairs R. V. Belt, begging for one thousand troops to suppress the Ghost Dance.

> Indians are dancing in the snow and are wild and crazy. I have fully informed you that employés [sic] and Government property at this agency have no protection and are at the mercy of these dancers. Why delay by further investigation? We need protection, and we need it now. The leaders should be arrested and confined in some military post until the matter is quieted, and this should be done at once. . . . Nothing short of 1000 troops will stop this dancing.

He needn't have bothered. On November 13, the same day that Royer received Little's note, President Harrison ordered troops to the Sioux Agencies to restore the Agents' authority and "prevent any outbreak that may put in peril the lives and homes of the settlers in the adjacent states." The military response would be the largest consolidated force of army troops since the Civil War; before the campaign ended, five to six thousand soldiers—nearly half of America's standing force—would be stationed in and around the Agencies. They came from as far away as California, Colorado, and Texas, all deploying by rail just as Sherman and Sheridan had envisioned when championing the expansion of the nation's rails. Units of the Nebraska National Guard were stationed at the southern borders of Pine Ridge and Rosebud; the federal government issued more than one hundred guns, with ammunition, to settlers around the Agencies.

Miles's actions are telling. In late October and early November, he did not regard the Ghost Dance as a serious threat and urged caution before calling in the military. But once the president gave him authority to summon troops, he magnified the danger. He issued a series of alarmist dispatches, claiming that nearly the entire West was "liable to be overrun by a hungry, wild, mad horde of savages." Critics later said that he magnified the threat for political gain—that he had a "Presidential bee." More certain, however, was a chance to prove the continued relevance of the western army. Only a massive buildup could prevent "another Indian war."

The greatest number of troops, under Brigadier General John R. Brooke, went to Rosebud and Pine Ridge. Two troops of cavalry and six companies of infantry hurried to Rosebud; five companies of infantry, three of cavalry, four Hotchkiss guns, and one Gatling gun were sent to Pine Ridge. Among the latter were African American soldiers of the Ninth Cavalry, known to the Indians as "buffalo soldiers" because their hair reminded them of buffalo fur. With them came the Seventh Cavalry, whose humiliation by the Sioux at the Greasy Grass was still a raw wound.

When the first two troop trains arrived at Rushville on November 19, Agent Royer was waiting. He'd arrived two days earlier: on November 17, after yet another Indian waved a knife, he loaded his family into a buggy, handed temporary charge of the Agency to a clerk, whipped the horses into a lather, and dashed to the rail junction to await the soldiers. According to witnesses, or rumormongers, Royer drove his team down the main street, crying, "Protect yourselves! The Sioux are rising!" He denied it afterward, saying he'd come at General Brooke's request. Whatever the truth, his flight to Rushville made national headlines, adding to the sense of panic as well as the impression that the agent was in control of neither his reservation nor his nerves.

With the soldiers came the first wave of newsmen. No fewer than twenty-five journalists would descend upon Pine Ridge from November 1890 to January 1891. In addition to the Associated Press, they represented some eighteen newspapers and journals published in St. Louis, New York, Denver, Chicago, Omaha, St. Paul, Lincoln, and Washington, DC. It was the largest number of reporters ever sent to an Indian war, far exceeding any previous campaign.

Yet when this pack arrived in the "war zone," they discovered that nothing was happening. A peculiar pattern emerged. Reporters with the "foreign" press—those newspapers outside the immediate region—became so desperate for daily copy that they resorted to rumor and fiction, demanded military action, and criticized the plans of Generals Brooke and Miles. *The New York Times* and *The Washington Post* printed articles about the Ghost Dancers almost every day. The local press, on the other hand, ran stories only when there was news, and much of their coverage was spent disproving "Sioux outbreak" stories of the exalted "foreigners." In a November 29 editorial in the *Aberdeen Saturday Pioneer*, L. Frank Baum—the paper's editor long before achieving fame for *The Wizard of Oz*—lamented this state of affairs: "The Indian scare was a great injustice, and when we realize that it was all the work of sensational newspaper articles, we are tempted to wish that the press was not so free."

One of the worst offenders was Charles "Will" Cressey, an *Omaha Bee* reporter whose stories were picked up by the Associated Press and circulated nationwide. His first dispatch, printed on November 20, was sent even as he barreled west to Rushville on the troop train: "Every officer on the ground, especially those in high command, looks on the situation as very critical. To be more specific, it is to say that the officers consider it likely that six or eight thousand Indians may sweep down on us at any moment."

Newspapers began running frequent retractions of Indian massacres that never occurred. On December 20, the Chicago *Inter Ocean* had to admit: "The Denver report that a company of the cavalry had been wiped out is false. There is no fighting except for the occasional exchange of shots along the Cheyenne."

The soldiers' arrival and newspaper stories created a panic that started first with the Sioux. At dawn on November 20, Royer returned to Pine Ridge with 170 cavalry troops, 200 infantry, a Hotchkiss gun, and a Gatling gun. At the same hour, another 110 cavalrymen and 120 infantry marched into Rosebud. It was the first time the Lakota had seen so many soldiers since 1877. Royer immediately issued an order for all "friendly" Indians to report to Agency headquarters; the Indian police rode all night to carry the order throughout the reservation. Whole villages erupted in panic: ponies were caught and watered, tents razed, goods packed onto wagons. Every day-school was closed, and every white teacher ordered to come in.

Throughout Pine Ridge and Rosebud, two streams of wagons left the villages after the order arrived. Non-dancers, once again called "friend-lies," camped by the thousands outside Agency headquarters. The second stream consisted of Ghost Dancers. Certain they would be killed for their belief, thousands of dancers and their families headed away from the soldiers. Some 364 lodges, representing 2,000 Sioux under Big Road, were camped at Pass Creek, and for the moment they did not move. But those camps under more militant leaders such as Short Bull headed north into the Badlands.

By November 27, 1,200 soldiers camped outside Agency headquarters. It was "a time of grim suspense," Elaine Goodale said. "We seemed to be waiting—helplessly waiting—as if in some horrid nightmare, for the inevitable catastrophe." It seemed the kind of situation where two or three people in positions of power could "break the evil spell," but no one seemed so inclined:

> We were practically under martial law. The infantry, in their neat Sibley tents, encamped in our midst, surrounded themselves with trenches and impromptu breastworks. A buffalo-coated sentinel, rifle on shoulder, met us at every turn. We gathered daily in little groups to watch the troops parade, but there was some unvoiced resentment, especially when the order was given to admit no Sioux within picket lines after half past four, putting a stop to Mr. Cook's nightly vesper service.

During this period, events finally caught up with Black Elk. Through October and November, he seemed nearly oblivious to the escalating panic: he shifted between the Rosebud camp and Wounded Knee, leading dances, making ghost shirts, interpreting the visions of others as they climbed from their swoons. He speaks of little else in the interview transcripts: he no longer seemed involved in his job as store clerk; no other troublesome doubts or visions plagued him. He worked hard to bring about Wovoka's vision, but he was not one of the more notorious

Ghost Dance leaders and his name never appeared in the newspapers. Despite the fact that Neihardt called him one of Pine Ridge's most important Ghost Dancers, he was probably seen more as the hardworking lieutenant to Good Thunder. Though he was known to the Lakota and to the Indian police, he was probably unknown to white authorities.

On November 20, one day after the army's arrival, the Indian Office ordered agents to list the names of the Ghost Dance leaders for possible arrest. At Rosebud, the agent submitted the names of twenty-one men; at Cheyenne River, five—Hump, Big Foot, and three others; at Crow Creek, no one. James McLaughlin at Standing Rock named Sitting Bull and five followers.

At Pine Ridge, Royer drew up a list of sixty-six Lakotas whom he considered "the prime leaders." They should be arrested, he wrote in his November 25 cover letter, and confined "for a certain period in some prison far off the reservation." He was apparently advised by the Indian police, who would have known the people involved but may also have used this opportunity to settle old scores. The list led off with Kicking Bear as the very worst of the "worst element," followed at positions four through six by Red Cloud, his son Jack, and Little, the cattle thief saved by the angry mob. Short Bull, Big Road, No Water, Iron Hawk, and Little Wound trailed them. Regarding "Old Red Cloud," Royer makes an odd comment: "I must say that I am not in possession of any evidence that goes to show that he is connected with the ghost dance, and since taking charge here he has given me no trouble of any character." Yet an informant "charged that Red Cloud belongs to the disturbing element." Based upon this vague accusation, Royer recommended him for arrest and incarceration.

Black Elk was listed as number sixty-five, almost as an afterthought, right after Good Thunder.

Soon after drafting the list, Royer sent fifty Indian police to Wounded Knee in the dead of night on a tip that Short Bull was there. The agent's information was wrong, but in one lodge a policeman found Black Elk and Good Thunder. What happened next demonstrates that even during the crisis, police were of divided loyalties. "We are looking for Short Bull now," the lone policeman said. "But for your own good I will tell you what I have heard—that soon they are going to arrest you two."

Who was this savior? Black Elk never says. But there are clues. Buffalo Bill's Indians often returned home convinced of the superior power of the white world; a great number of them joined the army scouts or Indian police, and in the crisis, wrote Royer, "stood by the government to the man." Black Elk was a conspicuous exception at Pine Ridge. Indians and non-Indians alike used personal connections to save their dancing friends and kinsmen during the crisis; for Black Elk, the most important was his companion Charles Picket Pin. They'd gotten lost in Manchester, missed the *Persian Monarch*, been interrogated by Scotland Yard, and supported each other through the madness of Mexican Joe. When Picket Pin bailed out first, he returned to Pine Ridge and joined either the scouts or the police. Royer would not have added Black Elk's name to his list if not for the Sioux operatives, yet the fact that he also got word of his pending arrest from the same body shows that friends in high places watched over him. Picket Pin fills these shoes.

That night, Black Elk and Good Thunder saddled their horses and joined the sea of Ghost Dancers migrating to the Badlands. They detoured first to the camp at Pass Creek, where they found Black Elk's mother. They turned north, stealing government cattle, the dancers' numbers growing to 3,500 by the time they reached the Badlands. There they made camp on an anvil-shaped plateau connected by an isthmus to the Cuny Table, high above the Badlands floor. It had freshwater springs on both sides, and the isthmus was so narrow that a few Lakotas could hold it against hundreds of soldiers. From this spot, they could see all the way south to White Clay Creek, a distance of fifteen miles. If any place in Pine Ridge seemed impregnable, this was it. They called it *Onáži*, or the "place of shelter," but to the world it was known as the Stronghold.

At first, claims of the Stronghold's impregnability seemed justified. The great camp forming there was probably the largest gathering of American Indians since the Little Bighorn. Tribes and bands camped separately, each forming part of a great hoop that spanned nearly a mile across the plateau. Camp criers rode through the hoop, shouting directions; horses were hobbled and grazed inside the camp circle. Cattle roamed freely. While men readied weapons, five hundred women dug rifle pits along the isthmus. If it came to a fight, the soldiers would pay dearly.

Yet Miles hoped to end the troubles without bloodshed. To do this, he tried to convince as many Ghost Dancers as possible to return home;

the army would then lay siege to the remnants, letting time and the cold take effect. He placed troops on three sides of the camp, at intervals of ten to twenty miles, but left the south end open back into Pine Ridge. While General Brooke maintained direct control of reservation forces, Miles moved his headquarters from Chicago to Rapid City to be close to the action.

The Ghost Dancers soon realized that although the Stronghold itself might be hard to breach, it had some real weaknesses. After several years of drought, the native grasses could no longer sustain the number of livestock necessary for 3,500 people. The two natural springs proved inadequate; unconfirmed reports suggest that at least one had dried up. The people loosed their cattle to graze outside on Cuny Table, hoping to round them up if a siege began. Yet even this was not enough, and raiders carved off livestock from government herds.

Brooke sent emissaries to the Stronghold almost daily after December 1: Indian scouts and progressive chiefs; the Black Robes John Jutz and Francis Craft. It was a dangerous job: sometimes they were shot at, and always they were subject to the fanatical harangues of Short Bull and Kicking Bear. Once, American Horse and an unidentified chief approached Black Elk "and asked me to put this ghost dance aside quickly." By now he had doubts, and agreed it might be for the best. Yet there were always eyes and ears at the Stronghold, and Kicking Bear, Big Road, and Good Thunder broke up the conversation.

Yet the combination of privations and visits wore at the dancers. On December 12, the subchief Crow Dog announced that the time for surrender had arrived; he would head back to the Agency, and anyone who wanted could go with him. This was a true crisis for the movement, and Short Bull demanded blood. A fight broke out and Black Elk found himself in the middle. He was knocked to the ground and beaten.

Crow Dog saved the day. "I cannot bear to see a Sioux shed the blood of another Sioux," he cried, a remarkable statement considering his murder of Spotted Tail nine years earlier. But in the heat of the moment, no one remembered. He sat in the circle of brawlers and pulled his blanket over his head. They could kill him first, he declared; he refused to fight his own people. The Ghost Dancers fell into stunned silence, suddenly aware that they'd been ready to kill one another. Was this, then, the final result of the Ghost Dance, turning brother against brother?

That day, more than half the Oglalas and some Brulés began to slowly move their lodges south toward the Agency. Black Elk went with them, presumably accompanied by Good Thunder. The Ghost Dancers' unity was broken: only a few holdouts remained behind in the Stronghold with Short Bull and Kicking Bear.

Black Elk never explained his reasons for turning back. He may have worried about his mother, who'd accompanied him to Cuny Table. More probably, the troubling dream of the eagle ate at him. If Wovoka's was the true path, why would his people turn on one another? He'd made a mistake, but it was not too late. If he went back now, he might still pick the right path through the shadows.

20

WOUNDED KNEE

The "inevitable catastrophe" feared by Elaine Goodale did not occur at the Stronghold, as many anticipated. It unfolded in two steps, and though the end came in Pine Ridge, it began to the north, distant from the soldiers and dancers so ready for war.

Though history would paint the trigger as the December 15 arrest of Sitting Bull, Kicking Bear loaded the gun. His October proselytizing mission to Standing Rock would be his key act that Ghost Dance autumn. "My brothers," he said upon arrival, "I bring you the promise of a day . . . when the red man of the prairie will rule the world and not be turned from the hunting grounds by any man."

In 1890, Sitting Bull approached his sixtieth year. Except for the season spent touring with Cody, he stayed in his isolated camp at Grand River and refused to visit headquarters, partly because he did not feel safe. Yet such isolation diminished his influence, and his followers at Grand River numbered only about 450. Participation in the Ghost Dance might be a way to regain his lost power.

James McLaughlin approached the Ghost Dance almost purely through Sitting Bull. The agent had been obsessed with the holy man since his return to Standing Rock; he saw in him the epitome of every old attitude blocking the Indians' entry into modernity. Before Kicking Bear's visit, McLaughlin saw no threat in the Ghost Dance. Afterward, the only way to stem it was by the arrest and transport of Sitting Bull.

When Kicking Bear came to Standing Rock, McLaughlin sent thirteen Indian police to throw him off the reservation. But they feared the apostle's powers and failed. On October 16, McLaughlin sent a larger force, which succeeded. The whole affair infuriated the agent: the next day, he wrote a long letter to the Indian Office calling Sitting Bull deceptive, vainglorious, and cunning; a coward, schemer, polygamist, and libertine. He was the chief mischief-maker at Standing Rock, the real power behind the Agency's Ghost Dancers, and McLaughlin urged his arrest. But the commissioner and secretary of war both decided that this might cause such mayhem that they ordered he be left alone.

Nevertheless, Sitting Bull knew he was vulnerable. In Canada, he'd predicted that whites would one day kill him as they had Tasunke Witko, but another prophecy was more troubling. One morning after his return to Standing Rock, he walked to a prairie hilltop to watch the daybreak when he heard a voice behind him. He turned and saw a meadowlark, a spirit messenger that he considered a friend. "Lakotas will kill you," it warned.

McLaughlin left Sitting Bull alone for two months, but on December 14 he heard that the prophet had received an invitation to join those in the Stronghold. Whether Sitting Bull intended to go is unknown: what matters is that McLaughlin believed he did. Just before daybreak on December 15, four volunteers and thirty-nine Indian police surrounded Sitting Bull's cabin; three miles away, a squad of cavalrymen waited in support if needed. The Indian police were commanded by Lieutenant Bull Head, with whom Sitting Bull had feuded. The police barged in and the old man, still bleary from sleep, agreed to go quietly. But when they tried to leave, they discovered the cabin surrounded by 150 supporters, screaming for their chief to be freed. As they led him out, Sitting Bull's fourteen-year-old son, Crow Foot, stood in the door. "Well, you always called yourself a brave chief," he chided. "Now you are allowing yourself to be taken."

Sitting Bull stopped and seemed lost in thought; he could see the gray circus horse, given to him by Cody, already saddled and set to go. Dogs howled in the village; his wives shrieked; his people shouted insults. "I shall not go," he said.

The crowd's hatred ignited with those words. A supporter raised his rifle and shot Lieutenant Bull Head in the right side. As Bull Head fell, he shot Sitting Bull in the chest; an officer behind them shot the old chief in the back of the head. A third officer was shot in the stomach.

All three fell in a heap and the battle disintegrated into close-quarters combat among family members. Policemen took cover where they could: an officer lying behind a chicken coop exchanged fire with his own father. The man who shot Bull Head was clubbed to the ground and shot; policemen pumped Crow Foot full of bullets.

Amid the shouting and gunfire, Buffalo Bill's circus horse began to perform. He danced to the sound of the shots, sat upright on his haunches, and raised one hoof as if to shake hands. The fighting stopped as both sides watched; when the horse ran through his act and wandered off, the firing resumed. The toll was quick and lethal: Sitting Bull and his son lay dead, as well as six other Hunkpapas. Four policemen were killed, and two others—including Lieutenant Bull Head—would die of their wounds. When the cavalry arrived, Sitting Bull's followers fled for their lives.

———————

The news reached Pine Ridge that afternoon. An Oglala named Corn-Man entered Drexel Mission, told the priests about the prophet's death, and told the boys to go home. When Father Perrig intervened, Corn-Man said he would "come again and kill us black-robes." For the moment, though, Corn-Man planned to "roam about and see where he could kill a white man."

Many of Sitting Bull's followers fled south to the Cheyenne River reservation. On December 17, thirty-eight made it to the camp of Big Foot, the last of the northern Ghost Dancing chiefs now that Sitting Bull was dead. Big Foot fed and clothed the refugees, yet their news deeply alarmed him. Despite his loss of influence in Standing Rock, Sitting Bull still commanded respect in the greater body of Lakota. Many saw his death as the latest in a string of assassinations of Indian leaders whom the *wasichu* did not consider "progressive." If the United States would kill such a prominent man to get what it wanted, all were vulnerable.

And Big Foot was definitely "non-progressive." An in-law of Kicking Bear, he was in one of the first Sioux bands to accept the Ghost Dance. But neither was he a fanatic—if anything, Red Cloud and other chiefs thought of him fondly as a peacemaker. Even before Sitting Bull's death, they'd invited him south to Pine Ridge to help mediate their troubles.

On the day that Sitting Bull died, Big Foot led his people down the Cheyenne River to Agency headquarters for their December 22 rations.

He'd promised Fort Bennett's commander that he'd bring his tribe to Soldiers' Town. Yet when the panicked Hunkpapas materialized en route, Big Foot grew keenly aware of his danger. He called a halt, and more refugees arrived. Soon his small band numbered 350 Indians. He seemed frozen by indecision. Not only was he a Ghost Dancer, but his ranks had swelled with Sitting Bull's people. He feared that if he stayed within striking distance of the fort, soldiers would enter his camp at night and either start shooting or send them all to an island in the sea. Their only hope was to seek protection with friends in Pine Ridge.

On December 23, they disappeared south into the frozen White River Badlands that separated the Cheyenne River Agency from Pine Ridge. They moved like ghosts, passing undetected by ranches, creeping unseen through pastures. But when they reached Pine Ridge's northern border, they had to slow down. Big Foot had contracted pneumonia; when he coughed up blood, his people put him in a wagon. The temperature dropped and his people starved. On December 24, they saw a strange light in the sky, and some thought it was the spirit of Sitting Bull guiding them to safety. On December 25, they stumbled across a log church and heard voices inside singing "Silent Night." This was the *wasichu* Christmas, Big Foot realized: he sent a woman to ask if the babies and old people could warm themselves inside. The door opened and the Lakota could see a tree strung with multicolored ribbons, small candles shimmering on each bough. Some mothers lowered their heads and ducked through. The minister rushed at them, raising his fist. "Go away, outlaws!" he cried, casting them from his small house of God.

Big Foot's disappearance worried Miles: fearing that the band was bound for the Stronghold, he sent patrols through the Badlands. Indeed, Big Foot would have welcomed any relief. Though the map of his route suggests that he originally aimed for Pine Ridge Village, he sent young men in all directions—some to the Stronghold, others to Red Cloud, another to the agent to report that he was coming in. The first messengers back reported that horse soldiers were camped to the south at Wounded Knee. Instead of trying to flee, Big Foot and his followers would meet the soldiers openly.

By Sunday, December 28, Big Foot's column had reached the foot of Porcupine Butte, east of Manderson and north of Wounded Knee. At 2:00 p.m., four troops of cavalry approached from the south, and Big Foot ordered a white flag run up over his wagon. He rose up to greet Major Samuel Whitside of the Seventh Cavalry; the blankets around him were black with blood. As he spoke in a hoarse whisper, drops of blood fell from his nose. It was obvious to Whitside that the man was dying. He told Big Foot that he had orders to take him to the cavalry camp at Wounded Knee Creek; Big Foot rasped that he'd been headed in that direction anyway, since he meant to take his people to the Agency. Whitside told his scout John Shangreau to disarm the band, but Shangreau advised that it might be safer once they settled Big Foot's people into camp. Food, warmth, and a little generosity might put them in a better mood. Whitside glanced at the dying chief and ordered his army ambulance brought forward.

That evening, Black Elk heard for the first time the exact location of Big Foot's people. Black Elk was camped outside the Agency stockade with the majority of the Oglala. Rumor had run rife for days—all that was known was that a band of three hundred to four hundred people was heading south through the snow. The first news materialized when Rough Feather, one of Big Foot's riders, galloped into the Agency. The soldiers were escorting them south, he said—they would camp overnight at Wounded Knee Creek, close to Bartlett's store, then come in tomorrow.

Black Elk had been here for two days, searching with a brother for ponies that had strayed while he was in the Stronghold. During this time, two policemen rode up and asked him to enlist as a scout; he declined, but his brother accepted. Now, as he watched, the soldiers camping outside the Agency lined up and marched north toward Wounded Knee. Big Foot was already guarded by 200 men, Rough Feather said—now more were going. When General Brooke learned of Big Foot, he sent the Seventh's commander, Colonel James W. Forsyth, with four more troops for reinforcement, plus a company of scouts and four Hotchkiss guns. By 9:00 that night, 470 soldiers guarded 350 Indians.

At the cavalry camp, Major Whitside tallied his prisoners. He counted 120 men, and 230 women and children. He decided to wait for morning to disarm them. He assigned them a camp area immediately south of the army bivouac, issued rations, and furnished canvas tents, since they had few tipis. He ordered a stove for Big Foot's tent, and sent the regimental surgeon to minister to the dying man. He positioned two cavalry troops around the Sioux camp, and posted two light mountain cannons on Black Elk's northern rise overlooking the basin. These rifled guns could fire exploding two-pound, ten-ounce, cartridges at a range of 4,200 yards, or slightly more than two and a third miles. They could easily rake the Indian camp if trouble started.

Big Foot's was the largest tent, and inside eight soldiers watched the ailing chief and six headmen. One of the headmen was Dewey Beard, who'd had a vision of the Red Christ similar to Black Elk's. All that night, he could hear soldiers celebrating Big Foot's capture. When one group tried to take Big Foot from the tent, they were stopped by the Little Big-horn veteran Myles Moylan, assigned this night as captain of the guard. Richard Stirk—a local freighter and former scout—later testified that a lot of drinking took place that night. "Whiskey was plentiful," he said.

All that night, Dewey Beard felt sick with worry. Something terrible was going to happen. "They wouldn't let us go to sleep," he said. "All night they tortured us by gunpoint. They asked us who all was in the Battle of the Little Bighorn, the battle with Custer. . . . 'Were you there?' . . . We told them we don't know. They were saying things to us in English, but we can't tell them what we don't know."

Black Elk had the same feeling. "When I saw the soldiers going out it seemed that I knew there would be trouble," he said. No warning voice was necessary. He could not sleep, and walked all night through the slumbering camp and into the prairie.

———•◦•———

Monday, December 29, dawned clear and sunny, so mild that it re-minded some of spring. Don't be fooled, warned native forecasters—a blizzard was coming. Yellow Bird, Big Foot's medicine man, had pre-dicted three days earlier that cold weather would roll in today. Even if the weather did change, Big Foot's people expected to be snug in their army-issue lodges outside Pine Ridge Agency by early afternoon. The women cooked bacon and hardtack, and sang as they loaded the wag-ons. Children played among the tents and tipis.

Colonel Forsyth pondered how best to disarm the Indians. He'd come up overnight with the reinforcements, taking charge from Major Whitside. His orders emphasized that he must disarm Big Foot's people completely, and he must not allow a single Indian to escape. Rather than stop at the Agency, as expected, he would escort the Indians to Rushville for transport and incarceration in Omaha.

Forsyth could claim twenty-three years of experience dealing with Plains Indians. Since 1867, he'd participated in campaigns against the

Comanche, Cheyenne, Arapaho, Bannock, and Kiowa. Although most of his troops had never been in battle and nearly 20 percent were green recruits, six officers were Custer survivors: Captains George D. Wallace, Myles Moylan, Charles Varnum, Edward Godfrey, Henry Nowlan, and Winfield Edgerly. A seventh, Lieutenant W. W. Robinson, Jr., had transferred into the Seventh one day after the Custer Massacre. Some Lakotas knew of this and feared vengeance, but at least one captain—the tall and lanky George Wallace—had learned to like and respect Indians, a feeling that was reciprocated. He was always quick with a joke, and was assigned to stand among the warriors to buffer tensions as they were disarmed. Another buffer was Father Craft, brought along as interpreter. Yet because he chose not to wear his black soutane that day, some Lakotas did not recognize him.

Thus, all should have gone well. Yet Forsyth's troop placement was so ill considered that when Miles later learned of it, he ordered Forsyth court-martialed. He interpreted "no escape" too literally, ringing the camp with soldiers, at close range and far off, mounted and afoot. Big Foot's people had camped overnight on the grassy flat west of Wounded Knee Creek; the dry ravine cut immediately south of their tipis. This ravine divided the basin in half, and measured thirty to forty feet wide and fifteen feet deep. Several cow trails crossed it; a north-south wagon road from the Agency bridged it near the creek. The hill from which Black Elk had studied Good Thunder's camp rose to the north; two Hotchkiss guns were placed atop, trained on the camp and ravine.

As a show of force, Forsyth's deployment was obvious and overwhelming. The fatal flaw lay at the center. The Indian men were assembled before Big Foot's tent and formed into a tight group to be disarmed. The troops lined up at right angles to them. If shooting started, both soldiers and Indians would be in the line of fire. Even Forsyth's officers were troubled. As Lieutenant Harry Hawthorne gazed across the camp from his aerie at the gun battery, he turned to his captain and said that, given a fight, soldiers could not shoot at the Indians without hitting one another. His captain assured him there was no reason to worry: "Big Foot wants to go to the agency, and we're the guard of honor to escort him."

At about 8:00 a.m., the warriors sat in a semicircle before Big Foot's tent. They were told to go, twenty at a time, to their lodges and return with their weapons. The first group returned with two guns. It became obvious this was not working. Forsyth ordered one set of troops to move closer to the Indians, while a second set searched the lodges for guns. As these soldiers moved through the tents, they overturned beds, threw around possessions, and pushed aside protesting squaws.

The warriors were clearly growing agitated. Since few understood English, they did not know what was happening. Were their women being attacked? Many carried knives beneath their blankets, and wondered if they should use them. In the midst of all this, Yellow Bird moved through the ranks until stopping at the western edge of the council ring. He stood close to the soldiers of B Company, arranged by their captain, Charles Varnum, in a line about two hundred feet long. The men were spaced at eleven-foot intervals. Yellow Bird faced them, stretched his arms to the west, and prayed for the strength of the ghost shirt. He danced in a circle and blew on an eagle-bone whistle; he threw dust in the air. "Look out!" he cried. "Something big is going to happen." He added, "I have lived long enough," a statement often made before a warrior entered battle. "Do not be afraid! There are lots of soldiers and they have lots of bullets, but the prairie is large and the bullets will not go toward you, but over the large prairies."

Even if the soldiers could not understand Yellow Bird, his meaning was clear. He wanted to "make mischief," witnesses later said. Forsyth told him to sit down. Yellow Bird did as commanded, but kept chanting about the bulletproof shirts. Big Foot, lying between relatives in his tent opening, tried to quiet Yellow Bird, but was too weak to be heard.

Yet the resentments raised by Yellow Bird were palpable. Lieutenant James Mann of K Company could feel it: his troops were stretched at right angles to B Company, east to west at the south arc of the council circle. A presentiment of danger passed over him, much like Black Elk's "queer feelings." Mann passed a warning down the line. His superior officer, Captain Wallace, felt it, too. Standing in the midst of the Indians, he turned to Joseph Horn Cloud, brother of Dewey Beard. "Joseph," he whispered, "you better go over to the women and tell them to let the wagons go and saddle up their horses and be ready to skip, for there is going to be trouble."

At this unlucky moment, the soldiers searching for weapons in the Indian lodges returned. The time was 9:30 a.m. They had gathered a pile of knives, awls, axes, crowbars, and other tools. They'd also uncovered thirty-eight rifles, but only a few of the Winchesters the Indians had flourished the previous day when Whitside first rode up. If the guns weren't in the tipis, that meant they were hidden under the blankets worn by the braves. Forsyth ordered that every warrior be searched: each man would pass through two facing lines formed by Wallace, Varnum, Whitside, and six enlisted men. The lines formed just west of Big Foot's tent. Twenty men walked through them and opened their blankets; all were unarmed. Yellow Bird started chanting again.

To this point, eyewitnesses basically agreed upon the course of events, but everything now becomes cloudy and accounts diverge. Whitside ordered another group of braves to come forward. After some hesitation, a few complied. Three passed through the facing lines, and two carried hidden rifles. At this moment, a young Indian leapt up and started to shout; he dragged a Winchester from under his blanket and held it over his head. Some Indians later said his name was Black Coyote; most said he was a troublemaker. He stomped through the crowd, crying that this was his gun, he'd paid good money for it, and he would not hand it over unless he got paid. The young men still waiting to be searched drifted quietly toward the east, the one escape route from the hollow box of soldiers. Two sergeants grabbed Black Coyote and tried to take his rifle. In the scuffle, it discharged.

In that instant, the firing began. A half-dozen or more young warriors threw off their blankets and leveled their rifles at K Company. "What can they be thinking of?" Lieutenant Mann thought a moment before their volley ripped into his line. "Fire! Fire on them!" he cried. Both lines fired into the Indians, filling the square with the smell of cordite and the yellow-gray smoke of gunpowder. Yellow Bird fell. Big Foot rose from his blankets and caught a bullet in the head; as he fell back, his daughter ran toward him, was shot in the back, and fell lifeless across his body. Big Foot's wife rose, holding a rifle; she was hit in the heart, pitched forward, and rolled down a slight incline. Captain Wallace ran to rejoin K Company and a second Indian volley tore off the top of his skull. Wallace was not the only Custer survivor to die; Sergeant Gustave Korn, one of Reno's abandoned men, was also cut down by the second volley. Father Craft moved among the fallen but was unrecognizable in the smoke without his black soutane. As he bent over Hugh McGinnis of K Company, an Indian stabbed him in the back, collapsing a lung.

It was now that Forsyth's troop deployment turned lethal. As B and K Companies fired into the Indians, the angles were such that they fired on their friends in the opposite line. Indians who fired into the soldiers fired into their lodges, killing or wounding their own. Twenty to thirty Indians dropped in that first instant, as well as a handful of soldiers.

Gunfire grew scattered. Men disappeared in the smoke; Indians and soldiers fought hand to hand.

During this phase of the fight, the soldiers in the outer ring and the gun battery on the hill did not fire. The smoke enveloped the small area like a thick fog. "Through rifts in the smoke, heads and feet would be visible," said Joseph Horn Cloud. After two or three minutes of close combat, a few Indians sprinted east to the creek or south toward the Indian village. Forsyth spurred his horse up the hill to the Hotchkiss battery; B and K Companies fell back to the protection of the cavalry tents. The square was empty: about thirty dead or wounded Indians and the same number of soldiers lay behind in the dust and pools of blood.

When the groups separated, the Hotchkiss guns came to life. The gunners fired at any Indian groups they could see shooting at soldiers. Some men, women, and children headed south down the Agency road, but cavalry and cannons blocked that route and they dropped down into the deep cut of Wounded Knee Creek. These were the ones who survived. Some wagons filled with women and children fled to the northwest. Some got through, others were shot down.

The majority of warriors, however, fled south to the village, and this was where the gun battery turned its attention. Shells exploded among the tents at about fifty per minute. Lodges burst into flame. Shrapnel whined and people fell. Most noncombatants had gathered at Bartlett's store and a hall to the immediate northeast, and they could see everything. Bartlett watched as a gunner sent a shell into a tent occupied by an armed Indian. The shell "blew the Indian to atoms," Bartlett recalled. "A more ghastly sight I never saw. His entrails were scattered over the ground for several feet distant and his whole body presented a very much burnt spectacle; chunks of flesh appeared to have been pulled out of different parts of his body."

When the Hotchkiss guns began demolishing the camp, the women and children fled south to the apparent safety of the dry ravine— followed quickly by the men. They raced down one bank and up the other, but at the top were greeted by withering fire from the mounted scouts and soldiers south of them. The Indians dropped back into the gulch and huddled in place or ran.

But others, in their panic, ignored even this slight cover and ran for their lives in the open. Bartlett watched as five young girls ran for a small hill, hoping to pass to the safety of the other side. Cavalrymen chased after them. When the girls knew there was no chance for escape, "they with seeming one accord sat down on the ground and quickly covering their faces and heads with their blankets, calmly awaited death which followed as soon as the soldiers could ride up to them." Bartlett watched in horror as two little boys he knew from the store "not even ten years old" ran up a road to the west. A soldier on a white horse rode close, dismounted, "and dropping to his knees shot both of the little boys."

Some soldiers grew horrified. Private Eugene Caldwell wrote to his father in Philadelphia that "some of the men went wild; they would shoot men or women." Second Lieutenant Sedgwick Rice of E Company plowed through the melee until coming to a woman standing by a group of bodies, the last person left alive of her little band. As Sedgwick watched, she cut her own throat, "and was in the last throes of death when I went up to her." Hugh McGinnis, the wounded private over whom Father Craft crouched when stabbed in the back, was surrounded by the bodies of Craft and others when he regained consciousness. "The moans of the wounded and dying were enough to give a man nightmares the rest of his life," he would recall.

Charles W. Arnet of *The New York Herald* was one of three reporters at the scene. He'd been with a search party when the shooting started; he picked his way back to the council ring in time to see Big Foot killed and his daughter fall over him. He made his way to a hill held by the Grey Horse Troop and contemplated the unfolding atrocity. Though he was an old Indian campaigner, the sight still made him "faint and ill." He found a supply box and sat down. "I drew out my old pipe—a never-failing friend in such emergencies—and concluded that those boys of the Seventh Cavalry were too excited to think of anything but vengeance."

———•◦•———

The distant thunder of big guns rolled into Pine Ridge Village by midmorning. Long afterward, one shared memory was how the Hotchkiss barrage sounded like the "long, continuous tearing of a blanket." All had been listening to the north. They knew where Big Foot was camped and that he was surrounded by soldiers; they knew he would surrender formally to Custer's old regiment and feared reprisals. The gunfire, which seemed to last a half hour, meant that something terrible was taking place at Wounded Knee.

Elaine Goodale was making Christmas gifts for children in the Episcopal church when she heard the gunfire eighteen miles away. The sound sent shivers down her back: shortly past noon, an Indian runner and a cavalry rider arrived almost simultaneously with the news. The children at the Oglala boarding school saw them first; scattered across the playground, they could read the runner's sign language as he passed and spread the word. "The children were panic stricken," recalled their teacher, Thisba Morgan, "for many of them knew that their parents must have been in the fray." The teachers hurried them into the building and battened the doors and windows; the school was two miles north of the Agency, and through the windows Morgan could see streams of vengeful Lakotas passing south toward the stockade. The occasional warrior called to the children to flee, for they planned to shoot fire arrows at the roof and burn the schoolhouse down. But the teachers would not let them leave: their survival depended on keeping the children virtual hostages, "as the Indians would not set fire to it so long as their children were inside."

"The resulting chaos and excitement was unmistakable," wrote Goodale's fiancé, Charles Eastman. The "friendly" Indians ran for the protection of the stockade; the "hostiles" departed quickly for the Badlands. Thousands of Oglalas were on the move; the brown hills surrounding the Agency were "instantly alive with galloping horsemen." Most soldiers were spread across the reservation; only a small detachment remained. Sentinels were placed, Gatling guns trained on various approaches; some hotheaded braves fired at the sentinels and wounded two.

The Jesuits also heard the thunder. That morning, an Indian named Calico came to them "out of breath" and told Father Jutz about the fighting, Perrig wrote. When the boarding-school boys heard the news, "most of them ran away." Jutz headed to the Agency to learn the truth, but the road was "crowded with Indians in warpaint rushing about and driving their ponies together." Two Indians told Jutz to go home, then followed "while occasionally urging him to hurry on."

Black Elk would have heard the guns before the rest, if only slightly. He'd risen at daybreak to round up his horses. They grazed in the open prairie between the Agency and Wounded Knee; he was culling them from the larger herd when he heard the guns so close that "I felt it right in my body." He did not need to go look: he knew the trouble had begun. He drove his horses back to the Agency, and as he reached camp a man rode up, his eyes wild. "Hey, hey son," he shouted, "those that are coming are fired upon, I know it." Black Elk didn't stop to talk; the man in his excitement rode on, slightly out of his head.

He saddled his fastest horse, ducked into his lodge, and did something telling. While others ran around in a panic, Black Elk dressed as ceremoniously as had Crazy Horse before charging Reno's men at the Little Bighorn. He donned his ghost shirt and painted his face red. He thrust a single eagle feather in his hair. He grabbed the sacred red stick that he used in the Ghost Dance, but not his gun. Instead, he grabbed his sacred bow, the one modeled after that in his Great Vision, ducked through the flaps, and mounted his buckskin.

He'd thought all night about what he would do if the worst happened; he considered his earlier doubts about "this Messiah business," and did not think it right to kill anyone, even a *wasichu*, in its name. He suspected that he'd been fooled by the promises, diverted from the goals set for him by the Grandfathers. After all, while preparing for the Horse Dance, the old *wicasa wakan* told him that his Great Vision was meant to save *all* people, not just Lakota. Still, he had to do *something*. Thus, he took his bow, but not his gun; he does not say whether he took arrows. It almost sounds like a suicide mission.

He started out alone on an old trail that cut east or east-northeast across the hills. It was not long before he heard horses coming up, and when he looked back saw a band of young men galloping after him. The first up were Loves War and Iron White Man; they were going to see the cause of the firing, they said. "I'm going to fight for my people's rights," Black Elk answered. "If you want, you can come along." He turned and rode fast, and others joined. Soon a tight knot of about twenty young warriors had coalesced around Black Elk, some wearing ghost shirts, some stripped for war. Strung out at a distance behind them were boys caught up in the excitement, just as he had been at the Little Bighorn.

They rode fast, and the shooting grew louder. A man charged over the hill, screaming "*Hey-hey-hey!* They have murdered them!" He whipped his horse and rode on. Where they emerged is slightly uncertain: according to family tradition Black Elk crested a ridge southwest of the killing zone, while according to the Neihardt transcripts he gazed from the heights almost two and a half miles due west of the dry ravine and the hill with the Hotchkiss guns. No matter: he could see it all— the low basin of Wounded Knee Creek, the hill where six months

Red Cloud, war chief of the Oglala Lakota during the 1865–1868 Red Cloud's War, when Black Elk was still a small child (Courtesy of the Library of Congress)

General William Tecumseh Sherman, general of the U.S. Army during the Indian wars and architect of the campaign against the Sioux (Courtesy of the Library of Congress)

Lieutenant General Philip H. Sheridan, commander of the Division of the Missouri and Sherman's chief lieutenant during the campaign against the Sioux (Courtesy of the Library of Congress)

Brigadier General George Crook, commander of the Department of the Platte during the campaign against the Sioux (Courtesy of the Library of Congress)

Major General Nelson A. Miles, commander of the Fifth U.S. Infantry Regiment during the 1876–1877 campaign to capture or kill Sitting Bull and Crazy Horse, and commander of the Division of the Missouri during the December 1890 Massacre at Wounded Knee (Courtesy of the Library of Congress)

Lieutenant Colonel George Armstrong Custer, commander of the Seventh Cavalry during the Battle of the Little Bighorn on June 25–26, 1876. This photograph was taken two years earlier, during the 1874 expedition into the Black Hills; Custer poses in his famous buckskin suit behind a bear he brought down in the Hills. To Custer's right sits his favorite Indian scout, Bloody Knife, later killed as he stood beside Major Marcus A. Reno in the Valley of the Little Bighorn; to Custer's left pose Private John Nunan (or Noonan) and Captain William Ludlow, neither of whom died in the battle. (Courtesy of the Library of Congress)

A promotional photograph of Sitting Bull and William F. "Buffalo Bill" Cody, taken for the 1885 North American tour of Cody's Buffalo Bill's Wild West. The photograph, taken in Montreal, was titled *Foes in '76, Friends in '85*. (Buffalo Bill Center of the West, Cody, Wyoming, U.S.A. [P.6.1564])

William F. Cody, as he appeared during the Wild West's 1887–1888 tour of England for Queen Victoria's Jubilee celebration, honoring her fiftieth year on the throne (Buffalo Bill Center of the West, Cody, Wyoming, U.S.A. [P.69.0136])

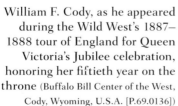

The young Black Elk, wearing his dance costume, as he appeared during the Wild West's 1887–1888 tour of England. Black Elk's arm is linked through that of a scowling fellow performer identified as Elk. (National Anthropological Archives, Smithsonian Institution [NAA INV 00506100])

Colonel Joseph "Mexican Joe" Shelley, whose Mexican Joe's Western Wilds of America toured England and Europe at the same time as Cody's Wild West show. Black Elk traveled with Shelley from 1888 to 1889. (The National Archives UK ref. COPY 1/381/278)

Frederic Remington magazine illustration of an 1890 Ghost Dance ceremony at Pine Ridge (Courtesy of the Library of Congress)

Corporal Paul Weinert and gunners of E Company, First Artillery, standing behind one of the Hotchkiss guns that caused such carnage during the Massacre at Wounded Knee (Courtesy of the Library of Congress)

The body of Chief Big Foot, photographed as it lay in the snow after Wounded Knee (Courtesy of the Library of Congress)

Mass burial of the Indian dead after the battle at Wounded Knee (Courtesy of the Library of Congress)

Black Elk and an unidentified woman, believed to be his first wife, Katie War Bonnet, ca. 1892. Black Elk appears older and sicker than in the 1887 London studio photograph, and may have already suffered from ulcers and tuberculosis.
(Photographer unknown; collection of Elenita Brown)

Black Elk's sponsor and advocate Henry I. Westropp, standing to the far right in front of the log cabin of the catechist John Foolhead. Westropp dubbed Black Elk an Indian "St. Paul," an image that would stick with later Catholic commentators. (Courtesy of Red Cloud Indian School and Marquette University [Holy Rosary Mission—Red Cloud Indian School Records, ID MUA_HRM_RCIS_02241])

Black Elk, his second wife, Anna Brings White, and their daughter, Lucy Looks Twice. By now, Black Elk is fully committed to his role as a Catholic catechist, and he even looks healthier than in his 1890s photograph with Katie War Bonnet. His vested suit became his uniform during these early years as a catechist. (Courtesy of the Denver Public Library, Western History Collection)

Black Elk teaching the rosary to his daughter, Lucy, ca. 1907–1910. The photograph was reportedly taken by Father Eugene Buechel. (Marquette University Archives, Bureau of Catholic Indian Missions Records [ID BCIM 09-1 47-14])

The cover of the fall 1926 *Indian Sentinel*, the monthly publication of the Bureau of Catholic Indian Missions. This is a repainting of Buechel's 1910 photograph of Black Elk teaching the rosary to his daughter; it came at a time when the Catholic Church often used the theme of an Indian dressed in traditional garb but engaged in Catholic ritual to symbolize the replacement of ancient traditional beliefs with modern Catholic ones. (Marquette University Archives, Bureau of Catholic Indian Missions Records, *Indian Sentinel* Collection, 1902–1962)

Eagle Elk and Black Elk standing before the altar of Our Lady of the Sioux chapel in Pine Ridge, ca. 1910–1915 (Courtesy of St. Francis Mission and Marquette University [Saint Francis Mission Records, ID SFM_6-6 1375])

Hilda Neihardt, Black Elk, Chase in the Morning, and John Neihardt, 1931. The photograph was taken during the 1931 interviews, presumably before the four engaged in a traditional hoops game. (With permission of the John G. Neihardt Trust)

The famous photograph, taken by John Neihardt, of Black Elk praying to the Grandfathers from atop Harney Peak in the Black Hills. This is the scene described at the end of *Black Elk Speaks*. (With permission of the John G. Neihardt Trust)

Black Elk's cousin Standing Bear, posing in traditional regalia before his cabin in Pine Ridge. This portrait was taken around the time of the 1931 interviews. (University of Nebraska Archives, Mari Sandoz Collection)

Father Placidus Sialm, around the time of the publication of *Black Elk Speaks* (Courtesy of Red Cloud Indian School and Marquette University [Holy Rosary Mission— Red Cloud Indian School Records, ID MVA_HRM_RCIS_00344])

Black Elk and John Neihardt, ca. 1940s. This photograph would have been taken during one of Neihardt's final visits to Pine Ridge. (With permission of the John G. Neihardt Trust)

Black Elk and Joseph Epes Brown, ca. 1947–1948. This photograph would have been taken during the winter that Brown collected material from Black Elk that would become *The Sacred Pipe: Black Elk's Account of the Seven Rites of the Oglala Sioux.* (Photographer unknown; collection of Elenita Brown)

Ben Black Elk, often called the "fifth face of Mount Rushmore." This was from a postcard available for sale at the national monument's gift store. (Author's collection; gift of Betty Black Elk O'Rourke)

Black Elk's Point at
Harney Peak today
(Author's collection)

The remains of Black Elk's log cabin, on his allotment near Manderson
on the Pine Ridge Reservation (Author's collection)

earlier he'd sat like this on horseback and gazed down at the dancers praying for the end of the world.

When history calls Wounded Knee a massacre, it means that period encompassing the moment that the cannons began firing to when Black Elk and others like him arrived. The fight in the council ring was a battle; though furious, fluid, and chaotic, both sides gave as well as they got and casualties were just about even. But when the Indians broke to the south and tried to hide in the gulch, the Hotchkiss guns turned Wounded Knee into a lake of blood. The dirt walls of the ravine, though eight to ten feet high, gave little protection from shell bursts; where the big guns could not reach, soldiers lined the sides and poured down gunfire, just as the Sioux had done in another deep ravine fourteen years earlier. The only escape was to run west, toward the flimsy cover of a clump of yellow pines. From there the ravine made a right-angle turn south, then opened to the plains. But those who made it found their way blocked by a screen of cavalry and Indian scouts, and in the heat of pursuit the soldiers did not distinguish among men, women, and children.

One who survived was twenty-five-year-old Dewey Beard. His father died beside Big Foot; his wife and infant son died in the tipis. He killed one soldier in the square and one more while fleeing toward the gulch, and there he saw his mother, badly wounded and weak, a pistol hanging in one hand. "My dear son," she cried, "pass me by!" A bullet struck her and she died. Bitter and grieving, he reached a spot where the guns could not focus and the last center of resistance fired at the Hotchkiss guns. A bullet hit the pocket watch of Lieutenant Hawthorne, who'd questioned Forsyth's deployment, sending its works scattering through his anatomy. "Oh my God," he cried, and dropped, leaving command of the Hotchkiss gun to his corporal, Paul H. Weinert, who went a little mad. "I said, by God! I'll make them pay for that!" Weinert later told investigators, and ran his gun off the hill and into the ravine's east opening, close to the road and bridge. It was a straight shot from there to the western terminus, where lay the pines and pocket of defenders. His mates kept yelling for him to come back; instead, he said, "I kept yelling for a cool gun!"

Weinert's Hotchkiss mowed down everything in its path, and the ravine was already clogged with women and children and warriors singing their death songs. A warrior at Dewey Beard's elbow was blown to bits when a shell hit him directly; he saw another man slumped against the bank, a hole in his stomach six inches wide. Corporal Weinert feared that he'd be court-martialed for lashing the gun to the ravine. Instead, he was awarded the Congressional Medal of Honor.

Black Elk and his followers arrived as the massacre entered this final stage. Smoke rose in columns from the burning camp; the screams of dying ponies and people could be heard even up here in the surrounding hills. Fewer than sixty Lakotas remained alive in the ravine. It is clear by this point that once the fighting started, officers lost control of their men. Horse soldiers rode atop the banks and shot into the gulch, reportedly calling each kill "Custer's Revenge!" Troopers stalked among the dead and dying and gave the coup de grace to anything that moved. A wounded man who'd almost made it over a western ridge rose up; a mounted platoon swept past at that moment and shot him down. "For God's sake!" cried Forsyth, already at the breaking point after losing control of his soldiers. "Stop shooting at them!"

Directly in front of Black Elk, down the ridge near the angle in the gulch, a tiny knot of women and children huddled against the bank as troopers aimed at them. C and D Companies were scattered between his ridge and the gulch, still rounding up escapees. Black Elk sang a sacred song of the Thunder-beings, then turned to the young men behind him. "Take courage!" he yelled. "These are our relatives! We shall try to take the captives back." His arm swept the field. "Our women and children are lying dead. Think about this and take courage."

"It is time to fight!" his men cried.

He'd been in more mock battles before American and European audiences than he could count; now this was in deadly earnest, a different kind of theater. Gone was the sickness he'd felt at the Greasy Grass, gone the unreal sense that he floated above it all. Black Elk and his men flew in a wedge down the slope, straight into the soldiers, while shouting the old Sioux war cry *Hoka hey! Hoka hey!*" The charge was so sudden that the soldiers panicked and ran east; those behind them, possibly convinced that more reinforcements were coming, fell back, too. Near the head of the ravine the Oglalas found a man shot through both legs; they draped him across a horse and one of Black Elk's troops carried him over a hill to safety. Near the man, Black Elk found an abandoned baby, still alive. He wrapped her in a bullet-riddled shawl, placed her gently in a sheltered spot, and rode on. A group of about twenty captives huddled to the north by the remnants of Big Foot's pony herd. Two of Black Elk's group and a third Indian, riding a black horse, loosed their restraints and told them to run.

But now, to the east, the troops that had fled were joined by others; they started to rally, jumped from their horses, and dug in. Black Elk realized that if they started shooting at this distance, they'd wipe out the captives and his men. "Wait!" he cried to his followers, knowing in that instant what he must do. He told them to hang back and lead the captives out of range; then he charged the line of soldiers alone.

Certainly he was inspired. He'd heard the tales of his cousin, how he'd charge a line of troops with nothing but his coup stick and every soldier fired—yet Crazy Horse emerged unscathed. At this moment, he became Tasunke Witko. He charged at the soldiers, armed only with his sacred bow. He held it before him as they aimed. Bullets snapped around him, but none found their mark. He rode within twenty yards of the line and some of the soldiers jumped up and ran. He shouted his defiance in their faces; with so much detail in the Neihardt transcripts, he could not remember his words. But often warriors in such transcendent moments screamed out their names so their enemy would always remember. "I am Black Elk!" he cried. He wheeled his horse sharply and charged back to the ridge at a dead run.

By now, other defenders had arrived, but they were strung out across the landscape and could only harass the soldiers in small groups. A band under the Brulé chief Two Strikes showed up; other stragglers, from Pine Ridge. Though soldiers would estimate this late force at 300 to 600, later evidence suggests a number closer to 150 to 200. In addition, the battle was starting to take a toll on Black Elk's men: one of his young men was shot; one broke his arm; a third broke his leg. The fire from the soldiers seemed to be growing more accurate: when Black Elk came to a stop and lowered his bow, he felt some bullets pass near his hip through his billowing ghost shirt. So much for "bulletproof," he realized; the sacred bow of his Vision was stronger medicine. He told his men to save the captives, then raised his bow and charged the soldiers again.

"It was a good day," he later said. Sunny and clear. Time slowed. He charged toward the burning village: "I could see children dying all over. . . . I could not get as far as Big Foot's body, though." Somehow, he did not feel sorry for the dead—even wrapped in the power of his Vision, part of him thought that a bullet would find him and "I would join them somewhere." He would probably die before this day ended and this was the kind of moment when one took revenge or died. From the corner of his eye he saw two boys, both about fifteen, firing at the soldiers from the gulch, and they'd already brought down a number with their repeating rifles. He rode up again with his bow held before him; the line of soldiers fired and missed again. Other enraged Oglalas did the same, hurling themselves at the dismounted cavalrymen, but it soon became evident that even in their fury they could not dislodge a regiment of troops. In addition, the Hotchkiss guns were being turned to rake the western ridgetops, making the fight untenable. The warriors split into small groups and melted off; the soldiers made no attempt to pursue.

Before he left, Black Elk fulfilled one last obligation. He plucked up the orphaned baby he'd stowed in a place of safety. He saw now it was a girl. He held her close and kept his buckskin at an easy gait so the girl would not be jostled. He rode back to the Agency and hunted for the family. In time, she would be adopted by the father of his future wife and named Blue Whirlwind. Other infants would be plucked up by warriors and taken home that day. Many would be adopted by the families of their saviors.

In later years, as Black Elk approached death, he would come to the battlefield and wonder if he could have done more. Though he'd gone to the battle unarmed, there *was* a way, in his mind, that he could have killed soldiers. By mystical means. The soldier weed: the deadly herb shown to him by the Grandfathers that grew only in the Black Hills. "There will be a dispute of nations," the Spirit of War had told him, "and you will defend your people with this herb." Anything that touched it died. Presumably, if the herb were ground up and tossed into the breeze, those who breathed it would die. But he did not use it, he said. Presumably he'd not even sought it out, for the Grandfathers told him not to use it until he turned thirty-seven, and he was only twenty-seven now. But what if he had? The world would tremble, and *wasichus* would die. And that would be terrible, for not only would these soldiers die, as they deserved, but *all* whites—including his friends: Mexican Joe; Buffalo Bill; his lover Charlotte; their child, if his suspicions were true. *Wasichu* infants would be butchered like the Lakota infants in the ravine.

So he made his choice, though he always wondered if he'd chosen wisely. Black Road and the other holy men had said that his powers were not for the Lakota alone. They were for all nations, even his enemy.

But hatred dies hard, and long afterward he could see in his mind the piles of dead. He'd wanted to die with them, but it was not to be. To the end of his life he would never think that he'd done enough to save his people, and the pictures of the dead would not go away. Sometimes the bodies lay in heaps; sometimes, scattered down the ravine. "Sometimes bunches of them had been killed and torn to pieces where the wagon guns hit them," he told Neihardt. "I saw a little baby trying to suck its mother, but she was bloody and dead."

What if he'd used his power? he would ask himself. Would it have saved the slaughtered and innocent?

Even those we call holy can dream of revenge.

21

"THERE WILL BE A BETTER DAY TO DIE"

That night, a frigid wind blew from the northwest, bringing a light cover of snow. At Wounded Knee, bodies began to freeze. Pools of blood iced over. The snow fell heavier as the night progressed, freezing the dead into grim statuary but softening the angles. Almost all the dead warriors were clustered around Big Foot's tent and down in the ravine, but the bodies of the women and children were scattered as far as two or three miles from this epicenter. Some still lived and would lie where they'd fallen until burial parties arrived. Most would die of their wounds or the cold; they included some infants, wrapped tight in shawls or sheltered by their mothers' corpses. Every infant suffered hypothermia, and only one survived. Indian women in camp called her Zitkalanoui, or "Lost Bird."

How many died at Wounded Knee? The army reported twenty-five soldiers killed and thirty-five wounded, though a 1933 report in the *Official Bulletin of National Indian War Veterans* said that about fifty coffins were needed for soldier fatalities. One explanation has been noted previously: the army at this time did not include in its casualty lists the deaths of Indian and mixed-blood scouts, and of civilians. One out of every eight soldiers at Wounded Knee was killed or wounded, a high rate in any conflict. The grim line of wagons and ambulances rolled into the Agency at 9:30 that night, escorted by the shocked and sobered survivors. They took the army wounded to the hospital, which soon filled up; thirty-eight wounded Lakotas also brought by the wagons were taken to the Episcopal church, where the Santee Sioux pastor, Thomas Cook, removed the pews and altar and covered the floor with blankets and straw.

Far more Indians died than were ever counted, and the exact number has been debated since the massacre. The final telegrams to Washington would tally 150 Indians killed, 30 wounded or captured; this would be modified in the Indian Office's final report as 84 men and boys killed, 44 women, and 18 children, for 146 dead. Another 33 were listed as wounded, "many of them fatally." But this only includes those whose bodies were found at the scene. The women and children later found scattered across the prairie never made it into the reports.

Such numbers do not bear scrutiny for very long. Miles totaled about 200 Indian dead in his report and in a confidential letter lamented that "I have never heard of a more brutal, cold-blooded massacre than that at Wounded Knee." He described "women with little children on their backs, and small children powder-burned by men being so near as to burn the flesh and clothing with the powder of their guns, and nursing babes with five bullet holes through them." Nebraska state troops put the Indian dead at 220, while Agent Royer, Dewey Beard, and the Smithsonian's James Mooney placed it around 300. Today, scholars believe the Seventh Cavalry killed between 270 and 300 of the 400 members of Big Foot's band, or nearly 75 percent. Of these, 170 to 200 were women and children.

The rage and despair over what the Lakota would call the Big Foot Massacre spread to all Sioux, traditional or progressive. As panic swept the villages, as many as four thousand Oglalas fled north from the Agency to No Water's camp at White Clay Creek, or even farther into the Badlands; they set fire to wasichu homes as they passed and took with them Red Cloud, aging and infirm but still a powerful symbol. He barely had time to lower the American flag before his house to half-mast; some accounts claim that he left after learning that an officer wanted to shell his home. To the progressive Lakota, the massacre stank of personal betrayal. When Luther Standing Bear—who'd attended Carlisle, adopted white ways, and now ran the Rosebud store—heard the guns, "it made my blood boil," he wrote. "I was ready to go and fight then: There I was, doing my best to teach my people to follow in the white men's road— even trying to get them to believe in their religion—and this was my reward for it! The very people I was following—and getting my people to follow—had no respect for motherhood, old age, or babyhood. Where was all their civilized training?"

Not everyone acted with the compassion of Elaine Goodale or the outrage of Nelson Miles. Many who'd lived in a state of panic believed the Lakota brought the suffering upon themselves. Emmy Valandry, the mixed-blood wife of a white Agency employee, could not tolerate the Indian wounded in the Episcopal church: "Smelling of blood, looking so dirty, they were spoiling our church; they were yelling so hard now, when really it was their own fault for being so intractable." While the eastern press deplored the bloodshed, the western press reveled in it. The *Deadwood Times* gloated over the Indian dead: "Among the 'good Indians' was Big Foot himself, dead as smelt." The massacre was little different from the corporal punishment meted out to unruly children, wrote *The Word Carrier*, the Protestant Sioux paper published in Nebraska: "It was needed that these people should feel in some sharp terrible way the just consequence of their actions and be held in wholesome fear from further folly."

It was nearly dark when Black Elk rode back to the now-deserted camp near the stockade. He clutched the orphan baby close; his friend the warrior Red Crow rode beside him. Red Crow had also found an infant beside its slain mother; they'd planned to turn them over to women with milk in their breasts, but the village was empty. They wondered where everyone had gone.

But first, they were hungry. They found an abandoned lodge with dried beef in a cookpot, so they crawled inside and began to eat. The hungry baby, no doubt, began to squall; soldiers on the barricades shot at their tipi and a bullet landed between them, spurting dust into the pot. They ate until full, then grabbed the babies, jumped astride their horses, and with a *whoop* followed the trail of their kin. They reached the main body later that night; as they rode among the families, Black Elk heard his mother singing his death song. The last she'd seen of him was that morning, when he'd ridden off. Now she was so happy to see him that she wept for the rest of the night.

The next morning, Black Elk and others wanted revenge. Before daybreak, Kicking Bear headed a huge party from the Ghost Dance camp, and Black Elk joined the throng. One group attacked an army supply train about two miles from the Agency; the buffalo soldiers of the Ninth Cavalry drove off the attackers. But most of the party rode upstream along White Clay Creek and soon commanded a ridge overlooking Drexel Mission. They set fire to some empty cabins, hoping to lure soldiers from the stockade.

It worked. Brooke ordered Forsyth to drive away the dancers; Forsyth led eight companies of the Seventh and one Hotchkiss gun past the mission and into a narrow valley. It was the old Oglala lure-and-ambush; the soldiers were trapped in the low ground around the creek while Sioux sniped at them from above. Forsyth sent back three times for help, and finally the buffalo soldiers, who'd just saved the supply train, rushed to the mission and rescued the Seventh Cavalry.

It was the last true engagement between the Lakota and the U.S. Army, and Black Elk was in the thick of it. This time he traded his sacred bow for a Winchester. His friends were firing at the soldiers from both sides of the creek, and one cried to him, "This is a day in which to do great things!" They were right, he thought: he jumped off his horse, rubbed dry earth all over himself in homage to the gods, grabbed his rifle, and remounted his little buckskin. He galloped up the high ridge even as friends cried for him to be careful.

He did not listen; he placed his life in the hands of the Grandfathers. He kicked his horse into a run and charged down the hill straight at the soldiers. He remembered from his Vision the geese of the north flying before the storm; he raised his hands in front of him, the Winchester in his right, and cried "*Br-r-r-p, br-r-r-p, br-r-r-p*," like a goose. It must have been a strange sight for the defenders. He charged within a few feet of their line and fired into their faces. They fired back, but he swung wide and galloped back uphill. The bullets buzzed around him as he rode over the crest to safety.

He charged again, but the soldiers had changed position and were only one hundred yards from the crest. This new position caught him by surprise. He charged anyway, but on the way back up his Vision's protection suddenly faded, as if he'd woken from a dream and he was afraid. He dropped his arms and quit making the call of the goose; bullets pattered around him and something hit his belt like an ax. The blow nearly pitched him to the ground. He grabbed the buckskin's mane to keep from falling; his little horse carried him to safety over the hill.

An old man named Protector grabbed him before he fell. He lifted Black Elk's shirt and saw that a bullet had furrowed through his abdomen so deeply that blood gushed out and his intestines began to protrude. He knew he was going to die. As Protector tore a blanket into strips and bound his wound so his bowels would stay in place, Black

Elk began to thrash. "Let me go," he cried. "Help me on my horse! It is a good day to die—let me over there."

"No, nephew," Protector said softly. "You must not die today. You must live. Your people need you. There will be a better day to die."

———•◦•———

Hostilities continued. Private Dominic Francischetti, a trooper left behind at the mission fight, was scalped to avenge the dead at Wounded Knee. Henry Miller, a government beef herder, was killed a few miles from the Agency by a son of No Water. When Miles arrived at the Agency on Thursday, January 1, 1891, an estimated four thousand Sioux had declared open war on the United States. In his mind it was a debacle. His first action was to relieve Forsyth of command. The second, to order a burial party for the Indians left at Wounded Knee.

Two parties set out that New Year's Day, though many histories have merged them. The first was the official burial detail headed by the scout Paddy Starr, paid two dollars for every body collected and interred. The party included thirty laborers, an escort of the Seventh, one wagon filled with tools, and two more with provisions. They left late on the 1st and by the time they arrived the ground was frozen. They pitched their tents by the store and waited for daybreak to start collecting bodies.

Not every laborer seems to have volunteered. Nineteen-year-old Frank French was "recruited" by a drunken army officer. French drove a mule team for a Northwestern Railroad contractor who hauled dirt; the soldiers seemed less interested in French than in his wagon.

French's tale of easy liquor and drunken soldiers was common at the Agency. The soldiers "had a bitter grudge against all Sioux for Custer's defeat, and as most of them were drunk on the day of the fight, they didn't need much reason to start a slaughter," French later said. William Peano, a mixed-blood Lakota who'd returned from touring with Buffalo Bill a week earlier, said that "liquor was free at the Agency." The officers "had all they could use," while the enlisted men could get "all they wanted."

Burial began the next morning and went on until sundown. The civilians collected the bloody corpses of Big Foot's folk, frozen after four days in the snow into eerie contortions, then loaded them in the wagons. The bodies collected by this group were strewn across two hundred acres, and the expressions on their faces could make one sick. "But, of course, you got used to it," said August Hettinger, one of the guards with H Company, Eighth Infantry. Once, he rounded a corner in the ravine and came face-to-face with a warrior, sitting upright, painted green, his finger pointed at the sky. He stared "with wide open, clear eyes straight at me." Hettinger grabbed his gun and was set to shoot when he realized the man was dead.

They rolled the wagons up the hill where the Hotchkiss guns had fired, then dug a long trench ten feet wide, six feet deep, and sixty feet long. The bodies were stripped of salable ghost shirts and dresses, and stacked three layers deep "like so much cordwood" until the pit was full. Earth was heaped over them and the burial was complete. There were no priests or preachers, but the Episcopal lay reader John Blunt Horn rang a bell so their spirits would enter Heaven.

The exact number of dead in that pit has forever been uncertain. William Peano would say that 146 bodies were buried—24 old men "to [sic] feeble to fight"; 6 boys, ages five to eight; 7 "cradle-board" babies; 7 old women; 102 other males and females, ages ten and older. Peano's tally became the official count. But Paddy Starr, who led the party, claimed that 168 bodies were stacked in the grave. Others would claim more.

In addition to those hunting for bodies, relic hunters combed the field. Anything that might be of value was scooped up by journalists, civilians, soldiers, and even local squaws who realized that the *wasichu* would pay for such things. The Washington *Evening Star* correspondent George H. Harries dubbed them all "busy men." They descended upon Big Foot's deserted camp like "Nebraska locusts," stripping it of anything that might be salable. Pipes were especially valuable, as were ghost shirts, but the most sought-after items were war clubs, many later advertised as the one that brained Captain Wallace (who'd been shot through the head). Will Cressey of *The Omaha Bee* was probably the busiest of the "busy men": his battlefield collection included the bracelets of Big Foot's slain wife, a belt and knife sheath, and a book of psalms. The *Omaha World-Herald* would later attest to their authenticity, saying all were "more or less blood-stained and all have the strong and disagreeable odor that is indisputable of the genuineness of the articles."

The second category of "busy men" consisted of two war photographers who ranged the field—German-born George (Gustave) Trager of nearby Chadron, Nebraska, and his business partner, Joseph Ford, an enterprising Agency barber. Trager snapped the only known photographs of the gruesome aftermath of Wounded Knee. He took the famous photo of Big Foot's frozen corpse, his hands up like claws. He shot the corpse of Yellow Bird, facedown, then flipped him over. When this exposed the medicine man's genitals, Trager inked them out so as to not offend his customers' sensibilities. On the back of each photograph a stamped "advert" proclaimed: "Everything of interest in the late Pine Ridge War are held by us for sale."

The last group did the most good. A party of about one hundred civilians, Indian and white, followed on the heels of the burial party. Dr. Charles Eastman led them: their goal was to find any who may have survived. Three miles from the battlefield, they found the body of a woman "completely covered with a blanket of snow." From this point on, Eastman's group found corpses scattered as if they had been hunted down like vermin. As members of his party began to find friends and relatives, wailing and mourning marked their slow passage. When they reached the council circle, Eastman counted eighty bodies sprawled in a weird, lifeless, frozen tableau.

By now, nearly every Indian in his group cried or sang his death song. "It took all of my nerve to keep my composure in the face of this spectacle," he wrote. Whites in his party grew nervous, and the only way to calm them was to find survivors, unlikely as that seemed. Eastman told his searchers to uncover and examine every corpse in the hope that some might still live.

Miraculously, a few had held on. They found an infant girl, warmly wrapped, on her head a little cap of buckskin with an American flag beaded in red, white, and blue. They found three other living babies, but of these four only the girl in the cap—the one soon called Lost Bird— would survive. They found an old woman under a wagon, totally blind. A mortally wounded man asked Eastman to fill his pipe before he died. A few other women and children were found in the abandoned store; they'd managed to crawl there after the Seventh had loaded their own wounded and departed for the Agency. They found eleven survivors— five women, four children, two men—but most died.

Days later, an impromptu memorial arose. It would be a dozen years before a granite obelisk, eerily similar to Custer's, rose atop the mass grave. Funded by Joseph Horn Cloud, it named the 146 people buried beneath it and was inscribed with forty-nine words. The last line was most poignant: "Many innocent women and children who knew no wrong died here." But before that, anonymous mourners brushed upon the posts marking the trench the red paint given to them by Wovoka. Those who wore it, he'd said, would enter a better world.

The mass burial seemed to take the heart out of the resistance, though it would sputter on, sometimes tragically, for a few more days. On January 3, 1891, a detachment of the Sixth Cavalry was attacked a few miles north of the Agency; Black Elk was able to walk by then, and during the skirmish stole five army horses, two of which he gave to warriors who had lost theirs. The next day, he left camp with three friends—One Side, Poor Buffalo, and Brave Heart—on a raiding party. They were heading east toward Manderson when they spotted cavalry riding up the creek toward them. They hid behind a hill close to the Manderson store. Black Elk wanted to ambush them: "Let's stay here and kill at least one," he pleaded. His friends argued against it: there were too many; the soldiers would rub them out. Black Elk was adamant and their voices grew loud. "We had quite an argument," he said in the Neihardt transcripts. "So, the three men led me away on my horse to stop me," the suggestion being that they had to restrain him to save their own lives.

Though Black Elk told Neihardt that no one was killed, he apparently told a different story to his family members. One was Aaron DeSersa, owner of *The Shannon County News*, married to his granddaughter Esther. DeSersa would write that the old man showed him the spot "where he killed two soldiers at Wounded Knee." According to the Jesuit priest Michael Steltenkamp, Black Elk told another in-law that he'd shot a soldier. Such persistence suggests that Black Elk may indeed have shot someone—either at the mission fight or in ambush close to Manderson.

At the end of *Black Elk Speaks*, Neihardt asked Black Elk to reflect on Wounded Knee. The old man remembered the dead women and children piled in heaps, the way he courted death as he rushed the soldiers. Finally his luck ran out and he only wanted to die. Every man faces death, and for some it can be a relief. But not for Black Elk. There would be no relief that day.

The struggle was winding down. Kicking Bear and Short Bull returned to the Stronghold and cried for revenge. Once again, soldiers surrounded the holdouts. Food was scarce. Winter was on them.

Chief Standing Bear of the Oglala—the author Luther's father—knew this on January 13 when he took a peace pipe there. The sight enraged believers, and the Ghost Dancer Ten Fingers leveled his rifle at

Standing Bear's heart. "The white people have killed our people without mercy!" he screamed. "We want no peace. We want to fight the soldiers—even if we all die." He fired and the bullet hit the ground between the chief's knees. Standing Bear sat quietly, regarding Ten Fingers with his pale blue eyes. Ten Fingers' face crumbled; he disappeared into the crowd of dancers and fled.

The tension broke, and others spoke, too. Red Cloud, still with the dancers, said that winter was coming; Kicking Bear admitted that the fight was out of him. The most eloquent was Young Man Afraid of His Horses, who took Black Elk into a tipi and addressed him with Kicking Bear, Good Thunder, and Short Bull. Young Man Afraid was one of the first Wild Westers, and so had a bond with Black Elk; he'd become chief of his clan when his famous father, Old Man Afraid of His Horses, had died in the terrible winter of 1889. He'd been a progressive, a member of the Indian police, but the massacre had saddened him, too. "Relatives," he said, "if this were in summertime it would not be so hard. If this were [not] winter, my people at Pine Ridge would have joined you and we would have had a fight to the finish, and I don't want my and your people to make us kill each other among ourselves. I don't care how many the soldiers are, without the Indian scouts they cannot fight and the camp will be helpless. So, relatives, if this were in summer I would have joined you and had it to the finish. But this is winter and it is hard on our children especially, so let us go back and make peace."

Black Elk and the others agreed. It was the end.

The next day, a caravan of about four thousand Lakotas, seven thousand horses, and five hundred wagons began the march south through Pine Ridge. They trudged along White Clay Creek to a campsite a half mile from Agency headquarters; Black Elk said the soldiers stood in two lines as they marched between them and presented arms. On a hill to the north, artillerymen stood beside their guns. The Oglala walked through the stockade gates, and there Kicking Bear surrendered his rifle to General Miles. The officers saluted them, Black Elk said. The Ghost Dance War had lasted thirty-two days, and cut short the lives of forty-eight soldiers and scouts, one civilian, and more than three hundred Sioux. The reservation's beef herd had been decimated, and several buildings burned down. The largest military operation in the United States since the Civil War was over, and it had cost the government $1.2 million, a staggering amount for the time.

On January 22, the three thousand troops who'd participated in the campaign passed in grand review outside the Agency walls. Miles sat astride a pitch-black horse and watched from atop a small hill. Twelve infantry, five cavalry, and four artillery companies marched past. The Seventh Cavalry played "Garry Owen" as it passed, followed by the black troops of the Ninth who'd saved them. When the last soldier passed, an awesome quiet settled over the field.

The Lakota watched in silence from the surrounding hills. A gentle snow was falling; they pulled their hoods up for protection from the icy wind. The hills funneled the gusts into the valley, kicking up clouds of snow that sometimes obscured the parade.

"The scene was weird and in some respects desolate, yet it was fascinating to me," Miles later wrote. The vast prairie covered in white—the frigid winds blowing before them sleet, ice, and snow. As he told his superiors in the War Department: "A more complete submission to the military powers has never been made by any Indians."

In distant Nevada, Wovoka was told of Wounded Knee. Realizing that his religion had failed and that further dancing must stop, he covered his head with his blanket and spoke for the last time in the Voice of God. "My children!" he moaned. In days past, he'd told believers to abandon all things of white society and find the trail back to the way of the Indian. "Now these trails are choked with sand," he said. They were so thickly overgrown that "the young men cannot find them." Only one choice remained. "My children, today I call upon you to travel a new trail, the only trail now open—the White Man's Road."

But even that would be hard to travel for the Oglala. After the soldiers had passed and the parade ended, wrote a correspondent for *Harper's Weekly*, thousands of Oglalas and Brulés "were still standing like statues on the crests of the hills."

PART IV

"WHAT IS AN INDIAN?"

The struggle of man against power is the struggle of memory against forgetting.   —Milan Kundera

22

THE UNDERGROUND

The year of surrender is a blank spot in Black Elk's memoirs. He disappears from the record, and may have gone into hiding. As happened earlier, friends in the Indian police may have advised him to go underground, for soon after surrender the primary Ghost Dance evangelists were arrested and imprisoned at Chicago's Camp Sheridan. Miles suggested to Cody that he take the prisoners with him to Europe in the next Wild West. Removing them from the country would cool tempers; exposure to Europe would convince them of the "power and numbers of the white race." Even Kicking Bear welcomed the idea: in late February or early March 1891, he greeted Cody in the prison stockade. "For six weeks I have been a dead man," he told his rescuer. "Now that I see you, I am alive again." On April 1, 1891, Kicking Bear and twenty-two other Ghost Dance prisoners sailed to Antwerp with seventy-five Wild West Lakotas.

They were the lucky ones. This year would be so dark, so bitter, that few records remain of it today: as if by consensus 1891 was expunged from memory. The Big Foot Massacre had sucked the heart and soul from Black Elk's people. Everyone knew the dead; many more were crippled in body and spirit. He heard the tales of a few bitter-enders who refused to give up; heartsick with grief, they'd rushed from their camps, shot down their horses and dogs, and disappeared into the Badlands. They were said to be out there still.

For Black Elk, the mass grave atop the hill at Wounded Knee held more than just 146 frozen corpses. It held his people's identity. He knew that the Ghost Dance had been at heart a last-ditch effort to remain Lakota. For that, they had been slaughtered. If they could not *act* Indian, they were not Indian. If they were not Indian, what were they?

It was a question asked at the highest levels of government, one that by the end of the century evolved to include an economic dimension. Commissioner of Indian Affairs Thomas Morgan stated it bluntly in his annual report of 1892. Although the 1889 Sioux Agreement assumed that allotting tribal lands would "privatize" the Indian and turn him "white," the process itself would not begin until the first decades of the twentieth century. Now was the time to iron out details. "What is an Indian?" Morgan mused: "One would have supposed that this question would have been considered a hundred years ago and been adjudicated long before this. Singularly enough, however, it has remained in abeyance, and the Government has gone on legislating and administering law without carefully discriminating as to those over whom it had a right to exercise such control."

It is a remarkable statement, since Morgan admits that neither he nor anyone else in the government could "define" the Indian. Morgan would be commissioner from June 10, 1889, to April 17, 1893, yet the man who presided over the first stages of the social experiment to determine the Indians' fate admitted he did not understand them. For the second time in three decades, a dominant force on the Northern Plains wrestled with identity. In 1864, the Lakota had asked, "What is the white? Is he like us?" In 1892, the Indian Office asked the same question of Indians. Everyone "knew" what the Indian had been in the past—brave, free, self-sufficient, unapologetic in his beliefs, ruthless in battle: in essence, the self-image adopted by Americans themselves. An Indian, said Morgan, was someone who owed allegiance first to his tribe "and secondarily, if at all, to the United States." But if the allotment experiment worked and eradicated the tribes, what did that mean? A new century approached and the wild days were over. In this new world, what was an Indian?

If anything, Morgan defined the Indian by what he had and what whites wanted: his land. How much land was an Indian worth? It was a question, Morgan said, that could be answered only by race and blood. The issue still rises today in the form of "blood quantum" laws, the percentage of "Indian blood" in a person's ancestry used to determine his or her eligibility for tribal membership: for example, a person whose father is a full-blooded Indian and whose mother is white has a blood quantum of one-half. No one disputed that a "full-blooded" Indian was "Indian," but what about "mixed-bloods," those joined through marriage, or those adopted into a tribe? For the purpose of landownership, such legal distinctions meant everything. But again, Morgan did not know the answer. "We must give the term 'Indian' a liberal and not a technological or restrictive construction," he ended, in essence passing the problem down to successors.

It was an existential limbo in which men fared worse than women. Women, at least, had their work—they went on as always, bearing and raising children, cooking and feeding the family, once setting and striking camp but now keeping house in these strange log squares. They remained who they were through their activity. Through the same reasoning, men became tragic figures. Their traditional work—war and the hunt—was a thing of the past; with its removal, the man "was left in a daze, unable to overcome this strange and passively powerful inertia that stayed him from doing anything else," wrote the ethnographer Ella C. Deloria, who grew up in that world. So he sat by the hour, "indifferent and inactive," called a "lazy Indian." He came to life only when the pipe was passed and stories of the old days told.

If anything, 1891 was a slow reshuffling of the deck, a sluggish drift from past to present as government officials came and went and the Lakota wandered aimlessly. On January 29, massacre survivors were rounded up and returned to Cheyenne River under military guard. Brulés from Rosebud were slated for roundup next, yet many Indian police had disappeared and no authority remained to enforce the dictates of Washington. More than forty sizable camps of Lakotas from other reservations wandered across Pine Ridge, absorbing stray Oglalas, cattle, and ponies into their slow-moving mass like amoebas. On February 10, Captain Jesse Lee brought back to Rosebud 635 Brulés, leaving an estimated 900 tribesmen still in Pine Ridge. An unrecorded number of Oglalas tried to escape; teachers and farmers were ordered to report absentees; lawmen and settlers on the borders, asked to look out for refugees.

The post-massacre world of Pine Ridge was "bad, wholly bad," wrote Royer's replacement, Charles Penney. Loss and hardship made the Oglalas "bitter and sore"; the memory of that awful day "rankles in their hearts and is an ever present source of discontent" that could spark again into bloodshed. They had not been "whipped" enough into complete and utter submission, he wrote, reflecting a sentiment that went as high as

Sherman: the old campaigner wrote to his niece on January 7, 1891, that her husband simply had not killed enough Indians. Miles was too softhearted: "The more he kills now, the less he will have to do later."

Sherman's blame-the-victim philosophy would be a common refrain, guiding Indian policy well into the twentieth century: the massacre, though unfortunate, was solely the fault of the Indian. The Lakota had not suffered enough on December 29, 1890: "Had they been thoroughly chastised," wrote the new agent on April 7, 1891, "the half of them killed and the remainder cowed into abject subjection, horrible and uncalled-for as such a thing would have been, they would have felt that they had been punished, and in crouching fear would have kissed the rod of correction, as these poor oppressed and down-trodden people have done so often before."

<hr />

In such a world, one surrenders one's soul completely, or goes underground.

The Jesuits, more privy to the nuances of the Lakota spirit, saw it first. "Now already since Easter there seems to be a dance-craze among the Indian women," Perrig wrote on April 14, 1891. "Lots of them have been dancing at least 3 or 4 times not far from the mission. What kind of dance I do not know."

It was probably the Ghost Dance, which experienced a quiet resurgence in the spring following Wounded Knee. Special Agent A. T. Lea reported that members of No Water's band had started dancing again at White Clay Creek; Superintendent of Indian Schools Daniel Dorchester observed several Ghost Dances that spring. The Fourth of July was set as the day of the New Millennium; some tribesmen watched from "the tops of hills in the expectation that when the Messiah comes the hills and mountain will move," Dorchester said.

The peyote cult also surfaced during this time. Known today as the Native American Church of Jesus Christ, a legally protected religion under amendments to the 1978 American Indian Religious Freedom Act, it was then more secretive, known as the "medicine-eating church," or *pejuta yuta okolakiye*. Mooney witnessed a peyote ceremony in 1891; the religion had drifted up from Mexico, passed from border Apaches to the Oklahoma Indian Territory, and by 1890 the rites were firmly established. Retreats started on Saturday nights and lasted until the next morning: worshippers cut the tops from *Lophophora williamsii*, a small, carrot-shaped cactus known as peyote, then ate the bitter-tasting "buttons" as a sacrament. Adherents claimed the "divine herb" possessed medicinal and spiritual properties; missionaries and the Indian Office saw its use as one of "orgiastic drunkenness" and condemned or arrested users. It had just drifted north and met in two underground churches: Allen in Bennett County, and Porcupine.

Black Elk would have known of these movements, though no evidence suggests that he participated. He'd been disillusioned by the Ghost Dance and would have steered clear of its resurgence; he'd been fooled once, and now trusted only his Vision. The peyote cult fell into the same context. Although he never publicly condemned it, he would not have believed it followed the one true path. It was instead one of those shadows that clouded men's minds.

This period saw a resurgence of missionary attempts to eradicate the old ways, given force by new government regulations. Bans on the funeral giveaway were enforced, new sanctions on the Sun Dance imposed, sanctions not limited to Pine Ridge. In 1910, the missionary J. B. Carroll begged the military to wipe out the Sun Dance at the Blackfoot Agency. To those who said a ban violated the freedom of religion, Carroll answered that the law applied only to religions that worshiped God, not the devil. The Indian response was to go underground: evidence suggests that the giveaway continued and a Sun Dance was held in 1910 at Rosebud, and from 1917 to 1919 at the village of Kyle in Pine Ridge.

Yet the greatest threat to what Black Elk represented was the Black Robes at Holy Rosary. More than any other group, the Catholic fathers filled the spiritual gulf created by Wounded Knee, and they did so by occupying a middle ground between the old world and the new. The original five Jesuits at Holy Rosary were Prussians or Austrians, and understood exile from one's native land. Fathers John Jutz, Aemilius Perrig, Joseph Lindebner, Aloysius Bosch, and Florentine Digmann came to Holy Rosary in the late 1880s, before Wounded Knee; some died and were buried there.

Unlike Protestant missionaries, whose approach to conversion was all-or-nothing, the Jesuits were more likely to mold Catholic doctrine to Sioux culture. The symbolism of the Sacred Pipe as a focus for all that was holy easily transferred to the Cross; the Sioux idea of a Great Spirit and watchful Grandfathers was not that different from a Catholic God, Trinity, and host of angels. Ritual sacraments were central to both religions. Pain and suffering—their acceptance and endurance—were the nexus of both Catholic and Lakota identity.

The Black Robes discovered that it was easier to convert women than men. The life of a Sioux woman after marriage was that of a work-horse, subject to unending toil. "Human life can scarcely present a stranger contrast than is experienced by an Indian woman as a maiden and as a matron," observed *The Illustrated American* of January 31, 1891. "Light-hearted happiness, free from care, wild independence mark the one; thorough-going wretchedness, constant drudgery, and slavish obedience, the other." The Lakota wife was the tribe's unsung manager: she carried water, cut wood, cooked, hitched horses to the wagon, and butchered and loaded beef on Issue Day. Now that the man no longer supported the tribe through the hunt, she'd also become an entrepreneur: she prepared hides for market, did beadwork for the "Indian trade," did most of the shopping at the stores, and, while it lasted, gathered bison skeletons for the bone trade. "Small wonder," observed the reporter, "they early begin to take on the appearance of age."

The priests did not know *why* it was easier to convert women, but they had theories. Among the Oglala, men engaged in religious rites while women rarely took leadership roles. While a man's religious life was prescribed by custom, a woman's was less clear-cut. Entry into the church was a less radical change for a woman than for a man. Her modest dress easily passed muster with the priests and nuns; her conversion brought her to the attention of government "matrons," a kind of home economics teacher supervised by the district farmer, which merely meant a tidier household. The man, on the other hand, had to cut off his hair, change his style of dress, and adopt a new work ethic—in essence, become more obviously "white" if he converted.

Once priests baptized a Lakota woman, they did everything possible to deepen her ties to her new faith. Native role models worthy of imitation became a kind of shorthand for the Church's universality. The Black Robes spoke often in their sermons of Kateri Tekakwitha, the Mohawk woman born in 1656 in New York near a Jesuit mission. Even during her life, they'd recognized her as a model Catholic: she'd endured persecution for her new faith, made a vow of chastity, and planned to enter a convent. Even though she died at age twenty-four of smallpox, the Church still elevated her as a model of sanctity. In their homilies, the priests spoke of her as a proper model for Sioux women, driving home the theme that all people were alike in the eyes of God. Indeed, the first full-blooded adult to be converted at Holy Rosary was a woman, but Catherine Mary Little Wolf was a special case. "Evidently her desire for baptism was intensified by sickness, for she died the same day," wrote Father Louis Gall. A review of the priests' diaries from 1890 to the 1930s reveals that their days and nights were filled with final sacraments and deathbed conversions. In these early decades, the majority seem to fall into this category. An ailing Indian might visit the native healer first, but when that failed, he called for the Black Robe and promised to convert should he work a miracle.

In essence, a struggle between rival shamans developed in Pine Ridge during the 1890s. The Jesuits would balk at such a portrait, but ever since the early Plains ministry of Pierre-Jean De Smet and his predecessor Pierre Biard, they never went anywhere if not dressed in their vestments of power: the crucifix hanging around their necks; the black soutane that gave them the name *Sina Sapa*, or Black Robe. What developed in the 1890s was a war of magicians battling for men's souls. Whose medicine was stronger? Whose God would prevail? Though the Pine Ridge Jesuits of this period did not seek to eradicate all traces of Sioux culture, they did try to wipe out the medicine men. Both *pejuta wicasa* and *wicasa wakan*, they believed, worked in league with the devil. Even more than the agent or the Indian police, the *Sina Sapa* stood at the forefront of a religious war. They seized and destroyed Sioux holy objects; quizzed informants—usually women and children—for the names of prophets and healers; gloried in the occasional conversion of a medicine man. Until the Big Foot Massacre, their successes were slight, but they saw the failure of the Ghost Dance as a blow to the medicine men. Now was the time to strike.

As Father Digmann would say with a smile, "The devil trimmed his own tail."

For Black Elk, the battle would be waged in both the deathbed and the marriage bed.

Little is known of Black Elk's first wife, Katie War Bonnet, known in Lakota as Wapota. According to the Pine Ridge census, they wed in 1892 when he was twenty-eight and she was twenty-four. The very last line of Black Elk's interview transcripts—after the long tale of his childhood, the florid complexity of his Vision, and the heartbreak of the massacre—was six words long and ended with blunt finality: "Two years later I was married." He never said anything of his new wife in letters or manuscripts. He never even spoke her name.

Family lore suggests she'd had more than her share of troubles before her marriage. Katie had been one of Sitting Bull's people, and had walked with the refugees to Big Foot's camp after the old prophet was killed. How she survived Wounded Knee is not a story that was passed along; the memory may have been too painful. It would be convenient if she were one of the hostages saved by Black Elk, but that is not known; she did, however, evade the army's roundup of survivors for transport back to Cheyenne River, and she remained in Pine Ridge. Black Elk began clerking at the Manderson store again sometime in 1892: the position made him visible, and she may have met him there. What is certain is that the couple soon had two sons: Never Showed Off, born in 1893; and Good Voice Star, in 1895.

During this time, Black Elk became one of the most prominent medicine men at Pine Ridge. This was no secret: in 1893, a large party of Oglalas visited the ranch of the cattleman James Cook; the rancher was a friend of Red Cloud's, and groups such as this gathered annually at his spread just to the south in Sioux County, Nebraska. This year the party included Red Cloud and his family, Little Wound, American Horse, Big Road, He Dog, and other famous old warriors. Such a collection of once-antagonistic progressives and traditionalists suggests that the anger and sadness of Wounded Knee smoothed over old divisions. Cook was intimate enough with the Lakota to also recognize healers: "Two prominent medicine men of the tribe—Black Elk and Corn Cob— were also there," he wrote in his memoirs.

Any curiosity Black Elk may have shown during his travels in Europe for either Christianity or the Catholic Church was eradicated by his bitterness over Wounded Knee. Instead, he devoted himself more fully to the old beliefs, and became known throughout Pine Ridge as the kind of specialized healer called a *yuwipi*. People knew him as "the *yuwipi* man." He was still a bear healer, a *wicasa wakan* versed in the nuances of the vision quest, and a *heyoka*, or sacred clown. Yet *yuwipi* was the most overtly magical of the healing arts, a conjuring ceremony used to tell the future, find lost objects, and contact the spirits of the dead. It is significant that he took it up during this period of spiritual war against the *Sina Sapa*; it was also the only practice that he would later disparage. "I was kind of good at it," he later told family, but when asked if he believed in it, he shot back, "No! That's all nonsense—just like the magicians you have in the white people." The *yuwipi* ceremony was a bag of tricks "trying to fool."

Though one part of him felt guilty, in the hands of an expert, *yuwipi* was effective. *Yuwipi* basically meant "they bind him," and fell within a complex of ceremonies known as *lowanpi*, or "sings." If the condition to be cured was serious, such as paralysis from a stroke, Black Elk was wrapped in a sacred blanket, tightly bound with a rope, and tied with special knots by an assistant, usually his old friend One Side. After Wounded Knee, One Side had assumed his old name, Kills Enemy: in humorous homage to his former name, he'd wear a hat crooked to one side of his head. The lights were doused and good or bad spirits announced their presence through flashes of light, pounding, voices, whispers, the beating of wings, or the growls of animals. In Black Elk's ceremonies, women could be heard singing all around the darkened room. Even within the practice, *yuwipi* specialized: Black Elk was famous for love potions. During a final song series, rattles shook, beds tilted, and sparks flew around the room. Then Black Elk answered questions. It was the closest thing in Lakota ceremony to the spiritualism then popular in Victorian society; just as in these settings, even skeptics experienced a chill. Then it was over: the assistant and ghostly chorus vanished. Black Elk stood by his bindings, as free as an Oglala Harry Houdini, the blanket and rope neatly bundled beside him.

This was the very tradition the Jesuits sought to eradicate, the kind of superstitious manipulation they felt kept the Lakota trapped in the Dark Ages. Black Elk would have been one of the "clever and cunning men" denounced from the pulpit by priests, accused of wielding "a baneful influence over the people."

Such pressure would have come at him from all sides. Sometime during this period, Katie War Bonnet converted to Catholicism. Though her baptismal records no longer exist, she had the boys baptized soon after the 1895 birth of Good Voice Star. Never Showed Off was christened William; Good Voice Star, John, though the census sometimes recorded him as James. The sudden christenings may have been due to a health scare: William was a sickly child and died sometime between 1895 and 1897. Soon afterward, on May 17, 1898, a third son, Benjamin, was born. Like his brothers, he was baptized. Unlike them, he survived into adulthood.

Katie would have wanted Black Elk to convert: she sat in the Wounded Knee or Manderson chapel every Sunday and listened to the circuit-riding priests rail against men like her husband. He was a good provider; he cared for his sons; he was not violent like other men. He spent so much time trying to help others. How could he be evil? Yet the seeds of doubt were planted every week on the hard wooden pews. After William's death, the doubt increased. Evil had entered the house, said the *Sina Sapa*, and in the doubt and agony of the confessional, she may have whispered her husband's name.

It need not have been Wapota who informed. Manderson was tight-knit; there were few secrets in a village that small. Sam Kills Brave lived close to Black Elk: with Lewis Shields and Black Elk, he was one of the main organizers of Manderson. He was an important man, by then a Catholic, but also Black Elk's friend. He would see Black Elk in the store or the town and come up to him. "Why don't you give up your *yuwipi* and join the Catholic church?" he would ask. "You may think it's best, but the way I look at it, it isn't right for you to do the *yuwipi*." This did not happen once, but almost every time Sam Kills Brave saw him.

In the end, it does not matter who informed to the priests; what is known is that by the turn of the century, Black Elk was targeted by the Black Robes. Once the Jesuits knew a medicine man's identity, they pursued him relentlessly and campaigned for his conversion. They destroyed his drums, rattles, and other instruments of healing; they published accounts of conversions in the Catholic press to spread word of their success against the devil. And if a man proved particularly difficult, they exposed him to the authorities.

Real consequences could follow. The medicine man could be hauled before the Indian Court and fined or sentenced to jail. His family could be hounded in the community, church, and schools. The most insidious sanction has no documentary support and appears almost exclusively in Oglala oral histories: priests acting in concert with agents consigned the most recalcitrant medicine men to an asylum for treatment of mental illness. The Lakota elder Wallace Black Elk (no relation to Hehaka Sapa) would write in his 1991 autobiography that in the 1930s a Jesuit priest, Father Bernard Fagan, colluded with reservation authorities to have him committed; he claimed he was beaten for refusing to stop his traditional practice, then thrown into a basement cell: "Then they slammed that steel-mesh door and locked it. There was a second door there that had a little window in it. They slammed that shut and locked it also. It had a big latch on it with a big padlock. So I looked around and began to crawl around in there. There was a bench in there,

so I pulled myself up onto it. I hurt everywhere." When told of the accusation by the Jesuit author Michael Steltenkamp, "Fagan good-
naturedly countered that nothing of the sort took place."

It all sounds far-fetched and conspiratorial—except that such a
place did in fact exist. From 1903 to 1934, the Indian Insane Asylum in
Canton, South Dakota—also known as the Hiawatha Insane Asylum—
would admit more than 350 Indian patients from across the nation and
keep them in abysmal conditions. According to a 1927 investigation by
the Bureau of Indian Affairs, barely a third were there for legitimate reasons: a large number showed no signs of mental illness and were admitted for offenses such as alcoholism, the continued practice of *yuwipi*
and the Sun Dance, refusing to send their children to Indian schools,
and impeding the plans of white businessmen. At least 121 patients—
or more than a third of those admitted—died there and were buried in
unmarked graves. No records survived or even seemed to be kept: no
one knows today why they died or why they were even admitted.

Thus, it could be dangerous to persist in *wakan* practices, fatal to
be an inconvenient man. In most cases, however, this did not happen:
very few Pine Ridge Oglalas claim, like Wallace Black Elk, that people
"disappeared." The Jesuits might be tough, relentless, and blinkered in
their pursuit of the devil, but they generally preferred live converts to
martyred medicine men.

The most frequent battleground was the deathbed, the field where
the priest faced the *wicasa wakan* to claim the soul of the dying. Such
meetings were inevitable. Family members would call both the priest
and the medicine man to the bedside to double the chances of survival.
Depending upon the priest, the two might work together—to a point.
Father Digmann wrote of telling the mother of the dying Jim Low Cedar,
"Call the physician and give his medicines. If you know of any good
Indian medicine, you may also give it, but do not allow any conjuration,
sacred songs, etc., of the medicine man."

The Jesuits were jealous about the final rites, and would intervene
violently if they happened upon a medicine man in the midst of "conjuring." According to Digmann, "We had a special eye on the sick, not
to let them go without baptism." This was a delicate point: the picture
of a priest hovering over a dying, unbaptized person seems ghoulish,
especially since the priest implied that without it the fading Lakota was
in danger of eternal damnation. Yet the Jesuits believed that this was
often the only way to save an Indian's soul. So often did they baptize

Lakotas near death that many Oglalas had an absolute horror of the rite, convinced that the sprinkling of the *mniyuwakanpi*, or holy water, would kill them. And medicine men such as Black Elk did their best to spread the idea.

Black Elk competed in this spiritual face-off at least twice, and probably more. Although the confrontations were similar, the endings were diametrically opposed. Both times, Black Elk was called in by grieving parents to minister to a dying child; the Jesuits' web of informants ran deep, and both times the *Sina Sapa* arrived mid-chant to disrupt the ceremony. The stories are so similar, in fact, that one wonders whether they might not have been variations of the same folkloric tale. As best as can be guessed, the first confrontation occurred sometime in 1901 or 1902. Black Elk told Neihardt that he was performing a holy rite when a Jesuit priest stormed in, tossed his sacred instruments from the tent, and then destroyed them. Though the Black Robe called him a fraud, the patient recovered, convincing the Oglala once again that Black Elk was a powerful sacred healer.

The priest, for his part, died.

Although Black Elk never named this priest, the only known fatal event for a Black Robe during this period was the death in 1903 of Father Aloysius Bosch, one of the five original Jesuits at Holy Rosary. It was said that during Bosch's fifteen years among the Indians, "he was always in the saddle." One day in the autumn or winter of 1902, an urgent sick call came to the mission, so he jumped upon an Indian pony. On the return trip, the horse stumbled and fell on Bosch, breaking his leg and possibly causing internal injuries. Bosch suffered for five months before he died.

Although Black Elk's tale could be taken as a warning to the arrogant, it did not come off that way. The tone was rather matter-of-fact, much different from priestly stories of vanquishing the heathen. If Father Bosch was the victim of anything, it was a clumsy horse, and bad karma.

———•—•———

By the turn of the century, Black Elk was tired. The struggle, plus the sadness of Never Showed Off's death, had worn him down. According to his Great Vision, 1900 was the year in which he must use the soldier weed to wipe out his enemies and set the Oglala free. But who was the enemy? Men such as Sam Kills Brave badgered him to abandon what he'd considered since childhood to be the core of his life—and Sam was a friend. His own wife probably pressured him to be baptized by the Black Robes, and he knew they considered him an agent of Satan. A picture of the period shows the once-handsome Black Elk, now a man in his late thirties who seems at least a decade older. His shoulders droop; his face is sad; heavy folds of skin have lodged beneath his eyes. He was plagued by a constant, painful stomach disorder that would be diagnosed as ulcers. Though he continued with his *yuwipi* work, his sense of purpose had suffered: we hear nothing of the Great Vision, replaced instead by a darker reality.

For Black Elk was going blind, the victim of corneal flash burns suffered during either a *yuwipi* or a *heyoka* ceremony. In one account, Black Elk and Kills Enemy pushed a cartridge into the ground to create some small explosive effects during a *heyoka* ceremony. But when they tamped the shell flush, it exploded into Black Elk's eyes. In a second account, Black Elk placed gunpowder beneath the dirt so the earth would rise up during a ceremony. Yet when he used a cigarette to light the powder, it ignited near his eyes. The third and final account contains elements of native folklore: Black Elk and Kills Enemy were persistently irritated by an owl that kept them awake at night. They decided to shoot it, but first had to make the cartridges. Black Elk was working near a fire when a spark ignited the powder near his eye.

Whatever caused the accident, his world was growing dark, but he could not give up. His people depended upon him. This was the great era of the "catching" diseases at Pine Ridge: pneumonia, measles, and whooping cough. Smallpox hit in the winter of 1901, taking with it the old chief Little Wound. Worst by far was "consumption." In 1899, the prevailing disease among the Oglala was tuberculosis: of the reservation's 6,788 full- and mixed-blood Indians, about 50 percent, or nearly 3,400, were infected. "The larger percentage is among the children," wrote the Agency physician James Walker, "and it appears to be increasing." The common wisdom during this period was that 75 percent of reservation deaths were caused by consumption, most occurring among those under age four. Thus, if 124 people died at Pine Ridge in 1896, 93 of those deaths would be attributed to TB.

Black Elk had discovered his own medicine for tuberculosis, a family member later said. He'd stand on a hill on a moonless night and scan the landscape for a plant that glowed. Two mushrooms like this could be found at Pine Ridge: the honey mushroom mycelium, *Armillaria ostoyae*, and the fox fire, *A. mellea*. Like most medicine men, he was secretive about his recipes, so the cure is not known today. It was also said that the roots of one of his most curative plants seemed to have arms and legs—possibly American ginseng, or *Panax quinquefolius*. He later said he was adept at fighting consumption, and was often on call. Yet in later life he, too, would suffer from the "coughing sickness"; it is not unusual for caregivers to contract the plagues of those they try to save.

But there were also diseases of the mind that could not be so easily cured—diseases rarely seen in the old days, but which now appeared with greater frequency. The Sioux doctors called a common one *wacinko*. People would clam up, refusing to talk or even react when their lives became unbearable. In the worst cases, *wacinko* would worm its way into some other physical illness "maybe in the heart or head or both," and never go away. Sometimes the sufferer just wandered off from home without warning. A few days later, he'd be found hanging by a rope or belt from a tree or in an abandoned shed.

Sometimes a man can only take so much before he reaches a breaking point. That point came for Black Elk in 1903. In the year that Red Cloud finally abdicated his chieftaincy, saying simply that "shadows are long and dark before me," Katie War Bonnet died of unknown causes at age thirty-four. Hers had been a short and unhappy life, with too much death in myriad guises. No doubt a Black Robe came and performed last rites; she would have wanted it, but whether her husband watched is unknown. He was alone, without a partner, responsible for two young sons.

It was finally too much. He converted to Catholicism the following year.

23

BLACK ROBE DAYS

Black Elk's conversion is probably the greatest mystery of his life. Whereas his Great Vision is a chimera, shifting with time and interpreters, it still left him with a singular purpose—to save his people. That never changed. Yet his baptism as Nicholas William Black Elk on December 6, 1904, seemed to run counter to everything he'd stood for, a repudiation of all he'd held holy. He chose as his name day the Feast of St. Nicholas, the fourth-century Greek bishop Nikolaos of Myra, "Nikolaos the Wonderworker," model for Santa Claus, and patron saint of children, students, prisoners, the poor, and the falsely accused. Black Elk took the name Nick, and at Pine Ridge today, he is remembered by that name.

Though Black Elk would relate his conversion with the skill of a showman, the main source for the account comes from Lucy Black Elk, his daughter by a later marriage. She revealed it in 1973 to Michael Steltenkamp, a teacher at the Red Cloud School who would become a Jesuit priest. Lucy was strongly Catholic, as was Steltenkamp's second informant, Olivia, daughter of Black Elk's son Benjamin. Thus, where Neihardt wrote nothing at all about Black Elk's second religious career, Steltenkamp, Lucy, and Olivia translated virtually everything Black Elk experienced in the twentieth century in light of Catholicism.

Black Elk's turning point came in November 1904, soon after the death of his wife. His sadness over her loss probably set the stage. He'd been called to doctor a sick little boy in Payabaya, a village seven miles north of Holy Rosary. Black Elk found the boy in a tent, covered by robes; he laid out his medicines, rattle, pipe, and tobacco offerings, then shed his shirt and pounded softly on his drum.

Because of Payabaya's proximity to Holy Rosary, a Black Robe had also been called. The boy had been baptized, and the priests jealously guarded their right to send the boy to a Catholic and not a Lakota god. The priest drove up in his buggy; the camp dogs started barking, and he could hear Black Elk calling on the spirits to heal the boy. The Black Robe barged into the tent, threw the Indian medicine into the stove, pitched the drum and rattle through the flap, grabbed Black Elk by the nape of the neck, and cried, "Satan, get out!" According to Lucy, Black Elk left willingly. The priest gave the boy Communion, administered last rites, cleaned up the tent, and prayed with the boy. "After he was through, he came out and saw my father sitting there looking downhearted and lonely—as though he lost all his powers," Lucy related. The priest gazed at him a moment and said, "Come on and get in the buggy with me." Black Elk climbed into the carriage and the two drove back to Holy Rosary.

There are problems with this story. First, the account is identical to that of the interruption by Father Aloysius Bosch—except for the outcome. It was the familiar battleground for the soul about which Father Digmann wrote: the archetypical contest between the "pagan" and the "civilized." The interchangeability of the two stories places it in a separate folk genre, wrote Steltenkamp: "an oral narrative telling a biographical truth via incidents that never actually happened quite as reported." The detail of barking dogs was also a giveaway: the expression *sungwapa*, or "dog barking," denotes any general commotion. The howling of dogs in the night heralds the presence not only of human interlopers but of spirits, too. By saying that dogs were barking, Black Elk framed the event as "something important, extraordinary, or mysterious," said Steltenkamp, a dramatic effect that might be lost on *wasichu* listeners, but not on the Sioux.

There is also the question of character. Although there is no proof, it was assumed among the Oglala that a *wicasa wakan* of Black Elk's stature would not allow himself to be pushed around in this manner. The same caveat held for the Black Robe of the incident—Father Joseph Lindebner, then forty-nine. One of the original German Jesuits at Pine Ridge, he was called by the Oglala Ate Ptecela, or "Little Father," for his short stature. By all accounts, Lindebner was not a zealot: like Father Jutz, he tried to understand the Oglala. The detail that does ring true is that moment when he left the tent: he saw Black Elk sitting by himself and understood the man was hurting. "Come on and get in the buggy with me" is something that Little Father would say.

Black Elk was indeed in pain. According to Lucy, her father had "suffered a lot" in those years after Wounded Knee. His wife and son had died. Sometime in the late 1890s, Good Thunder had first become an Episcopal, then died of a heart attack. Once again, Black Elk was responsible for his mother. Before this death, there had been Crazy Horse, his father, his friends at Wounded Knee. So many losses, and despite his best efforts, people continued to die. He had not saved his people, as the Grandfathers commanded; he was hunted and persecuted by the authorities, doubled over from ulcers, and going blind. Little made sense any longer. He was tired.

Come with me, said Little Father at this critical moment, and Black Elk followed him like a child. He stayed two weeks at Holy Rosary in preparation for baptism, but during this time his ulcers became unbearable. On the feast day of St. Nicholas, he was baptized and renamed Nicholas Black Elk, but he was in such bad shape that he was rushed to an Omaha hospital and placed on a strict diet for two or three months until the ulcers healed. He rose and came home—a new faith, a new name, a new man.

It was his second great resurrection, thirty-two years after receiving the secrets and powers of the Grandfathers. But something had happened, and their promised salvation did not come. Maybe this time would be different. Maybe this time he would find the key and get it right.

———•◦•———

Years later, people would ask why he converted when he did. The scholar Raymond DeMallie, in his painstaking examination of the Neihardt transcripts, concluded that by accepting Catholicism, Black Elk at last put himself beyond the onerous obligations of his Vision—at least for a while. When Neihardt gingerly asked why he'd joined "the white church," the old man paused, then answered, "Because my children have to live in this world." Lucy was convinced her father was too exhausted to continue in the old ways.

All are factors, yet the explanation that probably came closest to the truth was told to his nephew sometime after June 1917. Frank Fools Crow was on his way to becoming a powerful Pine Ridge *wicasa wakan*, one of the most important of the mid- to late twentieth century, and Black Elk often counseled him in the ways and duties of the medicine man. In later years, Fools Crow would say he was both a practicing Catholic and a traditionalist, but in 1917, when he was twenty-five, he said, "I gave in to the persuasion of the priest and decided to become a Catholic," which implies a struggle. He asked his uncle what had led to his own baptism in 1904: "Black Elk told me he had decided that the Sioux religious way of life was pretty much the same as that of the Christian churches, and there was no reason to change what the Sioux were doing. We could pick up some of the Christian ways and teachings, and just work them in with our own, so in the end both would be better."

Ecumenicism was not a new idea among the Sioux, but it was rare. As early as July 1892, when the Hunkpapa leader Gall was baptized in the Episcopal church, he told the priest that the idea of the Golden Rule was identical in both Christian and Lakota theology: "What this man Jesus says we must do unto others, I already know. Be kind to your neighbor, feed him, be better to him than to yourself, he says. All are brothers, he says. But that's an old story to me. Of course! Aren't we all Dakotas?"

But what *was* new for Gall in 1892 was new for Black Elk in 1904 and Fools Crow in 1914—the revelation, as Gall had said, that *Wakan Tanka* "is actually the Father of all men." White Buffalo Calf Woman had come to *them* with the Sacred Pipe. *They* were God's Chosen People, and all others were "common men." Why, then, should one "love one's enemies"? Turning the other cheek made no sense in a world of war.

At first, conversion was not easy for Black Elk. Although there are hints that he eventually resumed healing, he abandoned the practice of *yuwipi* and *heyoka*. By so doing, he lost an important source of income. He told how "people would scourge him with vicious words and make fun of him, since he had been a *yuwipi* medicine man," Lucy later said. Two or three times, he was chased from a house; he learned later that the owners belonged to the "peyote clan."

In truth, Black Elk's timing was bad. The previous year, Red Cloud had abdicated to his son Jack, and resentment still ran high. It was painful to watch the once-powerful chief led around by his little grandson. Such a symbol of lost glory was hard to ignore. Yet the old man's eloquence remained. "I was born a Lakota and I have lived a Lakota and I shall die a Lakota," he said. "We were as free as the winds and like the eagle, heard no man's commands. We fought our enemies and feasted our friends." Their children were many; herds, large; young men and women, vital and beautiful; old men, wise.

Those days were gone. "The white men try to make the Indians white men also," he said. "It would be as reasonable and just to try to make the Indian's skin white as to try to make him act and think like a white man. But the white man has taken our territory and destroyed our game so we must eat the white man's food or die." Red Cloud was eighty-three, old for a warrior, and ready to leave this world. "Then I will be with my forefathers," he said. "If this is not the heaven of the white man, I shall be satisfied."

But Black Elk was nothing if not adaptable, and during the first year of his conversion he attended Mass and learned the Catholic way. The Bible had been translated into Lakota in 1885, and from 1902 to 1904 Father Buechel translated several popular Bible tales. Catholic homilies were fairly standard, emphasizing the commission of sins, the sacraments, and the primacy of the soul over the body. In a place such as Pine Ridge, where death took many forms, sermons never strayed far from mortality. A priest would speak to his flock of the judgment that came after death and the horrors of Hell—its sights, sounds, and smells; its everlasting and unforgiving eternity. A 1917 childrens' sermon delivered by Father Buechel was nearly identical to 1907 discourses delivered to whites in Cleveland and Youngstown. Buechel told about a boy almost killed by snakes, and how close they all were to death and perdition: "We are not rocks, not bugs, not birds, not coyotes, not horses— we are men," he stormed. "Animals live and die and that's the end of them." But men belonged to God, were His property, and must do His will!

In 1905, Black Elk joined the St. Joseph Society, the companion "sodality" to the St. Mary Society for women. These groups filled the gap rent by the ban on all sacred and dancing societies, and were a new avenue for men and women to attain influence within the church and reservation. A new member must be Catholic, know or learn the basic prayers and precepts, attend Mass on Sundays and holy days, and promise not to attend Protestant services. He must go to confession, receive the sacraments four times a year, respect the bishops and priests, baptize his children, and educate them (if possible) in Catholic schools. He should visit the sick, assist in burials, and aid widows and orphans. He must not drink alcohol, and always behave responsibly.

It was time to settle down, and in 1906 Black Elk married again. Anna Brings White was a widow with three young daughters—Agatha, Mary, and Emma Waterman. She was named Between Lodges at birth and called Brings White Horses as a maiden; little else is known of her life before baptism or of her previous marriage. Yet by 1906, she was a member of the St. Mary Society and regularly described by priests as "congenial," something one never heard of the troubled Katie War Bonnet. She was "an attractive example of what a Catholic woman should be." Although Anna's older daughters apparently lived with relatives, she brought with her the youngest, five-year-old Emma. Black Elk brought his two sons by Katie War Bonnet—Johnnie Good Voice Star, age nine, and seven-year-old Benjamin—as well as his widowed mother. That made six in the crowded household. Later that year, Anna gave birth to Lucy, the daughter who became the principal source for information about Black Elk's Catholic days.

According to family lore, it was a good marriage. Black Elk and Anna Brings White built a three-room log house near Manderson; raised horses, pigs, and chickens; and grew potatoes and vegetables. They worked together in the home and church. There is evidence that, when asked, he still healed the sick in the traditional way. People who'd known him as a *wicasa wakan* and *pejuta wicasa* would still come for treatment; when they asked about his new church, he told them.

And he raised cattle. Black Elk would come closer to material wealth in the years 1906–17 than at any other time in his life, and it would all come on the backs of steers. Though no official records document his herd strength, letters suggest that he evolved, like several Oglalas of his generation, into a successful small-time rancher. Prior to conversion, he probably owned a number of horses, since medicine men were paid in ponies: as early as 1889, he spent the hours before the Big Foot Massacre rounding up his ponies that grazed in the hills. On January 29, 1909, a Jesuit priest wrote that Black Elk was "on the way to prosperity—eighty head of cattle coming to him within a year or so." The historian Joseph Agonito claimed that Black Elk owned "fifty head of cattle" in the years "prior to World War I," while in late 1914, he owned thirty-six head of cattle and sixty horses. As late as May 2, 1917, the Pine Ridge agent John R. Brennan indicated that he still owned some cattle. But by 1931, when Neihardt conducted his interviews, Black Elk was destitute, and no sign of a once-healthy herd remained.

———•◦•———

The story of the growth and disappearance of Black Elk's livestock is the story of almost every small-scale Oglala rancher during the first decades of the twentieth century. Pine Ridge was a stockman's paradise: 2.7 million acres of grazeable short-grass prairie that grew stirrup-high with gramma, buffalo, and slender wheat grasses, an especially nutritious forage that retained high protein content even after being cut for hay. There was more grassland at Pine Ridge than at all five other Sioux reservations added together. Immediately after Wounded Knee, in March 1891, the Indian Office contracted for ten thousand cows and four hundred bulls to be delivered to Pine Ridge by that summer. Within two years, stock-raising would be such a significant part of the reservation economy that when Teddy Roosevelt visited in 1893 he wrote: "All over the reservation I was stunned by seeing herds of cattle guarded by Indians, often boys. They locate their herds right around their own neighborhoods and watch over them carefully."

By 1895, the Oglala realized that ranching was the key to prosperity. Visitors saw hills crisscrossed by young Lakotas dressed in "cowboy hats and spurs." Many Oglalas owned large herds, while even the poorest families seemed to have a few head. The numbers exploded from 7,982 in 1891 to 41,000 in 1897, an 80 percent increase in six years. Hard winters winnowed the herd: in 1904, the range held 33,944 cattle and horses, increasing slightly to 34,256 in 1905. Then the herd boomed again, reaching a peak of 60,000 animals by 1910.

But even as the government's cattle initiative showed promise, a second federal program started up that would destroy it entirely. The year of Black Elk's conversion was the year that allotment surveys finally began on Pine Ridge. While most Sioux on the other reservations cooperated, the majority of Pine Ridge Oglala resisted. They distrusted the process and sensed that the division of tribal land into privately owned parcels would somehow destroy the tribes. Stories of resistance were common: one unidentified Lakota put on his war paint and took up his gun when he saw the survey party approach. Agents called such holdouts "kickers," yet when they were told they could also lose government support, such resistance waned.

Nevertheless, the kickers had good reason to suspect government intentions. A patchwork of small, scattered allotments would be unsuitable for the continuous acreage needed for ranching. From 1904 to 1916, the reservation's original 2.72 million acres would be split into 8,275 separate plats totaling 2.38 million acres, with the remainder assigned to the tribe or bought by the federal government for resale.

Black Elk started ranching in 1909 or 1910. He bought eighty head of cattle to augment his pony herd, in all likelihood raising money by selling off chunks of his land. After his marriage to Anna Brings White, this could have totaled 480 acres or more. He was not alone. From September 15, 1903, to June 30, 1904, Oglala landowners sold an average of 8,182 acres a month at $16.83 per acre, in essence selling off land as soon as they got it and using the proceeds to enter the cattle business. Black Elk, like his neighbors, almost certainly sold part of his land for a small windfall and invested that money in stock-breeding.

It seemed a good idea: he was, after all, devoid of income after abandoning his life as a medicine man. But doing so meant economic suicide. Less land meant fewer cattle. It was a given among Montana and Dakota cattlemen that thirty-five to forty acres of grassland were needed to support a cow and her calf. This was called the "carrying capacity of the land." Eighty acres would support 2 cows and 2 calves; 600 acres, 15 cows and 15 calves. Ranchers had learned the hard way that a family could not support itself on herds numbering fewer than 150 to 200 head; of this, only 10 percent annually were sufficiently mature to sell for beef.

The Oglala could not build a self-sustaining cattle business on individual allotments of land. The only way to succeed was to allow the unfettered, free-range grazing of large tribal herds, something their leaders understood quite early. On May 1, 1897, Kicking Bear, Little Wound, and two others wrote the interior secretary asking that "our reservation still be held in common [as] a free range for our cattle." Pine Ridge was perfect grazing land, they said. The White River flowed in the north, many southern creeks streamed into it, and "between these streams the land is high and rolling, and in some places [are] breaks of timber that offer shelter for our cattle during winter storms." All they asked for was government protection: "We want a free range, free water and an opportunity to learn our people to be self-sustaining or rely on their efforts to become men in every sense of the word"—the government's very definition of Indian assimilation. By 1910, when the herd peaked at sixty thousand, the numbers suggested that the government's plan might be working.

Yet others also wanted that land: stockmen grazing their herds to the north in the former "surplus land" above the White River, and to the west between Pine Ridge and the Black Hills. They considered the reservation unused land. Ranchers passed through the borders as if by osmosis: the lure of free grass sucked them in.

Even worse than the threat of illegal grazing was the legal practice of leasing. Hidden within the Dawes Act was language that allowed for an Indian's land to be leased to outside business interests "by reason of age, disability, or inability." "Inability" could mean anything, including simple lack of understanding of English or of the law. Such decisions were made by the agents; the judgments were vulnerable to fraud and graft, and tended to favor white over Indian interests. In 1906, the first land leases were sold—nine one-year leases that allowed the grazing of 969 non-Indian cattle. Little by little after that, the great sea of grass reserved for Indian ranchers was chipped away; in time, the secretary of the interior would admit that allotment had been a dismal failure, opening up the reservations to "white thieves."

When Black Elk entered the business, stock-raising was as good for the Oglala as it would ever get, yet after 1910 herd numbers began to slide. On March 13, 1913, a blizzard killed 30 percent of the herd. In 1916, Oglala ranchers owned 26,755 cattle and horses; in 1920, 13,460; in 1930, the year of Neihardt's arrival, 3,750. These were the years of the "Cattle Ring," which operated in Pine Ridge with a free hand. The Ring had many elements: the agent and his subordinates; white traders; squawmen on the reservation; and members of the Western South Dakota Stock Growers Association (WSDSGA). But the true power behind the Ring was the WSDSGA's vice president, Henry A. Dawson, who'd lived on the reservation and secured the government contract, with Paddy Starr, to bury the massacre victims in the mass grave.

Dawson reportedly knew beef better than anyone in southwest South Dakota, and by 1910 was the state's biggest cattle dealer. Under Dawson and the Ring, outside cattle interests had free rein in Pine Ridge. Their use of allotted and leased land increased from fifty thousand acres in 1913 to more than two million acres in 1918. By 1919, all Oglala land had been leased or applied for. The once-verdant pastures that sustained sixty thousand cattle now became an ecological disaster area under the daily assault of hundreds of thousands of head. Creeks used for drinking water and irrigation were fouled by organic waste; once-nutritious grasses were cropped and trampled out of existence. The devastation was monumental, as great as anything before or after in the nation. The long-term stampede of Ring cattle changed the very face of the land.

No one knows what happened to Black Elk's herd. He may have sold it in 1917–18, when America entered World War I and cattle prices skyrocketed. They may have been driven off to market during the annual roundups, when Indian cattle were mixed and sold with the huge herds of the Newcastle Land and Stock Company or the Matador Land and Cattle Company, both of which leased hundreds of thousands of acres. Of the thousands of Oglalas who'd made their living as ranchers in the early 1900s, only 368 would call themselves that by 1917.

The loss of their cattle was the greatest disaster to befall the Oglala since the destruction of the buffalo. For a second time, the economic foundation of their society was ripped out from under them. When John Neihardt arrived in 1930, all that remained of Black Elk's eighty cattle and sixty horses were a few cows kept on Ben's land in the north, and a big white horse named Baloney that followed Black Elk around like a dog.

———•◦•———

Ultimately, Black Elk's only real success during this period was lay preaching for the Black Robes. Just as his timing was abysmal for entering the cattle industry, it was perfect for ministering to his tribe's spiritual needs. He was as fervent a catechist as he had been a medicine man: once he learned the ritual, it is fair to say that he merely substituted one "church" for another. Black Elk served in this capacity from 1906 until sometime in 1928 or 1929; he traveled around Pine Ridge and to Indian reservations throughout the West, and "according to one of the old missionaries"—probably Eugene Buechel—was "responsible for at least four hundred conversions," statistics that led one Black Robe to declare that "he is the most prominent of all."

In 1906, the Jesuits on the Sioux reservations needed help. Though their missionary work since Wounded Knee had resulted in more converts than that of their Protestant rivals, this meant the priests had to travel long distances to visit every far-flung chapel on the reservation. In Rosebud and Pine Ridge, it took a month to complete this circuit;

the Jesuits could offer Mass only once a month in each tiny village. For the rest of the time, they depended upon Lakota catechists, unordained members of the laity certified to read sermons, conduct religious services, and instruct others in Church doctrines.

From 1900 to 1940, Holy Rosary and St. Francis maintained about ten catechists apiece. On those Sundays when the priest could not visit, the catechist would hold a service in which he preached a sermon, read from the Gospels, and led the worshippers in Lakota prayers and hymns. During Lent, catechists visited the house of each Catholic family to pray and say the rosary. During the rest of the year, they alerted priests about a member's sickness or impending death, gave funeral services when priests could not, exhorted parishioners to stay away from peyote and alcohol, and prayed with Catholics for myriad reasons. They baptized the dying, counseled people with marital problems, taught children about the Church, and tried to convert new Catholics. Showing up to help and pray during a serious illness proved especially effective: families appreciated that a catechist might stay for several days until the sickness passed or the ailing person died. Catechists were always older men, usually married, building upon the Lakota respect for elders. Their pay was small—only five to fifteen dollars a month—but they sometimes received free housing provided through fund drives heralded in the pages of *The Indian Sentinel*, the monthly publication of the Washington-based Bureau of Catholic Indian Missions (BCIM).

To deal with the distances and growing number of converts, the BCIM sent three new Jesuit priests to Pine Ridge and Rosebud in 1904–1906. By 1915, the three would bring the number of chapels from seven to forty, or twenty per reservation. The first two—Fathers Grothe and Grotegeers—suffered from the harsh conditions: Grotegeers would leave early, while Grothe died at age fifty-seven in 1929. The third priest, thirty-one-year-old Henry I. Westropp, had suffered from tuberculosis so badly that he was ordained early for fear that his days were numbered. Ironically, he regained his health in South Dakota, while the other two faded.

For the Oglala, Westropp seemed to represent a new direction among the Black Robes: young, clean-cut, and apparently athletic, he appreciated Lakota humor and tolerated their traditions better than the founding Germans. He felt right at home on Pine Ridge, he once said: the mournful wailing at Lakota funerals sounded like the keening at Irish wakes from his own childhood. Once, when he stayed in a village for Christmas dinner, his host served as the main dish a fat, roasted puppy. Westropp took a couple of ribs, and when he asked what he was eating, was told, "This is a young sheep." But the young priest knew better and after a couple of bites exclaimed: "This young sheep tastes very good; it is even barking in my stomach. Please give me more mutton!" Even the old long-hairs got a chuckle; because of his wit and good nature, the Oglala called Westropp "Little Owl."

Westropp was also able to gently joke with the Oglala women, something no other Black Robe at Pine Ridge seemed capable of during this time. At least, no other examples are recorded. Married women were famously reticent around whites, even more so than men, but Westropp would drive up late from the mission to outside Anna Brings White's tipi and cry "*Tunwin,*" or "Auntie!" She would wake and answer "*Han, mitoska,*" or "Yes, my nephew!"

"Aunt, the ghosts have pushed me here," Westropp would say in Lakota, an expression that conveyed the image of a tired and hungry Indian guided by his guardian spirit to a friendly place where he might get a bite to eat. His quips always amused his hostess, and regardless of the time, Brings White would find something to feed her "nephew" Little Owl.

Westropp would work with several prominent Lakotas during this period: Silas Fills the Pipe, White Crow, John Foolhead, and Joe Big Head, almost all of whom served as catechists for more than twenty years. Yet of them all, claimed Westropp, none was more prominent than the man he called Uncle Nick. "In the whole district where he works," he wrote, "Black Elk's word is law. Nobody can gainsay him."

The change in Black Elk was remarkable, and not a little troubling, for those who see in him a symbol of resistance to change. From the point of view of the Jesuits, Black Elk's rebirth as a catechist was a real coup. It validated everything they'd done since the 1880s. And here is the mystery: on one hand, there is the Black Elk of *Black Elk Speaks,* the proud, defiant, yet despairing warrior mourning all that has passed; on the other hand, Black Elk the Catholic agent, driven to usher the Indian into the white spiritual world. Some said he played a double game—the outward show of piety merely camouflage as he continued the old rites privately.

Yet the record is clear that during this first decade of his conversion, Black Elk was a man on fire. Neither the Ghost Dance nor his Great Vision had saved his people; maybe Catholicism would. The forms were different, but his trust in the holy had not changed. He'd merely cast his lot with a different group of *wicasa wakan*. Sometime in early 1906, little more than a year after conversion, he approached the Jesuits and "desired to become a catechist," Westropp recalled. "If he had done harm in his younger years, he was now going to make up for it, he said." He put away his drum and rattle. "He never talked about the old ways" during this period, said his fellow catechist John Lone Goose. "All he talked about was the Bible and Christ."

To be a catechist, Black Elk had to learn Catholic doctrine, and the first thing the Jesuits handed him was a teaching device called the Two Roads Map. First developed in the 1880s by a French missionary among the Canadian Blackfeet, this was a strip of paper measuring one foot wide and three feet long. Two roads ran along its length. The gold road led to Heaven; the black road, to Hell. Along the road to Heaven were depicted such things as the Creation, the life of Christ, Church milestones, and the Apostles' Creed. The black road was sprinkled with pictures of self-indulgent sinners, bat-winged demons, the Tower of Babel, and the Seven Deadly Sins. Crowds milled everywhere: caught in a natural disaster; consumed by Leviathan; embraced by the Creator; burning in a lake of fire.

The Two Roads Map appealed to the Lakota, since they'd always recorded their history in a similar pictographic fashion in their annual winter counts. It also mystified Black Elk, and probably succeeded in keeping alive for him the validity of his Great Vision. Along both routes were illustrations that seemed plucked from his transformative dream thirty-four years earlier. The parallels included thunder beings; flying men; circled villages, a place where people wept and mourned; the spread wings of angels or eagles; a sacred tree; and the Blue Man of his healing ceremonies, mysteriously surrounded by flames. How could the images be so similar, unless the Lakota and Catholic faiths were different expressions of the same thing? The Ghost Dancers had already gone down a similar path, exclaiming that God the Creator and *Wakan Tanka* were the same; that the Red Christ was simply the Second Coming of Christ as foretold in the Book of Revelations. They'd said as much, loudly, and look what happened to them.

Yet hints did leak out as he taught the Two Roads Map to others that Black Elk suspected the two faiths were similar. The first lay in his description of the two roads. Where other catechists advised potential converts to follow the "yellow" road to Heaven, Black Elk substituted the "good red road" of his vision. His daughter, Lucy, and friend John Lone Goose remembered that he always described the holy road as red. In time, the black road changed in his mind into the path of suffering, not the sure path to Hell. In the Two Roads Map, the parallel roads never touched, though sinners could cross to salvation and saints be tempted to damnation. But in Black Elk's cosmology, the roads *did* cross, and that spot was sacred. On Harney Peak, he later said to *Wakan Tanka*: "The good road and the road of difficulty you have made to cross; and where they cross, the place is holy."

According to Westropp, Black Elk descended upon an area like a whirlwind. "In his neighborhood, conversion follows conversion, and the Black Gown had all he could do to follow in the trail broken by the earnest neophyte," Westropp related. By the summer of 1906, he'd secured a horse and buggy and began traveling to the outlying districts. He proved so persuasive that "there was a great awakening" among the Lakota, and Uncle Nick became known "far and wide." He discovered a gift of oratory on the order of Red Cloud's, and when he preached, "people sat there and just listened to him," recalled Pat Red Elk, a young man during this period. "They could picture what he was talking about," pictures apparently derived from the Two Roads Map and his own Great Vision.

Part of this spontaneity came from his greater experience with the world outside Pine Ridge. He seemed interested in recent history, and would use the flow of events as metaphors in his sermons. In a pastoral letter published in the February 15, 1914, *Sina Sapa Wocekine Taeyanpaha*—or *Catholic Sioux Herald*, the Sioux-language newspaper printed on the Devil's Lake Reservation—he alluded to the sinking of the RMS *Titanic* approximately two years earlier. Rich men built a boat and "said never would the boat sink," but like so many they were blinded by greed and worldly honors, and destroyed. It was the same for his people, he warned: "You do not see when you are struck by something large. You wander about, a ghost that will wander about and sinks. There is a grave sin here. Then you will say 'Lord! Lord!'"

On November 12, 1906, he wrote his first pastoral letter to the *Catholic Sioux Herald*. He'd written open letters before, when in Europe and immediately after coming back, but these were printed in the Protestant *Iapi Oaye* and were mostly observational. This one, finally published in the Catholic organ on March 15, 1907, is significant for a number of reasons. It discusses the state of his health, and how he envisions his role. Most important, it shows how he imagines the state of his people. During the early part of a Catholic retreat, he said,

> I spoke mainly on Jesus—when he was on earth, the teachings and his sufferings. I myself do a lot of these things. I suffer and I try to teach my people the things that I wanted them to learn, but it's never done.
>
> In my sufferings, my eyes are failing, and also my health is failing. So I will tell you that all of you . . . are like sheep among the wolves ready to be eaten up. And you know when one sheep is surrounded by wolves, it has no place to go. That's how we are. We are ready to be eaten up.

"Like sheep among the wolves": the reference might be deliberately blurred, but his readers knew the identity of the circling predators. Red Cloud and Sitting Bull had used similar images—now it was his turn. The only true defense was to "stand together and do what is right and be patient." Take the red road. Endure.

It is interesting also how he describes himself: in constant motion and constant suffering. Not quite Christ-like, but apostolic. The name of the specific apostle will come with time.

"I am going to make this country all Black" like the Jesuits' robes, he would tell Westropp when talking about his work. "I will hammer the devil down tight."

"Yes, Uncle Nick," Westropp answered, "the devil is much afraid of you."

By 1907, Westropp realized the Church could make greater use of this firebrand former medicine man: "Such a man could do a vast amount of good among the other tribes, as well." On June 11, when he suggested to the BCIM director, William H. Ketcham, that Oglala catechists could be used to "missionize" other tribes, he clearly had Black Elk in mind. He claimed that the cost would be minimal, that they would speak to other tribesmen in sign language, and that they could found men's and women's societies like those in Pine Ridge. "I think they could do more good in a way than many a priest," he said.

That year, Black Elk and Westropp attended short conferences outside Pine Ridge, as if to acclimate the catechist to the role. The first was on July 14, 1907, at the annual meeting of the Federation of Catholic Societies in Indianapolis; the second, on September 20, to address newly formed St. Joseph and St. Mary societies in Montana. The second trip was especially difficult, since all communication would have been in sign.

One would expect Black Elk's 1907 letters to the *Sioux Herald* to brim with excitement. Instead, they are sad. On April 16, George Changing, a young man he'd converted, died, "and I really felt bad because his mother really loved him," he says. The next month, a woman named Julia White Crow died. The years and the deaths seem to press down on him: "Every one of us has to die some day," he writes from Manderson on October 20. Though only forty-four, he adds, "I'm very old now, and my days are numbered."

Suddenly, his tone modifies. Before, he'd been inspired, teaching his people a new way to pray. Now, as he visits more deathbeds, his letters grow somber. He did not pick this path, but was selected to it, he says. He once again was Chosen, and the weight that had lifted briefly has settled again. "Remember that I am just a common man like you," he pleads: "So if I should come to your house, don't be afraid of me— because I am one of you."

Westropp knew what he was going through. By 1908, the mission work at Pine Ridge extended over five thousand square miles and covered approximately seven thousand Indians, "nearly half of whom belong to the Catholic Church," Westropp said. This was due in no small part to the labors of Black Elk and his fellow catechists. But when they went out, what did they encounter? They saw "little babies [who] die off so fast when the nursing mothers have only tea to drink" and nothing to eat "but Indian bread and wild turnips." They'd be called to "some old lady of eighty or ninety, lying in an old shack on a squalid quilt or mattress, with hardly enough to eat."

On February 20, 1908, the BCIM sent Black Elk and his fellow catechist Joseph Red Willow to Wyoming's Wind River Reservation to "missionize" the Arapaho. Ketcham allocated a modest seventy dollars to the project; the two took with them their wives. Westropp hoped the little band would stay at least a year, but they returned to Pine Ridge at the end of two months. Black Elk indicated to Westropp and in his letters that they had difficulties at first, especially with language. When Black Elk spoke in Lakota, Red Willow would translate into English, for retranslation into Arapaho. It was a tedious process, foreshadowing

Neihardt's translation difficulties a decade later. There also seemed problems with trust: "We told the Arapaho that we, too, are very poor, and that there is no difference between them and us because we are both Indians," Black Elk wrote. Yet both men called the trip a success.

The assessment was too rosy. On March 29, 1908, Father William McMillen of St. Stephen's Mission in Wind River wrote Ketcham that Black Elk and Red Willow were on the reservation only about a week "when they became discouraged and wanted to leave." The two "could make no impression on our Indians," he said. The language barrier was too daunting. Black Elk left first, on March 19, followed by Red Willow eleven days later. Of the two, McMillen liked Red Willow better: he "shows more manliness, is very devout, not ashamed of his faith, and can command the respect of those he is instructing," he wrote. He thought Red Willow was the better catechist: "Still, you have seen more of them."

Around this period, Black Elk suffered what seems a crisis of confidence. Westropp does not give a date, but says that Black Elk quit his catechist's duties without explanation. Little Owl pressed him for a reason, but he would not say, so the chagrined Westropp accepted his resignation. After the letdown of Wind River, Black Elk may have thought he'd lost his newfound powers; given his bitter disappointment with the Ghost Dance and his Great Vision, he may have been extraordinarily sensitive to what he would consider spiritual failure. Yet in less than a week he bounced back: "He hunted me up and begged me to take him back," Westropp wrote, and the priest gladly reinstated him.

The mission work continued. He wanted to go to the Crow reservation, but the posting fell through. Instead, in early November 1908, Ketcham asked that Black Elk and Red Willow be sent to the Winnebago reservation in Nebraska. Once again, they returned within a month. Though Ketcham had allocated a mere sixty dollars, he wrote on December 12 that these supposed missionaries seemed to be taking advantage of free travel funds. "To the onlooker it would appear that I have become a bureau for traveling Indians," he penned in obvious frustration.

But after these false starts, Black Elk hit his stride. Between 1909 and 1916, he would be called away to missions among the Shoshone, the Omaha, the six Sioux tribes in the Dakotas, the Yankton reservation at Sisseton, South Dakota, and "the tribe living in California and Florida." During his year at Yankton, he and the catechist Ivan Star built the congregation to 138 members. The Assiniboine in Canada—who'd

once tried to kill him—asked him to visit, but Ketcham pled poverty.
Black Elk preached in New York, Boston, Washington, Chicago, Lincoln, and Omaha. In some white towns, people threw tomatoes or rot-
ten eggs, but in others *wasichus* listened. In 1913, he spoke to the
inmates of Sing Sing. "You white people, you came to our country," he
told the prisoners. "You came to this country, which was ours in the
first place. We were the only inhabitants. After we listened to you, we
got settled down. But you're not doing what you're supposed to do—
what our religion and our Bible tells us. I know this. Christ himself
preached that we love our neighbors as ourselves. Do unto others as you
would have others do unto you."

He was a "show man" again, this time for the Catholics, but he did
not mind. This was the period when he converted close to four hundred
people, and the sheer numbers told him that he'd been chosen to do
good. Westropp and he called these trips "spiritual scalping-tours."
Once, at the end of a trip, they were drawing close to the home of the
catechist Silas Fills the Pipe. "Little Owl," he said to Westropp, "let us
sing the war song, the song of victory." Black Elk sang the lyrics from a
former life; then Westropp and he ended with a few *whoop*s.

Silas threw open his door. "I thought the way you sang that you had
killed some people."

"Yes," Black Elk replied, "we have taken the scalps of a few devils."

<hr />

Yet during this period of triumph, he was severely tried. Beginning in
1909, most of his children would die, one by one. His first son by Katie
War Bonnet—William Never Showed Off—had died in 1895 or 1897;
now his second son by Katie, nine-year-old Good Voice Star, "died
quietly" of tuberculosis on March 17, 1909. "I have lost a good boy,"
he writes four months later, on July 15. That same summer, "my sister
died," he wrote in a letter dated September 7, 1909. He does not mention her name. One year later, Anna's daughters Agatha and Mary Waterman died of TB, as did Black Elk's newborn son, Henry. He sent his
surviving children, Ben and Lucy, to boarding schools as much to escape the "coughing sickness" as to prepare them for the white man's
world. This strategy must have worked, for neither contracted the disease. His mother died in 1915 at age seventy-one; she'd moved in with
Black Elk after the death of Good Thunder, and had probably converted
to Catholicism around the same time as her son.

Three sons, two stepdaughters, a wife, a sister, and a mother—eight deaths in fourteen years, the majority clustered in 1909–10. Near the end of this period, disease comes for him. On January 12, 1912, he wrote Ketcham that in six more days he would be checking into the Hot Springs Indian Sanitarium for the treatment of TB. He was in critical condition, he said: "I beg you to find me a little help and would like to hear from you, too." If he survived and regained his health, "I will again look into our business among my Catholic Sioux's."

But he was probably in despair. Forty percent of Pine Ridge's 7,000 Oglalas, or about 2,800, were tubercular, and the death rate was 35 per 1,000. It was estimated that 30 percent of all deaths among Indians in the United States were due to TB, while the death rate among whites was 11 percent. The disease lodged in the lungs; grew in the glands of the neck, which broke open to run with yellow fluid; grew in the bones of the back, hip, ankle, knee, wrist, and elbow, turning one into a cripple. For many, admittance to the sanitarium meant a death sentence.

Black Elk gave his letter to Father Buechel, who passed it to Ketcham after adding some comments of his own. Black Elk's personal entreaties to Ketcham for money would often draw an instant rebuke from the priests. They'd trained him to appeal for donations for the construction of new chapels, yet when he asked Ketcham for help, that was "begging." In 1909, when he'd petitioned the monsignor for extra funds for the Winnebago mission, Westropp advised, "To make him one present would plant a weed in his soul. . . . Begging has become a passion with many of these fellows." He added then that eighty head of cattle would be coming in about a year. Now Buechel pitched in, even more harshly: "He will always be a beggar, no matter how much one would give him. At the end of last [Catholic Indian] Congress, I gave him $10.00 for extra work done. The next day he begged again for he had distributed the money among the visitors from Standing Rock. He never has anything and always asks for something. Poor fellow! And yet he can do a great deal and has done much in the past." If Ketcham did send money, Buechel added, he should do so care of the hospital's sisters, since they would serve as Black Elk's money managers.

Buechel's letter shows a misunderstanding of Lakota ways. By giving his money to the "visitors from Standing Rock," Black Elk had practiced the Christian virtue of charity. Yet he'd also donned the traditional mantle of leadership: a chief helped his people and gained their respect by giving away almost everything. "In a significant sense," wrote the scholar Raymond DeMallie, "effective leadership for the Lakota shifted from the early reservation period from political to religious spheres." He was a chief without ever being named chief, one of the few hints that he hadn't abandoned the old values.

Black Elk survived the sanitarium, but he had changed. The stay in Hot Springs was his closest brush with death, at least in his eyes. The two long comas were not mortal, just periods of physical hibernation in which he visited the spirit world. The blood-sickness he'd felt at the Greasy Grass and the near-fatal wound he'd received after the Big Foot Massacre were merely part of the glory and madness of war. But death by the coughing sickness had ripped through his family and left it in tatters; he'd suffer from tuberculosis for the rest of his life, and it left him with a lingering sense of doom. Before his trip to Hot Springs, he'd always felt he could "whip the devil," whether as a catechist or a medicine man. But after Hot Springs he realized that nothing could beat the White Plague.

Now he began to write as never before, and again Westropp pointed him in a particular direction. "Ever since his conversion," Westropp wrote, Black Elk "has been a fervid apostle and he has gone around like a second St. Paul, trying to convert his tribesmen to Catholicity." In another article, Little Owl said the former medicine man had "the zeal of a St. Paul." It is easy to see how an eager young Jesuit such as Westropp would make the connection: how Saul—the zealous persecutor of Christians, reborn as Paul the Apostle—would resemble to Westropp Black Elk, the leading medicine man of Pine Ridge reborn as Nick Black Elk, the most effective Indian evangelist of his day. And Black Elk willingly assumed the role given to him by his friend.

In some ways, he was already primed. As far back as the fall of 1889 he'd shown curiosity in the apostle, soon after returning home from Paris. In his second open letter to *Iapi Oaye*, published finally in December 1889, he wrote of the *wasichus'* faith, which "I wanted to understand." He expressed a desire to visit the Holy Land "where they killed Jesus . . . but it was four days in the ocean and there was no railroad," and such a trip required more money than he could spare. Suddenly, in the middle of the letter, he wrestled with Christian precepts out of the Epistles of Paul. "Though I speak with the tongues of men and angels, and have not charity, I am become as a sounding brass, or a tinkling cymbal," he writes, quoting the famous passage from I Corinthians

13:1–3: "And though I have the gift of prophecy, and understand all mysteries, and all knowledge, and though I have all faith, so that I could remove mountains, and have not charity, I am nothing. And though I bestow all my goods to feed the poor, and though I give my body to be burned, and have not charity, it profiteth me nothing."

Though his early curiosity in Paul had been snuffed out by Wounded Knee, it was now rekindled by his new missionary zeal. Westropp's comparison would inspire the imaginations of later Catholic commentators, long after the young priest had left the scene. One wonders also whether it planted the seed for the current movement to deem Black Elk a saint; the contention by Westropp that the former medicine man was responsible for more than four hundred conversions certainly contributed. In 1947, Sister Mary Claudia Duratschek would write that "after his conversion, like a second St. Paul, Black Elk went around trying to convert his tribesmen whom, before his conversion, he had helped shackle in the fetters of paganism." Though Black Elk was indeed inspired by the image of shackles, the chains he imagined were not forged by his old religion.

One sees the Pauline influence throughout Black Elk's letters to the Sioux. From 1907 to 1916, he wrote at least twenty open pastoral letters in Lakota that were published in *Sina Sapa Wocekine Taeyanpaha*. Six of these have never been translated; another five are missing. The question of their exact production is difficult: Black Elk was a literate man, and could read the Bible and Catholic liturgy in Lakota. "Though half blind he had by some hook or crook learned to read and he knows his religion thoroughly," Westropp marveled. At another point he wrote, "He is nearly blind, and it was edifying to see him read the prayers with his eyes one or two inches from the book—for despite his poor sight, he has learned to read."

Yet his English was bad: "I do not talk English well," Black Elk wrote in 1908. And his self-written letters were garbled. Thus, he dictated his letters, and the elegance of the finished product depends upon his scribes. But if there is an inconstancy of style, there is over time a development of theme. He creates an epistolary persona modeled on Paul, and like the apostle's, his letters are pedagogic and avuncular. He appeals more to tradition than to theology, a commonsense approach the Lakota can understand. Religion was a means to power—over enemies, fate, the random blows of a cruel world. If one stood in the center of the sacred hoop, one was part of its flow. The Christian idea of agape might have seemed similar. Love "bears all things"—famine, death, the destruction of one's culture and land. It bears its own crucifixion and, passing through death, gains a power entirely new to the world.

In fact, Paul would be the only apostle either quoted or referenced in Black Elk's letters, and like Paul, he used himself as an example. "When I was given this job, I did not want it," he wrote in October 1909, "but you people here encouraged me to take on this job . . . so I need your help." On November 2, 1911, he writes in language reminiscent of Paul's letters to struggling Christians:

> Remember the words you have said in making declarations. You speak the words but your lives are lives of the old way. Therefore my relatives, unify yourselves. Perhaps you cannot live lives split in two, which does not please God. Only one church, one God, one Son, and only one Holy Spirit—that way you have only one faith, you have only one body, and you have only one life and one spirit. Thus we have three but really we have One—thus he who unifies himself will have victory.

As we do of Paul in his Epistles, we learn of Black Elk's trials. He loses his son, contracts TB, is slowly going blind. And just as the Great Vision examined that sacred place where the red and black roads crossed, Black Elk often returns, like Paul, to the crossing of salvation and suffering. The Christian who suffers shall be rewarded. The Indian *has* suffered, and will be consoled.

Oddly enough, the Pauline Epistle most similar to Black Elk's theme is the one he never directly references. Of Paul's thirteen Epistles, the least known is his letter to Philemon. Except for 2 John, it is the shortest book of the Bible, and is the Epistle in which Paul famously calls himself a "prisoner of Christ." It concerns the fate of Onesimus, a wayward slave who fled the household of Philemon, a fellow Christian and Paul's friend. Paul is in prison when he writes: he has met and converted Onesimus behind bars, calls him "a part of my own self," and sends him back to Philemon with the request that his friend accept him "not as a slave," but as something more—as a fellow Christian and "dear brother." Surprisingly, he does not ask Philemon to set Onesimus free.

Like Paul, Black Elk loved the grand metaphor: it was central to both men's rhetorical style. The sinking *Titanic* was the doomed ship of greed and pride. The plight of the newly baptized Indian was like the

first steps and spills of a toddler. The most significant Pauline metaphor
for the Christianized Indian was that of the prisoner: the reservation
was his jail; the *wasichu*, his jailer. In Paul's world, Romans are the
masters. In Black Elk's world, the Lakota must survive their white-
forged chains. Yet neither directly attacks the status quo. Both focus on
the slave.

In Paul's world, all men were equal in the eyes of God, just as all
slaves were equal in the eyes of the master. Black Elk concurred, with
one big change. If God leveled all men after death, suffering provided a
foretaste. All were alike in affliction, and the United States was a nation of pain. He had seen a "number of different people" in his travels,
he wrote: the "ordinary people of this earth," even the "white men living
in all these places [and] I have said prayers for their tribe." He'd counseled the prisoners in Sing Sing; he'd seen the insane at Blackwell's
Island; he'd come to know that the poor were everywhere. And he'd
reached a conclusion:

"We all suffer in this land."

Then it all stopped, another of those sudden shifts that so characterized
Black Elk's life. In 1916, all the things that made him famous among
Indian catechists came to an end—the trips to national conferences,
long missions to other reservations, even the pastoral letters. The cessa-
tion was as abrupt as his conversion in 1904. Part of the reason could
have been familial: the mission trips were of long duration, and Anna
Brings White bore a son, Nick Jr., in 1914. Black Elk's blindness could
have played a role: in 1917, Pine Ridge's agent, John Brennan, wrote to
the superintendent at Carlisle that Black Elk was "practically blind."
His last "foreign" posting was at Ravinia, on the Yankton reservation,
which he visited for long periods during 1913–16. After that, he stayed
at Pine Ridge.

The primary reason, however, was Westropp's reassignment to Patna,
India. During World War I, British authorities asked all German and
Austrian Jesuits to leave India, and in 1916 a wave of younger American
and British priests replaced the older pioneers. Little Owl was forty-one
and found himself in conditions much like those of Pine Ridge a decade earlier: India, he said, was a "burning land" of poverty, mysterious
spirituality, death, and disease.

To Black Elk, Little Owl's reassignment was a personal loss. His sadness may have shown: from now until 1930, Black Elk worked increasingly with Father Buechel and the Swiss-born Father Placidus Sialm, who came to Holy Rosary in 1901 as headmaster of the mission school. Finally ordained in 1906, Sialm bounced among western reservations before landing back in Pine Ridge in 1914. An early photo suggests an imposing man: he glares at the camera from horseback, face framed by heavy brows and a dark, square-cut beard. After Westropp left, Sialm's chief work became the supervision of Indian camps and outlying mission stations, yet he retained the post of children's confessor at Holy Rosary—which meant that Black Elk and his son Ben would get to know him well.

Yet diary entries suggest that Black Elk worked primarily with Buechel, who apparently handled most of the home visits during the late 1910s and the 1920s. The work could be tragic and harrowing, reminiscent of battlefield triage. On November 6, 1918, Buechel writes of a nighttime emergency call to baptize a dying "Mrs. Brass," but he got there too late: "I found her dead. As she was still warm, I gave Extreme U." On November 7–10, he gives last sacraments to a number of dying, one after the other, probably from the Spanish influenza. On June 21, 1921, he is called to the bedside of eighteen-year-old Leah Rook: "There she lay, all emaciated, nothing but skin and bone," he wrote. "Her face had grown quite small." He assures her that she will go to Heaven; when it was over, "I went home with a heart full of sorrow." In June 1923, he visits the scene of a woman murdered in her home; the next month, of a man poisoned by moonshine.

Black Elk is often beside him, exhorting, admonishing, praying, baptizing. The dead and dying pile up; the bedside prayers never end. In 1928 alone, Buechel records how the two of them exhort Joe Red Bear, "Rocky Mountain," James Thunder Club, Scabby Face, and Sarah Bear Horse. They baptize Clara Thunderbird and admonish the backsliding Joe Thunder Club. Black Elk sponsors the newborn babies Oliver Little and Wilbur John Blacksmith, and is well-known by the other faiths: on April 29, the Presbyterian catechist Blue Cloud asks his congregation, "Do you consider Black Eagle and Black Elk God?" It is hard to know this statement's context, but considering the fierce competition for converts among faiths, it is doubtful they were praising him. More likely, Blue Cloud "must be worked up," Buechel writes. "No reason for such a question."

Yet the Black Robes desperately wanted to keep Black Elk, and in

1921 Buechel appointed him permanent catechist at Oglala, a small village west of Manderson and north of Holy Rosary. He now had less supervision from the priests, more autonomy. Some of his old confidence must have returned, for during a three-day retreat during Holy Week 1922, he presented a resolution that read, "We catechists resolve never to commit a mortal sin." Black Elk would attend eight retreats, and play a prominent role in each one. That year saw the death of Father Lindebner, the Black Robe who'd converted Black Elk; the priest was famous for his spit-shined boots, which he changed every time he entered an Indian home. Black Elk asked if he could keep those boots as a way to remember Lindebner.

In 1925, the BCIM's *Indian Sentinel* published a 1910 photo taken by Buechel of Black Elk sitting before his cabin in Manderson. He is dressed in his worn vested suit with the stiff collar and tie; he sits on a split bench, displaying a rosary to Lucy and holding a crucifix out to her. Lucy kneels on the ground with her hands folded in prayer. With her cotton dress and braids, she represents the new generation of Catholic Indian; Black Elk, the old.

The next year, the editors made sure their readers got the message. The same photo was displayed on the cover of the Fall 1926 issue, but redrawn. Now, Black Elk wears a buckskin suit and large war bonnet of eagle feathers. Once again, he hands a rosary and crucifix to a child. The issue was widely circulated on the reservations, and the symbolism was blatant. The old Indian ways had passed, replaced by Christianity. The message must have been effective: the Sioux catechists' retreat that year attracted two dozen men, more than ever before.

That year, the Church built a new catechist's home in Oglala, far nicer than the one in Manderson: painted wood shingles rather than hand-hewn logs, white-trimmed windows with glass, a pitched tar-paper roof, and three rooms instead of one. Black Elk, Anna Brings White, and their younger children moved to the house, while their older children maintained the allotment near Manderson. Lucy Black Elk would grow up in Oglala and considered it home. The house became the center of missionary activity, where people came to sing and pray; where Black Elk acted as village priest and local chief, all rolled into one.

By 1930, the year John Neihardt pulled his dust-covered Gardner to a stop in front of "a sort of a preacher," the Jesuit fathers at Pine Ridge liked to point to Nicholas Black Elk as the perfect example of a "civilized savage."

24

VANISHING AMERICANS

Clearly something preyed on Black Elk the day Neihardt rolled to the end of the road. Although he was not specifically waiting for the poet, he *was* awaiting a sign—the same intuitive hint through which shamans interpreted meaning. Neihardt's arrival was phenomenologically no different from the cloud of butterflies dusting him on the hilltop or the thunderclouds booming approval at the Horse Dance. All was connected. There were no coincidences.

He'd been searching a long time, and by 1930 was no longer the unquestioning Catholic the Jesuits believed him to be. As early as 1916, the year Westropp left, Black Elk began performing the old ceremonial dances after a hiatus of twelve years. That year, fifty-two Pine Ridge Oglalas—thirty-two men, fifteen women, and five children—were selected to dance in the annual Cheyenne Frontier Days parade, then in its eighteenth year. At the time, this was the largest western celebration in existence; if this was not the first time Oglalas participated, it was apparently their largest showing. Black Elk took the train to Cheyenne with such long-hairs as Flying Hawk, White Bull, and Long Soldier. With them was Black Elk's nephew Frank Fools Crow.

Fools Crow was either twenty-four or twenty-six, and by the 1970s would be the ceremonial chief of the Oglala. In 1916, he was just starting his training as a medicine man, and Black Elk was one of his primary mentors. If Black Elk belonged to the first generation of *wicasa wakan* to convert to Christianity, Fools Crow was part of the first group raised in both Christian and traditional ways. Uncle and nephew were close: Black Elk "was also a father to me," Fools Crow said. He would have known of his nephew's involvement in the medicine underground, and encouraged it, even during his most fervent catechist period.

On this trip, Black Elk took him aside. "He told me that as a medicine man I would learn many sacred secrets and perform countless ceremonies for people." Travel such as this was important: as he participated in dance competitions and toured with Wild West shows, "word of my healing and prophetic power would spread." Doubters would challenge him to prove himself, but he must stay hidden from the eyes of the *wasichu*. The modern *wicasa wakan* must lead a double life. Even a glimpse of one's powers could be disastrous.

These were not secrets revealed to the Jesuits, even to Westropp. In fact, this suggests that even during those years when he converted four hundred Indians to the Church, Black Elk was a practicing, if well-hidden, *wicasa wakan*. If not, then 1916 can be seen as a pivotal year, and even then, he kept the truth hidden from the Jesuits until his first public performance in Pine Ridge.

Ironically, this occurred with the Church's full knowledge. In 1922, Father Sialm organized the first annual Corpus Christi Sunday procession at Oglala's mission church, where Black Elk presided. Over a thousand Lakotas attended. Sialm led the procession, dressed in full priestly garb; he carried the monstrance with the consecrated host, while four Lakota men bore a canopy overhead. Back in line, Black Elk led the long hairs, all dressed in native finery.

Though this union of the old and new was as blatant as the later *Indian Sentinel* photo of Black Elk presenting a rosary to Lucy, it indicated a dawning realization. The death of the old ways was killing the Sioux. Even the Church could see this after thirty years of repression. But the new, guarded openness did not come easily: the Indian Office proposed allowing "innocent" dances—those that did not last too long, encourage "licentiousness," or allow drinking—but limiting their frequency to three or four times a year. All did not agree. Father Henry Grotegeers, Holy Rosary's superior from 1916 to 1920, believed the dances led to sin and broken marriages. Father Louis Gall suggested that the best way for whites to discourage dancing was by mockery: "Where persuasion fails to have any effect," he wrote in January 1923, "ridicule often triumphs."

By now, Black Elk was already performing isolated "Indian shows" in the Black Hills. Exactly when these started is not known, yet his prominence as a catechist and legacy as a "show man" seemed to have worked an alchemy. In addition, as the Black Robes relaxed their strictures against Indian dances, Black Elk was repeatedly asked to perform.

Black Elk's rediscovery of the old ways coincided with the growth of tourism. The 1920s was the great decade of Black Hills boosterism, thanks to the growth of the automobile. In 1900, when South Dakota first considered turning Wind Cave into a national park, there were only 8,000 registered autos in the United States. By 1910, that number had jumped to 350,000; by 1920, to 7.5 million, and private ownership of autos had reached 7 percent of all households. By the end of that decade, when Highway 87 was built between Wind Cave and Custer State Park, the numbers had grown to 23 million cars and 20 percent of households. The American family could jump in its car and go anywhere, and suddenly the auto shortened the distance between the city and what people called "wild." With no sense of irony, a 1917 article in *Sunset* magazine extolled driving through a scenic area as "an elemental contact with the reality of nature."

Although the Black Hills had been a destination since the 1890s, the number of tourists now exploded. In 1916, when the National Park Service was established, Wind Cave received an estimated 9,000 annual visitors. By 1928, that number increased to 100,309. In 1910, most visitors hired motor coaches from Hot Springs to visit the cave; by 1923, 92 percent of its visitors arrived by private automobile, a number that rose to nearly 100 percent by 1929.

The big draw for this new breed of tourist was Mount Rushmore. First conceived in the early 1920s by the state historian Doane Robinson, it was seen as a way to draw tens of thousands of motorists to the Black Hills. Robinson had heard of a forty-eight-foot concrete Indian placed above Illinois' Rock River; he wondered if a larger monument could be carved into the twisted granite upthrusts called the Needles, and proposed that it be of "some notable Sioux as Redcloud, who lived and died in the shadow of these peaks." In 1924, he contacted the sculptor Gutzon Borglum, then carving Confederate generals into Stone Mountain, Georgia. Borglum took a train to Rapid City, and Robinson's original idea evolved into the pantheon of presidents at Mount Rushmore.

Like other Oglalas, Black Elk never discarded the faith in Sioux ownership of the Hills. In 1923, the Lakota tribal lawyer Richard Case argued in the U.S. Court of Claims that the 1877 seizure of Paha Sapa was illegal; that, in fact, the nation never made a legitimate purchase of the land. The Sioux would come to the Hills in spring and summer to pluck medicinal plants, harvest lodgepoles, and visit favorite places. Now, as tourist traffic increased, they saw that a new invasion had begun. Yet this time many turned it to their advantage. They found new ways to supplement their incomes: some sold handmade crafts, while others performed in informal "Indian shows" along heavily traveled routes, much like buskers today.

Mount Rushmore was the invasion's vortex, and Black Elk would bend the national monument to his own ends. When Rushmore was officially dedicated on October 1, 1925, a few hundred people watched as a lone Indian in headdress and buckskins was photographed at the top, his arms spread in benediction. Though the man remained unidentified, many think it was Black Elk atop the mountain. If so, it was the beginning of a forty-eight-year connection that would continue after his death and pass down to his son.

The next year, on June 25, 1926, Black Elk attended the fiftieth anniversary of the Custer Massacre. About eighty Sioux and Cheyenne veterans attended, including White Bull and his cousin Standing Bear, all dressed in traditional clothes. The Seventh Cavalry's military band hid out of sight in the ravine where Black Elk had taken his second scalp; they played a funeral dirge as two columns—army, led by General E. S. Godfrey, and Indian, led by White Bull—marched to the national cemetery near the top of Massacre Hill. White Bull gave the general his blanket; Godfrey gave White Bull a large American flag. Black Elk heard a roar and saw overhead a formation of army biplanes.

He gazed at the white gravestones, perfectly aligned. He could still smell the copper taint of blood of the soldiers slaughtered where the band now played; could hear the grinding of the soldier's teeth as he took that first scalp down in the valley. Historians and journalists swarmed like midges, bargaining for the tribesmen's memories. For some, this was the first time they'd dared reveal their role; others, like Standing Bear, had already broken that silence. But when the curious came to him, Black Elk shook his head. Beware the white man with his questions. They never stopped; they always wanted more.

It was during this period that Black Elk started down a path that he hoped held promise for his people. Unlike the other journeys, this was a return. After the benediction atop Rushmore and ceremonies at the Greasy Grass, the man whom the Jesuits called a perfect "civilized savage" regained in earnest what he'd abandoned. That same year as the Custer memorial, he danced again at Holy Week; that summer, he performed for the boys' camp at St. Francis Mission. The more he performed, the more he remembered how he'd excelled at these dances. It was only on the red road, when his people danced freely, that they had been happy and whole.

It was probably the beginning of doubt, a feeling he'd suppressed during his travels with Westropp as the "Indian St. Paul." Then, he'd had neither the time nor the inclination to consider the rightness of his work: his new religion seemed strong medicine, and his work with Little Owl brought peace to the converted. But Catholicism had also brought them an acceptance of poverty, sickness, and death, not a way to alleviate such ills.

Life had not improved for America's Indians after more than five decades on the reservation. Though their population had increased—from 244,000 nationwide in 1880 to 330,000 in 1930—in every other index the quality of life had plummeted. Existence was little more than a continual state of emergency. Food shortages were commonplace: severe droughts in 1925 and 1926 forced missions to order boxcarloads of potatoes, flour, and vegetables. Rosebud's St. Francis fed and clothed 450 children on a consignment for 380. From the fall of 1926 to the winter of 1927, "there was wholesale sickness and many deaths in Pine Ridge and Rosebud," noted the local *Province News Letter*.

The most damning assessment came from the government itself. A detailed seven-month survey in 1926 of conditions in ninety-five reservations, Agencies, hospitals, and schools by the Institute for Government Research (which the following year became known as the Brookings Institution), confirmed what people already suspected: life on the reservations was abysmal. The infant mortality and general death rates were high; incomes were among the lowest in the United States, with more than 71 percent of residents earning less than two hundred dollars annually; Indian schools were inadequate and often little better than prisons. The 847-page *The Problem of Indian Administration*, published in 1928 and called the "Meriam Report" after the project manager, Lewis Meriam, asked Indian Office employees: "How can these people eke out an existence?"

Several replied that it was hardly to be called an existence.
Others said that they did not know the answer; that they had
never been able to figure it out. The standard of living is often
almost unbelievably low. Almost nothing is spent for shelter
and firewood, and very little for clothing and food. Many homes
were visited where there was almost no food on hand. The
homes where a reserve of food had been accumulated were the
exception. Many Indians are just above the famine level, and if
anything goes wrong they must go without or fall back upon government rations.

Pine Ridge's 7,820 Indians made an annual average of eighty-six dollars in 1926, the twelfth-lowest rate among all reservations surveyed.
Buried near the end of the report was the brief observation that the
failure to utilize Indian religions and ethics was a "common failure"
throughout the nation.

In 1926, when the survey staff came through Pine Ridge, Black Elk
was living at Oglala with Anna Brings White, his nineteen-year-old
daughter, Lucy, and his twelve-year-old son, Nick Jr. By Pine Ridge
standards, life there was palatial. While recalling these days to Michael
Steltenkamp, Lucy painted the life and her sixty-three-year-old father
in pastels. Once, while returning to Ogala on the back of Father Grotegeers's motorcycle, they discovered that the brakes had failed. They
could not stop: they drove around a racetrack before crashing into a
bank down the road. Black Elk had wondered all the time why they
kept going: "You nearly killed me!" he cried. Blindness figured often in
her tales: her father stood ten feet from the house, crying for help
because he could not see; he grabbed Anna's coat instead of his own
and wore it while leading prayers. He came home on a dark night atop
their "big white horse Baloney" and dismounted to open the corral gate.
But when he turned, a "white ghost with big black eyes was right behind
him—looking at him. My father real quickly punched that ghost in the
nose, and was he surprised to see Baloney run off! You see, he didn't
realize that Baloney had followed him to the gate and had turned to
face him. That horse didn't come back until the next day."

Lucy saw these tales as little more than humorous incidents, and
painted her father as a kind of lovable, scatterbrained character—a
Mr. Magoo of Pine Ridge. Steltenkamp saw the stories hearkening back
to the intentional "contrary" humor of the *heyoka*. Yet there is another

interpretation. Things happened to Black Elk—whether due to blindness, bad engineering, or wandering ghosts—that were out of his control. Life was like that for many at Pine Ridge.

One theme haunting the nation's conscience during this period was the belief that the Indian was dying out—that he was the "Vanishing American." The idea had been a current in early American thought when disease and removal from tribal lands began to cut into native numbers; it gained traction from 1860 to 1920 as "assimilation" seemed destined to obliterate the tribes. Now, with the observance of Custer's defeat, the idea found new urgency among scholars. European and American anthropologists rushed to collect information on traditional tribal language, culture, and religion. Historians scoured the reservations in search of the last survivors of the Indian wars. Many households owned some version of Cyrus Dallin's 1908 *Appeal to the Great Spirit*, the famous sculpture in which a brave sits astride his horse, head thrown back, arms outspread and palms up, the message one of grief and supplication: it would be duplicated in postcards, prints, and plaster replicas. The message took further root with the publication of Zane Grey's *The Vanishing American*, first released in 1922–23 as a serial in *Ladies' Home Journal*, then as a novel by Harper & Brothers in 1925; it was the first work of fiction to paint a harsh picture of the treatment of Indians by government agencies. Grey portrayed missionaries as vultures preying upon a dying race, a depiction that sparked angry letters from Indian "friends" and the Bureau of Indian Affairs. The book was a bestseller, and spawned a 1925 silent film starring Richard Dix as the doomed Navajo leader Nophaie. The 1928 release of the Meriam Report cemented the impression that these were the last days of the American Indian.

A strange obsession among professional and armchair historians drew Black Elk into its orbit, through no fault of his own. As the Custer observance approached and more Indian combatants opened up, people began to realize how important Crazy Horse had been for the Indian victory. A hunt began for all things undisclosed about the war chief: two grail quests developed—one for his photo, one for his grave. At least five "authentic" photos and one full-face sketch of Crazy Horse would surface, and all would be proven frauds.

The grave was another matter. It was known to be located somewhere between Manderson and Wounded Knee. Various rumors had been published ever since Worm carried his son's body into the hills, but four in particular gained credence, and today a sign placed along U.S. Highway 18 about seven miles south of Wounded Knee indicates these possibilities. Yet when fortune hunters came to search, they ran into a wall of secrecy. When Eleanor Hinman and Mari Sandoz tried their luck in 1930, they learned that many of Crazy Horse's friends and descendants considered them "spies sent from Washington to fix the blame for the late Massacre." The old suspicions remained. Lakotas had heard that anyone who'd fought at the Little Bighorn would be fined ten thousand dollars, the funds deducted from any future settlement reached over Sioux claims to the Black Hills.

Up to this point, Black Elk hovered at the fringes of the *wascihus'* western narrative. He existed in the records, but was not widely known. He was barely acknowledged in the Ghost Dance records; identified as Choice in the Wild West rosters; lauded by the Jesuits, but only sporadically. He was not a historical presence in the national epic. Now, because of his blood relationship to Crazy Horse, experts called. The first was apparently the historian Walter M. Camp, who wrote to him around 1914; he sent a letter to Manderson, saying he was the man who took his photo among a bunch of catechists at the White River Congress "last year." He said he'd heard that Black Elk was Crazy Horse's cousin, and asked the name of his father and that of Tasunke Witko's. Black Elk never replied.

Sometimes other relatives spoke candidly about Crazy Horse, as shown by the 1930 response of Red Feather, the war chief's brother-in-law. "I will tell you the true facts about Crazy Horse because I am a Catholic now and it is part of my religion to tell the truth," Red Feather said. He implied that others usually lied. But Black Elk would simply clam up when a stranger approached, as can be seen in a portrait sketched by Eleanor Hinman in an undated letter to her friend the future author Mari Sandoz. She described Black Elk as tall, slender, and lithe, with a dark complexion and what she sensed to be a "forceful personality." He was chatting with the Manderson storekeeper when Hinman drove up, so she had a chance to observe him for a minute or two:

> The day before we called on him, Black Elk's farm wagon had broken down. So it happened that when I called, Black Elk was at a neighbor's, borrowing tools to fix the wagon. He either saw or was told of the fliver approaching his house, so he came running

across the flat and up the hill to meet us, a distance of about half a mile, his tools in his hands. Although he must have been nearly sixty years old at the time, he ran like a young man, and was scarcely even out of breath when he reached us. In his work overalls, smiling and waving a tire tool in greeting, he looked at the moment very modern—quite the friendly farmer, in fact. He had the same long mobile type of face which seems to have been characteristic of the men of this family, and fine eyes—very dark, very expressive, very Sioux—not the "beady" sort but long, liquid, straight, set to far distances, and deeply crows' footed at the corners. Neihardt insists that at this date he was already commencing to lose his vision, but it certainly did not show at this time, either in his appearance or in his manner.

Yet when she asked about Crazy Horse, the affability vanished. Then she saw a dark, sad look that reminded her of the legendary warrior. Either then or during the follow-up, he demanded two hundred dollars for his tale and Hinman turned him down. She later said she thought Neihardt "advised Black Elk to take this attitude," but this is mistaken, since, according to Flying Hawk, Hinman got to the old medicine man first.

He would adopt an entirely different attitude when Neihardt arrived.

———•◦•———

Life would change drastically for Black Elk in the course of a year. Census records suggest that in 1929, he still lived in the relatively spacious mission house in Oglala. Given that this was built by the Church, the lot almost certainly included a well and a privy. He enjoyed the prestige of the catechist's life, the extra income of five to fifteen dollars a month, and the donations filtering through Holy Rosary from the BCIM. He was an important man in the community.

But sometime before April 11, 1930, all that changed. Comments by priests suggest his eyesight had deteriorated to where he could no longer fulfill his catechist duties. He moved back to the one-room log cabin in Manderson. The 1930 census lists nine people living in this cabin; in addition to Black Elk, Anna, and Lucy, his son Benjamin lived there with his wife and their first four (of six) children—Henry, Katherine, Esther, and Olivia. Nick Jr. was not listed in the census, and probably tended what remained of the family herd at Cuny Table. When Neihardt arrived four months later, he saw only the single cabin on the allotment, partway up a barren hill. The interior was stark: a woodstove, table, and chairs; barrels of water at one end of the room; a tangle of iron beds. Drinking water was brought from White Horse Creek, poured into wooden barrels, and dragged to the house by a horse-drawn sledge. No outhouse existed.

Until Black Elk moved back, the allotment had been occupied by his oldest son, Ben. In 1930, Ben was thirty-one. He was of medium height, lean and muscular, with aquiline features and "a penetrating gaze," said Hilda Neihardt, the poet's daughter. Because of Ben's protruding front teeth, Hilda did not consider him handsome; his hair was cut short, in "white man's style." Yet the two forged a friendship that lasted decades, and she said he was "very friendly and likeable, and he laughed often."

In time, Ben Black Elk would become the backbone of the Black Elk clan and the keeper of his father's legacy. Even during hard times, he'd prove a steady, imaginative provider. He would be the unacknowledged coauthor of his father's famous memoirs, travel the world, act in three movies, and become as familiar at Rushmore as the four faces carved into stone. His image would be beamed into space via early satellite transmission. His wife, the twenty-eight-year-old Angelique "Ellen" Bisonette, was a small, quiet woman of Mexican and Oglala descent, her long black hair worn in braids. Ben did a little of everything to keep his family fed: he tended the cattle and jerked beef; grew corn on the allotment; gathered wild plums, honey, turnips, and "greenies," or wild clover; set traps and skinned coyote, mink, and beaver. Yet even with such versimilitude, Ben's children often remembered him at this time as sad.

Part of it was worry. The Great Depression came early to Pine Ridge, as to most reservations. "Our Sioux Indians are poorer now than ever," Father Sialm wrote in the summer that Neihardt conducted his interviews. "The crops are almost a complete failure. There is no wild fruit either to be found. Work or employment is scarce. It is good that the Indians don't worry too much about the future. God will provide even for these poor people through the charity of the Christians." Though the infamous dust storms that eclipsed the sun would not start until 1932, Pine Ridge had its own localized version: the erosion wreaked by cattle companies meant that with each breeze dust filled the air. The Lakota remembered Sitting Bull's prophecy—that the land itself would become a malevolent force, bringing doom to the whites. These days, it seemed, the Lakota would suffer with them.

Yet much of Ben's sadness was existential. Who was he? *What* was he? He was like those Indian children taken and raised by whites described by Sweet Medicine in his vision: they straddled two worlds, accepted by neither. "I led two lives," he later said—Christian and Indian—yet inhabited neither comfortably.

His was an unsettled childhood. In his earliest years, he never had a stable home. Born to Black Elk and Katie War Bonnet on May 17, 1899, he lost his mother when he was one. Then his two brothers and two stepsisters died. After his mother's death, he lived with his grandmother, Mary Leggings Down, and her husband. But Good Thunder died when Ben was five, and he remembered his grandmother cutting herself as she mourned. Ben and his grandmother then moved in with his father and new stepmother. In 1905, he attended the government-funded Day School No. 9, a quarter mile from Manderson. Thirty-three students came to the school, in all grades. But he only stayed there for two months: he entered Holy Rosary, where he remained for the next nine years.

More than anything else, Ben blamed his sadness on his education, both at Holy Rosary and later at Carlisle. The boarding schools—both government and private—were tasked with "taking the Indian out of the Indian" and assimilating the child into the white world. There were successes, the author/physician Charles Eastman and the author/actor Luther Standing Bear (the store clerk in Rosebud) perhaps the most notable Sioux examples. But on the whole the schools created a dismal record of shame, intimidation, abuse, and even death. Rather than ease Indian children into American society, they propagated generations of resentment toward the white world. As Sweet Medicine predicted, their emphasis on eradicating Indian identity produced graduates who, upon returning to the reservation, felt they would "never know anything"— especially themselves.

Many Oglala parents believed that the immersive environment of the boarding schools, away from home and tribe, was the only way that a child could learn to speak, read, or write English. But this came with a price: home visits were prohibited. In the beginning, children had been allowed home for weekends and holidays, but they would often not return to school and had to be retrieved by the Indian police. While back at home, the missionaries complained, the children fell victim to the "savage potency" of old ways.

Thus, from 1904 to 1915, Ben lived at Holy Rosary from fall to summer, with few family visits allowed. Half of the school day was devoted to reading, composition, and math; the rest, to learning the practical skills of "civilized" men and women. Boys were taught the essentials of agriculture, animal husbandry, shoe repair, carpentry, and painting; girls learned to milk cows, sew, cook, wash, and perform other facets of home management. All instruction was in English; Lakota was forbidden, and the punishment for a moment's slip could be harsh.

Many families whose members attended Holy Rosary from the early twentieth century to around 1960 still remembered how the priests and nuns "beat the Indian out of you," as Betty Black Elk said. Being hit on the hand ten times "to remind you of the Ten Commandments" was common, said Wallace Black Elk: "Sometimes they would break that ruler." The father of the noted Pine Ridge journalist Tim Giago, Jr., told his son how the Black Robes used rubber hoses on children for real or imagined infractions. When the younger Giago entered Holy Rosary, the rubber hose had been replaced by a leather strap, but the beatings continued.

Government schools could be just as cruel, if not more so. In 1929, Luke White Hawk of the Wounded Knee district testified before a Senate investigating committee that his children had been hitched to a plow by a district-school teacher: "I have two going to school there and one of them came back sick; he was sick still in the morning, and I ask him about it, and he said the teacher had eight of the larger boys hooked up to cultivate potatoes, and the teacher's boy had a punch and punch them along when they lag behind." When the grandfather of young Mary Rough asked a school official why Mary had been whipped, he was told, "What the hell are you going to do about it? We've got a right to give her a whipping."

According to the Meriam Report, corporal punishment was the national norm. In 1929, the construction engineer H. J. Russell described conditions at the Indian school in Leupp, Arizona: "I have seen Indian boys chained to their beds at night for punishment. I have seen them thrown in cellars under the building, which the superintendent called a jail. I have seen their shoes taken away from them and they then forced to walk through the snow to the barn to help milk. I have seen them whipped with a hemp rope, also a water hose." One Senate investigator who found a student jail in Wahpeton, North Dakota, wondered "if Dakota is not the Siberia of the Indian Service."

Humiliation was a more common punishment for girls. The first impression an Oglala girl got when entering school was that she was dirty. "Some teachers confess that they can't possibly hide their disgust at the Indian child's home smell," the child psychoanalyst Erik Erikson, who later coined the term "identity crisis," noted in his 1937 study of Pine Ridge schools. Students were deloused, a practice that persisted into the 1960s; according to Mary Crow Dog, nuns would "dump the children into tubs of alcohol . . . 'to get the germs off.'" The nuns addressed any breach with some form of social shaming. Tim Giago's sister Lillian told how once, during a meal, she accidentally spilled a bowl of sugar on the floor. "As punishment, she was forced by a nun to get down on her hands and knees and lick the sugar from the floor."

"Perfection" was the goal, but a perfection defined as white, Christian, and above all else, *not* Lakota. The nuns and priests might be tough, but the strictest disciplinarians were other Indians, said Albert White Hat, an early pioneer of Lakota studies. Like Ben Black Elk, White Hat's father was a well-known catechist; like Ben, White Hat attended Holy Rosary. The greatest pressure he ever felt, he said, was from his peers: the hatred of all things Oglala had been internalized to the point where "Indian kids at school were ridiculing me for being an Indian," he recalled. "Every time I spoke Lakota, I was a 'buck Indian' and they were making fun of me." White Hat quickly realized that "we were trained to be ashamed of who we were," and *that*, he concluded, was the cause of such high rates of alcoholism on the reservation. When White Hat finished school, he said, "I was so angry that I was born an Indian that I didn't want to live."

Ben would leave Holy Rosary in October 1914 to enter Carlisle Indian School. He was fifteen, and would stay three years. Richard Pratt's transformative school had been in operation for thirty-five years, and Ben's culture shock on the first day of arrival was as disorienting as for that first class in 1879. The boys were still issued military-style uniforms and organized into companies whose officers took charge of drill; they marched to and from classes, and to the dining hall for meals. When they violated the rules, they were sent to the old brick guardhouse built by Hessian prisoners during the Revolutionary War. For Luther Standing

Bear, who was part of that first class of 1879, the sudden change in diet was, for him, "doubtless the most injurious." Instead of the simple meals of meat, fruit, and vegetables that he'd eaten since infancy, his diet suddenly consisted of white bread, coffee, sugar, and other processed foods. Between this, the change in clothing and housing, the regimentation, and the loneliness, nearly one-half of the children he entered with had died within three years. The youngest died first; in time, 186 Indian children from nearly fifty tribes would be buried in the school cemetery outside the main entrance of the U.S. Army War College.

Ben's greatest shock was the initial trip to the barber. When a military or prison system inducts a new member, the first step is to dismantle identity—usually by shaving him bald. Ben was proud of his hair: it hung down to his waist and was tied in four braids. Even the priests at Holy Rosary had not shaved his hair. They may have understood the implications—in Lakota culture, to have one's hair cut meant one of two things, both of great gravity. Either one was publically exposed as a coward, or one was in the throes of grief after losing a loved one. The father of John Makes Enemy, who entered Carlisle one year after Ben, realized the humiliation this would cause his son and begged the commissioner of Indian affairs to change the policy. "My son, John Makes-Enemy, is about to start school," he wrote on September 4, 1906.

He has long and beautiful hair, which according to the regulations now in force he must cut off. I beg you to rescind this regulation, for I and this boys mother are proud of this boys hair, and I can not see why we should be compelled to cut it off. I have long since adopted the ways and customs of civilization in every particular, except that I have not yet cut off my hair. I want my boy to go to school, and live according to the teachings he may get there. But I do not see how he wears his hair will have anything to do with his learning, or living according to what this may teach at the school.

I have been among the white people, and have seen that they are permitted to wear their hair as they choose, and have seen boys, and even men among the whites that wear their hair long.

Cutting the hair does not make us Indians like they of the white man any better, and it does not keep us from being Indians,

for returned students let their hair grow long, for they like to be
like their people.

The plea was a small masterwork of logic, but it did no good. Makes
Enemy's hair was cropped as close as Ben's a year earlier.

The haircut would be the only thing Ben ever mentioned publicly
about his three years at Carlisle. Given this, one might think it was
a nightmare. Yet according to school records, Ben was a good student
who weathered his time there with a minimum of difficulty. He made
Bs in all academic subjects (English, math, geography, and history), Bs
in what was then physical education and health, and high Cs in pen-
manship and drawing. Every summer, he lived with one of three nearby
farm families in the "outing" program, which provided the farmer cheap
labor while giving Ben some experience in agriculture. His conduct and
adjustment both in the classroom and on the farm were consistently
rated Fair and Good, with two exceptions: a May 1915 drinking incident immediately after his transfer to a farm in Newton, Pennsylvania;
and six days in June 1916 when he ran away from a second farm. Tru-
ancy, said the 1934 *Boys' Adviser in the Government Boarding Schools
for Indians*, was the most persistent of all problems in Indian schools
such as Carlisle. By the time Ben attended, it was as if school officials
expected even the best student to be a "deserter" at least once: "They
just simply up and went," one advisor complained. Ben left, then came
back of his own accord; no punishment seems to have been levied against
him. One official wrote that he was transferred to a new farm following
this desertion, and "after his transfer he has been a splendid boy."

The oddest thing about Ben's stay at Carlisle was his communication with his father. There was very little. The relationship between
Black Elk and his son at times seemed distinctly cold. Black Elk's greatest concern about Ben during this period was his attendance at Catholic Church; he peppered school and BCIM officials with letters asking
whether his son attended Mass. Nick Black Elk was "a very devout
Christian," wrote William Ketcham to Carlisle's superintendent, and he
seemed "uneasy concerning the spiritual welfare of his boy." Yet no
letters show that he communicated such worry directly to Ben. In
March 1917, a relative mistakenly wrote to Ben that his father had died;
Ben asked the superintendent to write Pine Ridge's agent, J. R. Brennan, to inquire—not about the circumstances of his father's death, but
about the disposition of Black Elk's "36 head of cattle and 60 head of

horses." In essence, during this period, the two communicated only through intermediaries. It wasn't as if they were antagonistic; rather, it was as if neither knew how to act around the other.

Such detachment seems out of character for both men. Friends and extended family described Black Elk and Ben as warm, jovial, dependable, and eager to help or please others. But as Eleanor Hinman discovered, an emotional line existed that could not be crossed, and when it was, a protective curtain slammed down. The line, it seemed, was one of loss and pain. Hinman crossed the line by bringing up Crazy Horse. Ben was a reminder of a family that no longer existed: his mother, two older brothers, and two stepsisters were gone. Photos of this time always show Black Elk sitting beside Ben in the center of the family group, stiff, uncomfortable, unbending. As if he were afraid to get too close, since those he'd loved had all died.

But Black Elk did worry about his oldest son. In May and June 1917, he sent a flurry of letters to Agent Brennan and to Carlisle, begging that Ben be sent home. "The father is practically blind," wrote Brennan to Carlisle, "and needs the son to help him in what farming he is attempting, and in the care of his stock." This was not exactly true. Perhaps he did want his eighteen-year-old son to take over the herds and crops, but in 1917 Black Elk was still well enough to fulfill his duties as a catechist—and in fact was able to see well enough to climb Harney Peak in 1931. It is more likely that he feared the possibility of Ben's enlistment in the army, and his death overseas. America had declared war on Germany on April 6, 1917. In the boarding schools, the government pressed young Indians to volunteer for service with the promise that they'd be granted citizenship—a long-standing promise that would not come true until 1924.

Ben came home in July 1917 after three years at Carlisle. In 1918, he married Ellen Bisonette at Holy Rosary; the next year, she bore their first child—Henry, born on December 16, 1918. They moved into the allotment, farmed the sparse crops, tended the dwindling herd, did whatever it took to survive. He'd lived by the white man's rules since he was six. Soon that would change, and he'd learn to be an Indian.

————•◦•————

The man driving the creaking Gardner up the road that day in August 1930 apparently fascinated Black Elk from the moment he stepped from the car.

John Neihardt was a funny-looking man. He was shorter than many Oglala women, and like many short men, he made up for inches in attitude. Black Elk was probably reminded of Little Big Man—both were short, and both *thrust* themselves at the world.

Yet Neihardt had a big voice, and this may have sparked Black Elk's attention. Because of his blindness he depended as much upon sound as on sight, and he could tell from the way this newcomer talked that he was an expressive person. Neihardt did not hide his feelings. When surprised, he'd take a sharp intake of breath; his rising and falling inflections said as much as the words themselves. *Wasichu* men did not usually reveal themselves so freely, at least not through their voices, and Black Elk was intrigued.

Finally, Neihardt was extremely physical. A trained boxer and wrestler in his youth, he could lift his 125 pounds of weight overhead with one arm; friends said the force behind his fist was "surprising." A fight promoter, watching him ring a midway bell, offered to make him a featherweight boxing champ, but Neihardt was not interested. "What's the matter?" the man snapped. "Do you hate money?" Neihardt liked money well enough, but he had other plans. He had a broad chest, and his stanzas boomed forth loud and long. His voice was high and nasal, and he could draw out a vowel as if it were strummed. His wavy brown hair framed his sharp face like a helmet; it was as long as Custer's, but thicker, and his scalp would have adorned a trophy lance at the Little Bighorn. He would have taken a grim satisfaction in that; he never, to use his own phrase, saw himself as a "lily-fingered" aesthete haunting high society's salons.

Though his first success would be in prose, Neihardt saw himself first and foremost as a poet. The Sioux thought poetically, too, Neihardt said, but strictly out of necessity: "Their language was a poor language," he told Dick Cavett forty years later. "It lacked synonyms, so they needed figures of speech and images to express feelings." Black Elk seemed to recognize in Neihardt a kindred poetic spirit, yet no word existed in Lakota for "poet," so he called him a "sender of words": "This world is like a garden," he said. "Out from this garden go his words like rain, and where they fall they leave it a little greener. And when his words have passed, the memory of them shall stand long in the west like a flaming rainbow." He called the little man Pte Wigamuu Gke, or Flaming Rainbow.

The rest of the world saw Neihardt as a regional poet. He was born in a one-room Illinois prairie cabin on January 8, 1881—the year that

Black Elk returned to Pine Ridge to start his life as a medicine man. "If I write of hot winds and grasshoppers, of prairie fires and blizzards," exclaimed Neihardt, "I knew them early." His parents moved to a sod house in western Kansas, where, at age five, he witnessed a huge prairie fire; then to Kansas City, where in 1891, the family splintered and his father left, causing a sadness that never entirely disappeared. Neihardt, his mother, and his two sisters moved to Wayne, Nebraska, where, a year later at age eleven, he contracted a mysterious raging fever and nearly died.

"The world tottered and began to rotate," he wrote in his autobiography. "Then there was blackness." He woke in bed, floating dizzily; his mother stood above him pressing a cold rag to his head. But she dissolved and he found himself in vastness, "flying face downward, with arms and hands thrust forward like a diver's," traveling at a "dreadful speed." He wanted to go home, but the void was "terribly empty save for a few lost stars"; he cried out, but a Great Voice filled the emptiness and drove him on. "Faster!" cried the Voice. "Faster! faster!!" He woke three times that night and held tight to his mother, fearing that if he released his grip he would slip back into the great loneliness; three times he lost consciousness and reentered the dream. When he finally woke in the morning, "the world was still and the fever was gone."

The flying dream would be one of two key experiences that turned him into a mystic, he said. Before the dream, he wanted to become an inventor, but afterward he felt a need to understand this other world. Soon after his recuperation, he was hired by a tombstone maker named "Professor Durrin" to help polish marble. The Professor encouraged Neihardt's literary aspirations; a friend heard about the Professor's protégé and gave Neihardt a copy of the Hindu Upanishads. Around this time he had a second brush with death: he slipped while grabbing for the reins of a team of running horses and found himself upended, his face a few inches from the spinning wagon wheels. He realized he was about to die, when suddenly "an overwhelming sense of expanded being and clairvoyant awareness" overtook him; he was outside his body, looking on with "complete acceptance; and somehow it was good." Again he survived, and the Upanishads seemed to explain everything: there was more to the world than the "visible," and this "something more" was as real as the known. The dreams and near-death experiences became for Neihardt what visions were for Black Elk: a divine indication of the path he must follow.

To a point, the lives of Neihardt and Black Elk had followed similar lines. Both experienced visions of an alternate reality during sickness or a brush with death; both returned with a sense of higher purpose and obligation. But where Black Elk kept quiet about his vision for fear of ridicule, Neihardt announced his to the world. He was a smart, precocious child, and adults doted on him. His mother wrangled an early admission into the newly opened Nebraska Normal College, now Wayne State; he graduated from the regular course in 1896 at age fifteen, then from the scientific track one year later. Graduation, he proclaimed, lifted him "to a higher, creative level of being." He taught in country schools for a year, long enough to confirm to himself that writing, not teaching, would be his life's work. He privately published *The Divine Enchantment*, a book-length poem about Hindu deities that was so embarrassingly overwritten that he would later buy up and destroy almost every one of the five hundred printed copies.

In 1900, his mother and sisters moved to Bancroft, a small farming town in northeast Nebraska close to the Omaha Indian Reservation. He moved there a year later, co-owned and edited the *Bancroft Blade* until 1905, and began sending short stories to magazines such as *The Overland Monthly*, where he would be regularly accepted. He was a strange fit for the little midwestern town; people there remembered him as a "character" given to long, rambling walks and even more rambling flights of imagination. But finances were tight, and when he was approached by the local Indian trader J. J. Elkin to work as his firm's bookkeeper for about thirty dollars a month, Neihardt jumped at the opportunity.

It was his first real exposure to Indians, one that gave him a view of their lives much different from that commonly held. "It was two or three years before I came to know and respect the Omaha as an ancient people with a rich culture that was dying out," he wrote. As Neihardt befriended the Omahas, they took him under their wing, christening him Tae Nuga Zhinga, or Little Bull Buffalo, in honor of his build. His experiences prompted him to write the first of his "Indian tales," short fiction springing from Omaha folklore, a creative process that proved invaluable when he met Black Elk.

Yet poetry still had a grip on him. In 1907, he published *A Bundle of Myrrh*, a romantic collection of free verse. Though poems such as "If This Be Sin" were considered frank and sensual for the time, the collection's greatest accomplishment was to circulate among a group of American artists in Paris, one of whom—the young, wealthy Manhattan socialite Mona Martinsen—studied sculpture under Auguste Rodin. She sent Neihardt a letter, praying the young poet was not married. They began to correspond, and fell in love.

In the summer of 1908, Neihardt undertook a two-thousand-mile journey down the Missouri River, and wrote about his experiences in a series of articles for *The Outing Magazine* that would become *The River and I*. The fifty-six-day journey from Fort Benton, Montana, to Sioux City, Iowa, in an open boat was hard: the boat hit the rocks at the Dauphin Rapids and nearly cracked up; after that, the engine was always unreliable. Yet he and his boatmates persevered, and the resulting travelogue was well received. Many times, the language was ponderous and overblown: "We no longer write epics," he announced, "we live them." The westward expansion was a heroic epic: "We have the facts, but we have not a Homer," he said, implying that he would fill the blind poet's shoes.

But the endless trek humbled him, and with that his writing turned more honest and practical. "The monotony of the landscape was depressing," he admitted:

> It seemed a thousand miles to the sunrise. The horizon was merely a blue haze—and the endless land was sere. The river ran for days with a succession of regularly occurring right-angled bends to the north and east . . . until at last we cried out against the tediousness of the oft-repeated story, wondering whether or not we were continually passing the same point, and somehow slipping back to pass it again

He was twenty-seven, and the experience matured him as a writer. It also gave him his subject—the Vanishing West—to which he would devote the rest of his career. For a brief period he lived in New York, but felt ungrounded and returned home to Bancroft. He wrote his travelogue, and wrote to Mona in Paris. That November, the daughter of the international financier Rudolph Vincent Martinsen would step off the train at the Bancroft station, eyes shaded under a broad-brimmed velvet hat. Neihardt described the moment as terrifying; she recognized him from his photos and yelled "John!" before he could slip away. They married the next day, would bear four children—Enid, Sigurd, Hilda, and Alice—in quick succession, and stay together for fifty years.

About two years after they married, Neihardt experienced the second of his visionary experiences. One summer afternoon, while working in his yard, he caught from the corner of his eye something strange happening to a small syringa bush at the garden's edge. He turned toward it and saw that the bush had become "vibrantly alive with a colorless stuff like a diaphanous flame lacking heat." As he watched, the ghostly fire oozed from the buds and spread down the branches; the fire traced into emptiness, as if the spectral shapes tested possibilities for future branches and limbs. Finally the bush seemed to find its path and "burned tall in ghostly splendor." Neihardt awoke from a trance and found himself "leaning on the handle of my hoe and gazing vacantly at the ground."

Whether Neihardt's "burning bush" actually happened or not, it prepared him for the moment when Black Elk described his own Great Vision. "This was not a dream," he told Neihardt; "it actually happened." Neihardt would have no reason to doubt the old man, since he believed the same kind of thing had happened to him.

Over the next decade, Neihardt began assembling the material that would become the five epic "songs" of his *Cycle of the West*. He located and interviewed soldiers and warriors who survived the Battle of the Little Bighorn; he followed in the steps of the fur trapper Hugh Glass, the plainsman Jedediah Smith, Crazy Horse, and the Ghost Dancers. In 1915, he published *The Song of Hugh Glass*, and in 1919, *The Song of Three Friends*. With these first two Western "songs," the fame he'd sought so long finally found him. *The Song of Three Friends* won a five-hundred-dollar prize from the Poetry Society of America for the best volume of American poetry published in 1919. In 1920, he moved his family to Branson, Missouri, where he supported himself through writing, lecturing, and serving as literary editor of the *St. Louis Post-Dispatch*. In April 1921, he was named poet laureate of Nebraska, a title he would keep for the rest of his life. The 1925 *Song of the Indian Wars* was the most tragic of his epics, ending with the death of Crazy Horse and his secret burial by Worm. Three years later, in 1928, *Scribner's American Literature* dubbed him "the foremost representative of the epic in American Literature." By then, he was already being called the "Shakespeare of the Plains."

Yet even at the height of this success, he seemed to understand that the epic tradition was being left behind by new directions in American poetry. This was the era of Modernist experimenters such as T. S. Eliot,

William Carlos Williams, and Ezra Pound. In his own way, he, too, was a Vanishing American. As early as 1917, after the publication of *The Song of Hugh Glass*, he addressed at a poetry symposium the question of whether he and the epic were out of step with modern times:

> But I do not forget, as many of my contemporaries seem to do, that the world did not begin with the present decade. . . . By ignoring the past the poet deliberately sacrifices the chief source of poetic power. For it is mainly by appealing to memory that poetry works its magic: and the individual memory is too brief, too fragmentary. The racial memory, rich with the distilled experience of countless men and women, is necessary, and racial memory is literary tradition.

In March 1930, *Indian Wars* was chosen as one of five hundred books for Herbert Hoover's White House library. Five months later, the poet drove up a lonely dirt road in Indian Country where, at the very end, an old man seemed to know he was coming.

25

BLACK ELK SPEAKS

John Neihardt considered himself a worldly man. He'd seen the beauty and loneliness of the West, enjoyed success in literature and love; but this Black Elk confounded and fascinated him. From the moment they'd started talking that hot afternoon in August 1930, the old blind preacher had seemed to him possessed of an eerie, intuitive insight. He'd given him his father's hide-and-eagle-feather pendant, which he called the Morning Star, the kind of heirloom passed from father to son rather than to a complete stranger. He'd exacted from the poet a promise to return the following spring, when he would reveal to him something he called the Great Vision—a holy dream central to his life, which, he said, had been given by the gods to save his people. What started as a chance detour had turned instead into a surprising obligatory weight that settled firmly on the poet's shoulders.

After that first meeting, he returned home to Branson and wired his editor, William Morrow. He sensed that the old man's story promised something new: "A book truly *Indian* from the inside out," he said. Yet, something troubled him. On August 10, 1930, he wrote to Dr. Julius House, an English professor at his old college and one of his closest friends. He described his journey to Pine Ridge, and found it "very curious that everyone did not know Black Elk." The old man struck him as being "a bit uncanny in his intuitions; not that he favored me, but that he seemed to know what was inside the visitor. He told me—the sphinxlike old chap—that, as he sat there, he felt in my heart a very strong will to know the things of the other world and that a spirit, which stood behind me, had forced me to come to him that I might learn a little from him."

In October, Morrow contracted with Neihardt for a book on the life of Black Elk. He agreed to an advance on royalties of a thousand dollars, "an amount that was adequate for these times but now would seem laughable," his daughter Hilda later wrote. If Neihardt managed his money, he would be able to use the advance for operating expenses. On November 3, Black Elk wrote Neihardt, with the help of his children; he thanked him for sending a copy of his *Song of the Indian Wars*. Neihardt responded and told him of the contract:

> I would want you to tell the story of your life beginning at the beginning and going straight through to Wounded Knee. I would have my daughter, who is a shorthand writer, take down everything you would say, and I would want your friends to talk any time about, and share in, the different things that you would tell about. This would make a complete story of your people since your childhood. . . .
>
> So, you see, this book would be not only the story of your life, but the story of the life of your people. The fact that you have been both a warrior and a medicine man would be of great help in writing this book, because both religion and war are of great importance in history.

This is an important letter. Neihardt had written Black Elk a couple of times after leaving Manderson, keeping him apprised of his thinking. After the rerelease of *Black Elk Speaks* in the 1960s and its subsequent success, some critics would contend that, in effect, Neihardt fooled and victimized the old man. Some said he cheated Black Elk financially, when in fact he offered to let him make the terms. In another part of the letter, Neihardt said, "Write and tell me how much you think you should be paid for each meeting," an echo of Black Elk's demands to Eleanor Hinman. Considering that Neihardt spent almost all of the advance on expenses and that the book was remaindered soon after release, the poet proved prescient when he said this would not be a lucrative venture. "I can make money much faster and easier in other ways," he wrote. Although it is not known how much Black Elk was paid for the interviews, there is some indication that Ben was paid privately for his work as a translator. On the whole, Black Elk seemed satisfied.

Moreover, while critics said that Neihardt kept Black Elk in the dark about the book's intent, he in fact included the old man in all plans from the very beginning. Catholic critics in particular complained that Neihardt omitted Black Elk's conversion, but Neihardt plainly spelled out the scope—"the story of your life beginning at the beginning and going straight through to Wounded Knee." Black Elk did not disagree. Since Ben translated, Neihardt assumed that everything would be explained. This would be a narrative of traditional Sioux life and the Indian wars from the Oglala perspective, but what was unique was that it would be told not by a warrior, but by a holy man.

Finally, Neihardt asked Black Elk to invite "three or four of the fine old men" to the interviews. This would expand the narrative and make it more of a tribal history. Black Elk invited four Lakota contemporaries, all older warriors. Among them, they had survived every important engagement of the Sioux wars. At eighty-two, the Fetterman survivor Fire Thunder was the oldest, followed by Holy Black Tail Deer, seventy-four, and Standing Bear, age seventy-two. The fourth, Iron Hawk, was Black Elk's elder by one year.

Of the four, Black Elk's cousin Standing Bear would be most important for the book's production. He'd experienced many of the same events, but from the eyes of someone four years older—the fight at the Little Bighorn; travels in Europe with Cody; adaptation to the reservation. Both men had become Catholic, and just as Black Elk took the baptismal name of Nicholas, Standing Bear adopted that of the first Christian martyr, Stephen. He was an artist and would paint scenes from Black Elk's life and Vision on doe- or buckskin for the book. Besides the Neihardts and Ben, he would be the only one present when Black Elk related his Great Vision—an honor, since this would be the first time Black Elk had made it public since his youth, something he had not even told his wife and children.

In fact, Black Elk seemed to sense a weakness with his narrative. Until that point in 1886 when he signed Cody's two Wild West contracts, Black Elk had existed outside the historical record: though he was part of events, there was no way to prove participation outside his own observations of history. But Standing Bear was a man of substance and a chief, openhanded in these hard times, respected for his generosity. He'd sustained a serious injury during the Wild West's 1889–90 tour of Europe; as he recuperated in a Viennese hospital, he learned that his wife, twenty-four-year-old Red Elk, and daughter, seven-year-old Yellow, had died at Wounded Knee. The Austrian nurse who attended him, Louise Rieneck, also knew loss: she was a widow with two young daughters. During Standing Bear's grief and convalescence, the two fell in love. They wedded in the Austrian court in January 1891, and started back to Pine Ridge one month later.

Where Black Elk struggled with the new reality of Pine Ridge, Standing Bear and Louise Rieneck prospered. As Louise learned Lakota, Standing Bear's female kin taught her the nuances of an Indian household. Soon she was known as Across the Eastern Water Woman. At the same time, she brought to them her knowledge of European medicine, stock-raising, and crops, things they did not know. They had three daughters—Hattie, Lillian, and Christina—and all roved between the Indian and white worlds as if no chasm existed. Louise ordered a sewing machine from her merchant parents in Chicago, who'd accompanied her from Vienna; with this, she and her daughters turned their cabin into a small factory for Lakota and western wear. After 1900, they moved to White Horse Creek, west of Manderson; built a whitewashed log cabin with a shingled pitched roof and frame windows; and, according to a 1913 "Industrial Status Report" of their allotment, owned one hundred cattle, thirty horses, and 640 acres of land. At a time when the average annual salary was $621, Standing Bear and Louise had $1,000 in savings.

Thus, Standing Bear assured the truth of Black Elk's story. Such an upstanding and honorable man in Lakota society would not lie, and he would not allow a lie from others in his presence. His participation served as more than a notary's seal; it held behind it the honor of the tribe. With Standing Bear at his side, Black Elk might make the occasional chronological mistake while telling his story, but he could not and would not lie.

This is not the only example of how Black Elk took control of the proceedings. The letters show that he knew exactly where he wanted the story to go. He apparently had no problems with Neihardt's interest in the Ghost Dancers, but the real focus would be his Great Vision. He insisted that Ben translate: his son had gone to Carlisle, but more important, the old man planned to talk about sacred matters that could be heard only by those close to him.

For his part, Neihardt took a three-month leave from the *Post-Dispatch*, corresponded with Morrow about details, and received permission from the Indian Office for an extended stay at Pine Ridge. "Mr. Neihardt is not an investigator, an uplifter nor anything of that kind," wrote Malcolm McDowell, secretary of the Board of Indian Commissioners, to Agent Courtright, "and while I appreciate the fact that it would be unwise to grant wide open permission to strangers to hold meetings in your jurisdiction, I think you need have no fear whatever about helping Mr. Neihardt to get in touch with some of the old fellows up there."

By passing his Great Vision not only to Neihardt but also to Ben and Standing Bear, Black Elk "was tying together the ends of his life," wrote the scholar Raymond DeMallie. He was sixty-seven and worried that his days were numbered. He'd felt for a long time that his Vision *had* to be told: it was his last and final duty. If the poet had not come along, it would have been lost; that would have been the last and ultimate failure. Every route to salvation had been blocked; every attempt to save the Lakota thwarted. He believed absolutely in the separate existence of a higher truth; by telling his story to Neihardt, he'd make one last attempt to tap into that truth and save his people.

Within this context, Black Elk was doing something unprecedented. According to Charles Eastman, "Sometimes an old man, standing upon the brink of eternity, might reveal to a chosen few the oracle of his long-past youth." Yet Black Elk was not merely telling the story of his life. By sharing the details of his untold Vision, he passed along his power. By passing it to Neihardt, he gave it to another culture—the very one that had destroyed the Lakota! Yet a book meant permanence: what could be lost would be preserved. The truth of his Vision would remain long after he and the poet were gone.

Neihardt agreed with Black Elk about the existence of a higher truth. During this time, Hilda would wake at night and slip downstairs. A rising high school sophomore, she would become the chronicler of the book's production; a self-professed tomboy, she listened as her parents talked of a "tapestry" of ideas "whose meanings I could then hardly comprehend." Her father seemed to feel he stood on the brink of unexplored territory. Her parents discussed "art, poetry, the beauty and sorrows of life, and—above all—their unswerving belief that the pursuit of what they called 'the higher values' was worth all the desperate effort it might demand."

For Black Elk, this was that "desperate effort." His eyesight deteriorated more each year: in addition to the corneal burn, he'd been diagnosed with glaucoma. His tuberculosis plagued him. Lately, old friends had begun to die. Flying Hawk was not long for this earth. One Side disappeared from the records. Most sobering was a recent decision by his cousin. On February 1, 1929, a year and a half before Neihardt's appearance, Standing Bear and Louise visited Father Buechel. Standing Bear "really is sick," Buechel wrote: though he provides no details, his condition was serious enough that Buechel gave him the sacraments, including Extreme Unction, and christened him in the name of the first Christian martyr. Now he was Stephen Standing Bear. According to Buechel, the old man "was truly happy."

And now a new, unexpected problem arose, a family dispute that foreshadowed the later controversy about Black Elk's "true" identity. Lucy grew upset upon learning that Ben would translate. She'd thought that her father's fellow catechist Emil Afraid of Hawk would serve in that role. Afraid of Hawk was a good interpreter: he'd been Eleanor Hinman's when she'd asked Black Elk about Crazy Horse. Emil was a family friend.

More important, Lucy did not feel that her father's Catholicism would be properly emphasized with Ben at the helm. Given the later direction of his thought, he may have shown too much interest in the old ways to make Lucy comfortable. Would Neihardt focus only on her father's life before his conversion? Would he include his twenty-nine years as a catechist? In 1930, Lucy was twenty-three and could properly be considered part of that first generation of Lakota raised entirely in a Catholic environment. She'd come of age at a time when her father's old religion was banned and Lakota language and culture had been vigorously and violently suppressed in Catholic and government schools. She was proud of her catechist father: he was an honored man, and through him, she had community standing. Without Emil Afraid of Hawk in the strategic role, she feared she'd have no control over her father's legacy.

In the end, Lucy and Emil dissociated themselves from the project, allowing Ben free rein. The family dispute was either smoothed over or well hidden by the time Neihardt arrived: there is no indication in his commentary that he knew what was going on. Yet tensions still remained. During Black Elk's description of the carnage at Wounded Knee, he suddenly mused, "At this time I had no children and maybe if I had been killed then I would have been better off." The comment was so out of context that it suggests the family dispute was still going strong.

Neihardt left Branson for the interviews on Friday, May 1, 1931. He took with him his two oldest daughters: twenty-year-old Enid, an accomplished stenographer, and the excitable Hilda. They drove the zigzag route of Neihardt's memory: he gave a reading in Lincoln, visited the old family home in Bancroft, visited Julius House in Wayne. They got stuck on a slick, muddy road, were rescued by a man in a Chevy—what Enid called a true "Western type of man"—then turned north at Rushville for Pine Ridge. On May 9, they stopped briefly at the Wounded Knee gravesite—"what a lonely, windswept place," Hilda wrote—then hopped back in the Gardner for the few remaining miles to Manderson. They met Black Elk's oldest sons, Ben and Nick Jr., who were borrowing beds from the store for their visitors. Enid noted in her diary that two hundred to three hundred sheep roamed freely around Manderson and the surrounding hills, probably a communal herd. The Neihardts downed a quick lunch of crackers and Vienna sausages, then followed Ben's old Ford along the familiar one-lane road.

When they reached the allotment, Neihardt was surprised. As before, Black Elk's cabin squatted partway up the hill, surrounded by dry brown grass. But on a knoll before the house, the family had pitched a large new tipi of white army duck donated by the store owner. Black Elk had painted on it images from his Great Vision, including a flaming rainbow over the door like the one on the Grandfathers' cloud tipi. A new outhouse had been built; a circle of small, fresh-cut pines thrust into the ground around the house and lodge. Down the slope the Black Elks had built a circular dance bower, also made of freshly cut pines.

In essence, Black Elk had created a teaching space for what he considered one of the greatest events of his life. By doing so, he cast himself as guide and professor. It was too cold this night to sleep in the tipi, so the Neihardts crowded inside the already packed cabin on the borrowed beds. The next morning—Sunday, May 10—they started work at the break of day.

This first day was spent recording the tales of the elders: their presence validated Black Elk's narrative and placed it within the history of the tribe. This would be the general structure of the book: everything, even the Great Vision, revolved about the tribe's history and well-being. Neihardt passed around cigarettes, then told the old long-hairs what he hoped to accomplish. He said that they would be paid at a rate suggested by Black Elk and Ben: though the stipend was small by today's standards, Hilda said, it was "welcome and well-received" by the old men.

It soon became obvious that this would be a public event: other old men rode up and sat a respectful distance from the house with their backs to the speakers. Ben's wife, Ellen, would ask Neihardt if each new arrival could be fed; he couldn't say no, and the newcomer would join the group. This became a general pattern: the women of Black Elk's family ended up cooking three meals a day as others arrived. So many people showed up that first day that Enid Neihardt wondered whether her father would have "to feed the whole Sioux nation!"

It also became evident that the interview process would be slow and tedious. Blankets were spread in the pine shade and the participants sat in a circle: Ben sat between Black Elk and Neihardt, Enid beside them with her steno pad. Others fanned out from this center. Black Elk made a statement in Lakota; Ben translated it into idiomatic "Indian English"; Neihardt repeated Ben's words in Standard English; Ben would sometimes repeat Neihardt's words back to Black Elk in Lakota for clarification. When all were satisfied, Ben said, "That's it," and Enid jotted it down in Gregg shorthand. At first the process was clumsy. Enid wrote in her notebook on the first morning: "To begin with my father name Black Elk, his father name Black Elk, his son name Black Elk, 3rd one Black Elk, 4th of the name Black Elk. His father was Medicine Man as far back remember." But soon they all "got into the swing of things," Hilda said.

In effect, what appeared in Enid's notebook was one or two removes from Black Elk's original words. Yet such back-and-forth controlled for misunderstandings and ensured that Neihardt could be faithful to the intended meaning. When scholars criticized Neihardt for writing in his idiom rather than Black Elk's, they failed to understand the narrative's essential group nature. When Neihardt reshaped Ben's translation into Standard English, he was already writing the story. When Enid later transcribed her notes for her father, it served as the first revision.

Hilda, whom her father called the "official observer," saw this all as endless drudgery. Later, as the others worked, she rode on horseback around the prairie with Indian boys her age. But on this first day, as she sat with the others, she could not help but realize how important this was to the old men. "I looked around the circle, and in the intensity of the moment what I saw was stamped on my memory. All the men were dressed in white men's clothing that day, and several wore cowboy hats." Fire Thunder, the oldest, was "slim and strongly built"; Iron Hawk, "deep-chested"; Standing Bear, "kingly." She caught a glimpse of "how powerful they must have been as young warriors." In that brief moment, she understood the importance of what her father and Black Elk were trying to preserve.

The material that first day provided the historical context for Black Elk's birth and the existential threat to his tribe. The elders spoke of the white invasion of the Powder River Country and of the hated Bozeman Trail. Fire Thunder described the Fetterman Massacre, where Black Elk's father was permanently lamed. After they finished, Black Elk told of his earliest mystical experiences: the voices when he was barely four; the messengers flying toward him and veering off when he was five. The Neihardts had to leave the next morning for a May 12 speaking engagement at a college south of Chadron, Nebraska; they returned the next evening and spent their first night in the white tipi.

On May 14, a grand feast was planned. Neihardt financed it, an appropriate gesture since giving a feast was an honor, and generosity, in Sioux society, was considered the highest virtue. He bought a "fat little" Holstein bull from Lucy, and the men butchered it in the traditional way, gathering around to eat the freshly cut raw liver. Neihardt accepted a piece when offered, and pretended to love every bite. For the long-hairs this was a rare treat, reminding them of buffalo hunts when they were young. The women made *wojapi*, an Indian pudding of sweetened fruit thickened with flour; they served the meat in a soup boiled in the beef paunch suspended from a tripod, or roasted over the open fire. By the end of the night, the entire bull had been consumed, except for the hooves and horns. Later, the hooves were eaten, too.

Between two hundred and three hundred people came to the feast from throughout the district. The number was so great that Hilda remembered her father's thousand-dollar advance "melting like ice in the summertime"; she later calculated that the diminishing advance equaled the combined annual income of eight Oglala families, and thus must have seemed a fortune to them. Those who could dressed in their traditional garb. Black Elk wore a cerise shirt, beaded leggings, and a fur band around his head with a single eagle feather attached to the front. Standing Bear wore his beaded buckskin shirt and leggings, and a long, trailing war bonnet of eagle feathers. Black Elk began the festivities by presenting his pipe in six directions, invoking the blessings of the Six Grandfathers. He prayed aloud, smoked the pipe, then presented it to Neihardt, who took four puffs and passed it around the circle of old men.

In order to receive Black Elk's Great Vision, Neihardt and the girls had to be adopted into the tribe. The ceremony was performed on feast night: it started with kill-talks led off by Standing Bear. Black Elk stood to give the final speech, in which he told of his despair at Wounded Knee. They climbed to the top of the hill and bestowed new names on Neihardt and his daughters. Hilda was christened Ompo Wichach Pe Win, or Daybreak Star Woman; Enid, Ta Sa Okige Luta, or She Walks with Her Holy Red Stick. Neihardt was given a name he prized for the rest of his life: Peyta Wigimuu Ge, or Flaming Rainbow, the chief symbol of Black Elk's vision. From henceforth, Black Elk called Neihardt "son" or "nephew," and Neihardt called him "uncle." Neihardt was not only Oglala, but an Oglala with a sacred duty.

The Neihardts were not the only whites present at the feast. After the speeches came dancing—first the war dance, in which the men acted out their coups; then, by firelight, the Rabbit Dance. Though this had been banned, Neihardt received permission from the Indian Office and the agent gave his assent for this one time. The performance was more comical than licentious. Dorothy Cook of the *Lincoln Journal* wrote: "The sight of Nebraska's dignified poet laureate being dragged through the steps of the Rabbit Dance by a large and blandly smiling Indian woman brought shrieks of laughter from the bystanders." Standing Bear grabbed Enid for a spin, and Chase in the Morning, a cousin of Crazy Horse, grabbed Hilda.

An uninvited *wasichu* also appeared. Sometime during the celebrations, Hilda watched as "a rather obsequious man approached her father and confided that he could supply liquor for the feast and split the profits with him. Neihardt exploded. "If you come back," he yelled as the man hurried to his car parked at the bottom of the hill, "I'll have you arrested!"

The interviews renewed the next day, on May 16, though everyone moved slowly as they recuperated from the late night and excess food. From then until May 19, they worked morning to night on the Great Vision. The days started with Ben's breakfast announcement, "Come and get it or we'll throw it out!!" accompanied by a grin. Yet on May 16 a change was made: the interview was moved to Standing Bear's property. Black Elk's bestowal of the Vision was too sacred and private for a

public place: only Ben, Standing Bear, Black Elk, and the three Neihardts would be present. He said that no one else in the Oglala nation
had heard the entire Vision, not even his own family, but this was not
quite true. This would actually be the third telling: to Black Road before the Horse Dance; to Few Tails and the other holy men after his
vision quest; and now. But the listeners in the previous instances had
been medicine men, members of a select, initiate group, not outsiders
like Neihardt and his girls. Each private recantation had set him on a
course to stage a public ceremony, an unburdening that revealed his
Vision to his people. This time would be more demanding. With a book,
he would share his Great Vision with the world.

The party spread their cotton blankets on a grassy spot near some
young trees, and built a small fire for ceremonies that involved the burning of sweetgrass or sage and the lighting of the pipe. Hilda cooked the
noon meals, usually potatoes, corn bread, vegetables, and any meat if
available. The talks continued late into the evenings, often until ten or
eleven o'clock, and Enid sat by a kerosene lamp to see what she was
writing.

For the first time, Neihardt got a glimpse of Standing Bear's place in
the community. He owned a *real* house," Enid wrote—a large log house
painted white, with a shingled roof and wood ceilings. Hilda was told it
was the only shingled roof in Pine Ridge. The girls couldn't help but
compare it with Black Elk's log cabin, with the sod roof sprouting with
weeds and prairie grasses. By Agency standards, Standing Bear was
rich, or at least well-to-do. He owned a large garden, chickens, and a milk
cow, in addition to a herd of horses and cattle, which he drove seasonally
between the pastures of White Horse Creek and the higher meadows
of Red Shirt Table. His wealth was a communal affair: close cousins—
the Red Shirts and High Eagles—helped tend the herds. Yet with that
wealth came responsibility. Hilda could see it etched in the face of
Louise. "I remember feeling considerable sympathy for Mrs. Standing
Bear," she said, "because she looked work-worn." As a successful subchief, it was Standing Bear's obligation to feed the poor of his clan, especially during the Great Depression. Now that he thought his days were
numbered, a lot of that responsibility fell on Louise.

The Great Vision was the heart of Black Elk's narrative, and the
most exacting to transcribe. Black Elk returned not only to his youth,
but back to the spirit world he'd visited when he was nine. As Enid
wrote, "Black Elk is not very good at telling history, but he is very good

at telling his vision." The telling was laced with song: Black Elk would reach a part in the narrative where suddenly he'd stop and say "There's a song for that," then reach for his drum. His voice was cracked and "none-too-melodious," but one in particular resonated with Neihardt—the song of the sacred hoop, that point in his Vision when the young Black Elk had saved his people and righted the world:

> See where the holy tree is flowering,
> From the earth, bright with birdsong, it is flowering.
> Happy all who live beneath it.
> Hey-o-ha! Hey-o-ha!

Yet the effort exhausted the old man. Often he would tire and without warning drop his head on the blanket and fall asleep. At such times, the others would digest what they'd heard. Standing Bear grew quiet, humbled by the depths of the Vision. He remembered the cousin who'd lain "dead" for days, how he'd changed when he came back, and now everything made sense to him. Hilda was enthralled: like her father, she, too, had experienced vivid dreams. Although they were nothing like Black Elk's, she wrote, "I was already a believer."

Neihardt was amazed. He paced back and forth, trying to make sense of it all. "I just cannot *believe* the beauty and the meaning of what is coming out of that old man's head," he declared, the girls at his heels. "I know of no other vision in religious literature that is equal to this!" This is telling: where originally Neihardt had seen the book as a testament of a vanishing life, now suddenly it had grown into something new and holy. Like the writers of the Gospels, he saw himself introducing a new path to the world. Later, in a letter to Julius House, he described the Vision as "a marvelous thing, vast in extent, full of profound significance and perfectly formed. If it were literature instead of a dance ritual, it would be a literary masterpiece!" We can see with these words the poet's plans to shape Black Elk's history into literature.

Of them all, Ben seemed most affected. He'd known a little about his father's career as a medicine man, had heard how he'd experienced visions, but the old man had never hinted at their scope—a silence that once again indicated the gulf between father and son. Ben could barely come up with the proper English to explain to Neihardt what his father said. He seemed overcome. Once, while riding with Neihardt, Ben exclaimed, "Isn't it great? Isn't it *wonderful*?"

"What is wonderful, Ben?" Neihardt asked.

"What the old man is a-sayin'. I always knew he had *something*, but I didn't know what the hell it was!"

They all seemed deepened by what they'd heard, filled with the tragic scope of this land. Once, when Enid, Hilda, and Lucy's fiancé, Leo Looks Twice, rode past White Horse Creek, Leo reined up to water the horses. "You know, Crazy Horse is supposed to be buried somewhere near here," he said. "The old man said so, but I don't think he knows just where the grave is." They returned in the darkness and caught sight of the glow of their tipi, a tiny golden triangle "out in that vast loneliness." They stopped their horses on the hilltop and sat silently. It was strangely beautiful, Hilda thought, but how much more for the young Indian men and women they now called friends? What thoughts did they have of a life that was gone forever?

Black Elk completed his narration of the Great Vision on May 19; from May 20 to May 23, he continued his story through the Custer battle, the army's retribution, the flight to Canada, and his apprenticeship as a young medicine man. On the 24th, they drove to Wounded Knee and made camp in the bottomland; he completed his tale of the Horse Dance and told about the events of 1890, pointing to the hills where he'd charged the soldiers and the ravine where he'd seen the women and children piled in the snow. He told Enid about his "bullet proof" body, then showed her the scar where the bullet "had gone right through him and did not kill him." He survived, he said, "because he was sacred to the Great Spirit."

As the old man talked, Neihardt felt gripped by an odd feeling. Black Elk would be narrating some event of his life when suddenly it seemed as if the old man read Neihardt's thoughts and quoted from his poems. It was the most intense merger of consciousness with another person he'd ever experienced, even with Mona, whom he considered a soul mate. He listened as the silence descended on the day's dying light, and told Black Elk of something that once happened to him. While writing the 1915 *Song of Hugh Glass*, he'd needed to describe a spot on the Grand River where the title character had been mauled by a bear. Neihardt was too poor at that time to make the trip, so he sketched out the setting from his research and intuition. Eight years later, he was able to visit the spot, and the place was exactly as he'd described. Black Elk listened quietly, then said he was not surprised. This was no coincidence, he said.

When a man sits down making something, in his mind it will be full of all kinds of thoughts equal to the books you have written. You are what they call a man thinker. As you sit there, in your mind there is a kind of a power that has been sent to you by the spirits; and while you are doing this work in describing this land, probably there is a kind of power that did the work for you, although you think you are doing it yourself. Just like my vision; a man goes without food twelve days he'll probably die, and during this time probably they were feeding me. But all this while I was in a form of the vision. It seems that I was transformed into another world.

Neihardt told Black Elk about the vision of flying he'd had when he was eleven and in the same kind of comatose state as the old man at nine. Twenty years later, Neihardt had written a poem based upon this fever dream called "The Ghostly Brother." Black Elk listened and said he understood. This was a power vision, just like his own. The "brother ghost" who'd helped Neihardt survive, who would later describe to him places he'd never seen, was like those messengers who'd come for him from the clouds. "I think this was an Indian brother from the happy hunting grounds who is your guide." Their lives were not that different, he said. Maybe they'd been brought together by the same kind of spirit guide.

Maybe *this* was Neihardt's most important and sacred work, Black Elk softly continued, and it had to be done. He'd tried to do it on his own, and had failed. If he'd completed his task, as the Grandfathers wanted, his people would have prospered, but "because I did not do it I have been punished." He'd despaired—but, perhaps, too soon. Now he could see that all was not lost. The sacred tree of his Vision had faded as he grew older, "but the roots will stay alive, and we are here to make that tree bloom." Perhaps the gods had taken pity on him one last time:

This vision of mine ought to go out, I feel, but somehow I couldn't get anyone to do it. I would think about it and get sad. I wanted the world to know about it. It seems that your ghostly brother has sent you here to do this for me. You are here and have the vision just the way I wanted, and then the tree will bloom again and the people will know the true facts. We want this tree to bloom again in the world of true that does not judge.

Neihardt breathed out. "All great spiritual visions triumph in this world by being diffused," he finally answered.

Black Elk nodded. "Yes, that is true."

———•◦•———

They left at 8:00 a.m. the next day, Monday, May 25, for the Badlands. They would drive first to Black Elk's property on Cuny Table, the long, rectangular butte in the north that rose from the alkali wastes like a crumbling fortress, abandoned centuries past by the giants predating man. One road traced up from the east, and this could hardly be called a road. It was an "exceedingly steep" line in the rock, runneled with washouts, and the Gardner bounced from side to side as it strained in low gear.

Black Elk's land rested on the north side of the butte, close to the isthmus connecting Cuny Table to the Stronghold. The ground was pocked with dry brown grass, just like the vegetation throughout the rest of Pine Ridge that spring: no trees, just dust below and sky above. They could see in the west the humped blue silhouettes of the Black Hills, and Black Elk pointed out Harney Peak. Around noon they made camp at the edge of the precipice; they built a small fire and roasted some prairie chickens Neihardt had shot on the way. The poet wore a Colt revolver strapped to his hip for these daylong excursions, and had become a good shot over the years. He worried about the propriety of hunting on the reservation, but Ben assured him, "This is *our* land, and we can hunt whenever we want to!"

Black Elk continued his narrative for about four hours, then rose to visit the Stronghold; considering the state of the road, it was best to head back before darkness fell. Before they left, however, he wanted to lift his voice in prayer. He faced the Black Hills and placed Ben on his right, as a symbol of his future generations, and the Neihardts on his left, representing the coming generations of the white world. "Hey-a-a-hey!" he cried four times: "Grandfather, the Great Spirit, behold us on earth, the two-leggeds. The flowering stick that you have given to me has not bloomed, and my people are in despair." Yet now a new chance had materialized, this effort by "I myself, Black Elk, and my nephew, Mr. Neihardt," and maybe the Grandfathers would take pity this time. Help us, he asked, so "that our generation in the future will live and walk the good road with the flowering stick to success."

There was silence. Night was coming. They went home.

Two more days passed, and Black Elk's narrative wound down. The old man would grow quiet, as if the thread had almost run out; during this time Neihardt asked questions that he'd put off, tying up loose ends. He asked Black Elk about the *yuwipi* ritual: the old man described the ceremony in detail, but when Neihardt asked if he'd be willing to stage a demonstration, Black Elk firmly answered, "I do not care to do that anymore." He seemed to feel that he'd progressed spiritually beyond that point, so the subject was not broached again.

Another subject they did not press was Black Elk's Catholicism. Neihardt knew he'd been a successful catechist; he was curious why Black Elk had put aside his old ways to take up those of the Black Robes. "Because my children have to live in this world," he replied, and nothing more. Again, Neihardt did not press: he was not a journalist, burrowing into uncomfortable subjects, but a poet, and the beauty of Black Elk's Vision was complete for him. Neihardt always let Black Elk take the lead in the interviews: if he did not elaborate on something, that said to Neihardt that the old man no longer felt it was where his true beliefs lay.

The events of the next morning seemed to verify this to Neihardt. On Thursday, May 28, most of Black Elk's family went to the annual Catholic Indian Congress, held this year at Holy Rosary. Because the old man was one of the senior and most well-known catechists, his absence was probably noted; at the same time, he'd cut back on his activities to the extent that it may not have elicited much comment. At least for a little while Black Elk's world seems to have contracted, most probably because of his physical condition. Agency officials and the residents of Manderson were well aware of Neihardt's presence, but the Jesuits at Holy Rosary seem to have been left in the dark. Not even Lucy informed them—not yet, not now. Instead, when Hilda asked about Lucy, Ellen, and the others, the answer was vague and mysterious: "Not to be mentioned." Only Ben and the old man stayed behind.

That afternoon, in the relative quiet, Black Elk finished the story of his life up through the Ghost Dance and Wounded Knee. He grew melancholy when he had finished. Several times during the long interview he'd told Neihardt that by "giving away" his Great Vision, he gave away his power—which sounded ominously like he'd given away his life. He reiterated that now: "I have given you my power, and now I am just a poor old man."

Yet in the same breath, he'd ask Neihardt to take him to Harney

Peak. He would soon be "under the grass," but before that happened he wanted to visit the center of the earth one last time. It surprised Neihardt to learn that he'd apparently never been there, at least not in the flesh; his only visit was when he was nine and the Grandfathers took him there. But the spiritual and physical seemed the same to Black Elk, and such a visit would close the circle of his life, he said. There was something he wanted to tell the Six Grandfathers when he made it to the top, and then he would be at peace before he died. "We will go, Black Elk," Neihardt always promised. "We will all drive to Harney Peak in the Black Hills together just as soon as your story is finished!"

And now the story was over. The next morning, the Neihardts, Black Elk, and Ben drove to the center of the world.

———·•·———

They left early for the Black Hills on Friday, May 29, dismantling their prized tipi and stuffing it in the backseat, throwing everything else not already loaded in with it. The interviews were over, and they said good-bye to Lucy, Ellen, and the rest of their adopted family. In the future, when they wrote, they would address one another as uncle, nephew, or niece; later, Ben would write that it was lonesome on the allotment without them. Black Elk and Ben followed the Gardner in Ben's old Ford.

The trip took all day. They drove to Brennan, then followed Highway 18 to Hot Springs. There they stopped for lunch, and saw that a carnival had hit town. Enid and Hilda wanted to ride the Ferris wheel, and they urged Black Elk to join them. The old man was reluctant, but by now Enid was the sweetheart of the Indians: she was pretty, bright, and personable, and had worked the long hours of the interviews without the least complaint. Several of the young men seemed to be in love with her; in her diary she mentioned Joe Masters and George Sandix Ledoux, for whom she also seemed to harbor a crush. Even Standing Bear would present her with fresh milk from his milk cow—a delicacy. If Enid set her mind to it, she could make the Indian men do just about anything.

So Black Elk relented, and was immediately sorry. He was terrified by the swinging basket of the Ferris wheel. Every time the wheel stopped to let someone on or off, it seemed Black Elk and the girls were stuck at the top, holding tight to the precarious chair. Every time the chair passed the operator, Black Elk cried, "'top! 'top!," the only English the girls had heard him utter. It did not help: the carny did not pull back on his lever. Black Elk got the full ride.

They headed north on Highway 83 through Custer and on to Sylvan Lake, the smooth and deep blue body of water that sat at the foot of Harney Peak. This was weird, imposing country: one drove past the Needles, up into the elevations of towering Ponderosa pine. The Sylvan Lodge sprawled along the edge of the frigid lake, a white-frame resort that drew visitors from all over the central United States. A village of small cabins clustered near the lake's edge behind a general store, and Neihardt rented two.

At this point, Hilda's picture-perfect memory for once grew slightly fuzzy. Sometime during the day—whether in Hot Springs, Custer, or farther north in Rapid City—the five took in a movie. Neither could she remember the name of the picture. Several movies were playing that day in these towns, and all were Westerns—except one: a romantic comedy titled *The Naughty Flirt*, with Myrna Loy, later of *Thin Man* fame. On weekdays the movies only ran at night, and in Rapid City the comedy ran at 7:15 and 9:15 p.m. in a double feature with Rin Tin Tin.

Yet Hilda remembered Black Elk's reaction to the picture quite well. She sat beside him in the darkened theater and watched the tale of a young woman who was "brazen or forward or flirty." It is uncertain whether Black Elk disliked Loy or her costar Alice White, but every time one of them did something on-screen that "a good young woman should not do," Black Elk hissed "*Sheetsha! Sheetsha!*" or "Bad! Bad!" Hilda spent much of the picture calming him down.

The next morning, the five breakfasted at the Sylvan Lodge, then began their four-mile climb. The weather on May 30, 1931, was warm and pleasant: a high of 66 degrees Fahrenheit, with no mention of rain. At the higher elevations, however, it would have been brisk, and Enid kept her coat on the entire way.

The climb seemed a long one. One starts at Sylvan Lake at 6,000 feet; the altitude at the top of Harney Peak is 7,240. Though not necessarily mountain climbing, Hilda considered it a heavy hike, while Enid wrote, "That was some climb!" The rocky path went up, then down, over and over. One begins in meadows of daisies and thistle, then the path turns rocky. Lava fingers stand along the path like watchmen. Near the very top, rocky promontories build one upon the other, and one clambers hand over hand.

For Black Elk, the climb was a struggle. The group stopped several times to let him rest, and during one of these pauses Black Elk told Ben that if he still had any of his old power left, something should happen on the summit. Ben asked what that might be.

"A little lightning, a little thunder, and a little rain," the old man replied. Ben looked around—the day was bright and clear. Nevertheless, said Black Elk, his power had always come from the west. If he had any left, the Thunder-beings would send a greeting from that direction.

The last rocky ascent was precipitous, and to reach the top, said Hilda, "we just *climbed*." The summit was partially flat, and all grew silent: one could see in a huge circle, a view that extended seventy-five to one hundred miles before dissolving at the horizon into blue haze.

"Right over there is where I stood in my vision," said Black Elk, pointing to a high, jutting column of rock, Harney Peak's highest point, "but the hoop of the world about me was different, for what I saw was in the spirit." He'd prepared in advance for this address to the gods. In his Vision, he'd been naked except for his breechclout, his body painted red, the color of the right red road. But the girls were there and he didn't want to embarrass them, so he stepped behind an outcrop and a few minutes later emerged wearing a bright red union suit, commonly called long johns. Over that he wore a black or dark blue breechclout, trimmed in green, and on his feet high stockings and beaded moccasins. He'd donned a buffalo-hide headdress with a single eagle feather hanging in front and several more hanging behind. It looked very much like the headdress in Black Elk's photos from the Buffalo Bill Wild West, only older and a little crushed, and may very well have been the same.

He also carried in the crook of his arm his pipe, hung with an eagle feather representing *Wakan Tanka*, and four colored ribbons representing the earth's four corners. He looked around the rough peak and picked his way to a point directly beneath the high rock upon which he'd stood in his dream. He stretched upright, offering the pipe in one hand with the mouthpiece up, the other hand extended palm-out toward the sky. Neihardt had brought with him a Kodak 3A camera with a pull-out bellows that produced a photo about the size of a postcard. The others grew silent, transfixed. "*Tunkashila, Wakan Tanka*, you have been always, and before you nothing has been," the old man cried. "There is nothing to pray to but you." Neihardt focused his lens. "Grandfather, lean close to the earth, that you may hear the voice I send."

It was a long, eloquent prayer, similar to the one he'd sent out at Cuny Table, but now more impassioned, as if this was his last chance to be heard. "All over the world the faces of living things are alike," and now he prayed for them. He'd been told, when he was still young and believed in his ability and strength, "that in difficulty I should send a voice four times, one to each quarter of the earth, and you would hear me. To-day I send a voice for a people in despair."

He reiterated his Vision, as if the gods had forgotten. Tears ran from his eyes. Years ago he'd observed how hard it was to cry on cue during prayers and lamentations, but today it was not hard. He reminded the Grandfathers how, when they'd brought him to this spot, the world's sacred tree was blooming, a promise to shield his people for all time. Now the tree had withered, but he refused to believe it had died.

"It may be that some little root of the sacred tree still lives," he cried. Nourish it, he pleaded; let it live again. "Hear me, not for myself, but for my people; I am old. Hear me, that they may once more go back into the sacred hoop and find the good red road, the shielding tree."

As he prayed, the others watched what formed above them in the "bright, brassy, cloudless sky." A few thin clouds gathered, and a light, chill drizzle began to fall. Thunder muttered low, without lightning, like a familiar voice too distant to catch the words.

"Oh, make my people live," Black Elk cried. He grew quiet, his face uplifted, until the mist dissolved.

All awaited more. But there was only silence, and a final smattering of rain.

26

DEFENDERS OF THE FAITH

The little group descended in silence, each alone with his or her thoughts. Neihardt, for his part, was astounded. Black Elk's words upon that strange, lonely prominence . . . the light rain and distant thunder emerging from emptiness . . . all seemed fraught with mystery. How, he wondered, could it be anything but an acknowledgment to the old *wicasa wakan* of his plea?

They planned to eat dinner in the Lodge, but it was too late by the time they arrived, so they purchased ten roast beef sandwiches and downed them in the cabin. The mood was subdued. All felt they'd "been in the presence of something very large," said Hilda, "very mysterious, very meaningful." Something *numinous*, to recall Rudolf Otto. That feeling of mystery never left Hilda: the moment had rooted deep, and the sense of wonder grew.

The next morning, they packed up the two cars and began the trip home. They drove to Hill City, where Neihardt topped off Ben's Ford with oil and gas and father and son headed east to Manderson. "We told them good-bye," Enid wrote, "and sadly parted." Neihardt turned north to Deadwood, and took his girls to the saloon where Wild Bill Hickok had been killed. They camped at Spearfish, planning to continue west to the Custer Memorial, but discovered that "the rear end of the Gardner had gone out" and had to wait for repairs. After that, Neihardt and Enid drove two days straight home to Branson.

He was in a fever to start, but first Enid had to transcribe her four spiral notebooks of shorthand. It was a long, laborious process. She rearranged the material in rough chronological order, smoothed out the grammar, deleted redundancies, then typed it for her father. Although this added one more level of interpretation between Black Elk and the reader, Enid's transcript followed the notes almost exactly.

While she worked, Neihardt got his thoughts in order. Even before returning home, he'd written Julius House from Spearfish: "This is going to be the first absolutely Indian book thus far written," he claimed. "It is all out of the consciousness," almost exactly the same claim Carl Jung would make two decades later. Neihardt called the Great Vision "vast, in extent, full of profound significance and perfectly formed," and even then knew that the prayer on Harney Peak would be the book's closing chapter.

Neihardt was more pragmatic in his June 21 letter to William Morrow. He made suggestions about marketing, and said the material he'd gotten from Black Elk "is richer than I had expected it to be and there is much in [there] no white man has heard before." Then, as now, books sold better if made into a movie, and he asked Morrow whether "it might not be possible to interest some movie [studio] in producing it . . . especially the Horse Dance dream." When Neihardt had mentioned the same idea to Black Elk, the old man had grown excited and said he could probably drum up some willing Oglalas to act in the film. Within a day of receipt, Morrow wrote or wired back his excitement, but suggested making a movie of not only the Horse Dance, but Black Elk's entire story.

Neihardt had barely heard from Morrow when, on June 27, he wrote a letter to "Uncle Black Elk" and a second to Ben. He'd been greatly affected by what he'd seen on Harney Peak: he'd already told House that "the old man seemed broken and very sad." To Ben, he brought hope: "Morrow is a very knowing man and will do the best possible with our idea," he said. "There seems to be a good reason to believe that a great many people are going to know about your father in the next two years, and I think this book is going to make him a happier man." He echoed this to Black Elk: "My publisher means business," he said. "You can depend upon me to see that you get what is justified."

He was so taken with his experience that he mentioned moving to Pine Ridge. He planned to buy a section of land that abutted Black Elk's allotment and was filled with "Prairie Chickens and Jack Rabbits," he told House. Ben promised to get the section number so Neihardt could start the purchase process; Neihardt went so far as to write the agent. "We could all live very happy there and may do so," he exclaimed. His adoption into the tribe had been more than symbolic; he was part of the family and wanted to live in his new home. He felt more comfortable—more *at home*—in Manderson than anywhere else.

With Black Elk's story, Neihardt felt he had discovered an alternative to the American myth that the West could only have been "civilized" by means of "savage war." The typical account blamed Native Americans as instigators of a war of extermination; Neihardt rejected the national narrative, and hoped to show otherwise by exposing the real "savages" at Wounded Knee. The beauty and grace one found in life came from balance, not conflict, and he saw Black Elk's quest as a search for greater understanding in every sphere. Too many secrets had been lost in the national slaughter. Truth did not reside in a gun.

Neihardt worked at an inspired rate, writing in longhand on oversized sheets directly from Enid's transcripts. He set aside *The Song of the Messiah* while the experiences of Pine Ridge were still fresh. For historical material, he referred to the sources he'd already collected for his 1925 *Song of the Indian Wars*. He puzzled out the chronology, tried to make sense of the Great Vision, and spent a lot of effort editing text until he could "reflect an echo" of the rhythms of spoken Lakota.

Neihardt conceived the text as an elegy—a prose poem of lamentation for the dead and for a vanished age. The first six paragraphs are in his words, a paraphrase of Black Elk's words in the interviews that sum up his motives for telling his story. "My friend," he wrote, "I am going to tell you the story of my life, as you wish; and if it were only the story of my life I think I would not tell it; for what is one man that he should make much of his winters, even when they bend him like a heavy snow?" It begins, as it ends, on Harney Peak, thus completing the circle of Black Elk's life; it is the story not of a great warrior or chief, but of tragic failure—of a "mighty vision given to a man too weak to use it . . . and of a people's dream that died in bloody snow."

Black Elk's personal story was always set against that of his people. Their life is his life; his failure, theirs. Even though the second chapter begins with Black Elk's birth, it is framed within the apocalypses of Sweet Medicine and Drinks Water. From the moment of his birth, Black Elk follows in the tradition of the Old Testament prophets: he tries to save his people, but fails. All that remains in the end is a poetic lament that serves as a warning to the future.

None of this departs from the transcripts, and Neihardt adheres closely to Black Elk's words. There are omissions, but they are few: Neihardt omits a section in the origin of the Sacred Pipe that describes the birth of an old woman from a buffalo; he leaves out some kill-talks and that portion of the Great Vision describing the use of the soldier weed to wipe out the *wasichu*, believing that this distracted from its greater message of renewal for all men. Perhaps the greatest omission was Black Elk's Catholicism, yet in truth Black Elk did not dwell on that portion of his life in the interviews: he mentions the death of the priest who interfered with his healing ritual—without specifically naming Bosch—and tells Neihardt that he became Catholic because his children "have to live in the world." But other than this, it is only through Lucy and Catholic records that we learn of his conversion and career as a lay preacher.

One later criticism was that the book's "otherworldliness" detracted from the reality of Black Elk's daily life as a rancher, catechist, and family man. Yet the sixteen days of interviews show that Black Elk absolutely interpreted his life in terms of his Great Vision. All else was secondary. Both Black Elk and Neihardt made mysticism the very core of the old man's existence, and by so doing, created between them a Black Elk who was less an everyday person and more a tragic figure of mythic proportions.

Where Black Elk saw the book as a means to save and pass on his Vision, Neihardt always intended it as a work of art. But the two were not exclusive. Through Neihardt, Black Elk preserved his Vision; through Black Elk, Neihardt created a literary masterpiece that transcended ordinary "Indian biographies." In the process, it became not only an interpretation of the whole of Lakota culture, but also a tragedy symbolizing the greater tragedy of the Native American. It became a commentary on the ruthlessness of empire, and on the costs of the American Dream.

Neihardt finished the manuscript in October, and sent it to Morrow under the title *The Tree That Never Bloomed*. But soon bad news arrived. On November 11, 1931, the fifty-eight-year-old Morrow died suddenly of nephritis and related kidney problems following a three-week illness. Neihardt missed Morrow's support almost immediately. Soon after the publisher's death, a letter from an editor suggested to Neihardt that the Great Vision be excised from the narrative and slapped on the end of the book as an appendix. "Rarely had I seen my father so angry, so upset," Hilda said. Neihardt stormed about the house, threatening to withdraw the manuscript and go elsewhere. A flurry of letters passed back and forth, and in the end Neihardt prevailed. But neither did the new editor like Neihardt's original title, and so the poet searched for a new one. One day, his wife and he bandied titles when finally Mona sighed, "Oh, John, why don't you just call it *Black Elk Speaks?*," slowly emphasizing each word. Neihardt liked the suggestion, thinking it gave proper credit to the old holy man. Yet what seemed elegant and simple at the time would create misunderstandings about the book's authorship over the years.

There were other problems. Without Morrow's encouragement, the publishing house either made no effort to have a movie made or did not try very hard. On his own, Neihardt was unable to find financial backing. The plan to settle in Pine Ridge withered and died.

Black Elk Speaks: Being the Life Story of a Holy Man of the Oglala Sioux as told to John G. Neihardt was released in 1932 in a cloth edition that included Standing Bear's paintings. Though it received little publicity, it did garner strong reviews. Some critics called it the most insightful book ever published on Native American shamanism and "primitive psychology." *The New York Times* was impressed by the book's poetry, and said of the Wounded Knee episodes that "for such scarifying detail, at once prophetic and horrifying, one will have to go to Tolstoy's 'War and Peace' to find its equal." Others called it "beautiful" and "spiritual." But the reading public at the time was not interested in a strange Sioux visionary, and the book was a financial failure. *Black Elk Speaks* was soon out of print, and unsold volumes traded on the remainder table for forty-five cents a copy. Even at such a low price, Neihardt could not afford to buy many copies, and no record remains of what he told Black Elk.

If the publication of *Black Elk Speaks* did not gain much traction with the reading public, it caused a stir at Pine Ridge. Agent Courtright, who'd helped Neihardt find Black Elk two years earlier, called it "a beautiful work" when Neihardt sent him a signed copy. "I am writing to

Black Elk and Standing Bear to congratulate them on their material. The claim and delight of the book, however, remain distinctly yours."

A hint of the book's effect on others surfaced soon after publication. In 1932, the ethnographer Ella Deloria—herself a Yankton Sioux—wrote Neihardt after reading the first edition: "I have just finished 'Black Elk Speaks.' I want you to know that it makes me happy and sad all at once—sad for the days that are gone, and glad that a white man really lives who can enter into a right understanding of a Dakota's vision, and can translate it into so poetic a form."

The Black Elks were also pleased. In the year of the book's release, Ben and Ellen had a new baby boy; they named him John Neihardt Black Elk, and Ben wrote that he had "something of the blood of Crazy Horse in him." Neihardt realized that no more powerful symbol of respect existed in Sioux culture than such an act. On July 12, 1932, he wrote to Julius House: "I am genuinely thrilled by the idea that one of Crazy Horse's blood should bear my name."

One has to wonder what Black Elk felt when he held his book in his hands. No record of that moment has been preserved. No doubt he felt relieved that his Great Vision would live. Yet there must also have been some trepidation. He'd revealed his double life, and on a national stage. How would the Black Robes react? His fears of dying without leaving behind a record apparently overrode the caution he imparted to Frank Fools Crow during the 1916 train ride.

For their part, the Jesuit fathers were shocked, especially by the ending on Harney Peak. To suggest that one of their most valued catechists—the man they'd paraded to the world as an "Indian Saint Paul"—still practiced the old religion horrified them. To accept *Black Elk Speaks* at face value questioned their efforts in the four decades after Wounded Knee. The worst part for them was the representation of Black Elk as a still-practicing "pagan," praying to the Six Grandfathers when he knew that the Catholic God and Trinity were the only true source of salvation. The portrayal suggested that not only had the Jesuits failed in their mission, but they'd also been played for fools.

They certainly felt betrayed, and wondered whether they'd nurtured a snake in the garden. Their approach had been two-pronged: win souls while wiping out the medicine men. If Frank Fools Crow can be believed, they had good reason for concern. The medicine men had not disappeared, but adapted; at the same time that *wicasa wakan* such as

Black Elk held on to their old beliefs, they were Catholic, too. Frank Fools Crow discovered during this period that given the right rituals, he could heat sweat-lodge rocks without a fire; these "animated" rocks then helped him in his healing ceremonies, he said. Black Elk heard and came to his nephew for verification. When Fools Crow performed the ceremony, his uncle seemed impressed: "Black Elk held his hands out toward [the rocks] and said [they] might even be hotter than they are when heated in the usual way. When we were finished we were both perspiring as in a regular sweatbath. Afterward, he shook my hand, said he believed in me and in the power of my prayers, and went home thoroughly convinced." Thus, like the elders who'd counseled him in his youth, Black Elk was now helping to raise the next generation of *wicasa wakan*. The younger men honored him: Black Elk, said Fools Crow, had "earned a place above all of the other Teton holy men."

No one reacted more vehemently than Father Placidus Sialm. By now, Sialm wielded real power at Holy Rosary. He turned sixty in the year of the book's release, and he'd spent thirty-six years—more than half of his life—among the Sioux at Rosebud and Pine Ridge. His features softened as the dark black hair and beard turned white, but he felt a real ownership for the souls of his Lakota and age had made him "embittered against the Indians because he is disliked by them on account of his incorrigible nagging," wrote the more tolerant Father Buechel in his diary. Now Sialm attacked *Black Elk Speaks* and the authors, writing long screeds in "Camp Churches," a series of mimeographed sketches and musings on reservation life read by Catholics throughout Pine Ridge and clearly intended for wider publication.

Sialm fired broadsides on all fronts, and as Buechel said, the tone was embittered. Rather than accept *Black Elk Speaks* as a valid portrait of Black Elk's life, he called the old man an "ignorant Indian" before his conversion: "There is scarcely one Indian who went across the Ocean and got so little out of it as was Nick Black Elk." Indeed, before the arrival of Catholicism, the old ways praised in *Black Elk Speaks* had been sordid and vile. "The story of Black Elk clearly proves that the old times had more ways of starvation than the latter days," he said. "The buffalos did not run into the mouth of the Indian and did not cover the ground like Manna in the Indian camps." The bison, not the Sioux, controlled the Plains, dragging the tribes in their wake. The children were wild and the parents "not smart enough to stop their wild nature." Sialm concluded: "There is not much beauty in all the olden times."

Sialm's greatest animus was reserved for Neihardt, whom he condemned as a thief and a fraud. "Nic Black Elk could have finished the book with a fine chapter of his conversion," Sialm wrote. Instead, "Mr. N——," to whom he never referred by name, "seems to enjoy paganism more than Christianity. The last performance of Nic Black Elk on Harney Peak was rather theatrical than true. It was to satisfy the author who paid him for it," a contention unsupported by evidence. By ending *Black Elk Speaks* on Harney Peak, Neihardt had committed "one of the worst exploitations ever done to an honest Indian," Sialm said. "It could fairly be put into a class of not only Exploitation, but what is worse, of stealing—plagiarism—material for a book, cleverly done, a kind of kidnapping the very words of a man, of an Indian, and translated them into a new language to disguise the fraud."

If these had merely been the private rants of an irate priest, all well and good. That was his right. Instead, Sialm laid out a framework for pressure and attacks that would last at least through 1940, if not beyond. He insinuated himself into the feud that had started during the interviews between Lucy and Ben, and had everything to do with the old man's legacy. And Black Elk was worried about death, possibly more so than on Harney Peak. In the winter of 1933, he was driving a team of horses, which spooked and ran away with him. He was pitched from the wagon and run over, snapping two ribs. Though he was rushed to the hospital, his condition deteriorated through Christmas. By January 1934, his family and he believed that his last days were near.

Reminders of mortality were everywhere. In 1933, the year of his accident, his stalwart cousin died. By all accounts, Standing Bear took pride in the paintings that appeared in *Black Elk Speaks*, but whether he was hounded by the Jesuits is not known. Something in his generally unruffled demeanor suggests it would not have mattered much if he was. Earlier that year, Louise was involved in a traffic accident and died soon afterward. Standing Bear, who'd already been sick during the 1931 interviews, grew depressed with the passing of his beloved Across the Eastern Water Woman. His daughters tried to console him, but he seemed to feel no need to continue. Later that year he followed Louise.

On January 26, 1934, Black Elk was still recuperating in the hospital when he allegedly wrote and signed what has been titled "Black Elk Speaks Again—A Last Word." This sounds for all the world like a final declaration of faith; Black Elk says in the two-and-a-half-page letter that he'd just been given Extreme Unction and the Holy Eucharist—the "holy oil and the Holy Food, the 'Yutapi Wakan.'" It was, he said, his "last word." If anything, it appears to be a deathbed repudiation of *Black Elk Speaks.* "A white man made a book and told what I had spoken of older times, but the new times he left out," Black Elk said. "So I speak again, a last word." He summarizes his baptism at the hands of Father Lindebner, his years as a catechist and a missionary. In the last paragraph, he abjures the old Indian ways he celebrated in the 1931 interviews: "The medicine men looked for their own glory and for presents," he wrote. "Christ taught us to be humble and stop sin. Indian medicine men did not stop sin." He signs the document "Nick Black Elk" and it is witnessed by his daughter, Lucy Looks Twice, and the Jesuit father Joseph A. Zimmerman, a younger priest who has proved to be a close ally of Sialm's.

The letter was dictated and written in Lakota, then translated— apparently by Lucy. Typed copies of the Lakota and English versions were signed by Black Elk, witnessed, and preserved in the records of Holy Rosary. Sialm wrote in "Camp Churches" that "this Declaration should stand in every new Edition of Black Elk Speaks," and it was circulated around Holy Rosary and Pine Ridge. The general impression given by the priests was that Black Elk gave the statement of his own free will; even the scholar Raymond DeMallie said it had "all the indications of sincerity." Most Catholic commentators see this "last word" as the *final* word.

Yet evidence in the text suggests that the statement was composed under the threat of eternal damnation, and Black Elk, who genuinely thought he was dying, was terrified. "The church people frightened him to death when *Black Elk Speaks* came out," Hilda Neihardt said in a 1997 interview. "They had him so scared that for awhile he denied Neihardt," though in a couple of years he would write the poet again, addressing him as "My dear friend." It was the same technique described in the early 1900s in the diaries of Father Florentine Digmann: "We had a special eye on the sick, not to let them go without baptism," threatening an eternity in Hell if one held to the old ways. Medicine men, Sialm says in "Camp Churches," are "worthy of death," quoting Romans 1:32. In fact, much of Black Elk's declaration is straight from Sialm's pen. When Black Elk supposedly writes, "Your white friends should read 2 Peter 2-20, 2," Sialm spells it out explicitly in "Camp Churches": "He knows better than Neithard [*sic*] the Words of Peter II.2.22." One can hear this very passage quoted to Black Elk at what all believed to be his deathbed. It would have been better if those who converted to Christianity and then recanted had never converted at all: "The dog is turned to his own vomit again; and the sow that was washed to her wallowing in the mire."

This was strong medicine, especially for a man whose entire life had been a spiritual quest and who was convinced he would soon die. Ben was not there, and the bedside retraction was apparently orchestrated by Lucy. Yet Ben had apparently already been called on the carpet for his part in *Black Elk Speaks*, saying finally that "the last chapter was not in the intention of his father"—at least, according to Sialm. Though neither Ben nor his father ever denied the sincerity of Black Elk's appeal to the Grandfathers on Harney Peak, they lived in an impoverished world where the Church still controlled the resources for daily life, and knew that some compromise had to be made.

After Father Buechel, Sialm was the most veteran priest at Pine Ridge. Unlike Buechel, Sialm was not a scholar, nor enlightened in the sense of Westropp or the earlier Father Craft, all of whom tried to balance an understanding of Lakota ways with their own Christian beliefs. In fact, Buechel and Westropp may have been in the minority on the reservation: Buechel would later comment that Westropp was "the only other Jesuit out there with whom he felt and thought alike regarding their work as missionaries," and both worked closely with Black Elk. This suggests Sialm was merely the most vocal proponent of the dominant attitude regarding Sioux ways.

Trained as a disciplinarian, Sialm was revealed in his writings as he grew older to be a demagogue and scourge. No belief system is monolithic: if Buechel and Westropp were the kinds of Jesuits who elicited devotion and affection from the Oglala, Sialm was the portrait of the blinkered priest whom generations of Lakota would blame for forcing them to hate their very identity. Sialm was a defender of the faith. The Inquisition had descended upon Ben and his father, and the two stood alone.

Neither Black Elk nor Ben apparently ever told Neihardt what they endured. In some important ways it was a family matter—a philosophical tug-of-war between Lucy and Ben over their father's public identity—and had to be handled discreetly. It was not in the nature of Lakota culture to divulge such things to outsiders, even trusted ones. But Ben did drop hints. When he wrote to Neihardt on June 4, 1934, about Black Elk's recuperation, he said, "Father got well but he wasn't the old man he used to be." He referred in the same letter to Lucy's friend Emil Afraid of Hawk, and possibly to some community backlash sparked by what the priests called Black Elk's backsliding. "Emil A. Hawk has been loading the old man about a lot of things," Ben wrote. "The old man felt uneasy for awhile. But he is perfectly satisfied, very glad to hear you are coming again."

Neihardt did return later that summer with Hilda and his youngest daughter, Alice. They camped on Ben's land on Wounded Knee Creek; he hoped to finish up *The Song of the Messiah* in the area where the poem's final tragic act unfolded. The time the two families spent together does not suggest any belief on Ben's part that Neihardt had cheated his father: the poet bought a steer, which the Black Elks butchered and dried for the winter; at one point the Neihardts, Ben, Ben's oldest son, Henry, and daughter Esther all saddled up to drive in Ben's herd. Black Elk was not present: he was "working in Colorado," Hilda said. The timing suggests he was on a dance circuit, and part of the absence may have been spent in Cheyenne's Frontier Days.

It did not take long for the priests to learn of Neihardt's return. One day, Hilda recalled, an unidentified missionary came to call on the poet. The two "sat on the grass under a tree for an hour or so, chatting and expressing in a friendly fashion their differing views." At one point, the priest expressed concern about the poet's spiritual welfare. "But don't you fear God?" he asked.

"Fear God?" Neihardt shot back. "No! God and I are good friends!"

All seemed very civilized. Yet Neihardt's visit evidently alarmed Holy Rosary, for on September 20, 1934—soon after the poet's departure and Black Elk's return from the dance circuit—a second letter, purportedly written by the old holy man, appeared. This one, filled with grammatical and factual errors, makes accusations that ultimately run counter to the record and to Ben's extended hospitality to Neihardt and his girls:

Dear Friends—

Three years ago in 1932 a white man named John G. Neihardt came up to my place whom I have never met before and asked me to write a story book with him[.] I don't know whether he took out a permit from the agent or not[.] He promised me that if he completed and publish [*sic*] this book he was to pay half of the price of each book[.]

I trusted him and finished the story of my life for him[.] [A]fter he published the book I wrote to him and ask [*sic*] him about the price which he promise [*sic*] me on the books he sold[.] He answered my letter and told me that there was another white man who has asked him to make this book so he himself hasn't seen a cent from the Book which we made[.]

By this I know he was now deceiving me about the whole business[.] I also asked to put at the end of this story that I was not a pagan but have converted into the Catholic Church in which I work [*sic*] as a Catechist for more than 25 years[.] I've quit all these pagan works[.] But he didn't mention [these] last talks[.]

So if they cant put this Religion life in the last part of that Book also if he cant pay what he promised I ask you my dear friends that this Book of my life will be null & void[.] Because I value my soul more than my Body[.] Im awful sorry for the mistake I've made[.]

I also have this witnesses [*sic*] to stand by me[.]

"This is a difficult document to assess," said the scholar Raymond DeMallie. "It is not signed by Black Elk, and the motive for writing it is not clear." It is a troubling document, and many commentators today seem to think it was dictated by Black Elk to quiet the priests and then translated by Lucy. Yet neither Black Elk nor Ben ever showed evidence in their letters or actions of harboring the kind of anger against the poet expressed here. In addition, everything Black Elk wrote in his name bore his signature. Finally, Lucy's translation of the January 1934 "Black Elk Speaks Again" is far more polished and error-free. "It is possible," DeMallie speculates, that Lucy "was the actual author," but this would suggest that Lucy mimicked the unlettered style of her father—in effect committing outright fraud. This, too, is hard to believe.

One other explanation exists—one never suggested yet supported by evidence within the letter. Father Sialm committed the fraud. A comparison of the letter and Sialm's style in "Camp Churches" raises suspicions. The grammatical mistakes and run-on sentences are similar. Such English phrases as "he himself hasn't seen a cent," "null & void," and "I value my soul more than my Body," are not in Black Elk's idiom, while they are in Sialm's.

More damning than anything else is the letter's obsession with "paganism." Black Elk may have renounced the old ways when he converted in 1904, but never, in either his interviews or his letters, did he call his belief in *Wakan Tanka* "pagan." To do so in 1934 would be to renounce Frank Fools Crow and the young generation of *wicasa wakan* for whom Black Elk served as a mentor. But Sialm was prone to such diatribes, and denouncements of "pagans" pop up throughout his discussion of Black Elk in "Camp Churches." He writes: "Black Elk Speaks reveals only the pagan." Neihardt "seems to enjoy paganism more than Christianity." If Black Elk had died at Wounded Knee "with 'papa' in his mouth he would have been nothing better than the old pagans." And so on.

One other moment serves to indict Sialm. By 1935, Black Elk had grown fed up with the abusive old priest. He would not be pushed around anymore. One day that spring, his granddaughter Esther was visiting the cabin; Black Elk readied his pipe for his morning smoke when "here was Father Sialm knocking on the door." When he saw Black Elk smoking the pipe, he rushed inside:

> Father Sialm grabbed the pipe and said, "This is the work of the devil!" And he took it and threw it out the door on the ground.
>
> My grandfather didn't say a word. He got up and took the priest's prayer book and threw it out on the ground. Then they both looked at each other, and nobody said one word that whole time.

Finally, both men walked outside. Sialm picked up his prayer book; Black Elk, his pipe. They turned around, shook hands, and walked back in the house. Yet never again would Black Elk be bullied into making or signing statements renouncing the old faith.

And more than anything else, the abuse set him upon his final path to save his people.

27

DISCIPLES

In the spring of 1935, around the same time as the confrontation with Sialm, another dust-covered coupe rattled to a stop before Black Elk's cabin. This time the driver was no stranger—Alex Duhamel and Black Elk were old friends. They'd known each other since the turn of the century, when the teenage Alex punched cows around White River and Black Elk was still a medicine man. Since Alex spoke Lakota, no interpreter was necessary. It was a long drive from Rapid City to Manderson, so the two rarely saw each other. They scooted two cottonwood stumps into the shadows and caught up on old times.

The Duhamels were one of the oldest business families in the Black Hills, descendants of a French Canadian adventurer who'd trekked west in 1857 at age nineteen with seventy dollars in his pocket. Their holdings now included cattle, timber, and a sizable "Pioneer Western Store" in Rapid City, best known for its handmade saddles, "the Best on Earth." They also sold Native American crafts, and had traded with the Lakota for decades. Lately they'd hired a number of Indian craftsmen to handle the burgeoning tourist trade.

The Duhamels had recently bought a seven-hundred-acre plot of land nine miles south of Rapid City, in a place called Rockerville Gulch. The property included an extensive network of caverns, while the plateau above was known locally as the spot where Sitting Bull camped during his annual trip to cut jack pines for tipi poles. It was a smart investment: shortly after 1925, when work on Mount Rushmore started, the state built a road from Rapid City to the monument that ran right past the Duhamels' land.

Black Elk had an idea. He'd thought about it for a while, probably after hearing about the Duhamels' purchase and its "crystal cave." He told a Lakota with easier access to Duhamel—probably one of the hired craftsmen—that he wanted to speak with Alex about his notion.

Black Elk wanted to put on a show—but not just any show. He wanted to create a village and "pageant" modeled after the Indian segments of Cody's Wild West—a permanent fixture that would run daily during tourist season and provide regular employment for the Oglala. "I always want to come back to Holy Land," he told Duhamel, "a quiet place away from the non-believing Indians," or those who disparaged the old ways. Though the show never seemed an implicit break with Christianity, it was probably a way for Black Elk to escape the upheavals surrounding *Black Elk Speaks*. More important, such a show would be a means to preserve the old ways and teach the anticipated hordes of whites that the Lakota were not the savages depicted in novels and movies. Their culture was worthy of esteem. "Nick really wanted people to understand his people, that's why he did the pageant," said Alex's son Francis, better known as Bud. It was a way to keep his people alive.

It's possible that the idea of a dance project had been building in his mind for a while. He'd danced before the kings and queens of Europe; before tens of thousands of *wasichus* in New York, London, and Paris. With little more than a drumbeat, he'd held them in thrall. Grandmother England had blessed him when he'd performed for her. Performance bridged the cultures and awoke in the audience something profound.

He may also have been the first among the Oglala to understand the power of publicity. He'd already begun to make himself a fixture at these western celebrations, from Cheyenne's Frontier Days to the big anniversary at the Custer Memorial, yet the desire for a local event seemed to grow with the numbers of tourists. As early as 1927, a small group of Lakotas would pitch a summer camp in a part of Rapid City called Baken Park, which featured tourist cabins and a dance hall. The Duhamels rented the hall and the Lakotas danced for tourists before parading through town. Like pied pipers, they led them to the Duhamel store. They'd perform a few more dances, scoop up their tips, lead the tourists inside, and disappear out a back door.

But the publication of *Black Elk Speaks* made the old man aware of wider possibilities. His story had gone out to the nation; now, because of Mount Rushmore, thousands would be coming here. Manderson was in the middle of nowhere, but the route between Rapid City and the presidential mountain was in the middle of everything. "What shall we name it?" Alex asked, cutting into his thoughts.

After a pause, Black Elk answered: "Sitting Bull was a big Holy Man. White people know Sitting Bull." He'd learned a thing or two about marketing during his years as a showman.

So the Sitting Bull Indian Pageant was born, and the Duhamels named their cave the "Sitting Bull Crystal Caverns." The year of the first show is uncertain. A printed program said it began in 1927, but this probably refers to the earlier informal shows at Baken Park. Most sources place the opening at 1934 or 1935, and from the beginning Black Elk was the central figure. In the summer of 1935, the Duhamels built a huge wooden tipi for ticket sales that could be seen from the road; behind that, they built a large octagonal dance hall to Black Elk's specifications. This could hold several hundred people, and resembled the smaller Omaha dance halls once found in every Agency village until the Church and government tore them down.

From its opening until a few years before his death, Black Elk was key to the pageant's operation. In his role as "Medicine Man," he was the main performer: he planned the dances and recruited performers, and the Duhamels relied upon him in their dealings with the Indians. Every year, a core group of twenty-five to thirty Pine Ridge Oglalas would pitch their tents in a little wooded copse three miles from the pageant site. It was a summer paradise, with running water and laundry facilities, in many ways more pleasant than back home. Sometimes fifty to sixty performers might be present; families drifted in, pitched their tipis, participated for a few days or weeks, then moved on. The Duhamels prepared a lengthy booklet for sale to tourists detailing everything: the roots of the dances; tribal customs of birth, courtship, marriage, and death; the performers themselves; and the Sioux calendar. The Duhamels gave the Indians 25 percent of the daily gate. The pageant rarely broke even, Bud Duhamel claimed, but "it satisfied the Indians and it satisfied us, so what the heck? What's the difference if you make money or not?"

Every late spring, Black Elk and his wife would move to the Black Hills, gathering friends along the route and children from the boarding schools. Lucy and her family went, as did Ben and his: by this time, Black Elk had several grandchildren, and they went, too. Others who performed over the years included Dewey Beard and his wife; the Red Bears, Sioux Bobs, American Horses, and Crazy Thunders; Black Elk's fellow *wicasa wakan* Little Warrior; and John Sitting Bull, son of the famous Hunkpapa holy man. Though the latter was deaf, he danced for years. His fellow dancers never seemed to worry about a misstep; he apparently felt the drum's vibrations and watched the other performers.

The pageant was held mornings and evenings, rain or shine. A truck collected the dancers at their campsite and took them back when the performance ended. The morning show started at 8:30 a.m. and lasted forty-five minutes; two shows were held in the evening, at 7:30 and 8:30 p.m. Sometimes a promotional show was held in Rapid City. Just as in the Wild West, visitors were encouraged to stroll through the village afterward and see how the Oglala lived. It was here the performers made friends with audience members and families sold their crafts to collectors.

A typical show began with a pipe ceremony similar to that in the first chapter of *Black Elk Speaks*. Black Elk usually led this; then the Lakota launched into dances, ceremonies, and songs. Dances included the Sun Dance, Rabbit Dance, Buffalo Dance, Horse Dance, Grass Dance, and even the Ghost Dance, though rarely. Black Elk would reenact a healing ritual, then the troupe would demonstrate an Indian burial atop a scaffold, accompanied by lamentation: Ben's daughter Olivia and Lucy's son George would often portray the sick or the dead. The performers sang a tribute to Sitting Bull, and the pageant usually ended with the Omaha war dance, the most flamboyant of the dances. Like Cody's stentorian Frank Richmond, either Alex or Bud Duhamel would provide a running English commentary.

Although Black Elk performed healing rituals in the show, nothing suggests that he offered true healing to the audience. He did, however, doctor other members of the troupe. Bud Duhamel remembered the case of Henry Horse, a dancer who fell deathly ill. When the Duhamels took him to the Sioux Sanitarium, the doctors pronounced him incurable. He was at death's door, and they advised the Duhamels to take him to Pine Ridge to die with his family.

But Black Elk told the Duhamels he could cure the man. He went into the Hills and filled a gunny sack with roots and herbs that Bud Duhamel could not identify. He brewed these into a tea, poured the concoction down Henry Horse's throat, kept him covered in his tent, and watched him. Within three days, Horse danced with the troupe. Within a week, he was fully recovered.

Bud Duhamel, for one, believed in the old man's healing powers. "Once I had the worst toothache," he told the interviewer Dale Stover in 1994. Once again, Black Elk went into the Hills, and this time returned with a purple-and-white, cone-shaped flower with a long taproot that he'd plucked from a creek bank. Though Duhamel identified it as a purple cornflower, it also sounded like Black Elk's "daybreak herb." He sliced off a piece of root and placed it against the tooth. "I thought the top of my head had lifted off—I never felt such pain," Duhamel said. Yet he never again experienced the toothache: the cure was permanent, not just the topical numbing common to folk medicine. "Old Nick was no fake," Duhamel swore. "He was a true medicine man."

Lucy would later say that the dances were not serious—that they were "just a show." Bud Duhamel disagreed: Black Elk and the other participants were sincere in their beliefs, he said. The pageant "was no fake deal they did just for show." Black Elk wanted to prove to whites that his culture was as complex and spiritual as their own. Yet he also knew the effects of timing and artistry: he'd learned his lessons under Buffalo Bill and Mexican Joe, and a good deal of showmanship was involved. During the healing segment, for example, the "sick" boy was brought to Black Elk on a travois as the grieving parents followed. Black Elk assumed his old persona: he wore his buffalo hide headdress and sacred ornaments; painted himself red with yellow streaks resembling lightning. He sang his healing songs, beat a square drum, and touched the boy's body with a rattle until suddenly the patient leapt up and ran off, completely cured. In the Sun Dance segment, dancers were attached to the center pole by ropes ending in halters. They strained at the ropes and blew their eagle whistles, imitating a dancer struggling to break away. Suddenly the ropes would be loosed from the halters and the dancers would stagger off as if they'd torn free.

If the pageant was not "serious" in a sacred sense, Black Elk was serious in his intentions. Though *Black Elk Speaks* was apparently never offered for sale, the Duhamels advised the audience to find a copy so they could better understand what they saw. After his treatment by the Jesuits, he had something to prove: his was not a "pagan" religion, as Sialm had said. It was not a tool of Satan. He believed that now even more strongly than in 1931 when he told Neihardt, "The whites think we have the power from the devil, but I'll say that they probably have that themselves."

Word of the pageant soon spread. On August 28, 1936, Black Elk was asked to Mount Rushmore again, this time for the official unveiling of the head of Thomas Jefferson. The dedication was attended by President Franklin D. Roosevelt. Two days before the ceremony, Black Elk, Ben, and Ben's sister-in-law asked to take the wooden tramway up the mountain for a private ceremony, and permission was granted. Black Elk wore his buffalo headdress; he carried his pipe in his right hand and asked the Grandfathers for unity between the Sioux and whites and for the preservation of his people. He asked that these presidents whose faces were carved in granite would always be remembered. Since it was a dry summer, he also prayed for rain.

Of all the Duhamels, Bud apparently spent the most time around Black Elk and thus served as his chronicler during the pageant years. On July 10, 1939, a blaze started on the ranch of John and Ben McVey, seven miles northwest of Hill City. This soon transformed in the dry conditions into a huge and historic forest fire. The "McVey Burn" became a holocaust as "freakish, gale-like winds" whipped the flames into an uncontrollable crown fire. One thousand firefighters were assembled, but they could do nothing. The flames shot hundreds of feet and were visible for miles: on July 11, a forest official told the *Rapid City Journal* that "one hundred thousand men would not be enough to stop the fire at its present rate of burn." On July 12, lightning struck and killed a firefighter taking shelter under a rock. By July 14, the McVey Burn had consumed 21,857 acres, making it the largest fire in the Black Hills' recorded history.

The Burn was not far from the pageant—only thirteen to fourteen miles west. Massive pillars of black smoke joined heaven and earth; the night burned bright as day. By the second day of the fire, Black Elk approached Alex and Bud Duhamel and said the white firefighters did not seem to know how to fight this fire. He set up what Bud Duhamel called a "72-hour Sun Dance"—hours and hours of nonstop dancing, accompanied by prayer. In such an emergency, it seems the dancers ignored federal law. Years later, Bud Duhamel remembered a central pole topped with a flag, dancers wearing little more than thongs, and, he remarked with the shock of sudden memory, "there was piercing." Duhamel was convinced the dance made a difference—a storm rolled from the west, reducing the McVey Burn to manageable size.

As the new decade started, Black Elk could hope that the struggle had not been in vain. *Black Elk Speaks* had caused discord in his family and estranged him from the priests, yet he'd emerged with a new resolve. He turned seventy-seven in the summer of 1940, and rather than the sad, defeated old man portrayed by Neihardt, he felt renewed. Whatever his feelings about the Catholic omissions in *Black Elk Speaks*, the book and his treatment afterward brought into focus for him his purpose in his last years. He realized that, if nothing else, his collaboration with Neihardt finally allowed his Great Vision to "go out" into the world. The Duhamel Pageant was the second step, and brought back all the lessons he'd learned under Buffalo Bill. If you have a message, Cody had insisted, don't hide it under your hat.

On December 16, 1940, Black Elk wrote a letter to Neihardt after a silence of five or six years. There was no blame or guilt—life had simply carried both men in different directions. Now, back in Pine Ridge for the winter, he addressed the poet as "Dear Son":

> Well you'll be surprised to hear from you [*sic*] because I don't know why you never write to me but I still remember you folks so here I am writing to you and your family. First of all I will say we're all getting along fine even up to Ben & his family. Well the weather is pretty cold up here but quite a few snow. For 5 yrs successive I've been in the Bl[ack] Hills for the summer & pretty busy putting up a show for Duhamels so I really forget to write to my friends.
>
> Well theres [not] any news except that we're hearing about the war all the time. I hope you enjoy your holidays and may the Great Spirit bring lots of blessings.
> I'm yours truly father
> Nick Black Elk Sr.
> Oglala S.D.

The war years started sadly. On February 17, 1941, Anna Brings White died of unspecified causes. Now he'd buried two wives, five children, two parents, and untold siblings and relatives—and Black Elk took it hard. He began to stay on a rotating basis with Ben, Nick Jr., and Lucy; soon after Anna's death, he returned to the Sioux Sanitarium. He continued at the Sioux Pageant, yet even that was plagued by misfortune. On August 8, 1941, his old friend and business partner Alex

Duhamel died of complications from an earlier stroke; on Pearl Harbor Day, December 7, Alex's brother Pete died of a heart attack. Bud took over the show.

Because Black Elk spent so much time in the Black Hills, events in Pine Ridge passed him by. The war of true faith that once cast Black Elk as the enemy moved to other targets, partly due to a change of inquisitors. On April 7, 1940, the sixty-seven-year-old Father Sialm died of pneumonia contracted on a missionary trip. Father Zimmerman took up his mantle: the works of the devil were rising back up—the Lord's work was never done. Sun Dances had been held at Kyle from 1917 to 1919, and at least four men were pierced in 1917; rumor held that the dances had not stopped in the intervening quarter century. Far to the southwest, in Navajo country, a messianic cult resembling the Ghost Dance had resumed, and some priests worried that it might find a welcome in Pine Ridge. Zimmerman wandered the reservation, grasping his crucifix containing "small pieces of bone from the body of Kateri Tekakwitha and from the Jesuit Martyrs of North America," he said, bringing comfort to those of the True Faith before they died.

Zimmerman's greatest war during these years was not against Black Elk, but against a greater threat—the peyote cult, "masquerading," he said, as the Native American Church, "an innocent sounding name." The sound of drums at twilight called its adherents to worship; many were backsliding Catholics, and unless they repented, they were damned by both God and their addiction. Zimmerman narrated the fate of Peter Good Lance, a peyote "propagandist" who tempted members of his flock away from Catholicism. Yet justice came for Good Lance in what Zimmerman painted as divine retribution:

> Satisfied with his apparent success in spreading the peyote cult, Good Lance mounted his horse and rode away. Three days later a searching party found him lying dead beside his horse out in a kind of "no man's land." Man and beast had been struck down by one of those bolts of lightning that drop unexpectedly upon our prairie. Putrefaction was so far advanced that removal was impossible. Horse and rider were buried side by side.

Zimmerman blamed the government, at least implicitly. In 1934, the newly appointed Indian commissioner, John Collier, issued "Indian Religious Freedom and Indian Culture," a circular directing Indian

Office employees to steer a new course in Indian religious affairs. "No interference with Indian religious life or ceremonial expression will hereafter be tolerated," he wrote. "The cultural liberty of Indians is in all respects to be considered equal to that of any non-Indian group." In the same year that Sialm and Zimmerman threatened Black Elk with eternal damnation and probably drafted the January 1934 rebuttal to *Black Elk Speaks*, Collier's new policies lifted the long-held ban on the Sun Dance and opened the door for the legitimization of the peyote cult. Believers "masquerade under an aspect of religion," complained Zimmerman. After a few weeks of "worship," adherents "became mental, physical, and moral wrecks."

It was all part of the "Indian New Deal," reforms that had built slowly after publication of the 1928 Meriam Report and which were codified by the Indian Reorganization Act of 1934. Roosevelt's New Deal legislation attempted, at least for a short time, to reverse one hundred years of BIA policy. Within days of his April 21, 1933, Senate confirmation, Collier instituted reforms. He hoped to end the policy of assimilation: no longer was Washington in the business of "liquidating" the Indian, he said. He insisted that the federal government end allotments, set up tribal constitutions, end the suppression of ancient customs, and allow the tribes to govern themselves. Within days of his installment, he convinced Roosevelt to abolish by executive order the Board of Indian Commissioners, created in 1869 to oversee the BIA. The board was an obstacle to reform; its members remained committed to the Dawes Severalty Act and the breakup of the tribes. Roosevelt acted on Collier's request almost immediately.

Black Elk may have been unaware of the changes wrought by Collier's Indian New Deal. From spring to late fall during the mid- to late 1930s, during the same period when Pine Ridge elections were taking place and discussions on the new tribal constitution were under way, the Black Elks lived in their little wooded utopia in Paha Sapa and performed the old dances.

But if Black Elk knew nothing about John Collier, the new Indian commissioner knew a lot about him. *Black Elk Speaks* was published in 1932; Collier was made commissioner the next year, and his first significant act involved preserving and maintaining tribal customs and religions. He was an earnest man with round glasses, dark hair, and a forelock that hung down like Alfalfa's in the Hal Roach *Little Rascals* comedies. A transplanted Georgian who pursued social work in New

York, he knew nothing about Indian culture until a 1920 sojourn in a Taos pueblo, where he discovered a "Red Atlantis" that held secrets desperately needed by the white world. Like Neihardt, he became a mystic, espousing a mysticism centered on Indian folkways. Returning to New York, he founded the American Indian Defense Association, the reform group that challenged decades-old Indian policy and spearheaded the Meriam Report. Indians were not a vanishing race, he argued. When Roosevelt became president, Collier determined to reverse history.

Importantly, Collier and Neihardt would be friends, though they apparently did not meet until 1943 or 1944. Still, it is interesting to speculate how much effect *Black Elk Speaks* had on Collier's Indian policy, especially his call for greater religious freedoms. The timing was certainly right, and Collier was known as a voracious and up-to-date reader of Indian literature. The mystical vision of the young Black Elk would have appealed to the mystic in John Collier. Two family histories by Hilda Neihardt indicate that Collier and her father were good friends; she wrote that her father "was asked to work with a man he knew and admired."

The years following publication of *Black Elk Speaks* were hard ones for Neihardt. He published *The Song of the Messiah* in 1935; expectations ran high that he would win the 1936 Pulitzer Prize, but Robert P. Tristram Coffin's *Strange Holiness* won the poetry category instead. It was the second time one of his *Cycles of the West* had been passed over, and it took something out of him. He returned to the *St. Louis Post-Dispatch* and stayed with the paper until 1938, then quit to finish *The Song of Jed Smith*, published in 1941. It was the last of his Western epics and he was in debt; at age sixty, his eyesight was fading. In danger of losing the house in Branson, he moved to Chicago to look for a job. After a pair of minor positions, Neihardt interviewed with Collier, whose office had moved from Washington to Chicago for the duration of the Second World War. Collier hired him immediately and made him director of the BIA's Bureau of Information, responsible among other things for editing the monthly magazine *Indians at Work*. Collier also asked him to build upon his earlier work in *The Song of the Messiah* and *Black Elk Speaks* and produce a cultural history of the Oglala.

In November 1944, Neihardt came to Pine Ridge and stayed at "the Club," the modest brick hotel for BIA employees. He was accompanied by Hilda. It had been ten years since he'd set foot on the reservation, and things had changed. Where in the past the Agency village had been inhabited mostly by Indian Office staff, now it overflowed with Oglalas. Some had sold their land after being forced out by the ten-year drought and Great Depression; others bunked here at night, then spread out by day to finish the various road and bridge construction projects still lingering from Roosevelt's New Deal. The town was split down the middle by U.S. Highway 18. On the west side huddled the offices of the federal government, BIA, jail, courthouse, tribal offices, and the Oglala Community Hospital; on the east, the squat frame-and-stucco houses of the *ieska*—the mixed-bloods. His hotel stood in the amorphous middle, along with the supermarket, gas station, barber shop, a couple of cafés, and a pool hall.

Yet if the village was crowded, the reservation seemed empty. When the draft revived in 1940, Oglala men enlisted in droves. They would see action in all branches of the service, in both Europe and the Pacific; most joined the infantry, often as scouts, while in the South Pacific a unit of Sioux code talkers existed beside the better-known Navajos. Many Sioux women served as nurses or joined the auxiliary corps. Two of Ben's children entered the service: his oldest son, Henry, who became an army sergeant, and his daughter Katie, who became a WAC corporal. Of the 1,250 Indian casualties in the war, 300 were Sioux, 100 of them fatalities. The population emptied for jobs in defense plants; in early 1942, about 2,000 people left Pine Ridge and Cheyenne River to build depots and air training centers. As they drove across Pine Ridge, the Neihardts could see women assuming the workload— driving tractors, repairing windmills, herding cattle into shelter from the cold.

Neihardt scheduled the interviews in two segments. He and Hilda talked to Eagle Elk first, from November 27 to 29 and on December 1. At age ninety-three, Eagle Elk was probably the oldest long-hair still living in Pine Ridge. He was such an adamant traditionalist that he refused to live in a cabin and instead lived in a canvas tent pitched beside his daughter's house, its interior heated by a woodstove. His long, flowing hair was nearly white; he walked bent forward. A catechist interpreted as Eagle Elk told of his three-day participation in a Sun Dance and of his exploits against the Crow and the army. Hilda tapped out the notes on a portable typewriter. In a November 29 letter to his wife, Neihardt told how Eagle Elk had always carried a charmed buffalo-hide quirt into battle as protection against bullets and arrows. But when his wife died, he placed the quirt on her chest to protect her on the long journey through the spirit world.

They interviewed Black Elk on December 5–8 and 11–13. According to Hilda Neihardt, the poet had not seen the old holy man since 1931. Although the Neihardts had remained close to Ben and his family, the release of *Black Elk Speaks* and the reaction of the Jesuits had apparently strained relations between the "uncle" and "nephew." That all seemed to vanish now. They fell into the old storytelling rhythms as for the next seven days Black Elk narrated the cultural history of his people, exactly what Neihardt had been sent to find. Ben translated, as he had twelve years earlier, and it seemed to Hilda that father and son were much closer now. "When I think back to those times I often see Ben's earnest face, his penetrating eyes," she later wrote. "Ben really cared, and it showed."

On the surface, Black Elk's stories seemed more of a disjointed collection of myths and legends than any sort of legitimate history, but from his perspective it was the Oglala's sacred history, a sequence resembling Genesis and Exodus in the Bible. Beginning with the dispersion of the seven Lakota bands in the east, he moved through the discovery of the bow and arrow, the knife, and fire, and the origin of kinship relations, among other things. He added a number of hunting, war, and humorous stories, then told the long narrative of the hero Falling Star, the kind of *ohunkakan*, or traditional myth, that Oglalas felt should be told only in winter when snows piled deep around the tipi. He told of the prophecies of Drinks Water, thus ending where *Black Elk Speaks* began, creating a spiritual prequel for the story of his life and the last days of the Oglala Eden.

A different Black Elk emerges in these interviews. Instead of the vanquished old man of *Black Elk Speaks*, he appears confident and strong, the assured voice of tribal history and legend. The transmission of sacred history was one of a *wicasa wakan*'s most important duties in the final act of life. Rather than simply publish a compendium of folktales, Neihardt shaped the interviews into the fictional *When the Tree Flowered: An Authentic Tale of the Old Sioux World* as a way of re-creating a vanished way of life. Indeed, one can hear in the folktales the fulfillment of Black Elk's responsibility.

Neihardt would return twice more to Pine Ridge at the behest of the Indian Office. The first time was on September 15, 1945, for the

Great Sioux Victory Celebration marking the end of World War II. Neihardt gave the main address: the Lakota had never truly been defeated, he told them. They'd fallen only because of the destruction of the buffalo. They were still great warriors, proven by their service in the war. A photo shows Black Elk and Neihardt standing together, two aged men in rumpled suits, Neihardt's arm around the shoulders of the holy man. Afterward, Black Elk wrote his friend that "the Sioux sure did appreciate what you said."

The poet's final visit stretched for nearly a month, from September 19 to October 11, 1946. Though he no longer worked for the Indian Office, Collier asked him to conduct a special investigation of reservation conditions, focusing especially on tribal government, education, and law and order. An early blizzard cut his travel through Pine Ridge to eight days; the rest of his stay was spent interviewing residents and BIA staff in the more accessible Agency village.

What he saw disheartened him. It was as Black Elk had said: Indians no longer wanted to be Indian. Despite Collier's reforms, "the Oglalas simply are not any longer a tribe in the social sense," Neihardt wrote in his report. "Their old culture is dead. They recognize no leader. They are mostly just poor people living together in a land that cannot support them all, and laboring under psychological, social, and economic handicaps."

He saw the signs of cultural rejection everywhere. The young men especially spurned "Indian" identity. They dressed like cowboys, favoring large hats, bright, close-fitting shirts, and tight-fitting denim jeans. They tattooed their arms and the backs of their hands with initials and small designs. The only braided hair he saw was on girls, women, and old men; young men favored crew cuts, like cowboys. "Get rid of all this Indian stuff!" cried Ben American Horse, chairman of the Treaty and Eight-Reservation Councils. "Let them forget the Sioux language! They got to live with white people!" Time and again, said Neihardt, he heard the same refrain—from the young, mixed-bloods, and even full-bloods. Tribal identity was a thing of the past. "We have to become one people!"

It was as if the government's long drive to assimilate the Oglala had finally succeeded—at the very moment they were being encouraged to remain Indian. Yet if the Oglala wanted to be white, or at least enjoy the benefits of white society, white America wanted little to do with them except in menial and stereotypical roles. It was the same position in which black America found itself during the Jim Crow era and at the end of each world war. The whites in towns surrounding Pine Ridge simply did not want to deal with the Sioux except in prescribed circumstances, observed the sociologist Gordon Macgregor in his *Warriors Without Weapons*. If anything, their attitudes were the same as during frontier days: hostile, fascinated, mercantile, and cynical. "Employers want Indians to harvest corn and potatoes," he wrote:

> They are invited to participate in the summer fairs and rodeos, to which they add a great deal of color. The stores enjoy their trade, particularly in the fall, when Indians buy winter supplies and clothing before returning home from the harvest.
>
> On the other hand, the white people in the towns look down upon the Indians. Part of this feeling is a reaction to the fear in which the Indians were once held. It is also due to their present demoralized condition and occasional drunken brawls.

The mechanisms needed to fix the reservation were broken, Neihardt said. He called the tribal council a "comic opera," governed by the "jealousy and bickering" generated in any society characterized by "chronic need." Alcoholism was rampant, even among the tribal police, the one body tasked to enforce liquor laws. "When I asked if the Chief of Police drinks, the answer was, 'Everybody drinks.' If a policeman tried to arrest a drunk, the accused shot back, 'You cannot arrest me, you're as drunk as I am.'" Mixed-bloods and full-bloods jockeyed for scant resources, and "there is a feeling that things will get better if all the old-timers just die."

And so, Neihardt concluded, the Oglala once again found themselves in limbo. They could not survive on the reservation, but the outside world wanted nothing to do with them. "Two families left while I was in Pine Ridge," he wrote, but returned within a short period. When he asked why, they answered, "There is no opportunity here. We left once before and got homesick. We will not come back again."

Though Neihardt no doubt visited his old friend during that 1946 trip, no records attesting to this have been preserved. Nevertheless, the two were close, their lives and identities intertwined. If they did meet, it was their last reunion. The poet never saw his holy man again.

Time and age had finally caught up with Black Elk. He was eighty-three in 1946, and tuberculosis and old injuries shrank his world. The Duhamel Pageant began hemorrhaging money, and was discontinued sometime after the mid-1940s. Black Elk moved in with Ben; he walked with a cane and moved very slowly. He'd attend Sunday Mass in every season but winter, when it was too cold and slippery. He started early and would never catch a ride; he'd reach the store and meet with John Lone Goose, then they'd hobble to church while saying the rosary together.

A letter written in the 1970s by Father Joseph Sheehan, a Jesuit stationed at Manderson, called Black Elk "a figure of rejection" in his final days. While Catholic leaders suspected him because of *Black Elk Speaks*, medicine men distrusted him because of his Catholicism, Sheehan said. While some of this is probably true, some is wishful thinking. The priests were uncertain of his motives and watched for lapses, yet if Frank Fools Crow and Wallace Black Elk can be believed, the *wakan* men honored him. Nevertheless, Black Elk's ecumenical attempts to bridge the two religions were an unwelcome idea until the more liberal 1960s, and the ideas he represented would be deeply ambiguous or yet unborn. As he moved slowly through the Manderson hills, he may have seemed to many a fringe character, isolated, forgotten.

But in the world outside Pine Ridge, he was anything but ignored. Though *Black Elk Speaks* was out of print, old copies passed from hand to hand. One copy made it to Carl Jung during an American lecture tour, said Hilda Neihardt. If that is true, it would have been during his 1937 lectures "Psychology and Religion" at Yale University. Back in Zurich, he prevailed upon the Swiss publishing house Walter Verlag to publish the story in German, but war intervened.

After the war, Jung tried again. Black Elk's Great Vision haunted the famous psychiatrist on several levels. It seemed to support his hypothesis that revelation lay at the heart of all great religions. And at the heart of revelation pulsed those ingrained models called archetypes that Jung believed existed deep in humanity's unconscious—the collective reservoir of sense and image inherited from one's ancestors and shared by all mankind. "Archetypes," he wrote, "are images and at the same time emotions. One can speak of an archetype only if those two aspects coincide." Black Elk's Vision was filled with such archetypes—the warrior, hero, mother, wise old men. The Six Grandfathers, horses, cloud tipi, et cetera, said as much about the young boy who dreamed them, and the old man who cherished them, as they did about the revelatory truths of his tribe. "Myth is more individual and expresses life more precisely than does science," Jung wrote in his autobiographical *Memories, Dreams, Reflections*: "We are a psychic process which we do not control, or only partly direct." He thought enough of *Black Elk Speaks* to send a student to interview Neihardt and Black Elk, but whether this ever happened is unknown. Nevertheless, Jung was largely responsible for the postwar attention the book received in Europe. And once American scholars noticed, they slowly woke to the strange and forgotten tale of the old holy man in their own backyard.

The last disciple of note was a complex and seemingly lost spiritual seeker. Black Elk may have recognized that quality; after all, he'd traveled his own share of dead ends. By so doing, he opened the door for a man who would become one of the nation's strongest advocates of all Indian faiths and who, like Neihardt, helped the old holy man preserve the essentials.

Joseph Epes Brown, like Neihardt, was a mystic, but more by disposition than by any near-death peek at an alternate world. Perhaps because of that he did not have the poet's booming confidence; on first impression, he seemed painfully quiet and shy. Brown was handsome, dark, and lanky, and the Oglala girls at Pine Ridge often had a crush on him. Such attention made him uneasy: he stares at the camera in photos taken with Black Elk, his gaze unwavering but wounded—a tall, brooding lumberjack, uncertain what the future holds.

His life had been difficult before Pine Ridge. He was born into privilege on September 9, 1920, to a Quaker mother and Princeton professor of Shakespeare, but the idyll ended when his father contracted tuberculosis and was confined to a sanitarium in New Mexico. Brown spent summers in the Southwest, and like John Collier, he was changed by his exposure to the Indians there. But the Southwest did not save his father, who died in 1937 when Brown was seventeen.

The death hit him hard: one could tell it weighed on him, said his wife, Elenita, though he hid the scars. He graduated with a degree in literature from Bowdoin College, another in philosophy and art history from Haverford, then taught prep school English long enough to know it wasn't for him. Then the war began. Brown chose not to fight, and, channeling his Quaker roots, registered as a conscientious objector, or CO. But "everyone hated COs," said Elenita Brown, remembering the signs on front lawns—"No Dogs or COs"—an adaptable form of bigotry that morphed, given the place, into "No Dogs or Indians" out west and "No Dogs or Sailors" in navy towns. He washed bottles in a New York lab doubling as a malaria-research facility and morgue; was shipped cross-country by sealed Pullman coach; and ended up in the Nevada and California wilderness, clearing trails for the U.S. Forest Service, measuring the depth of shifting snowpacks, packing mules.

But the isolation appealed to him, and his thoughts turned inward. He took classes in Gregorian chant in New York, befriended Sufi dervishes on the Brooklyn docks, labored alone in the land of Wovoka. After the war, he tried to enter graduate studies in comparative religion, but few programs existed in the United States. Europe was different, he was told.

One stream then flourishing in European thought sounded very Native American: a transcendent reality underlay all earthly existence, an idea not that different from Black Elk's "truer reality" of the spirit world. One branch of religious philosophy, called the "perennialist" perspective, believed that an "eternal religion" linked all earthly beliefs, be they Christian, Islam, or Hindu: beyond the apparent reality of our earth lay something firmer, purer, more real. Existentialist thought was more popular—its intellectual stars would include the future Nobel laureates Jean-Paul Sartre, Samuel Beckett, and Albert Camus. But existentialism was a shifting creed, built on the war's despair, and to many perennialism seemed more life-affirming.

The chief figure in the Perennialist School was the Swiss metaphysician Frithjof Schuon. Like his contemporary Carl Jung, Schuon was fascinated by American Indians, whom he'd first seen as a teenager in Alsace in 1923 at "a big German circus with red Sioux Indians." He was inspired, as were many Europeans before him. But Schuon went further, coming to believe that he had the "character" of an Indian: "incredible courage—their self-domination and dignity—the cult of dignity." Like Jung, he came to think of Black Elk as "the repository of an authentic traditional wisdom," possibly after reading Jung's copy of *Black Elk Speaks* brought back from America. Sometime in 1946, during his postwar journey to Europe, Brown drifted into Schuon's orbit. Soon afterward, wrote Schuon's biographer, the metaphysician apparently asked Brown to return to America, find Black Elk, and record his "valuable testimony" as a font of primal truth.

If there is one part of Brown's life that seems ambiguous, it is this early fascination with Schuon. The perennialist leader was a polarizing figure: he progressed over time from a seeker—like Brown, Jung, and Black Elk—to someone who actively promoted himself as holy. Though Brown was not one to publicly denounce a past mentor, at some point he seemed to have disengaged from the man.

With Schuon's entry we see the first sign of the New Age frenzy that would envelop everything related to *Black Elk Speaks* in a warm and fuzzy nimbus—and in the process drive serious Oglala religionists mad with frustration. But Brown displayed no doubts; instead, he now had purpose and meaning. He homed in on Black Elk like Galahad on the Holy Grail. In 1947, he wrote Neihardt for an introduction, and in time the poet agreed; according to Hilda, her father asked Black Elk to speak to Brown. He seemed a "fine young man," Neihardt wrote, whose "interest in spiritual and religious matters was sincere."

In May 1947, Brown outfitted an old Ford truck with a camper shell and struck out for Dakota. It took him four months to find the old holy man. In early September, he found the Black Elks working with other Oglalas in a Nebraska potato field, part of the annual harvest migration to towns outside Pine Ridge. Black Elk himself was too blind to dig potatoes; he was sitting in the shade of the family's tent when Brown finally found him.

Brown hit the side of the tent, a custom dating from tipi days. "Well, it's about time you came," the old man answered from inside. "I've been waiting for you. What took you so long?"

Thus began Black Elk's final collaboration. After hearing of the young man from Neihardt, Black Elk planned two tasks he wanted Brown to help him with for the short period he had remaining. Brown felt honored. He stayed with the Black Elks for eight months, through the cold winter of 1947–48, then later during the summers of 1948 and 1949, digging potatoes, returning with the family to Pine Ridge.

One task did not succeed. At the time, there was concern among holy men about the future of the original Sacred Calf Pipe Bundle, by legend given to the Sioux by White Buffalo Calf Woman. The keepers belonged to the Red Water Sans Arcs of the north; the previous keeper—Martha Bad Warrior—was the first woman to hold that role. In the summer of 1936, a village in Cheyenne River asked that the pipe be used to end a crippling drought, and Martha Bad Warrior sat in the sun from dawn to dusk holding the pipe and praying. When her relatives begged her to get in the shade, she said that a sacrifice was necessary. She died three months later, in October 1936, and her family pointed to this as the cause.

Martha's death created a problem of succession. The bundle passed to her son, but he was not versed in the pipe's care or the details of its origin. By 1947, little had been heard of the pipe and the elders were worried. Black Elk hoped to reinstate the "Order of the Pipe," a society devoted to its safekeeping. Brown contacted long-hairs such as Spotted Crow, Stabber, Little Warrior, and the sons of Red Cloud, American Horse, and Kicking Bear. Black Elk hoped that each reservation would create its own Order, and these together would oversee the pipe's maintenance and succession.

But nothing happened. Though Brown attended one Pine Ridge meeting in the spring of 1948, the idea failed to take root elsewhere. Concerns about the pipe would prove well founded. In 1968, when the anthropologist J. L. Smith tracked down the Sacred Calf Pipe Bundle, he found it kept by a "not-so-knowledgeable fifteen year old boy and housed in a not-so-elaborate tool shed," a far cry from the specially constructed buffalo hide lodge of the past. "What the future of the Pipe bundle will be one can only guess," Smith wrote.

Brown's second task proved more successful. He recorded Black Elk's description of the Oglala's sacred rites, and these became *The Sacred Pipe: Black Elk's Account of the Seven Rites of the Oglala Sioux*. Ben again served as translator. Although *Black Elk Speaks* is more narrative and poetic, it is in *The Sacred Pipe* that Black Elk systematized Oglala religion. He ordered it into seven sacramental rites: this seems to represent the final synthesis of his thought, in that he structures Lakota ritual in parallel to the holy sacraments of Catholicism. These were the ceremonies he hoped to preserve for posterity. They included the purification of the pipe, the keeping of the soul, the vision quest, Sun Dance, adoption rite, preparations for womanhood, and a sacred game he called "the throwing of the ball." He did not include the *heyoka* ceremony, since its strange clownishness probably put it beyond the understanding of Christians as he knew them. Likewise, he omitted animal mysteries such as bear ceremonies, since he'd seen these derided as "savage" polytheism. His choices tried to bridge the two religions: he seemed to say that they could be professed together by his people, and the merger would make them stronger.

By describing these Oglala sacraments in detail, *The Sacred Pipe—*

more than *Black Elk Speaks* alone—made Black Elk what one analyst would call the prophet of the Sioux revitalization movement. Yet neither work stood alone. Though Black Elk's meeting with Neihardt was co-incidence, the poet's style and love of epic myth turned Black Elk into what might be the only tragic prophet in American letters. Black Elk came to terms with this, but saw a need to go further. In the Duhamel Pageant, he introduced Sioux culture to passing tourists; in the 1944 Neihardt interviews, he preserves Sioux sacred history. Yet a lifetime spent pursuing and comparing different religions finally gave him the insight that the Sioux, Americans, and Europeans were all children of one God. *Wakan Tanka* had sent an incarnation of holiness to each people—to the whites, a young man; to the Lakotas, a young woman. Each incarnation included unique symbols and rites, and with *The Sacred Pipe* he sought to define the Lakota sphere. In Black Elk's world, the Pipe and the Cross were equally holy.

Brown realized that he was lucky to be taking down the old man's words. In the past, *wicasa wakan* closely guarded the material contained in *The Sacred Pipe*: such secrets were "too sacred to be told indiscriminately," he wrote. Yet Black Elk sat at the center of a group of "old wise men" who believed that an intellectual apocalypse was certain if something was not done. Mankind was "nearing the end of a cycle" in which the truths revealed in the beginning were falling away. If they were lost, "disaster and chaos [would] reign in every sphere." Given that, it was permissible, even desirable, to set such knowledge loose. The truth, "by its very nature, will protect itself against profanation," Brown was told.

Brown came to believe completely in the old man's world. He was adopted into the tribe and named Channumpa Yuhan Mani, or Walks with the Sacred Pipe; he was given a red-stone pipe and a bag of sacred tobacco made long ago by the holy man Little Deer. Since he had a truck, he took the Black Elks on excursions. In October 1947, he took Black Elk to Denver and they spent several hours looking for lodging, since most hotels would not admit Indians. By the time they found a place, it was late and they were tired; they'd had to settle for a dilapidated room in the "run-down area" of the city. "When we entered the room," Brown wrote, "Black Elk announced that he sure felt dirty here in this city and that we must have a sweat to cleanse ourselves." As Brown watched, the old man built a sweat lodge in the middle of the floor. He covered a table with a blanket, pried some loose bricks from a crumbling fireplace, and heated the bricks with a pan of coals. "We felt better after our purification," Brown said.

During his stay, Brown told Black Elk that people knew of him in Europe. He told him of Frithjof Schuon, who'd sent a couple of letters, and of Carl Jung's attempts to publish *Black Elk Speaks* in German. But more than anyone else, it seems, he told him of Schuon's older brother, "Father Gall." Erich Schuon was born on January 26, 1906, in Basel, Switzerland, and became a Trappist monk in Belgium's Abbaye Notre Dame de Scourmont in 1921 at age fifteen. Sometime during Brown's European sojourn, he and Father Gall became close friends. Like his famous brother, Gall was amazed by the Indians in the 1923 Alsace Western circus. Unlike his brother, he had recurring dreams in which he roamed the Plains like an Indian. He came to believe he *was* an Indian, born into a European shell. When he heard that Brown was hunting down the famous Black Elk, he begged his friend to mention his suspicions. Maybe the Sioux shaman could bring him peace of mind.

Black Elk was transfixed. He'd always believed that he'd left a child behind in Paris; the rumor would circulate in his family long afterward that Gall was this lost son. Yet the birthdays were not right: the rumored child would have been born in 1890, while Gall was born sixteen years later. Nevertheless, Black Elk was intrigued. On Christmas in 1947, he dreamed that he visited Lakota Ishnala, or Lone Sioux, in Belgium, "had a good talk with him, and had just now returned," Brown later wrote in a letter to Gall. "He said that he had told you that you shall always be a Lakota, for when you die your body, which is of earth, shall remain with the white man, but your soul shall return to us." Black Elk named him "Two Men," since "in appearance you are a white man but in reality you are an Indian." Three months later, on March 4, 1948, Black Elk wrote to Gall himself and told him the story of his life. He adopted Gall into the tribe and signed the letter "Your Father, Black Elk."

The letter from Black Elk brought peace to the Trappist. Gall no longer thought he was crazy, and transformed himself into a Sioux as much as his order allowed. He dug a sweat lodge and created in a forest glade outside the monastery a place he called his "reservation." Once, he took to his hideaway the Belgian cartoonist Hergé, creator of *Tintin*. Gall dressed in Indian clothing from head to foot: feather headdress, loincloth, moccasins, and blanket. He suggested that Hergé smoke the pipe with him in the way Brown had instructed. "My name is Lakota Ishnala," he said, "which means the Solitary Sioux. I am solitary in two senses: not only does this allude to the solitary prayers of the Indians, since I am a man of religion, but it is also a reminder that I am all alone here, far from my people and my family."

Not every priest took so well to the collaboration between Black Elk and Brown. In mid-January 1948, Father Zimmerman caught word of Black Elk's newest project. Brown, Black Elk, and Ben were sitting outside the cabin when they saw a cloud of dust whirl up the road. "We've got to behave now," Black Elk said. Zimmerman emerged from the car and was quite irate, Brown recalled: it was all right if Black Elk "wanted to put on a show, but if we were serious, it was a terrible thing, for he could not have his people going back to 'savagery.'" That unleashed the Furies. "Ben launched out with quite an oration," Brown wrote, "defending and pointing out the truths of his own traditions—during which time the priest became more and more tense and red in the face." Then Black Elk joined in, lecturing Zimmerman for about thirty minutes in Lakota. Finally Zimmerman looked at his watch "and sped off in his automobile in great haste."

Brown left in March 1948, and though he would return over the next two summers, he would never stay long. The work on *The Sacred Pipe* was slow. The array of books written by and with Black Elk in the last half of the 1940s would be impressive, but he would not live to see a single one. Neihardt's *When the Tree Flowered* was published in 1951; *The Sacred Pipe*, "recorded and edited by" Joseph Epes Brown, appeared in 1953. And *Ich Rufe Mein Volk*, the German-language version of *Black Elk Speaks* championed by Carl Jung, was released in 1955.

He'd already been fading, even during the visits by Brown. Having weathered and sidestepped death so many times, he knew he could not do so again. Not at his age.

In the spring of 1948, after Brown left Pine Ridge, Black Elk slipped on the ice outside his cabin and broke his hip. He argued with Lucy that he was all right, but the family took him to the Sioux Sanitarium in Rapid City for X-rays. Once admitted, he told the nurses that he was fine and could take on Custer again, this time single-handedly. Nevertheless, while there he experienced a resurgence of his tuberculosis, followed by a small stroke. He remained hospitalized until September

1948, and though he recovered, he could no longer walk. For the rest of his life he would be bedridden or confined to a wheelchair, first at Lucy's house, then at Ben's. "There was never a day he complained about his suffering," Lucy said.

During the rest of 1948 and 1949, his condition deteriorated. At first, the family carried him from place to place as he prayed with the rosary; at times, he would seem to get better and be taken to the top of the western hill that formed the boundary of his land. He would sit upon a rug and pray with his sacred pipe until the sun melted into the horizon.

Sometimes he had visions. He told Lucy that every day at 3:00 p.m., he was visited by a "holy-man . . . from overseas." The two of them would pray together, he said. Only Black Elk could see this visitor, but a discussion started among friends and family about who it might be. Lucy thought it was a Jesuit priest, while Frithjof Schuon insisted that his wife and he said the rosary daily at 3:00 p.m., so most probably he was the unseen holy man. Black Elk himself referred to the visitor as a *wicasa wakan*, which would suggest a Lakota visitant, possibly someone from his past who'd sent him on his spiritual path so long ago.

One day in the summer of 1950, he called Lucy to his bedside. His days were ending, he whispered. "I am old, so don't take my death too hard. My sufferings will be over, and I will have no hurt. Pray for me as I taught you to pray in your early days." Do not let a day pass without a prayer of remembrance, he added.

In the old Lakota belief, one's spirit passed from the body upon death and, if judged worthy, set out across the Milky Way, or "spirit trail," for the "land of many lodges." An outpouring of prayer would keep his soul from becoming a wandering spirit—a version of the soul-keeping vigil that Black Elk performed for his father, and that Crazy Horse's father performed for his son.

That summer, he turned eighty-seven, another world and time from that day in the month of the chokecherries when his mother gave birth to little Kahnagapi on a riverbank in the Powder River Country. In a vision he'd received a gift, but the quest to unlock it had haunted him. Perhaps the secret was too deep for any man; the burden almost was. Now he was tired, and his worries were ending. He'd done his best to keep the sacred tree alive.

Shortly before his death, he told Ben and Lucy to watch the sky for a sign—just as he'd said to Ben when they climbed Harney Peak. But now, instead of a sprinkling of rain, they might see a brief display of celestial fire. "I have a feeling when I die, some sign will be seen," he told Lucy. "Maybe God will show something. He will be merciful to me and have something shown which will tell of his mercy." He received last rites for the fourth time on August 19, 1950, and died soon afterward in the little bunkhouse built next to Ben's home in Manderson.

His wake was held that night; he was laid in a coffin in front of the cabin, dressed in his familiar catechist's suit and tie, his big crucifix hung about his neck. It was about 10:30 p.m. and William Siehr, a Jesuit brother at Holy Rosary, walked up the dirt road with Father Zimmerman. A large group sat near the coffin. Siehr was impressed by how many people had assembled. They stayed and talked to the mourners, then started back in the dark up the old Manderson Road.

They could not help but notice the lights in the sky. "The sky was just one bright illumination," Siehr later said. "I never saw anything so magnificent." He'd seen the Northern Lights before, but this seemed totally different. The sky was in constant motion—rising spires of light "like tremendous points going up—then flashes." Though people later speculated it might be the Pleiades meteor shower, these "weren't stars or meteors," Siehr said. Instead, he compared what he saw to "a fountain of water where you see light reflecting on the water as it's being sprayed up." The whole sky seemed ablaze.

Lucy thought she saw figures in the sky. A ring, like a hoop; and the number 8, the symbol of infinity. "They were separated by a short distance, but they were there—an 8 and a circle," she said. "I always wondered what that meant."

The lights that night were seen in far parts of the United States and Canada. In Moline, Illinois, the light show lasted two successive nights and was characterized by "rayed bands" that formed a corona and then dissolved into brilliant "rapid pulsations." They lit "the landscape as bright as with the moon," observed the October 1950 issue of *Sky & Telescope*. Above Toronto, the sky filled with "shimmering, darting forms." *Sky & Telescope* identified the phenomenon as an unusually dramatic display of Northern Lights, officially known as the aurora borealis. A. B. Meinel, an astronomer at the Yerkes Observatory in Williams Bay, Wisconsin, wrote in *Science* that spectrographic tests of the lights established "for the first time that photons of probably solar origin are streaming into the upper atmosphere at velocities of the order of 2,500–3,000 km/sec." If the fireworks had been caused by the annual meteor shower, Black Elk might have been able to predict such pyrotechnics. But auroral spectacles were never as predictable.

Black Elk's old friend John Lone Goose also watched the sky. "Everything looked miracle-like," he recalled twenty-four years later. "I'm not the only one who saw it. Lots of people did. They were kind of afraid, and I was scared a little bit, but I knew it was God's will."

But there was nothing to fear, he said. The light show subsided to a gentle glow; the summer insect chorus started back up, and in the distance dogs barked, the sign that spirits were near and something extraordinary had occurred. "The night was still and warm with nothing fearsome about it—just nice and quiet," he added. People started talking to fill the silence, and someone quietly remarked, "God is sending those lights to shine on that beautiful man."

EPILOGUE: BESIEGED

In the summer that Black Elk recuperated in Rapid City from his stroke, his sixteen-year-old grandson Ben Jr. was admitted to the same facility with a fever. At first, its cause was a mystery, yet its progression was similar to the illness that had nearly killed Black Elk seventy-six years earlier.

Though the ailment that nearly killed Black Elk was never identified, doctors diagnosed his grandson's illness as meningitis. By early September, it was obvious that Ben Jr. was doomed. The role of a shaman was to stand between his people and death, but Black Elk could not halt the inevitable. He could tell his son about the rites of soul-keeping, thus assuring that the boy's death was not the end. In the days before the final word came from the hospital, family observed Ben's preparations. They listened as he sang his son's *icilowan*, or death song.

Ben Jr. died on September 10, 1948. "I should have went instead of my grandson who is so young, and me I have seen many days," Black Elk wrote to a Denver friend. As others grieved conventionally, Ben donned a buckskin suit, saddled his old bay horse, and rode into the Black Hills. His father had said that when you lose a loved one, his spirit goes up into the Hills. Ben went looking for his namesake's spirit, riding through the places they'd visited together, calling his name. Doing this kept his soul close, saving it from an eternity of wandering alone. He loaded a packhorse with provisions, a blanket, and a tent, and slept out in the open. He traveled alone for almost a week and, when he returned, said he was satisfied.

One place he visited during his mourning was Mount Rushmore. It was still tourist season, and the tourists were intrigued. They asked to snap his picture, often beside family, then offered to pay him. By then, Rushmore's identity was set in the eye of the beholder: while it symbolized to many the nation's greatness and permanence, it reminded the Lakota of broken treaties and stolen land. But Ben had been raised by a man who remembered Sitting Bull's definition of Paha Sapa as a "food pack." The 1940s had been hard for the Black Elks, but now Ben saw a way out. He turned Mount Rushmore into his family's personal food pack and thrived.

For the next quarter century, Ben and his family would move at the start of tourist season to Keystone at the head of Buffalo Gap, and Ben would spend his days at Rushmore in his regalia. He became so familiar that he would be called the "fifth face of Rushmore." Tour buses pulled up and drivers told his story; families packed together for the ritual cross-country road trip threw open the Ford or Chevy doors and kids charged to his side, begging for a photograph with a "real-live Indian." Ben regularly wore an elkskin suit with the single eagle feather in his hair; he told them the history and lore of his people, and what the Hills meant to the Sioux. It was sometimes demoralizing being "an Indian who made his living being an Indian," yet each night he came home with a buckskin pouch filled with cash, enough to see them through the lean winter months back at Pine Ridge.

By the mid-1950s, he was becoming well-known. He had a bit part in the 1951 Van Heflin movie *Tomahawk*, then played opposite Charlton Heston as a Crow chief in 1952's *The Savage*. In 1955, his face graced the cover of the Rotary International's *Rotarian*: the article said that his likeness was as "familiar to American tourists as the Indian-head nickel." The next year, Ellen and he went on a six-state tour of mid-America promoting South Dakota tourism, followed by a second tour and TV appearances.

It could be said that Ben was the public face of the Oglala in the 1960s. The decade started with the American rerelease of *Black Elk Speaks*, in 1961. In 1962, he played an angry Arapaho chief in MGM's Cinerama spectacle *How the West Was Won*; toured Paris, Brussels, Stockholm, and Copenhagen for promotion; gave a peace pipe to the

King of Sweden; and joked with Europeans who said they'd never heard of South Dakota until he arrived. That same year, he sang in Lakota about Tasunke Witko from atop Korczak Ziolkowski's Crazy Horse Memorial, which the sculptor carved and blasted into the granite face of the six-hundred-foot-high Thunderhead Mountain. On August 18, 1962, the one-millionth visitor to Rushmore—part of an Illinois family en route to Yellowstone—was treated to lunch and a bag of gifts, but the photo with Ben proved "an especially big treat for the children." Six years later, he sang his own composition, "The Sioux National Anthem," in a ninety-minute documentary narrated by Henry Fonda.

By now he was in his sixties, and like his father before him, probably the best-known Oglala in Pine Ridge. He'd worked hard and overcome much, but sometimes in unguarded moments family members found him sunk into melancholy. His grandson Aaron DeSersa, Jr., once came upon him like that, as the old man was tanning hides. "Grandpa, how come you're so sad?" he asked. His grandfather held Aaron's gaze.

"Well, my people don't understand their way anymore," Ben finally said. "We want to bring back the Indian way. See, these things that we do here," and he motioned to the tanning rack, "it's good for our people by doing all this." But Aaron knew his grandfather meant more than the hides. He might only be in third grade, but he wasn't dumb. He asked his mother—Ben's daughter Esther—what Grandpa meant by *their way*. But when she tried to answer, he noticed that she looked sad, too.

His grandfather's sadness shocked the eight-year-old boy. What did his grandfather mean? Soon afterward, he climbed the hill to the crowded cemetery overlooking Holy Rosary and sat by Red Cloud's grave. He wrote a poem for his class, and though he could not remember the words as he grew older, he remembered their meaning. He realized that everything he thought and believed seemed forced on him from outside—from the Church, the government, TV. All he seemed to know came from whites; he knew very little that was Lakota. *He* was Lakota, but besides the random accident of birth, what made him so? When he tried to find out, there were no answers. He grew up, entered the military, starting drinking and taking drugs, came home and seemed lost like so many young Oglala men his age. Finally his mother gazed at him steadily, just like his grandfather that day by the tanning racks. "You're ready," she said.

He turned, surprised. "What?"

She'd already contacted an *ikcéka wicasa*, a kind of sacred counselor, whom Ben had said could "straighten out" lost children. She said simply, "You're ready to go up on the hill."

It was as if Aaron was besieged on two fronts: assaulted from without by white America, plagued from within by patchwork images of what had once been. During the same period, Aaron's contemporary Sister Marie Therese Archambault wrote of her own split and trials. A Hunkpapa Sioux who became a Franciscan nun, she tried to reconcile in her writings Lakota identity and Catholic faith, which she acknowledged had tried for decades to extinguish Sioux spirituality. One night, she had a dream: in it, she watched as an alcoholic relative stared at herself in the mirror. But as she drew closer, "it was me looking in the mirror," she said. The face looking back had two sides: "one side was clear and ordinary . . . and the other side was beaten, bruised and misshapen." She drew back in horror, then awoke and reflected on the dream. She'd always shown her "good" white face in public, but ignored the Lakota face, enabling it to "be beaten and hidden." In the process, "my heart was violent." She felt disinherited and filled with rage.

It was this that made Ben sad. After his father's death, the Pine Ridge schools called upon him to tell the traditional tales. He was shocked by what he found. Educational philosophy for Oglala children had not changed much since his sojourn in Carlisle. In 1907, Commissioner Francis E. Leupp put it bluntly: "Sordid as it may sound, it is the dollar that makes the world go around, and we have to teach the Indians at the onset of their careers what a dollar means." Six decades later, the same philosophy prevailed. Living in the white world trumped everything else. Indian identity was anathema. It felt to Ben as if he'd never been away.

"We who are Indians today live in a world of confusion," he told the Senate Subcommittee on Indian Education on December 14, 1967. "We love Indian ways. But to get along in this world, the white man tells us that we cannot be what we were born to be." He told the committee, which included Senator Edward Kennedy of Massachusetts and Senator George McGovern of South Dakota, of young people at Pine Ridge who'd lost their Indian heritage but did not understand the ways of the whites. "So our young people have lost their pride. They are Indians who are ashamed of their birthright when they should be proud of it as First Americans."

He told friends that despite his best efforts, it felt like a lost cause.

In the 1950s, after Black Elk's death, Jesuit priests seemed divided about the holy man's legacy. While older priests such as Zimmerman said he was forgotten, his books inconsequential, younger Jesuits tried to construct a form of Christianity more relevant to Oglalas. Membership had declined in local chapels, and these priests redesigned ritual in ways that seemed taken almost entirely from *The Sacred Pipe*. The Reverend Paul Steinmetz, the parish priest at Sacred Heart Mission in Pine Ridge Village, was one of these. To the consternation of his superiors, he participated in native ceremonies and designed a new church that merged Catholic symbolism with Oglala. Most important, he used the Sacred Pipe in Mass. "The pipe is a type of Christ," he wrote. Praying with the pipe was as valid as praying with the rosary.

The medicine men were amazed—something Steinmetz did not know until later. As they sat in the front pews of his church, they marveled that a priest had finally seen the light. As the Jesuits tried to create a new relationship between the Church and the flock, medicine men said the priests finally recognized the potency of *Wakan Tanka*. The medicine men had been right all along.

In 1961, *Black Elk Speaks* was reissued in paperback in the United States after a nearly thirty-year absence, and was enthusiastically received by the young. The 1960s and '70s saw the rise of the counterculture, ecological worries, and a new interest in Native Americans. In such a milieu, the book was taken seriously. As "crises mounted and, as we understood the implications of future shock, the silent spring, and the greening of America," wrote Vine Deloria, Jr., "people began to search for a universal expression of the larger, more cosmic truths which industrialization and progress had ignored and overwhelmed." In 1968, Ben would write to Joseph Epes Brown that every year "the Sundance continues bigger." Young men were starting to practice *yuwipi* and Sacred Pipe ceremonies again.

By the late 1960s, *Black Elk Speaks* and the spiritualism it made famous released a New Age flood upon the reservations, the likes of which the tribes had rarely seen. "Medicine men" with no right to the title except an ability to make a sweat lodge and the adoption of an "Indian" name offered instant enlightenment. False shamans such as Carlos Castaneda (aka Carlos Arania) cashed in on the Black Elk craze. Neihardt's granddaughter Coralie Hughes, a trustee of the Neihardt

Foundation, watched as people "adopted *Black Elk Speaks* as their own, but changed it to their own belief system." The anthropologist William K. Powers noted, "Today, when Black Elk speaks, everybody listens, and everybody hears precisely what he or she feels inclined to hear with little regard for the meanings of the Lakota words." Vine Deloria, Jr., bemoaned the "tide of abuse and misuse of Indian ceremonies" typified by "sweat lodges conducted for $50, peyote meetings for $1,500, medicine drums for $300, weekend workshops and vision quests for $500." Suddenly, the interest in Indian spirituality grew mercenary and bizarre.

There would be a backlash, much of it directed against Neihardt and his memory. Other than the two questionable letters "written by" Black Elk but in all likelihood dictated by Placidus Sialm, there was no documentary evidence that the poet used or cheated Black Elk or his son. The rancor seems to spring from two old racial stereotypes: whites will always cheat the Indian and profit from his land, history, or religion; and the Indian is easily cheated. Critics claimed that *Black Elk Speaks* was not what it seemed. Rather than the undiluted memories of a Sioux medicine man, it was a translation by a white poet writing for white readers. They questioned how much of the final work was Black Elk's and how much Neihardt's: though mostly confined to academic circles, the question addresses validity. Whose vision inspired so much fervor: the white man's or the Indian's? Neihardt always said he composed *Black Elk Speaks* in the old man's spirit, and except for the question of his Catholic conversion, Black Elk and Ben concurred. Nevertheless, the process led to confusion and accusations.

On April 27, 1971, Neihardt appeared on the prime-time broadcast of *The Dick Cavett Show*. He was ninety, near the end of his days, and such criticism no longer bothered him. It seemed he had addressed the critics a hundred times, and he knew it would continue after his death; a rancor can run through academia that is sometimes contrary to evidence and hard to understand. His literary reputation would plummet from his being named the "finest representative of the epic in American literature" to a "minor anachronism of a poet"—to no mention at all in contemporary poetry anthologies. He did not seem to care. He knew by then he'd helped usher into life an American classic, and he seemed satisfied.

Cavett would later say that he knew when the old man sat across from him that "this was it—this was good." Neihardt was dapper as ever, white hair swept back, eyes shaded beneath heavy brows. He was a presence, and Cavett, a fellow Nebraskan, said he felt an "electric contact" between them. The dominant theme of his life was endurance, Neihardt said, as it was for the Sioux. Yet endurance was made possible only through some connection with the holy. "I am profoundly religious, and the human animal is profoundly religious and can't live without it," the old poet said. The Sioux couldn't do anything if not under "spiritual auspices."

Most of the interview had to do with Neihardt's old friend. He told of that first meeting with Black Elk, the long interview process, Black Elk's Great Vision, and the final trip up Harney Peak. "We had to restrain him on the way up—he said he had something to tell the Six Grandfathers," he recalled. "He walked ahead of us and we had to tell him to come back and sit down." But when they got to the top and it rained for two or three minutes, Neihardt turned in a circle, "couldn't see any other rain for seventy miles around," and was amazed.

Near the end, Cavett asked him to read his poetry, and Neihardt recited the "Death of Crazy Horse," the last stanza describing Tasunke Witko's burial in his *Song of the Indian Wars*:

> Who knows the crumbling summit where he lies
> Alone among the badlands? Kiotes prowl
> About it, and the voices of the owl
> Assume the day-long sorrow of the crows
> These many grasses and these many snows.

It grew quiet in the studio when he finished, and Cavett would say it was the closest thing to a religious experience he could remember in his life. The TV host cleared his throat and asked the old poet what was next for him. Neihardt grinned.

"I'm sure what's coming will be very interesting."

———•◦•———

Ben Black Elk and John Neihardt both died in 1973—Ben in February, Neihardt in November, neatly bracketing the second engagement between U.S. forces and Indians at Wounded Knee.

This time, instead of a massacre, it was a seventy-one-day siege. The trouble began a year earlier. Although it can be argued it started as far back as the broken Treaty of Laramie, the Siege of Wounded Knee was sparked by the beating death in Gordon, Nebraska, of a quiet ranch hand named Raymond Yellow Thunder. One night in February 1972, four whites assaulted the fifty-one-year-old Oglala in a used-car lot and took his clothes; an autopsy showed that he died a few days later of his injuries. In response, the American Indian Movement (AIM) came to Gordon. Begun in 1968 and most famous to this point for its 1969 occupation of Alcatraz Island in San Francisco Bay, AIM and its sympathizers crowded the town; meanwhile, the chairman of the Oglala Sioux Tribe ordered the transfer of more than a million dollars from Gordon's banks, a considerable sum for that place and time. Faced with such pressures, the city attorney charged the suspects with manslaughter, but only two—the brothers Leslie and Melvin Hare—were convicted and sentenced to six and two years behind bars, respectively.

The rest of 1972 would be a busy one for AIM. It marched on Washington to protest the "Trail of Broken Treaties," occupied the BIA building, and kept itself in the news. One year after Yellow Thunder's killing, AIM returned to Pine Ridge. During the Gordon protests, members had forged close ties with traditionalist Oglalas at the reservation. Now AIM entered a dispute between the traditionalists and the new Oglala Sioux Tribe chairman, Richard Wilson, accused of favoring mixed-bloods in hiring and using his private militia to squelch dissent. During a meeting on February 27, 1973, two Oglala women dared their men to stand up for their rights and become warriors again. Frank Fools Crow—now the Oglalas' ceremonial chief—urged the protestors to "go to Wounded Knee and make your stand there."

It was an inspired move. By now, Wounded Knee was familiar to millions because of *Black Elk Speaks* and Dee Brown's 1969 *Bury My Heart at Wounded Knee*. The AIM leaders Russell Means and Dennis Banks saw this as a chance to publicize their hatred for the Indian Office while taking a public stand for a return to tribal sovereignty.

What toxic geography creates such a place, an empty landscape turned somehow into a watchword for hatred and blood? It is empty today, save for a roadside sign and the mass grave on the hill. The view from that hilltop is one of dry washes and scattered clumps of cottonwoods; it takes a leap of faith to imagine the dramas played out here. One remembers the old Sioux proverb "A people without history is like the wind through the buffalo grass," as dry vegetation rustles in the eternal breeze. But on February 28, 1973, a fifty-four-vehicle caravan stuffed with urban and Pine Ridge activists descended on the Wounded Knee Trading Post and the quiet surrounding village of about sixty people. As the leaders demanded Senate hearings on broken treaties and reservation conditions, about three hundred federal, state, and tribal lawmen formed a loose ring around the occupiers, blocking the few roads in and out with their armored vehicles.

The standoff lasted more than two months, and firefights erupted as both sides tried to iron out a deal. On two occasions, federal authorities considered an assault, a move that probably would have ended in a second massacre. But cooler heads prevailed. Still, sniper fire was a constant threat, and by the end of the standoff one federal marshal was critically wounded and two Indians, Frank Clearwater and Buddy Lamont, were killed. Yet most of that period, wrote the activist Mary Crow Dog, "was spent in boredom, just trying to keep warm and find something to eat." Between the fear and excitement of sporadic gun battles, Wounded Knee was a closed world where, she said, "people made love, got married Indian style, gave birth, and died."

It was also a major media event, with reporters arriving from print and broadcast outlets around the world. The more unsympathetic press called it "guerilla theater." Once, a young man stood in the middle of a firefight to pose for cameras. Russell Means, who later took movie roles, told photographers, "Be sure to get my good side." Veterans of other protest movements, such as William Kunstler and Angela Davis, showed up to proclaim their support, as well as hundreds of college students and Indians from Denver, Los Angeles, New York, and New Mexico. Supporters arranged two food airdrops using Piper Cherokees. As the days dragged past, Mary Crow Dog's husband, Leonard, one of AIM's two spiritual advisors, called for a four-day Ghost Dance, the first time one had been held in this spot in eighty years. When the dance ended, Means turned to the press and announced that the 1890 massacre was not the "end of the Indian," as many whites had said. "Here we are at war, we're still Indians, and we're Ghost Dancing again!"

Once again, the Black Elks found themselves drawn into the vortex of Wounded Knee. Black Elk's legacy was evoked for the cause; the most prominent relative was Frank Fools Crow. Despite his original call "to go to Wounded Knee," he was stunned by the coverage, shocked by the bloodshed. Most of his time was spent trying to broker peace, yet history repeated itself when he found himself at the end of a rifle just like another peacemaker eighty-three years earlier. "Let's wipe them all out!" cried a "furious Sioux youth from Porcupine" who shoved a gun deep into Fools Crow's belly. And like his predecessor, Fools Crow kept his head. "My son," he said, "I have lived many years; more than enough. If you are man enough, pull the trigger." But think of this, he added: if he did, all the justice they sought would be blown away. The young man's head fell and his shoulders drooped. He lowered the rifle and walked away.

There was also Black Elk's great-grandson Clifton DeSersa, son of Ben's daughter Esther. He'd survived Vietnam just to find himself in a new Indian war. He'd lived in sandbagged bunkers and in-country camps; followed a Montagnard scout though jungles and rice paddies; caught shrapnel from a grenade. The scout used a crossbow and carried in his pack an American comic book of cowboys and Indians. "Me and you is the same thing," the scout said. Now Clifton led reporters through night gullies and coulees to interview the occupiers, then led them out by a different way. He did this six or seven times, taking in groups of a dozen or more. The journalists impressed him with their ability to hide and sneak, though he did have to warn the women to remove their high heels.

The occupation ended on May 5 with the government's promise to investigate abuses by the tribal government and discuss the 1868 treaty. There was a meeting, but the government refused to open treaty talks and no action was taken against President Dick Wilson. The end of the siege did not end the violence, and in October 1973, BIA police shot and killed the AIM leader Peter Bissonette. In 1977, the AIM member Leonard Peltier was found guilty and sentenced to two life sentences for the 1975 murder of two FBI agents at Pine Ridge; Peltier's conviction remains controversial, and in 2010 Amnesty International called it unjust due to numerous doubts about the fairness of his trial. Arsons, beatings, and murders continued in Pine Ridge that have never been solved. The little village at Wounded Knee was destroyed and never rebuilt; the people who lived there moved elsewhere. The federal government arrested numbers of AIM members, including Banks and Means, and although it lost most prosecutions, the trials eventually bankrupted AIM.

It is hard to say what long-term effects were nurtured by the siege. Hard feelings still exist, yet many reformers in positions of responsibility today were, forty years ago, in their teens or twenties. The movement sparked their imagination and showed them that change was possible.

In 1979, Marvin Buzzard, director of Nebraska's Indian Commission, mused how the events followed the historical pattern of most minority groups seeking justice: they first "go through the process of taking drastic action to direct national attention" to their problems, much like the Civil Rights Movement of the 1950s and '60s. After that, the battles take place in court. The new Indian warrior "is the Indian lawyer with his briefcase, pressing legitimate claims in court, and at the same time concentrating more and more on the issue of tribal sovereignty."

The strategy has produced results. In 1980, the U.S. Supreme Court upheld the Indian Claims Commission's award of $102 million to the Lakota for the Black Hills. Interest accrues on the award: by 2007, the figure neared $750 million. But the tribes have refused to accept the decision: they say that taking the money would endorse the government's original seizure. Like Black Elk and Crazy Horse before them, they don't want the money. Paha Sapa is not for sale.

Perhaps the greatest paradox in American history has been the failure and the success of its Indian policy. Native Americans have been blocked in their attempts to thrive by the nation's very success at taking their resources and lands. At the same time, Washington has never succeeded in stamping out what made them Indian, because it never knew. Who can truly know an individual's heart, much less an entire people's? "What is an Indian?" asked Commissioner Thomas Morgan two years after the Wounded Knee Massacre. And his answer?

Blood and land.

He was right, but not in a way he understood. If the U.S. Army and government had spent more in the ruthless elimination of the tribes, "root and branch," as Sherman hoped, then strangled off their resources as Congress wanted, the "Indian Problem" would have been "solved." But nothing is straightforward in American history, not even ruthlessness, and the nation's better angels prevented total genocide. Their hearts were right, but their methods were mad. To save the Indian, they reasoned, they must kill the Indian inside.

Thus began decades of social engineering rivaling the darkest visions of Aldous Huxley and George Orwell. The reservation was the laboratory where new and often contradictory policies were introduced and tested—much like those classic social experiments where lab rats are shocked and rewarded, but always randomly. Each era had its own

philosophy—"assimilation," "reeducation," "Christianization," and "ter-
mination" of the tribes. Yet the purpose of each was similar: strip the
Indian of his "Indianness," then reshape him as an idealized American,
stamped and milled as if in a machine. It is easy to see why the young
rebels of AIM felt such loathing for the BIA and Washington. In the
parlance of the counterculture, they saw it as the Machine.

How does one survive in such a world? The Machine is overwhelming and unstoppable, larger than any one woman or man. Black Elk saw
it early, though he never used such dystopian terms. Perhaps the only
true defense is the most intimate—preservation of one's soul. Seen that
way, his life is more than just another tale of Indian versus white. It
becomes instead a parable of modern man.

Pine Ridge has ostensibly been at peace since the 1970s, but disqui-
eting signs remain. The reservation is just as poor, and life is just as
tough, as when Black Elk revealed his Vision in June 1931. Sheer numbers tell the tale. Recent state and federal statistics paint a stark profile:
the annual income per capita at Pine Ridge is $9,728, compared with
$27,334 in the nation overall; 48.3 percent of the residents live in pov-
erty, compared with the national average of 13.8; 80 percent of the residents are unemployed. Life expectancy at Pine Ridge is 66.6 years,
compared with the U.S. average of 76.5. The life expectancy of women
is even worse—52 years. Infant mortality is nearly triple the nation's.
Alcoholism is still the leading cause of death, disease, and abuse,
affecting eight out of ten Oglala families. A 2010 report by the U.S.
Department of Health and Human Services rated alcoholism as 674
percent greater in Indian communities than anywhere else. Since selling
or possessing alcohol is still illegal on the reservation, the closest place
to buy it is conveniently right across the border at White Clay, Nebraska,
population twelve. Four liquor stores operate in town, selling among them
12,329 cans of beer daily, or slightly more than 4.5 million cans a year.

Violent death is also common: Indians were 265 percent more likely
to die in accidents than other groups, 62 percent more likely by homicide. The suicide rate is nearly four times the national average, while
about 15 percent of the high school population attempts suicide each
year. Between December 2014 and March 2015 a true crisis gripped the
reservation when 9 people between the ages of twelve and twenty-four
committed, and 103 attempted, suicide; that March, a reservation pastor discovered a group suicide planned in the woods outside Pine Ridge
Village. When he arrived, "it was cold, it was dark, and there were a row

of trees with ropes hanging off the branches," said the pastor, John Two Bulls. There were no bodies, yet, but some teenagers had already congregated and they told him that "they were tired of the lives they led at home, no food, with parents all intoxicated, and some were being abused, mentally or sexually," he told *The New York Times*. It is no surprise that cemeteries are filled with the graves of the young, and small crosses dot the sides of the roads.

The boundary between Pine Ridge and border town may not be inscribed in steel and wire, but crossing over can still be as dangerous for the Oglala as when Raymond Yellow Thunder faced four townies in Gordon, Nebraska. On August 2, 2011, Daniel Tiger, a twenty-two-year-old Oglala, killed two Rapid City police officers, wounded a third in the face, then was killed himself in the shootout that followed. Though South Dakota's attorney general called the attack "unprovoked," Lakota journalists countered that provocation is still rife in these border towns. Rapid City was one of the worst, wrote Nick Estes in *Indian Country Today Media Network*, earning it the nickname "Racist City, S.D."

Residents were friendly when I traveled through Paha Sapa the following summer, but the tensions were still there. When I mentioned I'd be doing research for a week on the reservation, a strange pattern emerged: they said, like a broken record, "Be careful out there." These were hardworking whites—motel clerks, librarians, waitresses, an old man helping me find my bearings. There was no string of racial epithets, but when I pressed for details, to a soul they mentioned Daniel Tiger. Even a year later, they said, the entire region was "on edge."

Peter Heffron glanced off sadly when I mentioned this, then shook his head. The great-grandson of Alex Duhamel, he runs the Sitting Bull Crystal Caverns; he took me inside the old dance hall, still standing near the entrance at the top of the gorge. "There's a lot of anger and stereotyping on both sides," he said. "The Indians said [Tiger] was provoked. The cops say otherwise." He gazed around wistfully at the interior of the eight-sided dance hall: at the physical representation of a two-family friendship that withstood the resentments of history and ravages of time. "I haven't been in here for a while, you know." Murals depicting Oglala life on the Plains glowed softly in the muted light. "It wouldn't take a lot to fix this up," he stated in surprise. "I'd like to refurbish it and bring the dances back—the real ones, like Black Elk put on." His family had nothing but respect for the old holy man, he added.

"That was Black Elk's show. After he died, that was pretty much the end." But they never tore the building down.

It was the week before the Annual Powwow when I entered Pine Ridge; the normally empty reservation was filling fast with families, craftsmen, dancers, bull riders, bronco busters, and the occasional way-ward biker far from the Sturgis motorcycle rally. One is wise to arrange accommodations months in advance. "Oh man," laughed a craftsman selling dream catchers who helped me find a place. "This place gets crazy. Next time bring a tent. No one cares."

Black Elk is still a presence, though in the decades since his death it's sometimes hard to separate fact from fiction, disparagement from praise. When he died in 1950, the Jesuit priests wrote that he was forgotten, but after the re-publication of *Black Elk Speaks*, the old man began showing up in many forms: as Old Lodge Skins in Thomas Berger's *Little Big Man*, as well as Chief Dan George's portrayal in Arthur Penn's 1970 film adaptation; in the 1979 theatrical adaptation by Christopher Sergel that opened in Washington, DC's Folger Theatre; as William Least Heat-Moon's "inspirational touchstone" in his 1982 travel epic *Blue Highways*. "There is no interest in Black Elk on the reservation as a philosopher or spokesman for the traditional way of life," wrote the scholar William Powers in 1990, yet even as he claimed this, sculptures, greeting cards, poetry chapbooks, a novel, a children's book, prayer cards, and a hilltop park in Blair, Nebraska, were being inspired by or dedicated to the old holy man. Responding to a petition circulated by Black Elk's great-grandson Myron Pourier, the U.S. Board of Geographic Names is weighing whether to rename Harney Peak after the old *wicasa wakan*.

Lately the legacy has taken some strange turns. There was the portrayal of Black Elk as religious conspirator, an interpretation given to Professor Lee Irwin when he attended a Sun Dance at Pine Ridge. "You know," an unidentified ceremonial leader told him,

> Black Elk was part of a conspiracy, a cover up here among the Lakota. What he says there about the Indian religion being dead, over, was part of a plan to stop the oppression here at Pine Ridge. It worked too. After that book came out, things got better; we just said it was over, dead, a thing of the past. We had to still do it secretly, but things have gotten better. Now we can do it more openly and bring other people in. . . . I don't believe our religion

is something that should be hidden or kept from other people who are not Lakota or Indian. But for a long time, we had to keep everything hidden, even from other Lakota.

And there is Black Elk the saint, the newest permutation. When Kateri Tekakwitha was canonized by the Catholic Church as the first Native American North American saint on October 21, 2012, many thought Black Elk should follow. As "Native America's premier philosopher of religion and culture," Black Elk "is the pre-eminent candidate" for canonization, wrote Michael Steltenkamp, the Jesuit priest who revealed Black Elk's career as a lay preacher. In 2014, Steltenkamp's letter was sent to the Reverend Charles J. Chaput, archbishop of Philadelphia, along with the petition now circulating through South Dakota. Though such petitions gauge popular support, they also act as a means for tracking down miracles. "Ultimately, as for Saint Kateri," said Mark Thiel, Marquette University's archivist for the Tekakwitha Conference and the Bureau of Catholic Indian Missions, "two miracles authorized by Rome will be required."

Though Betty Black Elk never knew her great-grandfather Nick, she certainly keeps his legacy. She owns Bette's Kitchen in Manderson, and serves up the best lunch for miles. Her diner takes up half of a trailer set at the top of old Nick's allotment—children, grandchildren, and great-grandchildren run through the place, and on the walls hang black-and-white photos of Black Elk, Ben Black Elk, Neihardt, and Joseph Epes Brown. Down the hill one sees a circle of cottonwoods; Black Elk's cabin nestles in its shade.

"Nick didn't die in here, you know," she said as we circled the cabin. He died overnight in a bunkhouse built next to it, and her mother discovered the body the next morning. Still, it's the cabin that was famous, and she'd once considered registering it as a state or national historic site until discovering the cost of repairs. So it sits untended in the shade of the trees.

Was Black Elk's quest to save his people successful? Betty Black Elk thinks it was. "My great-grandfather's books made it okay for us to be Indians," she said. "I went to Catholic school, graduated in 1962. They wouldn't let you be Indian. They cut my hair short, made me wear these awful long dresses down to here," pointing at her feet. "If one of the girls in the class spoke a Lakota word, they made us all run the length of a football field. It was like Communists—it was like Hitler. Now, after those books, they want you to be Indian, but it's too late, the language is dying, no one speaks Lakota anymore."

Ted Hamilton, then superintendent of the Red Cloud School, agreed with her assessment of history. Red Cloud is what used to be Holy Rosary, still nestled in a valley of cottonwoods and overlooked by the cemetery where Red Cloud lies. It is the school Betty talked about, the place where nuns and priests did not want one to be Sioux. A lot of anger and resentment still lingers: against whites, Catholics, the federal government, and the Tribal Council.

But not against Black Elk. "Ask me how many copies of *Black Elk Speaks* we lose each year," Hamilton laughed. "We just bought eighteen copies for the school library, and we expect to lose many, if not all of them. That tells you something right there."

It's all about identity, said Hamilton, who is himself Lakota. "In the 1980s, ninety percent of the kids on the reservation dropped out of school; the rate now is more like thirty-five to forty percent." College attendance has increased, especially with the rise of reservation colleges such as Oglala Lakota. Many who graduate come back for jobs on the reservation, a trend previously unheard of.

"Every generation on the reservation has to reinvent itself," Hamilton said. He believed that kids today are stronger in their traditional culture than were their parents, and because of that he's hopeful for their future—despite the statistics, despite the crosses along the road. "Right now," during Powwow Week, "there is a Sun Dance taking shape"—a traditional one, with incisions through the chest and hours of staring at the sun. It was a private affair, not a watered-down tourist version. "It's all dancers in their twenties," he added proudly. "This was inconceivable a generation ago. It empowers them. . . . Identity is at the center of their existence."

Hamilton was not alone in such hopes. "It would be helpful to return to the old religions in a new form," postulated a present-day healer in 1990's *The Medicine Men*. "It would help the Indian people and give them a sort of spiritual strength they need." This seems to be happening, yet assessing the extent is nearly impossible. Some non-native scholars have estimated twenty-first-century membership in traditional native religions as hovering around nine thousand people, but spiritual leaders say the numbers are substantially higher. Native American "religion" often does not orbit around a church; the forms of worship can be as diverse as the nation's 567 legally recognized tribes or its 5.22 million full- and mixed-blood individuals.

Ultimately, this kind of worship depends in large part upon the preservation of what Richard Henry Pratt said "made the Indian, Indian." Native American intellectuals have coined the term "survivance," but this is a cold and distant word for a struggle waged on the black road. One thinks of Faulkner's oft-repeated line—"The past is never dead. It's not even past"—and here on the Great Plains one can feel the relentless grind of history. To Hamilton and others, Black Elk lay at the heart of this resurgence when he chose to save the ancient ways. Yet every path threw up another obstacle, and too often he thought he'd failed.

Out here, where just surviving to adulthood is a gamble, Black Elk's struggle somehow speaks to Hamilton's kids. Without a soul, you die—but where and how can one find such a nebulous thing? The superintendent turns from the window and shakes his head. His cheerful voice is subdued, his expressive eyes sad. "I often wonder about that, what went through that old man's mind," he sighs. "Had he learned something from all the disappointment? Was it a recognition that you can get swallowed by the Machine?"

All querents demand enlightenment when they find their holy men. But what special Truth would Black Elk convey? When Frank Fools Crow, Joseph Epes Brown, and other seekers like them described the debt and reverence they owed to Black Elk, they rarely spoke as if he'd imparted arcane knowledge—the kind of world-shaking secrets for which he'd searched so long and fruitlessly. Instead, he seemed a life-affirming presence for those who sought him out—almost as if, as John Fire Lame Deer said in another context, he represented "a state of mind."

What had Black Elk learned? This was the Great Mystery for John Neihardt, and continues to be so for the light-fingered scholars of Ted Hamilton's school. The boy of nine rose from his coma endowed with purpose, certain that an incorruptible and saving Truth awaited down the right road. There would be so many roads. Even the Great Vision itself, as Black Elk described it to Neihardt, was an unending journey of conflict and concord, struggle and repose. Was it wisdom or madness to go on? This was the fool's journey, to rise up only to be knocked flat, not once but repeatedly; the eternal tragic comedy that only the *heyoka* dared to lampoon. Who would accept such a burden? Who could continue such a dance and not despair? Only a fool. But at least twice Black Elk told his children that the gods sometimes acknowledge such struggles. Yet, one must be vigilant. One must watch carefully for the quiet nod from above.

The trek up Harney Peak is still hard. I climbed it on a clear sunny day. The trail still leads past daisies and thistles, weird granite columns, and stands of ponderosa pine. It grows colder as one ascends. At the very top, one can see in a circle for seventy to one hundred miles. Crowded into a fire lookout built eight years after Black Elk's visit, about twenty members of a girl's soccer team huddle against one another to ward off the chill. Far to the west I can see a single small circle of rain. Black Elk's point is blocked off; the girls yowl in the cold and scramble back down. I wait for the rain, but it sails north over the Badlands and disappears.

It is right and just that the son surpass the father, and on July 23, 1962, three decades after accompanying his father on that famous climb of Harney Peak, Ben Black Elk did that very thing. He climbed atop Mount Rushmore, as had his father before him, and a TV camera trained upon his craggy face, filling the screen. He wore his traditional buckskin suit, his long hair pulled back in braids, a single eagle feather stuck near the crown. He was being shot for the first commercially broadcast satellite image via Telstar I; his face would beam from Rushmore to the satellite, orbiting somewhere from 592 to 3,687 miles up, then bounce back down to the BBC ground station at Goonhilly Downs in southwest England. He'd be the first person to appear in the first live TV broadcast transmitted from America to Europe, a Space Age echo of his father's own European journey, and he'd carefully considered his words. He'd chosen a greeting from the Lakota, "*Mitakuye oyasin*," or "All are related," a common Sioux prayer of the interconnectedness of all people, all life, all things.

At 3:00 p.m., the signal came through and the cameraman dropped his hand. Ben looked at the lens, and one wonders what he thought in that instant. He certainly thought of his people, their endurance through so much, but he probably also thought of that moment thirty years earlier when his father similarly cast his voice to the sky. Both men's voices were loud and strong. "*Nahaȟči unkupi*," Ben said in Lakota.

In English it means, "We are still here."

TIME LINE

NOTES

ACKNOWLEDGMENTS

INDEX

TIME LINE

LAKOTA MONTHS

January—Moon of Frost in the Tipi
February—Moon of the Dark Red Calf
March—Moon of the Snow-Blind
April—Moon of the Red Grass Appearing
May—Moon When the Ponies Shed
June—Moon of the Blooming Turnip
July—Moon of Red Cherries
August—Moon of Black Cherries
September—Moon of the Black Calf
October—Moon of the Changing Seasons
November—Moon of Falling Leaves
December—Moon of Popping Trees

CHRONOLOGY

1862: Gold is discovered in Bannack, Virginia City, and other towns in present-day Montana, bringing thousands of gold seekers.

1863: Black Elk is born on the bank of the Little Powder River in what is today upper Wyoming. Although he would later say that he was born in December, the month of his Catholic baptism, his mother said he was born in "the Moon of Red Cherries," thus setting his birthdate on an unknown day in late June or July.

Although most commentators cite December as his birthdate, this narrative follows his mother's memory.

1864: The Bozeman Trail is established, envisioned as a short route from the south to the Montana gold fields. It cuts through the Powder River Country and brings the Oglala into direct conflict with whites. For the first time, they officially regard the *wasichu* as a viable foe.

November 29, 1864: The Sand Creek Massacre: U.S. Army colonel John M. Chivington and a 750-man force of Colorado militia ride upon a sleeping Cheyenne camp at Sand Creek near Fort Logan, killing 150 men, women, and children. In March 1865, survivors arrive in Lakota camps to the north, bringing news of the massacre and sparking what will be called Red Cloud's War. Scholars consider this the true turning point in white-and-Sioux relations.

December 21, 1866: The Fetterman Massacre, known to the Sioux as "the Battle of the Hundred Slain." Black Elk's father is seriously wounded and will remain lame in his right leg for the rest of his life. Black Elk is three or three and a half years old.

1867: Black Elk begins to hear voices. He is four.

1868: The Fort Laramie Treaty of 1868, ending Red Cloud's War. The army agrees to abandon the forts on the Bozeman Trail; the treaty creates the Great Sioux Reservation and agrees that the Sioux do not cede their hunting grounds in the Wyoming and Montana territories. The Indians, for their part, agree to become "civilized."

1869: Completion of the Transcontinental Railroad divides the buffalo into two herds—the *Pte Waziyotz*, or Buffalo North, and the *Pte Itokagotz*, or Buffalo South.

May 22, 1870: The first Red Cloud delegation departs for Washington, D.C. Around the same period, Crazy Horse loses his status as a Shirt Wearer because of the scandal involving No Water and his wife.

June 1870: Crazy Horse marries Black Shawl and moves in with her relatives in Big Road's band. For the first time, he becomes a daily presence in the life of Black Elk, now seven.

1871: Crazy Horse's daughter, Kokipapi—or They Are Afraid of Her— is born.

June 1871: The first Red Cloud Agency close to the Platte River is established. Though Red Cloud and his followers will move there to be closer to the regular distribution of rations and annuities, other Oglalas under Crazy Horse and Big Road do not follow.

Summer 1872: Black Elk has his Great Vision. He is nine.

July 1873: Black Elk's family slowly heads east to visit relatives at the second Red Cloud Agency. They zigzag lazily through the hunting grounds and will not reach the Agency until early spring of 1874.

August 1873: The majority of Black Elk's people remain with Crazy Horse in the Powder River and Yellowstone Country. In August, they encounter the Yellowstone Expedition of 1873, notable for the fact that it is the first battle between Crazy Horse and George Custer.

Fall 1873: The Panic of 1873 is followed by the collapse of the U.S. economy. At the same time, Crazy Horse's two-year-old daughter dies of fever.

March 8, 1874: Camp Robinson (later Fort Robinson) is established at the second Red Cloud Agency, near Crawford, Nebraska, on the White River in Sand Hills country. Black Elk's band arrives at Red Cloud after its slow trek east. It is the first time he has ever seen whites, and though he is afraid of them at first, he becomes used to them.

April 1874: Black Elk's family and about thirty others travel north and spend the rest of the spring in Buffalo Gap, at the foot of the Black Hills. For the first time, Black Elk reveals his powers to his family. They remain in the southeast area of the Black Hills through early summer.

July–August 1874: Black Elk's idyll in the Black Hills comes to an abrupt end. This is the summer of Custer's Black Hills Expedition, and the Black Elks flee before advancing soldiers back to the Red Cloud Agency. Word spreads nationwide that Custer discovered gold in the Hills.

Summer 1874: During the annual Sun Dance, Sitting Bull calls the Black Hills the Sioux's "meat pack," which must not be relinquished to the *wasichu*.

Fall 1874–Winter 1875: Black Elk's family stays with relatives outside Red Cloud Agency.

September 20–28, 1875: Commissioners, led by Senator William Allison, come to the Red Cloud Agency to negotiate the sale of the Black Hills. Black Elk is present, but does not understand what is happening. The Sioux are unwilling to sell.

Fall 1875: Black Elk leaves the Agency to join Crazy Horse on the Powder River.

December 6, 1875: The Commissioner of Indian Affairs orders all nontreaty Indians to return to their Agencies by January 31, 1876. Those violating the order will be considered hostile.

December 20, 1875: The directive arrives at the Red Cloud Agency. Runners from the Agency come to the bands of Crazy Horse and Big Road to warn that they must return to Soldiers' Town. Black Elk and others know that this is impossible: the cold is so intense that many would die on the journey.

February 1876: Black Elk's band starts for Soldiers' Town during an early thaw, but the cold returns and they button up tight for the rest of the winter. They are now considered "hostiles."

March 17, 1876: Troops under Colonel Joseph Reynolds attack He Dog's camp in the Powder River Country. The Great Sioux War begins.

March–May 1876: Black Elk's family lodges outside Camp Robinson. They leave in May, and Black Elk's aunt gives him a six-shooter. They depart at night, and gather with other families at War Bonnet Creek north of the Agency; the next day, scouts report a wagon train filled with miners headed to the Black Hills. Black Elk is twelve; he participates in a raid on the wagon train, his first action against the *wasichu*.

May–June 1876: Black Elk's family becomes part of the flood of Lakotas headed for the Great Camp of Sitting Bull and Crazy Horse, located on Rosebud Creek. The village is the largest Black Elk has ever seen. In mid-June, Sitting Bull has a vision during a Sun Dance in which he sees conquered soldiers falling from the sky. Scouts report that General George Crook approaches from the south; the village heads northwest to the Valley of the Little Bighorn.

June 17, 1876: The Battle of the Rosebud.

June 25, 1876: The Battle of the Little Bighorn. Both Black Elk and Standing Bear participate in the fighting and kill their first soldiers. Black Elk is probably twelve years old.

July 7–August 2, 1876: The Great Camp moves south after the Custer Massacre, drawing within thirty miles of Crook's base camp, then loops north, following the buffalo herd. The three soldier col-

umns under Crook, Terry, and Gibbon stay in camp, licking
their wounds.

August–September 1876: The Great Camp heads east toward the
Little Missouri, where deer herds migrate in the fall. Crook follows: the chase is known today as the Horsemeat March.

September 9, 1876: The Battle of Slim Buttes, the first army victory in
the Great Sioux War. Both Crazy Horse and Black Elk are
present.

Late September 1876: The bands of Crazy Horse and Sitting Bull
divide in search of food, putting an end to the Great Camp.
Black Elk and the Oglala follow Crazy Horse into the Powder
River Country. An early hard winter brings famine.

January 8, 1877: The Battle of Wolf Mountain. Crazy Horse opposes
General Nelson Miles, while Black Elk watches from a hilltop
with other boys.

Late February or early March 1877: Spotted Tail arrives at Crazy
Horse's camp to negotiate for his surrender. Black Elk watches
his arrival.

May 6, 1877: Crazy Horse and his people surrender at Camp Robinson. Black Elk's family signs what today is known as the Crazy
Horse Surrender Ledger.

Summer 1877: All summer long, rumors swirl around Crazy Horse.
The army wants him to visit the president in Washington, D.C.,
but advisors, including Black Elk's father, warn that if he leaves
the Agency, he will never be allowed to return to his people.

September 5, 1877. Crazy Horse is bayoneted to death at Camp
Robinson during an attempt to force him into a jail cell. Black
Elk is back in the crowd when this occurs.

Late October 1877: The tribes of Red Cloud and Spotted Tail leave
their Agencies and head north to their new winter quarters. On
November 7, while en route, the family of Crazy Horse breaks
away from the column, dragging Crazy Horse's coffin with them.
They bury his body in an unknown location on what is today the
Pine Ridge Reservation. Two days later, Black Elk and six hundred
others also leave the column; most head to Canada to join Sitting Bull.

January 1878: Black Elk's family crosses the "Medicine Line" separating the United States from Canada. They stay in "Grandmother's

Land" for two years, during which time Black Elk experiences increased premonitions and hears spirit voices.

May 1880: Black Elk's family returns to the United States and surrender at Fort Keogh. That winter he hears the Thunder-beings calling for him to fulfill his Great Vision, but does not know what is necessary and lives in constant fear of annihilation.

Spring 1881: Black Elk's fear grows so intense that he finally seeks relief in the medicine man Black Road; for the first time, Black Elk reveals his Great Vision. Black Road realizes that Black Elk is a thunder dreamer; the Horse Dance from his Great Vision must be staged if he hopes to be cured.

June 1881: The last great Sun Dance is held at Pine Ridge. About twelve thousand Lakotas from different Agencies attend.

September 1881: Black Elk and three companions leave Standing Rock on foot to reach the Rosebud and Pine Ridge Reservations, new home of the Brulé and the Oglala. The journey takes a week; his companions stay in Rosebud, while he heads on to Pine Ridge. He turns eighteen that year.

1882: Black Elk's family returns to Pine Ridge. Black Elk performs the vision quest; his mentor Few Tails realizes he must perform a *heyoka* ceremony.

1882–1886: Black Elk's power and influence grows. He performs the elk and buffalo ceremonies, and restages the Horse Dance from Fort Keogh. He successfully performs his first cure. At a time when the U.S. government is trying to stamp out medicine men, Black Elk becomes one of the most powerful and sought-after spiritual healers at Pine Ridge.

1883: The government establishes the Court of Indian Offenses, outlawing the Sun Dance and other dances, the giveaway, polygamy, and medicine men, and establishing sanctions. Punishment is harshest for medicine men, including imprisonment, commitment to the "Indian asylum," and suspension of rations for dependents.

Fall 1886: The hardships of reservation life winnow the Sioux. Black Elk signs two contracts with the Buffalo Bill Cody's Wild West show, hoping to learn the secrets of the power of the whites.

Winter 1886–1887: Black Elk performs with the Wild West at Madison Square Garden in New York. In spring 1887, Cody signs a contract to perform in London at Queen Victoria's Golden Jubilee.

1887: The Dawes Severalty Act, also known as the General Allotment Act, is passed by Congress.

1887–1888: Black Elk performs in London, Birmingham, and Manchester with the Wild West. He dances before the Queen.

February 15, 1888: Black Elk writes the first of his open letters to his people, this one published in the Sioux-language paper *Iape Oaye*. He writes from the Wild West's winter camp in Manchester, and shows his first signs of curiosity in Christianity.

May 6, 1888: Black Elk and three Sioux companions miss the steamship taking Cody's Wild West back to the United States. They are stranded in England.

1888–1889: Black Elk and his companions come to London, where they are investigated in the Whitechapel Murders and join "Mexican Joe" Shelley's Western Wilds of America. From then until spring 1889, he drifts with the troupe through England, Paris, Belgium, and Italy; he falls in love in Paris with a girl named Charlotte, possibly the daughter of a rich merchant. He is injured during a performance in England, and comes to Paris to recuperate; while staying with Charlotte and her family, he falls into his second near-death coma, and has a vision in which he travels by cloud back to Pine Ridge.

May 1889: Black Elk reunites with Buffalo Bill's Wild West, which has come to Paris as part of the Centennial Exposition. Cody pays for Black Elk's return ticket to Pine Ridge.

June 1889: Black Elk returns to Pine Ridge. The Holy Rosary Mission has opened during his absence; friends and family are starving and ill, the Sioux sell their lands to the government, and official boundaries are set for the five smaller Sioux reservations. Close to one percent of the Pine Ridge population dies each month; he resumes his duties as a healer and medicine man.

1889–1890: Word of the Ghost Dance and the Messiah drifts from the west. Kicking Bear, Short Bull, and Good Thunder travel to the land of the Paiutes to investigate. Black Elk becomes a store clerk in Manderson; his father dies, and he assumes responsibility for his mother.

October 1890: Kicking Bear, Short Bull, and Good Thunder bring the Ghost Dance to the Sioux.

November 8, 1890: The new Pine Ridge agent, Dr. Daniel Royer, calls a council of chiefs and tells them to give up the Ghost Dance.

He fails. Thus begins a series of increasingly panic-stricken letters and telegrams to Washington to put down what he calls a "Sioux rebellion."

November 20, 1890: Troops—including Custer's old regiment, the Seventh Cavalry—arrive at Pine Ridge.

November 25, 1890: Royer recommends the arrest and transportation of sixty-six Pine Ridge Ghost Dance leaders, including Black Elk.

December 15, 1890: Sitting Bull is killed by Indian police during an attempted arrest at Standing Rock.

December 17–28, 1890: The flight to Pine Ridge of Chief Big Foot and his people.

December 29, 1890: The Massacre at Wounded Knee. Black Elk and young men who coalesce around him arrive as soldiers are still shooting survivors in a ravine. They charge and free a number of hostages.

January 1891: The aftermath of Wounded Knee. Black Elk is seriously wounded during an attack on the Seventh Cavalry outside Holy Rosary; he survives, and seeks revenge. The Ghost Dancers prepare for a siege in the Stronghold, but the winter is harsh and they surrender to Nelson Miles.

1891–1904: Black Elk continues to serve his people as a traditional Indian healer, even as the government and Church try to stamp out the old ways. He becomes a *yuwipi*, and is known by his contemporaries as "the *yuwipi* man." His healing brings him in conflict with Jesuit priests, often over the deathbed of fellow Oglalas.

1892: Black Elk marries Wounded Knee survivor Katie War Bonnet.

1893: Black Elk's first son, Never Showed Off (later baptized "William"), is born.

1895: Black Elk's second son, Good Voice Star (baptized "John"), is born. Never Showed Off dies.

1899: Black Elk's third son, Benjamin Black Elk, is born. Of his three sons by Katie War Bonnet, Benjamin will be the only one to survive into adulthood.

1900: Black Elk turns thirty-seven. According to his Great Vision, this is the year he is supposed to use the "Soldier Weed," a force of destruction that will annihilate all *wasichus,* but he refuses to take responsibility for such slaughter. He later tells John Neihardt that this is part of the reason he turned to Catholicism.

1901: Katie War Bonnet dies, leaving Black Elk with two young sons.

November 1904: Black Elk converts to Catholicism, supposedly after a confrontation with Father Joseph Lindebner at the deathbed of a dying child.

December 6, 1904: Black Elk is baptized in the Catholic Church as "Nicholas William Black Elk." He will be remembered around Pine Ridge as "Nick."

1906: Black Elk marries Anna Brings White, a widow with two daughters. He becomes a member of a Catholic men's sodality, and is recommended as a catechist.

1907–1916: Black Elk travels throughout the United States and to Indian reservations in the west as a catechist; one priest writes that he is responsible for over four hundred conversions. His main sponsor is Father Henry I. Westropp, who publicizes Black Elk in the Catholic press as an "Indian St. Paul."

1907–1916: Black Elk writes a series of open pastoral letters in La-kota for *Sinasapa Wocekiye Taeyanpaha*, or "The Catholic Herald." They are modeled in tone and intent after Paul's epistles in the Bible.

1909: Black Elk's son Johnnie Good Voice Star dies of tuberculosis, leaving only Ben from his first marriage. This same year, Red Cloud dies.

1910: A son, Henry, is born, but dies in infancy. This same year, his step-daughters die.

January 13, 1912: Black Elk enters the Indian tuberculosis sanitarium in Hot Springs. He will be plagued by recurring bouts of TB for the rest of his life.

1914: A son, Nicholas Jr, is born. Benjamin Black Elk enters the Carlisle Indian School in Carlisle, Pennsylvania.

1915: Black Elk's mother, Mary Leggings Down, dies. Thus, from 1905 to 1915, he marries a second time, two children are born, three children die (including two stepdaughters), he contracts and is treated for TB, and his mother dies. According to Pine Ridge Census records, there was also an infant named Charlotte who was born and died, possibly in childbirth.

1916: Father Westropp is reassigned to missionary work in India. Black Elk ends his missionary travels around the nation, and limits his work as a catechist to Pine Ridge.

1917: Black Elk requests that Ben be released from the Carlisle Indian

School; the Agent writes that Black Elk is "practically blind" and that Ben would take over the family farm and cattle herd.

1921–1929: Black Elk is reassigned as catechist in Oglala, west of Manderson; in 1926, Holy Rosary builds a catechist's home in the village, and Black Elk moves his family there. Ben and his growing family take over the allotment in Manderson.

June 1923: Although Black Elk probably begins practicing the old ways before this point, he publicly performs the old dances in traditional dress for the first time at the Feast of Corpus Christi at Oglala.

1925 and 1926: *The Indian Sentinel* publishes on its cover a 1910 photo of Black Elk, dressed in his familiar vested suit, instructing his daughter Lucy in the rosary. The next year, the magazine publishes the same photo, but now as a stylized drawing with Black Elk dressed in buckskins and a feathered headdress. This was widely circulated on the reservations.

1930: The Jesuits point to Black Elk as a perfect example of an Indian convert and a "civilized savage."

August 1930: John Neihardt comes to Pine Ridge, hoping to interview a holy man for his epic poem about the Ghost Dance. The Agent directs him Black Elk; Neihardt is warned that the old *wicasa wakan* has turned down previous requests for interviews. But Black Elk sees something in the poet, and tells him he will relate the story of his life, his people, and his Great Vision if Neihardt returns the following spring.

May 1931: John Neihardt interviews Black Elk for nearly a month at his allotment and at the home of Standing Bear. Ben translates. Neihardt's daughter Enid transcribes Ben's translation into shorthand; his younger daughter, Hilda, observes.

May 30, 1931: Black Elk, his son Ben, and the Neihardts climb Harney Peak in the Black Hills.

1932: *Black Elk Speaks* is published by William Morrow; it opens to good reviews and poor sales, and is soon remaindered and out of print.

1933: Black Elk is seriously injured in a wagon accident and hospitalized.

August 8, 1936: Black Elk makes his first formal visit to Mount Rushmore, though it is believed he gave a benediction at Rushmore's dedication in October 1925.

1936–1945: Black Elk manages the Duhamel Indian Pageant at the Sitting Bull Crystal Caverns near Rapid City. His wife Anna Brings White dies in 1941.

1945–1946: The visits and interviews of Joseph Epes Brown.

1948: Black Elk is disabled by a broken hip and can no longer walk.

August 17, 1950: Black Elk dies at age eighty-seven.

1953: *The Sacred Pipe* is published.

1961: *Black Elk Speaks* is reprinted in the United States.

1973: Ben Black Elk and John Neihardt die; Siege of Wounded Knee.

NOTES

A NOTE ON SOURCES

Although the starting point for any study of Black Elk is the 1932 *Black Elk Speaks*, the primary source for *this* is the stenographic notes of the May 1931 interviews of the Oglala holy man by the poet John G. Neihardt. These exist in two forms: Enid Neihardt's original shorthand notebooks archived at the State Historical Society of Missouri in Columbia, Missouri; and, more accessibly, the anthropologist Raymond J. DeMallie's transcription of these notes, released in 1984 as *The Sixth Grandfather: Black Elk's Teachings Given to John G. Neihardt* (Lincoln: University of Nebraska Press, 1984).

Both sources are equally important for an understanding of the life and times of the Oglala holy man. Yet they are quite different. The transcripts are rough, repetitive, and at times confusing, as oral interviews tend to be; they also contain a wealth of detail about Oglala culture and history, Black Elk's place in this, and his psychology. *Black Elk Speaks* is a literary translation of the transcripts, and a powerful work in that, but in order to tell the holy man's story Neihardt necessarily compressed and omitted details. There has also been some academic debate about the validity of Neihardt's translation, some of it centered around a "postcolonial" critique of whether any white writer can understand and convey the Oglala experience. Instead, the final word would have to go to Black Elk's family and to DeMallie himself. Both generally agree, through their actions and words, that Neihardt was faithful to Black Elk's words and intent, especially regarding his Great Vision.

Nevertheless, Neihardt was an artist, trying to make sense of what he saw as a tragic story in a vast historical milieu. Thus, there are changes, which DeMallie often points out in the footnotes to *The Sixth Grandfather*. Although I make use of both sources in this biography, I generally depend first upon the interview transcripts for a more direct window into Black Elk's mind. I do make liberal use of *Black Elk Speaks*, for Neihardt is often able to cut to the chase when making sense of the old man's meaning. But at those times when there are differences in the texts, I defer to the transcripts in *The Sixth Grandfather*.

Although both texts end with the Wounded Knee Massacre on December 29, 1890, and its immediate aftermath throughout January 1891, Black Elk's story continues for another sixty years. Other sources are necessary to fill in the details of those decades. They are spread all over the West and Midwest, in archives and on battlefields, but the sites with the most comprehensive collections pertaining to Black Elk are: Marquette University's Department of Special Collections and University Archives; the State Historical Society of Missouri in Columbia; the John Neihardt Center in Bancroft, Nebraska; and the archives of Oglala Lakota College on Pine Ridge Reservation, South Dakota. The archives of the University of Nebraska–Lincoln and the private collection of the family of Joseph Epes Brown are also invaluable. The story of Black Elk's journeys with William Cody and "Mexican Joe" Shelley would not be possible without the resources of the Buffalo Bill Historical Center's McCracken Research Library in Cody, Wyoming; the first stop for resources on the Battle of the Little Bighorn is the White Swan Library at the Little Bighorn Battlefield National Monument. Finally, a more general understanding of Oglala culture, the Indian wars, and life on the reservation can be gleaned from the stacks of the Smithsonian's National Anthropological Archives and National Museum of the American Indian, the National Archives and Records Administration I, and the manuscript division of the Library of Congress, all in Washington, DC.

After the first reference, those resources frequently cited will be abbreviated as follows:

6GF: *The Sixth Grandfather: Black Elk's Teachings Given to John G. Neihardt.*
BES: *Black Elk Speaks.*
BBHC: Buffalo Bill Historical Center, McCracken Research Library, Cody, WY.
EB: Elenita Brown Collection, Stevensville, MT.
JNC: John Neihardt Center, Neihardt Foundation Archives, Bancroft, NE.
MARQ: Marquette University, Milwaukee, WI: Department of Special Collections and University Archives.
NAA: Smithsonian Institution, National Anthropological Archives, Washington, DC.
NARA I: National Archives and Records Administration I, Washington, DC.
NMAI: Smithsonian Institution, National Museum of the American Indian (NMAI), Washington, DC.
OLC: Oglala Lakota College Library and Archives, Kyle, Pine Ridge Agency, SD.
SHSM: State Historical Society of Missouri, Columbia, MO.
SSWT: *Sina Sapa Wocekiye Taeyanpaha* [The Catholic Sioux Herald].
UNL: University of Nebraska–Lincoln, Archives and Special Collections, Lincoln, NE.

PROLOGUE: "A SORT OF A PREACHER"

There are many accounts of Neihardt's first meeting with Black Elk, including Neihardt's letters in the Neihardt Collection at the State Historical Society of Missouri (hereafter SHSM), but the most comprehensive are: Neihardt, "Preface to the 1961 Edition," *Black Elk Speaks, Being the Life Story of a Holy Man of the Oglala Sioux, the Premier Edition, as Told Through John G. Neihardt (Flaming Rainbow)*, annotated by Raymond J. DeMallie, illustrations by Standing Bear (Albany: State University of New York Press, 2008; first published 1932 by William Morrow; hereafter *BES*), xxi–xxii; and Hilda Neihardt, *Black Elk and Flaming Rainbow: Personal Memories of the Lakota Holy Man and John Neihardt* (Lincoln: University of Nebraska Press, 1995), 12–16. Hilda was present at the historic interviews in 1931 between her father and Black Elk; she outlines the first meeting in the chapter "An Accidental Meeting."

4 *the horsemen descended upon Claire Trevor*: *Stagecoach*, directed by John Ford, United Artists, 1939.
4 *"brewery-distributed cromolithographic fantasies"*: Ralph K. Andrist, *The Long Death: The Last Days of the Plains Indian* (New York: Collier Books, 1993; first published by Macmillan, 1964), 2.
4 *Comanche carved out a 240,000-square-mile empire*: S. C. Gwynne, *Empire of the*

Summer Moon: Quanah Parker and the Rise and Fall of the Comanches, the Most Powerful Indian Tribe in American History (New York: Scribner, 2010).

4 *"It was mostly a battle, partly a massacre, and entirely a tragic blunder"*: Rex Alan Smith, *Moon of Popping Trees* (Lincoln: University of Nebraska Press, 1981; first published by Reader's Digest Press, 1975), 1.

5 *Moses Flying Hawk*: Wikipedia's "Flying Hawk" entry, http://en.wikipedia.org/wiki/Flying-Hawk.

6 *thirty-year-old Eleanor Hinman*: Eleanor H. Hinman, "Oglala Sources on the Life of Crazy Horse," *Nebraska History* 57 (Spring 1976, reprint, originally published in 1930), 6. Other Oglala, like Luke Little Hawk, took the position that since no questions had been asked about Crazy Horse at the time of his death, "he did not care to answer any now." Hinman never wrote her book, and instead gave her notes to the Nebraska Historical Society and later to Mari Sandoz; these became the initial basis for Sandoz's famous *Crazy Horse: The Strange Man of the Oglalas*, published in 1942.

6 *Hinman told the story differently*: Ibid.

7 *The near-extinction of the buffalo*: Andrew C. Isenberg, *The Destruction of the Bison: An Environmental History, 1750–1920* (Cambridge: Cambridge University Press, 2000), 24, 25.

7 *1.8 to 18 million*: Wikipedia's "Population history of indigenous peoples of the Americas" entry, http://en.wikipedia.org/wiki/Population-history-of-indigenous-peoples-of-the-Americas; and Russell Thornton, *American Indian Holocaust and Survival: A Population History Since 1492* (Norman: University of Oklahoma Press, 1990), 26–32.

8 *600,000*: Michael R. Haines and Richard H. Steckel, eds., *A Population History of North America* (Cambridge: Cambridge University Press, 2000), 24.

8 *332,397*: U.S. Bureau of the Census, *Fifteenth Census of the United States: 1930; Population, Volume II: General Report/Statistical Subjects* (Washington, DC: Government Printing Office, 1933), 25.

8 *When the Puritans*: Charles C. Mann, "1491," *The Atlantic*, March 2002, www.theatlantic.com/magazine/archive/2002/03/1491/302445/.

8 *25 to 50 percent of the population died*: Carl Waldman, *Atlas of the North American Indian* (New York: Checkmark Books, 2009), 206; Charles C. Mann, *1491: New Revelations of the Americas Before Columbus* (New York: Vintage Books, 2006), 118–23; William H. McNeill, *Plagues and Peoples* (Garden City, NY: Anchor Books, 1976), 181; and James Mooney, *The Aboriginal Population of America North of Mexico* (Washington, DC: Government Printing Office, 1928), 13.

8 *"where little else but weather"*: BES, xxxiii

8 *"fine eyes"*: University of Nebraska–Lincoln, Archives and Special Collections, Lincoln, NE (hereafter UNL), Mari Sandoz Collection, Part II, Research Files, Box 27, "Notes on Sioux and Cheyenne Indians, Part I," Folder 24. "Correspondence between Eleanor Hinman and Mari Sandoz, re: Sioux and Cheyenne," Folder 24–8: letter from Eleanor Hinman to Mari Sandoz, n.d.

9 *Swiss psychologist Carl Jung was talking*: Carl Jung, *Modern Man in Search of a Soul* (New York: Harcourt, Brace & World, 1933), 213.

10 *nine people lived in the one-room cabin*: National Archives and Records Administration I, Washington, DC (hereafter NARA I), "Indian Census Rolls, 1885–1940 [microform]: Indians of North America—Census; Native American Census—Pine Ridge (Oglala Sioux Indians)," Reel 376, "1930," 57–58.

11 *"The poultry and the pigs shriveled up"*: Thomas E. Mails, assisted by Dallas Chief Eagle, *Fools Crow* (Garden City, NY: Doubleday, 1979), 149.

11 *the average annual family income was $152.80*: Esther S. Goldfrank, "Historic Change and Social Character: A Study of the Teton Dakota," *American Anthropologist* 45 (1943): 68; and Raymond J. DeMallie, "Pine Ridge Economy: Cultural and Historical Perspectives," in *American Indian Economic Development*, ed. Sam Stanley (The Hague: Mouton, 1978), 259.

11 *Flying Hawk was sick*: *Wikipedia*'s "Flying Hawk" entry, and *Voices of the American West: The Indian Interviews of Eli S. Ricker, 1903–1919*, vol. 1, ed. Richard E. Jensen (Lincoln: University of Nebraska Press, 2005), 307.

12 *"strangely beautiful"*: Neihardt, "Preface to the 1972 Edition," *BES*, xxvii.

12 *"remarkable parallel vision"*: Carl G. Jung, *Mysterium Coniunctionis: An Inquiry into the Separation and Synthesis of Psychic Opposites in Alchemy*, vol. 14, *The Collected Works of C. G. Jung*, Bollingen Series XX (Princeton, NJ: Princeton University Press, 1963), 205–206, 205n.

13 *Vine Deloria, Jr.*: Quotes by Deloria, N. Scott Momaday, and Philip Zaleski from Raymond DeMallie, "Introduction," *The Sixth Grandfather: Black Elk's Teachings Given to John G. Neihardt*, ed. Raymond J. DeMallie (Lincoln: University of Nebraska Press, 1984; hereafter *6GF*), xx; and Philip Zaleski, "*Black Elk Speaks* in the Top Ten Spiritual Books of the Century," *Neihardt Journal* 2 (2000): 9.

13 *"a key statement in the understanding of myth and symbols"*: Joseph Campbell, *When People Lived Legends: American Indian Myths*, documentary (William Free Productions and Mythology, 1989); and *Joseph Campbell and the Power of Myth*, TV documentary miniseries (PBS, 1988).

14 *"numinous"*: Rudolf Otto, *The Idea of the Holy*, trans. John W. Harvey (New York: Oxford University Press, 1958; first published in German, 1917), 12–13.

15 *"because my children have to live in this world"*: Hilda Neihardt, *Black Elk and Flaming Rainbow*, 88.

15 *"a male counterpart ought to be close behind her"*: Michael F. Steltenkamp, S.J., "American Indian Sainthood and the Catholic Church," *American Catholic Studies* 124, no. 1 (2013): 93.

15 *"shaman sickness"*: Lawrence Wright, *Going Clear: Scientology, Hollywood, and the Prison of Belief* (New York: Vintage Books, 2013), 102–103.

16 *"When I look back now out from this high hill of my old age"*: *BES*, 218.

17 *"the sacred tree is dead"*: Ibid.

1. CHOSEN

This chapter encompasses events described in *Black Elk Speaks*, 7–16; and *The Sixth Grandfather*, 101–10. Other general sources include Smithsonian Institution, National Anthropological Archives, Washington, DC (hereafter NAA), Philleo Nash Papers, Series 3, Box 17, "Miscellaneous Papers of Others," Robert E. Daniels, "Cultural Identities Among the Oglala Sioux," February 1965, typescript, 40; Stephen R. Riggs, *Grammar and Dictionary of the Dakota Language*, Smithsonian Contributions to Knowledge, vol. 4 (Washington, DC: Smithsonian Institution, 1852), 34; Joseph S. Karol, ed., *Everyday Lakota: An English-Sioux Dictionary for Beginners* (St. Francis, SD: Rosebud Educational Society, 1997, first published 1971), 110; and Kingsley M. Bray, "Teton Sioux: Population History, 1655–1881," *Nebraska History* 75 (Summer 1994): 174–75.

21 *disappearance of the buffalo*: Jeffrey Ostler, *The Lakotas and the Black Hills: The Struggle for Sacred Ground* (New York: Viking, 2010), 70–71; and Paul Robertson, *The Power of the Land: Identity, Ethnicity, and Class Among the Oglala Lakota* (New York: Routledge, 2002), 13–14.

21 *Pte had drained underground*: James Owen Dorsey, "A Study of Siouan Cults," extract from the *Eleventh Annual Report of the Bureau of Ethnology* (Washington, DC: Government Printing Office, 1894), 476–77.

21 *Kahnigapi, or "Chosen"*: William K. Powers, "When Black Elk Speaks, Everybody Listens," in *Religion in Native North America*, ed. Christopher Vecsey (Moscow: University of Idaho Press, 1990), 138.

22 *"They are coming closer all the time"*: Richard G. Hardorff, ed., *Cheyenne Memories of the Custer Fight* (Lincoln: University of Nebraska Press, 1995), v–vi.

22 *Sweet Medicine*: D. M. Dooling and Paul Jordan-Smith, eds., *I Become Part of It: Sacred Dimensions in Native American Life* (New York: Parabola Books, 1989), 255–58.

22 *Drinks Water*: 6GF, 290, 338–41; and BES, 9.

22 *Iktomi*: Robert H. Ruby, *The Oglala Sioux: Warriors in Transition* (Lincoln: University of Nebraska Press, 1955), 72.

22 *"shape and direct"*: Richard Slotkin, "Dreams and Genocide: The American Myth of Regeneration Through Violence," *Journal of Popular Culture* 5, no. 1 (Summer 1971): 38.

22 *a tipi was warm in the winter*: M. I. McCreight, trans., *Firewater and Forked Tongues: A Sioux Chief Interprets U.S. History* (Pasadena, CA: Trail's End, 1947), 61. This was the second of Flying Hawk's books, translated by the Pennsylvania banker and conservationist McCreight. All of Flying Hawk's books were translated or edited by McCreight, who was the chief's good friend, and published posthumously.

23 *"alongside of those gray houses"*: 6GF, 338–41.

24 *the year of Black Elk's birth*: Michael F. Steltenkamp, S.J., *Nicholas Black Elk: Medicine Man, Missionary, Mystic* (Norman: University of Oklahoma Press, 2009), 15–16; Joseph Campbell, *When People Lived Legends: American Indian Myths*, documentary (William Free Productions and Mythology, 1989); and NARA I, "Indian Census Rolls, 1885–1940 [microform]: Indians of North America—Census; Native American Census—Pine Ridge (Oglala Sioux Indians)," Reel 368, "1900–1903." Black Elk's year of birth is corroborated by the 1900 Pine Ridge Reservation Census, which lists his age as thirty-seven in 1900. However, there are discrepancies in the records. Neihardt in his interview notes said Black Elk was seventy-two when they talked, making 1859 the year of his birth. His granddaughter said he was born in 1858; his later disciple Joseph Epes Brown, 1862; archives at Holy Rosary Mission, 1865; Black Elk's daughter Lucy and friend and business partner Bud Duhamel, 1866. Joseph Campbell would say Black Elk was "over ninety" when the Neihardt interviews took place, but this seems a kind of shorthand on Campbell's part for the fact that, as a man born in a time and place outside official records, his was the wisdom of the ages.

24 *"winter count"*: UNL, Mari Sandoz Collection, Part II, Research Files, Box 11, File 9.1: "Indian Chronology (Indian Wintercounts)," Folder 9.1-1: "Calendar of Oglala Sioux Names for Years from A.D. 1759 to A.D. 1908," Folder 9.1-15, "A Minneconjou Calendar or Wintercount, 1781–1932," Folder 9.1-16: "A Hunkpapa Sioux Calendar."

24 *seventh of nine children*: In addition to *Black Elk Speaks* and *The Sixth Grandfather*, notes on Black Elk's genealogy can be found in Michael F. Steltenkamp, S.J., *Black Elk: Holy Man of the Oglala* (Norman: University of Oklahoma Press, 1993), 17–18; Steltenkamp, *Nicholas Black Elk*, 19–21; and UNL, Mari Sandoz Collection, Part II, Research Files, Box 33, "Notes on Indian Tribes," Folder 28.1, "Sioux Relationship List," Folder 28.1-26: Black Elk. Charlotte Black Elk, Black Elk's famous great-granddaughter, does not believe that Runs in the Center was a half brother— that this was the kind of honorific the Sioux would assign to those close to them, just like "uncle" or "cousin." But statements by Black Elk's daughter Lucy—and the fact that his mother was actually his father's second wife—seem to suggest otherwise. In addition to those individuals listed in the text, Black Elk was the cousin of Black Wasichu, who was shot in the right shoulder at the Little Bighorn, and of Hard to Hit, who went with Sitting Bull to Canada in 1878. Black Elk's uncle on his mother's side was Running Hawk, who also went north with Sitting Bull.

25 *"on call"*: Vine Deloria, Jr., *The World We Used to Live In: Remembering the Powers of the Medicine Men* (Golden, CO: Fulcrum, 2006), 13–14.

25 *possessed by the spirit of the bear*: Raymond J. DeMallie, "Lakota Belief and Ritual in the Nineteenth Century," in *Sioux Indian Religion*, ed. Raymond J. DeMallie and Douglas R. Parks (Norman: University of Oklahoma Press, 1987), 41; Deloria, *World We Used to Live In*, xxiv; and Thomas E. Mails, *Dog Soldiers, Bear Men and Buffalo Women: A Study of the Societies and Cults of the Plains Indians* (Englewood Cliffs, NJ: Prentice Hall, 1973), 263–64.

25 *the* Zuya-Wakan, *or war prophets, and the* Wapiya: Gideon H. Pond, "Power and Influence of Dakota Medicine-Men," in *Information Respecting the History, Conditions and Prospects of the Indian Tribes of the United States,* ed. Henry R. Schoolcraft, vol. 4 (Philadelphia, 1854), 642.

25 pejuta wicasa: *6GF,* 102n3.

26 *"often passed down through the family":* Francis La Flesche, "Who Was the Medicine Man?" *Journal of American Folk-Lore* 18 (1905): 273.

26 *Catherine Wabose:* Henry R. Schoolcraft, *The Indian Tribes of the United States: Their Histories, Antiquities, Customs, Religion, Arts, Language, Traditions, Oral Legends, and Myths,* vol. 1 (Philadelphia: J. B. Lippincott, 1884), 391–93.

26 *Black Elk's mother:* Steltenkamp, *Nicholas Black Elk,* 19.

27 *secret ingredients:* Deloria, *World We Used to Live In,* 14–15.

27 *his mother's labor pains:* Account of an Oglala birth from Kingsley M. Bray, *Crazy Horse: A Lakota Life* (Norman: University of Oklahoma Press, 2006), 5.

27 *washed by an old woman:* Raymond J. DeMallie, "Teton," *Handbook of North American Indians* 13, no. 2 (Washington, DC: Smithsonian Institution, 2001): 808.

27 *Memory is history:* Katherine Nelson, "The Psychological and Social Origins of Autobiographical Memory," *Psychological Science* 4, no. 1 (January 1993): 9; David Thelen, "Memory and American History," *The Journal of American History* 75, no. 4 (March 1989): 1120; Richard Sennett, "Disturbing Memories," in *Memory,* ed. Patricia Fara and Karalyn Patterson (Cambridge: Cambridge University Press, 1998), 12; "Rewriting Memory," *The Week,* February 21, 2014, 17; and "Your Memory Is No Video Camera: It Edits the Past with Present Experiences," *ScienceDaily,* February 4, 2014, www .sciencedaily.com/releases/2014/02/140204185651.htm.

27 *"the children of the forest":* Charles Eastman is quoted in William Bloodworth, "Varieties of American Indian Autobiography," *MELUS* 5, no. 3 (Autumn 1978): 72.

27 *"a beautiful country":* Luther Standing Bear, *My Indian Boyhood* (Lincoln: University of Nebraska Press, 1931), 5.

28 *"as a man might remember some bad dream": BES,* 7–8.

28 *"troubled and afraid":* Ibid., 8.

28 *John M. Bozeman:* "A Brief History of the Bozeman Trail," www.wyohistory.org /encyclopedia/brief-history-bozeman-trail.

29 *The Sioux first appeared:* Ostler, *Lakotas and the Black Hills,* 6–7; James H. Howard, *The Dakota or Sioux Indians: A Study in Human Ecology* (Lincoln, NE: J and L Reprints, 1980; first published by University of South Dakota, 1966), 2; Richard White, *"It's Your Misfortune and None of My Own": A New History of the American West* (Norman: University of Oklahoma Press, 1993), 23; and Joseph Agonito, *Lakota Portraits: Lives of the Legendary Plains People* (Guilford, CT: TwoDot, 2011), xn. "Nátawèsiwok" most likely meant "speaks a foreign language," rather than "snake" or "enemy," as is usually suggested.

29 *The tribe preferred "Dakota":* Helen Hunt Jackson, *A Century of Dishonor* (Mineola, NY: Dover, 2003; first published by Harper & Bros., 1881), 136.

29 *the "Seven Council Fires":* Raymond J. DeMallie, "The Sioux at the Time of European Contact: An Ethnohistorical Problem," in *New Perspectives on Native North America: Cultures, Histories, and Representations,* ed. Sergei Kan and Pauline Turner Strong (Lincoln: University of Nebraska Press, 2006), 257; and Catherine Price, *The Oglala People: 1841–1879: A Political History* (Lincoln: University of Nebraska Press, 1996), 6.

29 *"Lakota" for their dialect:* Ostler, *Lakotas and the Black Hills,* 7; Howard, *Dakota or Sioux Indians,* 3; DeMallie, "Teton," 799; Steltenkamp, *Black Elk,* 6; and Agonito, *Lakota Portraits,* x. Where the other six Council Fires, called the "Dakota," used a "d" when they spoke, the Lakota used an "l." Where Lakota said *kola* for "friend," Dakotas said *koda.*

29 *The Oglala were the westernmost:* UNL, Mari Sandoz Collection, Part II, Research Files, Box 32, "Notes on Indian Tribes," Folder 31: "Sioux Indians," 31.14, "The Teton

Sioux," 31–54; and DeMallie, "Teton," 804. The Lakota names are as follows: Oglala; Sicangu, best known as Brulé; Mnikowoju, best known as Minneconjou; Hunkpapa; Oohenunpa, or Two Kettles; Sihasapa, or Blackfoot; and Itazipcos, or Sans Arc.

29　*Southern Oglala . . . Northern Oglala*: Price, *Oglala People*, 5; and George Hyde, *Red Cloud's Folk: A History of the Oglala Sioux Indians* (Norman: University of Oklahoma Press, 1967, first published 1937), 98. The Southern Oglala were known as the Bear People, the Northern Oglala as the Smoke People. Although the Bear People included the oldest leading Oglala bands, they began to lose members and influence because they tended to be more friendly with whites.

29　*"Bad Faces"*: Hyde, *Red Cloud's Folk*, 87. The origin of the name "Bad Faces" was typical of Lakota humor. According to a story told by He Dog, the son of one of Red Cloud's sisters, the chief of the band had a jealous wife who often quarreled with him. She was so loud the entire camp could hear her. Her favorite barb was to tell her husband he had a "bad face." She repeated this so often, and shrilly, that it became a standing joke.

29　*their true origin*: DeMallie, "Teton," 799–800; *6GF*, 283–85.

30　*That changed between 1750 and 1820*: Smithsonian Institution, National Museum of the American Indian, Washington, DC (hereafter NMAI), exhibit: "A Song for the Horse Nation"; *Wikipedia*'s "Evolution of the Horse" entry, http://en.wikipedia.org /wiki/Evolution_of_the_horse; and S. C. Gwynne, *Empire of the Summer Moon: Quanah Parker and the Rise and Fall of the Comanches, the Most Powerful Indian Tribe in American History* (New York: Scribner, 2010), 28–31.

30　*In 1630, no tribes anywhere were mounted*: Gwynne, *Quanah Parker*, 30–31; NMAI, "Song for the Horse Nation"; and White, *"It's Your Misfortune,"* 24.

30　*They did not catch one until 1809*: "A Song for the Horse Nation," NMAI; Howard, *Dakota or Sioux Indians*, 20–21.

30　*At early 1800s trading posts*: Ibid. In addition to these more exceptional horses, a plain, nondescript horse could bring the following: one gun and one hundred rounds of ammunition; or three pounds of tobacco; or fifteen eagle feathers; or ten weasel skins; or five tipi poles; or one skin shirt and leggings, decorated with human hair and porcupine quills.

30　*signified strength of character*: "A Song for the Horse Nation," NMAI; and Esther S. Goldfrank, "Historic Change and Social Character: A Study of the Teton Dakota," *American Anthropologist* 45 (1943): 72–73.

31　*By 1839, the Oglala and Brulé had pushed south*: Price, *Oglala People*, 21.

31　*right of conquest*: White, *"It's Your Misfortune,"* 95.

31　*By the time of Black Elk's birth*: Ostler, *Lakotas and the Black Hills*, 13, 17; Goldfrank, "Historic Change," 73; and "A Brief History of the Bozemah Trail."

31　*the Oglala were the richest*: Goldfrank, "Historic Change," 73.

32　*the Oglala had a reputation*: Howard, *Dakota or Sioux Indians*, 24–25.

32　*prosperity did not bring peace*: Prince Maximillian of Wied, *Travels in the Interior of North America*, quoted in Goldfrank, "Historic Change," 73.

32　*violence among peers*: Goldfrank, "Historic Change," 69–72; George Catlin, *North American Indians* (New York: Penguin, 2004), 242–44; and Francis Parkman, Jr., *The California and Oregon Trail* (New York: Penguin, 1985; first published by G. P. Putnam, 1849), 124.

32　*a two-thousand-mile set of wheel ruts*: Rex Alan Smith, *Moon of Popping Trees* (Lincoln: University of Nebraska Press, 1981; first published by Reader's Digest Press, 1975), 10–12.

33　*the first Treaty of Fort Laramie*: Ibid., 13–14.

34　*The "Grattan Massacre" . . . Battle of Blue Water Creek*: Ibid., 31–32.

35　*The Indian Agents noticed first*: U.S. Government Report, Department of Indian Affairs, 1862, 31; and U.S. Government Report, Department of Indian Affairs, 1866, quoted in Goldfrank, "Historic Change," 75.

35 *cooperative values began to replace*: U.S. Government Report, Department of Indian Affairs, 1854 and 1872, both quoted in Goldfrank, "Historic Change," 75–76. Of fifty-three thousand Sioux from all tribes, forty-six thousand were said to be "uncivilized." Of these, ten thousand—mostly Lakota—were hostile.

35 *two most-vaunted values*: H. Scudder Mekeel, *The Economy of a Modern Teton Dakota Community*, Yale University Publications in Anthropology 6 (New Haven, CT: Human Relations Area Files Press, 1970, first published 1936).

2. A CASUALTY OF THE HUNDRED SLAIN

This chapter encompasses events described in *Black Elk Speaks*, 9–12; and *The Sixth Grandfather*, 103–104.

36 *began a debate*: Douglas R. Parks and Raymond J. DeMallie, "Plains Indian Native Literatures," *boundary 2* 19, no. 3 (Fall 1992): 127.

37 *turn him into an equal*: Lt. Col. Dave Grossman, *On Killing: The Psychological Cost of Learning to Kill in War and Society* (Boston: Back Bay Books, 1996), 160–67.

37 *had relied extensively upon military success*: Francesco Duina, *Winning: Reflections on an American Obsession* (Princeton, NJ: Princeton University Press, 2011), 44, 65.

37 *"Away, away, with all these cobweb tissues"*: Richard White, *"It's Your Misfortune and None of My Own": A New History of the American West* (Norman: University of Oklahoma Press, 1993), 73.

37 *the Santee Sioux had risen*: Scott W. Berg, *38 Nooses: Lincoln, Little Crow, and the Beginning of the Frontier's End* (New York: Pantheon Books, 2012), 6; letter, Thos. S. Williamson to T. J. Galbraith, Sioux agent, June 2, 1862, in Board of Commissioners, *Minnesota in the Civil and Indian Wars: 1861–1865, Official Reports and Correspondence* (St. Paul, MN: Pioneer Press, 1893), 162–63; Rex Alan Smith, *Moon of Popping Trees* (Lincoln: University of Nebraska Press; first published by Reader's Digest Press, 1975), 34–35; and Dee Brown, *Bury My Heart at Wounded Knee: An Indian History of the American West* (New York: Henry Holt, 1970), 64–65. The spark for the "Minnesota Massacre" occurred on Sunday, August 17, 1862, when four young warriors stopped at a farm near Acton. They found a hen's nest filled with eggs and argued about stealing some. This led to accusations of cowardice and a dare to shoot the whites; when the smoke cleared that Sunday, they'd killed three white men, a woman, and a fifteen-year-old girl.

38 *Sitting Bull*: Brown, *Bury My Heart*, 65.

38 *an image of the Sioux*: Smith, *Moon of Popping Trees*, 35.

38 *John Milton Chivington and 750 men*: White, *"It's Your Misfortune,"* 95–96; Smith, *Moon of Popping Trees*, 37–39; and Ralph K. Andrist, *The Long Death: The Last Days of the Plains Indians* (New York: Collier Books, 1993; first published by Macmillan, 1964), 88–89.

39 *Red Cloud was the most driven*: Joseph Agonito, *Lakota Portraits: Lives of the Legendary Plains People* (Guilford, CT: TwoDot, 2011), 33.

39 *well placed for leadership*: Ibid., 31.

40 *dramatic and instant eloquence*: Ibid., 33–34; and Doane Robinson, "The Education of Red Cloud," *Collections of the South Dakota Department of History* 12 (1924): 166–67.

41 *From July 1 to December 21, 1866*: U.S. Indian Commissioner's Report, 1867, 269.

41 *"The races of mammoths"*: Henry E. Fritz, *The Movement for Indian Assimilation, 1860–1890* (Philadelphia: University of Philadelphia Press, 1963), 123–24.

41 *people cease to be themselves*: Martin van Creveld, *The Culture of War* (New York: Ballantine, 2008), 116.

41 *How can one unravel Crazy Horse*: Richard S. Grimes, "The Making of a Sioux Legend: The Historiography of Crazy Horse," *South Dakota History* 30, no. 3 (Fall 2000): 277–78; *Wikipedia*'s "Crazy Horse" entry, http://en.wikipedia.org/wiki/Crazy_Horse;

"The Death of Crazy Horse," *The Sun* (New York), September 14, 1876, 1; *BES*, 9, 67; Agonito, *Lakota Portraits*, 81–91; SHSM, John G. Neihardt Papers (1881–1973), c. 1858–1974, C3716, Folder 431, "Transcription, 1944, Eagle Elk, November 27, 1944: 'Crazy Horse'"; UNL, Mari Sandoz Collection, Part II, Research Files, Box 27, "Notes on Sioux and Cheyenne Indians, Part I," Folder 1: "Miscellaneous Notes on Crazy Horse," 1.17, "Crazy Horse," Box 28, "Notes on Sioux and Cheyenne Indians, Part II," Folder 9: "Information and Misinformation on Crazy Horse," Folder 9.2: "Indian Haircut," letter from Stanley Vestal to *New York Herald Tribune*, July 15, 1948; Kingsley M. Bray, *Crazy Horse: A Lakota Life* (Norman: University of Oklahoma Press, 2006), 84, 94–95; John H. Monnett, *Where a Hundred Soldiers Were Killed: The Struggle for the Powder River Country in 1866 and the Making of the Fetterman Myth* (Albuquerque: University of New Mexico Press, 2008), 210–19; Oliver Knight, "War or Peace: The Anxious Wait for Crazy Horse," *Nebraska History* 54 (1973): 521; "Chipp's Interview," in *Voices of the American West: The Indian Interviews of Eli S. Ricker*, vol. 1, ed. Richard E. Jensen (Lincoln: University of Nebraska Press, 2005), 273; Ian Frazier, *Great Plains* (New York: Picador, 1989), 96, 102; and Paul L. Hedren, *After Custer: Loss and Transformation in Sioux Country* (Norman: University of Oklahoma Press, 2011), 136. Regarding the year of Crazy Horse's birth: While census records support 1845, Chips said he was born in the year the Oglala "Stole One Hundred Horses," or the winter count for 1840–41. His father, also originally named Crazy Horse, said his son was born "on the South Cheyenne River in the fall of 1840." Black Elk said that during the fall and winter of 1866, Crazy Horse was "only about 19 years old," but this would put his birth in 1847, outside the accepted range, and is probably mistaken.

43 *Worm*: Edward Kadlecek and Mabell Kadlecek, *To Kill an Eagle: Indian Views on the Last Days of Crazy Horse* (Boulder, CO: Johnson Books, 1981), 26.

43 *his cousin Standing Bear*: Ricker, *Voices of the American West*, vol. 1, 57n. Standing Bear is a common Lakota name, and should not be confused with *Luther* Standing Bear (1863–1936), a Brulé Lakota and the author of *My People the Sioux* and several other books on Lakota life.

43 *"When we were young"*: Ricker, *Voices of the American West*, 273.

44 *a second vision*: Bray, *Crazy Horse*, 65.

45 *Fort Phil Kearny*: Cyrus Townsend Brady, *Indian Fights and Fighters* (Lincoln: University of Nebraska Press, 1971; first published by McLure, Phillips, 1904), 15–18; Margaret Carrington, *Ab-sa-ra-ka, Land of Massacre* (Philadelphia: Lippincott, 1878), 141, 165; and Dee Brown, *The Fetterman Massacre*, originally published as *Fort Phil Kearny: An American Saga* (Lincoln: University of Nebraska Press, 1962), 67. "But for the presence of hostile Indians, the country around Fort Philip Kearny would be a charming field for hunting and picnic purposes," wrote Margaret Carrington in *Ab-sa-ra-ka, Land of Massacre*.

46 *"A horseback could ride through our villages"*: George Hyde, *Red Cloud's Folk: A History of the Oglala Sioux Indians* (Norman: University of Oklahoma Press, 1967, first published 1937), 145; and *BES*, 9.

46 *The best place for an ambush*: 40th Congress, 1st session, S. Doc. 13, 37–38.

46 *The Sioux tried twice*: Carrington, *Ab-sa-ra-ka*, 197; and Brown, *Fetterman Massacre*, 164.

46 *On December 21, Red Cloud tried again*: Sources for the account of the Fetterman Massacre include *BES*, 9–12; Evan S. Connell, *Son of the Morning Star: Custer and the Little Bighorn* (New York: Harper & Row, 1984), 128–32; Hyde, *Red Cloud's Folk*, 146–49; Smith, *Moon of Popping Trees*, 42–49; Brown, *Fetterman Massacre*, 165–66, 198; Monnett, *Where a Hundred Soldiers Were Killed*, 210–19; John Guthrie, "The Fetterman Massacre," *Annals of Wyoming* 9, no. 2 (October 1932): 714–18; Peter D. Olch, "Medicine in the Indian-Fighting Army," *Journal of the West* 21, no. 3 (July 1982): 39; Stanley Vestal, *Warpath: The True Story of the Fighting Sioux Told in a Biography of Chief White Bull* (Lincoln: University of Nebraska Press, 1984), 55–68;

and Bruce A. Rosenberg, *Custer and the Epic of Defeat* (University Park: Pennsylvania State University Press, 1974), 111. Considerable debate still exists regarding Crazy Horse's role in the decoy party. Though many writers place him there, it is hard to support this from primary sources.

3. THE GREAT VISION

This chapter encompasses events described in *Black Elk Speaks*, 12–38; and *The Sixth Grandfather*, 109–42.

49 *that winter*: BES, 12–13; 6GF, 104–105; and Royal B. Hassrick, *The Sioux: Life and Customs of a Warrior Society* (Norman: University of Oklahoma Press, 1964), 176.

49 *the pasqueflower bloomed*: Jeffrey Ostler, *The Lakotas and the Black Hills: The Struggle for Sacred Ground* (New York: Viking, 2010), 15.

49 *losses cut too deep*: Ralph K. Andrist, *The Long Death: The Last Days of the Plains Indians* (New York: Collier Books, 1993; first published by Macmillan, 1964), 126–27.

49 *People had grown tired of war*: Ibid., 125–26.

50 *"I did not feel so much afraid"*: BES, 12.

50 *A cozy place in the lodge*: Melvin R. Gilmore, "The Old-Time Method of Rearing a Dakota Boy," *Indian Notes: Museum of the American Indian, Heye Foundation* 6, no. 4 (1929): 367–72.

50 *daydreams were dangerous*: Vine Deloria, Jr., *The World We Used to Live In: Remembering the Powers of the Medicine Men* (Golden, CO: Fulcrum, 2006), 6.

50 handloglaka: Ibid., 15.

51 *500 to 600 Cheyennes under Two Moon and Dull Knife*: George Hyde, *Red Cloud's Folk: A History of the Oglala Sioux Indians* (Norman: University of Oklahoma Press, 1967, first published 1937), 159.

51 *Hayfield and Wagon Box Fights*: Andrist, *Long Death*, 127–31; Dee Brown, *Bury My Heart at Wounded Knee: An Indian History of the American West* (New York: Henry Holt, 1970), 140–41; Hyde, *Red Cloud's Folk*, 159; 6GF, 107–108; BES, 13–14; and Joseph Agonito, *Lakota Portraits: Lives of the Legendary Plains People* (Guilford, CT: TwoDot, 2011), 90. At the Wagon Box Fight, it has been estimated that the Lakota dead totaled between 50 and 120, many buried in the surrounding hills.

52 *halted the steady western progress*: Richard G. Hardorff, *Cheyenne Memories of the Custer Fight* (Lincoln: University of Nebraska Press, 1995), 173–74, 174n20.

52 *the Treaty of 1868*: Brown, *Bury My Heart*, 142–46; and Rex Alan Smith, *Moon of Popping Trees* (Lincoln: University of Nebraska Press; first published by Reader's Digest Press, 1975), 46–52.

53 *Now he was five*: Black Elk's first vision is drawn from 6GF, 109–10; and BES, 15–16.

54 *"until the summer I was nine years old is not a story"*: BES, 17.

54 *administration of President Ulysses S. Grant*: Brown, *Bury My Heart*, 178, 180.

54 *Philip Henry Sheridan*: Paul A. Hutton, "Phil Sheridan's Frontier," in *The Great Sioux War, 1876–1877: The Best from Montana, The Magazine of Western History*, ed. Paul L. Hedren (Helena: Montana Historical Society Press, 1991), 91–105; Henry E. Fritz, *The Movement for Indian Assimilation, 1860–1890*, 125; and Brown, *Bury My Heart*, 170–71.

55 *"Buffalo Bone Days"*: M. I. McCreight, *Buffalo Bone Days* (Sykesville, PA: Nupp Printing Co., 1939), 8–10.

55 *new Agencies*: Agonito, *Lakota Portraits*, 39; and Brown, *Bury My Heart*, 183–88.

56 *thousands followed Red Cloud*: Hyde, *Red Cloud's Folk*, 194.

56 *"non-treaty Indians"*: Brown, *Bury My Heart*, 183–84; and Doane Robinson, "The Education of Red Cloud," *Collections of the South Dakota Department of History* 12 (1924): 174–75.

56 *midsummer of 1872*: Sources for this account of the Great Vision include 6GF, 111–42;

BES, 17–36; and Lynn Woods O'Brien, *Plains Indian Autobiographies*, Boise State College Western Writers Series 10 (Boise, ID: Boise State College, 1973), 24–27.

57 *Symptoms alter over time*: William H. McNeill, *Plagues and Peoples* (Garden City, NY: Anchor Books, 1976), 54.

57 *childhood meningitis*: "Meningitis Symptoms Checklist," http://patient.info/health /meningitis-symptoms-checklist.

58 *"I was high up in space"*: Carl Jung, *Memories, Dreams, Reflections* (New York: Random House, 1963), 289.

4. RESURRECTION

This chapter encompasses events described in *Black Elk Speaks*, 37–48; and *The Sixth Grandfather*, 143–54.

63 *"You can't put that wine back into the bottle"*: "Connecticut Q & A: Kenneth Ring; 'You Never Recover Your Original Self,'" *The New York Times*, August 28, 1988, www .nytimes.com/1988/08/28/connecticut-q-a-kenneth-ring-you-never-record-your -original-self.html.

63 *Carl Jung felt a similar sense of loss*: Carl Jung, *Memories, Dreams, Reflections* (New York: Random House, 1963), 292.

64 *young Kahnigapi*: BES, 37–39; and 6GF, 149–50.

65 *"He is not the boy he used to be"*: 6GF, 143–44.

65 Wasichu: BES, 8, 12n18; and 6GF, 150–52, 4n. This note refers to a discussion of *wasichu* in George Bushotter, "Lakota Texts," nos. 93 and 101, trans. J. Owen Dorsey, NAA. The etymology of the word is somewhat confusing. Black Elk says that *"wasi-chu"* at one point seemed to mean either "big talker" or "fat taker," but Bushotter, a Lakota, wrote in 1887 that the Lakota believed whites were some kind of water spirit when they first saw them in ancient times. Such spirits were called *mniwasicu*.

66 *a wren flitted from branch to branch*: BES, 39; 6GF, 152.

66 *They traveled in two types of groups*: Andrew C. Isenberg, *The Destruction of the Bison: An Environmental History, 1750–1920* (Cambridge: Cambridge University Press, 2000), 66–67.

66 *black horned ground beetle*: Luther Standing Bear, *Land of the Spotted Eagle* (Lincoln: University of Nebraska Press, 1933), 76.

67 *the band rode out to the herd*: Sources for this account of the buffalo hunt include BES, 41–44; 6GF, 145–47; Royal B. Hassrick, *The Sioux: Life and Customs of a Warrior Society* (Norman: University of Oklahoma Press, 1964), 200–201, Luther Standing Bear, *My Indian Boyhood* (Lincoln: University of Nebraska Press, 1931), 170–56, and Luther Standing Bear, *My People the Sioux* (Lincoln: University of Nebraska Press, 1928), 60–66.

68 *a tipping point*: BES, 47; and 6GF, 152–53.

69 *Red Cloud Agency No. 2*: George Hyde, *Red Cloud's Folk: A History of the Oglala Sioux Indians* (Norman: University of Oklahoma Press, 1967, first published 1937), 219.

69 *streams of antagonism*: Ibid., 194–95.

70 *Dr. J. J. Saville*: Ibid., 195.

70 *customary to seek revenge*: Kingsley M. Bray, *Crazy Horse: A Lakota Life* (Norman: University of Oklahoma Press, 2006), 174–75; *Report of the Special Commission Appointed to Investigate the Affairs of the Red Cloud Indian Agency, July, 1875* (Washington, DC: Government Printing Office, 1875), 807–808.

70 *Appleton paid no heed*: 6GF, 154; "The Garnett and Wells Interviews: Killing of Frank Appleton," in *Voices of the American West: The Indian Interviews of Eli S. Ricker, 1903–1919*, vol. 1, ed. Richard E. Jensen (Lincoln: University of Nebraska Press, 2005), 7–8.

70 *"out here among the infernal Red skins"*: Frank Appleton's 1874 Letter from Red Cloud Agency," *Nebraska History* 90 (2009): 2–4; and Bray, *Crazy Horse*, 175.

71 *The Battle of the Washita*: Dee Brown, *Bury My Heart at Wounded Knee: An Indian History of the American West* (New York: Henry Holt, 1970), 167–70; and Edward S. Godfrey, "Cavalry Fire Discipline," *Journal of the Military Service Institution of the United States* 19 (1896): 256.

72 *the Yellowstone Expedition*: Ralph K. Andrist, *The Long Death: The Last Days of the Plains Indians* (New York: Collier Books, 1993; first published by Macmillan, 1964), 240–43; and Bray, *Crazy Horse*, 165–69.

72 *"he is a cold-blooded, untruthful and unprincipled man"*: Evan S. Connell, *Son of the Morning Star: Custer and the Little Bighorn* (New York: Harper & Row, 1984), 234.

73 *Bear Butte*: Henrietta Whiteman, "White Buffalo Woman," in *The American Indian and the Problem of History*, ed. Calvin Martin (New York: Oxford University Press, 1987), 163; Jeffrey Ostler, *The Lakotas and the Black Hills: The Struggle for Sacred Ground* (New York: Viking, 2010), 5.

73 *"big-hearted"*: UNL, Helen Blish MSS Notes, "Crazy Horse—He Dog description of Shirt Wearers," *Interview with Short Bull*, 7-33-29, 27-25-1; and Bray, *Crazy Horse*, 122.

73 *he invited Black Buffalo Woman*: Sources for the shooting of Crazy Horse by No Water include: Joseph Agonito, *Lakota Portraits: Lives of the Legendary Plains People* (Guilford, CT: TwoDot, 2011), 93; Ricker, *Voices of the American West*, 75–76, 234; and Joseph C. Porter, "Crazy Horse, Lakota Leadership, and the Fort Laramie Treaty," in *Legacy: New Perspectives on the Battle of the Little Bighorn*, ed. Charles E. Rankin (Helena: Montana Historical Society Press, 1996), 52.

74 *"I'd rather be a plain warrior"*: Agonito, *Lakota Portraits*, 94.

74 *Crazy Horse married Black Shawl*: Ricker, *Voices of the American West*, 399, 91n.

74 *The move brought Crazy Horse*: Michael F. Steltenkamp, S.J., *Nicholas Black Elk: Medicine Man, Missionary, Mystic* (Norman: University of Oklahoma Press, 2009), 40; *6GF*, 203; and *BES*, 68.

75 *younger brother, Little Hawk, was killed*: SHSM, John G. Neihardt Papers (1881–1973), c. 1858–1974, C3716, Folder 431: "Transcription, 1944, Eagle Elk, November 27, 1944: 'Crazy Horse,'" 431n.

75 *Death demanded death*: M. I. McCreight, *Chief Flying Hawk's Tales: The True Story of Custer's Last Fight* (New York: Alliance Press, 1936), 21.

75 *"to make his warriors feel good"*: *BES*, 68.

75 *Crazy Horse's . . . daughter died*: Bray, *Crazy Horse*, 169–71; Ian Frazier, *Great Plains* (New York: Picador, 1989), 104.

5. THE BLACK HILLS

This chapter encompasses events described in *Black Elk Speaks*, 47–51 and 61–62; and *The Sixth Grandfather*, 155–64.

77 *annual spring migration*: Royal B. Hassrick, *The Sioux: Life and Customs of a Warrior Society* (Norman: University of Oklahoma Press, 1964), 174–75.

77 *Paha Sapa resembles a forested black island*: Jeffrey Ostler, *The Lakotas and the Black Hills: The Struggle for Sacred Ground* (New York: Viking, 2010), 3–5; Linea Sundstrom, "The Sacred Black Hills: An Ethnohistorical Review," *Great Plains Quarterly* 17 (Summer/Fall 1997): 185–200; and Sven G. Froiland, *Natural History of the Black Hills and Badlands* (Sioux Falls, SD: The Center for Western Studies, 1978), 1–11.

78 *the groans of a Great White Giant*: Edwin Denig, *Five Indian Tribes of the Upper Missouri* (1854), quoted in Sundstrom, "Sacred Black Hills," 186. Scholars believe today that the story about the giant was meant to scare off whites.

78 *Paha Sapa's first mention*: George Hyde, *Red Cloud's Folk: A History of the Oglala Sioux Indians* (Norman: University of Oklahoma Press, 1967, first published 1937), 23; and Linea Sundstrom, "Mirror of Heaven: Cross-Cultural Transference of the

Sacred Geography of the Black Hills," *World Archaeology* 28, no. 2 (October 1996): 179–80.

78 *traveled three days*: 6GF, 155.

78 *Pte Tali Yapa*: Sundstrom, "Sacred Black Hills," 195, 194.

78 *Black Elk and his father went hunting*: 6GF, 155.

80 *It happened suddenly*: Ibid., 158; and Hassrick, *The Sioux*, 267–69.

81 *Army Special Orders No. 17*: Ralph K. Andrist, *The Long Death: The Last Days of the Plains Indians* (New York: Collier Books, 1993; first published by Macmillan, 1964), 244; and Ostler, *Lakotas and the Black Hills*, 82.

81 *sheer massiveness*: Jerry Keenan, "Exploring the Black Hills: An Account of the Custer Expedition," *Journal of the West*, 6, no. 2 (April 1967): 250–51; Evan S. Connell, *Son of the Morning Star: Custer and the Little Bighorn* (New York: Harper & Row, 1984), 236–37; Ostler, *Lakotas and the Black Hills*, 82–83; and Hyde, *Red Cloud's Folk*, 218.

81 *"squat, humorless" Stanley*: Connell, *Son of the Morning Star*, 234.

81 *"perfumed with cinnamon oil"*: Ostler, *Lakotas and the Black Hills*, 81–82; and Connell, *Son of the Morning Star*, 235–36.

81 *The expedition left Fort Lincoln*: Ostler, *Lakotas and the Black Hills*, 83; Keenan, "Exploring the Black Hills," 251–57; and Connell, *Son of the Morning Star*, 236.

82 *some abandoned camps*: Ostler, *Lakotas and the Black Hills*, 83.

82 *climbed Harney Peak*: Keenan, "Exploring the Black Hills," 258–59; Connell, *Son of the Morning Star*, 236–37; and Ostler, *Lakotas and the Black Hills*, 83–84.

82 *another two troops southeast*: Keenan, "Exploring the Black Hills," 258.

82 *two "better pleased" officers*: Connell, *Son of the Morning Star*, 246–47.

82 *"the yellow metal that makes the Wasichus crazy"*: BES, 62.

83 *"Killed by Inds beyond the high hills"*: Connell, *Son of the Morning Star*, 238–39.

83 *The metaphor of lunacy*: Richard White, *"It's Your Misfortune and None of My Own": A New History of the American West* (Norman: University of Oklahoma Press, 1993), 191–92; and E. S. "Rocky" LeGage, *Gold . . . ABCs of Panning* (Denning, NM: Carson Enterprises, 1975), 9, 17–18.

83 *"Humanitarians may weep"*: *The Bismarck Tribune*, June 17, 1875, quoted in Connell, *Son of the Morning Star*, 241.

84 *"I have upon my table forty or fifty particles"*: Keenan, "Exploring the Black Hills," 260; Ostler, *Lakotas and the Black Hills*, 85; Walter P. Jenney, *Report on the Mineral Wealth, Climate, and Rain-Fall, and Natural Resources of the Black Hills of Dakota, 1875–1876*, 44th Congress, 1st session, H.R. Doc. 125, February 14, 1876, 12.

84 *The column returned to Fort Lincoln*: Keenan, "Exploring the Black Hills," 261; Ostler, *Lakotas and the Black Hills*, 85; Richard Slotkin, *The Fatal Environment: The Myth of the Frontier in the Age of Industrialization, 1800–1890* (Norman: University of Oklahoma Press, 1994, first published by Atheneum, 1985), 355.

84 *"I have been captured and sent out from the Hills four times"*: Col. Richard Irving Dodge, *The Black Hills: A Minute Description* (New York: J. Miller, 1876), 111.

85 *"just like a food pack"*: 6GF, 103–104.

85 *"we have now to deal with another race"*: M. I. McCreight, *Firewater and Forked Tongues: A Sioux Chief Interprets U.S. History* (Pasadena, CA: Trail's End, 1947), 142; and Kingsley M. Bray, *Crazy Horse: A Lakota Life* (Norman: University of Oklahoma Press, 2006), 187.

86 *Iktomi men*: U.S. Department of the Interior, *Report of the Commission to Treat with the Sioux Indians for the Relinquishment of the Black Hills* (Washington, DC: Government Printing Office, 1875), 4.

86 *this was as good a time as any to start a war*: Andrist, *Long Death*, 246–47.

86 *War was averted, but not old antagonisms*: Ostler, *Lakotas and the Black Hills*, 91–92; and BES, 64n15.

86 *soldiers crept between camps*: 6GF, 169, 169n7. According to DeMallie, this was a

persistent rumor in Lakota tradition and also showed up in Stanley Vestal's *Warpath*, the "as-told-to" autobiography of Chief White Bull.

87 *"Our Great Father has a big safe"*: Ostler, *Lakotas and the Black Hills*, 92; Andrist, *Long Death*, 247; and U.S. Department of the Interior, *Report of the Commission to Treat with the Sioux*, 7–8.

87 *the Sioux "would demand an exorbitant sum for the Hills"*: Ostler, *Lakotas and the Black Hills*, 92; and U.S. Department of the Interior, *Report of the Commission to Treat with the Sioux*, 6.

87 *"absolutely nothing but eat, drink, smoke, and sleep"*: Ostler, *Lakotas and the Black Hills*, 92–93; and U.S. Bureau of Indian Affairs, *Annual Report of the U.S. Commissioner of Indian Affairs to the Secretary of the Interior, 1875* (Washington, DC: Government Printing Office, 1875), 188, 193, 199.

87 *"I am going away to see my people"*: SHSM, John G. Neihardt Papers (1881–1973), c. 1858–1974, C3716, Folder 431, "Transcription, 1944, Eagle Elk, November 27, 1944: 'Crazy Horse,'" 2.

88 *"a 'Paradise' for Indians"*: Library of Congress Manuscript Division, Washington, DC, Philip Henry Sheridan Collection, "Subject File, 1863–1891, n.d.": Reel 88, "Indian affairs (2 vols.), 1869–1877," Frames 527–28, report by E. C. Watkins, U.S. Indian Inspector General, November 9, 1875.

88 *"one thousand men"*: Ibid., Frame 529.

88 *Winter hindered*: Paul A. Hutton, "Phil Sheridan's Frontier," in *The Great Sioux War, 1876–1877: The Best from Montana, The Magazine of Western History*, ed. Paul L. Hedren (Helena: Montana Historical Society Press, 1991), 102.

89 *A final report by Watkins*: Hyde, *Red Cloud's Folk*, 250–51.

6. "IT IS WAR"

This chapter encompasses events described in *Black Elk Speaks*, 63–71; and *The Sixth Grandfather*, 164–74.

90 *New Year's Day 1876*: Dee Brown, *The Year of the Century: 1876* (New York: Charles Scribner's Sons, 1966), 1–4; and Lally Weymouth, ed., *America in 1876: The Way We Were* (New York: Random House, 1976), 7.

90 *George Custer and his wife*: Brown, *Year of the Century*, 172–73.

91 *Agent James S. Hastings at Red Cloud Agency*: George Hyde, *Red Cloud's Folk: A History of the Oglala Sioux Indians* (Norman: University of Oklahoma Press, 1967, first published 1937), 250–51.

91 *massacred a party of Loafers*: Ibid., 251–52.

91 *Crow Nose*: BES, 69–70; and 6GF, 166–67.

92 *in February about thirty-five families*: 6GF, 168; and BES, 70.

92 *Sheridan hoped to squeeze*: Ralph K. Andrist, *The Long Death: The Last Days of the Plains Indians* (New York: Collier Books, 1993; first published by Macmillan, 1964), 248; and John Keegan, *Fields of Battle: The Wars for North America* (New York: Vintage Books, 1997), 288–89.

92 *"Three Stars"*: Cyrus Townsend Brady, *Indian Fights and Fighters* (Lincoln: University of Nebraska Press, 1971; first published by McLure, Phillips, 1904), 74; and Andrist, *Long Death*, 249.

92 *On March 17, 1876*: Sources for the Battle of Powder River include Hyde, *Red Cloud's Folk*, 254–55, 254n3, 259n5; BES, 69, 71; Keegan, *Fields of Battle*, 289; Robert E. Strahorn, "The Battle of Powder River, March 17, 1876," in *Battles and Skirmishes of the Great Sioux War, 1876–1877: The Military View*, ed. Jerome A. Greene (Norman: University of Oklahoma Press, 1993), 3–19; and Andrist, *Long Death*, 251–52.

93 *obvious cracks were showing*: "Small Pox—Wicahanhan Tanka," *Iapi Oaye* (*The Word Carrier*) 2, no. 11 (November 1873): 48; "Indian Appropriation Bill," *Iapi Oaye* (*The Word Carrier*) 2, no. 4 (April 1873): 16; and Michael P. Malone and Richard B. Roeder, "1876 on the Reservations: 'The Indian Question,'" in *The Great Sioux War, 1876–1877: The Best from Montana, The Magazine of Western History*, ed. Paul L. Hedren (Helena: Montana Historical Society Press, 1991), 57.

93 *a "summons" from Sitting Bull*: Hyde, *Red Cloud's Folk*, 257–59.

93 *"It is war"*: Kingsley M. Bray, *Crazy Horse: A Lakota Life* (Norman: University of Oklahoma Press, 2006), 202.

93 *They were going to have to fight*: BES, 73; and Hyde, *Red Cloud's Folk*, 257.

93 *gave Black Elk a six-shot revolver*: Hyde, *Red Cloud's Folk*, 257. While *Black Elk Speaks*, p. 74, states that it was an aunt who gave Black Elk his revolver, the transcripts claim it was a sister (6GF, 170).

94 *engraved with the words "Red Cloud"*: Bray, *Crazy Horse*, 202; and Evan S. Connell, *Son of the Morning Star: Custer and the Little Bighorn* (New York: Harper & Row, 1984), 88.

94 *"were bad like ours"*: Hyde, *Red Cloud's Folk*, 257; and BES, 73.

94 *Little Big Man always liked a brawl*: Joseph Agonito, *Lakota Portraits: Lives of the Legendary Plains People* (Guilford, CT: TwoDot, 2011), 87–88.

94 *to attack the wagon train*: 6GF, 170–71; and BES, 74.

95 *three great columns*: Keegan, *Fields of Battle*, 290.

96 *a valley of tipis*: BES, 75; and Bray, *Crazy Horse*, 203.

96 *Sitting Bull received a sign*: Robert M. Utley, *The Lance and the Shield: The Life and Times of Sitting Bull* (New York: Henry Holt, 1993), 136–37.

96 *The dance would be held in June*: BES, 75–77; and Utley, *Lance and the Shield*, 137.

97 *the "dance looking at the sun"*: UNL, Mari Sandoz Collection, Part II, Research Files, Box 32, "Notes on Indian Tribes," Folder 29: "Sioux Sun Dance," Folder 29.1: "Pine Ridge Sioux Will Recreate Wiwanyag Wachipi," *Sunday World-Herald Magazine* (Omaha, NE), July 13, 1960, 5; *Wikipedia*'s "Mortification of the Flesh" entry, http://en.wikipedia.org/wiki/Mortification-of-the-flesh; and Vine Deloria, Jr., *Custer Died for Your Sins: An Indian Manifesto* (Norman: University of Oklahoma Press, 1988; first published by Macmillan, 1969), 89.

98 *"Each candidate in turn was laid at the foot of the Sun Pole"*: UNL, Mari Sandoz Collection, Part II, Research Files, Box 32, "Notes on Indian Tribes," Folder 29: "Sioux Sun Dance," Folder 29.6: "Sioux Sun Dance," *Gordon Journal*, August 21, 1963, n.p.

98 *Sitting Bull entered the circle*: Sources for Sitting Bull's Sun Dance vision include Bray, *Crazy Horse*, 203–204; Utley, *Lance and the Shield*, 137–39; and Stanley Vestal, *Warpath: The True Story of the Fighting Sioux Told in a Biography of Chief White Bull* (Lincoln: University of Nebraska Press, 1984), 96–97.

7. WHEN THE *WASICHUS* COME

This chapter encompasses events described in *Black Elk Speaks*, 73–98; and *The Sixth Grandfather*, 174–94.

100 *A gathering as large*: Stanley Vestal, *New Sources of Indian History, 1850–1891: The Ghost Dance—A Prairie Miscellany* (Norman: University of Oklahoma Press, 1934), 162–63; Robert M. Utley, *The Lance and the Shield: The Life and Times of Sitting Bull* (New York: Henry Holt, 1993), 139; and 6GF, 134.

100 *On May 27, Lieutenant J. H. Bradley*: George Hyde, *Red Cloud's Folk: A History of the Oglala Sioux Indians* (Norman: University of Oklahoma Press, 1967, first published 1937), 262n7.

100 *On June 7 or 8, Major Marcus A. Reno*: Ibid., 262.

101 *"Stay and look at the helpless"*: 6GF, 174.

101 *"I was too little to do much"*: BES, 29.

101 *morning of June 17*: Sources for the Battle of the Rosebud include Evan S. Connell, *Son of the Morning Star: Custer and the Little Bighorn* (New York: Harper & Row, 1984), 88–89, 141; J. W. Vaughn, *With Crook at the Rosebud* (Harrisburg, PA: Stackpole, 1956), 102–103, 136; 6GF, 174–76; Vestal, *New Sources*, 141; Stanley Vestal, *Warpath: The True Story of the Fighting Sioux Told in a Biography of Chief White Bull* (Lincoln: University of Nebraska Press, 1984), 190; Jerome A. Greene, ed., *Battles and Skirmishes of the Great Sioux War, 1876–1877: The Military View* (Norman: University of Oklahoma Press, 1993), 33; Kingsley M. Bray, *Crazy Horse: A Lakota Life* (Norman: University of Oklahoma Press, 2006), 209, 211; Utley, *Lance and the Shield*, 141; and BES, 78–81.

102 *Crazy Horse said thirty-six*: Doane Robinson, "Crazy Horse's Story of Custer Battle," *South Dakota Historical Collections* 6 (1912): 228. This interview was reportedly conducted soon after Crazy Horse's surrender at Camp Robinson in May 1877.

102 *Standing Bear and twenty friends*: 6GF, 177.

103 *How big was this "Great Camp"*: Gregory F. Michno, *Lakota Noon: The Indian Narrative of Custer's Defeat* (Missoula, MT: Mountain Press, 1997), 3–11; Utley, *Lance and the Shield*, 142; Michael N. Donahue, *Drawing Battle Lines: The Map Testimony of Custer's Last Fight* (El Segundo, CA: Upton & Sons, 2008), 17, 23; and Robert P. Hughes, "The Campaign Against the Sioux in 1876," *Journal of the Military Service Institution of the United States* 18, no. 79 (January 1896): 15, 16–17.

103 *"we couldn't count them"*: 6GF, 178.

104 *The tipis were arranged*: BES, 83; and Hyde, *Red Cloud's Folk*, 267.

104 *For six days*: Bray, *Crazy Horse*, 212.

104 *Hairy Chin*: 6GF, 178–79; and BES, 84–85.

105 *three exhausted riders*: Bray, *Crazy Horse*, 213.

105 *the news distressed Crazy Horse*: Ibid.

105 *"always taciturn"*: John G. Bourke, *On the Border with Crook* (New York: Charles Scribner's Sons, 1892), 299–300.

105 *Sitting Bull presented to* Wakan Tanka: Utley, *Lance and the Shield*, 144.

106 *Makoto Fukui, the Japanese commissioner*: Lally Weymouth, ed., *America in 1876: The Way We Were* (New York: Random House, 1976), 19.

106 *Every thirty seconds*: Dee Brown, *The Year of the Century: 1876* (New York: Charles Scribner's Sons, 1966), 112–15, 134.

106 *Watch for something strange*: BES, 85; and 6GF, 179–80.

106 *"If anything happens"*: 6GF, 180.

106 *"I was so young yet"*: 6GF, 178.

107 *Where were the soldiers?*: Ralph K. Andrist, *The Long Death: The Last Days of the Plains Indians* (New York: Collier Books, 1993; first published by Macmillan, 1964), 268–70; E. A. Brininstool, *Troopers with Custer: Historic Incidents of the Battle of the Little Big Horn* (Harrisburg, PA: Stackpole, 1952), 11; and Hughes, "Campaign Against the Sioux," n.p.

107 *Estimates vary on the size of Custer's force*: "Ten Myths of the Little Bighorn," www .historynet.com; Douglas D. Scott, P. Willey, and Melissa A. Connor, *They Died with Custer: Soldiers' Bones from the Battle of the Little Bighorn* (Norman: University of Oklahoma Press, 1998), 26–29. Four members of Custer's family rode with him: his eighteen-year-old nephew, Harry "Autie" Armstrong Reed; his younger brothers, Boston, employed as a civilian guide, and Captain Tom Custer, who commanded C Company; and his brother-in-law James Calhoun.

107 *"Look for worms in the grass"*: Andrist, *Long Death*, 271–72.

107 *In the valley, it was 8:00 or 9:00 a.m.*: 6GF, 180–81.

108 *By every sign, it was another lazy, windless day*: Sources for the Valley Fight and the Custer Massacre include: 6GF, 180–95; BES, 86–97; "Copy of the Revised Draft of

Reno Report," in Donald W. Moore, *Where the Custer Fight Began: Undermanned and Overwhelmed—The Reno Valley Fight* (El Segundo, CA: Upton & Sons, 2011), 173–74; Moore, *Where the Custer Fight Began*, 39–102; John Keegan, *Fields of Battle: The Wars for North America* (New York: Vintage Books, 1997), 300–301; Andrist, *Long Death*, 276–86; Richard Allan Fox, Jr., "West River History: The Indian Village on Little Bighorn River, June 25–26, 1876," in *Legacy: New Perspectives on the Battle of the Little Bighorn*, ed. Charles E. Rankin (Helena: Montana Historical Society Press, 1996), 151–52; Little Bighorn Battlefield Tour, August 5, 2012; Michno, *Lakota Noon*, 23–89; Bray, *Crazy Horse*, 215–39; David Humphreys Miller, *Custer's Fall: The Indian Side of the Story* (Lincoln: University of Nebraska Press, 1957), 93–107; Col. Richard Irving Dodge, *Our Wild Indians: Thirty Three Years' Personal Experience Among the Red Men of the Great West* (Hartford, CT: A. D. Worthington, 1884), 512–13; Everett Ellis, "To Take a Scalp," in Ralph W. Andrews, *Indians as Westerners Saw Them* (Seattle: Superior, 1963), 50; and author's interview with Gerald Jasmer, chief historian, Little Bighorn National Park, Agency, MT, August 6–7, 2012.

112 *"Fire is everything"*: Edward S. Godfrey, "Cavalry Fire Discipline," *Journal of the Military Service Institution of the United States* 19 (1896): 252–54.

112 *"They were never drilled at firing on horseback"*: Lt. Edward Maguire, "Annual Report of Lieutenant Edward Maguire, Corps of Engineers, for the Fiscal Year Ending June 30, 1876: Explorations and Surveys in the Department of the Dakota," *Annual Report of the Chief of Engineers to the Secretary of War for the Year 1876, Part III*, 44th Congress, 2nd session, Doc. No. 1, part 2, vol. 2 (Washington, DC: Government Printing Office, 1876), Appendix OO, 704.

116 *Then he saw a soldier*: Sources for account of Black Elk's first kill include Bruce R. Liddic and Paul Harbaugh, eds., *Custer & Company: Walter Camp's Notes on the Custer Fight* (Lincoln: University of Nebraska Press, 1995), 123; Richard G. Hardorff, *The Custer Battle Casualties: Burials, Exhumations, and Reinterments* (El Segundo, CA: Upton and Sons, 2002), 103–104, 105 106, 113–14, 117; and Scott, Willey, and Connor, *They Died with Custer*, 173–75. There are several clues, often by omission, that help identify Black Elk's first victim during the Battle of the Little Bighorn. Black Elk does not describe any facial hair. A bullet hole to the forehead would be a forensic giveaway, but unfortunately no such injuries were ever noted among the haphazard burial notes or the scant archaeological remains that washed up or were unearthed over the decades. At this point, one begins to eliminate the known dead who fell in this area. Eyewitnesses recalled finding the stripped, scalped, or mutilated bodies of several soldiers along that stretch of river, on both sides of the deadly ford: Privates John E. Armstrong and William Moodie, both of A Company, and Sergeant Edward Botzer, Saddler Crawford Selby, and Farrier Benjamin Wells, all of G Company. Private Henry Seafferman of G Company is sometimes mentioned as dying at the river, but most eyewitnesses saw him slain during the rout from the timber and along the plain. Others of these men can also be eliminated. Armstrong had dark, curly hair, not cut short like Black Elk's man; in addition, he was later decapitated and his head set on a pole in the Indian village, a detail Black Elk probably would have mentioned. Sergeant Botzer's body lay on the east bank; however, he sported a mustache and goatee, and a skull, later unearthed and thought to be his through forensic reconstruction, did not show any signs of a gunshot wound. The horse of Farrier Benjamin Wells panicked during the rout, carrying him directly into the hands of the Indians; two people later said he was killed *in* the river, and one said his body was found floating facedown. No eyewitnesses recalled either the death or the remains of Saddler Selby, but at five feet five and a half, he was one of the shortest men in Reno's battalion. Black Elk says nothing about his first scalp coming from an exceptionally short man. In fact, five feet eight was the average height for the men of the Seventh Cavalry.

117 *their fragile redoubt*: Connell, *Son of the Morning Star*, 52–53; and William O. Taylor, *With Custer on the Little Bighorn: A Newly Discovered First Person Account* (New York: Viking, 1996; first published 1923), 47.

120 *Kate Bighead*: Connell, *Son of the Morning Star*, 418–19.

8. THE BURNING ROAD

This chapter encompasses events described in *Black Elk Speaks*, 98–108; and *The Sixth Grandfather*, 194–202.

123 *How many Indians died*: Richard G. Hardorff, *Hokahey! A Good Day to Die!: The Indian Casualties of the Custer Fight* (Spokane, WA: Arthur H. Clark, 1993), 211; Stanley Vestal, *New Sources of Indian History, 1850–1891: The Ghost Dance—A Prairie Miscellany* (Norman: University of Oklahoma Press, 1934), 136; Evan S. Connell, *Son of the Morning Star: Custer and the Little Bighorn* (New York: Harper & Row, 1984), 418, 420; and Don Russell, "How Many Indians Were Killed? White Man Versus Red Man: The Facts and the Legend," *American West* 10, no. 4 (July 1973): 47.

124 *"Custer was coming at last"*: William O. Taylor, *With Custer on the Little Bighorn: A Newly Discovered First Person Account* (New York: Viking, 1996; first published 1923), 53–54; and Connell, *Son of the Morning Star*, 54–55.

124 *Carlo Camilius DeRudio*: BES, 99; 6GF, 194–95; Taylor, *With Custer on the Little Bighorn*, 49; Donald W. Moore, *Where the Custer Fight Began: Undermanned and Overwhelmed—The Reno Valley Fight* (El Segundo, CA: Upton & Sons, 2011), 97–100; Connell, *Son of the Morning Star*, 384–85; and "Lieutenant Charles DeRudio's Letter," *The New York Herald*, July 30, 1876, in W. A. Graham, *The Custer Myth: A Source Book of Custeriana* (New York: Bonanza Books, 1953), 253–56.

124 *For this act of bravado*: A Hunkpapa named Hawk Man was also killed for coming too close to Reno's position.

125 *"there was not an Indian in view anywhere"*: Paul L. Hedren, *We Trailed the Sioux: Enlisted Men Speak on Custer, Crook, and the Great Sioux War* (Mechanicsburg, PA: Stackpole Books, 2003), 24; UNL, Mari Sandoz Collection, Part II, Research Files, Box 12.1, "Pamphlets and Articles—Frontier Life," Folder 2.1: "Pamphlets and Articles—Military"; and Thomas B. Marquis, *Two Days After the Custer Battle* (Hardin, MT: Custer Battle Museum, 1935), 1.

125 *the remains turned disheartening*: Hedren, *We Trailed the Sioux*, 24–25; Marquis, *Two Days After*, 2–3; Thomas R. Buecker, ed., "A Surgeon at the Little Big Horn," *Montana, The Magazine of Western History* 32, no. 4 (Autumn 1982): 43.

126 *and burying the dead*: Hedren, *We Trailed the Sioux*, 26–27; Marquis, *Two Days After*, 5–6; and Connell, *Son of the Morning Star*, 287–88.

126 *Custer's body was undisturbed*: Connell, *Son of the Morning Star*, 40; and Marquis, *Two Days After*, 7.

126 *June 28 was spent burying the dead*: Hedren, *We Trailed the Sioux*, 27–28; Edward S. Godfrey, "After the Custer Battle," ed. Albert J. Partoll, *Frontier and Midland* 19, no. 4 (1939): 279; and "Interview with John Lattman," in *Custer in '76: Walter Camp's Notes on the Custer Fight*, ed. Kenneth Hammer (Provo, UT: Brigham Young University Press, 1976), 80.

127 *the seventeen-mile trek to the river's mouth*: Buecker, "Surgeon at the Little Big Horn," 46.

127 *"It is my painful duty"*: Library of Congress Manuscript Division, Washington, DC; Philip Henry Sheridan Collection, "Subject File, 1863–1891, n.d.," Reel 88, "Indian affairs (2 vols.), 1869–1877," Frames 751–57, telegram from Gen. Alfred Terry, Camp at Little Bighorn River, to Headquarters, Department of Dakota, June 27, 1876.

127 *citing Terry's belief that Custer disobeyed orders*: Robert P. Hughes, "The Campaign Against the Sioux in 1876," *Journal of the Military Service Institution of the United*

States 18, no. 79 (January 1896): 18–19; and Ralph K. Andrist, *The Long Death: The Last Days of the Plains Indians* (New York: Collier Books, 1993; first published by Macmillan, 1964), 293.

127 *word had leaked by then*: Dee Brown, *Year of the Century: 1876* (New York: Charles Scribner's Sons, 1966), 169–70.

128 *Western papers howled for revenge*: Henry E. Fritz, *The Movement for Indian Assimilation, 1860–1890* (Philadelphia: University of Philadelphia Press, 1963), 171–77; "Extermination," *The New York Times*, July 12, 1876, in Robert Hays, *Editorializing "The Indian Problem": The New York Times on Native Americans, 1860–1900* (Carbondale: Southern Illinois University Press, 1997), 273–76; "The Custer Massacre," *Frank Leslie's Illustrated Newspaper*, Saturday, July 29, 1876, 338; and Kingsley M. Bray, *Crazy Horse: A Lakota Life* (Norman: University of Oklahoma Press, 2006), 245.

128 *The encomiums to Custer*: Brown, *Year of the Century*, 177–79; Bruce A. Rosenberg, *Custer and the Epic of Defeat* (University Park: Pennsylvania State University Press, 1974), 10; Frederick Whittaker, "General George A. Custer," *Galaxy* 22, no. 3 (September 1876): 367, 368; and "Custer's Last Battle," *New-York Tribune*, July 13, 1876, 1. Whitman's "Death Song for Custer" was the first of hundreds of inaccurate portrayals of the Battle of the Little Bighorn.

130 *"A charger, he is coming"*: BES, 100–101; and 6GF, 196–98.

130 *"he gained a greater prestige"*: Bray, *Crazy Horse*, 236–37.

130 *the Great Camp wandered*: Ibid., 241; and 6GF, 199–200.

130 *"Buffalo Bill"*: Louis S. Warren, *Buffalo Bill's America: William Cody and the Wild West Show* (New York: Alfred A. Knopf, 2005), x, 112–13, 127–28; Joy S. Kasson, *Buffalo Bill's Wild West: Celebrity, Memory, and Popular History* (New York: Hill & Wang, 2000), 12–15; John Neihardt interview, *The Dick Cavett Show*, aired April 27, 1971; and *Wikipedia*'s "Buffalo Bill" entry, http://en.wikipedia.org/wiki/Buffalo_Bill,

131 *Cody would scout in the summer and act in the winter*: Kasson, *Buffalo Bill's Wild West*, 135.

132 *a young Cheyenne subchief named Yellow Hair*: Charles King, *Campaigning with Crook* (Norman: University of Oklahoma Press, 1964), 34.

132 *"The first scalp for Custer"*: Warren, *Buffalo Bill's America*, 118–19; and Kasson, *Buffalo Bill's Wild West*, 136.

132 *often played a role*: UNL, Mari Sandoz Collection, Part II, Research Files, Box 30, "Notes Relating to Sioux and Cheyenne Indians, Part IV," Folder 33: "Yellow Hand," letter from E. S. Sutton to Mari Sandoz, n.d.

133 *"Why, where on earth are the Indians?"*: King, *Campaigning with Crook*, 75.

133 *most densely populated sections of real estate*: Bray, *Crazy Horse*, 243.

133 *set fire to the grass*: BES, 104.

133 *Horsemeat March*: Jerome A. Greene, *Slim Buttes, 1876: An Episode of the Great Sioux War* (Norman: University of Oklahoma Press, 1982), 23, 40, 88. "Cavalry horse meat, played out, sore-backed . . . [and] fried without salt, [is] stringy, leathery, blankety, and nauseating," wrote John F. Finerty, one of the four journalists unlucky enough to cover the ordeal.

134 *Mills discovered the soggy camp*: Sources for account of the Battle of Slim Buttes include: Greene, *Slim Buttes*, 50; Bray, *Crazy Horse*, 243–45; and Hedren, *We Trailed the Sioux*, 53.

135 *"They were chasing us now"*: BES, 105.

135 *statistics began to circulate*: Andrist, *Long Death*, 295.

135 *nearly one-quarter of America's regular army*: Hedren, *We Trailed the Sioux*, 8.

135 *Great Camp disbanded*: Bray, *Crazy Horse*, 246.

135 *The Word Carrier*: Articles from the Lakota-language newspaper published at the Yankton Sioux Reservation include "The Snow Banks," in vol. 2, no. 7, July 1873, 28; "Small Pox—Wicahanhan Tanka," in vol. 2, no. 11, November 1873, 48; and "Grasshoppers," in vol. 5, no. 8, September 1876, 32.

136 *nothing but doom for the Indians*: "Report of Commissioner of Indian Affairs, J. Q. Smith, October 30, 876," in Lally Weymouth, ed., *America in 1876: The Way We Were* (New York: Random House, 1976), 70–71.

136 *"What then is the American"*: J. Hector St. John de Crèvecœur, "What Is an American?," *Letters from an American Farmer*, Letter III (1784), in "Making the Revolution: America, 1763–1791," *America in Class*, National Humanities Center, http://americainclass.org/sources/makingrevolution/independence/text6/crevecoeuramerican.pdf.

136 *new commission of Iktomi men*: Jeffrey Ostler, *The Lakotas and the Black Hills: The Struggle for Sacred Ground* (New York: Viking, 2010), 100–101; and Robert M. Utley, *The Lance and the Shield: The Life and Times of Sitting Bull* (New York: Henry Holt, 1993), 167.

136 *Fourteen papooses were later found frozen to death*: P. E. Byrne, *Soldiers of the Plains* (New York: Minton, Balch, 1926), 209; and *BES*, 105–106.

9. KILLING CRAZY HORSE

This chapter encompasses events described in *Black Elk Speaks*, 112–14; and *The Sixth Grandfather*, 202–204.

137 *Nelson Appleton Miles*: Robert Wooster, *Nelson A. Miles and the Twilight of the Frontier Army* (Lincoln: University of Nebraska Press, 1996), 50–58; "Nelson Appleton Miles," *The West* Film Project, PBS/WETA, www.pbs.org/weta/thewest/people/i_r/miles.htm; *Serving the Republic: Memoirs of the Civil and Military Life of Nelson A. Miles* (New York: Harper & Bros., 1911), 144–45; and Dee Brown, *Bury My Heart at Wounded Knee: An Indian History of the American West* (New York: Henry Holt, 1970), 303.

137 *This was not friendly country*: Miles, *Serving the Republic*, 146–47.

137 *"I want to know what you are doing on this road"*: Brown, *Bury My Heart*, 304.

138 *the two men met*: Source for the meeting between Miles and Sitting Bull include Miles, *Serving the Republic*, 148–52; Brown, *Bury My Heart*, 304–305; Ralph K. Andrist, *The Long Death: The Last Days of the Plains Indian* (New York: Collier Books, 1993; first published by Macmillan, 1964), 298; and Joseph Agonito, *Lakota Portraits: Lives of the Legendary Plains People* (Guilford, CT: TwoDot, 2011), 307.

139 *"The chief fighting man is Crazy Horse"*: Schuyler's interview in the May 3, 1877, *Chicago Tribune* is quoted in Oliver Knight, "War or Peace: The Anxious Wait for Crazy Horse," *Nebraska History* 54 (1973): 522.

139 *Crazy Horse was thirty-six*: Kingsley M. Bray, "Crazy Horse and the End of the Great Sioux War," *Nebraska History* 79, no. 3 (Fall 1998): 96.

139 *The Crows "approached them in a friendly manner"*: Library of Congress Manuscript Division, Washington, DC, Philip Henry Sheridan Collection, "Subject File, 1863–1891, n.d.," Reel 91, "Indian Affairs, 1868–1878, 1885–1891, n.d.," Frames 755–62, letter from Bvt. Maj. Gen. Nelson A. Miles, Tongue River, MT, to Assistant Adjutant General, Department of Dakota, December 17, 1876; and *6GF*, 199–200. Most of the eight were Minneconjou and Sans Arc headmen, but one was the Oglala Drum on His Back, known to the whites as Sitting Bull the Good.

140 *The murder solidified*: Kingsley M. Bray, *Crazy Horse: A Lakota Life* (Norman: University of Oklahoma Press, 2006), 251; *6GF*, 200; and Bray, "Crazy Horse and the End of the Great Sioux War," 97.

140 *Agency Sioux called Crazy Horse "big trouble"*: Richard S. Grimes, "The Making of a Sioux Legend: The Historiography of Crazy Horse," *South Dakota History* 30, no. 3 (Fall 2000): 297–98.

140 *Former allies came to the camp*: Bray, "Crazy Horse and the End of the Great Sioux War," 97.

140 *his guerillas drove off 150 cattle*: Miles, *Serving the Republic*, 153–54; and ibid., 97–98.

140 *he caught up with Crazy Horse*: Sources for account of the Battle of Wolf Mountain include: *6GF*, 202; Jerome Greene, *Yellowstone Command: Colonel Nelson A. Miles and the Great Sioux War, 1876–1877* (Lincoln: University of Nebraska Press, 1991), 147–82; Bray, *Crazy Horse*, 255–59; Miles, *Serving the Republic*, 154–56; Jerome Greene, ed., *Lakota and Cheyenne: Indian Views of the Great Sioux War, 1876–1877* (Norman: University of Oklahoma Press, 1994), 125–33; Jerome Greene, ed., *Battles and Skirmishes of the Great Sioux War, 1876–1877: The Military View* (Norman: University of Oklahoma Press, 1993), 186–203; and *BES*, 107–108.

141 *the changes Black Elk saw in his cousin*: Bray, "Crazy Horse and the End of the Great Sioux War," 102–103; and *BES*, 106–107.

141 *A political skirmish*: Greene, *Yellowstone Command*, 183; and Knight, "War or Peace," 531.

141 *Spotted Tail*: Brown, *Bury My Heart*, 124–25, 308; Agonito, *Lakota Portraits*, 59–63, 76; Bray, *Crazy Horse*, 207, 269–70; *BES*, 108; and Bray, "Crazy Horse and the End of the Great Sioux War," 105.

142 *"Uncle, you might have noticed me"*: *6GF*, 202; and Bray, *Crazy Horse*, 275.

142 *In the end, the gods did not come*: *6GF*, 203; and Bray, *Crazy Horse*, 271.

143 *a thousand Indians had gathered at Devils Tower*: Bray, *Crazy Horse*, 275.

143 *Crook sent Red Cloud*: Sources for account of Red Cloud's delegation to Crazy Horse include Agonito, *Lakota Portraits*, 47; Knight, "War or Peace," 531–37; Bray, "Crazy Horse and the End of the Great Sioux War," 111–12; Bray, *Crazy Horse*, 278; and Robert M. Utley, *The Lance and the Shield: The Life and Times of Sitting Bull* (New York: Henry Holt, 1993), 181–82.

143 *Crazy Horse rose from his council seat*: Sources for account of the surrender of Crazy Horse include Bray, *Crazy Horse*, 281–83; Knight, "War or Peace," 538, 540; Brown, *Bury My Heart*, 333; and *Chicago Tribune*, May 8, 1877, in Thomas R. Buecker, "The Crazy Horse Surrender Ledger: A New Source for Red Cloud Agency History," *Nebraska History* 75, no. 2 (Summer 1994): 193.

144 *the Crazy Horse Surrender Ledger*: Buecker, "The Crazy Horse Surrender Ledger," 191–94; Thomas R. Buecker, and R. Eli Paul, eds., *The Crazy Horse Surrender Ledger* (Lincoln: Nebraska State Historical Society, 1994), xii, 159, 162; *BES*, 108–109; *6GF*, 203; and "The Complete Crazy Horse Surrender Ledger from May 6, 1877," www .astonisher.com/archives/museum/crazy_horse_surrender.html.

145 *"We had enough to eat now"*: *BES*, 109.

145 *The last battle of the Great Sioux War*: Paul Hedren, *After Custer: Loss and Transformation in Sioux Country* (Norman: University of Oklahoma Press, 2011), 22–23.

146 *What unfolded that summer*: Ibid., 24; Edward and Mabell Kadlecek, *To Kill an Eagle: Indian Views on the Last Days of Crazy Horse* (Boulder, CO: Johnson Books, 1981), 37; Robert A. Clark, ed., *The Killing of Chief Crazy Horse: Three Eyewitness Views by the Indian, Chief He Dog; the Indian-white, William Garnett; the White doctor, Valentine McGillycuddy* (Lincoln: University of Nebraska Press, 1988; first published by A. H. Clark, 1976), 77.

146 *Valentine T. McGillycuddy*: Wikipedia's "Valentine McGillycuddy," entry, http://en .wikipedia.org/wiki/Valentine_McGillycuddy; "Valentine Trant McGillycuddy," www .rapidcitylibrary.org/bhkm/knowledgenetwork/includes/bios/mcgillycuddy-bio.asp; and Julia B. McGillycuddy, *Blood on the Moon: Valentine McGillycuddy and the Sioux* (Lincoln: University of Nebraska Press, 1990; first published as *McGillycuddy, Agent* by Stanford University Press, 1941), 75–76.

146 *the largest Sun Dance ever seen*: Clark, *Killing of Chief Crazy Horse*, 37–42; and "William Garnett Interview," in *Voices of the American West: The Indian Interviews of Eli S. Ricker, 1903–1919*, vol. 1, ed. Richard E. Jensen (Lincoln: University of Nebraska Press, 2005), 55.

147 *Crazy Horse tried to get along with old foes*: Agonito, *Lakota Portraits*, 104–105.

147 *the Great Father*: Bray, *Crazy Horse*, 278. The Republican Rutherford B. Hayes was elected in November 1876. Crazy Horse was pleased by the news. Hayes was "a very good man," said Crazy Horse, conceding him a bond of kinship, something he had never done with a *wasichu*.

147 *How did one use a fork?*: Ibid., 105; and "Garnett Interview," in Ricker, *Voices of the American West*, 59.

147 *swamp of intrigue*: McGillycuddy, *Blood on the Moon*, 76–77.

148 *Friends and family advised against a visit*: "Garnett Interview," in Ricker, *Voices of the American West*, 59–60; and Bray, *Crazy Horse*, 326.

148 *Helen "Nellie" Larrabee*: Mari Sandoz, *Crazy Horse: The Strange Man of the Oglalas* (Lincoln: University of Nebraska Press, 1992; first published by Alfred A. Knopf, 1942), 409; Bray, *Crazy Horse*, 324; Agonito, *Lakota Portraits*, 106; and "Garnett Interview," in Ricker, *Voices of the American West*, 59–60.

148 *"there was no Great Father between him and the Great Spirit"*: Bray, *Crazy Horse*, 325; and Agonito, *Lakota Portraits*, 107.

149 *he'd just woken from a troubling dream*: Sources for Crazy Horse's dream include John G. Bourke, *On the Border with Crook* (New York: Charles Scribner's Sons, 1892), 299; Bray, *Crazy Horse*, 325; and UNL, Mari Sandoz Collection, Part II, Research Files, Box 28, "Notes on Sioux and Cheyenne Indians, Part II," Folder 9: "Information and Misinformation on Crazy Horse," Folder 9.13: "Vision of Crazy Horse," *Gordon Journal*, July 10, 1963, n.p.

149 *"I am no white man"*: Jeffrey V. Pearson, "Tragedy at Red Cloud Agency: The Surrender, Confinement, and Death of Crazy Horse," *Montana, The Magazine of Western History* 55 (Summer 2005): 24; Agonito, *Lakota Portraits*, 108.

149 *People "talked to him too much"*: Quoted in Bray, *Crazy Horse*, 326.

150 *the final, most damaging incident*: Ibid., 341–42; James N. Gilbert, "The Death of Crazy Horse: A Contemporary Examination of the Homicidal Events of 5 September 1877," *Journal of the West* 32 (January 1993): 9.

151 *"Tell my friend that I thank him"*: Pearson, "Tragedy at Red Cloud Agency," 21.

151 *Woman's Dress*: Sources for this account include: "Garnett Interview," in Ricker, *Voices of the American West*, 61, 66; McGillycuddy, *Blood on the Moon*, 81; and Pearson, "Tragedy at Red Cloud Agency," 6, 22. William Garnett appeared to distrust Woman's Dress from the first, but he did not have the proof until later. His initial uncertainty appears in an early report: "Report of William Garnett, Interpreter to General H. L. Scott and James McLaughlin," copy in Burgess Memorial Collection, Holland Library, Washington State University, Pullman, WA, 3, and quoted in Pearson, "Tragedy at Red Cloud Agency," 22.

151 *"We broke camp"*: BES, 111; and McGillycuddy, *Blood on the Moon*, 81. Black Elk did not talk about the death of Crazy Horse in the interview transcripts, so the passages on pages 111–14 of *Black Elk Speaks* were largely added by Neihardt. Yet comments made later by Black Elk to Neihardt and to his own family show that Black Elk's part in the tragedy essentially followed the events narrated in *Black Elk Speaks*.

152 *Spotted Tail began screaming*: Pearson, "Tragedy at Red Cloud Agency," 23; and E. A. Brininstool, "Chief Crazy Horse: His Career and Death," *Nebraska History Magazine* (December 1929): 19, 20, 23.

152 *They left the next morning*: Sources for the death of Crazy Horse include BES, 112–13; Pearson, "Tragedy at Red Cloud Agency," 24–27; Bray, *Crazy Horse*, 380–90; McGillycuddy, *Blood on the Moon*, 83–87; Gilbert, "Death of Crazy Horse," 11–17; "He Dog's History of Crazy Horse," in Clark, *Killing of Chief Crazy Horse*, 64–67; "Garnett Interview," in Ricker, *Voices of the American West*, 68–73; NAA, MS 2932, H. L. Scott, "Notes on Sign Language and Miscellaneous Ethnographic Notes on Plains Indians," File: "Sioux," Folder: "The Death of Crazy Horse, as told to Gen H. L. Scott and James Mclaughlin by interpreter Wm Garnett," 13–14; "He Dog Interview," in Eleanor H. Hinman, "Oglala Sources on the Life of Crazy Horse," *Nebraska History*

57 (Spring 1976, reprint; originally published in 1930): 19–22; "Interview with White Calf," in Hinman, "Oglala Sources," 42–43; Hedren, *After Custer*, 146–49; and "Louis Bordeaux and the Death of Crazy Horse," in Bruce R. Liddic and Paul Harbaugh, eds., *Custer & Company: Walter Camp's Notes on the Custer Fight* (Lincoln: University of Nebraska Press, 1995), 146–49.

10. GRANDMOTHER'S LAND

This chapter encompasses events described in *Black Elk Speaks*, 115–21; and *The Sixth Grandfather*, 204–209.

159 *Crazy Horse's father made*: Sources for Crazy Horse's funeral and his eventual burial include *BES*, 113–14; *6GF*, 204; "William Garnett Interview," in *Voices of the American West: The Indian Interviews of Eli S. Ricker, 1903–1919*, vol 1., ed. Richard E. Jensen (Lincoln: University of Nebraska Press, 2005), 72–74; and "Chipp's Interview," in Ricker, *Voices of the American West*, 276–77; Kingsley M. Bray, *Crazy Horse: A Lakota Life* (Norman: University of Oklahoma Press, 2006), 391–98; UNL, Mari Sandoz Collection, Part II, Research Files, Box 30, "Notes Relating to Sioux and Cheyenne Indians, Part IV," Folder 1: "Crazy Horse," Folder 1.1: "The Burial of Chief Crazy Horse, by Lone Eagle"; Bruce R. Liddic and Paul Harbaugh, eds., *Custer & Company: Walter Camp's Notes on the Custer Fight* (Lincoln: University of Nebraska Press, 1995), 150–51; Edward Kadlecek and Mabell Kadlecek, *To Kill an Eagle: Indian Views on the Last Days of Crazy Horse* (Boulder, CO: Johnson Books, 1981), 57–68, 143–44; and *The Sacred Pipe: Black Elk's Account of the Seven Rites of the Oglala Sioux*, recorded and edited by Joseph Epes Brown (Norman: University of Oklahoma Press, 1953), 11.

160 *Crazy Horse's journey was not over*: Bray, *Crazy Horse*, 394; Paul L. Hedren, *After Custer: Loss and Transformation in Sioux Country* (Norman: University of Oklahoma Press, 2011), 149; James O. Gump, *The Dust Rose Like Smoke: The Subjugation of the Zulu and the Sioux* (Lincoln: University of Nebraska Press, 1994), 108; and Kingsley M. Bray, "'We Belong to the North': The Flights of the Northern Indians from the White River Agencies, 1877–1878," *Montana, The Magazine of Western History* 55 (Summer 2005): 37.

162 *Sitting Bull's messengers*: Bray, "'We Belong to the North,'" 40.

162 *one hundred lodges, or about six hundred people*: Ibid., 41. Lt. Clark counted forty-five lodges of Sans Arcs; thirty of Minneconjous; and twenty-five of Oglalas.

162 *the "Medicine Line"*: Hedren, *After Custer*, 151, 153–54.

163 *Canadian tribes*: Ibid., 154–55; and Robert M. Utley, *The Lance and the Shield. The Life and Times of Sitting Bull* (New York: Henry Holt, 1993), 199. The Canadian tribes included the northern branches of the Blackfoot, Cree, Assiniboine, Piegan, Sarsi, Salteaux, and Métis.

163 *Major James M. Walsh*: Utley, *Lance and the Shield*, 183–89; and Hedren, *After Custer*, 154–55.

164 *The Canadians should either adopt the Sioux*: Utley, *Lance and the Shield*, 191–92. Utley quotes a letter from Sherman to SW George W. McCrary, Cantonment on Tongue River, July 16, 1877 (NARA I, RG 94, AGO LR 1871–80, File 4163, AGO 1876, M666, Roll 282, Frame 184).

164 *costs of the Sioux War*: Paul L. Hedren, *Great Sioux War Order of Battle: How the United States Army Waged War on the Northern Plains, 1876–1877* (Norman, OK: Arthur H. Clark, 2011), 171; and "Inflation Calculator," DaveManuel.com, www.davemanuel.com/inflation-calculator.php,

164 *Indian casualties*: Hedren, *Great Sioux War*, 172, 211–12.

165 *More insidious and long-lasting*: Don Russell, "How Many Indians Were Killed? White Man Versus Red Man: The Facts and the Legend," *American West* 10, no. 4 (July 1973): 62; Hedren, *After Custer*, 25; Rex Alan Smith, *Moon of Popping Trees* (Lincoln:

University of Nebraska Press, 1981; first published by Reader's Digest Press, 1975), 43–44; and "Report of Captain Mills," in Jerome A. Greene, *Slim Buttes, 1876: An Episode of the Great Sioux War* (Norman: University of Oklahoma Press, 1982), 132–35.

165 *"What can you do if even Sitting Bull can do nothing?"*: BES, 115–16.

165 *a pattern had formed*: Hedren, *After Custer*, 160; and David G. McCrady, *Living with Strangers: The Nineteenth-Century Sioux and the Canadian-American Borderlands* (Lincoln: University of Nebraska Press, 2006), 90.

165 *One day he rode alone with his uncle Running Horse*: BES, 116–17; and 6GF, 204–205.

166 *"This showed that my power was growing"*: BES, 117.

166 *The voices found him again*: Ibid., 118; and 6GF, 206–207.

169 *attacks by the Crow were just the beginning*: McCrady, *Living with Strangers*, 93–94.

169 *autumn of 1879*: Ibid., 91.

170 *They started west*: Sources for account of the winter buffalo hunt include BES, 118–21; 6GF, 207–209; Michael F. Steltenkamp, S.J., *Nicholas Black Elk: Medicine Man, Missionary, Mystic* (Norman: University of Oklahoma Press, 2009), 41; and Hedren, *After Custer*, 161–62.

11. THE FEAR

This chapter encompasses events described in *Black Elk Speaks*, 123–27; and *The Sixth Grandfather*, 210–14.

173 *the decade when the frontier died*: James O. Gump, *The Dust Rose Like Smoke: The Subjugation of the Zulu and the Sioux* (Lincoln: University of Nebraska Press, 1994), 108.

174 *"The story of one tribe is the story of all"*: Helen Hunt Jackson, *A Century of Dishonor* (Mineola, NY: Dover Publications, 2003; first published by Harper & Bros., 1881), 337–38.

174 *he saw two men crawl forward on their bellies*: 6GF, 210–11; and BES, 123–25.

174 *"make a hole so that the Buffalo can come in"*: David G. McCrady, *Living with Strangers: The Nineteenth-Century Sioux and the Canadian-American Borderlands* (Lincoln: University of Nebraska Press, 2006), 91.

175 *Instead of welcoming*: Account of the events at Fort Peak from 6GF, 211–12.

176 *three male buffalos challenging an older bull*: Ibid.; and Michael F. Steltenkamp, S.J., *Nicholas Black Elk: Medicine Man, Missionary, Mystic* (Norman: University of Oklahoma Press, 2009), 47.

177 *the days of the warrior were ending*: Steltenkamp, *Nicholas Black Elk*, 43; and 6GF, 212–13.

178 *"A terrible time began for me then"*: BES, 125.

178 *Miles City had grown up*: Kathy Grauman, "Fort Keogh," in *Montana Memory Project*, http://milescity.com/forum/posts/view/124524; and Josef James Warhawk, "Fort Keogh: Cutting Edge of a Culture," master's thesis, California State University, 1983, www.ars.usda.gov/SP2userfiles/place/30300000/history/ftkeogh.pdf.

179 *He thought he was going mad*: BES, 125–27; and 6GF, 213–14.

181 *Black Elk's nephew Frank Fools Crow*: Thomas E. Mails, assisted by Dallas Chief Eagle, *Fools Crow* (Garden City, NY: Doubleday, 1979), 79–81.

181 *To dream of thunder*: Royal B. Hassrick, *The Sioux: Life and Customs of a Warrior Society* (Norman: University of Oklahoma Press, 1964), 272.

12. DANCES WITH THUNDER

This chapter encompasses events described in *Black Elk Speaks*, 129–34; and *The Sixth Grandfather*, 215–26.

182 *"Indian religion appears to many of us"*: Vine Deloria, Jr., *Custer Died for Your Sins: An Indian Manifesto* (Norman: University of Oklahoma Press, 1988; first published by Macmillan, 1969), 119.

183 *Lakota concept of power*: *The Sacred Pipe: Black Elk's Account of the Seven Rites of the Oglala Sioux*, recorded and edited by Joseph Epes Brown (Norman: University of Oklahoma Press, 1953), 95; and Raymond J. DeMallie, "Wakan: Plains Siouan Concepts of Power," in *The Anthropology of Power: Ethnographic Studies from Asia, Oceania and the New World*, ed. Richard Adams and Raymond D. Fogelson (New York: Academic Press, 1977), 157.

183 *"a state of mind"*: John Fire Lame Deer and Richard Erdoes, *Lame Deer, Seeker of Visions* (New York: Simon & Schuster, 1972), 162.

184 *shamans*: Mircea Eliade, *Shamanism: Archaic Techniques of Ecstasy*, trans. Willard R. Trask (Princeton, NJ: Princeton University Press, 1972; first published by Bollingen Foundation, 1951), 5, 8, 13, 16, 42–43, 133, 297–99.

185 *"It is time"*: 6GF, 214; and Dee Brown, *Bury My Heart at Wounded Knee: An Indian History of the American West* (New York: Henry Holt, 1970), 420.

185 *dance was humanity's first "high art"*: Richard Drinnon, "The Metaphysics of Dancing Tribes," in *The American Indian and the Problem of History*, ed. Calvin Martin (New York: Oxford University Press, 1987), 109–10; and Bruce Kapferer, "Performance and the Structuring of Meaning and Experience," in *The Anthropology of Experience*, ed. Victor W. Turner and Edward M. Bruner (Urbana: University of Illinois Press, 1986), 188.

185 *"Dream Dances"*: NAA, Philleo Nash Papers, Series 2, Box 10; Box 11: "Dream Dancing," File "KA-Dream Dancing: CD," Folder: "Cora DuBois' Notes: Dream Dance."

185 *Black Elk's dance*: 6GF, 215–26; BES, 129–39; and Michael F. Steltenkamp, S.J., *Nicholas Black Elk: Medicine Man, Missionary, Mystic* (Norman: University of Oklahoma Press, 2009), 46–49.

13. THE LAND OF DARKNESS

This chapter encompasses events described in *Black Elk Speaks*, 141–43; and *The Sixth Grandfather*, 216–27.

193 *sent by steamboat down the Missouri*: BES, 144nn3–4. Black Elk apparently left Fort Keogh in the second wave: in late May, 1,125 Sioux were sent, followed by another 1,640 on June 13. Paul L. Hedren, *After Custer: Loss and Transformation in Sioux Country* (Norman: University of Oklahoma Press, 2011), 162.

193 *Sitting Bull's clothing was ragged*: Robert M. Utley, *The Lance and the Shield: The Life and Times of Sitting Bull* (New York: Henry Holt, 1993), 231–32; P. E. Byrne, *Soldiers of the Plains* (New York: Minton, Balch, 1926), 33

194 *the soldiers had taken their ponies*: BES, 144nn3–4. Although the government promised to pay for the horses, it would not be until 1928 that Washington considered the claims.

194 *The winnowing of the Great Sioux Reserve*: Dee Brown, *Bury My Heart at Wounded Knee: An Indian History of the American West* (New York: Henry Holt, 1970), 416.

194 *Cattle ranching*: Ian Frazier, *Great Plains* (New York: Picador, 1989), 60–62; and Utley, *Lance and the Shield*, 234–35.

195 *promised to homesteaders*: Utley, *Lance and the Shield*, 235.

195 *Black Elk would have seen much of this*: 6GF, 226–27; and BES, 142.

196 *the new homes of the Oglala and Brulé*: Brown, *Bury My Heart*, 416–17.

196 *a plateau that plummeted into a deep valley*: Herbert Welsh, *Four Weeks Among Some of the Sioux Tribes of Dakota and Nebraska* (Philadelphia: Office of the Indian Rights Association, 1882), 16.

196 *Spotted Tail had been murdered*: Sources for the account of Spotted Tail's death, burial, and the aftermath of the killing include Joseph Agonito, *Lakota Portraits: Lives*

of the Legendary Plains People (Guilford, CT: TwoDot, 2011), 78–80, 80n15; Esther S. Goldfrank, "Historic Change and Social Character: A Study of the Teton Dakota," *American Anthropologist* 45 (1943): 80–81; and Hedren, *After Custer*, 165–66.

197 *He rode at a leisurely pace*: BES, 142; and Welsh, *Four Weeks Among the Sioux*, 16–18.

197 *Pine Ridge Agency was a testament to contention*: BES, 142, 142n7; and Gayla Twiss, "A Short History of Pine Ridge," *The Indian Historian* (Winter 1978): 36.

198 *One thing that Pine Ridge was* not: *Wikipedia's* "Pine Ridge Indian Reservation" entry, http://en.wikipedia.org/wiki/Pine_Ridge_Indian_Reservation; author's notes.

198 *the Badlands*: Twiss, "Short History of Pine Ridge," 3–7.

198 *The Agency was in flux*: George Hyde, *Red Cloud's Folk: A History of the Oglala Sioux Indians* (Norman: University of Oklahoma Press, 1967, first published 1937), 307; and Kingsley M. Bray, "Teton Sioux: Population History, 1655–1881," *Nebraska History* 75 (Summer 1994): 174–75. Bray attributes Hyde's 1882 figures as being due to "inflationary factors," but does not explain.

199 *"just like one long night"*: BES, 143.

199 *some Oglalas tried to imitate whites*: Ella DeLoria, *Speaking of Indians* (New York: Friendship Press, 1944), 90–91, 92.

200 *titular faith*: Richard Ellis, ed., *The Western American Indian: Case Studies in Tribal History* (Lincoln: University of Nebraska Press, 1972), 96–97; and James S. Olson and Raymond Wilson, *Native Americans in the Twentieth Century* (Urbana: University of Illinois Press, 1986), 51.

200 *"whisky-sellers, bar-room loungers, debauchers"*: Flora W. Seymour, *Indian Agents of the Old Frontier* (New York: Appleton-Century, 1941), 1–2.

200 *the two clashed*: Sources for account of McGillycuddy's meeting with the chiefs include "Valentine Trant McGillycuddy," www.rapidcitylibrary.org; "Interview with McGillycuddy," by Elmo Scott Watson, professor of journalism, University of Illinois, first published in the Oakland *Tribune Magazine*, December 2, 1923, n.p., quoted in Doane Robinson, "The Education of Red Cloud," *Collections of the South Dakota Department of History* 12 (1924): 176; George Hyde, *A Sioux Chronicle* (Norman: University of Oklahoma Press, 1956), 26–28; James C. Olson, "Red Cloud vs. McGillycuddy," in *The Western American Indian: Case Studies in Tribal History*, ed. Richard N. Ellis (Lincoln: University of Nebraska Press, 1972), 98–99; U.S. Government Report, "1883–1884, Condition of Indian Tribes in Montana and Dakota," 174–75; Will H. Spindler, *Tragedy Strikes at Wounded Knee* (Vermillion, SD: Dakota Press, 1972), 30–31; Mark R. Ellis, "Reservation Akicitas: The Pine Ridge Indian Police, 1879–1885," *South Dakota History* 29 (Fall 1999): 187–88, 193; and *U.S. Statutes at Large*, vol. 20, Act of 27 May 1878, 86.

202 *proposed other expedients*: Robert M. Utley, *The Indian Frontier of the American West, 1846–1890* (Albuquerque: University of New Mexico Press, 1984), 240.

202 *the Pine Ridge Lakota were divided into two camps*: Ibid., 233–34.

203 *Captain Richard Henry Pratt*: Olson and Wilson, *Native Americans*, 61; Agonito, *Lakota Portraits*, 51; Utley, *Indian Frontier*, 245, 247; Wilbert H. Ahern, "Assimilationist Racism: The Case of the 'Friends of the Indian,'" *Journal of Ethnic Studies* 4, no. 2 (Summer 1976): 24; and *Wikipedia's* "American Indian Boarding Schools" entry, http://en.wikipedia.org/wiki/American_Indian_boarding_schools.

203 *Pierre De Smet*: George E. Tinker, *Missionary Conquest: The Gospel and Native American Cultural Genocide* (Minneapolis: Fortress Press, 1993), 92. During an 1864 peace commission, General David Stanley had written of De Smet: "The Reverend Father is known among the Indians by the name of 'Black-Robe' and 'Big Medicine Man.'"

203 *a Catholic mission would be well received*: Julia McGillycuddy, *McGillycuddy, Agent: A Biography of Dr. Valentine T. McGillycuddy* (Palo Alto, CA: Stanford University Press, 1941), 106, 108–109; William K. Powers, *Oglala Religion* (Lincoln: University of Nebraska Press, 1975), 112–13; Clyde Holler, *Black Elk's Religion: The Sun Dance*

and Lakota Catholicism (Syracuse, NY: Syracuse University Press, 1995), 129–30; and Olson, "Red Cloud vs. McGillycuddy," 100.

204 demanded McGillycuddy's instant removal: Ralph W. Andrews, Indians as Westerners Saw Them (Seattle: Superior, 1963), 113; Olson, "Red Cloud vs. McGillycuddy," 104; Robinson, "Education of Red Cloud," 176; Seymour, Indian Agents, 321; and Utley, Indian Frontier, 241.

204 suspicion of . . . Indian schools: Twiss, "Short History of Pine Ridge," 38; Utley, Indian Frontier, 245; and Ralph H. Ross, The Pine Ridge Reservation: A Pictorial Description (Pine Ridge, SD, 1909), 2.

205 Why the sudden turn?: Ellis, "Reservation Akicitas," 195–96; and Utley, Indian Frontier, 243–44.

14. THE MAKING OF A MEDICINE MAN

This chapter encompasses events described in Black Elk Speaks, 143–69; and The Sixth Grandfather, 227–44.

206 "last great Sun Dance": Will H. Spindler, Tragedy Strikes at Wounded Knee (Vermillion, SD: Dakota Press, 1972), 36.

207 dire winter of 1881: William T. Hagan, "The Reservation Policy: Too Little and Too Late," in Indian-White Relations: A Persistent Paradox, ed. Jane F. Smith and Robert M. Kvasnicka (Washington, DC: Howard University Press, 1976), 161, 163.

207 "do the work of your Grandfathers": BES, 143.

207 cry for a vision: Sources for Black Elk's vision quest include 6GF, 227–32; BES, 144–48; William Stolzman, How to Take Part in Lakota Ceremonies (Pine Ridge, SD: Red Cloud Indian School, 1986), 43, 45, 49–50; The Sacred Pipe: Black Elk's Account of the Seven Rites of the Oglala Sioux, recorded and edited by Joseph Epes Brown (Norman: University of Oklahoma Press, 1953), 44, 66; and Lynn Woods O'Brien, Plains Indian Autobiographies, Boise State College Western Writers Series 10 (Boise, ID: Boise State College, 1973), 27.

211 the ceremony of the heyoka: 6GF, 232–35, 234n13; BES, 149–53; Thomas Lewis, The Medicine Men (Lincoln: University of Nebraska Press, 1990), 140–52; and Joseph Epes Brown, "The Wisdom of the Contrary," Parabola 4, no. 1 (1979): 56–63.

213 Crazy Horse's people had relocated there: Ian Frazier, On the Rez (New York: Farrar, Straus and Giroux, 2000), 120.

213 he needed a powerful herb: Sources for account of the search for the daybreak herb include BES, 156–57; 6GF, 235–36; "USDA: Poisonous Plant Research: Lupine (Lupinus spp.)," USDA Agricultural Research Service, www.ars.usda.gov/News/docs.htm ?docid-9950; "Cambridge University Botanic Garden: Lupinus sp. (Lupin)," www.botanic.cam.ac.uk/Botanic/TrailPlace.aspx?p=27&ix=290&pid=11&pid=27&ppid=2693. George W. Linden and Fred W. Robbins, "Mystic Medicine: Black Elk's First Cure," Dakota History Conference, 1982 (Dakota State College, 1982), 393–94; Wikipedia's "Cynoglossum officinale" entry, http://en.wikipedia.org/wiki/Cynoglossum_officinale; and Wikipedia's "Pertussis" entry, http://en.wikipedia.org/wiki/Pertussis. In the Andes, lupine is grown as food; the beans are soaked in water, which removes the bitter alkaloid.

215 Cuts to Pieces appeared: Account of Black Elk's first cure from 6GF, 231, 235–40; BES, 157–61. Black Elk would say that the boy lived another twenty-six years, until 1908, when he died at the age of thirty: "I was not there, and if I had been I would probably have cured him again, for he was sick another time after this."

215 "Ignorance is emphatically the mother of credulity": Gideon H. Pond, "Power and Influence of Dakota Medicine-Men," in Information Respecting the History, Conditions and Prospects of the Indian Tribes of the United States, ed. Henry R. Schoolcraft, vol. 4 (Philadelphia, 1854), 646.

216 *group therapy*: Thomas Lewis, "Group Therapy Techniques in Shamanistic Medicine," *Journal of Group Psychotherapy, Psychodrama, and Sociometry* 35, no. 1 (Spring 1982): 29.

218 *"advanced in every respect in civilization"*: Flora W. Seymour, *Indian Agents of the Old Frontier* (New York: Appleton-Century, 1941), 319–20.

218 *His people weren't thriving*: Ella C. Deloria, *Speaking of Indians* (New York: Friendship Press, 1944), 87–88.

218 *If anything thrived at Pine Ridge, it was dogs*: U.S. Congress, Sen., Select Committee to Examine into the Conditions of the Sioux and Crow Indians, *Report on the Condition of Indian Tribes of Montana and Dakota*, Sen. Report 283, serial set 2174, 48th Congress, 1st Session, 1884, 177–78.

218 *the common ownership of all Lakota*: Robert W. Larson, "A Victor in Defeat: Chief Gall's Life on the Standing Rock Reservation," *Prologue* 40, no. 3 (Fall 2008): n.p., www.archives.gov/publications/prologue/2008/fall/gall.html.

219 *"The religion of our blessed Savior"*: Clyde Holler, *Black Elk's Religion: The Sun Dance and Lakota Catholicism* (Syracuse, NY: Syracuse University Press, 1995), 112.

219 *"Another great hindrance to the civilization"*: Quoted in Holler, *Black Elk's Religion*, 119–20.

219 *"Rules for Indian Courts"*: Thomas J. Morgan, "Rules for Indian Courts," in *Documents of United States Indian Policy*, ed. Francis Paul Prucha (Lincoln: University of Nebraska Press, 2000), 185, in "The Storm: Guns, Bibles, and Governments," exhibit, National Museum of the American Indian, March 23, 2012.

220 *"I heard it from a halfbreed"*: Letter from Richard Pratt to Secretary Teller quoted in Holler, *Black Elk's Religion*, 9A, 123–24. It is interesting that Pratt, a supposedly enlightened educator, would use the more pejorative "halfbreed" here, instead of the more neutral "mixed-blood." The former often seemed to imply untrustworthiness, while "mixed-blood" was closer to a statement of ancestry; in this case, however, Pratt presents the statement of the "halfbreed" as legitimate fact and worthy of action. By this point, the two terms may have gotten so mixed up in white usage that they were interchangeable, though the same connotations are not as immediately evident in Indian usage.

220 *"but a last bid for authority"*: Ibid., 131.

220 *"July was devoted to the Sun Dance"*: Ibid., 133.

220 *a small, underground performance held in outlying areas*: Ibid., 132.

221 *all that was left was a void*: Oglala Lakota College Library and Archives, Kyle, Pine Ridge Agency, SD (hereafter OLC), MS1, Jeanne Smith Collection, Box 6, Group 2, "Pine Ridge Reservation Family and Community Histories, August 1993, File #72-98," Folder 10: "Dr. James Walker Papers: Frinks, Maurice. *Pine Ridge Medicine Man* (unpublished manuscript with photos and captions)," 20. Frinks quotes LaVonne Three Stars in the *Pine Ridge Bulletin*, no. 9, p. 21, who suggested that the loss of the Sun Dance led to the ready acceptance of the Ghost Dance nine years later.

221 *"the crumbling of Dakota culture"*: Holler, *Black Elk's Religion*, 135.

15. THE "SHOW MAN"

This chapter encompasses events described in *Black Elk Speaks*, 171–77; and *The Sixth Grandfather*, 245–50.

222 *They did not trust the white way of medicine*: George W. Linden and Fred W. Robbins, "Mystic Medicine: Black Elk's First Cure," *Dakota History Conference*, 1982 (Dakota State College, 1982), 395, 398; and Louis Kemnitzer, "Whiteman Medicine, Indian Medicine and Indian Identity on the Pine Ridge Reservation," *Pine Ridge Research Bulletin* 8 (1969a): 15, 16.

222 *eight government day schools were built*: Jonathan B. Harrison, *The Latest Studies on Indian Reservations* (Philadelphia: Indian Rights Association, 1887), 21.

223 *They always wanted more*: Stanley Vestal, *Warpath: The True Story of the Fighting Sioux Told in a Biography of Chief White Bull* (Lincoln: University of Nebraska Press, 1984), 241; Harrison, *Latest Studies*, 16, 21; and William Barrows, *The Indian's Side of the Indian Question* (Boston: D. Lothrop, 1887), 132–33.

223 *"brick in the sun"*: Harrison, *Latest Studies*, 17–18.

223 *"I made up my mind I was going away from them"*: 6GF, 245.

224 *William F. Cody had not been idle: The Life of Hon. William F. Cody, Known as Buffalo Bill*, ed. Frank Christianson (Lincoln: University of Nebraska Press, 2011; first published as *The Life of Hon. William F. Cody, Known as Buffalo Bill, the Famous Hunter, Scout, and Guide: An Autobiography*, by F. E. Bliss, 1879), 470, 473; Louis S. Warren, *Buffalo Bill's America*, 358–61, 363–70, 495; Joy S. Kasson, *Buffalo Bill's Wild West: Celebrity, Memory, and Popular History* (New York: Hill & Wang, 2000), 552; and Bill O'Neal, James A. Crutchfield, and Dale L. Walker, *The Wild West* (Lindenwood, IL: Publications International, 2002), 334–35.

225 *Oglalas for his first show*: Sarah J. Blackstone, *The Business of Being Buffalo Bill: Selected Letters of William F. Cody, 1879–1917* (New York: Praeger, 1988), 8–9; and L. G. Moses, "Wild West Shows, Reformers, and the Image of the American Indian, 1887–1914," *South Dakota History* (Fall 1984): 197.

226 *"Fate if there is such a thing is against me"*: Kasson, *Buffalo Bill's Wild West*, 452–53.

226 *Cody calculated his losses at about sixty thousand dollars*: *Story of the Wild West and Camp Fire Chats, by Buffalo Bill* (Chicago: R. S. Peale, 1888), 669.

226 *"incidents that are passing away"*: Kasson, *Buffalo Bill's Wild West*, 16.

226 *she helped recruit Sitting Bull*: Sources for Sitting Bull's tour with Cody include ibid., 169–81, 453–54; Buffalo Bill Historical Center, McCracken Research Library, Cody, WY (hereafter BBHC), MS6, William F. "Buffalo Bill" Cody Collection, File "Native Americans," Baldwin, J. Tyler, "Sitting Bull Signed Contract Discovered," typescript, 1–5; Joseph Agonito, *Lakota Portraits: Lives of the Legendary Plains People* (Guilford, CT: TwoDot, 2011), 131; Robert M. Utley, *The Lance and the Shield: The Life and Times of Sitting Bull* (New York: Henry Holt, 1993), 264–66.

227 *the temptations to go were legion*: Sarah J. Blackstone, *Buckskins, Bullets, and Business: A History of Buffalo Bill's Wild West* (Westport, CT: Greenwood Press, 1986), 87; William Urban, "When 'The Wild West' Went to Florence," *Illinois Quarterly* 40, no. 3 (Spring 1978): 5–21, 6GF, 245; and *Story of the Wild West and Camp-Fire Chats, by Buffalo Bill*, 700.

227 *He could also make good money*: Moses, "Wild West Shows," 202n16; and Blackstone, *Buckskins, Bullets, and Business*, 87.

228 *no impediments*: David Humphreys Miller, *Ghost Dance* (New York: Van Rees, 1959), 82; 6GF, 7–8; Michael F. Steltenkamp, S.J., *Nicholas Black Elk: Medicine Man, Missionary, Mystic* (Norman: University of Oklahoma Press, 2009), 53; and *Letters Sent to the Office of Indian Affairs by the Pine Ridge Agency, 1875–1914* (Washington, DC: National Archives Trust Fund Board, 1985), 9.

228 *119 Pine Ridge Lakotas signed up*: Moses, "Wild West Shows," 201–202; BBHC, MS6, William F. "Buffalo Bill" Cody Collection, File "Native Americans," "Indians in the Wild West Who Traveled to Europe," typescript list, compiled by the McCracken Research Library, of Indians who traveled to Europe with the Buffalo Bill Wild West (BBWW) in 1887, 1891, 1892, and 1905; NARA I, "Indian Census Rolls, 1885–1940 (microform) Indians of North America—Census; Native American Census—Pine Ridge (Oglala Sioux Indians)," Reel 363, "1887–1888."

229 *time itself was divorced from reality*: James F. Stover, *American Railroads* (Chicago: University of Chicago Press, 1961), 157–58.

230 *"everything in the flow style"*: 6GF, 246; "Wild West in New York," online supplement to "Annie Oakley," *American Experience*, PBS/WGBH, 2006, www.pbs.org/wgbh /americanexperience/features/primary-resources/oakley-new-york/.

230 *"drafty, combustible old shell"*: Isabelle S. Sayers, *Annie Oakley and Buffalo Bill's Wild West* (Mineola, NY: Courier Dover, 2012), 25; *Wikipedia's* "Madison Square Garden (1879)" entry, http://en.wikipedia.org/wiki/Madison-Square-Garden-(1879).

230 *estimates ranged from five to fifteen thousand*: "They All Like the Indians," *The World* (New York), November 25, 1886; and *Story of the Wild West and Camp-Fire Chats, by Buffalo Bill*, 700. Where New York's *The World* estimated a crowd of "more than five thousand," Cody said fifteen thousand.

230 *twelve-dollar box seats*: Stella Adelyne Foote, *Letters from "Buffalo Bill"* (Billings, MT: Foote, 1954), 27. Regular seats sold from $.75 to $1.50; box seats, from $5 to $12.

230 *a spectacle of American expansion*: "Buffalo Bill in Drama for Wild West Epoch at Madison-Square Garden," *The New York Times*, November 25, 1886; and untitled article, *The New York Times*, November 28, 1886.

231 *"The dancing of the Indians"*: "The Opening Performance," *The New York Herald*, November 25, 1886.

231 *Opening night*: "They All Like the Indians," *The World*.

231 *"the show was not paying well"*: Sayers, *Annie Oakley*, 25.

232 *Custer Reborn*: Richard Slotkin, *Gunfighter Nation: The Myth of the Frontier in Twentieth-Century America* (Norman: University of Oklahoma Press, 1998; first published by HarperPerennial, 1992), 76–77.

232 *"the bullet is the pioneer of civilization"*: BBHC, MS6, William F. "Buffalo Bill" Cody Collection, File "1886 Program, New York."

233 *threw away the key*: BES, 174.

233 *they might cross the Atlantic*: William F. Cody, *The Wild West in England*, ed. Frank Christianson (Lincoln: University of Nebraska Press, 2012, first published as part of *The Story of the Wild West*, 1888), xix–xx.

234 *"prominent persons of America"*: *Story of the Wild West and Camp-Fire Chats, by Buffalo Bill*, 700.

234 *"you can remove that reproach"*: Cody, *The Wild West in England*, xxi, xix.

234 *the show's Americanness*: Christian F. Feest, "Europe's Indians," in *The Invented Indian: Cultural Fictions and Government Policies,* ed. James A. Clifton (New Brunswick, NJ: Transaction, 1990), 317, 325.

234 *not the first Native Americans*: Ibid., 319, 320.

234 *"My Indians are the principal feature of this show"*: Luther Standing Bear, *My People the Sioux* (Lincoln: University of Nebraska Press, 1928), 201.

234 *SS State of Nebraska*: "S/S State of Nebraska, State Line," Norway-Heritage: Hands Across the Sea, www.norwayheritage.com/p_ship.asp?sh=stane; BBHC, MS6, William F. "Buffalo Bill" Cody Collection, File "Cody, W. F.—European Views of," Monty Mickelson, "Disneyland, Paris," *Cowboys & Indians*, n.d., 48–53.

235 *at the foot of the gangway*: *Story of the Wild West and Camp-Fire Chats, by Buffalo Bill*, 704; and Alan Gallop, *Buffalo Bill's British Wild West* (Phoenix Mill, UK: Sutton, 2001), 41.

235 *Red Shirt*: *Story of the Wild West and Camp-Fire Chats, by Buffalo Bill*, 701–702; *Wikipedia's* "Red Shirt (Oglala)" entry, http://en.wikipedia.org/wiki/Red_Shirt_(Oglala); and "Red Shirt," www.american-tribes.com/Lakota/BIO/RedShirt.htm.

236 *hallmarks of forced gaiety*: Warren, *Buffalo Bill's America*, 282; 6GF, 247; and *Story of the Wild West and Camp-Fire Chats, by Buffalo Bill*, 704.

236 *good reason for concern*: Joe Jackson, *Atlantic Fever: Lindbergh, His Competitors, and the Race to Cross the Atlantic* (New York: Farrar, Straus and Giroux, 2012), 23–24.

236 *The winds came for them that evening*: 6GF, 248; and Mickelson, "Disneyland, Paris," 48–53.

237 *entered the Thames*: 6GF, 248; and "America Comes to London: Buffalo Bill Cody and His Wild West Show," *Victorian History* (blog), http://vichist.blogspot.com/2008/07/america-comes-to-london-buffalo-bill.html.

237 *Life moved quickly*: *Story of the Wild West and Camp-Fire Chats, by Buffalo Bill*, xxii–xxiii; Cody, *Wild West in England*, 30–34; and Paul Reddin, *Wild West Shows* (Urbana: University of Illinois Press, 1999), 90.

238 *The performers did not rest*: Cody, *Wild West in England*, 34–35; and Reddin, *Wild West Shows*, 86–87.

239 *Opening Day was set for May 9*: Reddin, *Wild West Shows*, 89–90.

239 *"gilt-edge advertising"*: "London News & Gossip," *New York Dramatic Mirror*, May 21, 1887, 10.

239 *services at Westminster Abbey*: L. G. Moses, *Wild West Shows and the Images of American Indians, 1883–1933* (Albuquerque: University of New Mexico Press, 1996), 44–45; *Wikipedia's* "Red Shirt (Oglala)" entry; and "The Sioux Chief Red Shirt Interview," *Brisbane Courier*, June 23, 1887.

239 *A steady procession of distinguished visitors*: Cody, *Wild West in England*, 61–62; and Antonia Fraser, *The Life and Times of Edward VII* (London: Weidenfeld and Nicolson, 1972), 31.

240 *"no reason why he should be treated as a brute"*: Letter from Edward to Lord Granville, November 30, 1875, quoted in Dana Bentley-Cranch, *Edward VII: Image of an Era 1841–1910* (London: Her Majesty's Stationery Office, 1992), 101–102.

240 *"you have fetched 'em!"*: Cody, *Wild West in England*, 62–63.

240 *He'd fetched 'em all right*: Ibid., 63–65; Reddin, *Wild West Shows*, 90–91; BES, 176; Gallop, *Buffalo Bill's British Wild West*, 115.

241 *Victoria had occupied the British throne for nearly fifty years*: Joe Jackson, *The Thief at the End of the World: Rubber, Power, and the Seeds of Empire* (New York: Viking, 2008), 235; Lytton Strachey, *Queen Victoria* (London: Penguin, 1971; first published by Chatto & Windus, 1921), 176, 206; and Cody, *Wild West in England*, 34.

242 *She arrived on the hour*: Cody, *Wild West in England*, 35; and untitled article in *The World* (UK), May 18, 1887, 15.

242 *Dance, in the Lakota world*: "Origins of the Grass Dance," *Indian Country Today Media Network*, http://indiancountrytodaymedianetwork.com/2011/04/06/origins-grass-dance-26738; James H. Howard, "Notes on the Dakota Grass Dance," *Southwestern Journal of Anthropology* 7, no. 1 (Spring 1951): 82–85; and Cody, *Wild West in England*, 78–79.

243 *And then the drumbeat ended*: BES, 176–77; 6GF, 249–50; Cody, *Wild West in England*, 78–79; William E. Deahl, Jr., "A History of Buffalo Bill's Wild West Show, 1883–1913," Ph.D. diss., Southern Illinois University, 1974, 64–65.

16. THE ENTRANCE TO HELL
This chapter encompasses events described in *Black Elk Speaks*, 177–80, and *The Sixth Grandfather*, 250–52.

244 *It was a rebuke*: James O. Gump, *The Dust Rose Like Smoke: The Subjugation of the Zulu and the Sioux* (Lincoln: University of Nebraska Press, 1994), 23–24; Byron Farrell, *Queen Victoria's Little Wars* (New York: W. W. Norton, 1972), 226–28.

245 *"Colonel, did you ever hold four kings"*: Helen Cody Wetmore, *Buffalo Bill: The Last of the Great Scouts* (New York: Grosset & Dunlap, 1918, first published 1899), 268–69; and Paul Reddin, *Wild West Shows* (Urbana: University of Illinois Press, 1999), 92.

245 *"It's up to you to come and see me now"*: 6GF, 250–51.

246 *"but very happy"*: Lytton Strachey, *Queen Victoria* (London: Penguin, 1971; first published by Chatto & Windus, 1921), 223–24.

246 *Londoners could not get enough*: Alan Gallop, *Buffalo Bill's British Wild West* (Phoenix Mill, UK: Sutton, 2001), 114–18; Reddin, *Wild West Shows*, 95; and Kate Flint, *The*

Transatlantic Indian, 1776–1930 (Princeton, NJ: Princeton University Press, 2009), 230.

247 *"Sometimes we would growl"*: John G. Neihardt, *Eagle Voice Remembers: An Authentic Tale of the Old Sioux World* (Lincoln: University of Nebraska Press, 1991; first published as *When the Tree Flowered: An Authentic Tale of the Old Sioux World* by Macmillan, 1951), 239–40.

247 *time dragged*: Stella Adelyne Foote, *Letters from "Buffalo Bill"* (Billings, MT: Foote, 1954), 30; Louis S. Warren, *Buffalo Bill's America: William Cody and the Wild West Show* (New York: Alfred A. Knopf, 2005), 319; and "America Comes to London: Buffalo Bill Cody and His Wild West Show," *Victorian History* (blog), http://vichist .blogspot.com/2008/07/america-comes-to-london-buffalo-bill-html.

247 *the Wild West moved to Birmingham*: James Noble, *Around the Coast with Buffalo Bill: The Wild West in Yorkshire & Lincolnshire* (Beverley, UK: Hutton, 1999), 47; Flint, *Transatlantic Indian*, 247; and 6GF, 8–9.

247 *"the introduction of a little scalping"*: Reddin, *Wild West Shows*, 92–93.

247 *the Indians were given considerable freedom*: Gallop, *Buffalo Bill's British Wild West*, 115; Rita G. Napier, "Across the Big Water: American Indians' Perceptions of Europe and Europeans, 1887–1906," in *Indians and Europe, an Interdisciplinary Collection of Essays*, ed. Christian F. Feest (Lincoln: University of Nebraska Press, 1989), 386–87; and Luther Standing Bear, *My People the Sioux* (Lincoln: University of Nebraska Press, 1928), 261–62.

248 *the issue of Indians and alcohol*: J. Beals, P. Spicer, C. M. Mitchell, et al., "Racial Disparities in Alcohol Use: Comparison of 2 Native American Reservation Populations with National Data," *American Journal of Public Health* 3, no. 10 (October 2003): 1683–85; "Study: 12 Percent of Indian Deaths Due to Alcohol," *USA Today*, August 28, 2008, http://usatoday30.usatoday.com/news/health/2008-08-28-308489977 _x.htm; Traci M. Krause, "A Potential Model of Factors Influencing Alcoholism in American Indians," *Journal of Multicultural Nursing and Health* (Fall 1998); Tamara L. Wall, Lucinda G. Carr, and Cindy L. Ehlers, "Protective Association of Genetic Variation in Alcohol Dehydrogenase with Alcohol Dependence in Native American Mission Indians," *American Journal of Psychiatry* 160, no. 1 (2003): 41–46; and Fred Beauvais, "American Indians and Alcohol," *Spotlight on Special Populations* 22, no. 4 (1998): 256.

248 *"foaming at the mouth, and very drunk"*: "Wild West Indians at Police Court," *The Birmingham Daily Post*, November 30, 1887; "Buffalo Bill's Indians in Trouble," *The Sheffield & Rotherham Independent*, December 1, 1887; and untitled article, *The Huddersfield Chronicle and West Yorkshire Advertiser*, December 1, 1887.

249 *Manchester*: William F. Cody, *The Wild West in England*, ed. Frank Christianson (Lincoln: University of Nebraska Press, 2012; first published as part of *The Story of the Wild West and Camp-Fire Chats, by Buffalo Bill*, R. S. Peale, 1888), 96–97, 98–99; Noble, *Around the Coast*, 47; G. J. Symons, "On the Meteorology of 1888, with Notes of Some of the Principal Phenomena," in *British Rainfall, 1888* (London: G. Shield, 1889), 3–8.

249 *tragedy struck the week before opening*: "Could Building Site Be Burial Ground of the Lost Warrior from Buffalo Bill's Show?" *Daily Mail*, www.dailymail.co.uk/news/article -475572/Could-building-site-burial-ground-lost-warrior-Buffalo-Bills-show.html; "Surrounded by the Enemy," Find a Grave Memorial, www.findagrave.com/cgi-bin/fg .cgi?page=gr&GRid=64846422.

250 *"Now I know the white man's customs well"*: 6GF, 8–9, 9n5. Black Elk's first open letter in Oglala was published in *Iapi Oaye* (*The Word Carrier*), vol. 17, no. 3, March 1888, 9. It was translated into English by Raymond DeMallie and Vine Deloria, Sr.

250 *an extended standing ovation*: Noble, *Around the Coast*, 49.

250 *a financial and critical success*: William E. Deahl, Jr., "A History of Buffalo Bill's Wild West Show, 1883–1913," Ph.D. diss., Southern Illinois University, 1974, 65–66.

251 *"We roamed around there"*: 6GF, 251.

251 *Black Elk was not with them*: Noble, *Around the Coast*, 49, 72; Cody, *Wild West in England*, n.p.; "An Enthusiastic Farewell" and "Farewell Performance of the Wild West," *Manchester Weekly Times*, May 5, 1888; "Round the Coast with Buffalo Bill," *The Hull News*, May 12, 1888; and author's interview with Tom F. Cunningham, Scottish Buffalo Bill scholar, August 5, 2013.

252 *last guests cast off*: "Round the Coast with Buffalo Bill."

252 *"English speaker"*: 6GF, 251.

252 *"more Cowboy Colonels"*: *North-Eastern Daily Gazette*, August 16, 1887, quoted in unedited proof of Tom F. Cunningham, *Black Elk, Mexican Joe & Buffalo Bill: The Real Story* (London: English Westerners' Society, 2015). Doc Carver, who'd toured Europe as a sharpshooter in the 1870s, arrived with new partners in 1889 for a show called "Wild America." That same year, P. T. Barnum came to England with a host of Western acts woven into his "Greatest Show on Earth." Warren, *Buffalo Bill's America*, 289–90.

253 *"Mexican Joe's Western Wilds of America"*: Cunningham, *Black Elk, Mexican Joe & Buffalo Bill*, chap. 2, n.p.; 6GF, 251; and BBHC, MS6, William F. "Buffalo Bill" Cody Collection, File "Mexican Joe's Wild West—Correspondence," "Mexican Joe—Outline of dates and venues," typescript calendar of Mexican Joe European venues from February 1888 to June 1889, compiled by the McCracken Research Center.

253 *"probably blamed us with something that had happened"*: 6GF, 251–52; description of Whitechapel in *The Pall Mall Gazette*, November 4, 1889, quoted in Stewart P. Evans and Keith Skinner, *The Ultimate Jack the Ripper Sourcebook: An Illustrated Encyclopedia* (Stroud, UK: Sutton, 2001), 516.

253 *Jack the Ripper*: Sources for Black Elk, Jack the Ripper, and the American connection include: Alexander Chisholm, Christopher-Michael DiGrazia, and Dave Yost, *The News from Whitechapel: Jack the Ripper in The Daily Telegraph* (London: McFarland & Company, 2002), 162–63; Robert D. Keppel, Joseph G. Weis, Katherine M. Brown, and Kristen Welch, "The Jack the Ripper Murders: A *Modus Operandi* and Signature Analysis of the 1888–1891 Whitechapel Murders," *Journal of Investigative Psychology and Offender Profiling* 2 (2005): 1–2, 3–4, 14–17; *Wikipedia*'s "Whitechapel Murders" entry, http://en.wikipedia.org/wiki/Whitechapel_murders; Patricia Cornwell, *Portrait of a Killer: Jack the Ripper—Case Closed* (New York: G. P. Putnam's Sons, 2002), 57, 165; Stewart P. Evans and Keith Skinner, *Jack the Ripper: Letters from Hell* (Stroud, UK: Sutter, 2001), n.p.; *The Daily Telegraph* (London), October 5, 1888, reports supported on *Casebook: Jack the Ripper*, www.casebook.org/press_reports/daily _telegraph/dt881005.html; Stephen Knight, *Jack the Ripper: The Final Solution* (London: Grafton Books, 1977), 58–60; Warren, *Buffalo Bill's America*, 319; and Cunningham, *Black Elk, Mexican Joe & Buffalo Bill*, n.p. "Observer's" letter was posted in Edinburgh on October 3, which means it would have been written around the same time that the *Atlanta Constitution* story appeared, but one day before the letter from Spring Heel Jack was first published.

254 *the belief in Indian cruelty*: Daniele Florentino, "'Those Red-Brick Faces': European Press Reactions to the Indians of Buffalo Bill's Wild West Show," in *Indians and Europe, An Interdisciplinary Collection of Essays*, ed. Christian F. Feest (Lincoln: University of Nebraska Press, 1989), 410; and Warren, *Buffalo Bill's America*, 316.

255 *Black Elk and his original companions*: Cunningham, *Black Elk, Mexican Joe & Buffalo Bill*, n.p.; "Mexican Joe—Outline of dates and venues"; and 6GF, 252. These three companions are Two Elk, High Bear, and Charles Picket Pin. Black Elk never mentions the fate of the two "English speakers" who joined them in Manchester.

255 *"Dear Boss" letter*: Quoted in Knight, *Jack the Ripper*, 220–21.

257 *On October 21*, The Echo: "Colorado Charley's Explanation," *The Echo* (London), October 21, 1888.

258 *the chaos surrounding Mexican Joe*: Tom F. Cunningham, "Mexican Joe: 'The Red Eagle of the Sierras,'" *The English Westerner's Society: The Tally Sheet* 59, no. 2 (Spring

2013): 1–7; Cunningham, *Black Elk, Mexican Joe & Buffalo Bill*, n.p.; *BES*, 179–80; *6GF*, 252; Warren, *Buffalo Bill's America*, 290; BBHC, MS6, William F. "Buffalo Bill" Cody Collection, File "Mexican Joe's Wild West," "Mexican Joe–Newspaper Transcripts" (typescript collection of newspaper accounts of the Mexican Joe Shelley Wild West Show from July 5, 1887, to October 19, 1889, including newspapers in England, Ireland, Scotland, New York, and Paris); BBHC, MS6, William F. "Buffalo Bill" Cody Collection, File "Mexican Joe's Wild West—Correspondence," "Mexican Joe in the Census Records," census records for "1891 Census Jarrow" and "1901 Census Jarrow"; untitled article, *North-Eastern Daily Gazette*, August 16, 1887; "Provincial Theatricals," *The Era*, June 15, 1889; "Mexican Joe," *Hampshire Telegraph & Sussex Chronicle*, March 3, 1888; "A Life's Romance," *Sheffield Evening Telegraph*, November 30, 1887; "A Life of Peril and Adventure," *The Anglo-American Times*, June 2 and 9, 1894; "'Mexican Joe' and His Troupe in Liverpool," *Liverpool Mercury*, August 12, 1887; "Mexican Joe at the Exhibition," *Liverpool Mercury*, August 18, 1887; untitled article, *The Whitstable Times and Herne Bay Herald*, September 24, 1887; untitled article, *The Citizen* (Gloucester, UK), August 11, 1887; "At Home and Abroad," *Pall Mall Gazette*, December 24, 1887; *The Fort Wayne Sentinel*, February 19, 1887, and *San Antonio Daily Light*, August 2, 1888, both quoted in Cunningham, "Mexican Joe," n.p.

261 *"A spirit of chaotic malignance was its presiding genius"*: Cunningham, *Black Elk, Mexican Joe & Buffalo Bill*, n.p.

261 *Mexican Joe had cast a toxic fascination*: "Gleanings," *Liverpool Mercury*, August 17, 1887; "Lively Scene at the Liverpool Exhibition," *Hampshire Telegraph & Sussex Chronicle*, September 3, 1887; "Street Accident in Liverpool," *The Scotsman*, October 1, 1887; untitled article, *North Devon Journal*, October 6, 1887; "Boy Killed at the Liverpool Exhibition," *Aberdeen Daily Post*, October 10, 1887; "Lasso Mack in Trouble," *Birmingham Daily Post & Journal*, November 4, 1887; "Mexican Joe," *The Era*, October 29, 1887; "Accident at 'Wild West' Show," *Leeds Mercury*, November 29, 1887; "Mexican Joe Shot by an Indian," *The Sheffield & Rotherham Independent*, November 30, 1887; untitled article, *The Sheffield & Rotherham Independent*, December 3, 1887; untitled article, *Sheffield Evening Telegraph*, December 1, 1887; and "Attempt to Murder Mexican Joe," *The Illustrated Police News*, January 21, 1888.

262 *boys were drawn into Mexican Joe's orbit*: Cunningham, *Black Elk, Mexican Joe & Buffalo Bill*, n.p.; "Boys' Freak with Firearms," *Liverpool Mercury*, November 7, 1887; "Birmingham Police Court," *Birmingham Daily Post & Journal*, October 20, 1888; and "Young Liverpool and the Wild West," *Birmingham Daily Post & Journal*, October 13, 1887.

262 *young women could not control themselves*: Untitled article, *Sheffield Evening Telegraph*, October 22, 1887; "Departure of Mexican Joe and His Troupe," *Liverpool Mercury*, October 17, 1887; "Young Liverpool and the Wild West," *Birmingham Daily Post & Journal*, October 13, 1887; "Gleanings," *Birmingham Daily Post & Journal*, November 17, 1887; and "Mexican Joe and His Satellite," *The Sheffield & Rotherham Independent*, November 18, 1887.

263 *reckless with life and love*: "Mexican Joe, or Buffalo Bill's Rival," *Liverpool Mercury*, August 10, 1887; "'Mexican Joe' and His Troupe in Liverpool," *Liverpool Mercury*, August 12, 1887; Cunningham, *Black Elk, Mexican Joe & Buffalo Bill*, n.p.; and BBHC, File "Mexican Joe's Wild West—Correspondence," letter and flyer sent to Buffalo Bill Historical Center, March 26, 1992.

263 *opened at Alexandra Palace*: Cunningham, *Black Elk, Mexican Joe & Buffalo Bill*, n.p.; "Alexandra Palace," *The Evening Standard*, May 22, 1888; "Accident to a Cowboy," *Sheffield Evening Telegraph*, May 29, 1888.

263 *"pyrotechnical representation"*: *The Fair-Trade*, May 25, 1888, quoted in Cunningham, *Black Elk, Mexican Joe & Buffalo Bill*, n.p.

264 *"some people had disappeared on the earth"*: *6GF*, 252.

264 *the Paris reception was so overwhelming*: Untitled article, *The Blackburn Standard*, June 23, 1888; Cunningham, *Black Elk, Mexican Joe & Buffalo Bill*, n.p.

264 *Eagle Eye*: "Eagle Eye's Romance," *The New York Times*, July 4, 1888.

264 *The sexual attraction that young white women*: Flint, *Transatlantic Indian*, 238–39; and Florentino, "'Those Red-Brick Faces,'" 407.

264 *"She liked me and took me home"*: BES, 179.

265 *"we went to the place where the earth was on fire"*: 6GF, 252; untitled article, *Local Government Gazette*, September 6, 1888, quoted in Cunningham, *Black Elk, Mexican Joe & Buffalo Bill*, n.p.

265 *He felt the heat on his face*: James Logan Lobley, *Mount Vesuvius: A Descriptive, Historical, and Geographical Account of the Volcano and Its Surroundings* (London: Roper and Drowley, 1889), 140–42, 160; J. F. Christie is interviewed in the *Eau Claire Leader* (Wisconsin), June 22, 1891, quoted in Cunningham, *Black Elk, Mexican Joe & Buffalo Bill*, n.p.

17. *LA BELLE ÉPOQUE*

This chapter encompasses events described in *Black Elk Speaks*, 180–83; and *The Sixth Grandfather*, 252–55.

267 *The pace was killing him*: Unedited proof of Tom F. Cunningham, *Black Elk, Mexican Joe & Buffalo Bill: The Real Story* (London: English Westerners' Society, 2015), n.p.

267 *nonpayment of wages*: Ibid., n.p.

267 *Charles Picket Pin*: "Red Cow Comes Home," *The New York Times*, March 1, 1889. Edward Moffatt, commissioner of agriculture, wrote a letter for Picket Pin to carry, explaining that the man was destitute and had asked to go home.

268 *tragedy befell his former employer*: Sources for the Manchester fire include Cunningham, *Black Elk, Mexican Joe & Buffalo Bill*, n.p.; "A Circus Destroyed by Fire," *The Belfast News-Letter*, February 27, 1889; "Burning of a Circus in Manchester," *Daily News* (Manchester), February 27, 1889; "A Circus Destroyed by Fire in Manchester," *Leeds Mercury*, February 27, 1889; "Gleanings," *The Birmingham Daily Post & Journal*, March 1, 1889; "A Circus Destroyed by Fire," *The Manchester Times*, March 2, 1889; and "A Circus Destroyed by Fire in Manchester," *The Illustrated Police News*, March 9, 1889.

269 *An eight-year-old boy named John Hancock*: "A Watch with a History," *The Scotsman*, March 1, 1889, and "Stealing Mexican Joe's Watch," *The Illustrated Police News*, March 9, 1889. The story about John Hancock's theft crossed the Atlantic and on March 22 the *San Antonio Daily Light* once again denounced Shelley as a fraud.

270 *a paper manufacturer named John Fletcher*: "Manchester Cab Tragedy," *The Penny Illustrated Paper and Illustrated Times*, March 9, 1889; and "Idareata," *The Echo* (London), March 9, 1889.

270 *"We went back to Paris again"*: 6GF, 252; and BES, 180.

271 *"Mr. Black Elk"*: "Black Elk's Accident," *The Pittsburg Dispatch*, June 18, 1889.

271 *Her name was Charlotte*: Author's telephone interview with Charlotte Black Elk, February 25 and 28, 2013; Ian Frazier, *On the Rez* (New York: Farrar, Straus and Giroux, 2000), 117–21; Elizabeth Manning, "There's a Notion That Indians Practicing Their Religion Are Less Than Religious," *High Country News*, May 26, 1997, www.hcn.org /issues/109/3425.

272 *"A man gets respect"*: Marilyn Yalom, *How the French Invented Love: Nine Hundred Years of Passion and Romance* (New York: HarperPerennial, 2012), 235–37.

272 *"She came out of the shadow"*: John G. Neihardt, *Eagle Voice Remembers: An Authentic Tale of the Old Sioux World* (Lincoln: University of Nebraska Press, 1991; first published as *When the Tree Flowered: An Authentic Tale of the Old Sioux World* by Macmillan, 1951), 240.

273 *"Her mouth was over my face"*: Ibid., 241.

273 *He looked overhead*: Account of Black Elk's Parisian vision from *6GF*, 252–53; and *BES*, 180–81.

275 *"I would have had a good coffin"*: *6GF*, 253; and *BES*, 181–82.

275 *"I told my girl that I would go first"*: *6GF*, 254.

276 *"I am coming!"*: Paul Reddin, *Wild West Shows* (Urbana: University of Illinois Press, 1999), 86–87.

276 *They came like famous Americans*: BBHC, MS6, William F. "Buffalo Bill" Cody Collection, Buffalo Bill Cody Scrapbooks, 1883–1895, "Bits from 1883–1886–1888; William F. Cody—France, 1889," Roll 2/Copy 2, "They're Seasick by Now," *The Sun* (New York), April 28–29, 1889, n.p.; "'Wild West' on the Ocean," *The New York Herald*, April 28–29, 1889, n.p.; and Neihardt, *Eagle Voice Remembers*, 238–42.

276 *The Wild West set up in the Parc du Neuilly*: BBHC, Buffalo Bill Scrapbooks, untitled article from *Home Journal* (New York), July 12, 1889, n.p.; Reddin, *Wild West Shows*, 96–97, 98–100; and "Carnot Was There: Buffalo Bill Plays to Celebrities," *San Francisco Chronicle*, n.d., n.p. (dateline Paris, May 15, 1889).

276 *Opening Day was held*: James Noble, *Around the Coast with Buffalo Bill: The Wild West in Yorkshire and Lincolnshire* (Beverley, UK: Hutton, 1999), 17.

278 *Did he want to travel with the show*: *6GF*, 254–55; *BES*, 182; interview with Charlotte Black Elk; BBHC, MS6, William F. "Buffalo Bill" Cody Collection, File "Native Americans," "Indians Known to have traveled with Buffalo Bill's Wild West 1889–1890," typescript list.

278 *"B. Elk," age twenty-five, sailed from Le Havre*: *BES*, 182; Cunningham, *Black Elk, Mexican Joe & Buffalo Bill*, n.p.; and "Black Elk's Accident."

18. THE MESSIAH WILL COME AGAIN

This chapter encompasses events described in *Black Elk Speaks*, 185–90; and *The Sixth Grandfather*, 257–58.

279 *he did not waste time*: 6GF, 254.

279 *funeral "giveaway"*: James R. Walker and Raymond J. DeMallie, eds., *Lakota Society* (Lincoln: University of Nebraska Press, 1982), 150–51.

279 *Military forts*: Rani-Henrik Andersson, *The Lakota Ghost Dance of 1890* (Lincoln: University of Nebraska Press, 2008), 129.

280 *now awaited passage*: Sources for Indian allotment debates include: Louis S. Warren, *Buffalo Bill's America: William Cody and the Wild West Show* (New York: Alfred A. Knopf, 2005), 375; James O. Gump, *The Dust Rose Like Smoke: The Subjugation of the Zulu and the Sioux* (Lincoln: University of Nebraska Press, 1994), 111; Henry Warner Bowden, *American Indians and Christian Missions: Studies in Cultural Conflict* (Chicago: University of Chicago Press, 1981), 193; Robert M. Utley, *The Indian Frontier of the American West, 1846–1890* (Albuquerque: University of New Mexico Press, 1984), 247–48, 249; OLC, Pine Ridge Agency Records, 1904+, SC 54, Box 2: RG 75, Box 2: Folder 1, "Great Sioux Reservation Council Proceedings, 1889 (Box 779, Pine Ridge Agency Proceedings)," 26–30, 32; Marquette University, Milwaukee, WI, Department of Special Collections and University Archives (hereafter MARQ), Holy Rosary Mission/Red Cloud Indian School Collection, Series 7-1, Box 19, Folder 7, "Perrig, Aemilius, Diary, 1886–1894," typescript (this is a facsimile; the original is in the Saint Francis Mission Collection, Series 7, Box 5); and Jerome A. Greene, "The Sioux Land Commission of 1889: Prelude to Wounded Knee," *South Dakota History* 1, no. 1 (Winter 1970): 55.

281 *4,463 signed away their land*: "The Sioux Nation Consents," *The New York Herald*, August 6, 1889; BBHC, Buffalo Bill Scrapbooks, "Sioux Sign Away All Their Lands," probably *The New York Times*, August 6, 1889.

281 *Washington reduced the annual beef issue*: Greene, "Sioux Land Commission," 65; Warren, *Buffalo Bill's America*, 375; Utley, *Indian Frontier*, 249–50; and Paul L. Hedren, *After Custer: Loss and Transformation in Sioux Country* (Norman: University of Oklahoma Press, 2011), 167–68.

281 *Black Elk returned to Pine Ridge*: *6GF*, 254–55. The Crook Commission left Pine Ridge on June 28 or 29 for Lower Brulé; Black Elk arrived in Rushville on June 21, and returned to Pine Ridge that day. Greene, "Sioux Land Commission," 54–55.

282 *"The little land that is arable"*: U.S. Department of the Interior, Census Office, *Report on Indians Taxed and Not Taxed in the United States (Except Alaska) at the Eleventh Census, 1890* (Washington, DC: Government Printing Office, 1894), 589.

282 *famine gripped Pine Ridge*: *6GF*, 256; Department of the Interior, *Indians Taxed and Not Taxed*, 589; Jerry Green, *After Wounded Knee: Correspondence of Major and Surgeon John Vance Lauderdale While Serving with the Army Occupying the Pine Ridge Indian Reservation, 1890–1891* (East Lansing: Michigan State University Press, 1996), 21; Roger L. DiSilvestro, *In the Shadow of Wounded Knee: The Untold Final Chapter of the Indian Wars* (New York: Walker, 2005), 62; and John D. McDermott, "Wounded Knee: Centennial Voices," *South Dakota History* 20, no. 4 (Winter 1990): 249.

282 *disease killed as many as forty-five people per month*: James Mooney, *The Ghost-Dance Religion and the Sioux Outbreak of 1890* (New York: Dover, 1976, first published by Government Printing Office, 1896), 826–27; Department of the Interior, *Indians Taxed and Not Taxed*, 589; *BES*, 186; and *6GF*, 256.

283 *One brother escaped*: *6GF*, 259.

283 *Then came the hardest blow*: Ibid.; Michael F. Steltenkamp, S.J., *Nicholas Black Elk: Medicine Man, Missionary, Mystic* (Norman: University of Oklahoma Press, 2009), 60–61.

284 *clerk at the Manderson store*: "Warren King Moorehead at Wounded Knee," *Ohio History Connection Archaeology Blog*, https://ohioarchaeology.wordpress.com/2011/12/29/warren-king-moorehead-at-wounded-knee; Eli Seavey Ricker, *Voices of the American West: The Settler and Soldier, 1903–1919*, vol. 2, ed. Eli S. Ricker and Richard E. Jensen (Lincoln: University of Nebraska Press, 2005), 30.

284 *good position for a young medicine man*: DiSilvestro, *In the Shadow*, 62; and U.S. Bureau of Indian Affairs, *Fifty-Ninth Annual Report of the Commissioner of Indian Affairs to the Secretary of the Interior, 1890* (Washington, DC: Government Printing Office, 1890), 49.

284 *"are some of the most dangerous Indians on the American continent"*: Department of the Interior, *Indians Taxed and Not Taxed*, 575.

285 *"Where Jesus stood, there the dust flew up"*: MARQ, "Perrig, Aemilius, Diary," September 9, 1889.

285 *Catholics officially arrived*: Christopher Vecsey, "A Century of Lakota Sioux Catholicism at Pine Ridge," in *Religious Diversity and American Religious History: Studies in Traditions and Cultures*, ed. Walter H. Conser, Jr., and Sumner B. Twiss (Athens: University of Georgia Press, 1997), 266; Harvey Markowitz, "The Catholic Mission and the Sioux: A Crisis in the Early Paradigm," in *Sioux Indian Religion: Tradition and Innovation*, ed. Raymond J. DeMallie and Douglas R. Parks (Norman: University of Oklahoma Press, 1987), 121; and Andersson, *Lakota Ghost Dance*, 165.

286 *"teach our people how to read and write"*: Vecsey, "Lakota Sioux Catholicism," 265–66.

286 *"God's Marines"*: "The Jesuits: 'God's Marines,'" *The Week*, March 26, 2013, 11; Ross Enochs, "The Catholic Mission to the Native Americans," in *American Indian Studies: An Interdisciplinary Approach to Contemporary Issues*, ed. Dane Morrison (New York: Peter Lang, 1997), 209; and Vecsey, "Lakota Sioux Catholicism," 266, 267–68, 273.

286 *America has always been a millennial land*: Bernard Barber, "Acculturation and Messianic Movements," *American Sociological Review* 6, no. 5 (October 1941): 663; Anthony F. C. Wallace, "Revitalization Movements," *American Anthropologist* 58, no. 2 (April 1956): 267; and Frank K. Flinn, "Millennial Visions Have Ranged from Armageddon to Spiritual Growth," *St. Louis Post-Dispatch*, December 30, 1999.

287 *revitalization and messianic movements*: Author's interview with Frank K. Flinn, July 7, 2011; Wallace, "Revitalization Movements," 267; and Kathleen Stewart, "Bad Endings: American Apocalypsis," *Annual Review of Anthropology* 28 (1999): 289.

287 *The* wasichu *God was a god of time*: *The New York Times,* November 30, 1890, n.p., quoted in H. Scudder Mekeel, "Messianic Excitements Among White Americans," *The Journal of American Folklore* 4, no. 13 (April–June 1891): 163–65.

287 *The Indian God was a god of space*: Frank K. Flinn, "Question: Is Apocalyptic Religion Bad for America?" *The Washington Times*, June 19, 1995, 18.

287 *Indian Messiahs in the past*: Mooney, *Ghost-Dance Religion*, 662; Joel W. Martin, "Before and Beyond the Sioux Ghost Dance: Native American Prophetic Movements and the Study of Religion," *Journal of the American Academy of Religion* 59, no. 4 (Winter 1991): 683; Rex Alan Smith, *Moon of Popping Trees* (Lincoln: University of Nebraska Press, 1981; first published by Reader's Digest Press, 1975), 64; DiSilvestro, *In the Shadow*, 65–66; and R. David Edmunds, *The Shawnee Prophet* (Lincoln: University of Nebraska Press, 1983), 28–41.

288 *Jack Wilson*: Smith, *Moon of Popping Trees*, 65–66, 70–71; Mooney, *Ghost-Dance Religion*, 820; Barber, "Acculturation and Messianic Movements," 665; Ake Hultkrantz and Walter H. Capps, eds., *Seeing with a Native Eye: Essays on Native American Religion* (New York: Harper & Row, 1976), 201; NAA, Philleo Nash Papers, Series 2, Box 10, File "Cora DuBois' Notes: Origin of 1870 Ghost Dance"; Lt. N. P. Phister, "The Indian Messiah," *American Anthropologist* 4, no. 2 (April 1891): 105; and Russell Thornton, *We Shall Live Again: The 1870 and 1890 Ghost Dance Movements as Demographic Revitalization* (Cambridge: Cambridge University Press, 1986), 1–2.

289 *Black Elk was related directly or by marriage*: Joseph Agonito, *Lakota Portraits: Lives of the Legendary Plains People* (Guilford, CT: TwoDot, 2011), 156; *6GF*, 154; Elaine Goodale Eastman, *Sister to the Sioux: The Memoirs of Elaine Goodale Eastman, 1885–91*, ed. K. Graber (Lincoln: University of Nebraska Press, 1978), 143; and NARA I, RG 75, Records of the Bureau of Indian Affairs, "Irregularly Shaped Papers, 1849–1907," Box 76, Entry 310, "Papers Relative to Sioux Outbreaks, Messiah Craze, and Ghost Dance, 1890," Folder 1, "B.I.A. Correspondence Re: Build-Up to Wounded Knee," letter from D. F. Royer, agent, Pine Ridge Agency, to secretary of the interior, November 8, 1890 (also included as "Armaments of Certain Indians," 5th Congress, 2nd session, S. Doc. No. 9, 14).

289 *The delegates started west, by train*: Mooney, *Ghost-Dance Religion*, 820.

289 *the delegates' journey*: Dee Brown, *Bury My Heart at Wounded Knee: An Indian History of the American West* (New York: Henry Holt, 1970), 432; and Omer C. Stewart, "Contemporary Document on Wovoka (Jack Wilson) Prophet of the Ghost Dance in 1890," *Ethnohistory* 24, no. 3 (Summer 1977): 221.

290 *It was Wovoka, the Cutter*: Smith, *Moon of Popping Trees*, 66–67; and L. G. Moses, "'The Father Tells Me So!' Wovoka: The Ghost Dance Prophet," *American Indian Quarterly* 9, no. 3 (Summer 1985): 337.

290 *That night, God came to him again*: Moses, "'The Father Tells Me So!,'" 337.

290 *When the ice floated past*: Smith, *Moon of Popping Trees*, 67.

290 *the year "a sun died"*: Ibid., 68; Mircea Eliade, *Shamanism: Archaic Techniques of Ecstasy* (Princeton, NJ: Princeton University Press, 1972; first published by Bollingen Foundation, 1951), 142; and Michael Hittman, *Wovoka and the Ghost Dance* (Lincoln: University of Nebraska Press, 1997; first published by Grace Dangberg Foundation, 1990), 63–64.

291 *gathering of the tribes*: Mooney, *Ghost-Dance Religion*, 795; Malcolm Gladwell, "Sacred and Profane," *The New Yorker*, March 31, 2014, 23.

291 *delegates would debate*: Mooney, *Ghost-Dance Religion*, 795, 796; Brown, *Bury My Heart*, 432; John D. McDermott, "Wounded Knee: Centennial Voices," *South Dakota History* 20, no. 4 (Winter 1990): 250–51; Thomas W. Overholt, "Seeing Is Believing: The Social Setting of Prophetic Acts of Power," *Journal for the Study of the Old*

Testament 23 (1982): 15; Herbert Welsh, "The Meaning of the Dakota Outbreak," *Scribner's Magazine* 9, no. 4 (April 1891): 447; and *6GF*, 257.

292 *read his letter to the tribes*: Excerpts from Wovoka's letter quoted in Mooney, *Ghost-Dance Religion*, 781:

> When you get home you must make a dance to continue five days. Dance four successive nights, and the last night keep up the dance until the morning of the fifth day, when all must bathe in the river and then disperse to their homes. You must do all in the same way.
>
> I, Jack Wilson, love you all, and my heart is full of gladness for the gifts you have brought me. When you get home I shall give you a good cloud which will make you feel good. I give you a good spirit and give you all good paint. I want you to [come] again in three months, some from each tribe. . . .
>
> There will be a good deal of snow this year and some rain. In the fall there will be such a rain as I have never given you before.
>
> Grandfather says, when your friends die you must not cry. You must not hurt anybody or harm to anyone. You must not fight. Do right always. It will give you satisfaction in life. . . .
>
> Do not refuse to work for the whites and do not make any trouble with them until you leave them. When the earth shakes [at the coming of the new world] do not be afraid. It will not hurt you.
>
> I want you to dance every six weeks. Make a feast at the dance and have food that everybody may eat. Then bathe in the water. That is all. You will receive good words again from me some time. Do not lie.

292 *Wovoka's Ghost Dance spread*: L. G. Moses and Margaret Connell Szasz, "'My Father, Have Pity on Me!' Indian Revitalization Movements of the Late-Nineteenth Century," *Journal of the West* 23, no. 1 (January 1984): 11–12.

292 *James Mooney*: Sources for Mooney's estimates of Ghost Dancers include Mooney, *Ghost-Dance Religion*, 926–27.

293 *Then there were the Sioux*: Moses and Szasz, "'My Father, Have Pity on Me!'" 12–13; Mooney, *Ghost-Dance Religion*, 926–27; Andersson, *Lakota Ghost Dance*, 75–77; and DiSilvestro, *In the Shadow*, 66.

293 *Black Elk heard talk*: *6GF*, 257.

293 *Good Thunder came to the store*: David Humphreys Miller, *Ghost Dance* (New York: Van Rees, 1959), 57–58.

19. DANCES WITH GHOSTS

This chapter encompasses events described in *Black Elk Speaks*, 190–204; and *The Sixth Grandfather*, 258–69.

295 *No one knew how the creek got its name*: "Warren King Moorehead at Wounded Knee," *Ohio History Connection Archaeology Blog*, https://ohioarchaeology.wordpress.com /2011/12129/warren-king-moorehead-at-wounded-knee.

296 *"Here we shall hunt the buffalo"*: Elaine Goodale Eastman, "The Ghost Dance War and Wounded Knee Massacre of 1890–1891," *Nebraska History* 26 (1945): 32; and Joseph Agonito, *Lakota Portraits: Lives of the Legendary Plains People* (Guilford, CT: TwoDot, 2011), 161.

296 *Black Elk rode close*: *6GF*, 258–59.

296 *The Ghost Dance had transformed both men*: David Humphreys Miller, *Ghost Dance* (New York: Van Rees, 1959), 81–82.

297 *Black Elk dressed in white*: *6GF*, 259.

297 *"What is it that comes to us now?"*: Miller, *Ghost Dance*, 38.

297 *dances proceeded similarly*: Michael F. Steltenkamp, S.J., *Nicholas Black Elk: Medi-cine Man, Missionary, Mystic* (Norman: University of Oklahoma Press, 2009), 61.

298 *Kicking Bear gave the invocation*: 6GF, 260.

298 *nearing exhaustion*: Ibid., 260–61; and Miller, *Ghost Dance*, 78–79.

299 *"ghost shirts"*: Sources for the origin of the ghost shirts include: Miller, *Ghost Dance*, 79–80; James Mooney, *The Ghost-Dance Religion and the Sioux Outbreak of 1890* (New York: Dover, 1976; first published by Government Printing Office, 1896), 791, 792, 916; Agonito, *Lakota Portraits*, 162–63; Rani-Henrik Andersson, *The Lakota Ghost Dance of 1890* (Lincoln: University of Nebraska Press, 2008), 68–73; Rex Alan Smith, *Moon of Popping Trees* (Lincoln: University of Nebraska Press, 1981; first pub-lished by Reader's Digest Press, 1975), 75; Steltenkamp, *Nicholas Black Elk*, 62; and John D. McDermott, "Wounded Knee: Centennial Voices," *South Dakota History* 20, no. 4 (Winter 1990): 257. Though Black Elk said the shirts originated with his vision, their appearance among the Sioux seems more widespread. Mooney claimed that the original idea came from the sacramental vestments used by the Mormons, whose in-fluence among the tribes near the Ghost Dance's birthplace had been strong. Their first white mention comes from an eyewitness account at White Clay Creek on June 20, 1890; in this case, the shirts were stitched together based upon the vision of Return from Scout's wife. But others claim that date is in error. Most sources suggest that the shirts originated with the Shoshone and Arapaho, who lived closest to Wo-voka. Kicking Bear studied the Arapaho dance in the late summer of 1890 as he re-turned from that first meeting with Wovoka. The idea that they were bulletproof seems to have started with him.

300 *He led the dance on the fourth day*: BES, 196; and 6GF, 262.

300 *Against the tree, he saw a man*: BES, 197; 6GF, 262–63; Steltenkamp, *Nicholas Black Elk*, 65; Herbert Welsh, "The Meaning of the Dakota Outbreak," *Scribner's Magazine* 9, no. 4 (April 1891): 447; and Miller, *Ghost Dance*, 81.

301 *His innate spirituality blossomed*: Marie Therese Archambault, O.S.F., *A Retreat with Black Elk: Living in the Sacred Hoop* (Cincinnati: St. Anthony Messenger, 1998), 23.

301 *The Ghost Dance spread*: George Bird Grinnell, "Account of the Northern Cheyennes Concerning the Messiah Superstition," *The Journal of American Folklore* 4, no. 12 (January–March 1891): 64.

301 *competing Messiahs*: "The Messiah Craze," *Report of the Secretary of the Interior*, 52nd Congress, 1st session, H.R. Doc. No. 1, part 5 (Washington, DC: Government Print-ing Office, 1892), 123.

301 *nowhere were the dances as prevalent as at Pine Ridge*: Jeffrey Ostler, *The Lakotas and the Black Hills: The Struggle for Sacred Ground* (New York: Viking, 2010), 119; and Luther Standing Bear, *My People the Sioux* (Lincoln: University of Nebraska Press, 1928), 218–19.

302 *This family split was not uncommon*: Ostler, *Lakotas and the Black Hills*, 119.

302 *missionaries*: MARQ, "Perrig, Aemilius, diary," August 24, 1890; MARQ, Holy Rosary Mission/Red Cloud Indian School Collection, Series 7-1, Box 18, "Jesuit Papers," Folder 3: Jutz, John B. "Historical Data on the Causes of the Dissatisfaction Among the Sioux Indians in 1890." Even more than the Catholics, Protestant missionaries viewed the Ghost Dance as an existential threat. The Presbyterian pastor C. G. Ster-ling complained that the Sunday dances held two miles away from his chapel at White Clay Creek had "drawn away nearly all the members of our congregation." Todd Kerstetter, "Spin Doctors at Santee: Missionaries and the Dakota-Language Re-porting of the Ghost Dance and Wounded Knee," *The Western Historical Quarterly* 28, no. 1 (Spring 1997): 59–60.

302 *belief would dissipate, as it had in 1870*: Smith, *Moon of Popping Trees*, 90.

302 *more than six hundred Indians danced at No Water's camp*: Miller, *Ghost Dance*, 82–85; Smith, *Moon of Popping Trees*, 91; "Messiah Craze," *Report of the Secretary of*

the Interior, 124; "Ghost Dances in the West," *The Illustrated American*, January 17, 1891, 327.

303 *He surfaced troubled*: BES, 201–202; 6GF, 265–66; Miller, *Ghost Dance*, 85–86; and Thomas Overholt, "Short Bull, Black Elk, Sword and the 'Meaning' of the Ghost Dance," *Religion* 8 (Autumn 1978): 178.

304 *The September 1890 lull proved deadly*: Smith, *Moon of Popping Trees*, 93–95; and Robert M. Utley, *The Lance and the Shield: The Life and Times of Sitting Bull* (New York: Henry Holt, 1993), 282.

304 *Dr. Daniel F. Royer*: Roger L. DiSilvestro, *In the Shadow of Wounded Knee: The Untold Final Chapter of the Indian Wars* (New York: Walker, 2005), 72–73; Smith, *Moon of Popping Trees*, 120–21; Richard E. Jensen, R. Eli Paul, and John E. Carter, eds., *Eyewitness at Wounded Knee* (Lincoln: University of Nebraska Press, 1991), 69; and Jerry Green, *After Wounded Knee: Correspondence of Major and Surgeon John Vance Lauderdale While Serving with the Army Occupying the Pine Ridge Indian Reservation, 1890–1891* (East Lansing: Michigan State University Press, 1996), 24.

305 *a man dominated by fear*: James H. Cook, *Fifty Years on the Old Frontier, as Cowboy, Hunter, Guide, Scout, and Ranchman* (Norman: University of Oklahoma Press, 1957; first published by Yale University Press, 1923), 200; Jensen, Paul, and Carter, *Eyewitness*, 69; Smith, *Moon of Popping Trees*, 125; Paul L. Hedren, *After Custer: Loss and Transformation in Sioux Country* (Norman: University of Oklahoma Press, 2011), 171; "Letter, Agent D. F. Royer to Commissioner Morgan," October 12, 1890, 51st Congress, 2nd session, S. Doc. No. 9, 5; and "Messiah Craze," *Report of the Secretary of the Interior*, 123.

305 *Miles arrived at Pine Ridge*: Peter R. Montravel, "General Nelson A. Miles and the Wounded Knee Controversy," *Arizona and the West* 28 (Spring 1986): 24; Jeffrey Ostler, "Conquest and the State: Why the United States Employed Massive Military Force to Suppress the Lakota Ghost Dance," *Pacific Historical Review* 65, no. 2 (May 1996): 233, 233n33; *Sister to the Sioux: The Memoirs of Elaine Goodale Eastman, 1885–91*, ed. K. Graber (Lincoln: University of Nebraska Press, 1978), 145–46; Green, *After Wounded Knee*, 24; and Kerstetter, "Spin Doctors at Santee," 60.

306 *the investigation itself disturbed the system observed*: Flora W. Seymour, *Indian Agents of the Old Frontier* (New York: Appleton-Century, 1941), 109; Mooney, *Ghost-Dance Religion*, 788–89; and Andersson, *Lakota Ghost Dance*, 73.

307 *"there is absolutely nothing in what you believe"*: MARQ, Jutz, "Historical Data," 316.

307 *the first snow of the season*: MARQ, "Perrig, Aemilius, diary," November 9, 1890.

307 *Daniel Royer's fears*: Seymour, *Indian Agents*, 110; and Smith, *Moon of Popping Trees*, 123.

307 *beef-issue day*: Sources for account of "Big Issue" day and the conflict with Little include Smith, *Moon of Popping Trees*, 124–25; Eastman, *Sister to the Sioux*, 146–47; and Andersson, *Lakota Ghost Dance*, 74–75.

308 *Royer's panic*: NARA I, RG 75, Records of the Bureau of Indian Affairs, "Irregularly Shaped Papers, 1849–1907," Box 76, Entry 310, "Papers Relative to Sioux Outbreaks, Messiah Craze, and Ghost Dance, 1890," Folder 5, "B.I.A. Correspondence Re: Build-Up to Wounded Knee," telegram from Royer to the Commissioner of Indian Affairs, November 15, 1890: "Indians are dancing in the snow and are wild and crazy"; "The Messiah Craze," *Report of the Secretary of the Interior*, 128; and Smith, *Moon of Popping Trees*, 125.

308 *President Harrison ordered troops*: Ostler, *Lakotas and the Black Hills*, 120, 122; Ostler, "Conquest and the State," 235; Green, *After Wounded Knee*, 25–27; and "The Messiah Craze," *Report of the Secretary of the Interior*, 128. In Miles's dispatches about the Ghost Dance threat, he said that Nebraska, Montana, North and South Dakota, Wyoming, Colorado, Nevada, Idaho, and the Utah Territory were all in danger from Ghost Dancers.

309 *When the first two troop trains arrived*: Smith, *Moon of Popping Trees*, 126; and Seymour, *Indian Agents*, 112–13.

309 *the first wave of newsmen*: Susan Forsyth, *Representing the Massacre of American Indians at Wounded Knee, 1890–2000* (Lewiston, NY: Edwin Mellen Press, 2003), 32–33; William Munn Colby, "Routes to Rainy Mountain: A Biography of James Mooney, Ethnologist," Ph.D. diss., University of Wisconsin–Madison, 1977, 192; Elmo Scott Watson, "The Last Indian War, 1890–91—A Study of Newspaper Jingoism," *Journalism Quarterly* 20, no. 3 (September 1943): 31; and Green, *After Wounded Knee*, 25.

310 *Charles "Will" Cressey*: Forsyth, *Representing the Massacre*, 34.

310 *a panic that started first with the Sioux*: DiSilvestro, *In the Shadow*, 75; Eastman, "Ghost Dance War," 33; Eastman, *Sister to the Sioux*, 151; and MARQ, "Perrig, Aemilius, diary," November 23, 1890.

311 *two streams of wagons*: Miller, *Ghost Dance*, 136–37; Eastman, "Ghost Dance War," 33; Will H. Spindler, *Tragedy Strikes at Wounded Knee* (Vermillion, SD: Dakota Press, 1972), 14; and Green, *After Wounded Knee*, 26.

311 *"We were practically under martial law"*: MARQ, "Perrig, Aemilius, diary," November 27, 1890; and Eastman, *Sister to the Sioux*, 152.

312 *list the names of the Ghost Dance leaders*: Green, *After Wounded Knee*, 24.

312 *Royer drew up a list of sixty-six Lakotas*: NARA I, RG 75, Records of the Bureau of Indian Affairs, "Irregularly Shaped Papers, 1849–1907," Box 76, Entry 310, "Papers Relative to Sioux Outbreaks, Messiah Craze, and Ghost Dance, 1890," Folder 1, "B.I.A. Correspondence Re: Build-Up to Wounded Knee," letter from D. F. Royer to commissioner of Indian affairs, November 25, 1890 (list of the sixty-six leaders of the "Messiah Craze" on Pine Ridge, including Black Elk).

312 *Who was this savior?* Miller, *Ghost Dance*, 137–38; NARA I, RG 75, Box 699, "Letters Received, 1881–1907," letter from D. F. Royer to commissioner of Indian affairs, January 10, 1891, no. 3186. Royer said in his letter that almost every Indian veteran of Buffalo Bill's Wild West joined either the Indian police or the army scouts. The two white cowboys who'd performed with Black Elk in the Wild West were Hank Clifford and John W. Nelson. The latter had received notoriety when the Prince of Wales gave him a medal for being "the Champion Liar of the World."

313 *Black Elk and Good Thunder saddled their horses*: Miller, *Ghost Dance*, 154–55; Andersson, *Lakota Ghost Dance*, 80; *6GF*, 268–69; and Robert H. Ruby, *The Oglala Sioux: Warriors in Transition* (Lincoln: University of Nebraska Press, 1955), 79.

313 *the Stronghold*: Green, *After Wounded Knee*, 26–27; Andersson, *Lakota Ghost Dance*, 82–83; Miller, *Ghost Dance*, 156–57, 172–73; *6GF*, 268–69; Forsyth, *Representing the Massacre*, 32; and Reneé S. Flood, *Lost Bird of Wounded Knee: Spirit of the Lakota* (New York: Scribner, 1995).

20. WOUNDED KNEE

This chapter encompasses events described in *Black Elk Speaks*, 204–12; and *The Sixth Grandfather*, 269–75.

316 *Sitting Bull approached his sixtieth year*: Roger L. DiSilvestro, *In the Shadow of Wounded Knee: The Untold Final Chapter of the Indian Wars* (New York: Walker, 2005), 68–69; Jerry Green, *After Wounded Knee: Correspondence of Major and Surgeon John Vance Lauderdale While Serving with the Army Occupying the Pine Ridge Indian Reservation, 1890–1891* (East Lansing: Michigan State University Press, 1996), 28; Robert M. Utley, *The Lance and the Shield: The Life and Times of Sitting Bull* (New York: Henry Holt, 1993), 3, 284–85; and NARA I, RG 75, Records of the Bureau of Indian Affairs, "Irregularly Shaped Papers, 1849–1907," Box 76, Entry 310, "Papers Relative to Sioux Outbreaks, Messiah Craze, and Ghost Dance, 1890," Folder 1, "B.I.A. Correspondence Re: Build-Up to Wounded Knee," letter from Agent James

McLaughlin, Standing Rock Reservation, ND, to the Commissioner of Indian Affairs, November 19, 1890.

317 *Sitting Bull knew he was vulnerable*: Sources for the last days of Sitting Bull include Flora W. Seymour, *Indian Agents of the Old Frontier* (New York: Appleton-Century, 1941), 114; Dee Brown, *Bury My Heart at Wounded Knee: An Indian History of the American West* (New York: Henry Holt, 1970), 475; Utley, *Lance and the Shield*, 285, 290; and NARA I, letter from James McLaughlin to the Commissioner of Indian Affairs, November 19, 1890.

317 *surrounded Sitting Bull's cabin*: Sources for the death of Sitting Bull include Utley, *Lance and the Shield*, 297, 299–305; DiSilvestro, *In the Shadow*, 82–84; Seymour, *Indian Agents*, 115–16; Rex Alan Smith, *Moon of Popping Trees* (Lincoln: University of Nebraska Press, 1981; first published by Reader's Digest Press, 1975), 157–59, 160; Louis S. Warren, *Buffalo Bill's America: William Cody and the Wild West Show* (New York: Alfred A. Knopf, 2005), 380; and Thomas Lawrence Riggs, "Sunset to Sunset: A Lifetime with My Brothers, the Dakotas," *South Dakota Historical Collections* 29 (1958): 261.

318 *Corn-Man*: MARQ, "Perrig, Aemilius, diary," December 15, 1890.

319 *He called a halt*: Sources for Big Foot's decision include Green, *After Wounded Knee*, 29; DiSilvestro, *In the Shadow*, 67, 85; Smith, *Moon of Popping Trees*, 168–75; and James O. Gump, *The Dust Rose Like Smoke: The Subjugation of the Zulu and the Sioux* (Lincoln: University of Nebraska Press, 1994), 114.

319 *"Go away, outlaws!"* Reneé S. Flood, *Lost Bird of Wounded Knee: Spirit of the Lakota* (New York: Scribner, 1995), 36–37.

319 *Big Foot's disappearance worried Miles*: Rani-Henrik Andersson, *The Lakota Ghost Dance of 1890* (Lincoln: University of Nebraska Press, 2008), 90; and Green, *After Wounded Knee*, 29.

320 *Black Elk heard for the first time*: 6GF, 269–70, 270n21; Ralph K. Andrist, *The Long Death: The Last Days of the Plains Indians* (New York: Collier Books, 1993; first published by Macmillan, 1964), 348; and Smith, *Moon of Popping Trees*, 179.

320 *Whitside tallied his prisoners*: Brown, *Bury My Heart*, 441.

321 *a lot of drinking took place*: Flood, *Lost Bird*, 38–39.

321 *"They wouldn't let us go to sleep"*: Ibid., 39.

321 *"I knew there would be trouble"*: BES, 207; and 6GF, 271.

321 *Monday, December 29*: Sources for the prelude to the massacre include Smith, *Moon of Popping Trees*, 179–84, 187, 188, 189–90; Brown, *Bury My Heart*, 441, 442; Flood, *Lost Bird*, 40–41; Andrist, *Long Death*, 348–50; and John D. McDermott, "Wounded Knee: Centennial Voices," *South Dakota History* 20, no. 4 (Winter 1990): 288.

324 *In that instant, the firing began*: Sources for account of the Wounded Knee Massacre include Bruce R. Liddic and Paul Harbaugh, eds., *Custer & Company: Walter Camp's Notes on the Custer Fight* (Lincoln: University of Nebraska Press, 1995), 74; Smith, *Moon of Popping Trees*, 190–91, 192–93; Hugh McGinnis quoted in O. M. Glasgow, "I Was There: The Wounded Knee Massacre," *True West*, March–April 1961, 52; Elton Howard, "Remember Custer!" *True West*, May–June 1959, 15; Flood, *Lost Bird*, 40–41, 42; Andrist, *Long Death*, 351–52; James Mooney, *The Ghost-Dance Religion and the Sioux Outbreak of 1890* (New York: Dover, 1976; first published by Government Printing Office, 1896), 872; "Joseph Horn Cloud Interview," *Voices of the American West: The Indian Interviews of Eli S. Ricker 1903–1919*, vol. 1, ed. Richard E. Jensen (Lincoln: University of Nebraska Press, 2005), 201; Joseph Agonito, *Lakota Portraits: Lives of the Legendary Plains People* (Guilford, CT: TwoDot, 2011), 170–71; Ralph W. Andrews, *Indians as Westerners Saw Them* (Seattle: Superior, 1963), 34; 6GF, 395; and Charles Arnet quoted in McDermott, "Wounded Knee: Centennial Voices," 272–80.

326 *The distant thunder of big guns*: David Humphreys Miller, *Ghost Dance* (New York: Van Rees, 1959), 232; Thisba Hutson Morgan, "Reminiscences of My Days in the

Land of the Ogallala Sioux," *South Dakota Historical Collections* 29 (1958): 54–56; *Sister to the Sioux: The Memoirs of Elaine Goodale Eastman, 1885–91*, ed. K. Graber (Lincoln: University of Nebraska Press, 1978), 160; and Charles A. Eastman, *From the Deep Woods to Civilization: Chapters in the Autobiography of an Indian* (Boston: Little, Brown, 1916), 107–108.

327 *The Jesuits also heard the thunder*: MARQ, "Perrig, Aemilius, diary," December 29, 1890.

327 *He'd risen at daybreak*: Miller, *Ghost Dance*, 232–33; author's telephone interview with Charlotte Black Elk, February 25 and 28, 2013; *6GF*, 271–73; and *BES*, 207–208.

329 *the Hotchkiss guns turned Wounded Knee*: "Dewey Beard Interview," in Ricker, *Voices of the American West*, 219–26; Smith, *Moon of Popping Trees*, 194–95; Miller, *Ghost Dance*, 236–39; McDermott, "Wounded Knee: Centennial Voices," 284–85; and Flood, *Lost Bird*, 42.

330 *Black Elk and his followers arrived*: Smith, *Moon of Popping Trees*, 195; and Miller, *Ghost Dance*, 239.

330 *"It is time to fight!"*: *6GF*, 272–73; Christer Lindberg, ed., "Foreigners in Action at Wounded Knee," *Nebraska History* 71, no. 4 (1990): 177; and Miller, *Ghost Dance*, 238–39.

330 *Black Elk and his man flew*: Sources for account of Black Elk at Wounded Knee include *6GF*, 272–73; *BES*, 209–12; Lindberg, "Foreigners in Action," 177; Miller, *Ghost Dance*, 239–42; Mooney, *Ghost-Dance Religion*, 873; and Smith, *Moon of Popping Trees*, 193–95.

332 *wonder if he could have done more*: *6GF*, 136–37.

332 *But hatred dies hard*: *BES*, 210.

21. "THERE WILL BE A BETTER DAY TO DIE"

This chapter encompasses events described in *Black Elk Speaks*, 213–18; and *The Sixth Grandfather*, 276–82.

334 *scattered as far as two or three miles*: James Mooney, *The Ghost-Dance Religion and the Sioux Outbreak of 1890* (New York: Dover; 1976; first published by Government Printing Office, 1896), 877–79.

334 *How many died at Wounded Knee?*: C. W. Ames, "Winners of the West," *Official Bulletin of the National Indian War Veterans USA* 10 (1933): 3; Rex Alan Smith, *Moon of Popping Trees* (Lincoln: University of Nebraska Press, 1981; first published by Reader's Digest Press, 1975), 199; and "The Messiah Craze," *Report of the Secretary of the Interior*, 52nd Congress, 1st session, H.R. Doc. 1, Part 5 (Washington, DC: Government Printing Office, 1892), 130.

335 *Far more Indians died*: "The Messiah Craze"; NARA I, RG 75, Box 76, Folder 5, "B.I.A. Correspondence Re: Build-Up to Wounded Knee," telegram from T. J. Morgan, commissioner of Indian affairs, to secretary of the interior, December 31, 1890.

335 *Such numbers do not bear scrutiny*: Miles's letter is quoted in Jerry Green, *After Wounded Knee: Correspondence of Major and Surgeon John Vance Lauderdale While Serving with the Army Occupying the Pine Ridge Indian Reservation, 1890–1891* (East Lansing: Michigan State University Press, 1996), 33; Mooney, *Ghost-Dance Religion*, 871; Michael F. Steltenkamp, S.J., *Nicholas Black Elk: Medicine Man, Missionary, Mystic* (Norman: University of Oklahoma Press, 2009), 71; and Jeffrey Ostler, *The Lakotas and the Black Hills: The Struggle for Sacred Ground* (New York: Viking, 2010), 123.

335 *lower the American flag*: Rani-Henrik Andersson, *The Lakota Ghost Dance of 1890* (Lincoln: University of Nebraska Press, 2008), 94; *Sister to the Sioux: The Memoirs of Elaine Goodale Eastman, 1885–91*, ed. K. Graber (Lincoln: University of Nebraska Press, 1978), 162; and Charles A. Eastman, *From the Deep Woods to Civilization: Chapters in the Autobiography of an Indian* (Boston: Little, Brown, 1916), 114.

335 *personal betrayal*: Luther Standing Bear, *My People the Sioux* (Lincoln: University of Nebraska Press, 1928), 224.

336 *Lakota brought the suffering upon themselves*: "Emmy Valendry Recalls Wounded Knee," in Julian Rice, "'It Was Their Own Fault for Being Intractable': Internalized Racism and Wounded Knee," *American Indian Quarterly* 22, no. 1/2 (Winter–Spring 1998): 79; Susan Forsyth, *Representing the Massacre of American Indians at Wounded Knee, 1890–2000* (Lewiston, NY: Edwin Mellen, 2003), 30; untitled article, *The Word Carrier*, vol. 1, January 1891, 1; and "The Indian Massacre," *The New York Times*, December 31, 1891, editorial quoted in Robert Hays, *Editorializing "The Indian Problem": The New York Times on Native Americans, 1860–1900* (Carbondale: Southern Illinois University Press, 1997), 227–29.

336 *Black Elk rode back to the now-deserted camp*: David Humphreys Miller, *Ghost Dance* (New York: Van Rees, 1959), 250.

336 *Black Elk and others wanted revenge*: Ibid., 251; and Mooney, *Ghost-Dance Religion*, 875.

337 *Black Elk was in the thick of it*: Sources for account of Black Elk's injury at Drexel Mission include: *BES*, 214–15; *6GF*, 276–78; and Miller, *Ghost Dance*, 251–52.

338 *Hostilities continued*: "The Messiah Craze," *Report of the Secretary of the Interior*, 132.

338 *the official burial detail*: "William Peano Interview," in *Voices of the American West: The Indian Interviews of Eli S. Ricker, 1903–1919*, vol. 1, ed. Richard E. Jensen (Lincoln: University of Nebraska Press, 2005), 235–36; "Paddy Starr Interview," in Ricker, *Voices of the American West*, 239; UNL, Mari Sandoz Collection, Box 25, "Notes on Indians, Part I," Folder 28: "Wounded Knee," 28–31; Elton Howard, "Remember Custer!" *True West*, May–June 1959, 15, 64; Agonito, *Lakota Portraits: Lives of the Legendary Plains People* (Guilford, CT: TwoDot, 2011), 174; Mooney, *Ghost-Dance Religion*, 878–79; "Ed Janis Interview," in Ricker, *Voices of the American West*, 273; and John D. McDermott, "Wounded Knee: Centennial Voices," *South Dakota History* 20, no. 4 (Winter 1990): 288.

339 *"busy men"*: R. Eli Paul, "Wounded Knee and the 'Collector of Curios,'" *Nebraska History* 75, no. 2 (Summer 1994): 209–10, 211–12.

339 *war photographers*: Christina Klein, "'Everything of Interest in the Late Pine Ridge War Are Held by Us for Sale': Popular Culture and Wounded Knee," *Western Historical Quarterly* 25, no. 1 (Spring 1994): 55–58.

340 *The last group did the most good*: Eastman, *Deep Woods to Civilization*, 111–19; letter from Charles Eastman to a Mr. Wood, quoted in McDermott, "Wounded Knee: Centennial Voices," 289–91; Agonito, *Lakota Portraits*, 174n24, and Roger L. DiSilvestro, *In the Shadow of Wounded Knee: The Untold Final Chapter of the Indian Wars* (New York: Walker, 2005), 91.

341 *"Let's stay here and kill at least one"*: *6GF*, 279

341 *Aaron DeSersa*: Elenita Brown Collection, Stevensville, MT (hereafter EB), Folder: "Correspondence with Steltenkamp," letter from Michael Steltenkamp to Joseph Epes Brown, October 24, 1971; Esther Black Elk DeSersa, Olivia Black Elk Pourier, Aaron DeSersa, Jr., and Clifton DeSersa, *Black Elk Lives: Conversations with the Black Elk Family*, ed. Hilda Neihardt and Lori Utecht (Lincoln: University of Nebraska Press, 2000), 151; Steltenkamp, *Nicholas Black Elk*, 71.

341 *The struggle was winding down*: "The Messiah Craze," *Report of the Secretary of the Interior*, 132; and Agonito, *Lakota Portraits*, 188–92.

341 *Ten Fingers leveled his rifle*: Miller, *Ghost Dance*, 265.

342 *"if this were in summertime"*: *6GF*, 280–81.

342 *a caravan*: Sources for account of the final surrender of the Ghost Dancers include Ibid., 281–82; Andersson, *Lakota Ghost Dance*, 98–99, 161; Miller, *Ghost Dance*, 268; Todd Kerstetter, "Spin Doctors at Santee: Missionaries and the Dakota-Language Reporting of the Ghost Dance and Wounded Knee," *The Western Historical Quarterly* 28, no. 1 (Spring 1997): 61; Charles G. Seymour, "The Sioux Rebellion, the Final

Review," *Harper's Weekly*, vol. 35, February 7, 1891, 106; *Serving the Republic: Memoirs of the Civil and Military Life of Nelson A. Miles* (New York: Harper & Bros., 1911), 246; and Smith, *Moon of Popping Trees*, 200.

343 *Realizing that his religion had failed*: Michael Hittman, *Wovoka and the Ghost Dance* (Lincoln: University of Nebraska Press, 1997; first published by Grace Dangberg Foundation, 1990), 102–103.

22. THE UNDERGROUND

Except for individual citations, noted below, both *Black Elk Speaks* and *The Sixth Grandfather* end with Black Elk's surrender after Wounded Knee.

347 *take the prisoners with him to Europe*: Louis S. Warren, *Buffalo Bill's America: William Cody and the Wild West Show* (New York: Alfred A. Knopf, 2005), 382–83.

347 *1891 was expunged from memory*: NARA I, Box 76, Folder 1, "B.I.A. Correspondence Re: Build-Up to Wounded Knee," letter from J. Geo. Wright, agent, Rosebud Agency, to commissioner of Indian affairs, May 18, 1891. The Indian Office lost considerable influence after Wounded Knee. On January 8, Royer was relieved as agent; he circulated a petition for reinstatement, but few people signed. A temporary agent, F. E. Pierce, arrived at Pine Ridge on January 12, but he immediately fell ill with pneumonia and on February 5 was replaced by Captain Charles G. Penney. He stayed until October 27, when he was replaced by Captain George LeRoy Brown—who stayed in office for only two years. This revolving door hit the Oglala where it hurt most—in the belly. Without a strong advocate to argue their case, the Sioux could starve and no one would care. That January 1891—soon after Royer left—Congress did in fact appropriate a hundred thousand dollars for beef, a deficit of which is justly blamed as the cause of the Ghost Dance War. But there was no power behind the measure, and though it passed the Senate on April 26, 1891, it died in the House—and so the Sioux continued to starve.

348 *"What is an Indian?"*: Jeffrey Ostler, *The Lakotas and the Black Hills: The Struggle for Sacred Ground* (New York: Viking, 2010), 125; "What Is an Indian?" *Sixty-First Annual Report of the Commissioner of Indian Affairs to the Secretary of the Interior, 1892* (Washington, DC: Government Printing Office, 1892), 31–37; and Ella DeLoria, *Speaking of Indians* (New York: Friendship Press, 1944), 95–96. The rhetoric and solutions arising in response to the "Indian" and "Negro" problems were remarkably similar. Both groups were seen as children needing to be led. Both would be segregated until they were "ready to become citizens": Indians, on the reservations; blacks, in a parallel if poorer simulacrum of Caucasian society. Whites saw both as slaves to their passions, in need of rigid controls. When segregation did not maintain order, threats or outright violence would. Education was believed the only long-term solution: what would "raise up" the former slave would "civilize" the Indian, and black and Indian schools during this period were often housed together. Even so, many doubted that either group would ever achieve true equality. "The negro is not the equal of the white man," claimed the *Norfolk Free Lance* as late as September 30, 1905, "and a thousand years of civilization will not make him so." Identical claims were made of Indians in the very same language. Robert E. Bieder, *Science Encounters the Indian, 1820–1880: The Early Years of American Ethnology* (Norman: University of Oklahoma Press, 1986), 162; "The Negro Problem," *Norfolk Free Lance*, September 30, 1905, 1–2.

349 *"bad, wholly bad"*: NARA I, Box 76, Folder 2, letter from Charles G. Penney, acting Indian agent, Pine Ridge, to the Commissioner of Indian Affairs, April 7, 1891; and Peter R. Montravel, "General Nelson A. Miles and the Wounded Knee Controversy," *Arizona and the West* 28 (Spring 1986): 35.

350 *"a dance-craze among the Indian women"*: MARQ, "Perrig, Aemilius, diary," April 14, 1891.

350 *a quiet resurgence*: Accounts of the continuing Ghost Dance from Richmond L. Clow, "The Lakota Ghost Dance After 1890," *South Dakota History* 20, no. 4 (Winter 1990): 330–32.

350 *The peyote cult also surfaced*: L. G. Moses and Margaret Connell Szasz, "'My Father, Have Pity on Me!' Indian Revitalization Movements of the Late-Nineteenth Century," *Journal of the West* 23, no. 1 (January 1984): 13–14; Emerson Spider, Sr., "The Native American Church of Jesus Christ," in *Sioux Indian Religion*, ed. Raymond J. DeMallie and Douglas R. Parks (Norman: University of Oklahoma Press, 1987), 189–209; and S. C. Gwynne, *Empire of the Summer Moon: Quanah Parker and the Rise and Fall of the Comanches, the Most Powerful Indian Tribe in American History* (New York: Scribner, 2010), 313–14.

351 *resurgence of missionary attempts*: Clyde Holler, *Black Elk's Religion: The Sun Dance and Lakota Catholicism* (Syracuse, NY: Syracuse University Press, 1995), 136–37; Mark Clatterbuck, *Demons, Saints, & Patriots: Catholic Visions of Native America Through* The Indian Sentinel *(1902–1962)* (Milwaukee, WI: Marquette University Press, 2009), 72–73; Ross Enochs, *The Jesuit Mission to the Lakota Sioux: Pastoral Theology and Ministry, 1886–1945* (Kansas City, MO: Sheed and Ward, 1996), 108; and Raymond J. DeMallie, "The Lakota Ghost Dance: An Ethnohistorical Account," *Pacific Historical Review* 51, no. 4 (November 1982): 401.

351 *the Black Robes*: Louis Goll, S.J., *Jesuit Missions Among the Sioux* (St. Francis, SD: St. Francis Mission, 1940), 25–27.

352 *it was easier to convert women*: "Sioux Women at Home," *The Illustrated American*, January 31, 1891, 481–84.

352 *a less radical change for a woman*: Robert F. Berkhofer, Jr., *Salvation and the Savage: An Analysis of Protestant Missions and American Indian Response, 1787–1862* (Lexington: University of Kentucky Press, 1965), 114–15.

352 *deepen her ties*: Ross Enochs, "The Catholic Mission to the Native Americans," in *American Indian Studies: An Interdisciplinary Approach to Contemporary Issues*, ed. Dane Morrison (New York: Peter Lang, 1997), 207.

353 *"she died the same day"*: Berkhofer, *Salvation and the Savage*, 115; MARQ, author's review of the diaries of the Jesuit fathers Perrig, Buechel, Digmann, Westropp, and Lindebner.

353 *a struggle between rival shamans*: George E. Tinker, *Missionary Conquest: The Gospel and Native American Cultural Genocide* (Minneapolis: Fortress Press, 1993), 91–92; Michael F. Steltenkamp, S.J., *Black Elk: Holy Man of the Oglala* (Norman: University of Oklahoma Press, 1993), 33; Goll, *Jesuit Missions*, 16; and Enochs, "Catholic Mission," 206–207.

354 *He never even spoke her name*: 6GF, 282; NARA I, "Indian Census Rolls, 1885–1940 [microform]: Indians of North America—Census; Native American Census—Pine Ridge (Oglala Sioux Indians)," Reel 365, "1893"; Native American Census—Pine Ridge, Reel 368, "1900–1903," 72.

354 *Family lore suggests*: Don Doll, S.J., *Vision Quest: Men, Women, and Sacred Sites of the Sioux Nation* (New York: Crown, 1994), 59; Esther Black Elk DeSersa, Olivia Black Elk Pourier, Aaron DeSersa, Jr., and Clifton DeSersa, *Black Elk Lives: Conversations with the Black Elk Family*, ed. Hilda Neihardt and Lori Utecht (Lincoln: University of Nebraska Press, 2000), 151.

354 *one of the most prominent medicine men*: James H. Cook, *Fifty Years on the Old Frontier, as Cowboy, Hunter, Guide, Scout, and Ranchman* (Norman: University of Oklahoma Press, 1957; first published by Yale University Press, 1923), 208; Joseph Agonito, "Young Man Afraid of His Horses: The Reservation Years," *Nebraska History* 79 (Fall 1998): 125; Joseph Agonito, *Lakota Portraits: Lives of the Legendary Plains People* (Guilford, CT: TwoDot, 2011), 220; and Damian Costello, *Black Elk: Colonialism and Lakota Catholicism* (Maryknoll, NY: Orbis Books, 2005), 9.

354 *"yuwipi man"*: Steltenkamp, *Black Elk: Holy Man*, 26–27; Michael F. Steltenkamp, S.J., *Nicholas Black Elk: Medicine Man, Missionary, Mystic* (Norman: University of

Oklahoma Press, 2009), 51–52; *6GF*, 13; William Stolzman, *How to Take Part in La-kota Ceremonies* (Pine Ridge, SD: Red Cloud Indian School, 1986), 58–59; Wesley R. Hurt, "A Yuwipi Ceremony at Pine Ridge," *Plains Anthropologist* 5, no. 10 (November 1960): 48; Louis Kemnitzer, "Yuwipi," *Pine Ridge Research Bulletin* 10 (1969b): 26; and Goll, *Jesuit Missions*, 15.

355 *Katie War Bonnet converted to Catholicism*: *6GF*, 13; NARA I, RG 75, Reels 365, 368, 369, Pine Ridge Census Rolls—1893, 1896, 1900, 1904; and LaDeane Miller, *Fami-lies of Pine Ridge, Book 1* (Cody, WY: self-published, n.d.), 522.

356 *Sam Kills Brave lived close to Black Elk*: Steltenkamp, *Black Elk: Holy Man*, 32.

356 *Real consequences could follow*: Wallace H. Black Elk and William S. Lyon, *Black Elk: The Sacred Ways of a Lakota* (San Francisco: Harper & Row, 1990), 124; and Steltenkamp, *Nicholas Black Elk*, 94.

357 *the Indian Insane Asylum*: *Wikipedia*'s "Canton Indian Insane Asylum" entry, http://en.wikipedia.org/wiki/Canton_Indian_Insane_Asylum; "Hiawatha Diary," www.hiawathadiary.com; and "Canton Indian Historical Society," National Park Service, http://crm.cr.nps.gov/archive/22-9/22-09-16.pdf.

357 *The most frequent battleground was the deathbed*: Steltenkamp, *Black Elk: Holy Man*, 38.

357 *The Jesuits were jealous*: Ibid., 39; Harvey Markowitz, "Converting the Rosebud: Sicangu Lakota Catholicism in the Late Nineteenth and Early Twentieth Centuries," *Great Plains Quarterly* 32, no. 1 (Winter 2012): 7–8; and Enochs, *Jesuit Mission*, 106–107.

358 *The priest, for his part, died*: *6GF*, 12.

358 *the death in 1903 of Father Aloysius Bosch*: Goll, *Jesuit Missions*, 27.

358 *Black Elk was tired*: Marie Therese Archambault, O.S.F., *A Retreat with Black Elk: Living in the Sacred Hoop* (Cincinnati: St. Anthony Messenger, 1998), 24.

359 *Black Elk was going blind*: Steltenkamp, *Nicholas Black Elk*, 89–90; Joseph Epes Brown, "The Wisdom of the Contrary," *Parabola* 4, no. 1 (1979): 58; and "Corneal flash burns: Causes, symptoms, and treatments," WebMD, www.webmd.boots.com/eye-health/guide/corneal-flash-burns.

359 *the great era of the "catching" diseases*: Louis Kemnitzer, "Whiteman Medicine, Indian Medicine and Indian Identity on the Pine Ridge Reservation," *Pine Ridge Research Bulletin* 8 (1969a): 15; Dr. James Walker's report in *Annual Report of the Department of the Interior, 1899* (Washington, DC: Government Printing Office, 1899), 336, 337; James R. Walker, "Tuberculosis Among the Oglala Sioux Indians," *The American Journal of the Medical Sciences* 132, no. 4 (October 1906): 600; and James R. Walker and Raymond J. DeMallie, eds., *Lakota Society* (Lincoln: University of Nebraska Press, 1982), 154.

359 *He'd stand on a hill on a moonless night*: Steltenkamp, *Nicholas Black Elk*, 87; and Steltenkamp, *Black Elk: Holy Man*, 26.

360 wacinko: Thomas Lewis, "A Syndrome of Depression and Mutism in the Oglala Sioux," *American Journal of Psychiatry* 132, no. 7 (1975b): 754.

360 *"shadows are long and dark before me"*: "I Was Born a Lakota," in James R. Walker, Raymond J. DeMallie, and Elaine A. Jahner, eds., *Lakota Belief and Ritual* (Lincoln: University of Nebraska Press, 1980), 140; NARA I, "Indian Census Rolls," Reel 369: "1900–1903," Wounded Knee District, 67; and Miller, *Families of Pine Ridge*, 522.

23. BLACK ROBE DAYS

361 *Nikolaos of Myra*: "People: St. Nicholas—Nearly Everybody's Saint!" St. Nicholas Center, www.stnicholascenter.org/pages/people; "Holy Rosary Mission—Red Cloud Indian School Records," www.marquette.edu/library/archives/Mss/HRM/HRM-sc.shtml.

361 *the main source for the account*: Sources for Black Elk's conversion narrative include: Michael F. Steltenkamp, S.J., *Black Elk: Holy Man of the Oglala* (Norman: University

of Oklahoma Press, 1993), 33–35, 40, 41–42; *6GF*, 14; William K. Powers and Marla N. Powers, "Putting on the Dog," *Natural History* 95, no. 2 (1986): 7; and Acts 22:6–12. It must be remembered that the ultimate source of the narrative was Black Elk himself, and that he passed it down to Lucy and the rest of his family.

363 *people would ask why he converted*: *6GF*, 14; Hilda Neihardt, *Black Elk and Flaming Rainbow: Personal Memories of the Lakota Holy Man and John Neihardt* (Lincoln: University of Nebraska Press, 1995), 88; and Steltenkamp, *Black Elk: Holy Man*, 36.

364 *just work them in with our own*: Frank Fools Crow is quoted in Thomas E. Mails, assisted by Dallas Chief Eagle, *Fools Crow* (Garden City, NY: Doubleday, 1979), 45.

364 *"is actually the Father of all men"*: Ella DeLoria, *Speaking of Indians* (New York: Friendship Press, 1944), 100–101; and Robert W. Larson, "A Victor in Defeat: Chief Gall's Life on the Standing Rock Reservation," *Prologue* 40, no. 3 (Fall 2008): 1, www .archives.gov/publications/prologue/2008/fall/gall.html.

364 *conversion was not easy for Black Elk*: Steltenkamp, *Black Elk: Holy Man*, 89; and Damian Costello, *Black Elk: Colonialism and Lakota Catholicism* (Maryknoll, NY: Orbis Books, 2005), 11.

365 *"The white men try to make the Indians white men"*: Joseph Agonito, *Lakota Portraits: Lives of the Legendary Plains People* (Guilford, CT: TwoDot, 2011), 57–58; James R. Walker, Raymond J. DeMallie, and Elaine A. Jahner, eds., *Lakota Belief and Ritual* (Lincoln: University of Nebraska Press, 1980), 137–41. Red Cloud would live for another five years after giving his abdication speech. He died on December 10, 1909.

365 *"We are not rocks, not bugs"*: Christopher Vecsey, "A Century of Lakota Sioux Catholicism at Pine Ridge," in *Religions Diversity and American Religious History: Studies in Traditions and Cultures*, ed. Walter H. Conser, Jr., and Summer B. Twiss (Athens: University of Georgia Press, 1997), 270–71.

366 *It was time to settle down*: William Stolzman, *The Pipe and Christ: A Christian-Sioux Dialogue* (Pine Ridge, SD: Red Cloud Indian School, 1986), 183; *6GF*, 9–10; "Rules for the St. Joseph Society," *Sina Sapa Wocekiye Taeyanpaha* [Catholic Sioux Herald] 5, no. 18 (November 1, 1936): 7; MARQ, Bureau of Catholic Indian Missions Collection, Series 4-1: "The Indian Sentinel, Hardbound," Stephen McNamara, S.J., "Black Elk and Brings White," *The Indian Sentinel*, November 1941, 139; Esther Black Elk DeSersa, Olivia Black Elk Pourier, Aaron DeSersa, Jr., and Clifton DeSersa, *Black Elk Lives: Conversations with the Black Elk Family*, ed. Hilda Neihardt and Lori Utecht (Lincoln: University of Nebraska Press, 2000), 151; NARA I, "Indian Census Rolls, 1885–1940 [microform]: Indians of North America—Census; Native American Census—Pine Ridge (Oglala Sioux Indians)," Reel 269: "1900–1903," 1903 Census, p. 72, frame 0362, Wounded Knee District. DeMallie noted that Anna Brings White lived with her five-year-old daughter, Emma.

366 *it was a good marriage*: Agonito, *Lakota Portraits*, 221; and Paul Steinmetz, *Pipe, Bible, and Peyote Among the Oglala Lakota*, Stockholm Studies in Comparative Religion 19 (Stockholm: Motala, 1980), 185.

366 *And he raised cattle*: Agonito, *Lakota Portraits*, 221; MARQ, Bureau of Catholic Indian Missions Collection, Series 1: "Records 1848, 1852. Correspondence, 1853, 1862–; Washington–North Dakota, 1908–1909," Box 63, Folder 3, "Correspondence Dakota, South, Pine Ridge Reservation Holy Rosary Mission, 1909," letter, January 29, 1909, from Fr. Westropp to Rev. Fr. Wm. F. Ketcham, director of the Bureau of Indian Catholic Missions; NARA I, RG 75, Records of the Bureau of Indian Affairs: "Black Elk, Benjamin," File 4806: letter from supt., Carlisle School, to J. R. Brennan, agent-in-charge, Pine Ridge Reservation, March 27, 1917, and letter from Agent John Brennan to John Francis, Jr., supt., Carlisle School, May 2, 1917.

367 *the growth and disappearance of Black Elk's livestock*: Vernon D. Malan, *The Dakota Indian Economy: Factors Associated with Success in Ranching* (Brookings: South Dakota State College, 1963), Bulletin 509, 7–8; Paul Robertson, *The Power of the Land: Identity, Ethnicity, and Class Among the Oglala Lakota* (New York: Routledge,

2002), 48–51, 88–89, 104, 123–35, 138–39; *Sixty-First Annual Report of the Commission of Indian Affairs to the Secretary of the Interior, 1892* (Washington, DC: Government Printing Office, 1892), 91; OLC, MS1, Jeanne Smith Collection, Box 4, Group 2: "Pine Ridge Reservation Family and Community Histories, August 1993," Folder 36: "Ellison, Robert S. Papers (selections from)," Denton, Luther, "Early Days at Pine Ridge Recalled," *Sheridan County Star* (Rushville, NE), July 29, 1954, n.p.; Jeffrey Ostler, *The Lakotas and the Black Hills: The Struggle for Sacred Ground* (New York: Viking, 2010), 126; U.S. Bureau of Indian Affairs, *Annual Report of the Commissioner of Indian Affairs to the Secretary of the Interior, 1899* (Washington, DC: Government Printing Office, 1900), 335; U.S. B.I.A., *Annual Report of the Commissioner of Indian Affairs to the Secretary of the Interior, 1901* (Washington, DC: Government Printing Office, 1902), 366; U.S. B.I.A., *Annual Report of the Commissioner of Indian Affairs to the Secretary of the Interior, 1904,* part I (Washington, DC: Government Printing Office, 1905), 62, 328–29; U.S. B.I.A., *Annual Report of the Commissioner of Indian Affairs to the Secretary of the Interior, 1906* (Washington, DC: Government Printing Office, 1907), 106; George Bird Grinnell, "Tenure of Land Among the Indians," *American Anthropologist* 9, no. 1 (January–March 1907), 9; author's interview with Ted Hamilton, supt., Red Cloud School, Pine Ridge, SD, July 31, 2012; "Clarence Three Stars Interview," in *Voices of the American West: The Indian Interviews of Eli S. Ricker, 1903–1919,* vol. 1, ed. Richard E. Jensen (Lincoln: University of Nebraska Press, 2005), 353–55; M. K. Sniffen, "Observations Among the Sioux," *Indian Rights Association, Twenty-Third Annual Report* (Philadelphia: Office of the Indian Rights Association, 1906), 18; William Red Cloud Jordan, "80 Years on the Rosebud," *South Dakota Historical Collections* 35 (1970): 356–58; Deborah Gangloff, "Trail Drives and Roundups: The Western South Dakota Cattle Industry, the Closing of the Open Range and the Round Up of 1902," http://moh.tie.net/content/docs/TrailDrivesandRoundups.pdf; Walker, DeMallie, and Jahner, *Lakota Belief,* 154–56; NARA I, RG 75, Records of the Bureau of Indian Affairs, "Letters Received by the Commissioners of Indian Affairs," 75216-1907 (File 031): "Annual Report of Agent John R. Brennan, Pine Ridge, September 3, 1907"; Reneé S. Flood, *Lost Bird of Wounded Knee: Spirit of the Lakota* (New York: Scribner, 1995), 50–54; "Perrig, Aemilius, diary, 1886–1894," August 16, 1892, and September 20, 1892; Mary Antonio Johnson, *Federal Relations with the Great Sioux Indians of South Dakota, 1887–1933, with Particular Reference of Land Policy Under the Dawes Act* (Washington, DC: Catholic University Press, 1948), 116; "Matador Land and Cattle Company," *The Handbook of Texas Online,* Texas State Historical Association, www.tshaonline.org/handbook; W. M. Pearce, "The Matador Ranch: Range Operations from Texas to Canada," *Journal of Range Management* 15, no. 3 (May 1962): 127–34; Steltenkamp, *Black Elk: Holy Man,* 58; and Gordon Macgregor, *Warriors Without Weapons: A Study of the Society and Personality Development of the Pine Ridge Sioux* (Chicago: University of Chicago Press, 1946), 39.

368 *Black Elk started ranching*: The exact details of Black Elk's original allotment are hard to determine. If he signed the paperwork in 1904, his allotment would have totaled 240 acres, yet later comments by Black Elk and his son Benjamin suggest the total exceeded this. If he waited one more year, his situation would have changed: in 1905, when he married a widow with three children, his allotted acreage could have doubled.

369 *"white thieves"*: In Pine Ridge, more than half the allotted land would be sold or leased to non-Indians, most of these cattle barons, while across the West leases were obtained for mining and other corporate business purposes. From 1887 to 1934 (when allotment was finally reversed), whites acquired more than 60 percent of the land held across the nation by Indians before severalty, reducing native holdings from 138 million to 48 million acres.

370 *as fervent a catechist as he had been a medicine man*: McNamara, "Black Elk and Brings White," 139; Henry Westropp, S.J., "Catechists Among the Sioux," *Catholic Missions* 2 (1908): 113; and Costello, *Black Elk: Colonialism*, 12.

371 *they depended upon Lakota catechists*: Ross Enochs, *The Jesuit Mission to the Lakota Sioux: Pastoral Theology and Ministry, 1886–1945* (Kansas City, MO: Sheed and Ward, 1996), 74–76; MARQ, Marquette League for Catholic Indian Missions Records, *The Calumet*, "Catechists and Meeting Houses Needed at Holy Rosary," October 1928, 2.

371 *Westropp seemed to represent a new direction*: McNamara, "Black Elk and Brings White," 139–40; Louis Goll, S.J., *Jesuit Missions Among the Sioux* (St. Francis, SD: St. Francis Mission, 1940), 61–62; and Westropp, "Catechists Among the Sioux," 113–14.

372 *The change in Black Elk was remarkable*: Marianna Bartholomew, "The Search for Black Elk," *Our Sunday Visitor*, May 29, 1994, 10–11; and Costello, *Black Elk: Colonialism*, 13–18.

372 *Black Elk was a man on fire*: Westropp, "Catechists Among the Sioux," 114; and Bartholomew, "Search for Black Elk," 10.

373 *the Two Roads Map*: Enochs, *Jesuit Mission*, 112–13; Scott J. Howard, "Incommensurability and Nicholas Black Elk: An Exploration," *American Indian Culture and Research Journal* 23, no. 1 (1999); 122; and Steltenkamp, *Black Elk: Holy Man*, 94–95.

373 *hints did leak out*: Howard, "Incommensurability," 122; and *BES*, 220.

374 *descended upon an area like a whirlwind*: Westropp, "Catechists Among the Sioux," 114; and Costello, *Black Elk: Colonialism*, 12.

374 *"a ghost that will wander about and sinks"*: MARQ, Bureau of Catholic Indian Missions Records, Series 14-1: "*Sina Sapa Wocekiye Taeyanpaha* (vol. 10–20)" (hereafter SWT), St. Michael's Mission, Devil's Lake Reservation, Fort Totten, North Dakota, Box 26, vol. 18, no. 7 (February 15, 1914), 4; and Pine Ridge Agency (Holy Rosary Mission), South Dakota, January 17, 1914.

375 *"I suffer and I try to teach my people"*: Marie Therese Archambault, O.S.F., *A Retreat with Black Elk: Living in the Sacred Hoop* (Cincinnati: St. Anthony Messenger, 1998), 54; and MARQ, SWT, vol. 10, no. 8 (March 15, 1907), 2.

375 *"I will hammer the devil down tight"*: Westropp, "Catechists Among the Sioux," 114.

375 *"Such a man could do a vast amount of good"*: 6GF, 18, 18n22. In the footnote, DeMallie quotes a letter from Westropp to Ketcham, June 11, 1907.

376 *Black Elk's 1907 letters*: MARQ, SWT, Box 25, vol. 10, no. 11 (June 15, 1907), 2, and vol. 11, no. 5 (December 15, 1907), n.p.

376 *"Remember that I am just a common man like you"*: MARQ, SWT, Box 25, vol. 10, n.d. (ca. 1907–1908). The exact date and issue of publication are unknown.

376 *Westropp knew what he was going through*: MARQ, Holy Rosary Mission/Red Cloud Indian School Collection, Series 7-1, Box 23, Folder 12: Westropp, Henry I., "In the Land of the Wigwam: A Few Missionary Notes from the Pine Ridge Reservation, Printed Entirely by Sioux Indian Boys" (Pine Ridge, SD: The Oglala Light Press, ca. 1910), 11. This is a short, fifteen-page pamphlet, basically serving as a fund-raising tool for the mission.

377 *both men called the trip a success*: 6GF, 18–19; MARQ, SWT, Box 25, vol. 12, no. 12 (July 15, 1908).

377 *The assessment was too rosy*: MARQ, Bureau of Catholic Indian Missions Collection, Series 1: "Records 1848, 1852. Correspondence, 1853, 1862–; Washington–North Dakota, 1908–1909," Box 62, Folder 10, "Correspondence, Wyoming, Wind River Reservation, St. Stephen's Mission 1908," letter, March 29, 1908, from William McMillen, S.J., to Ketcham, and letter, March 30, 1908, from William McMillen to Fr. Westropp.

377 *a crisis of confidence*: Westropp, "Catechists Among the Sioux," 114; and *6GF*, 19.

377 *Black Elk hit his stride*: *6GF*, 24; MARQ, *SWT*, Box 25, vol. 13, no. 12 (July 15, 1909); and Steltenkamp, *Black Elk: Holy Man*, 66–69, 106.

378 *He was a "show man" again*: Author's interview with Mark Thiel, Native American archivist, MARQ, July 12, 2012; MARQ, Holy Rosary Mission/Red Cloud Indian School Collection, Series 7-1, Box 23, Folder 13: Westropp, Henry I., "Missionary Life Among the Sioux: A Few Pages Picked Up Here and There on the Sioux Indian Mission and Printed Entirely by Indian Boys of the Oglala Sioux Tribe" (ca. 1912), 8.

378 *he was severely tried*: Steltenkamp, *Black Elk: Holy Man*, 18; and letter from Black Elk to William Ketcham, September 7, 1909, quoted in Steltenkamp, *Black Elk: Holy Man*, 70.

379 *He was in critical condition*: MARQ, Bureau of Catholic Indian Missions Collection. Series 1, "Records 1848, 1852. Correspondence, 1853, 1862–; Washington–North Dakota, 1908–1909," Box 78, "Correspondence, California-Dakotas, 1912," Folder 13, "Correspondence, HRM, 1912," letter, January 9, 1912, from Nicholas Black Elk to Rev. Wm. Ketcham, dictated.

379 *about 2,800, were tubercular*: M. Friedman, "More Physicians Needed in the Indian Service," *The Oglala Light* 14, no. 4 (January 1913): 5–7; M. Friedman, "A Few Statistics of the Medical Department of the Indian Service," *The Oglala Light*, 14, no. 4 (January 1913): 16–17; and William R. Bebout, "Our Fight Against Trachoma and Tuberculosis at Rosebud Agency," *The Oglala Light*, 14, no. 1 (September–October 1912): 8–10.

379 *"begging"*: MARQ, Bureau of Catholic Indian Missions Collection, Series 1, "Records 1848, 1852. Correspondence, 1853, 1862–; Washington–North Dakota, 1908–1909," Box 63, Folder 3, "Correspondence, Dakota, South, Pine Ridge Reservation Holy Rosary Mission, 1909," letter, January 29, 1909, from Fr. Westropp to Rev. Fr. Wm. F. Ketcham, director of the Bureau of Indian Catholic Missions, and Box 78, "Correspondence, California-Dakotas, 1912," Folder 13, "Correspondence, HRM, 1912," letter, January 19, 1912, from Fr. Eugene Buechel to Wm. Ketcham.

380 *"from political to religious spheres"*: *6GF*, 23.

380 *"he has gone around like a second St. Paul"*: Westropp, "In the Land of the Wigwam," 12–13; Westropp, "Catechists Among the Sioux," 114; I Corinthians 13:11–12; Galatians 3:28; and Mails, *Fools Crow*, 45. Black Elk's fall 1889 letter in *Iapi Oaye* is quoted in DeMallie's introduction to *6GF*, 9–10.

381 *the Pauline influence*: Claudia Duratschek, O.S.B., *Crusading Along Sioux Trails: A History of the Catholic Indian Missions in South Dakota* (Yankton, SD: Benedictine Convent of the Sacred Heart, 1947), 207; Westropp, "Catechists Among the Sioux," 114; MARQ, *SWT*, vol. 10, n.d. (ca. 1907–1908), *SWT*, vol. 13, no. 12 (July 15, 1909), 3, *SWT*, vol. 14, no. 4 (November 15, 1909), 4, *SWT*, vol. 16, no. 6 (January 15, 1912), 4, signed Manderson, South Dakota, November 2, 1911.

383 *"We all suffer in this land"*: MARQ, *SWT*, vol. 13, no. 12 (July 15, 1909, 3; the Epistle of Paul to Philemon 1:9; Jonathan Galassi, "The Epistle of Paul to Philemon: A Prisoner of Christ," in *Incarnation: Contemporary Writers on the New Testament*, ed. Alfred Corn (New York: Viking, 1990), 257, 260–64.

383 *Then it all stopped*: MARQ, Holy Rosary Mission/Red Cloud Indian School Collection, Series 7-1, Box 18, "Jesuit Papers," Folder 3: Jutz, John B., "Native Catechists and Lay Preachers," n.d.; NARA I, RG 75, Records of the Bureau of Indian Affairs, "Black Elk, Benjamin," File 4806; letter from Agent John Brennan to John Francis, Jr., supt., Carlisle School, May 2, 1917.

383 *Westropp's reassignment to Patna, India*: *6GF*, 24; "Anxious to Do Big Things," *The Catholic Journal*, August 11, 1916, 1; "The Pen Is Mightier," *The Observer*, April 21, 1946, 2.

383 *Little Owl's reassignment was a personal loss*: Mark Clatterbuck, *Demons, Saints, & Patriots: Catholic Visions of Native America Through* The Indian Sentinel *(1902–1962)* (Milwaukee, WI: Marquette University Press, 2009), 155; MARQ, Holy Rosary

Mission/Red Cloud Indian School Collection, Series 7-1, Box 28, "Sialm, Placidus. Correspondence," Folder 4, "Correspondence, 1925," letter, Sept. 17, 1925, to Miss Ray A. Smith. "The work they do is often quite considerable," wrote Sialm on September 25, 1925, to the young donor. "They lead the prayers on holidays when the priest cannot come to their church. They visit and pray over the sick, they bury the dead when the missionary cannot be present."

384 *Black Elk worked primarily with Buechel*: MARQ, Saint Francis Mission Collection, Series 7-1, "Facsimiles," Box 1: "Diary of Rev. Eugene Buechel, S.J. (St. Francis Mission Records, Series 7), vol. 1, 1900–1924," n.p., and Box 2: "Diary of Rev. Eugene Buechel, S.J. (St. Francis Mission Records, Series 7), vol. 2, 1925–1931," n.p. The entries include: vol. 2, 1925–1931, 36; Nov. 6–10, 1918; June 21, 1921; April–July, 1923; January–December, 1928, all n.p.

385 *permanent catechist at Oglala*: Steltenkamp, *Nicholas Black Elk*, 157; Agonito, *Lakota Portraits*, 224; and Karl Markus Kreis, ed., *Lakotas, Black Robes, and Holy Women: German Reports from the Indian Missions in South Dakota, 1886–1900* (Lincoln: University of Nebraska Press, 2007), 63–64.

385 *a 1910 photo taken by Buechel*: *The Indian Sentinel* 5, no. 2 (Spring 1925): 81, and 6, no. 4 (Fall 1926): front cover. By the late 1930s, the number of Indian catechists serving in Catholic missions across the United States would grow to a record 222.

385 *"civilized savage"*: Clatterbuck, *Demons, Saints, & Patriots*, 155.

24. VANISHING AMERICANS

386 *annual Cheyenne Frontier Days parade*: 6GF, 25.

386 *Fools Crow*: Thomas E. Mails, assisted by Dallas Chief Eagle, *Fools Crow* (Garden City, NY: Doubleday, 1979), 53, 87–88.

387 *allowing "innocent" dances*: Grotgeers and Goll are quoted in Ross Enochs, *The Jesuit Mission to the Lakota Sioux: Pastoral Theology and Ministry, 1886–1945* (Kansas City, MO: Sheed and Ward, 1996), 132–33.

388 *the growth of tourism*: Mark David Spence, *Historic Context Report for Potential Linear Historic Road Corridors Along South Dakota (SD) 87 in Wind Cave National Park* (Midwest Regional Office, National Park Service, U.S. Department of Interior, 2011), 9–11.

388 *the number of tourists now exploded*: Ibid., 12.

388 *Mount Rushmore*: Jeffrey Ostler, *The Lakotas and the Black Hills: The Struggle for Sacred Ground* (New York: Viking, 2010), 145–46. The 1923 U.S. Court of Claims suit originally argued by Richard Case would not be decided until June 3, 1979, when the court ruled 5–2 that the nation's seizure of the Hills was in violation of the Fifth Amendment.

389 *bend the national monument to his own ends*: Alice Beck Kehoe, *The Ghost Dance: Ethnohistory and Revitalization* (Washington, DC: Thompson, 1989), 67–68.

389 *fiftieth anniversary of the Custer Massacre*: Richard Upton, "Custer's Last Fight: Remembered by Participants at the Tenth Anniversary, June 25, 1886, and the Fiftieth Anniversary, June 25, 1926," Friends of the Little Bighorn Battlefield, www.friends littlebighorn.com/upton50anniversary.htm.

390 *the boys' camp at St. Francis Mission*: Enochs, *Jesuit Mission*, 134.

390 *Life had not improved for America's Indians*: Russell Thornton, Table 4.2: "American Indian Population in the United States: 1800–1910," in *We Shall Live Again: The 1870 and 1890 Ghost Dance Movements as Demographic Revitalization* (Cambridge: Cambridge University Press, 1986), 24; *Historical Census Statistics on Population by Race, 1790 to 1990, and by Historic Origins, for the United States, Regions, Divisions, and States*, www.census.gov; MARQ, Saint Francis Mission Collection, Series 8, Box 1, Archambault, Marie Therese, Folder 8. "Newsclippings—1915–1970," *Province News Letter*, vol. 8, no. 7 (November 1926), and *Province News Letter*, June 1927.

390 *The most damning assessment*: Brookings Institution, Institute for Government Research, *The Problem of Indian Administration: Report of a Survey Made at the Request of the Honorable Hubert Work, Secretary of the Interior, and Submitted to Him, February 21, 1928* (Baltimore: Johns Hopkins University Press, 1928), 448–50, 845.

391 *life there was palatial*: Michael F. Steltenkamp, S.J., *Black Elk: Holy Man of the Oglala* (Norman: University of Oklahoma Press, 1993), 58–61; and NARA I, "Indian Census Rolls, 1885–1940 [microform]: Indians of North America—Census; Native American Census—Pine Ridge (Oglala Sioux Indians)," Reel 375: "1929," 56.

391 *a Mr. Magoo of Pine Ridge*: Steltenkamp, *Black Elk: Holy Man*, 61.

392 *the "vanishing American"*: Robin and Jilian Ridington, "Review of *The Vanishing American: White Attitudes and U.S. Indian Policy*," *Great Plain Quarterly* (Winter 1994): 52–53; and *Wikipedia*'s "*The Vanishing American*" entry, http://en.wikipedia.org/wiki/The_Vanishing_American.

392 *five "authentic" photos*: "Bogus Portraits of Crazy Horse, his wives, Black Shawl Woman and Helen 'Nellie' Lavarie, and his personal belongings . . . ," *Conversations with Crazy Horse*, www.astonisher.com/archives/museum/crazy_horse_bogus_pics.html.

392 *The grave was another matter*: Ostler, *Lakotas and the Black Hills*, 142; and Veryl Walstrom, *My Search for the Burial Sites of the Sioux Nation Chiefs* (Lincoln, NE: Dageforde, 1995), 133–34.

393 *Black Elk hovered at the fringes*: OLC, MS1, Jeanne Smith Collection, Box 4, Group 2: "Pine Ridge Reservation Family and Community Histories, August 1993," Folder 36: "Ellison, Robert S. Papers (selections from)," letter from Walter M. Camp to Black Elk, April 29, 1914.

393 *"it is part of my religion to tell the truth"*: Michael F. Steltenkamp, S.J., *Nicholas Black Elk: Medicine Man, Missionary, Mystic* (Norman: University of Oklahoma Press, 1993), 106.

393 *a portrait sketched by Eleanor Hinman*: UNL, Mari Sandoz Collection, Part II, Research Files, Box 27, "Notes on Sioux and Cheyenne Indians, Part I," Folder 24: Correspondence Between Eleanor Hinman and Mari Sandoz, re: Sioux and Cheyenne," Folder 24–8: letter from Hinman to Sandoz, n.d.

394 *sometime before April 11, 1930*: NARA I, "Indian Census Rolls, 1885–1940 [microform]: Indians of North America—Census; Native American Census—Pine Ridge (Oglala Sioux Indians)," Reel 375: "1929," 56, 57, Reel 376: "1930," 57–58; Hilda Neihardt, *Black Elk and Flaming Rainbow: Personal Memories of the Lakota Holy Man and John Neihardt* (Lincoln: University of Nebraska Press, 1995), 31–32.

395 *his oldest son, Ben*: Ibid., 30–31, 33.

395 *the backbone of the Black Elk clan*: Esther Black Elk DeSersa, Olivia Black Elk Pourier, Aaron DeSersa, Jr., and Clifton DeSersa, *Black Elk Lives: Conversations with the Black Elk Family*, ed. Hilda Neihardt and Lori Utecht (Lincoln: University of Nebraska Press, 2000), 5, 23–24, 27–31, 151; NARA I, "Indian Census Rolls," Reel 376: "1930," 57–58. Ben's children at this time were Henry, age eleven; Katherine, eight; Esther, six; and Olivia, a newborn. Two other children—Ben Jr. and Grace, mother of Betty Black Elk (who lives on the allotment today and runs the diner)— would be born later.

395 *"Our Sioux Indians are poorer now than ever"*: MARQ, Holy Rosary Mission/Red Cloud Indian School Collection, Series 7-1, Box 28: "Sialm, Placidus. Correspondence," Folder 6, "Correspondence, 1927–1932, n.d." letter, August 14, 1931, to Mrs. R. A. O'Mara of Montclair, NJ; and Timothy Egan, *The Worst Hard Time* (Boston: Houghton Mifflin, 2006), 121–23.

396 *"I led two lives"*: DeSersa et al., *Black Elk Lives*, 5, 82.

396 *an unsettled childhood*: *Ben Black Elk Speaks*, audio recording, executive producer Warfield Moose, Jr. (Omaha: Yellow Spider, 2002); NARA I, RG 75, Records of the Bureau of Indian Affairs: "Black Elk, Benjamin," File 4806, "Application for Enrollment

in a Non-Reservation School"; and U.S. Bureau of Indian Affairs, *Statistics of Tribes, Agencies, and Schools, 1903* (Washington, DC: Government Printing Office, 1903), 72–73.

396 *boarding schools*: Thomas G. Andrews, "Turning the Tables on Assimilation: Oglala Lakotas and the Pine Ridge Day Schools, 1889–1920s," *The Western Historical Quarterly* 33, no. 4 (Winter 2002): 417; and Harvey Markowitz, "The Catholic Mission and the Sioux: A Crisis in the Early Paradigm," in *Sioux Indian Religion: Tradition and Innovation*, ed. Raymond J. DeMallie and Douglas R. Parks (Norman: University of Oklahoma Press, 1987)," 122.

397 *real or imagined infractions*: Author's interview with Betty Black Elk, July 30, 2012, Manderson, SD; Wallace H. Black Elk and William S. Lyon, *Black Elk: The Sacred Ways of a Lakota* (San Francisco: Harper & Row, 1990), 25; and Tim A. Giago, Jr., *The Aboriginal Sin: Reflections on the Holy Rosary Mission School (Red Cloud Indian School)* (San Francisco: The Indian Historian Press, 1978), 2.

397 *hooked up to cultivate potatoes*: Hearings before a subcommittee of the Committee on Indian Affairs, 1929, Part 7, 2836–37, quoted in Robert Gessner, *Massacre: A Survey of Today's American Indian* (New York: Jonathan Cape & Harrison Smith, 1931), 110.

397 *corporal punishment was the national norm*: Quoted in Gessner, *Massacre*, 108.

398 *she was dirty*: Erik Homburger Erikson, "Observations on Sioux Education," *Journal of Psychology* 7 (January 1939): 126; Giago, *Aboriginal Sin*, 2; and Mary Crow Dog, quoted in Debra K. S. Barker, "Kill the Indian, Save the Child: Cultural Genocide and the Boarding School," in *American Indian Studies: An Interdisciplinary Approach to Contemporary Issues*, ed. Dane Morrison (New York: Peter Lang, 1997), 55.

398 *"Perfection" was the goal*: Giago, *Aboriginal Sin*, 2–3; MARQ, Albert White Hat interview in *Ma'Lakota*, "I Am Lakota," in Saint Francis Mission Collection: Series 8, Box 1, and Archambault, Marie Therese, Folder 1: "Back to Back: Roman Catholicism Among the Brulé at St. Francis Mission, South Dakota," 23.

398 *Richard Pratt's transformative school*: Luther Standing Bear, *Land of the Spotted Eagle* (Lincoln: University of Nebraska Press, 1933), 234; NARA I, RG 75, Records of the Bureau of Indian Affairs: "Black Elk, Benjamin," File 4806; Barbara Landis, "About the Carlisle Indian Industrial School," www.english.illinois.edu/maps/poets/a_f/erdrich /boarding/carlisle.htm; and Jacqueline Fear-Segal, "Institutional Death and Ceremonial Healing Far from Home: The Carlisle Indian School Cemetery," *Museum Anthropology* 33, no. 2 (2010): 157.

399 *"My son, John Makes-Enemy"*: NARA I, RG 75, Records of the Bureau of Indian Affairs, "Council Proceedings, 1904–1907," Box 780, "Pine Ridge Agency Records," Folder 2: letter, Makes Enemy to U.S. commissioner of Indian affairs, September 4, 1906

400 *a good student who weathered his time*: NARA I, RG 75, "Black Elk, Benjamin"; and J. C. McCaskIll, *The Boys' Adviser in the Government Boarding Schools for Indians* (Lawrence, KS: Haskell Institute, United States Indian School, 1934), 36.

400 *The oddest thing about Ben's stay*: NARA I, RG 75, "Black Elk, Benjamin," letter from supt., Carlisle School, to J. R. Brennan, agent-in-charge, Pine Ridge Reservation, March 27, 1917, and letter from William Ketcham, BCIM, to O. H. Lipps, supt., Carlisle School, November 23, 1915.

401 *But Black Elk did worry*: NARA I, RG 75, "Black Elk, Benjamin," letter from Agent John Brennan to John Francis, Jr., supt., Carlisle School, May 2, 1917; *6GF*, 24; Joseph G. Jorgensen, "A Century of Political Economic Effects on American Indian Society 1880–1980," *Journal of Ethnic Studies* 6, no. 3 (Fall 1978): 15; and Dennis M. Christafferson, "Sioux, 1930–2000," in *Handbook of North American Indians* (Washington, DC: Smithsonian Institution, 2001), 13:2 "Plains," 821.

402 *Yet Neihardt had a big voice*: Author's interview with Coralie Hughes, July 10, 2012, Coatesville, IN.

402 *"Do you hate money?"*: Hilda Neihardt Petri, ed., *The Giving Earth: A John G. Neihardt Reader* (Lincoln: University of Nebraska Press, 1991), xiii.

402 *"This world is like a garden"*: John Neihardt interview, *The Dick Cavett Show*, aired April 27, 1971; and Hilda Neihardt, *Black Elk and Flaming Rainbow*, 47–48.

403 *"If I write of hot winds"*: Vine Deloria, Jr., "Neihardt and the Western Landscape," in *A Sender of Words: Essays in Memory of John G. Neihardt* (Salt Lake City: Howe Brothers, 1984), 85–86; Helen Stauffer, "Two Authors and a Hero: Neihardt, Sandoz, and Crazy Horse," *Great Plains Quarterly* (Winter 1981): 57; John Neihardt, *A Cycle of the West: The Song of Three Friends; The Song of Hugh Glass; The Song of Jed Smith; The Song of the Indian Wars; The Song of the Messiah*, fiftieth anniversary ed. (Lincoln: University of Nebraska Press, 1991), xi.

403 *"The world tottered and began to rotate"*: John Neihardt, *All Is But a Beginning: Youth Remembered, 1881–1901* (New York: Harcourt Brace Jovanovich, 1972), 48.

403 *a need to understand this other world*: John Neihardt, *Patterns and Coincidences: A Sequel to All Is But a Beginning* (Columbia: University of Missouri Press, 1978), 34; Reece Pendleton, "A Ghostly Splendor: John G. Neihardt's Spiritual Preparation for Entry into Black Elk's World," *American Indian Culture and Research Journal* 19, no. 4 (1995): 219; and W. E. Black, "Ethic and Metaphysic: A Study of John G. Neihardt," *Western American Literature* 2, no. 3 (1967): 205.

404 *the lives of Neihardt and Black Elk*: Black, "Ethic and Metaphysic," 205; and "John G. Neihardt," *Neihardt!* http://neihardt.com/john-g-neihardt-biography.

404 *Bancroft, a small farming town*: Pendleton, "Ghostly Splendor," 230; *Wikipedia*'s "John Neihardt" entry, http://en.wikipedia.org/wiki/John_Neihardt; Hilda Neihardt, *Giving Earth*, xiii–xiv; John Neihardt Center, Neihardt Foundation Archives, Bancroft, NE (hereafter JNC), Neihardt Foundation Collection, Folder, "Neihardt, John G., Miscellaneous," "Neihardt had 'big impact,'" *Norfolk* (NE) *Daily News*, February 26, 1998, 7F.

404 *"the Omaha as an ancient people"*: John Neihardt, *Patterns and Coincidences*, 34; Pendleton, "Ghostly Splendor," 220–21; and Michael Castro, *Interpreting the Indian: Twentieth Century Poets and the Native American* (Albuquerque: University of New Mexico Press, 1983), 80.

405 *a two-thousand-mile journey down the Missouri River*: John Neihardt, *The River and I* (Albany: State University of New York Press, 2008, first published by G. P. Putnam, 1910), 23.

405 *"The monotony of the landscape"*: Ibid., 239–40.

405 *the experience matured him*: Hilda Neihardt, *Giving Earth*, xiv; and interview with Coralie Hughes.

406 *"a diaphanous flame lacking heat"*: John Neihardt, *Patterns and Coincidences*, 101.

406 *"This was not a dream"*: 6GF, 42–43.

406 *"Shakespeare of the Plains"*: Interview with Coralie Hughes.

407 *"by appealing to memory"*: "Neihardt on Oral Tradition," *Neihardt Journal* 16 (2014): 3. This was originally quoted in Lloyd R. Morris, ed., *The Young Idea* (New York: Duffield, 1917), 188–93.

407 *Herbert Hoover's White House library*: JNC, Aly Collection, "Neihardt: Correspondence, Outgoing. 1905–1958," J4c: J4c.15, "Neihardt Correspondence Outgoing, 1931," letter from Neihardt to unknown recipient, September 25, 1928.

25. BLACK ELK SPEAKS

This chapter encompasses events described in *Black Elk Speaks*, 219–28; and *The Sixth Grandfather*, 30–48.

408 *"A book truly Indian"*: The telegram to Morris is quoted in Hilda Neihardt, *Black Elk and Flaming Rainbow: Personal Memories of the Lakota Holy Man and John Neihardt* (Lincoln: University of Nebraska Press, 1995), 17–18.

408 *"a bit uncanny in his intuitions"*: SHSM, John G. Neihardt Papers (1881–1973), c. 1858–1974, C3716, Folder 38, "Correspondence, 1930," letter from Neihardt to Dr. Julius House, August 10, 1930.

409 *"your life beginning at the beginning"*: Ibid., Folder 39, "Correspondence, 1930," letter from Neihardt to Black Elk, November 6, 1930. Neihardt's letter to Black Elk continues:

> Now I have something to tell you that I hope and believe will interest you as much as it does me. After talking with you four and a half hours and thinking over many things you told me, I feel that the whole story of your life ought to be written truthfully by somebody with the right feeling and understanding of your people and of their great history. My idea is to come back to the reservation next spring, probably in April, and have a number of meetings with you and your old friends among the Oglalas who have shared the great history of your race, during the past half century or more. . . .
>
> The book that I sent you at Manderson is a poem dealing only with the wars between the Sioux and white men and does not tell everything that ought to be told. This book about you would be written in prose, and I would use as much of your language in it as possible. My publisher is eager to have me do this, for I have told him all about it.
>
> I would, of course, expect to pay you well for all the time that you would give me. [It] would probably be necessary for us to have eight or ten meetings. Does this plan seem a good one to you, and if it seems good to you, will you not be willing to help me make it successful? I do feel that so much is known by you Indians that our white people do not know and should know. . . . This is not a money-making scheme for me. I can make money much faster and easier in other ways. I want to do this book because I want to tell the things you and your friends know, and I can promise you that it will be an honest and a loving book.

409 *"both religion and war"*: Ibid.; and Hilda Neihardt, *Black Elk and Flaming Rainbow*, 18–20.

409 *apprised of his thinking*: Hilda Neihardt, *Black Elk and Flaming Rainbow*, 19; 6GF, 29–30; SHSM, John G. Neihardt Papers (1881–1973), c. 1858–1974, C3716, Folder 38, "Correspondence, 1930," letter from Neihardt to Dr. Julius House, n.d., Folder 39, "Correspondence, 1930," letter from Neihardt to Black Elk, November 6, 1930, and Folder 40, "Correspondence, January 20–June 1931," letter from M. M. Dowell, Secretary of the Board of Indian Commissioners, to B. C. Courtright, supt., Pine Ridge Agency, n.d.

410 *Standing Bear would be most important*: Louis S. Warren, *Buffalo Bill's America: William Cody and the Wild West Show* (New York: Alfred A. Knopf, 2005), 390–96; NARA I, "Indian Census Rolls, 1885–1940 [microform]: Indians of North America—Census; Native American Census—Pine Ridge (Oglala Sioux Indians)," Reel 363: "1887–1888," 142; and David Humphreys Miller, *Ghost Dance* (New York: Van Rees, 1959), 268.

412 *"Mr. Neihardt is not an investigator"*: MO: John G. Neihardt Papers (1881–1973), c. 1858–1974, C3716: Folder 40, "Correspondence, January 20–June 1931," letter, Malcolm McDowell, Secretary of the Board of Indian Commissioners, to B. C. Courtright, supt., Pine Ridge Agency, n.d.

412 *"was tying together the ends of his life"*: 6GF, 31, 43; and George W. Linden, "Dakota Philosophy," in *The Black Elk Reader*, ed. Clyde Holler (Syracuse, NY: Syracuse University Press, 2000), 213.

412 *"Sometimes an old man"*: Charles A. Eastman, *The Soul of the Indian: An Interpretation* (Boston: Houghton Mifflin, 1911), 2.

412 *"'the higher values'"*: Hilda Neihardt, *Black Elk and Flaming Rainbow*, 19.

413 *Stephen Standing Bear*: MARQ, Saint Francis Mission Collection, Series 7-1, "Facsimiles," Box 2: "Diary of Rev. Eugene Buechel, S.J. (St. Francis Mission Records, Series 7), vol. 2, 1925–1931," n.p., diary entry for "Feb. 1, 1929."

413 *a family dispute*: 6GF, 275; Clyde Holler, *Black Elk's Religion: The Sun Dance and Lakota Catholicism* (Syracuse, NY: Syracuse University Press, 1995), 13; Michael F. Steltenkamp, S.J., *Nicholas Black Elk: Medicine Man, Missionary, Mystic* (Norman: University of Oklahoma Press, 2009), 141–42.

414 *Neihardt left Branson for the interviews*: Sources for account of the production of *Black Elk Speaks* include 6GF, 30–47; SHSM, John G. Neihardt Papers (1881–1973), c. 1858–1974, C3716, Folder 430, "Transcription, 1980, Enid Neihardt Fink, 'My Diary,' May 1–28, 1931," 1–18; Hilda Neihardt, *Black Elk and Flaming Rainbow*, 30–89; Raymond J. DeMallie, "John G. Neihardt's Lakota Legacy," in *A Sender of Words: Essays in Memory of John G. Neihardt* (Salt Lake City: Howe Brothers, 1984), 114–25; Joseph Agonito, *Lakota Portraits: Lives of the Legendary Plains People* (Guilford, CT: TwoDot, 2011), 225–26; Brian R. Holloway, *Interpreting the Legacy: John Neihardt and Black Elk Speaks* (Boulder: University of Colorado Press, 2003), 66; Lucille Aly, *John Neihardt: A Critical Biography*, Melville Studies in American Culture, ed. Robert Brainard Pearsall (Amsterdam: Rodopi, 1977), 170–71; H. David Brumble III, *American Indian Autobiographies* (Berkeley: University of California Press, 1988), 169; Clyde Holler, "Lakota Religion and Tragedy: The Theology of *Black Elk Speaks*," *Journal of the American Academy of Religion* 52, no. 1 (1984): 25–28; Carol T. Holly, "*Black Elk Speaks* and the Making of Indian Autobiography," *Genre* 12, no. 1 (1979): 126–29; John Neihardt, "Preface to 1961 Edition," *BES*, xxv–xxvi; Damian Costello, *Black Elk: Colonialism and Lakota Catholicism* (Mary Knolls NY: Orbis Books, 2005), 142.

424 *They left early for the Black Hills*: Hilda Neihardt, *Black Elk and Flaming Rainbow*, 90–91; and movie advertisements for the Ellis, Rex, and State theaters, *Rapid City Journal*, Friday, May 29, 1931, 8. The Sylvan Lodge burned to the ground in 1936 and was rebuilt on a high overlook a mile away.

425 *began their four-mile climb*: Sources for account of the climb up Harney Peak include *Rapid City Journal*, May 30, 1931, 1; *BES*, 219–21; 6GF, 48, 294–96; Hilda Neihardt, *Black Elk and Flaming Rainbow*, 92–95; SHSM, John G. Neihardt Papers (1881–1973), c. 1858–1974, C3716, Folder 406, "Enid Neihardt's personal diary," March 28, 1931, 17; author's observations on climb up Harney Peak; SHSM, John G. Neihardt Papers (1881–1973), c. 1858–1974, C3716, Folder 40, "Correspondence, January 20–June 1931," letter from Neihardt to Julius House, June 3, 1931, and Folder 41, "Correspondence, 21 June–December 1931," letter from Neihardt to William Morrow, June 21, 1931.

26. DEFENDERS OF THE FAITH

428 *"very mysterious, very meaningful"*: Hilda Neihardt, *Black Elk and Flaming Rainbow: Personal Memories of the Lakota Holy Man and John Neihardt* (Lincoln: University of Nebraska Press, 1995), 96.

428 *"and sadly parted"*: Enid Neihardt is quoted in ibid., 97.

429 *He was in a fever to start*: 6GF, 50. Raymond DeMallie's observation of Enid's transcriptions are quoted in 6GF, xiv–xxvi.

429 *"It is all out of the consciousness"*: SHSM, John G. Neihardt Papers (1881–1973), c. 1858–1974, C3716, Folder 40, "Correspondence, January 20–June 1931," letter from Neihardt to Julius House, June 3, 1931.

429 *"no white man has heard before"*: Ibid., Folder 41, "Correspondence, 21 June–December 1931," letter from Neihardt to William Morrow, June 21, 1931.

429 *a letter to "Uncle Black Elk" and a second to Ben*: Ibid., letter from Neihardt to Ben Black Elk, June 27, 1931, and letter from Neihardt to Black Elk, June 27, 1931.

429 *moving to Pine Ridge*: 6GF, 51.

430 *beauty and grace*: Author's interview with Coralie Hughes, July 10, 2012, Coatesville, IN; and Richard Slotkin, *Gunfighter Nation: The Myth of the Frontier in Twentieth-Century America* (Norman: University of Oklahoma Press, 1988; first published by HarperPerennial 1992), 12–13.

431 *"reflect an echo"*: 6GF, 52–53; Hilda Neihardt, *Black Elk and Flaming Rainbow*, 99–100; author's interview with Coralie Hughes; Sally McCluskey, "Black Elk Speaks: And So Does John Neihardt," *Western American Literature* 6 (1972): 241; and BES, 1. One place to observe Neihardt's developing style is in chapter 1. Whereas his first draft read, "Then a foolish one among the scouts had had bad thoughts and spoke bad words," Neihardt tightened this to read, "Then one of the scouts, being foolish, had bad thoughts and spoke them." The dignified idiom that Neihardt created for Black Elk echoed that of the King James Bible, commented McCluskey. SHSM, John G. Neihardt Papers (1881–1973), c. 1858–1974, C3716, Folders 248–76, "Manuscript Series, *Black Elk Speaks*," 4a.

431 *Neihardt adheres closely to Black Elk's words*: 6GF, 56; SHSM, John G. Neihardt Papers (1881–1973), c. 1858–1974, C3716, Folders 248–76, "Manuscript Series, *Black Elk Speaks*."

431 *bad news arrived*: Raymond J. DeMallie, "John G. Neihardt's Lakota Legacy," in *A Sender of Words: Essays in Memory of John G. Neihardt* (Salt Cake City: Howe Brothers, 1984), 119–20; 6GF, 50–51; "Notable Book Publisher Dies," *The Sun* (New York), November 11, 1931, 29; and Hilda Neihardt, *Black Elk and Flaming Rainbow*, 100.

432 *There were other problems*: 6GF, 51; and Hilda Neihardt, *Black Elk and Flaming Rainbow*, 101.

432 *strong reviews*: 6GF, 57; Hilda Neihardt, *Black Elk and Flaming Rainbow*, 100–101; and Blair Whitney, *John G. Neihardt*, Twayne's United States Author Series, ed. Sylvia E. Bowman (Boston: Twayne, 1976), 90.

432 *"a beautiful work"*: SHSM, John G. Neihardt Papers (1881–1973), c. 1858–1974, C3716, Folder 42, "Correspondence, 1932," letter, B. G. Courtright to Neihardt, February 22, 1932; and 6GF, 58.

433 *"it makes me happy and sad"*: SHSM, John G. Neihardt Papers (1881–1973), c. 1858–1974, C3716, Folder 42, "Correspondence, 1932," letter from Ella Deloria to Neihardt, March 18, 1932.

433 *The Black Elks were also pleased*: UGT, HT, JNC, MJ Collection, "Neihardt: Correspondence, Outgoing. 1905–1958," J4c: J4c.16, letter from Neihardt to Julius House, July 12, 1932.

433 *the Jesuit fathers were shocked*: 6GF, 58.

434 *"he believed in me and in the power of my prayers"*: Thomas E. Mails, assisted by Dallas Chief Eagle, *Fools Crow* (Garden City, NY: Doubleday, 1979), 102.

434 *"earned a place above all of the other Teton holy men"*: Ibid., 53.

434 *Father Placidus Sialm*: MARQ, Saint Francis Mission Collection, Series 7-1, "Facsimiles," Box 2: "Diary of Rev. Eugene Buechel, S.J. (St. Francis Mission Records, Series 7), vol. 2, 1925–1931," 36; and MARQ, Holy Rosary Mission/Red Cloud Indian School Collection, Series 7-1, Box 20, Folder 12, Sialm, Placidus E., "Camp Churches."

434 *"ignorant Indian"*: MARQ, Sialm, "Camp Churches," 52.

435 *Sialm's greatest animus*: Ibid., 52–53.

435 *pitched from the wagon and run over*: 6GF, 58–59.

435 *Louise was involved in a traffic accident*: Louis S. Warren, *Buffalo Bill's America: William Cody and the Wild West Show* (New York: Alfred A. Knopf, 2005), 394.

435 *"Black Elk Speaks Again—A Last Word"*: Michael F. Steltenkamp, S.J., *Black Elk: Holy Man of the Oglala* (Norman: University of Oklahoma Press, 1993), 82–84.

436 *letter was dictated and written*: 6GF, 59; and MARQ, Sialm, "Camp Churches," 63.

436 *composed under the threat of eternal damnation*: Harvey Markowitz, "Converting the Rosebud: Sicangu Lakota Catholicism in the Late Nineteenth and Early Twentieth Centuries," *Great Plains Quarterly* 32, no. 1 (Winter 2012): 7–8; Hilda Neihardt and R. Todd Wise, "Black Elk and John G. Neihardt," in *The Black Elk Reader*, ed. Clyde Holler (Syracuse, NY: Syracuse University Press, 2000), 97–98; MARQ, Sialm, "Camp Churches," 62, 64; and 2 Peter, 2:20–22.

437 *"the last chapter was not in the intention of his father"*: MARQ, Sialm, "Camp Churches," 64.

437 *the most veteran priest at Pine Ridge*: Francis J. Coffey, S.J., "Rev. Placidus F. Sialm, S.J.," *The Indian Sentinel* 20, no. 5 (May 1940): 71–72. The comment by Buechel was included in an e-mail, July 22, 2012, from Markus Kries to Marcia Poole, cc Mark Thiel.

437 *philosophical tug-of-war*: SHSM, John G. Neihardt Papers (1881–1973), c. 1858–1974, C3716, Folder 44, "Correspondence, 1934," letter from Benjamin Black Elk to Neihardt, June 4, 1934.

438 *"working in Colorado"*: Hilda Neihardt, *Black Elk and Flaming Rainbow*, 106–109; and ibid.

438 *"God and I are good friends!"*: Hilda Neihardt, *Black Elk and Flaming Rainbow*, 108.

438 *"Dear Friends"*: MARQ, Holy Rosary Mission/Red Cloud Indian School Collection, Series 7-1, open letter, Nick Black Elk, September 20, 1934, reprinted in Marie Therese Archambault, Mark G. Thiel, and Christopher Vecsey, eds., *The Crossing of Two Roads, Being Catholic and Native in the United States*, American Catholic Identities: A Documentary History 9 (Maryknoll, NY: Orbis Books, 2003), 139–40.

439 *"This is a difficult document to assess"*: 6GF, 62–63, 93n.

439 *the letter's obsession with "paganism"*: MARQ, Sialm, "Camp Churches," 61, 62.

440 *"here was Father Sialm knocking on the door"*: Esther Black Elk DeSersa, Olivia Black Elk Pourier, Aaron DeSersa, Jr., and Clifton DeSersa, *Black Elk Lives: Conversations with the Black Elk Family*, ed. Hilda Neihardt and Lori Utecht (Lincoln: University of Nebraska Press, 2000), 137.

27. DISCIPLES

442 *Black Elk wanted to put on a show*: Sources for the beginnings of the Sitting Bull Indian Pageant include David O. Born, "Black Elk and the Duhamel Sioux Indian Pageant," *North Dakota History: Journal of the Northern Great Plains* 61 (1994): 24–25, 24n9; and Dale Lewis, *Duhamel: From Ox Cart . . . To Television* (Rapid City, SD: Francis A. Duhamel, 1993), 117–19.

443 *a large octagonal dance hall*: 6GF, 64; and author's observations and interview with Peter Heffron, great-grandson of Alex Duhamel and owner of the Sitting Bull Crystal Caverns, Rapid City, SD, July 23, 2012.

443 *Black Elk was key*: Interview with Peter Heffron; 6GF, 63; Born, "Black Elk and the Duhamel Sioux Indian Pageant," 25–26; Lewis, *Duhamel*, 125–26; and Alice Beck Kehoe, *The Ghost Dance: Ethnohistory and Revitalization* (Washington, DC: Thompson, 1989), 69.

444 *mornings and evenings, rain or shine*: Lewis, *Duhamel*, 127–28; and Born, "Black Elk and the Duhamel Sioux Indian Pageant," 26–27.

445 *the old man's healing powers*: JNC, Neihardt Foundation Collection, Francis "Bud" Duhamel interview by Dr. Dale Stover, 1998; and Brian R. Holloway, *Interpreting the Legacy: John Neihardt and Black Elk Speaks* (Boulder: University of Colorado Press, 2003), 78.

445 *"just a show"*: 6GF, 64–65; Joseph Agonito, *Lakota Portraits: Lives of the Legendary Plains People* (Guilford, CT: TwoDot, 2011), 230; and Born, "Black Elk and the Duhamel Sioux Indian Pageant," 29.

445 *Black Elk was serious in his intentions*: 6GF, 289, 380–81.

446 *Word of the pageant soon spread*: 6GF, 65–66.

446 *The "McVey Burn"*: "Fires Changing in Black Hills Forest," July 26, 2002, *Rapid City Journal*, n.p., http://rapidcityjournal.com/fires-changing-in-black-hills-forest/article_3dc61dbe-b85-52e5-9a80-410d966fc47a.html; Duhamel interview by Stover, 1998; Born, "Black Elk and the Duhamel Sioux Indian Pageant," 27–29; and Holloway, *Interpreting the Legacy*, 78.

447 *"here I am writing to you"*: Letter from Black Elk to John Neihardt, December 16, 1940, quoted in Raymond J. DeMallie, "John G. Neihardt's Lakota Legacy," in *A Sender of Words: Essays in Memory of John G. Neihardt* (Salt Lake City: Howe Brothers, 1984), 127.

447 *The war years started sadly*: Michael F. Steltenkamp, S.J., *Black Elk: Holy Man of the Oglala* (Norman: University of Oklahoma Press, 1993), 114–15; 6GF, 68; and author's personal correspondence with Peter Heffron, great-grandson of Black Elk's friend and business partner Alex Duhamel.

448 *The war of true faith*: Francis J. Coffey, S.J., "Rev. Placidus F. Sialm, S.J.," *The Indian Sentinel* 20, no. 5 (May 1940): 71; Clyde Holler, *Black Elk's Religion: The Sun Dance and Lakota Catholicism* (Syracuse, NY: Syracuse University Press, 1995), 136; Bernard Barber, "Acculturation and Messianic Movements," *American Sociological Review* 6, no. 5 (October 1941): 667; and Joseph Zimmerman, "My Dear Friends," *Wanbli Wankatuya* (The Month of St. Joseph 1939), quoted in author's personal correspondence from Marcia Poole and Mark Thiel, July 12, 2012.

448 *"Good Lance mounted his horse and rode away"*: Joseph Zimmerman, "The True Faith Versus Paganism," *The Calumet* (May 1944): 17.

448 *Zimmerman blamed the government*: Ibid.; and John Collier, quoted in Holler, *Black Elk's Religion*, 137.

449 *"Indian New Deal"*: Richard Ellis, ed., *The Western American Indian: Case Studies in Tribal History* (Lincoln: University of Nebraska Press, 1972), 108–13, 145; and John Collier, "The Genesis and Philosophy of the Indian Reorganization Act," in *The Western American Indian*, 147–48.

449 *changes wrought by Collier's Indian New Deal*: William K. Powers, *Oglala Religion* (Lincoln: University of Nebraska Press, 1975), 108.

449 *the new Indian Commissioner knew a lot about him*: Kenneth R. Philip, "John Collier and the Controversy over the Wheeler-Howard Bill," in *Indian-White Relations: A Persistent Paradox*, ed. Jane F. Smith and Robert M. Kvasnicka (Washington, DC: Howard University Press, 1976), 171–72; and Peter Iverson, "Neihardt, Collier and the Continuity of Indian Life," in *A Sender of Words*, 103–04.

450 *Collier and Neihardt would be friends*: Hilda Neihardt, *The Broidered Garment: The Love Story of Mona Martinsen and John G. Neihardt* (Lincoln: University of Nebraska Press, 2006), 284; and Hilda Neihardt, *Black Elk and Flaming Rainbow: Personal Memories of the Lakota Holy Man and John Neihardt* (Lincoln: University of Nebraska Press, 1995), 110.

450 *hard ones for Neihardt*: 6GF, 68; and Lucille Aly, *John Neihardt: A Critical Biography*, Melville Studies in American Culture, ed. Robert Brainard Pearsall (Amsterdam: Rodopi, 1977), 227–39.

450 *cultural history of the Oglala*: SHSM, John G. Neihardt Papers (1881–1973), c. 1858–1974, C3716, Folder 36, "Correspondence, 1930s," letter from Neihardt to "Uncle Black Elk," n.d.

450 *Neihardt came to Pine Ridge*: Powers, *Oglala Religion*, 107, 117; Dennis M. Christafferson, "Sioux, 1930–2000," in *Handbook of North American Indians*, vol. 13, no. 2 (Washington, DC: Smithsonian Institution, 2001), 821; Gayla Twiss, "A Short History of Pine Ridge," *The Indian Historian* (Winter 1978): 39; and Hilda Neihardt, *Black Elk and Flaming Rainbow*, 110–11. The reservation actually shrank during World War II when, in early 1942, the army acquired 340,000 acres of the Badlands to use as a practice range for aerial bombing and gunnery. Though the tribe itself leased the land

for a minimal payment, individual owners were forced to sell. The Black Elks lost their grazing land on Cuny Table, while 128 families who actually lived in the north were forcibly moved. Though the army promised to return the land after the war, some was later deemed unusable due to unexploded bombs. No financial compensation would be awarded until 1956, and it would not be until 1975 that nearly three-quarters of this land, or 248,000 acres, would be returned to the Oglala. Christafferson, "Sioux, 1930–2000," 82; and 6GF, 69.

451 Neihardt scheduled the interviews in two segments: SHSM, Neihardt Collection, letter from John Neihardt to Mona Neihardt, quoted in DeMallie, "John G. Neihardt's Lakota Legacy," 128; and Hilda Neihardt, Black Elk and Flaming Rainbow, 110–12.

453 "the Sioux sure did appreciate what you said": Hilda Neihardt, Black Elk and Flaming Rainbow, 113; and 6GF, 70.

453 The poet's final visit: SHSM, John G. Neihardt Papers (1881–1973), c. 1858–1974, C3716, Folder 516, "Neihardt, Miscellaneous, 1945," John Neihardt, "Report to the Indian Bureau on a Field Trip to Pine Ridge in 1945," 3, 7; and Robert H. Ruby, The Oglala Sioux: Warriors in Transition (Lincoln: University of Nebraska Press, 1955), 27.

454 "to which they add a great deal of color": Gordon Macgregor, Warriors Without Weapons: A Study of the Society and Personality Development of the Pine Ridge Sioux (Chicago: University of Chicago Press, 1946), 82–83.

454 "comic opera": Neihardt, "Report to the Indian Bureau," 4, 7, 10.

454 Time and age had finally caught up: Michael F. Steltenkamp, S.J., Nicholas Black Elk: Medicine Man, Missionary, Mystic (Norman: University of Oklahoma Press, 2009), 122; and Lewis, Duhamel, 136.

455 "a figure of rejection": Marie Therese Archambault, O.S.F., A Retreat with Black Elk: Living in the Sacred Hoop (Cincinnati: St. Anthony Messenger, 1998), 85–86.

455 anything but ignored: Hilda Neihardt, Black Elk and Flaming Rainbow, 101.

455 Jung tried again: Carl Jung, Memories, Dreams, Reflections (New York: Random House, 1963), 3–4; Jung is quoted in Paul B. Steinmetz, S.J., "New Missiology and Black Elk's Individuation," in The Black Elk Reader, ed. Clyde Holler (Syracuse, NY: Syracuse University Press, 2000), 264; Aly, John G. Neihardt, 172; and John Neihardt, "The Book That Would Not Die," Western American Literature 6 (Winter 1972b): 229.

456 Joseph Epes Brown: Author's interview with Elenita Brown and Marina Weatherly, wife and daughter of Joseph Epes Brown, Kootenai Valley, MT, August 12, 2012; and "Biography of Joseph E. Brown," in Joseph Epes Brown, The Spiritual Legacy of the American Indian: With Letters While Living with Black Elk (Bloomington, IN: World Wisdom, 2007, first published by Crossroad, 1982), 127.

457 Swiss metaphysician Frithjof Schuon: Jean-Baptiste Aymard and Patrick Laude, Frithjof Schuon: Life and Teachings (Syracuse, NY: SUNY Press, 2012), 28; Michael Fitzgerald, "Frithjof Schuon and the American Indian Spirit: Interview with Michael Fitzgerald," Vincit Omnia Veritas, The Journal of Perennial Studies 111:2, 3–4, 6, n.d., http:religioperennis.org/documents/Fitzgerald/Indian.pdf.

457 this early fascination with Schuon: Interview with Elenita Brown and Marina Weatherly.

458 he now had purpose and meaning: Hilda Neihardt, Black Elk and Flaming Rainbow, 113–14; and 6GF, 71.

458 struck out for Dakota: Macgregor, Warriors Without Weapons, 83.

458 Brown hit the side of the tent: Joseph Epes Brown, Animals of the Soul: Sacred Animals of the Oglala Sioux (Rockport, MA: Element, 1992), viii.

458 Sacred Calf Pipe Bundle: Brown, Spiritual Legacy, 103–104, 107–108, 10n, 116; J. L. Smith, "The Sacred Calf Pipe Bundle: Its Effect on the Present Teton Dakota," Plains Anthropologist 15, no. 48 (May 1970): 89–90.

459 The Sacred Pipe: Nicholas Black Elk, The Sacred Pipe: Black Elk's Account of the Seven Rites of the Oglala Sioux, recorded and edited by Joseph Epes Brown (Norman: University of Oklahoma Press, 1953), ix–xiii, and in total; Kehoe, Ghost Dance, 69–71; 6GF, 71; and Agonito, Lakota Portraits, 231–32.

459 *seven sacramental rites*: Kehoe, *Ghost Dance*, 70–71.

460 *"nearing the end of a cycle"*: Black Elk, *Sacred Pipe*, xii.

460 *Walks with the Sacred Pipe*: Brown, *Spiritual Legacy*, 103–104.

461 *"Father Gall"*: Brown, *Animals of the Soul*, ix, 113; MARQ, Holy Rosary Mission/Red Cloud Indian School Collection, Series 1-1: Box 9, Correspondence," Folder 3, "A Letter by Black Elk to an Anonymous Trappist Monk, in Rome, Italy," March 4, 1948. Black Elk's letter to Father Gall was published in *Lakota Times*, November 2, 1983, with commentary by Charlotte Black Elk.

461 *Gall no longer thought he was crazy*: Interview with Elenita Brown and Marina Weatherly; Benoit Peeters, *Hergé, Son of Tintin* (Baltimore: Johns Hopkins University Press, 2011), 32, 204–205; and Steltenkamp, *Nicholas Black Elk*, 193–94.

462 *"We've got to behave now"*: Interview with Elenita Brown and Marina Weatherly; and Brown, *Spiritual Legacy*, 116.

462 *He'd already been fading*: Sources for the death of Black Elk include Steltenkamp, *Black Elk: Holy Man*, 122–23, 128–35; Archambault, *Retreat with Black Elk*, 66; MARQ, Sister Marie Therese Archambault O.S.F. Collection, Papers, Box 2, Folder 25, "Published Writings, 1999," "The Night the Sky Danced: A Hidden Life of Greatness," in *National Center Cross and Feather News*," n.d.; Agonito, *Lakota Portraits*, 231–32; Steltenkamp, *Nicholas Black Elk*, 193–96; interview with Betty Black Elk, July 30, 2012, Manderson, SD; Damian Costello, *Black Elk: Colonialism and Lakota Catholicism* (Maryknoll, NY: Orbis Books, 2005), 13; "August Auroral Displays Are Widely Observed," *Sky & Telescope*, October 1950, n.p., quoted in Steltenkamp, *Nicholas Black Elk*, 201; and A. B. Meinel, "Evidence for the Entry into the Upper Atmosphere of High-Speed Protons During Auroral Activity," *Science* 112, no. 2916 (November 17, 1950): 590.

EPILOGUE: BESIEGED

467 *icilowan, or death song*: Mircea Eliade, *Shamanism: Archaic Techniques of Ecstasy*, trans. Willard R. Trask (Princeton, NJ: Princeton University Press, 1972; first published by Bollingen Foundation, 1951), 508–11; Denver Public Library—Western History and Genealogy Department, Denver, CO: Black Elk Collection, 1945–1951, letter from Nick Black Elk to Claude and Frances Hansen, November 19, 1948; and Michael F. Steltenkamp, S.J., *Black Elk: Holy Man of the Oglala* (Norman: University of Oklahoma Press, 1993), 126–27.

467 *Ben Jr. died*: Esther Black Elk DeSersa, Olivia Black Elk Pourier, Aaron DeSersa, Jr., and Clifton DeSersa, *Black Elk Lives: Conversations with the Black Elk Family*, ed. Hilda Neihardt and Lori Utecht (Lincoln: University of Nebraska Press, 2000), 40–41; and JNC, Neihardt Foundation Collection, Folder, "Black Elk, Ben," Babcock, Calene, "The 'Fifth Face' on the Mountain: What Mount Rushmore Represented to Ben Black Elk," typescript copy.

468 *set in the eye of the beholder*: Babcock, "The 'Fifth Face' on the Mountain."

468 *he was becoming well-known*: *The Rotarian* is quoted in ibid., 305; and Will H. Spindler, *Tragedy Strikes at Wounded Knee* (Vermilion, SD: Dakota Press, 1972), 130–31.

468 *the public face of the Oglala*: "Documentary on Indians Has Finale in the Hills," *Rapid City Journal*, December 11, 1968, quoted in Babcock, "The 'Fifth Face' on the Mountain," 308–309; and Ian Frazier, *Great Plains* (New York: Picador, 1989), 115–17.

469 *"Grandpa, how come you're so sad"*: DeSersa et al., *Black Elk Lives*, 82.

470 *"You're ready to go up on the hill"*: Ibid., 82–83.

470 *"it was me looking in the mirror"*: MARQ, Sister Marie Therese Archambault O.S.F. Collection, Papers, Box 1, Folder 1, "Albuquerque—Women's Church Conference: 'Remarks on My Spirituality as a Lakota Woman,'" 1–2.

470 *"a world of confusion"*: "Indian Face Stirs Cog of Memory," *The Reading Eagle*, January 1, 1970, 5; Ben Black Elk's testimony before the Senate Subcommittee on Indian

Education quoted in JNC, NE, Neihardt Foundation Collection, Folder, "Black Elk, Ben," Brinkman, Grover, "A Sioux named Black Elk: The Saga of a Great American," *Midwest Roto*, March 1977, fold-in newspaper supplement, n.p.

471   *Jesuit priests seemed divided*: Paul Steinmetz, *Pipe, Bible, and Peyote Among the Oglala Lakota*, Stockholm Studies in Comparative Religion 19 (Stockholm: Motala, 1980), 20.

471   *a priest had finally seen the light*: William K. Powers, *Oglala Religion* (Lincoln: University of Nebraska Press, 1975), 116.

471   *"a universal expression"*: Deloria is quoted in Richard F. Fleck, "*Black Elk Speaks*: A Native American View of Nineteenth-Century American History," *Journal of American Culture* 17, no. 1 (March 1994): 69; and E B, Folder: "Correspondence from Ben Black Elk & Family," letter from Ben Black Elk to Joseph Epes Brown, September 10, 1968.

472   *"tide of abuse and misuse of Indian ceremonies"*: Author's interview with Coralie Hughes, July 10, 2012; Vine Deloria, Jr., *The World We Used to Live In: Remembering the Powers of the Medicine Men* (Golden, CO: Fulcrum, 2006), xvii; Ward Churchill, "A Little Matter of Genocide: Native American Spirituality and New Age Hucksterism," *The Bloomsbury Review* (Sept./Oct. 1988): 23–24; and William K. Powers, "When Black Elk Speaks, Everybody Listens," in *Religion in Native North America*, ed. Christopher Vecsey (Moscow: University of Idaho Press, 1990c), 148.

472   *prime-time broadcast of* The Dick Cavett Show: John Neihardt interview, *The Dick Cavett Show*, aired April 27, 1971; "Cavett Entranced by Neihardt During Famous 1972 Interview," *Norfolk Daily News*, August 4, 1997, n.p.; "John G. Neihardt," http://neihardt.com; JNC: Neihardt Foundation Collection: Folder, "Neihardt, John G., Interviews," Hull, Dr. Ron, "John Neihardt . . . All Is But a Beginning," unattributed article, n.d.; and Hilda Neihardt, *Black Elk and Flaming Rainbow*, 118.

472   *"minor anachronism of a poet"*: Mick McAllister, "Native Sources: American Indian Autobiography," in *Updating the Literary West*, ed. Western Literature Association (Ft. Worth: Texas Christian University Press, 1997), 143.

473   *The dominant theme of his life was endurance*: Regarding Neihardt's trials after 1948 and his growing mysticism: In mid-April 1958, a few months before their fiftieth wedding anniversary, Neihardt and Mona were involved in a minor auto accident that left Neihardt unscathed but Mona with a bump on the head. Within a day this developed into a hematoma; she checked into a hospital, where it was drained. She seemed on the mend. But the next morning, on April 17, she was chatting with a visitor when she collapsed, killed by a blood clot to the brain.

      For months, Neihardt gave the appearance of someone struck with a sledgehammer. But then, strange things began to happen. Neihardt's lifelong mysticism blossomed almost desperately after Mona died. At first there were séances and bouts of "automatic writing" with mediums brought to his farm. And then there was the matter of the levitating table. Throughout the 1960s, Neihardt held what he called an "experimental class" in mysticism and extrasensory perception. A December 9, 1966, report described the scene: a group of four sat around the table and grew quiet until the medium, Joe Mangini, went into "his usual state of trance" with deep, regular breathing and "occasional snores." A cool breeze blew from Mangini's direction "as though a small fan were working behind him." The table "began to vibrate violently, tipping in various directions. Then it arose rapidly to the ceiling, striking the ceiling light several times."

      Hilda Neihardt, *The Broidered Garment*, 290–91; SHSM, John G. Neihardt Papers (1881–1973), 1908–1974, C3778, Folder 82, "Camp Chesterfield, June 26, 1958," transcript of a séance, Stanley C. Smith Papers (1928–1999), 1951–1971, C3607, Folder 26, "Report on a Seance, December 9, 1966"; and Victoria McCargar, "Mizzou Mail: Spooky Seances," *Mizzou*, Spring 2002, 4.

473   *"Alone among the badlands?"*: John Neihardt, "The Song of the Indian Wars," in *A Cycle of the West: The Song of Three Friends; The Song of Hugh Glass; The Song of Jed*

Smith; The Song of the Indian Wars; The Song of the Messiah, fiftieth anniversary ed. (Lincoln: University of Nebraska Press, 1991), 418.

473 *the second engagement*: Sources for account of Wounded Knee II include Jeffrey Ostler, *The Lakotas and the Black Hills: The Struggle for Sacred Ground* (New York: Viking, 2010), 169–73; "Indians Go from Guns to Lawbooks," *Omaha World Herald*, December 16, 1979, 6G; Richard Ellis, ed., *The Western American Indian: Case Studies in Tribal History* (Lincoln: University of Nebraska Press, 1972), 172–73; Tim A. Giago, Jr., "Who Were the Real Victims of Wounded Knee 1973?" *Huffington Post*, www.huffingtonpost.com/tim-giago/who-were-the-real-victims_6_170866.html; Tim A. Giago, Jr., *Notes from Indian Country*, vol. 1 (Pierre, SD: State Publishing, 1984), 35–36; Mary Crow Dog, with Richard Erdoes, *Lakota Woman* (New York: HarperPerennial, 1991), 131–43; Thomas E. Mails, assisted by Dallas Chief Eagle, *Fools Crow* (Garden City, NY: Doubleday, 1979), 193; and DeSersa et al., *Black Elk Lives*, 65–67.

474 *a quiet ranch hand named Raymond Yellow Thunder*: "Jury in Nebraska Convicts 2 Brothers in Death of Indian," *The New York Times*, May 27, 1972, 60.

476 *Hard feelings still exist*: "Indians Go from Guns to Lawbooks."

477 *$102 million to the Lakota*: Ostler, *Lakota and the Black Hills*, 188.

478 *The reservation is just as poor*: Most recent statistics available, 2005–2010, from the U.S. Census Bureau, U.S. Department of Health and Human Services, and South Dakota Department of Health, compiled and published in Alexandra Fuller, "In the Shadow of Wounded Knee," *National Geographic* 222, no. 2 (August 2012): 30–38, 48, 51, 54–55; "Hope Air," brochure for the Red Cloud Indian School, 2013; MARQ, Sister Marie Therese Archambault O.S.F. Collection, Papers, Box 2, Folder 14, "Non-published writing after 1997," "The State of Native American Health," 5, quoting from *U.S. Dept. of Health and Human Services Developing Objectives for Healthy People 2010.*

478 *a true crisis gripped the reservation*: "Pine Ridge Indian Reservation Struggles with Suicides Among Its Young," *The New York Times*, May 1, 2015, www.nytimes.com.

479 *Pine Ridge and border town*: Account of Daniel Tiger and Rapid City from Nick Estes, "Racist City, S.D.: Life Is Violent, and Often Deadly, in Rapid City," *Indian Country Today Media Network*, http://indiancountrytodaymedianetwork.com/2014/09/05/racist-city-sd-rapid-city-where-life-violent-and-often-deadly-156754. Though Indians made up 12 percent of Rapid City's 2013 population of 68,000, they accounted for 48 percent of those in the county jail. In 2014, Indians comprised 75 percent of the homeless population.

479 *Peter Heffron glanced off sadly*: Author's interview with Peter Heffron, July 23, 2012.

480 *"There is no interest in Black Elk"*: Powers, "When Black Elk Speaks," 110.

480 *sculptures, greeting cards, poetry chapbooks*: These include a bronze monument to Black Elk by the sculptor Marshall M. Fredericks; greeting cards sold nationally with quotes by Black Elk (Leanin' Tree and Sunrise Publications); prayer cards sold on Catholic and New Age websites; *Bay Is the Land (To Black Elk)*, by the poet Donna Duesel de la Torriente (1982); a children's book—Carol Green, *Black Elk: A Man with a Vision* (Chicago: Children's Press, 1983); and a novel—Kate Horsley, *Black Elk in Paris* (Boston: Trumpeter Books, 2006).

480 *"Black Elk was part of a conspiracy"*: Lee Irwin, "Freedom, Law, and Prophecy: A Brief History of Native American Religious Resistance," *American Indian Quarterly* 21, no. 1 (Winter 1997): 46–47.

481 *Black Elk the saint*: Michael F. Steltenkamp, "American Indian Sainthood and the Catholic Church," *American Catholic Studies* 124:1 (2013), 93, 97; letter, Mark Thiel, archivist for the Tekakwitha Conference and the Bureau of Catholic Indian Missions, to Charles J. Chaput, Archbishop of Philadelphia, n.d., including "Nicholas Black Elk Petition" (in author's possession).

481 *"My great-grandfather's books made it okay"*: Author's interview with Betty Black Elk, July 30, 2012.

482 *"Every generation on the reservation has to reinvent itself"*: Author's interview with Ted Hamilton, superintendent, Red Cloud Indian School, Pine Ridge, SD, July 31, 2012. Hamilton retired from Red Cloud in April 2015 to care for an ailing family member.

482 *"It would be helpful to return to the old religions in a new form"*: Thomas Lewis, *The Medicine Men* (Lincoln: University of Nebraska Press, 1990), 96.

482 *Native American "religion"*: John Wybraniec and Roger Finke, "Religious Regulation and the Courts: The Judiciary's Changing Role in Protecting Minority Religions from Majoritarian Rule," in *Regulating Religion: Case Studies from Around the Globe*, ed. James T. Richardson (New York: Springer, 2004), 543; *Federal Register* 80, no. 9 (January 14, 2015); Department of the Interior, Bureau of Indian Affairs, "Final Determination for Federal Acknowledgment of the Pamunkey Indian Tribe," July 2, 2015, www.bia .gov/cs/groups/public/documents/text/idcl-030831.pdf; "Overview of Race and Hispanic Origin: 2010," *2010 Census Briefs*, March 2011, www.census.gov/prod/cen2010/briefs /c2010br-02.pdf.

484 "Mitakuye oyasin": The entire prayer is commonly translated as "There is a word meaning 'All my relations.' We will live by this word. We are related to everything. We are still here. We shall live." Translated by Tawa Ducheneaux, Michelle May, and Agnes Gay, archivists, Oglala Lakota College, Pine Ridge (private e-mail in author's possession, March 13, 2015); Don Doll, S.J., *Vision Quest: Men, Women, and Sacred Sites of the Sioux Nation* (New York: Crown, 1994), 25; Spindler, *Tragedy Strikes*, 131; and *Wikipedia*'s "Telstar" entry, http://en.wikipedia.org/wiki/Telstar.

ACKNOWLEDGMENTS

What would a writer do without the patience of others? Sometimes they're strangers, sometimes not, but you appear out of the blue and invade their lives, asking all sorts of questions. Black Elk's Jesuit sponsor, Father Henry Westropp, would do something very similar when, after a week of riding through Pine Ridge, he'd appear in the night at Black Elk's cabin. "Auntie," he would cry to Black Elk's wife, Anna Brings White, "the ghosts have pushed me here." And Brings White would always find a bite for her tired "nephew." This is the seventh nonfiction narrative in which I've appeared in people's doors like a ghost in the night, and few have pushed me away.

Most of my research centered either in federal archives or in the endless and beautiful west, so I'll start with the latter. And what better place to begin than Black Elk's home on Pine Ridge Reservation, South Dakota? Betty Black Elk O'Rourke lives on her great-grandfather's allotment near Manderson and keeps the holy man's memory: she showed me his cabin, told me of his life and death, and drove me to various points while singing the "Sioux National Anthem," penned by her grandfather Ben. Black Elk's legacy is safe in her hands. I'm also grateful for my phone conversations with Charlotte Black Elk, also a great-granddaughter, who proved herself an able detective when she found the Parisian descendants of Black Elk's great love Charlotte—for whom, she said, she was named.

All kinds of educators came to my aid in Pine Ridge. At Red Cloud School (formerly Holy Rosary Mission), then–school superintendent Ted Hamilton was gracious with his time and thoughts concerning Black Elk's place in the history of the Lakota Nation. Peter Strong of the Red Cloud Heritage Center was my first contact at the school and paved the way for my visit. To the north, three wonderful and brilliant librarians/archivists at Oglala Lakota College came to my aid more often than I can say. Head librarian Michelle May, head archivist Tawa Ducheneaux, and assistant librarian Agnes Gay heaped resources upon me, and occasionally even fed me. If there's a heaven for archivists, I'm sure they've got a spot reserved. Two others in the general area that I'd like to thank are Marie Kills in Sight, general manager of the Buechel Memorial Lakota Museum on Rosebud Reservation, and Peter Heffron, general manager of the Sitting Bull Crystal Caverns and the great-grandson of Black Elk's friend Alex Duhamel.

To understand Black Elk, one must understand the man who "discovered" him: Nebraska's poet laureate John G. Neihardt. Coralie Hughes is his granddaughter and trustee of the John Neihardt Foundation; she spent a day with me in tiny Coatesville, Indiana, where she pointed to a cemetery and quipped, "There are more people in there than are living in this town." Her grandfather was prone to similar observations. Much of Neihardt's work and ephemera is kept at the John Neihardt Historical Center in Bancroft, Nebraska: then–executive director Nancy Gillis and her assistants Norma Farrens and Mary Petersen helped me wade through reams of material. In addition, I'd like to thank Paul Hammel, Lincoln bureau chief of the *Omaha World-Herald*, for the use of his family farm during my week in the archives and cornfields of Bancroft. The second great repository for resources on Neihardt, Black Elk, and *Black Elk Speaks* is the State Historical Society of Missouri in Columbia, Missouri. Senior manuscript specialist Laura R. Jolley guided me through the sometimes complex labyrinth of the society's vast holdings.

One absolutely could not hope to grasp Black Elk's career as a Catholic catechist—nor the current drive to have him named a saint—without diving into Marquette University's Raynor Library and University Archives. If anyone knows his way through its holdings on the Bureau of Catholic Indian Missions, Black Elk, and the world of the Jesuits at Pine Ridge, it is archivist Mark G. Thiel. He also seems to know just about everyone in the west. One acquaintance I'd like to mention is Dominican sister Mary Ewens, O.P., Ph.D., who helped explain the mechanics and politics of canonization, especially regarding Native Americans.

To understand Black Elk's goals in his final years, one must understand the work of his admirer Joseph Epes Brown. Brown became one of the most respected professors of Native American studies in the United States, and it is amazing how many people said they'd been his student as I drove to his home in western Montana. Unfortunately, Brown died in 2000 after a long battle with Alzheimer's, but his wife, Elenita Brown, and his daughter, Marina Brown Weatherly, maintain his private library. They were gracious to let me spend a day in their collection.

At the McCracken Research Library of the Buffalo Bill Historical Center in Cody, Wyoming, I'd like to thank: Housel director Mary Abernathy; cataloguing librarian Karling Abernathy; curatorial assistant Lynn Houze; assistant librarian Charlotte Gdula; and associate editor Chris Dixon. Through them I also met the Scottish Buffalo Bill scholar and author Tom F. Cunningham, who probably knows more about the checkered career of "Mexican Joe" Shelley than anyone in the world.

Other deserving kudos go out to Josh Caster, Carter Hulinsky, and Brian Hobbes at the archives and special collections of the University of Nebraska–Lincoln; Gerald Jasmer, park ranger and chief historian at the Little Bighorn National Monument; Tim Bernardis, library director at Little Big Horn College, Crow Agency, Montana; and Chris Kortlander of the Custer Battlefield Museum in Garryowen, Montana.

The archives and libraries in Washington, D.C., became my second home. At the library and archives of the Smithsonian's National Museum of the American Indian I'd like to thank: Michael Pahn, head archivist; Elayne Silversmith, librarian; Heather Shannon, photo archivist; and Rachel Menyuk, archives technician. At the Smithsonian's National Anthropological Archives I'd like to thank archivist Gina Rappaport; at the National Anthropological Library, I'm beholden to librarian Maggie Dittemore and library technician Brandee Worsham.

Then there are those "free agents" whose help and expertise were invaluable. My optometrist, Dr. Marcia K. Leverett, helped me piece together the probable causes of Black Elk's blindness. Steve Coen, city councilor of Manchester, UK, helped me with the story of Buffalo Bill's "Salford Sioux" during their winter in England. My friend and French electronic artist Carine Masutti helped guide me through the huge and somewhat Kafkaesque French national library. And last but not least, my multilingual son, Nick Merlock Jackson, helped translate French reviews of Buffalo Bill's 1889 visit to the City of Light.

As always, I'd like to thank my literary agent, Noah Lukeman, who keeps me honest. And I'd like to thank my editors at Farrar, Straus and Giroux, Jonathan Galassi, Alex Star, and Scott Borchert, who struggled with me through the Great Sioux War.

INDEX

A NOTE ABOUT THE AUTHOR

Joe Jackson is the author of one novel and six works of nonfiction, including, most recently, *Atlantic Fever: Lindbergh, His Competitors, and the Race to Cross the Atlantic* (FSG, 2012). His book *The Thief at the End of the World: Rubber, Power, and the Seeds of Empire* was one of *Time*'s Top 10 Nonfiction Books of 2008. He is the Mina Hohenberg Darden Endowed Professor of Creative Writing in the M.F.A. creative writing program at Old Dominion University in Norfolk, Virginia.